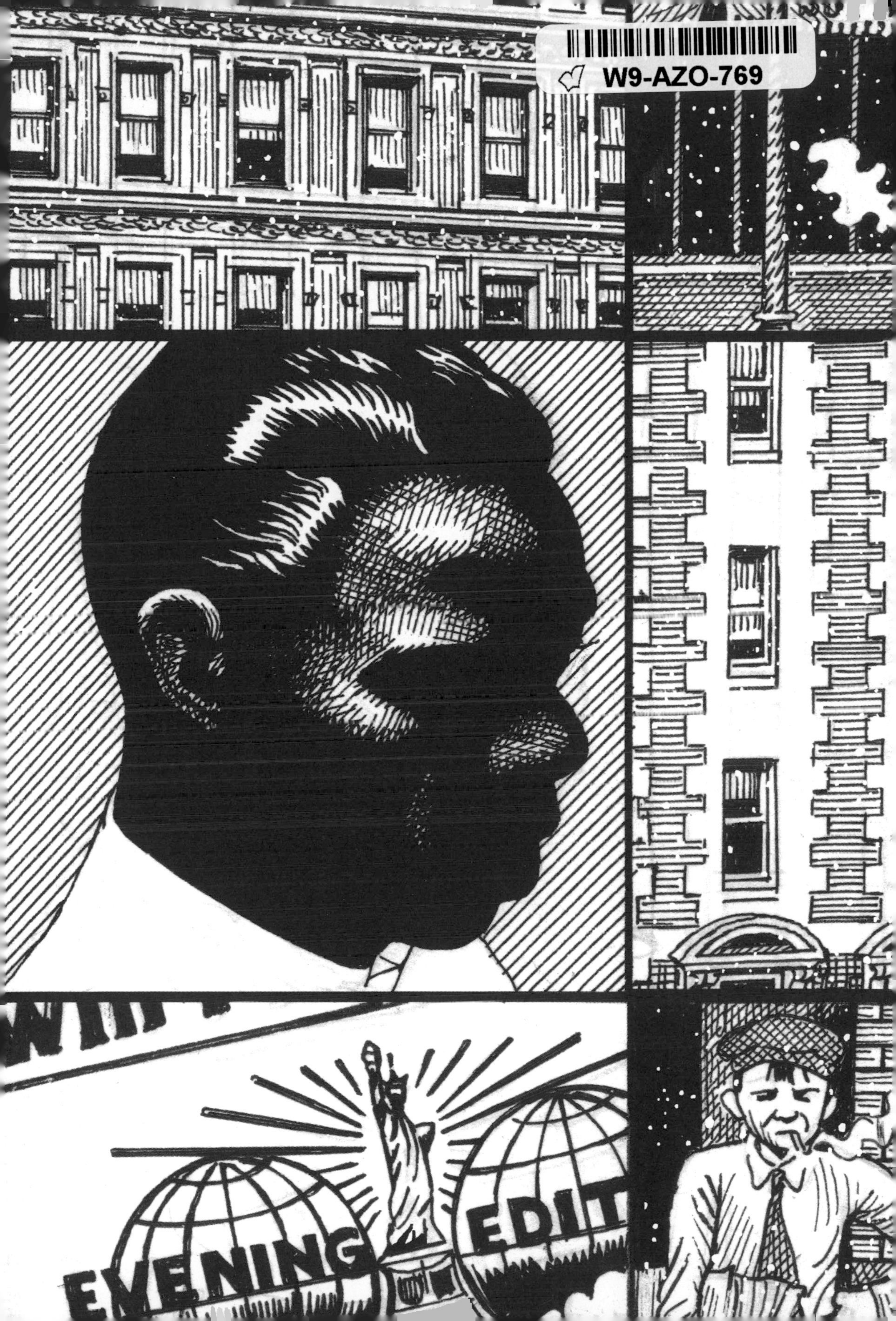
EVENING
EDIT

SELF
MADE
HERO

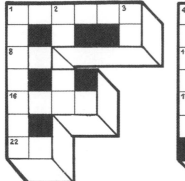

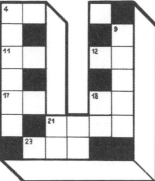

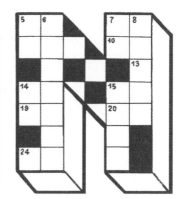

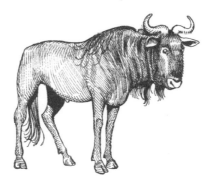

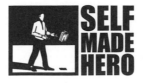

PAOLO BACILIERI

FUN

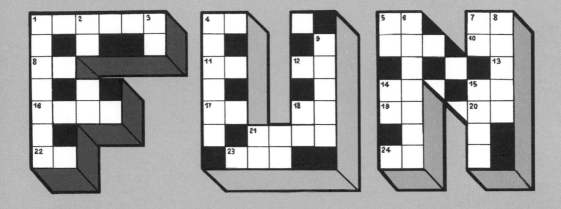

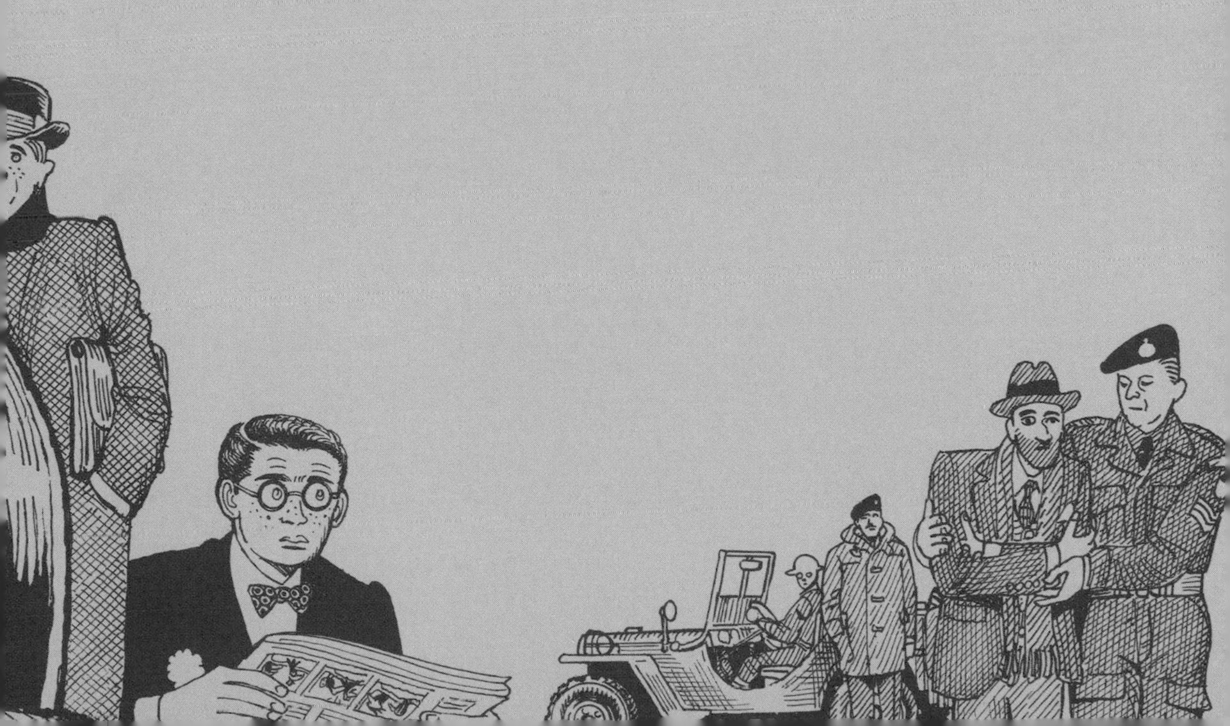

First published in English in 2017
by SelfMadeHero
139-141 Pancras Road
London NW1 1UN
www.selfmadehero.com

Written and illustrated by Paolo Bacilieri
Translated from Italian by Jamie Richards

English edition
Publishing Director: Emma Hayley
Sales & Marketing Manager: Sam Humphrey
Editorial & Production Manager: Guillaume Rater
UK Publicist: Paul Smith
US Publicist: Maya Bradford
Designer: Txabi Jones
With thanks to Dan Lockwood and Nick de Somogyi

A CIP record for this book is available from the British Library

ISBN: 978-1-910593-25-7

10 9 8 7 6 5 4 3 2 1

Printed and bound in Slovenia

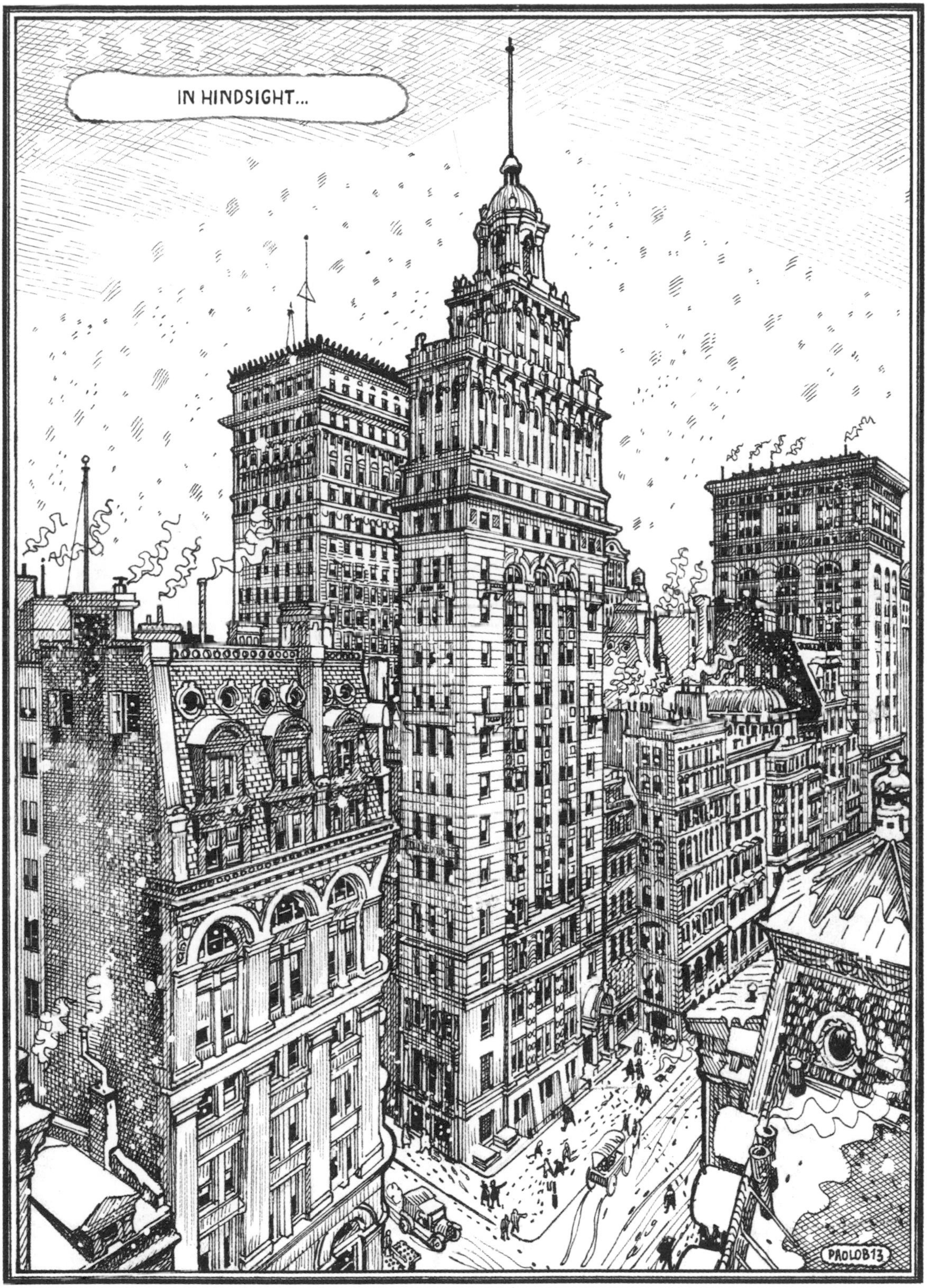
IN HINDSIGHT...
PAOLOB13

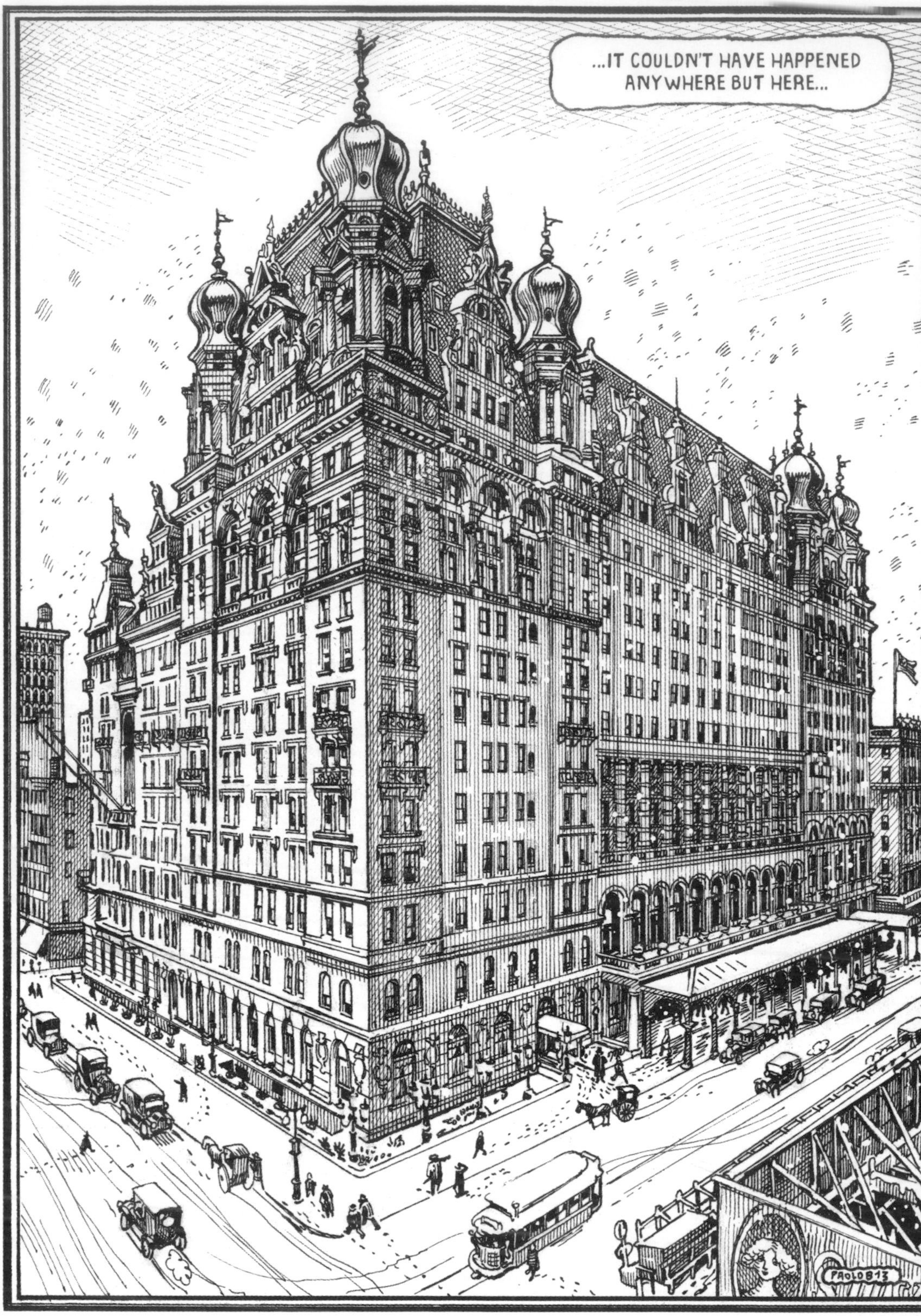
...IT COULDN'T HAVE HAPPENED ANYWHERE BUT HERE...
PAOLO 813

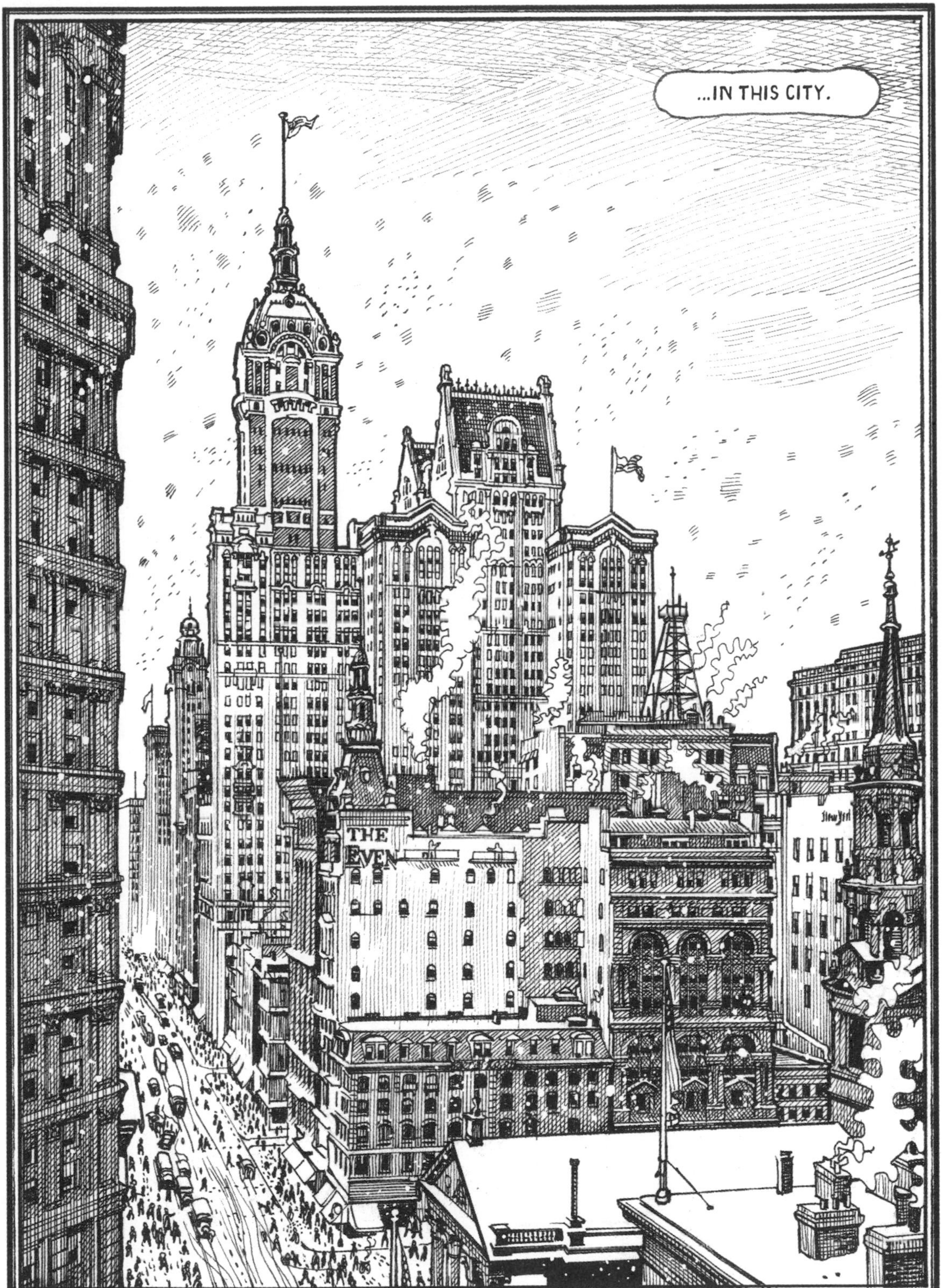
...IN THIS CITY.
THE
EVEN

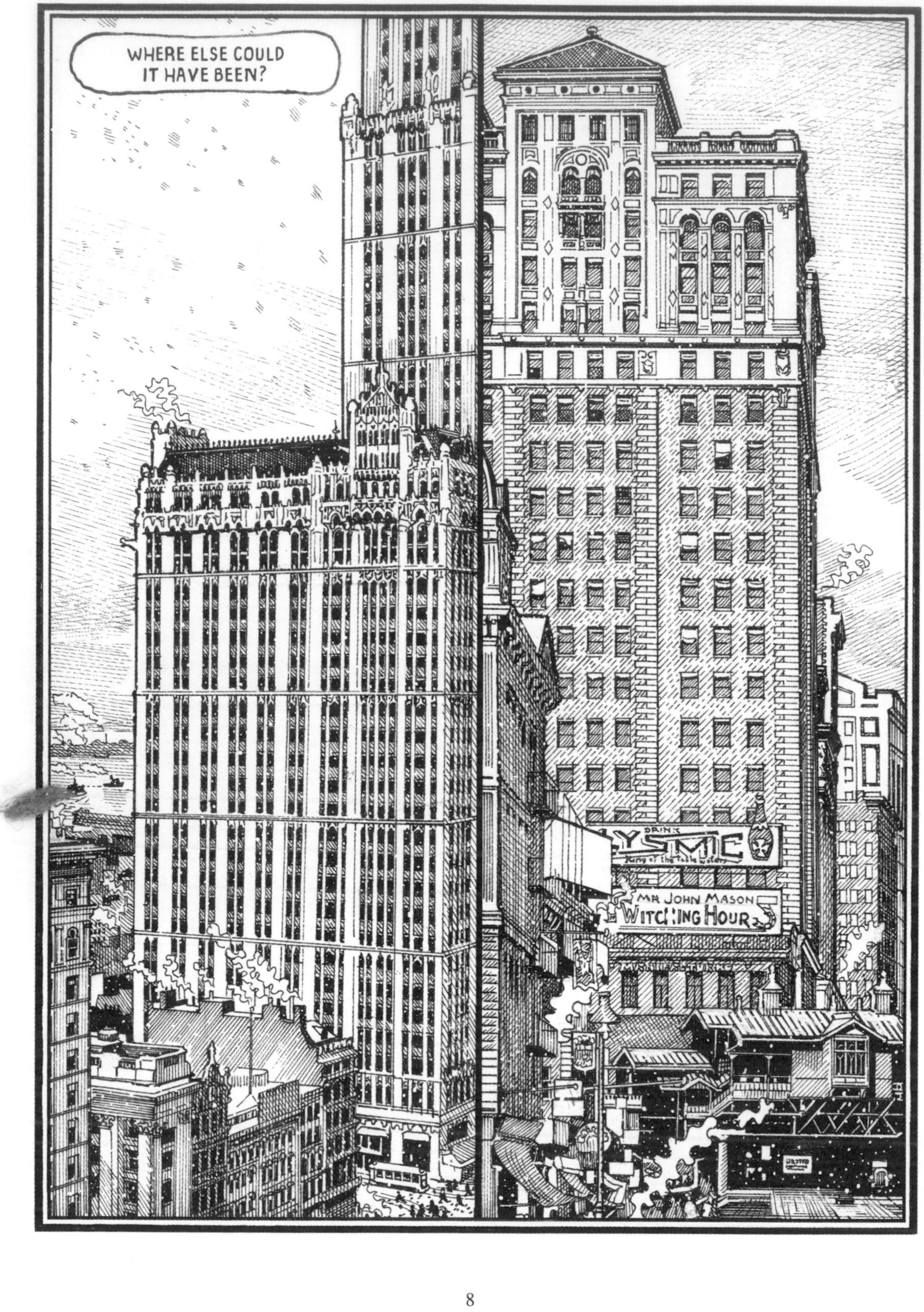
WHERE ELSE COULD IT HAVE BEEN?
DRINK
YSMIC
King of the table waters
MR JOHN MASON
WITCHING HOUR

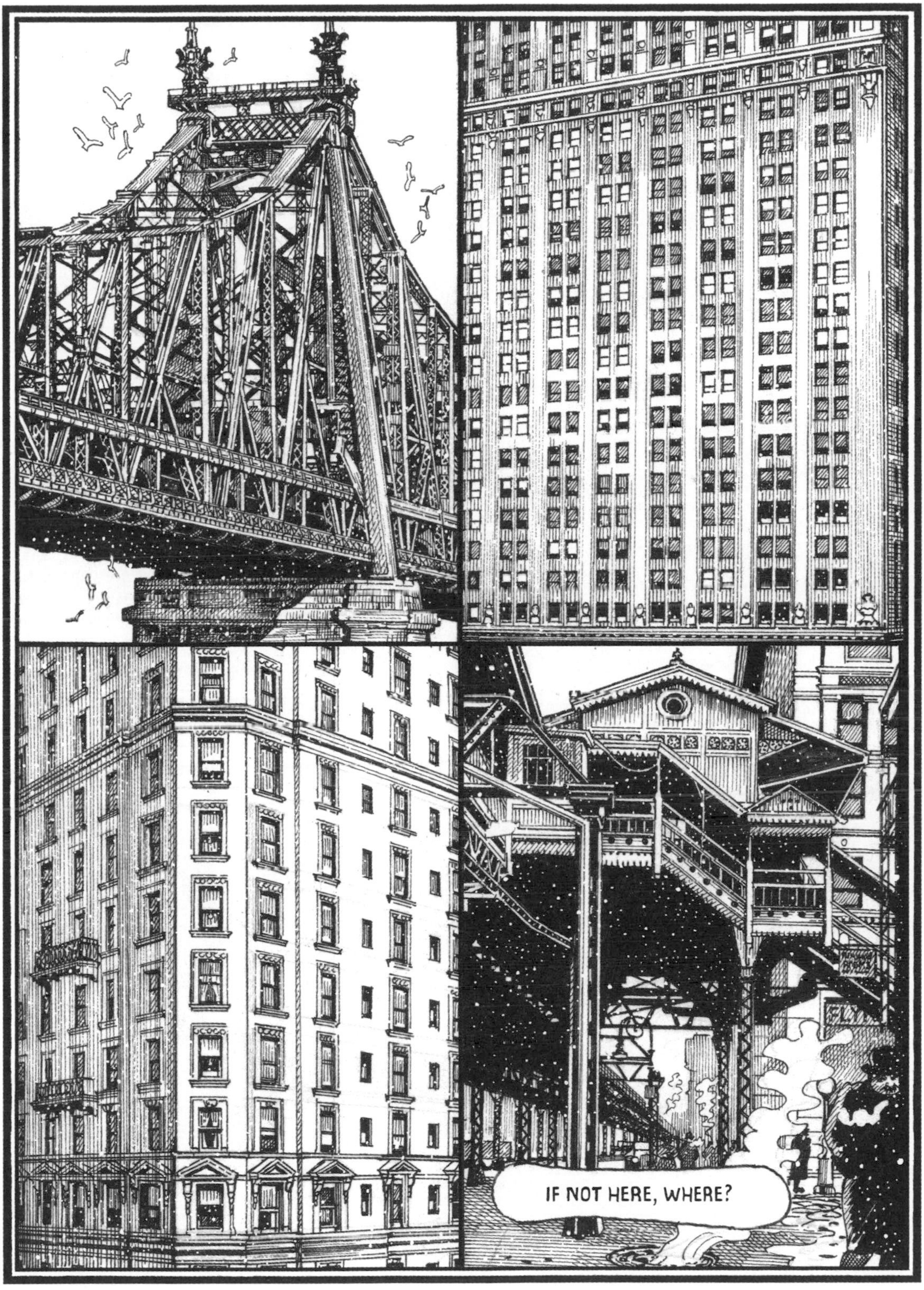
IF NOT HERE, WHERE?

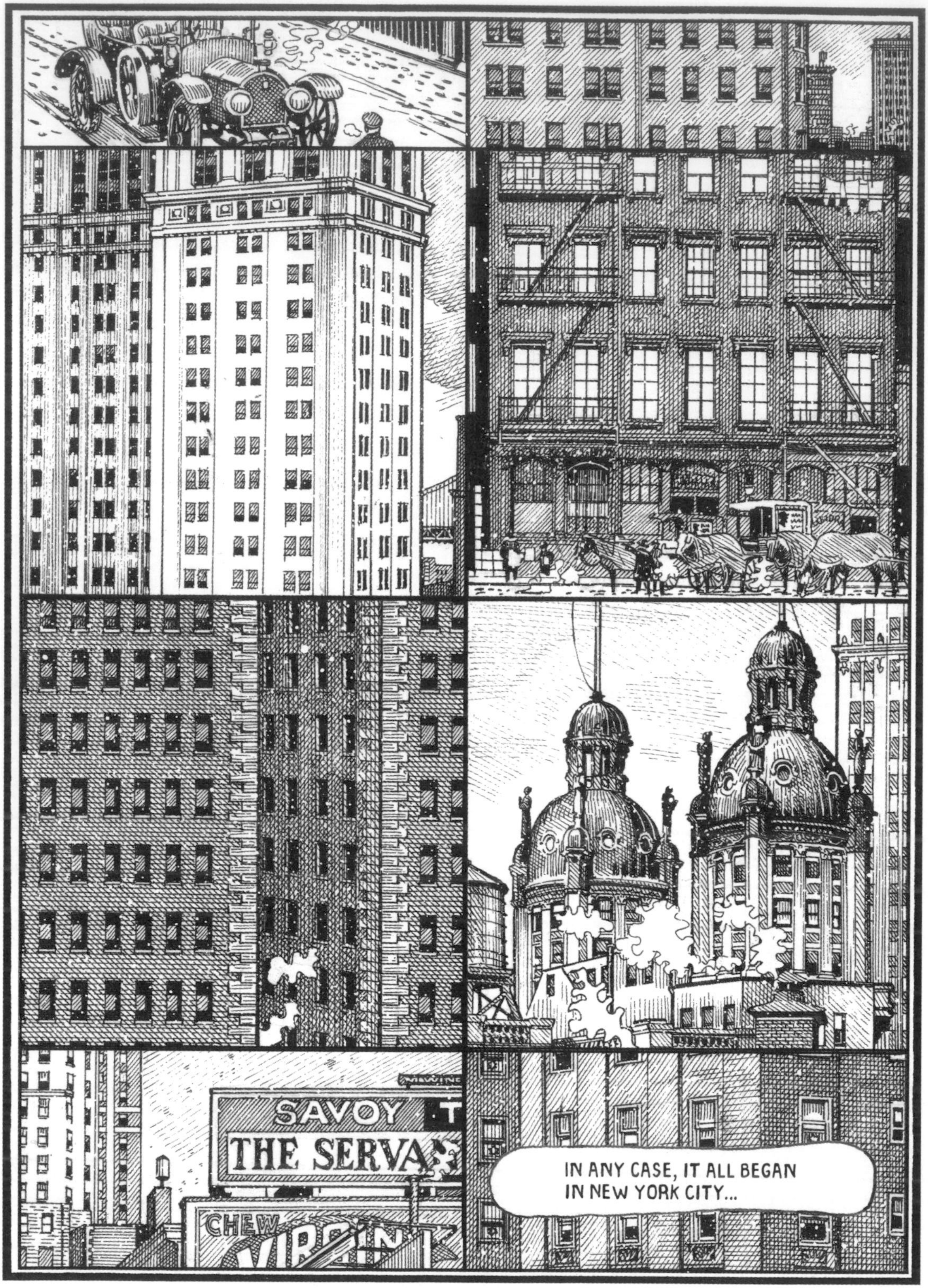
SAVOY
THE SERVA
CHEW
IN ANY CASE, IT ALL BEGAN IN NEW YORK CITY...

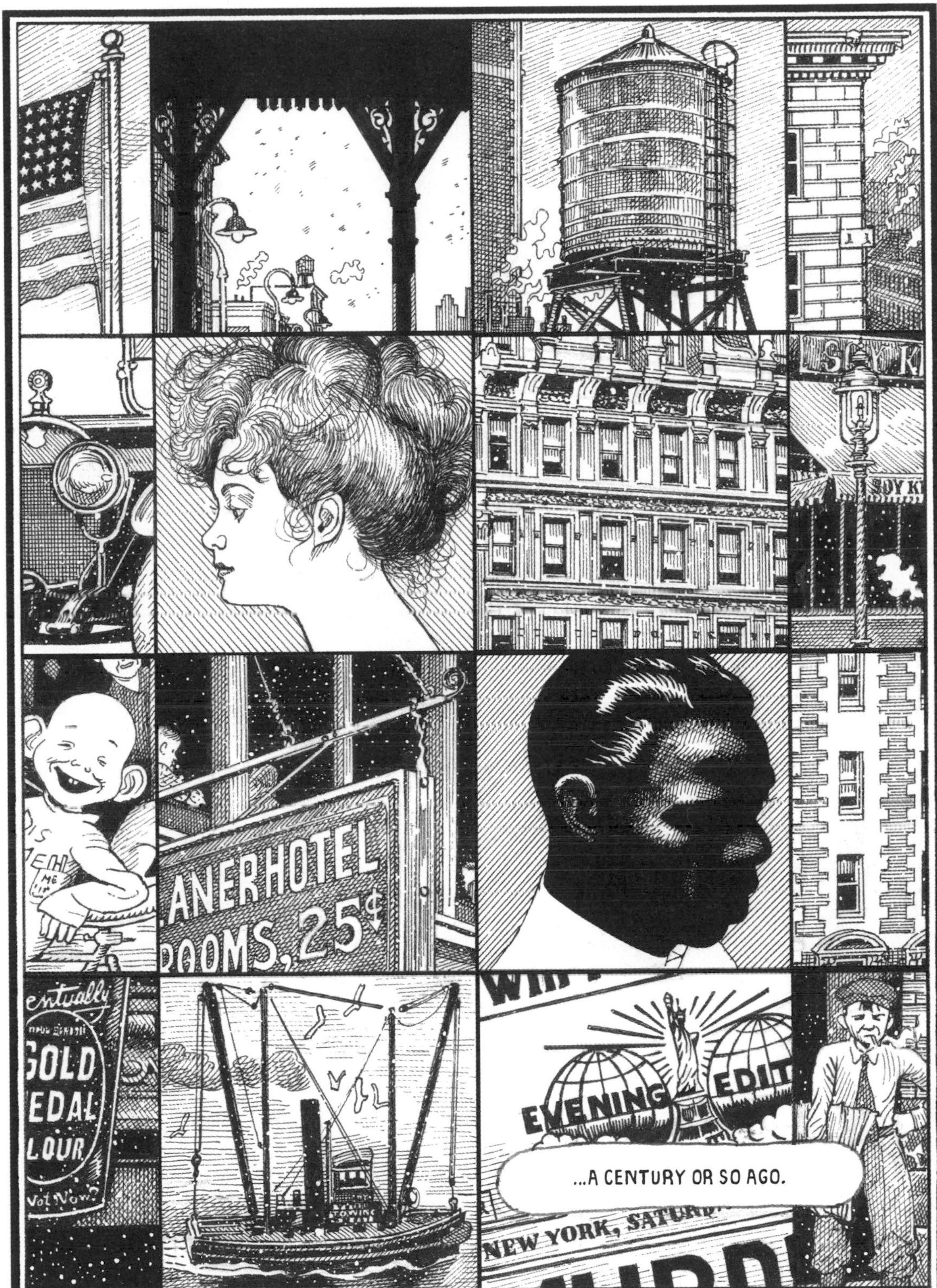

ANERHOTEL
ROOMS, 25¢
GOLD
EDAL
LOUR
EVENING
EDIT
NEW YORK, SATURD
...A CENTURY OR SO AGO.

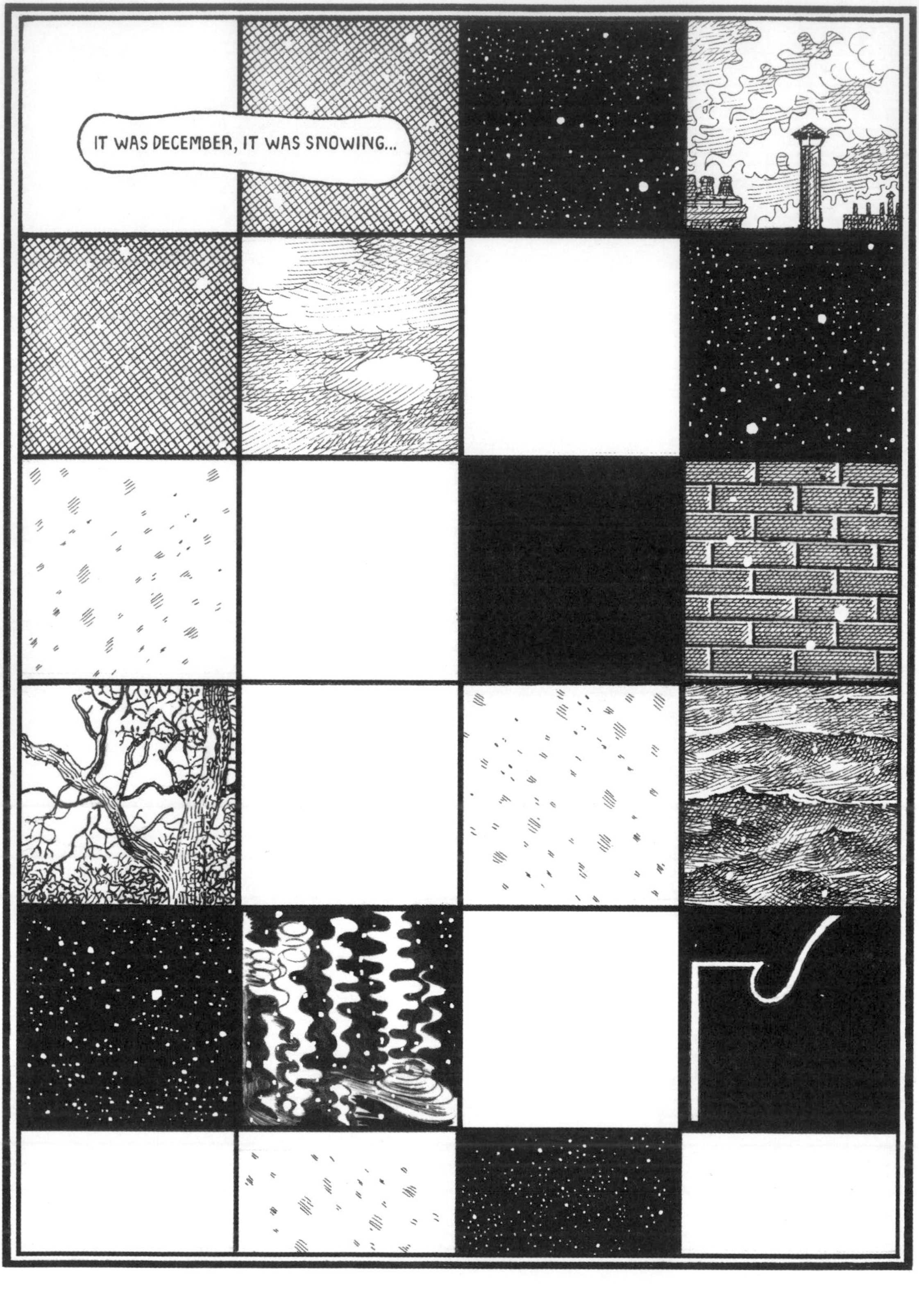
IT WAS DECEMBER, IT WAS SNOWING...

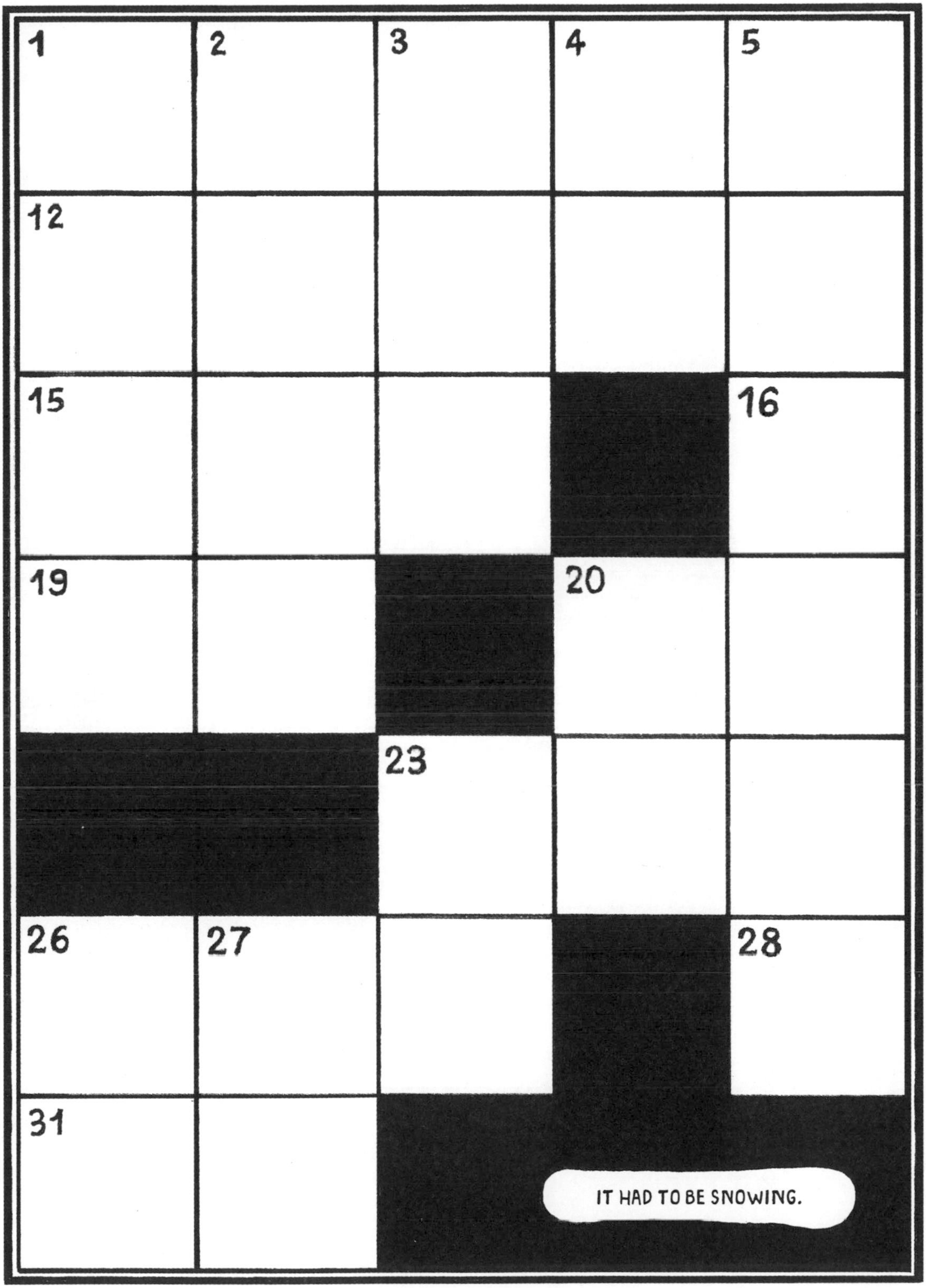
IT HAD TO BE SNOWING.

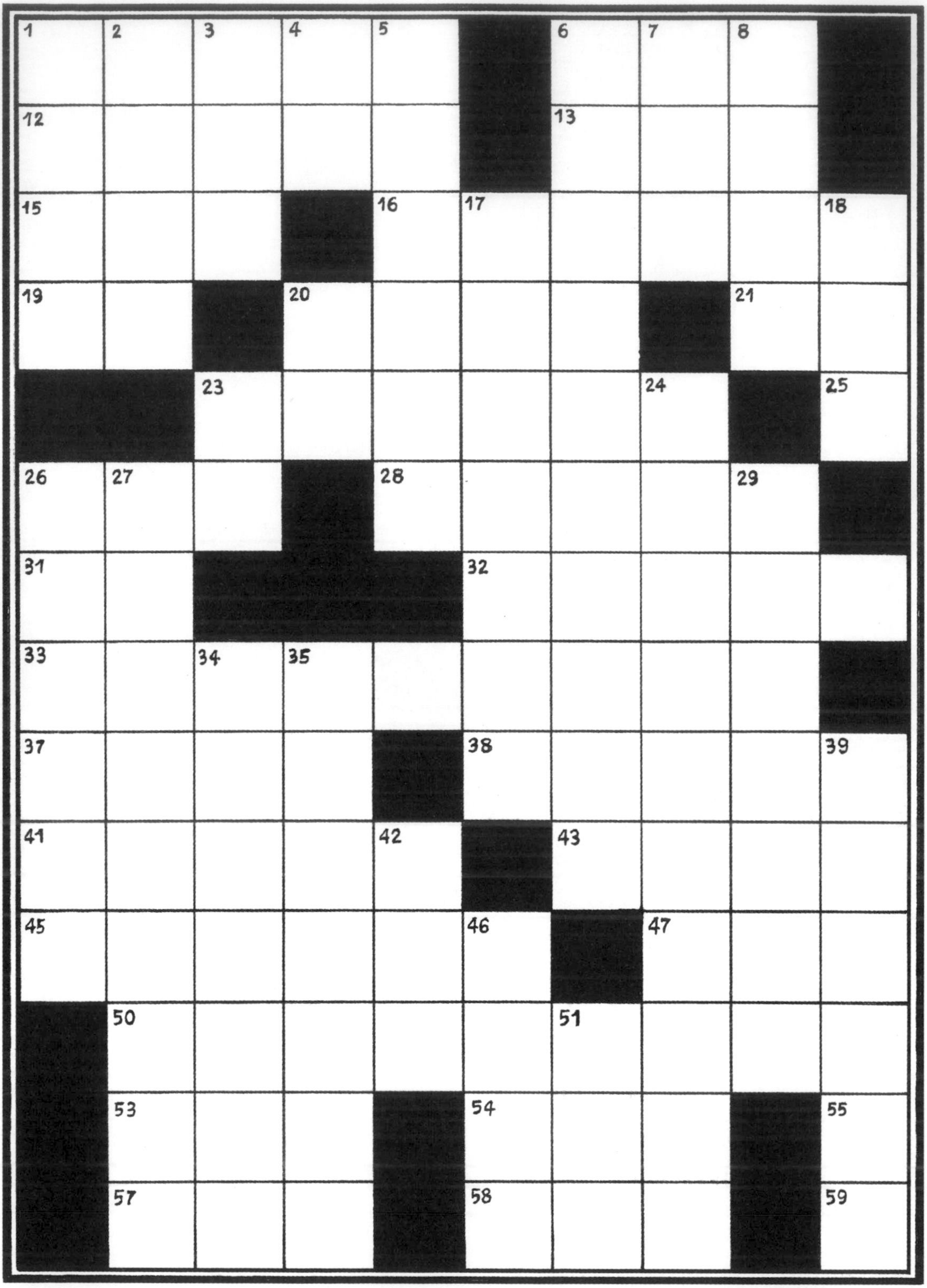

9
10
11
14
22
30
36
40
44
48
49
52
56

PAOLO BACILIERI

FUN

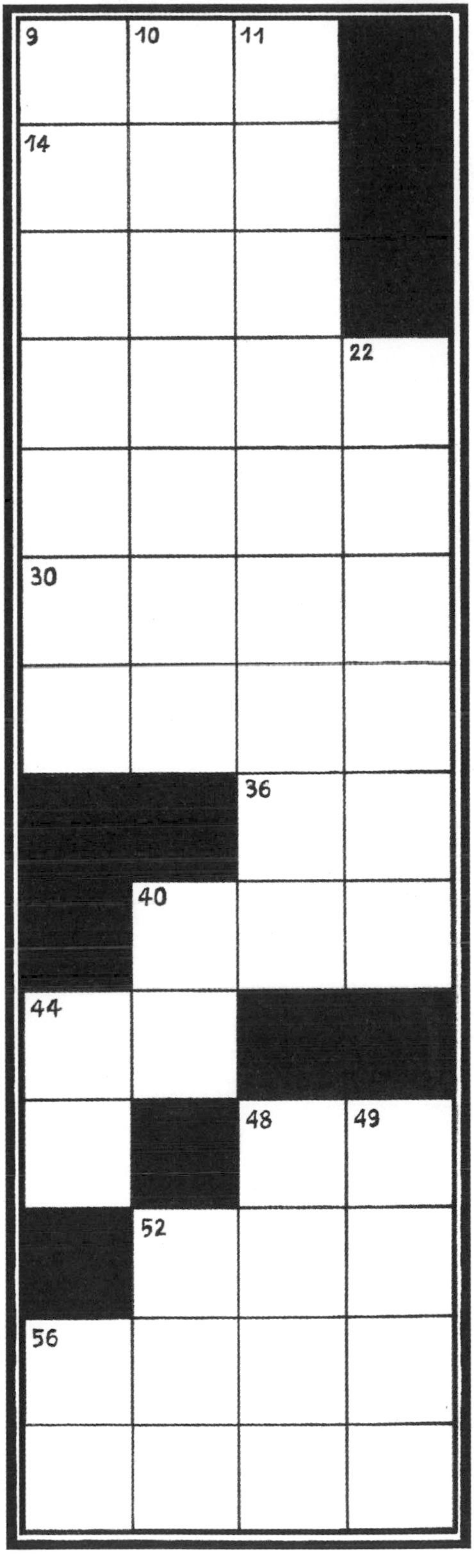

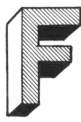

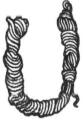

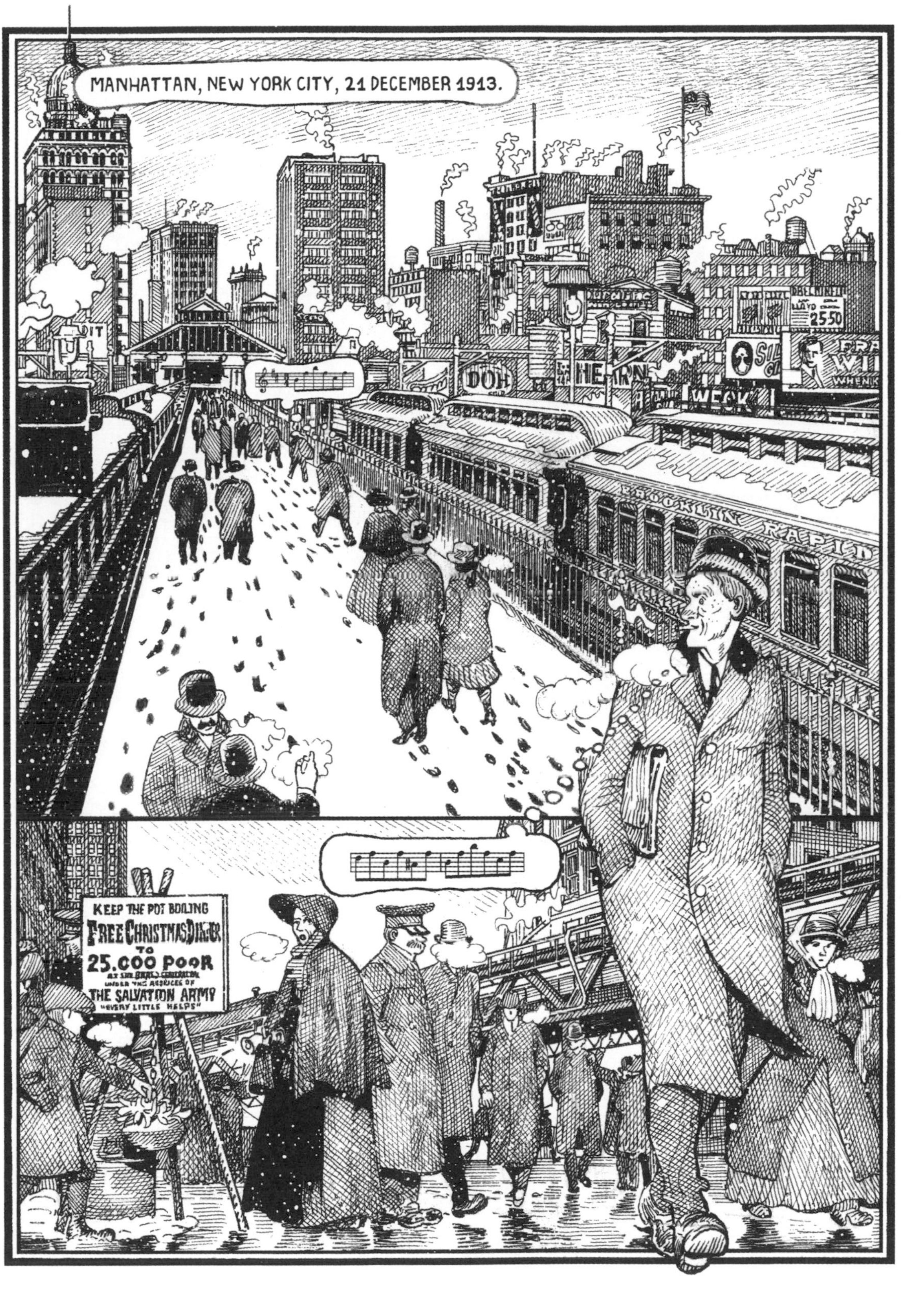
MANHATTAN, NEW YORK CITY, 21 DECEMBER 1913.
BROOKLYN RAPID
KEEP THE POT BOILING
FREE CHRISTMAS DINNER
TO
25,000 POOR
UNDER THE AUSPICES OF
THE SALVATION ARMY
"EVERY LITTLE HELPS"

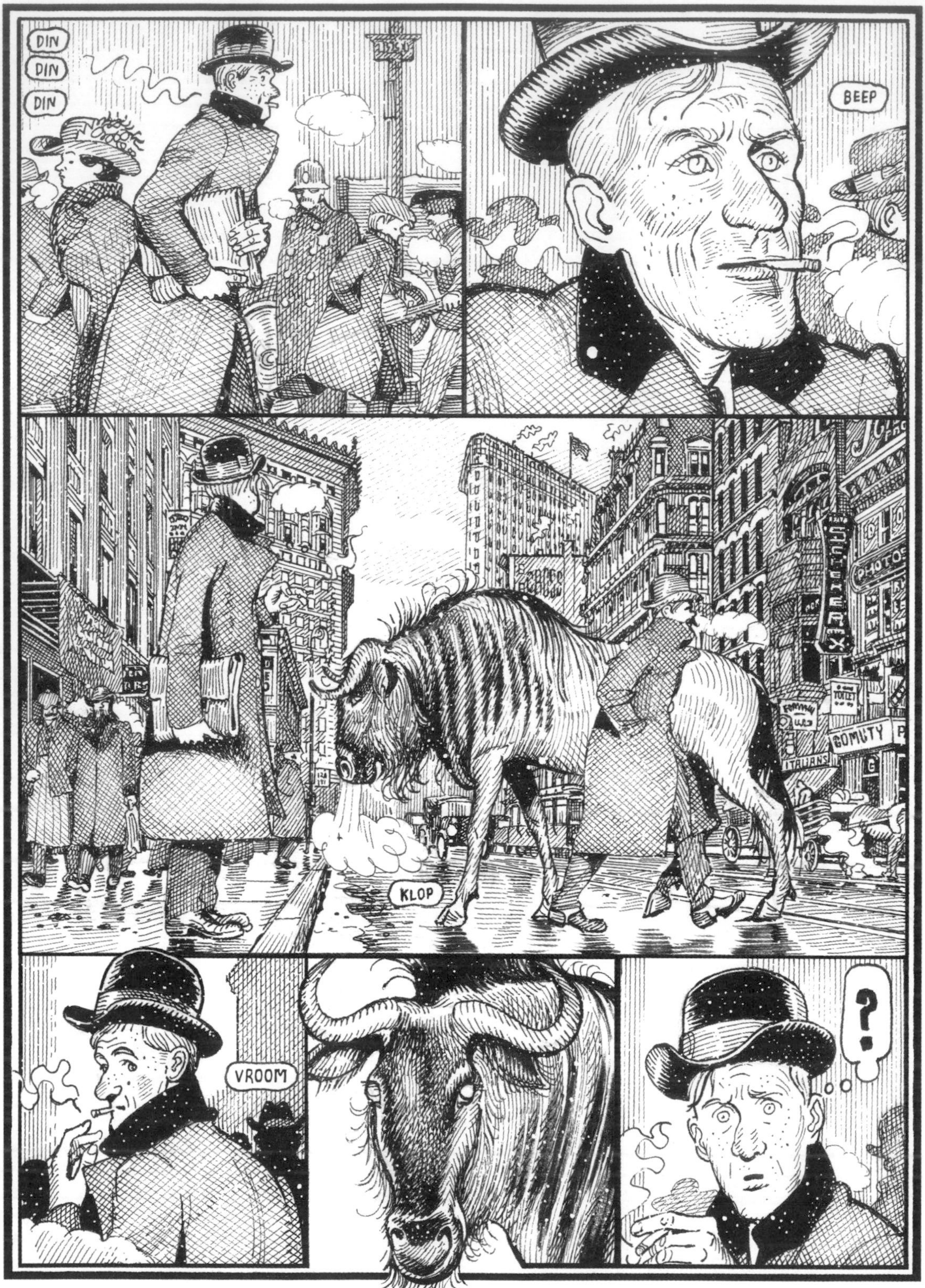
DIN
DIN
DIN
BEEP
PHOTOS
KLOP
VROOM
?

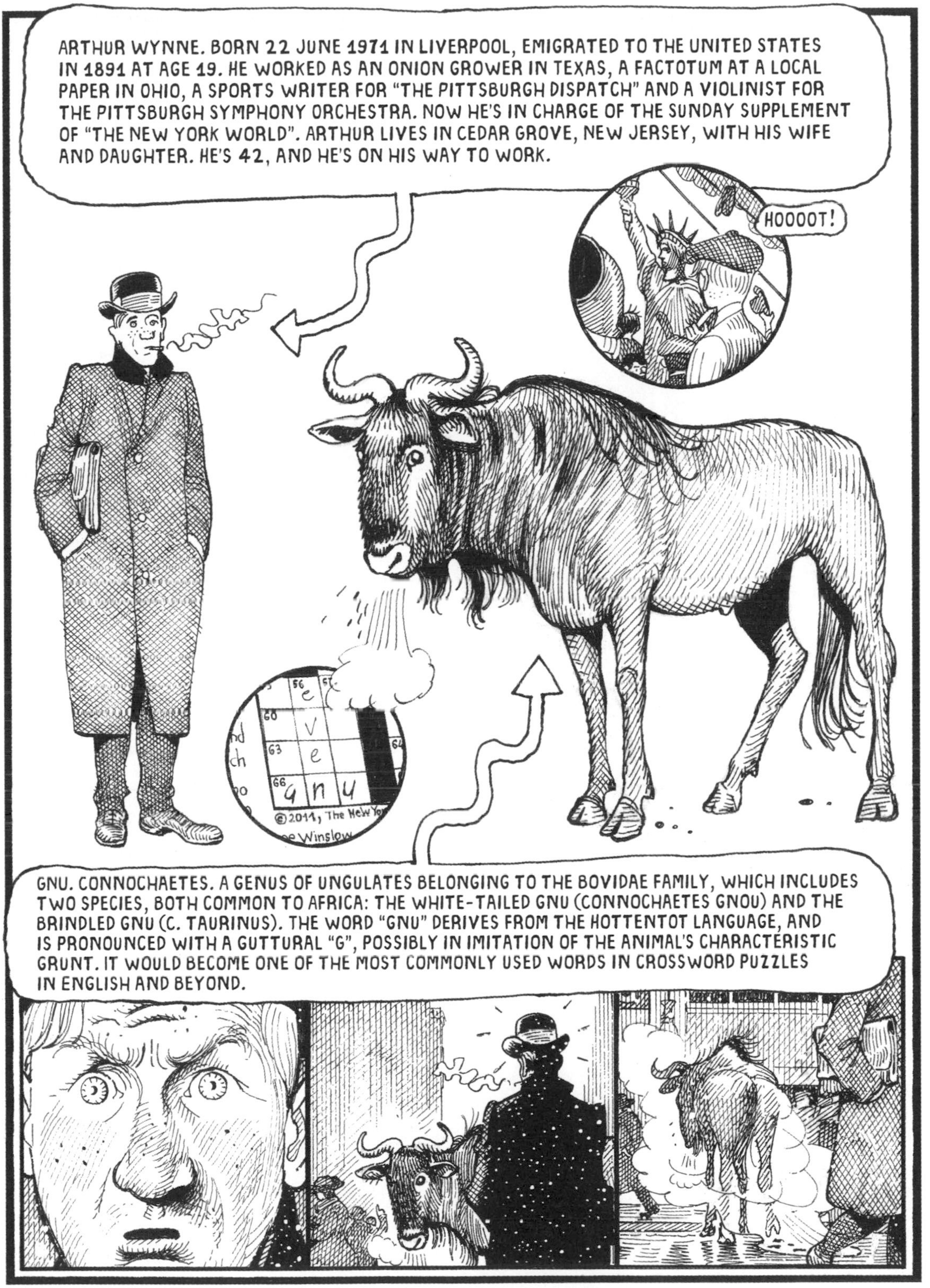
ARTHUR WYNNE. BORN 22 JUNE 1971 IN LIVERPOOL, EMIGRATED TO THE UNITED STATES IN 1891 AT AGE 19. HE WORKED AS AN ONION GROWER IN TEXAS, A FACTOTUM AT A LOCAL PAPER IN OHIO, A SPORTS WRITER FOR "THE PITTSBURGH DISPATCH" AND A VIOLINIST FOR THE PITTSBURGH SYMPHONY ORCHESTRA. NOW HE'S IN CHARGE OF THE SUNDAY SUPPLEMENT OF "THE NEW YORK WORLD". ARTHUR LIVES IN CEDAR GROVE, NEW JERSEY, WITH HIS WIFE AND DAUGHTER. HE'S 42, AND HE'S ON HIS WAY TO WORK.
HOOOOT!
GNU. CONNOCHAETES. A GENUS OF UNGULATES BELONGING TO THE BOVIDAE FAMILY, WHICH INCLUDES TWO SPECIES, BOTH COMMON TO AFRICA: THE WHITE-TAILED GNU (CONNOCHAETES GNOU) AND THE BRINDLED GNU (C. TAURINUS). THE WORD "GNU" DERIVES FROM THE HOTTENTOT LANGUAGE, AND IS PRONOUNCED WITH A GUTTURAL "G", POSSIBLY IN IMITATION OF THE ANIMAL'S CHARACTERISTIC GRUNT. IT WOULD BECOME ONE OF THE MOST COMMONLY USED WORDS IN CROSSWORD PUZZLES IN ENGLISH AND BEYOND.

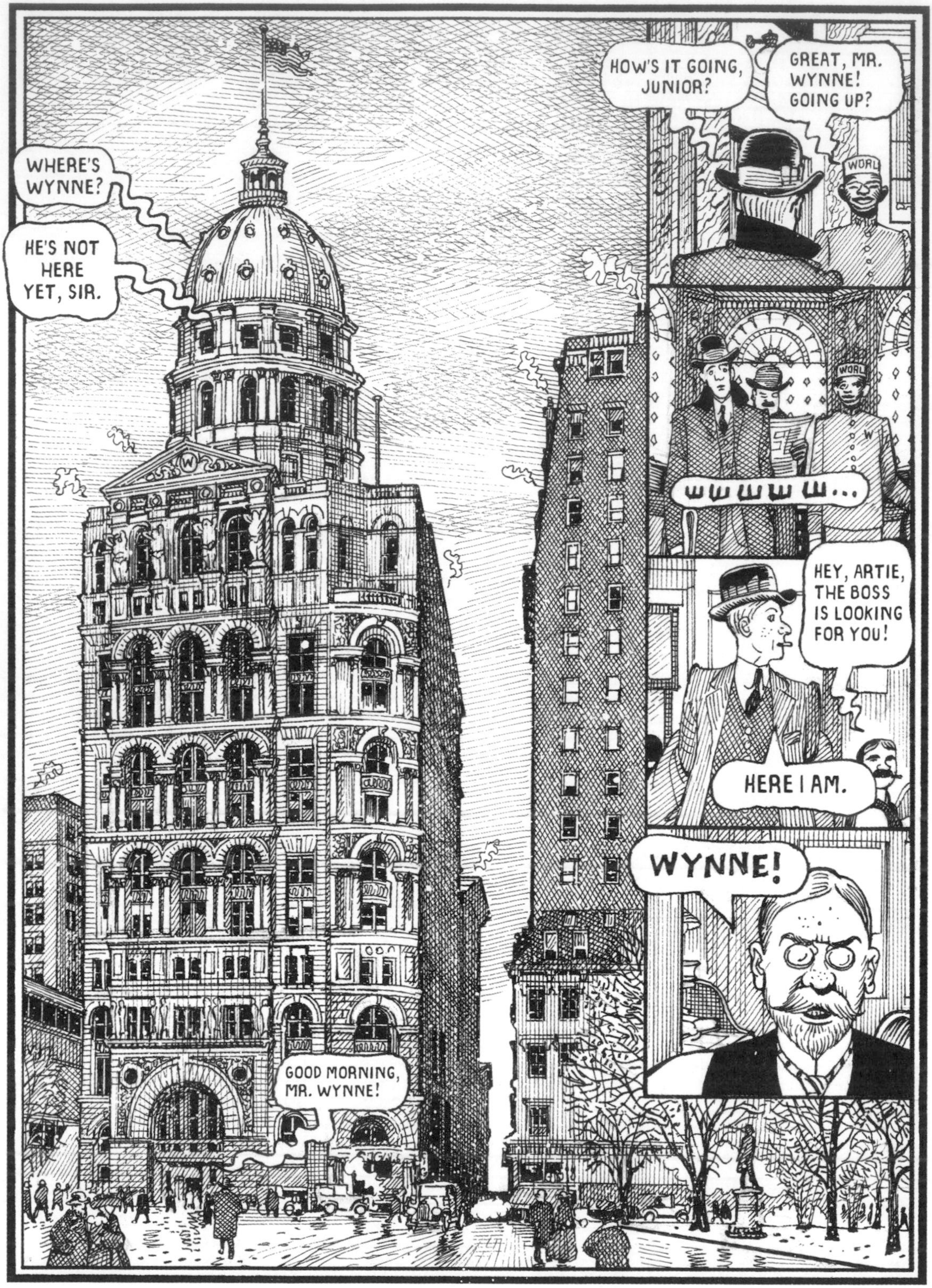
WHERE'S WYNNE?
HE'S NOT HERE YET, SIR.
GOOD MORNING, MR. WYNNE!
HOW'S IT GOING, JUNIOR?
GREAT, MR. WYNNE! GOING UP?
WWWWW...
HEY, ARTIE, THE BOSS IS LOOKING FOR YOU!
HERE I AM.
WYNNE!

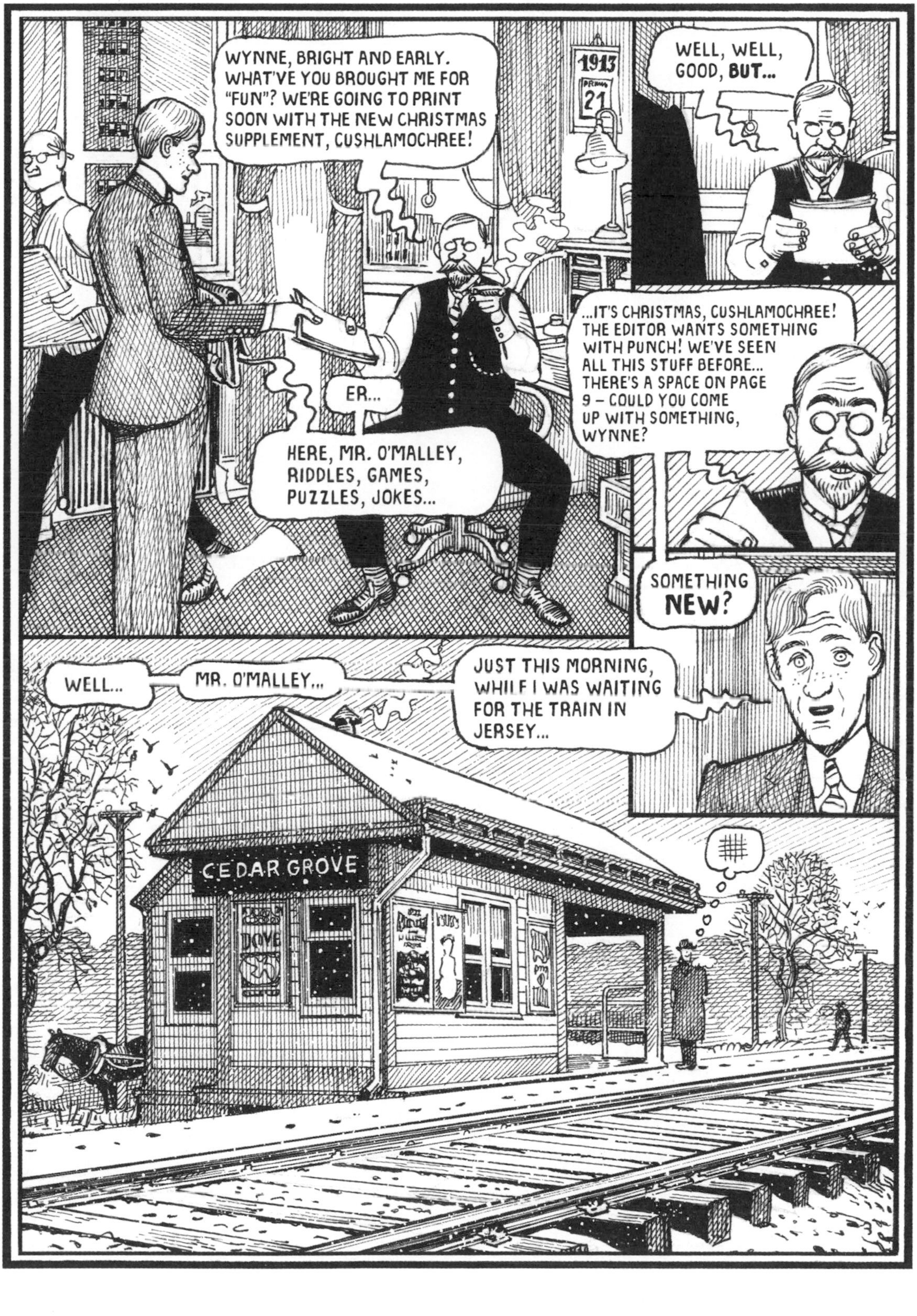
WYNNE, BRIGHT AND EARLY. WHAT'VE YOU BROUGHT ME FOR "FUN"? WE'RE GOING TO PRINT SOON WITH THE NEW CHRISTMAS SUPPLEMENT, CUSHLAMOCHREE!
1913
21
ER...
HERE, MR. O'MALLEY, RIDDLES, GAMES, PUZZLES, JOKES...
WELL, WELL, GOOD, BUT...
...IT'S CHRISTMAS, CUSHLAMOCHREE! THE EDITOR WANTS SOMETHING WITH PUNCH! WE'VE SEEN ALL THIS STUFF BEFORE... THERE'S A SPACE ON PAGE 9 – COULD YOU COME UP WITH SOMETHING, WYNNE?
SOMETHING NEW?
WELL...
MR. O'MALLEY...
JUST THIS MORNING, WHILE I WAS WAITING FOR THE TRAIN IN JERSEY...
CEDAR GROVE
DOVE

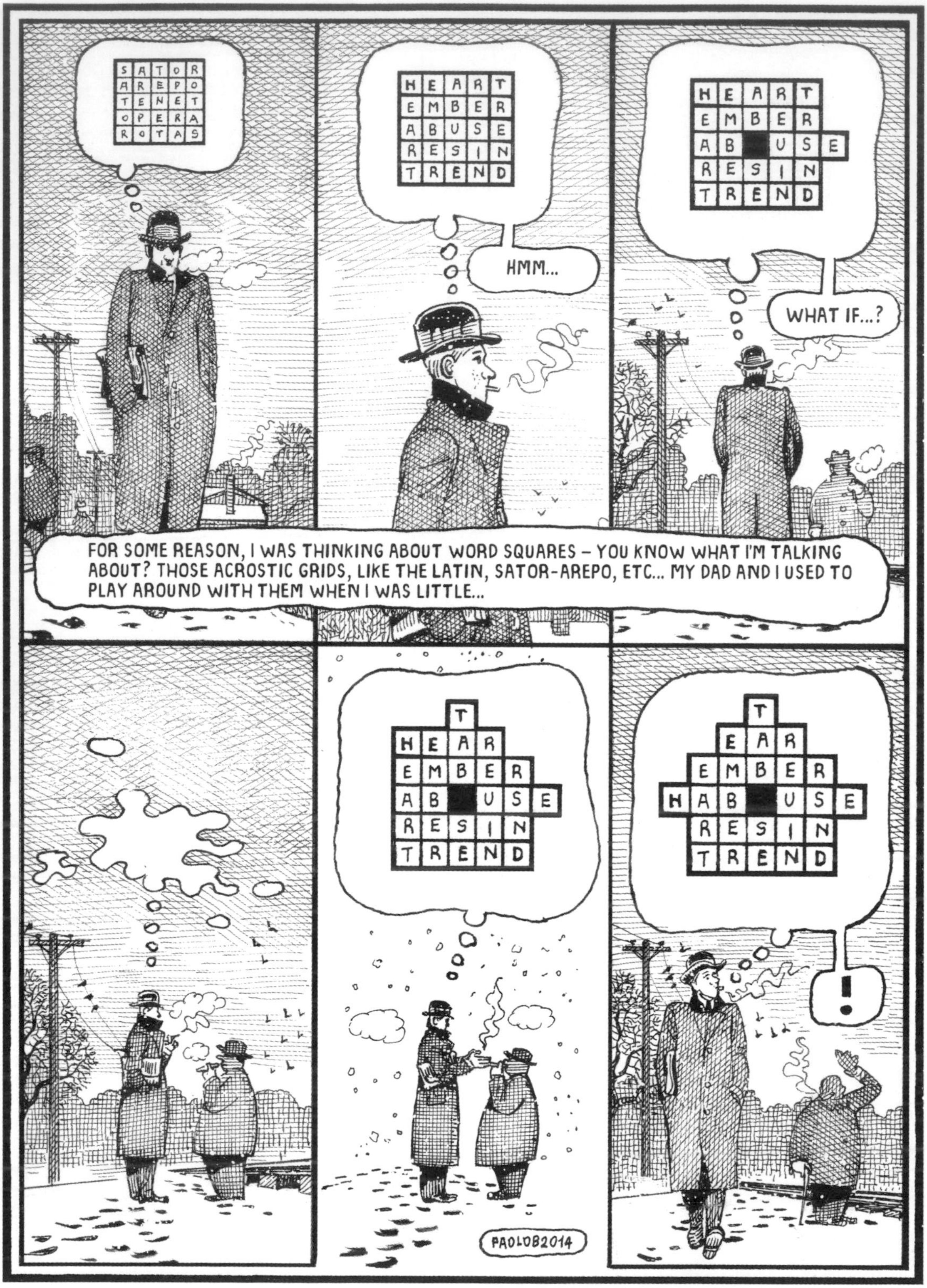

SATOR
AREPO
TENET
OPERA
ROTAS
HEART
EMBER
ABUSE
RESIN
TREND
HMM...
HEART
EMBER
AB USE
RESIN
TREND
WHAT IF...?
FOR SOME REASON, I WAS THINKING ABOUT WORD SQUARES – YOU KNOW WHAT I'M TALKING ABOUT? THOSE ACROSTIC GRIDS, LIKE THE LATIN, SATOR-AREPO, ETC... MY DAD AND I USED TO PLAY AROUND WITH THEM WHEN I WAS LITTLE...
T
HEAR
EMBER
AB USE
RESIN
TREND
T
EAR
EMBER
HAB USE
RESIN
TREND
!
PAOLOB2014

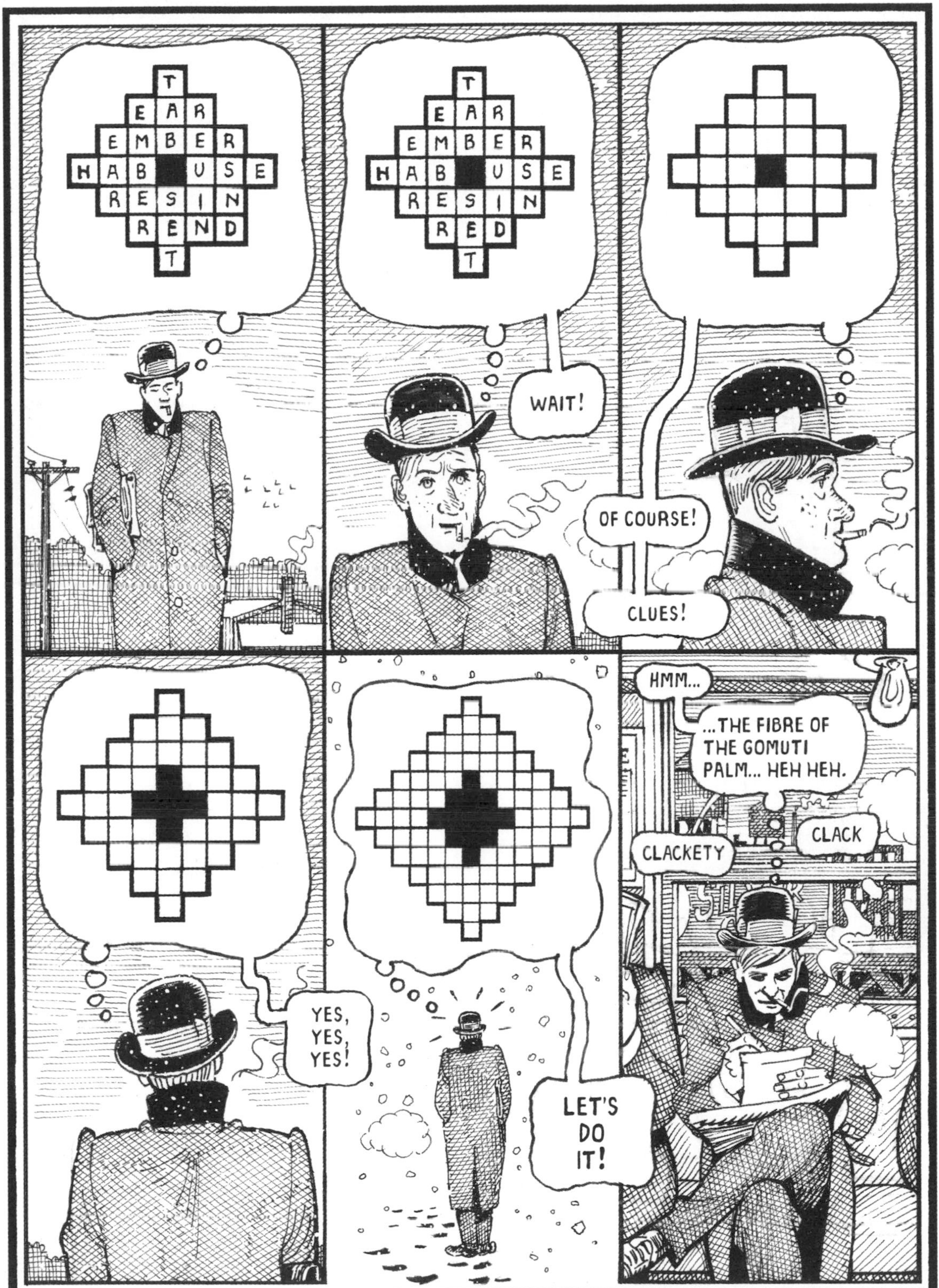
WAIT!
OF COURSE!
CLUES!
YES, YES, YES!
LET'S DO IT!
HMM...
...THE FIBRE OF THE GOMUTI PALM... HEH HEH.
CLACKETY
CLACK

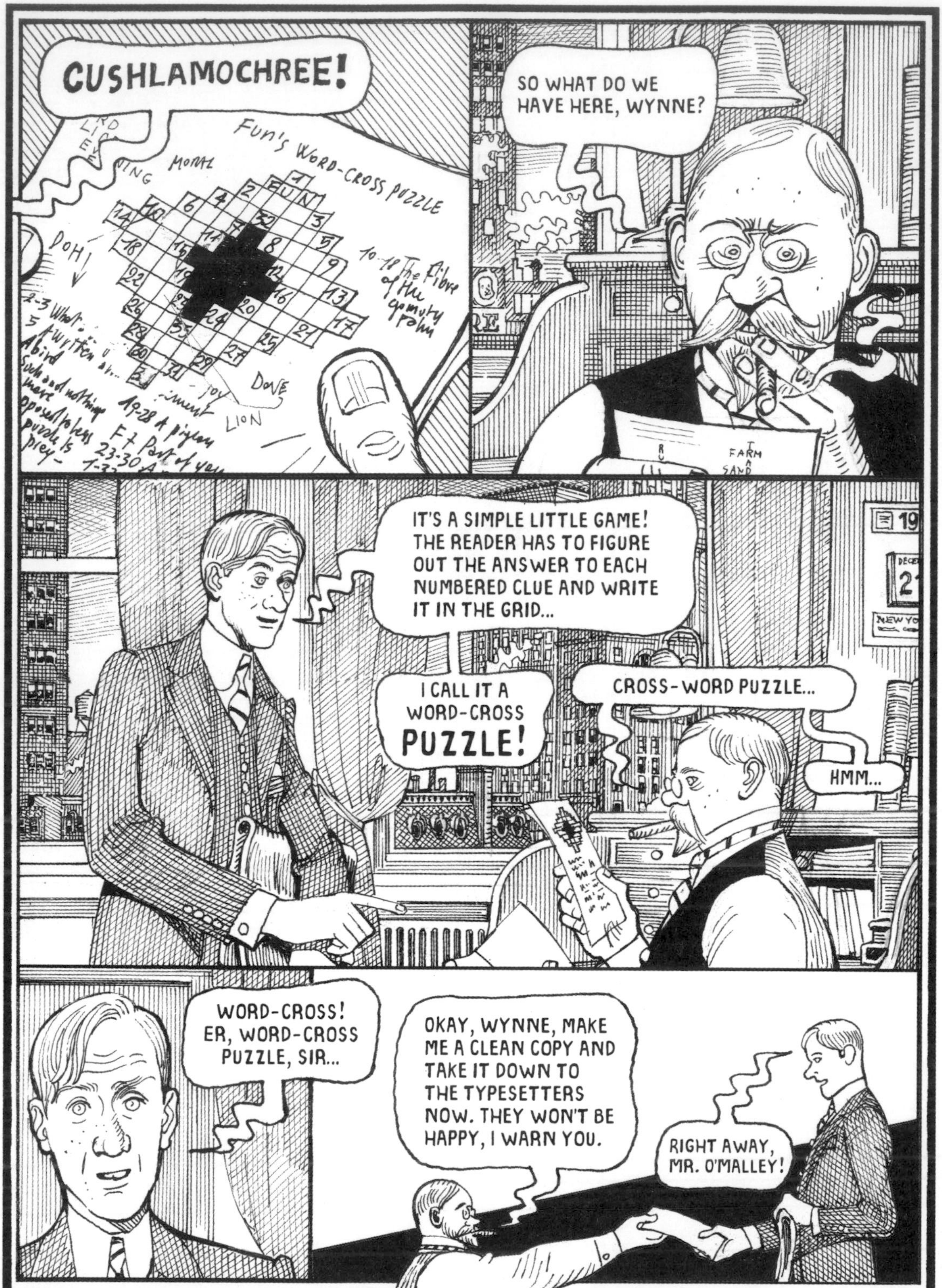
CUSHLAMOCHREE!
Fun's Word-Cross Puzzle
SO WHAT DO WE HAVE HERE, WYNNE?
IT'S A SIMPLE LITTLE GAME! THE READER HAS TO FIGURE OUT THE ANSWER TO EACH NUMBERED CLUE AND WRITE IT IN THE GRID...
I CALL IT A WORD-CROSS PUZZLE!
CROSS-WORD PUZZLE...
HMM...
WORD-CROSS! ER, WORD-CROSS PUZZLE, SIR...
OKAY, WYNNE, MAKE ME A CLEAN COPY AND TAKE IT DOWN TO THE TYPESETTERS NOW. THEY WON'T BE HAPPY, I WARN YOU.
RIGHT AWAY, MR. O'MALLEY!

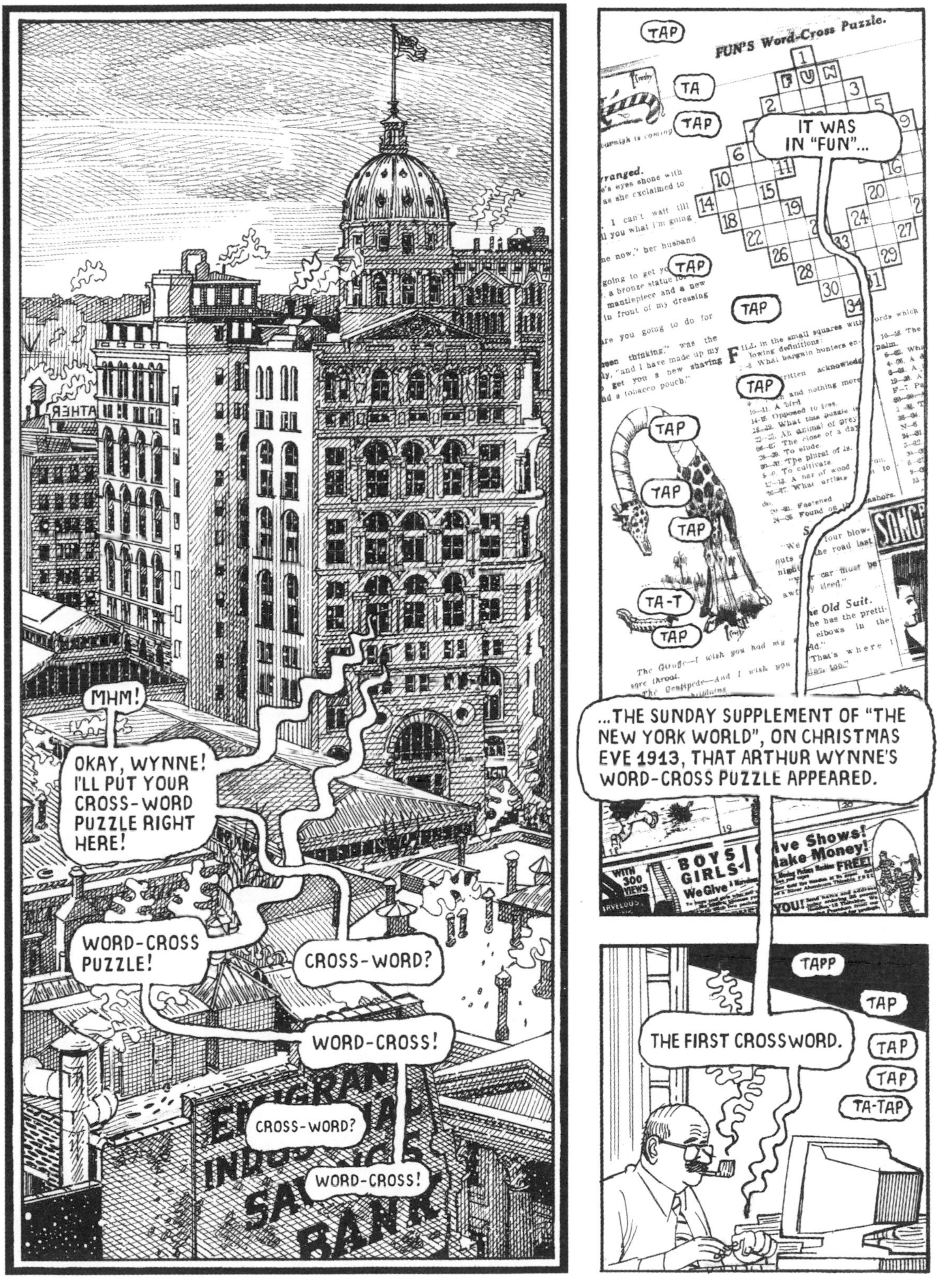
MHM!
OKAY, WYNNE! I'LL PUT YOUR CROSS-WORD PUZZLE RIGHT HERE!
WORD-CROSS PUZZLE!
CROSS-WORD?
WORD-CROSS!
CROSS-WORD?
WORD-CROSS!
TAP
FUN'S Word-Cross Puzzle.
TA
TAP
IT WAS IN "FUN"...
TAP
TAP
TAP
TAP
TAP
TAP
TA-T
TAP
...THE SUNDAY SUPPLEMENT OF "THE NEW YORK WORLD", ON CHRISTMAS EVE 1913, THAT ARTHUR WYNNE'S WORD-CROSS PUZZLE APPEARED.
TAPP
TAP
THE FIRST CROSSWORD.
TAP
TAP
TA-TAP

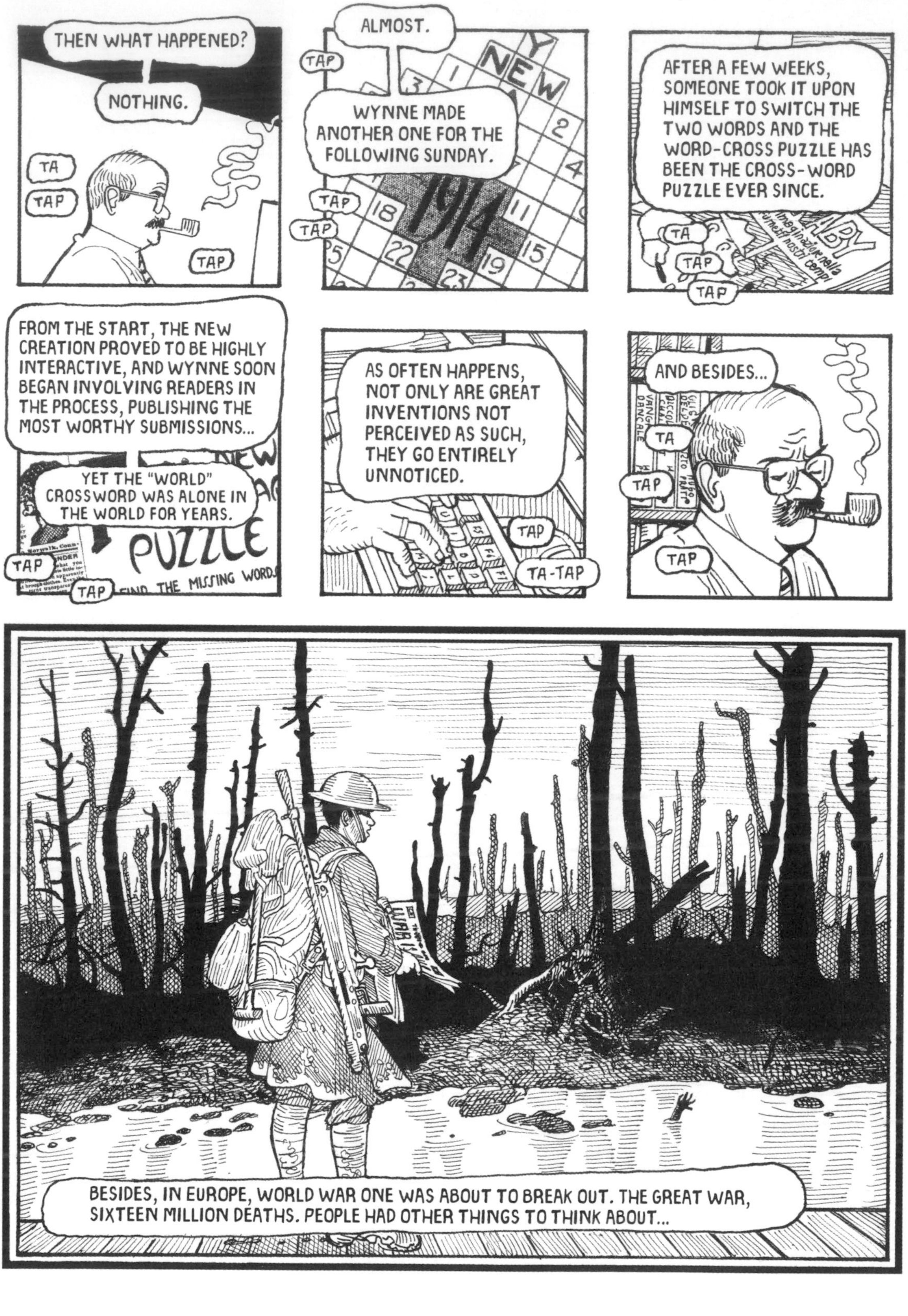
THEN WHAT HAPPENED?
NOTHING.
TA
TAP
TAP
ALMOST.
TAP
WYNNE MADE ANOTHER ONE FOR THE FOLLOWING SUNDAY.
TAP
TAP
NEW
1914
AFTER A FEW WEEKS, SOMEONE TOOK IT UPON HIMSELF TO SWITCH THE TWO WORDS AND THE WORD-CROSS PUZZLE HAS BEEN THE CROSS-WORD PUZZLE EVER SINCE.
TA
TAP
TAP
FROM THE START, THE NEW CREATION PROVED TO BE HIGHLY INTERACTIVE, AND WYNNE SOON BEGAN INVOLVING READERS IN THE PROCESS, PUBLISHING THE MOST WORTHY SUBMISSIONS...
YET THE "WORLD" CROSSWORD WAS ALONE IN THE WORLD FOR YEARS.
PUZZLE
FIND THE MISSING WORDS
TAP
TAP
AS OFTEN HAPPENS, NOT ONLY ARE GREAT INVENTIONS NOT PERCEIVED AS SUCH, THEY GO ENTIRELY UNNOTICED.
TAP
TA-TAP
AND BESIDES...
TA
TAP
TAP
BESIDES, IN EUROPE, WORLD WAR ONE WAS ABOUT TO BREAK OUT. THE GREAT WAR, SIXTEEN MILLION DEATHS. PEOPLE HAD OTHER THINGS TO THINK ABOUT...

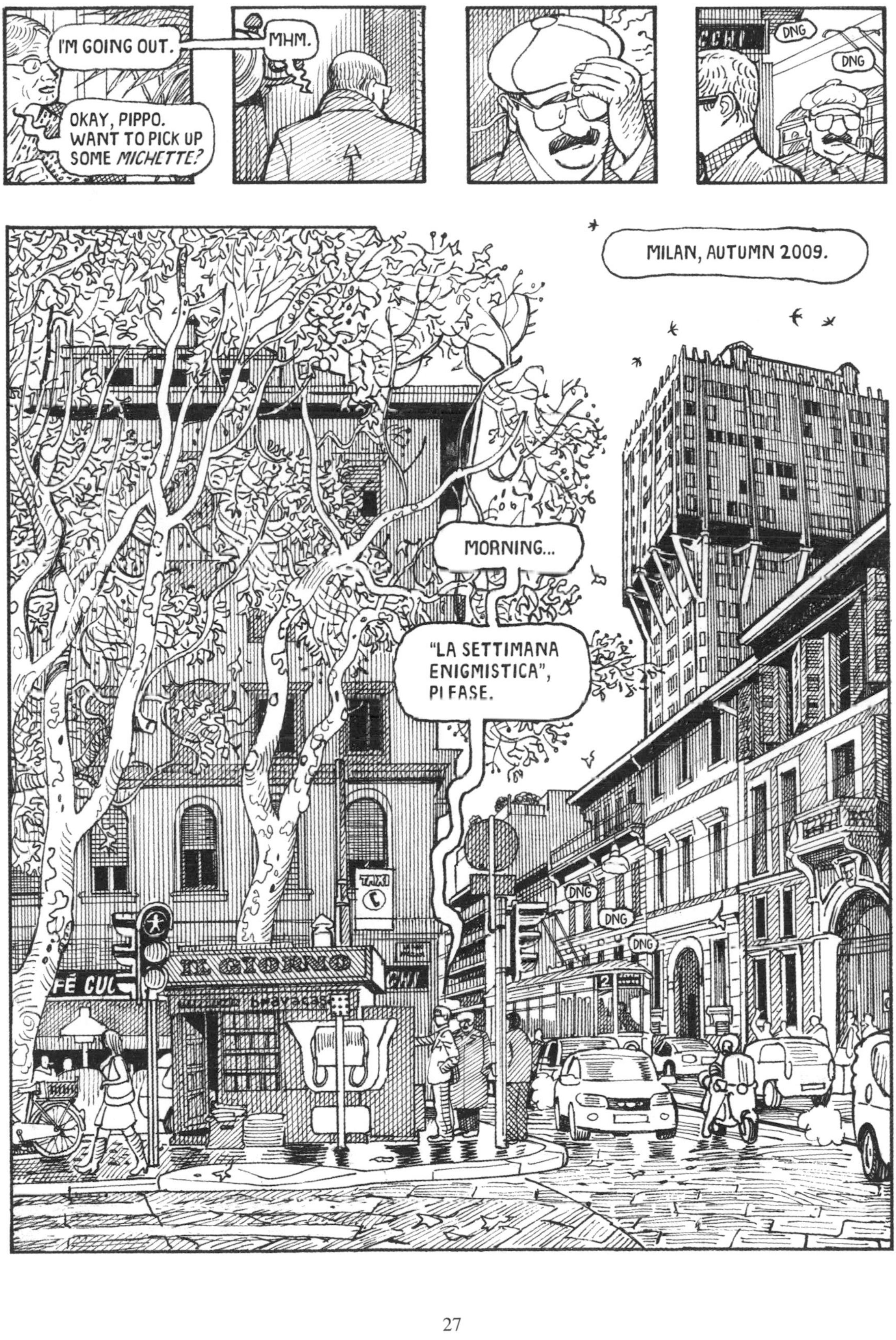
I'M GOING OUT.
MHM.
OKAY, PIPPO. WANT TO PICK UP SOME *MICHETTE?*
DNG
DNG
MILAN, AUTUMN 2009.
MORNING...
"LA SETTIMANA ENIGMISTICA", PLEASE.
TAXI
IL GIORNO
DNG
DNG
DNG
2

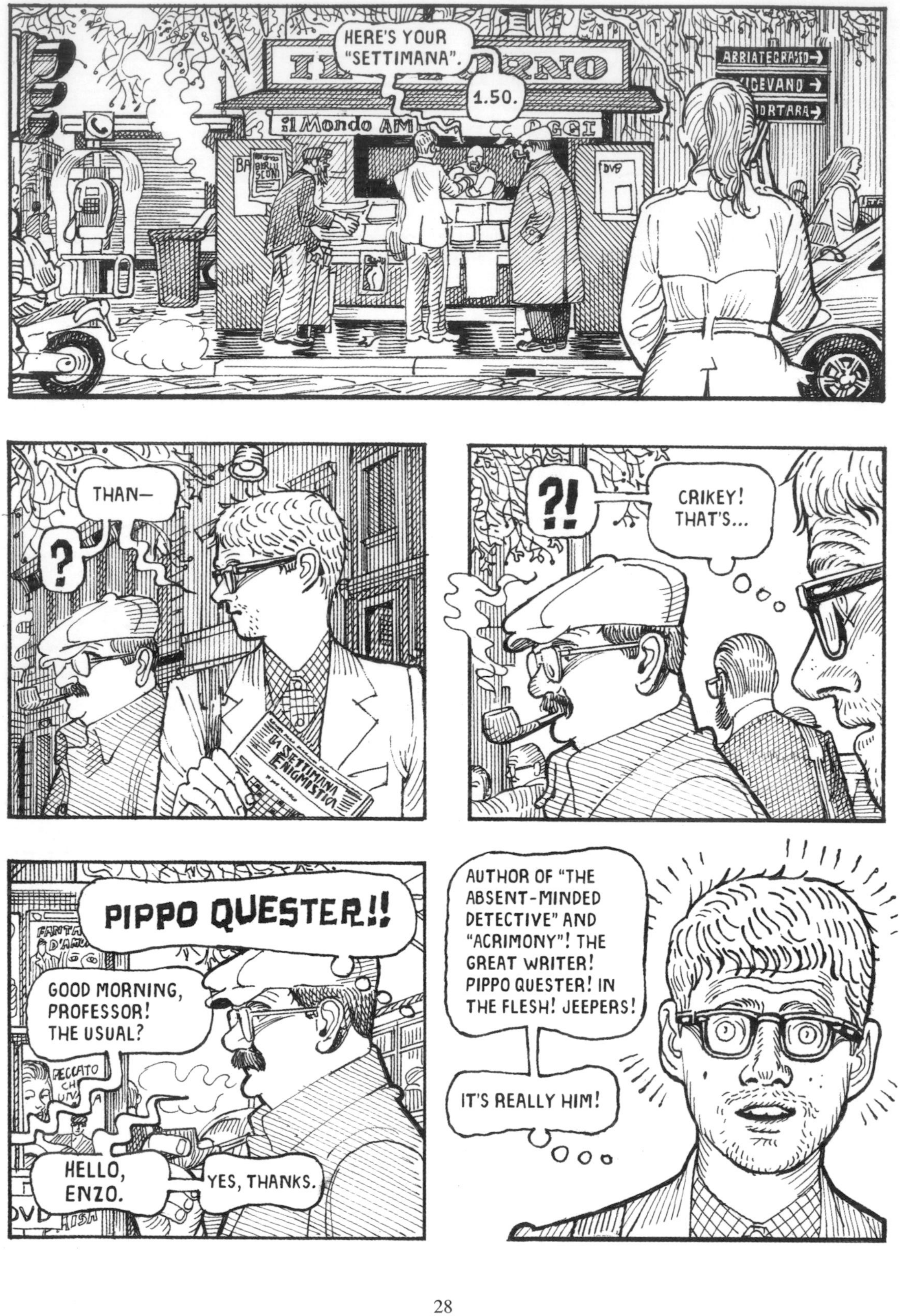
HERE'S YOUR "SETTIMANA".
1.50.
il Mondo AM
OGGI
THAN—
?
LA SETTIMANA ENIGMISTICA
?!
CRIKEY! THAT'S...
PIPPO QUESTER!!
GOOD MORNING, PROFESSOR! THE USUAL?
HELLO, ENZO.
YES, THANKS.
AUTHOR OF "THE ABSENT-MINDED DETECTIVE" AND "ACRIMONY"! THE GREAT WRITER! PIPPO QUESTER! IN THE FLESH! JEEPERS!
IT'S REALLY HIM!

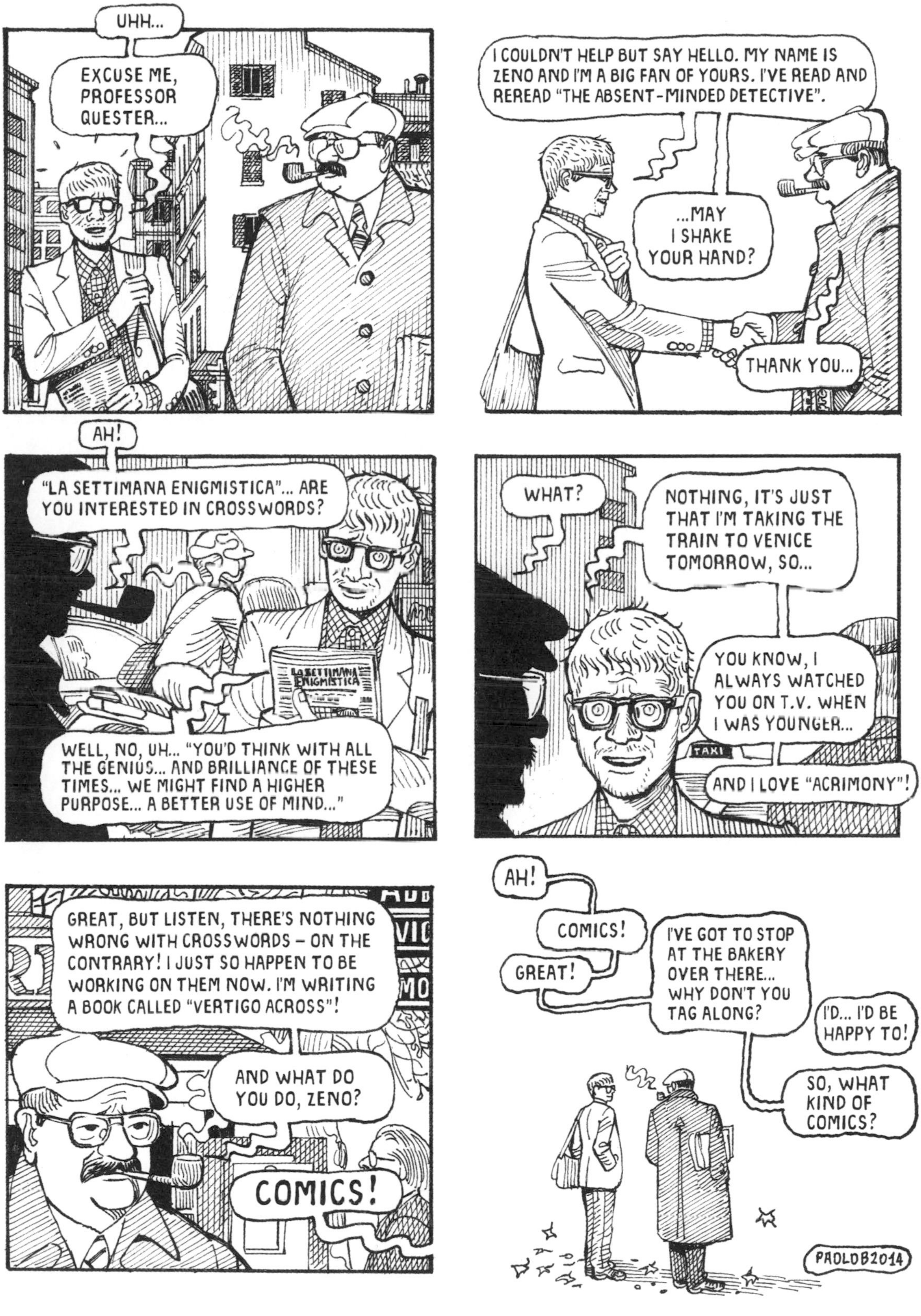
UHH...
EXCUSE ME, PROFESSOR QUESTER...
I COULDN'T HELP BUT SAY HELLO. MY NAME IS ZENO AND I'M A BIG FAN OF YOURS. I'VE READ AND REREAD "THE ABSENT-MINDED DETECTIVE".
...MAY I SHAKE YOUR HAND?
THANK YOU...
AH!
"LA SETTIMANA ENIGMISTICA"... ARE YOU INTERESTED IN CROSSWORDS?
LA SETTIMANA ENIGMISTICA
WELL, NO, UH... "YOU'D THINK WITH ALL THE GENIUS... AND BRILLIANCE OF THESE TIMES... WE MIGHT FIND A HIGHER PURPOSE... A BETTER USE OF MIND..."
WHAT?
NOTHING, IT'S JUST THAT I'M TAKING THE TRAIN TO VENICE TOMORROW, SO...
YOU KNOW, I ALWAYS WATCHED YOU ON T.V. WHEN I WAS YOUNGER...
TAXI
AND I LOVE "ACRIMONY"!
GREAT, BUT LISTEN, THERE'S NOTHING WRONG WITH CROSSWORDS – ON THE CONTRARY! I JUST SO HAPPEN TO BE WORKING ON THEM NOW. I'M WRITING A BOOK CALLED "VERTIGO ACROSS"!
AND WHAT DO YOU DO, ZENO?
COMICS!
AH!
COMICS!
GREAT!
I'VE GOT TO STOP AT THE BAKERY OVER THERE... WHY DON'T YOU TAG ALONG?
I'D... I'D BE HAPPY TO!
SO, WHAT KIND OF COMICS?
PAOLO B 2014

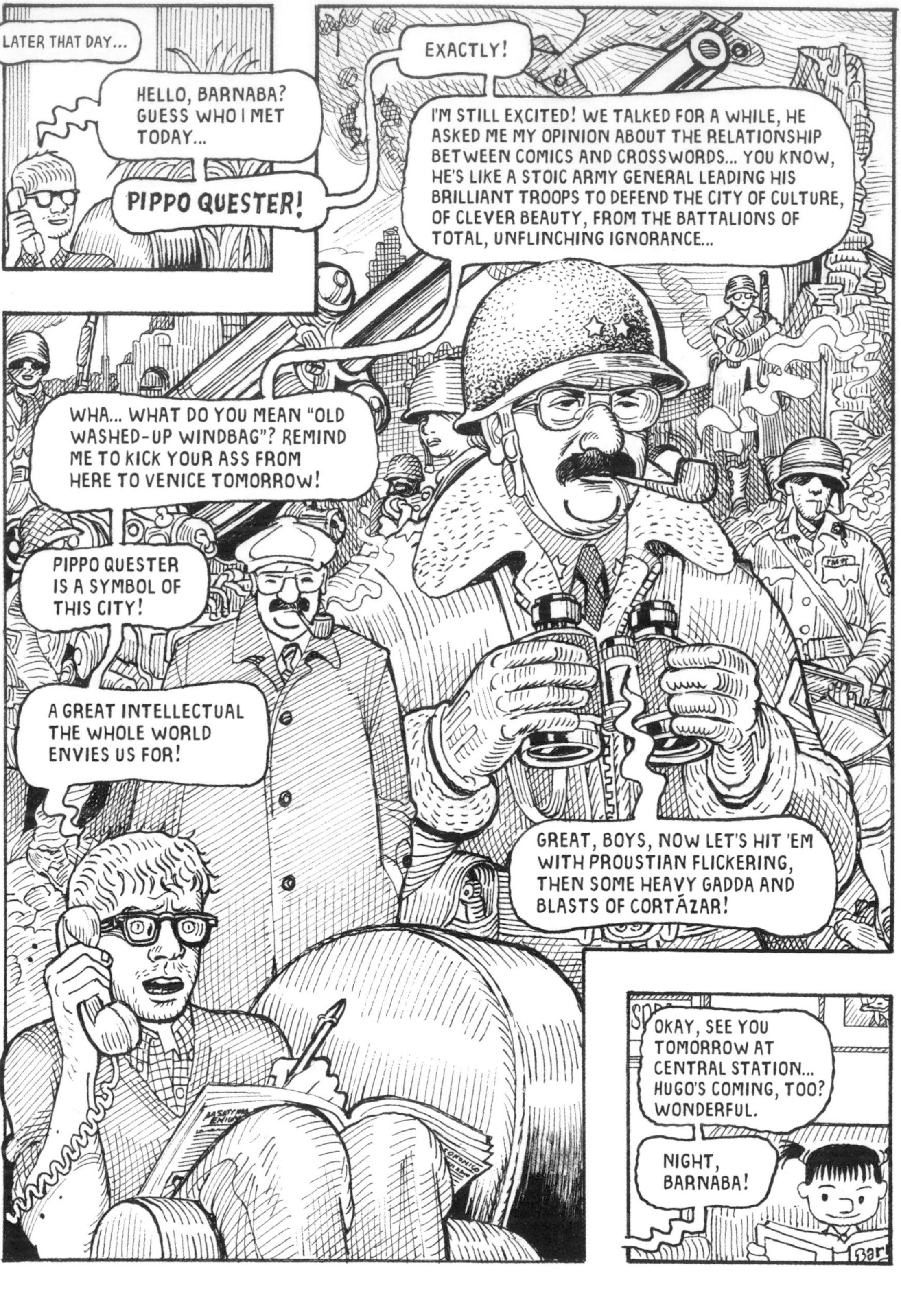

LATER THAT DAY...
HELLO, BARNABA? GUESS WHO I MET TODAY...
PIPPO QUESTER!
EXACTLY!
I'M STILL EXCITED! WE TALKED FOR A WHILE, HE ASKED ME MY OPINION ABOUT THE RELATIONSHIP BETWEEN COMICS AND CROSSWORDS... YOU KNOW, HE'S LIKE A STOIC ARMY GENERAL LEADING HIS BRILLIANT TROOPS TO DEFEND THE CITY OF CULTURE, OF CLEVER BEAUTY, FROM THE BATTALIONS OF TOTAL, UNFLINCHING IGNORANCE...
WHA... WHAT DO YOU MEAN "OLD WASHED-UP WINDBAG"? REMIND ME TO KICK YOUR ASS FROM HERE TO VENICE TOMORROW!
PIPPO QUESTER IS A SYMBOL OF THIS CITY!
A GREAT INTELLECTUAL THE WHOLE WORLD ENVIES US FOR!
GREAT, BOYS, NOW LET'S HIT 'EM WITH PROUSTIAN FLICKERING, THEN SOME HEAVY GADDA AND BLASTS OF CORTÁZAR!
OKAY, SEE YOU TOMORROW AT CENTRAL STATION... HUGO'S COMING, TOO? WONDERFUL.
NIGHT, BARNABA!

the BLUE WIDOW

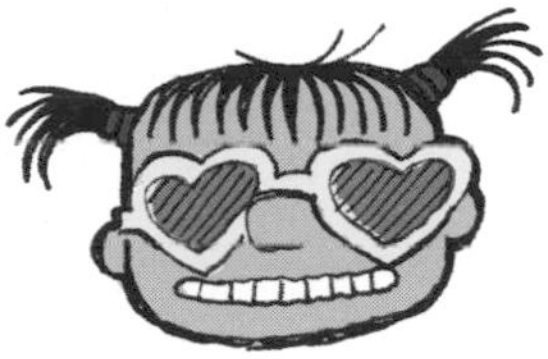

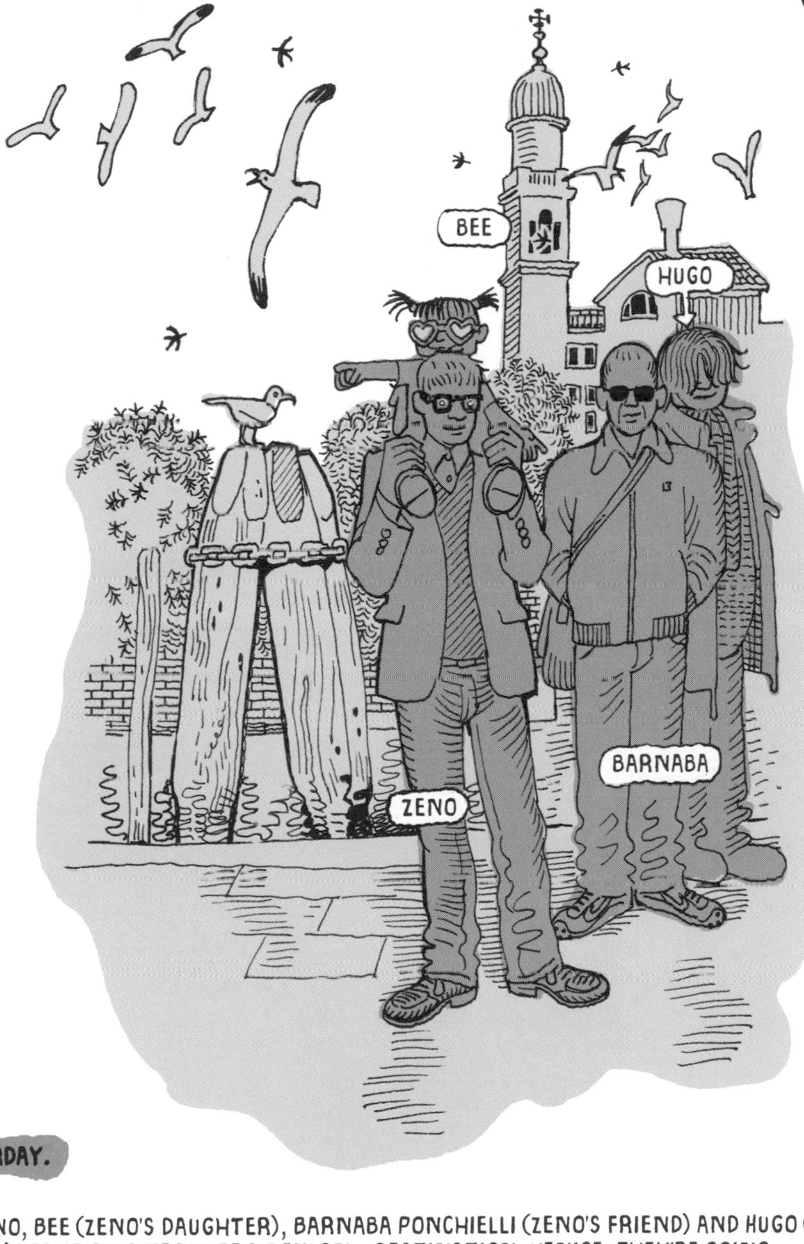
BEE
HUGO
BARNABA
ZENO

SATURDAY.

ZENO PORNO, BEE (ZENO'S DAUGHTER), BARNABA PONCHIELLI (ZENO'S FRIEND) AND HUGO (BARNABA'S BOYFRIEND) LEAVE ON A TRAIN FROM MILAN – DESTINATION: VENICE. THEY'RE GOING TO SEE THE EXHIBIT/*italics*/AT PALAZZO GRASSI.

PAOLOB.2009

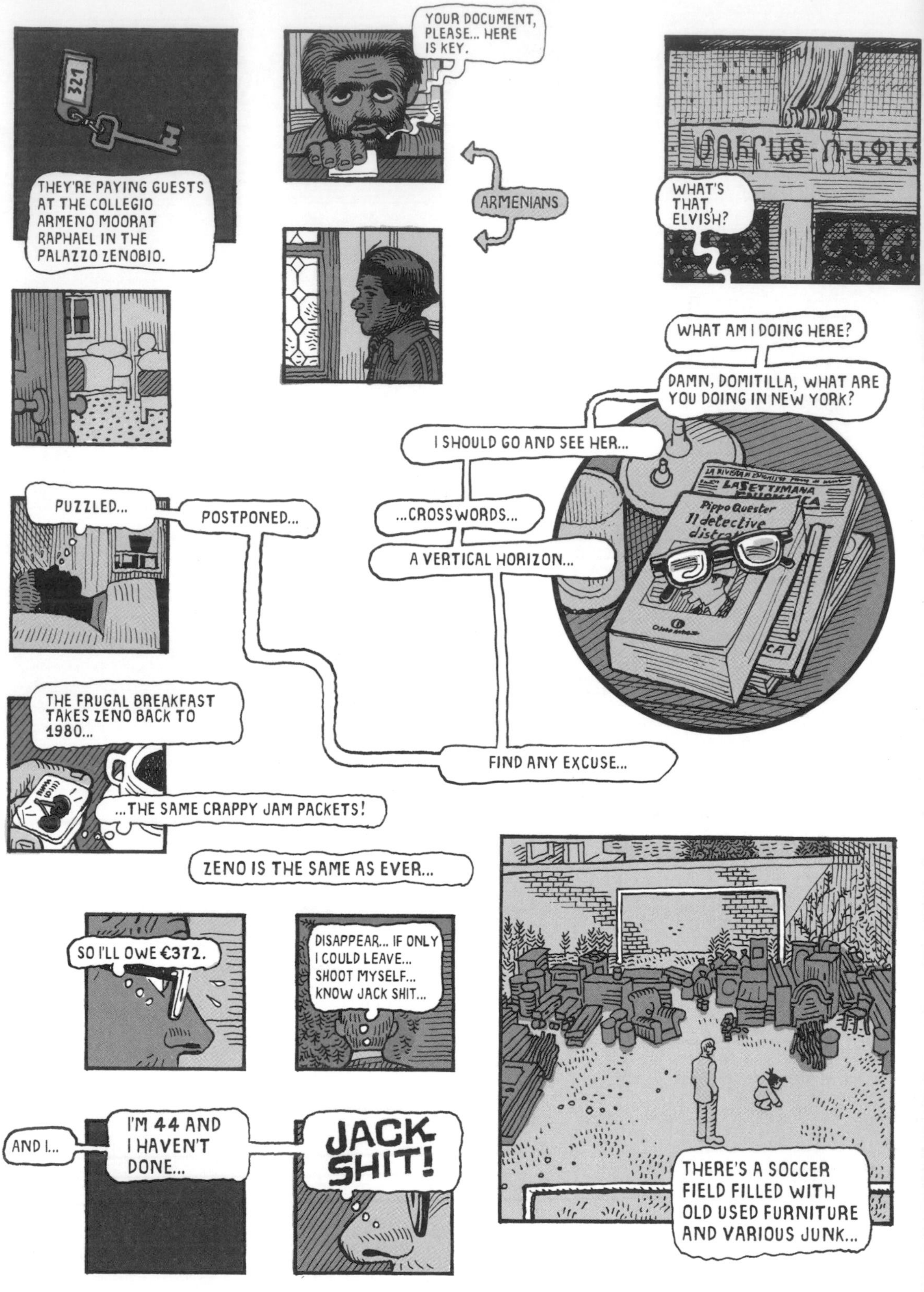
THEY'RE PAYING GUESTS AT THE COLLEGIO ARMENO MOORAT RAPHAEL IN THE PALAZZO ZENOBIO.
YOUR DOCUMENT, PLEASE... HERE IS KEY.
ARMENIANS
WHAT'S THAT, ELVISH?
WHAT AM I DOING HERE?
DAMN, DOMITILLA, WHAT ARE YOU DOING IN NEW YORK?
I SHOULD GO AND SEE HER...
PUZZLED...
POSTPONED...
...CROSSWORDS...
A VERTICAL HORIZON...
Pippo Quester
Il detective distratto
LA SETTIMANA
FIND ANY EXCUSE...
THE FRUGAL BREAKFAST TAKES ZENO BACK TO 1980...
...THE SAME CRAPPY JAM PACKETS!
ZENO IS THE SAME AS EVER...
SO I'LL OWE €372.
DISAPPEAR... IF ONLY I COULD LEAVE... SHOOT MYSELF... KNOW JACK SHIT...
AND I...
I'M 44 AND I HAVEN'T DONE...
JACK SHIT!
THERE'S A SOCCER FIELD FILLED WITH OLD USED FURNITURE AND VARIOUS JUNK...

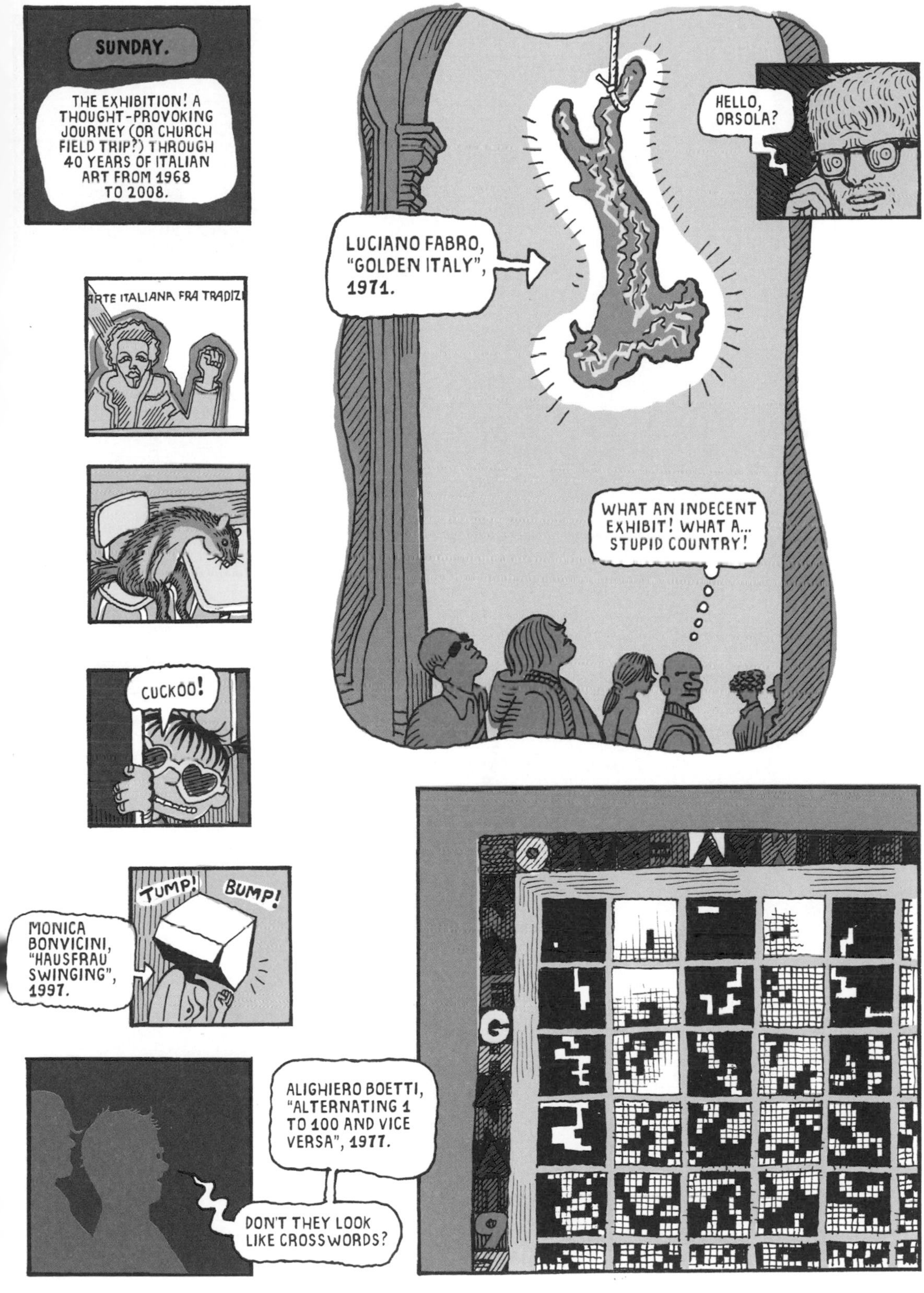
SUNDAY.
THE EXHIBITION! A THOUGHT-PROVOKING JOURNEY (OR CHURCH FIELD TRIP?) THROUGH 40 YEARS OF ITALIAN ART FROM 1968 TO 2008.
ARTE ITALIANA FRA TRADIZI
CUCKOO!
MONICA BONVICINI, "HAUSFRAU SWINGING", 1997.
TUMP!
BUMP!
LUCIANO FABRO, "GOLDEN ITALY", 1971.
HELLO, ORSOLA?
WHAT AN INDECENT EXHIBIT! WHAT A... STUPID COUNTRY!
ALIGHIERO BOETTI, "ALTERNATING 1 TO 100 AND VICE VERSA", 1977.
DON'T THEY LOOK LIKE CROSSWORDS?

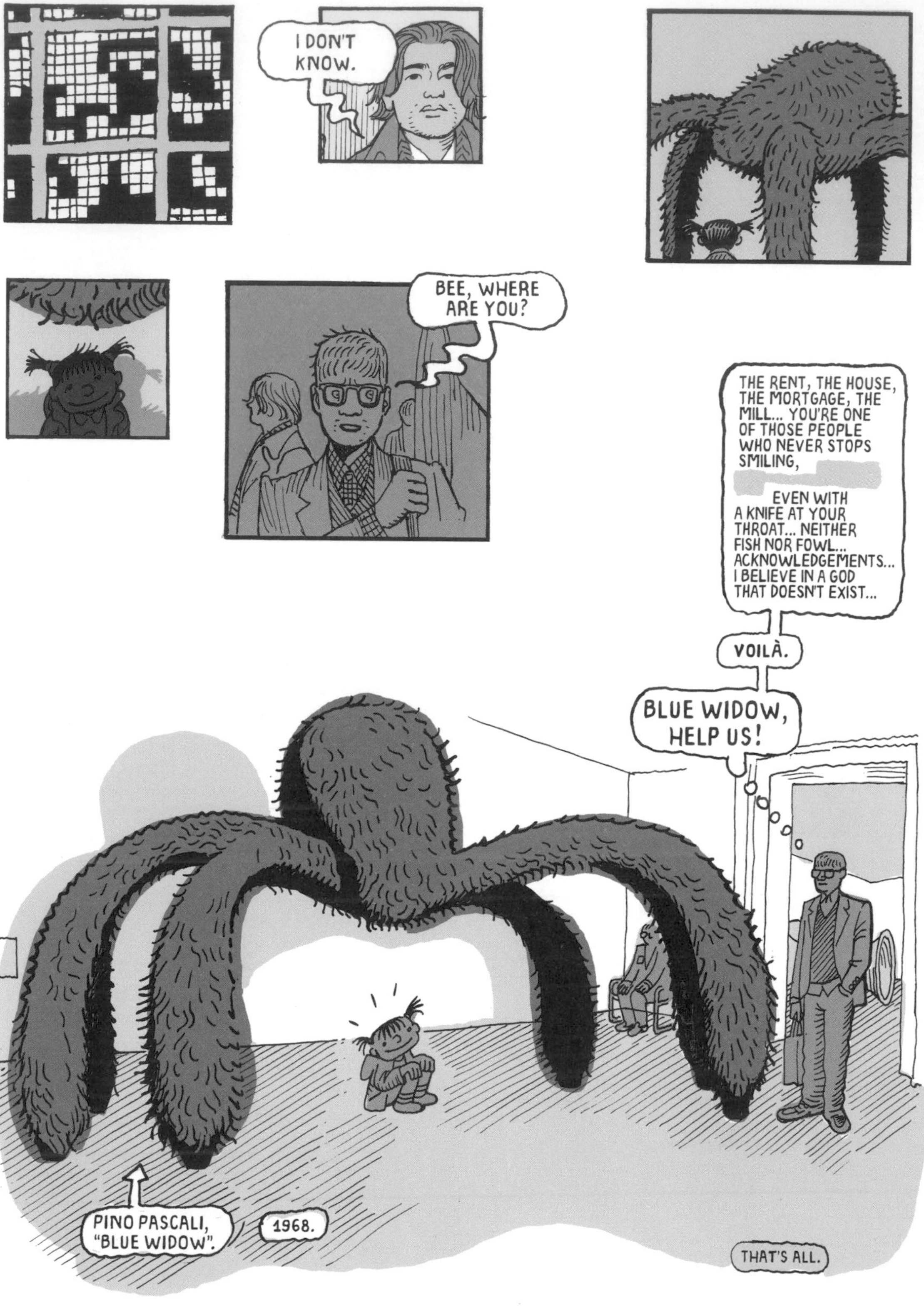
I DON'T KNOW.
BEE, WHERE ARE YOU?
THE RENT, THE HOUSE, THE MORTGAGE, THE MILL... YOU'RE ONE OF THOSE PEOPLE WHO NEVER STOPS SMILING,
EVEN WITH A KNIFE AT YOUR THROAT... NEITHER FISH NOR FOWL... ACKNOWLEDGEMENTS... I BELIEVE IN A GOD THAT DOESN'T EXIST...
VOILÀ.
BLUE WIDOW, HELP US!
PINO PASCALI, "BLUE WIDOW".
1968.
THAT'S ALL.

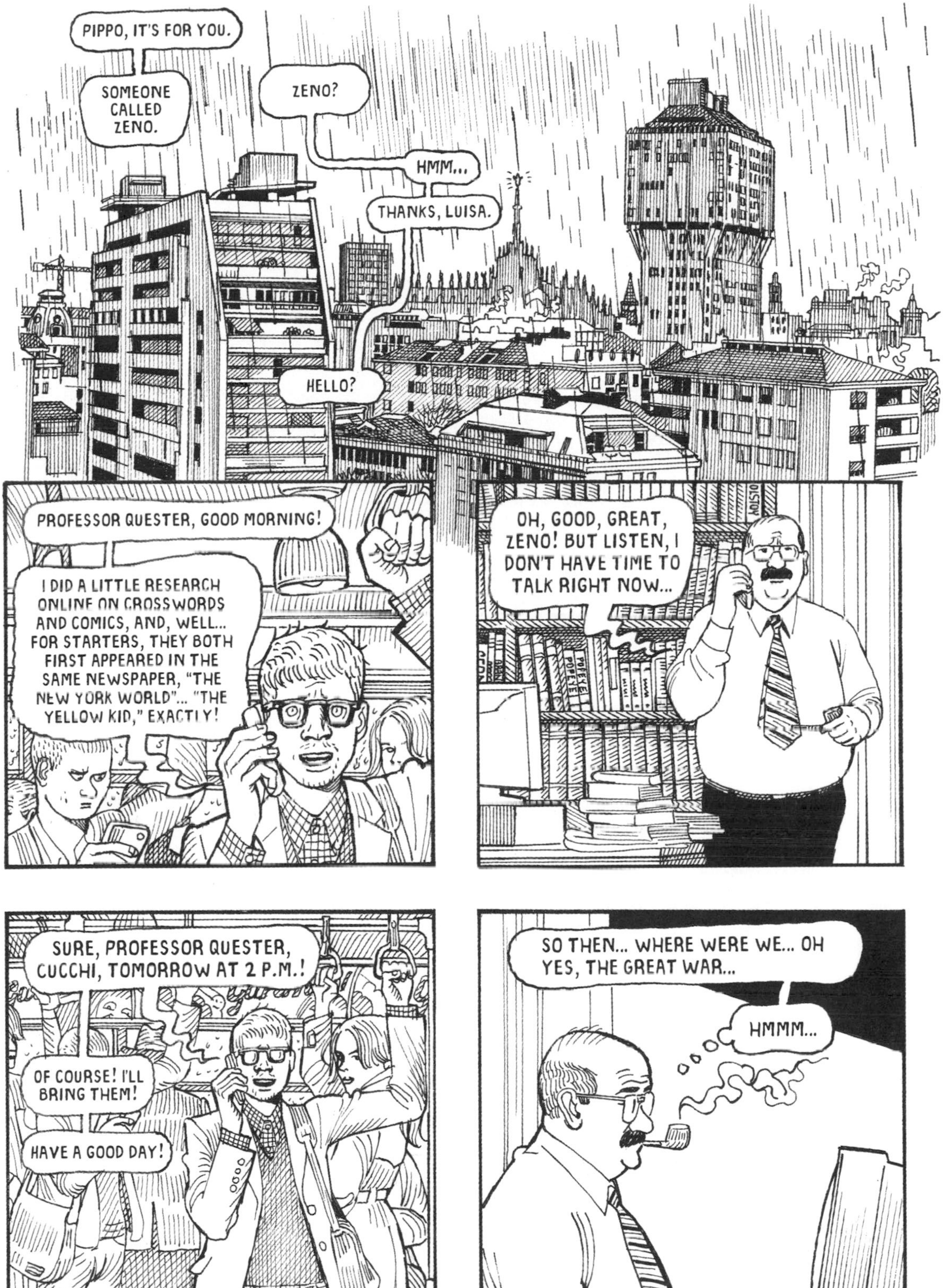
PIPPO, IT'S FOR YOU.
SOMEONE CALLED ZENO.
ZENO?
HMM...
THANKS, LUISA.
HELLO?
PROFESSOR QUESTER, GOOD MORNING!
I DID A LITTLE RESEARCH ONLINE ON CROSSWORDS AND COMICS, AND, WELL... FOR STARTERS, THEY BOTH FIRST APPEARED IN THE SAME NEWSPAPER, "THE NEW YORK WORLD"... "THE YELLOW KID," EXACTLY!
OH, GOOD, GREAT, ZENO! BUT LISTEN, I DON'T HAVE TIME TO TALK RIGHT NOW...
SURE, PROFESSOR QUESTER, CUCCHI, TOMORROW AT 2 P.M.!
OF COURSE! I'LL BRING THEM!
HAVE A GOOD DAY!
SO THEN... WHERE WERE WE... OH YES, THE GREAT WAR...
HMMM...

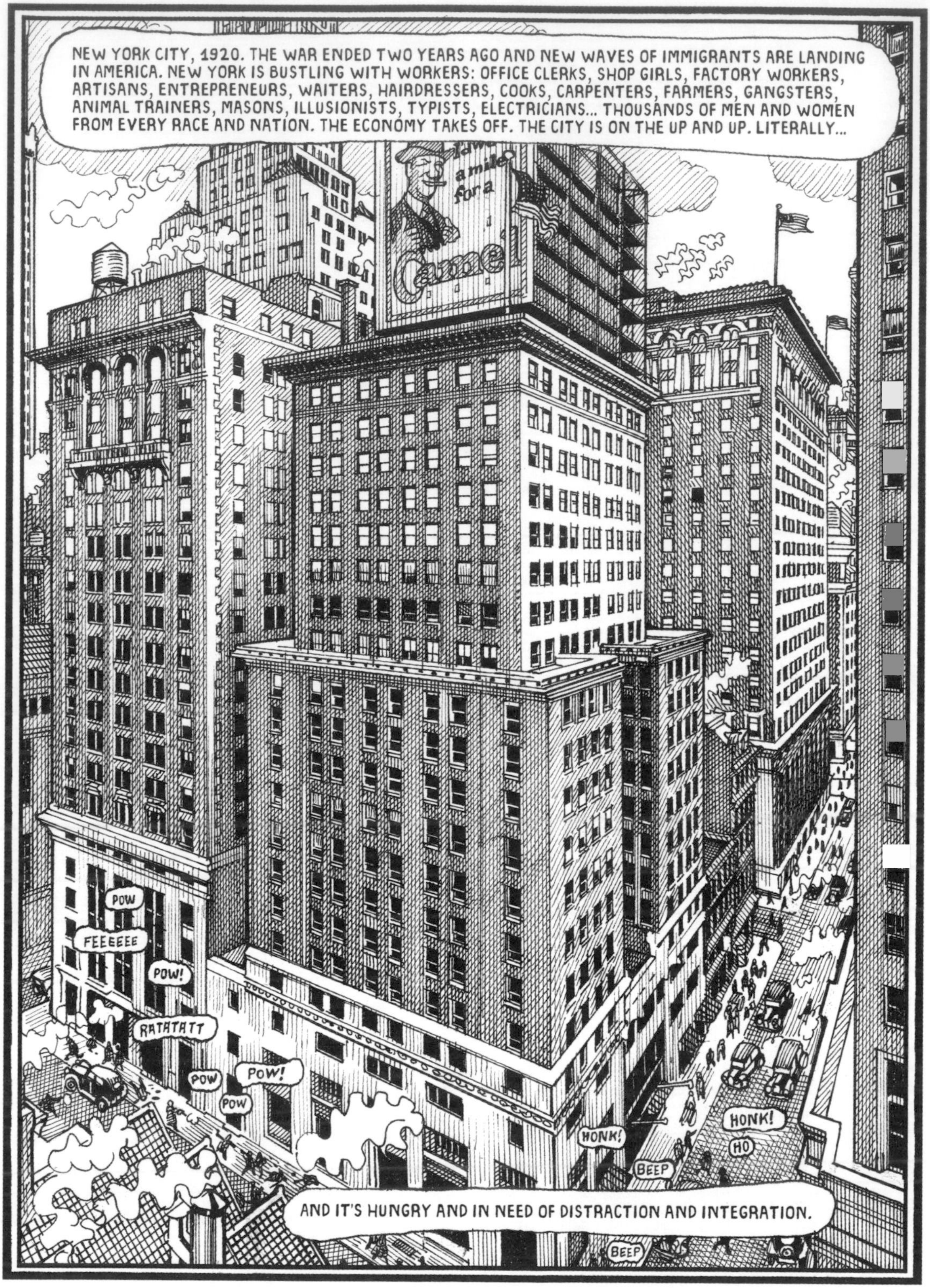
NEW YORK CITY, 1920. THE WAR ENDED TWO YEARS AGO AND NEW WAVES OF IMMIGRANTS ARE LANDING IN AMERICA. NEW YORK IS BUSTLING WITH WORKERS: OFFICE CLERKS, SHOP GIRLS, FACTORY WORKERS, ARTISANS, ENTREPRENEURS, WAITERS, HAIRDRESSERS, COOKS, CARPENTERS, FARMERS, GANGSTERS, ANIMAL TRAINERS, MASONS, ILLUSIONISTS, TYPISTS, ELECTRICIANS... THOUSANDS OF MEN AND WOMEN FROM EVERY RACE AND NATION. THE ECONOMY TAKES OFF. THE CITY IS ON THE UP AND UP. LITERALLY...
POW
FEEEEEE
POW!
RATATATT
POW
POW!
POW
HONK!
BEEP
HONK!
HO
AND IT'S HUNGRY AND IN NEED OF DISTRACTION AND INTEGRATION.
BEEP

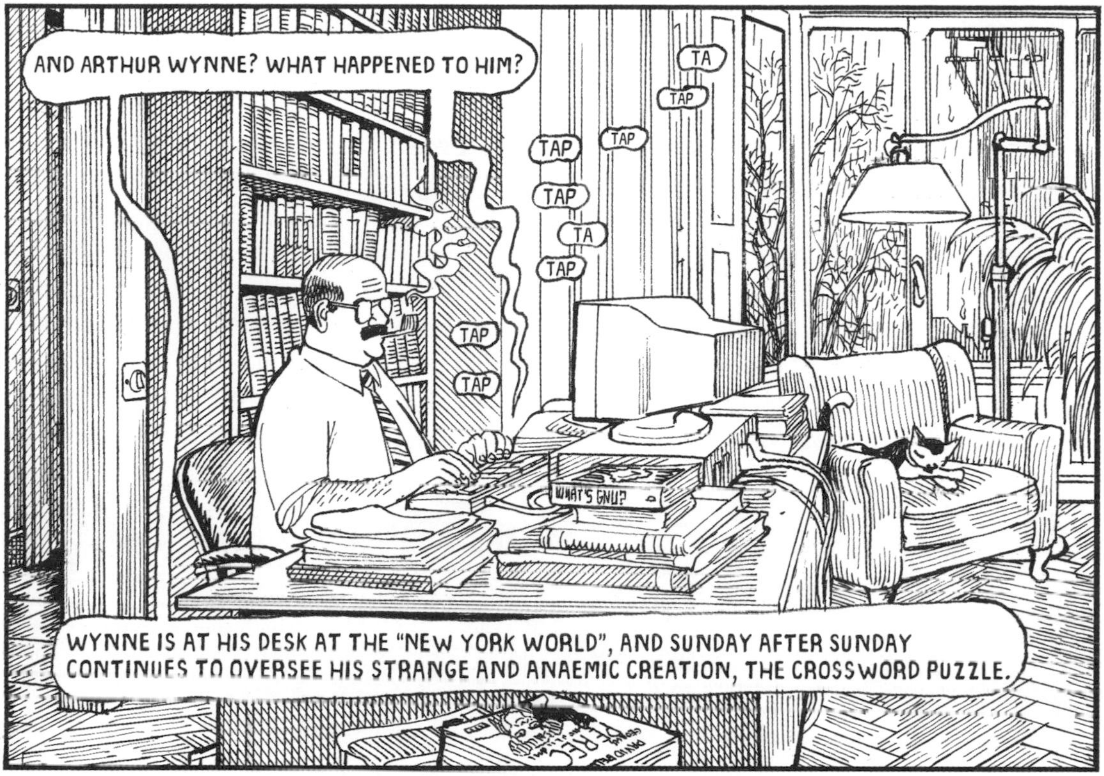
AND ARTHUR WYNNE? WHAT HAPPENED TO HIM?
TA
TAP
TAP
TAP
TAP
TA
TAP
TAP
TAP
WHAT'S GNU?
WYNNE IS AT HIS DESK AT THE "NEW YORK WORLD", AND SUNDAY AFTER SUNDAY CONTINUES TO OVERSEE HIS STRANGE AND ANAEMIC CREATION, THE CROSSWORD PUZZLE.

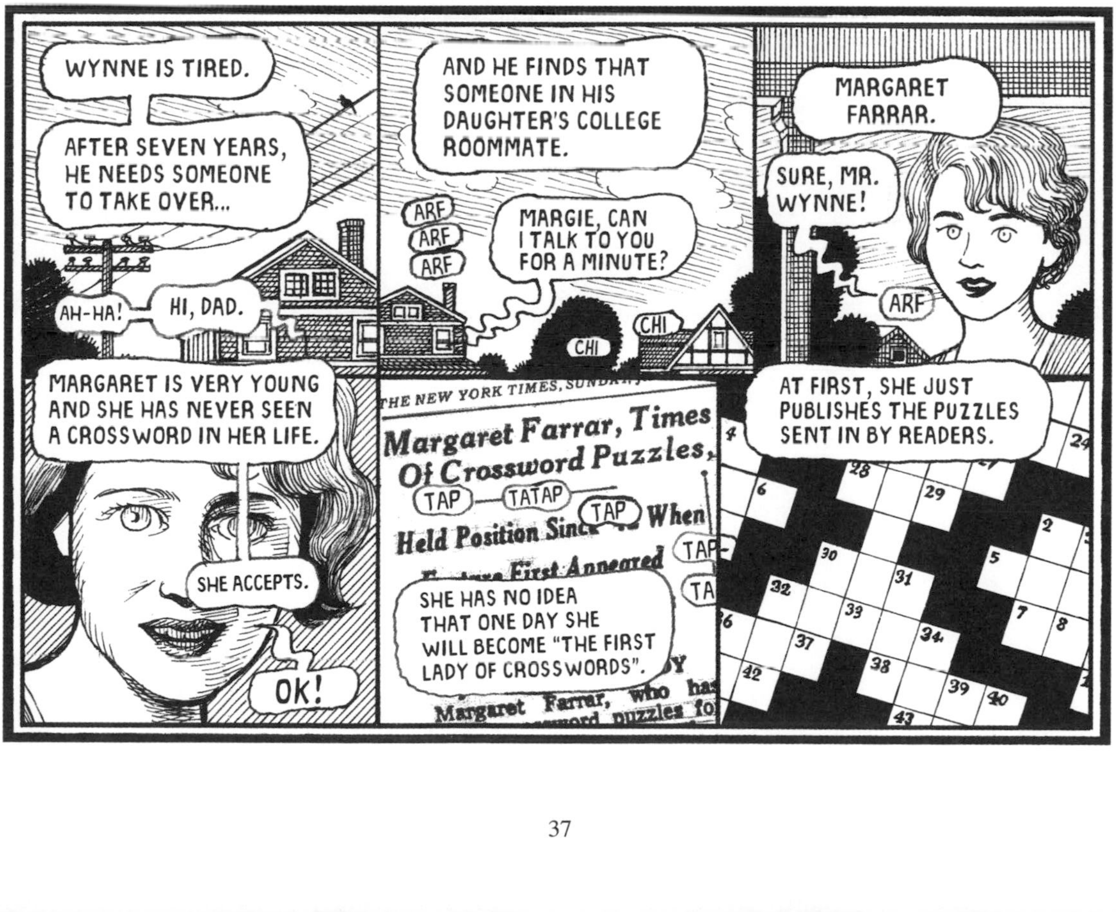
WYNNE IS TIRED.
AFTER SEVEN YEARS, HE NEEDS SOMEONE TO TAKE OVER...
AH-HA!
HI, DAD.
AND HE FINDS THAT SOMEONE IN HIS DAUGHTER'S COLLEGE ROOMMATE.
ARF
ARF
ARF
MARGIE, CAN I TALK TO YOU FOR A MINUTE?
CHI
CHI
MARGARET FARRAR.
SURE, MR. WYNNE!
ARF
MARGARET IS VERY YOUNG AND SHE HAS NEVER SEEN A CROSSWORD IN HER LIFE.
SHE ACCEPTS.
OK!
THE NEW YORK TIMES, SUNDAY
Margaret Farrar, Times
Of Crossword Puzzles,
TAP
TATAP
TAP
When
Held Position Since
TAP-
TA
SHE HAS NO IDEA THAT ONE DAY SHE WILL BECOME "THE FIRST LADY OF CROSSWORDS".
Margaret Farrar, who has
AT FIRST, SHE JUST PUBLISHES THE PUZZLES SENT IN BY READERS.

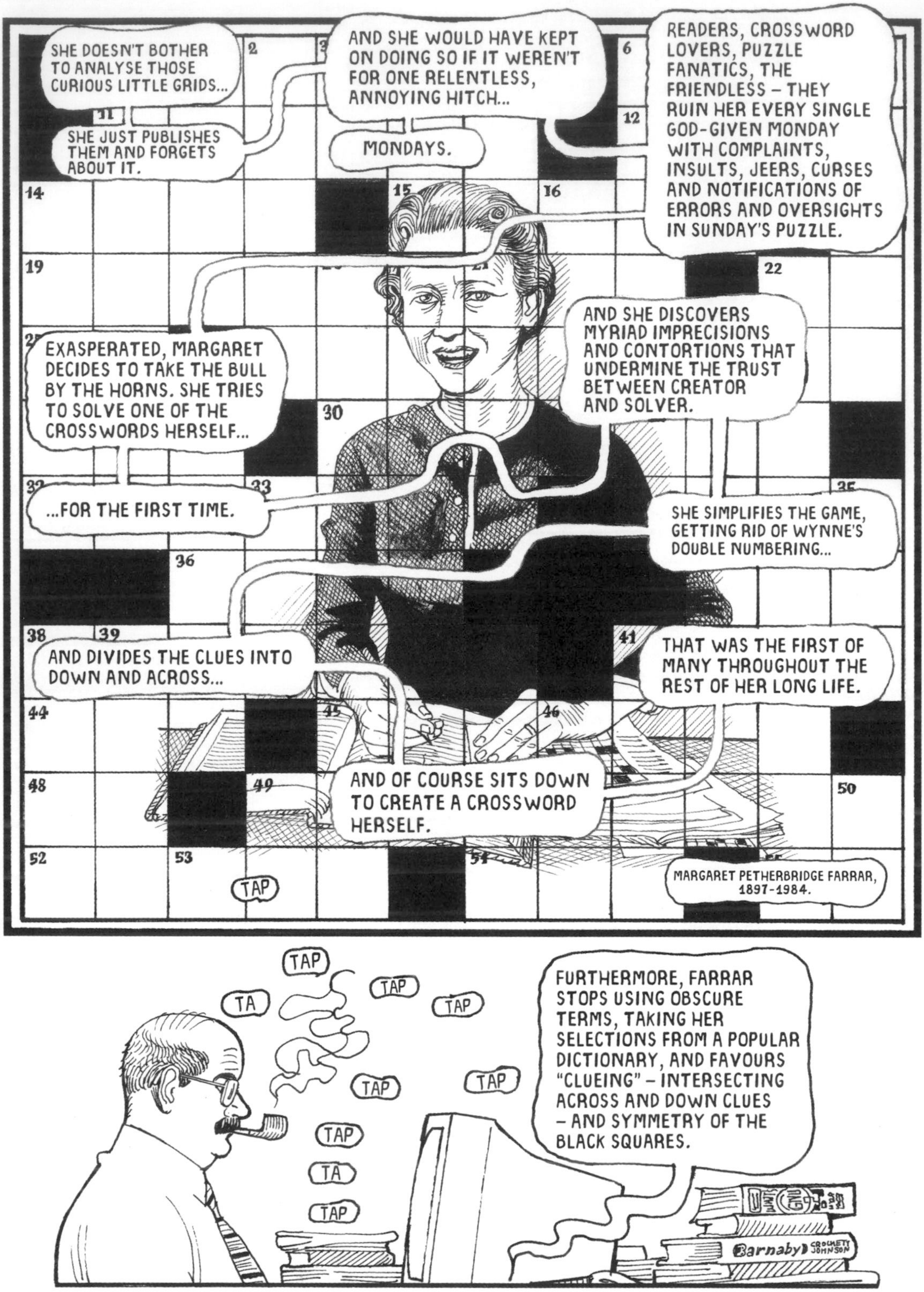

SHE DOESN'T BOTHER TO ANALYSE THOSE CURIOUS LITTLE GRIDS...
SHE JUST PUBLISHES THEM AND FORGETS ABOUT IT.
AND SHE WOULD HAVE KEPT ON DOING SO IF IT WEREN'T FOR ONE RELENTLESS, ANNOYING HITCH...
MONDAYS.
READERS, CROSSWORD LOVERS, PUZZLE FANATICS, THE FRIENDLESS – THEY RUIN HER EVERY SINGLE GOD-GIVEN MONDAY WITH COMPLAINTS, INSULTS, JEERS, CURSES AND NOTIFICATIONS OF ERRORS AND OVERSIGHTS IN SUNDAY'S PUZZLE.
EXASPERATED, MARGARET DECIDES TO TAKE THE BULL BY THE HORNS. SHE TRIES TO SOLVE ONE OF THE CROSSWORDS HERSELF...
...FOR THE FIRST TIME.
AND SHE DISCOVERS MYRIAD IMPRECISIONS AND CONTORTIONS THAT UNDERMINE THE TRUST BETWEEN CREATOR AND SOLVER.
SHE SIMPLIFIES THE GAME, GETTING RID OF WYNNE'S DOUBLE NUMBERING...
AND DIVIDES THE CLUES INTO DOWN AND ACROSS...
THAT WAS THE FIRST OF MANY THROUGHOUT THE REST OF HER LONG LIFE.
AND OF COURSE SITS DOWN TO CREATE A CROSSWORD HERSELF.
MARGARET PETHERBRIDGE FARRAR, 1897-1984.
TAP
TAP
TA
TAP
TAP
TAP
TAP
TAP
TA
TAP
FURTHERMORE, FARRAR STOPS USING OBSCURE TERMS, TAKING HER SELECTIONS FROM A POPULAR DICTIONARY, AND FAVOURS "CLUEING" – INTERSECTING ACROSS AND DOWN CLUES – AND SYMMETRY OF THE BLACK SQUARES.
Barnaby CROCKETT JOHNSON

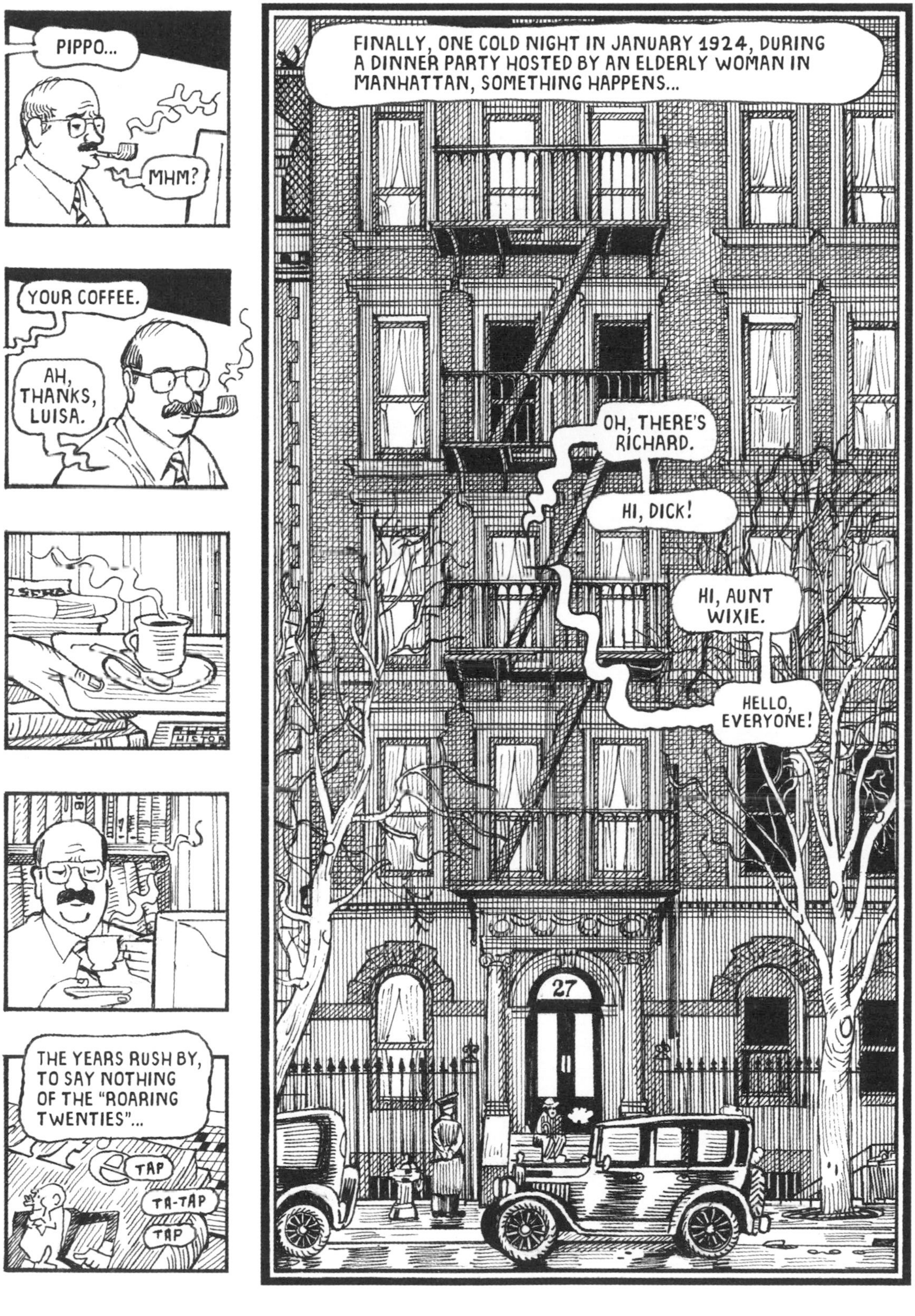
PIPPO...
MHM?
YOUR COFFEE.
AH, THANKS, LUISA.
THE YEARS RUSH BY, TO SAY NOTHING OF THE "ROARING TWENTIES"...
TAP
TA-TAP
TAP
FINALLY, ONE COLD NIGHT IN JANUARY 1924, DURING A DINNER PARTY HOSTED BY AN ELDERLY WOMAN IN MANHATTAN, SOMETHING HAPPENS...
OH, THERE'S RICHARD.
HI, DICK!
HI, AUNT WIXIE.
HELLO, EVERYONE!
27

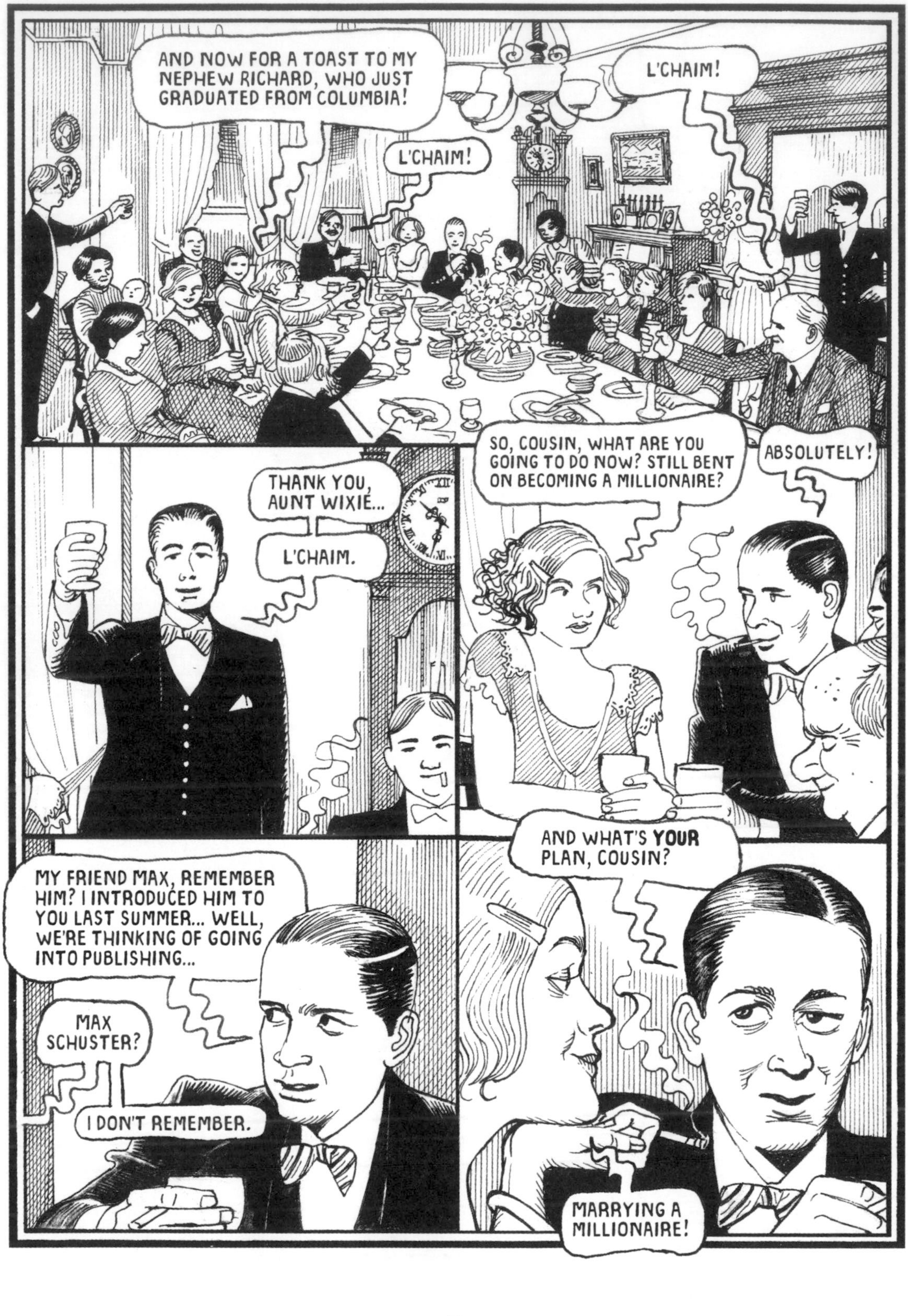
AND NOW FOR A TOAST TO MY NEPHEW RICHARD, WHO JUST GRADUATED FROM COLUMBIA!
L'CHAIM!
L'CHAIM!
THANK YOU, AUNT WIXIE...
L'CHAIM.
SO, COUSIN, WHAT ARE YOU GOING TO DO NOW? STILL BENT ON BECOMING A MILLIONAIRE?
ABSOLUTELY!
MY FRIEND MAX, REMEMBER HIM? I INTRODUCED HIM TO YOU LAST SUMMER... WELL, WE'RE THINKING OF GOING INTO PUBLISHING...
MAX SCHUSTER?
I DON'T REMEMBER.
AND WHAT'S **YOUR** PLAN, COUSIN?
MARRYING A MILLIONAIRE!

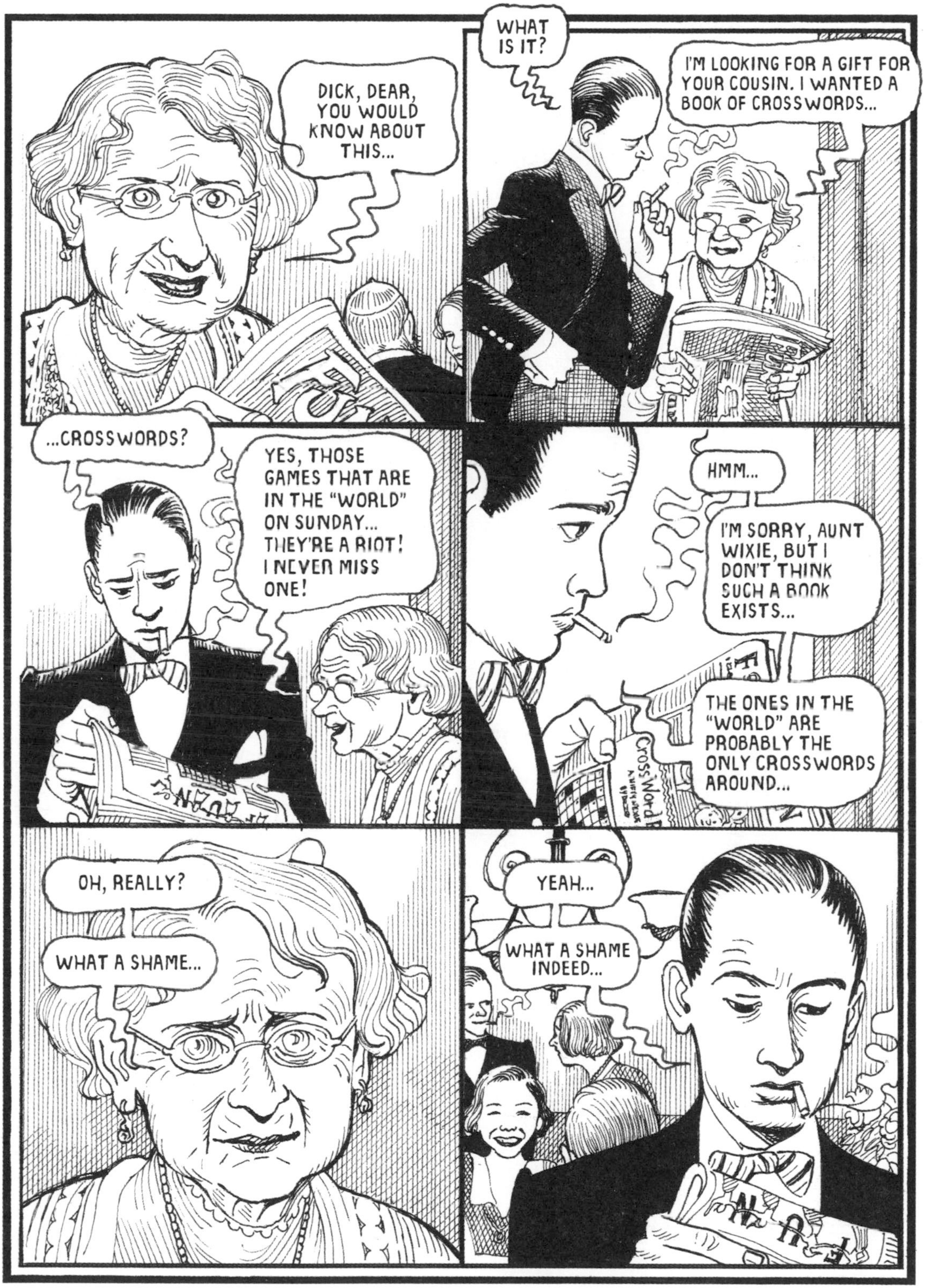
DICK, DEAR, YOU WOULD KNOW ABOUT THIS...
WHAT IS IT?
I'M LOOKING FOR A GIFT FOR YOUR COUSIN. I WANTED A BOOK OF CROSSWORDS...
...CROSSWORDS?
YES, THOSE GAMES THAT ARE IN THE "WORLD" ON SUNDAY... THEY'RE A RIOT! I NEVER MISS ONE!
HMM...
I'M SORRY, AUNT WIXIE, BUT I DON'T THINK SUCH A BOOK EXISTS...
THE ONES IN THE "WORLD" ARE PROBABLY THE ONLY CROSSWORDS AROUND...
OH, REALLY?
WHAT A SHAME...
YEAH...
WHAT A SHAME INDEED...

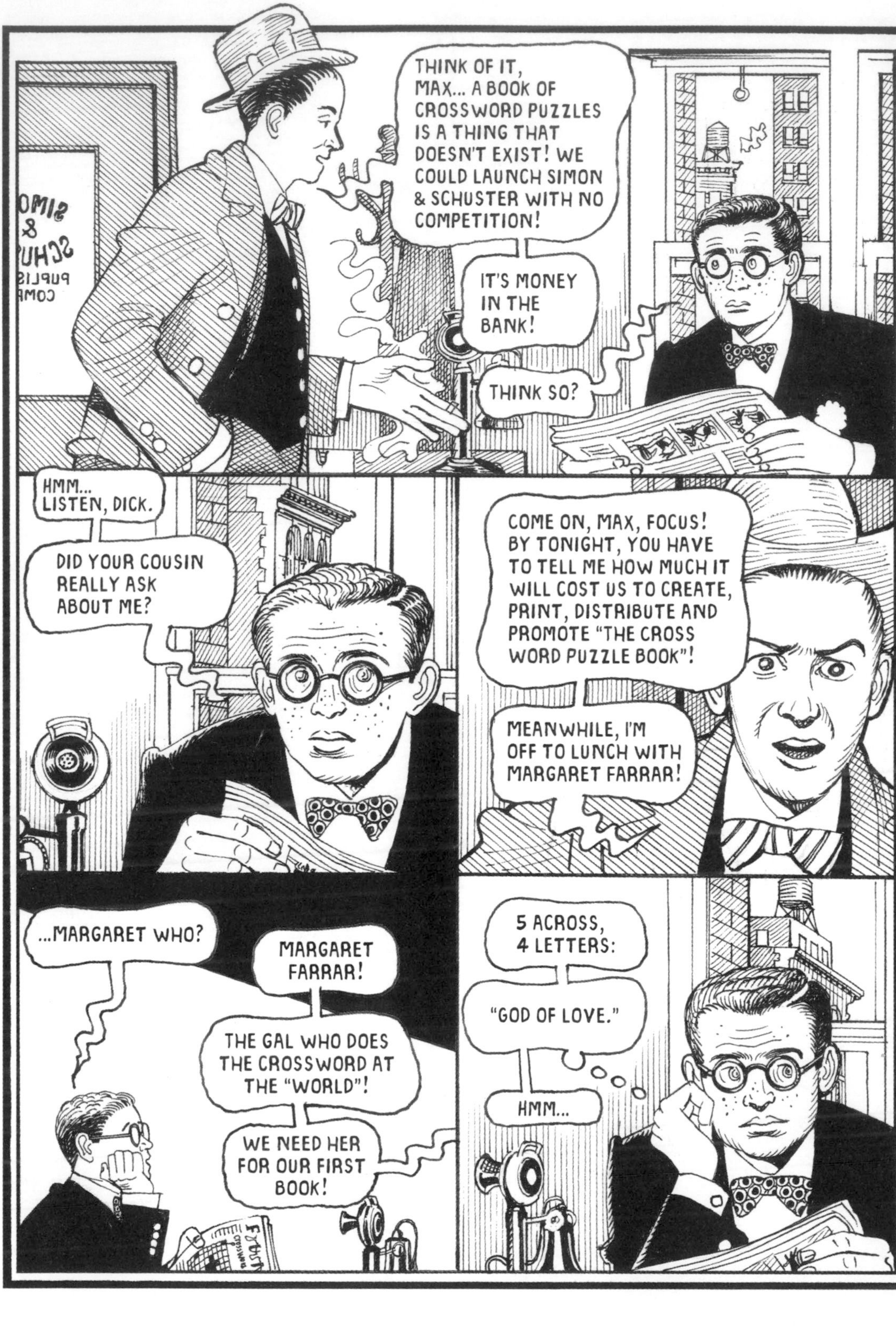
THINK OF IT, MAX... A BOOK OF CROSSWORD PUZZLES IS A THING THAT DOESN'T EXIST! WE COULD LAUNCH SIMON & SCHUSTER WITH NO COMPETITION!
IT'S MONEY IN THE BANK!
THINK SO?
HMM... LISTEN, DICK.
DID YOUR COUSIN REALLY ASK ABOUT ME?
COME ON, MAX, FOCUS! BY TONIGHT, YOU HAVE TO TELL ME HOW MUCH IT WILL COST US TO CREATE, PRINT, DISTRIBUTE AND PROMOTE "THE CROSS WORD PUZZLE BOOK"!
MEANWHILE, I'M OFF TO LUNCH WITH MARGARET FARRAR!
...MARGARET WHO?
MARGARET FARRAR!
THE GAL WHO DOES THE CROSSWORD AT THE "WORLD"!
WE NEED HER FOR OUR FIRST BOOK!
5 ACROSS, 4 LETTERS:
"GOD OF LOVE."
HMM...

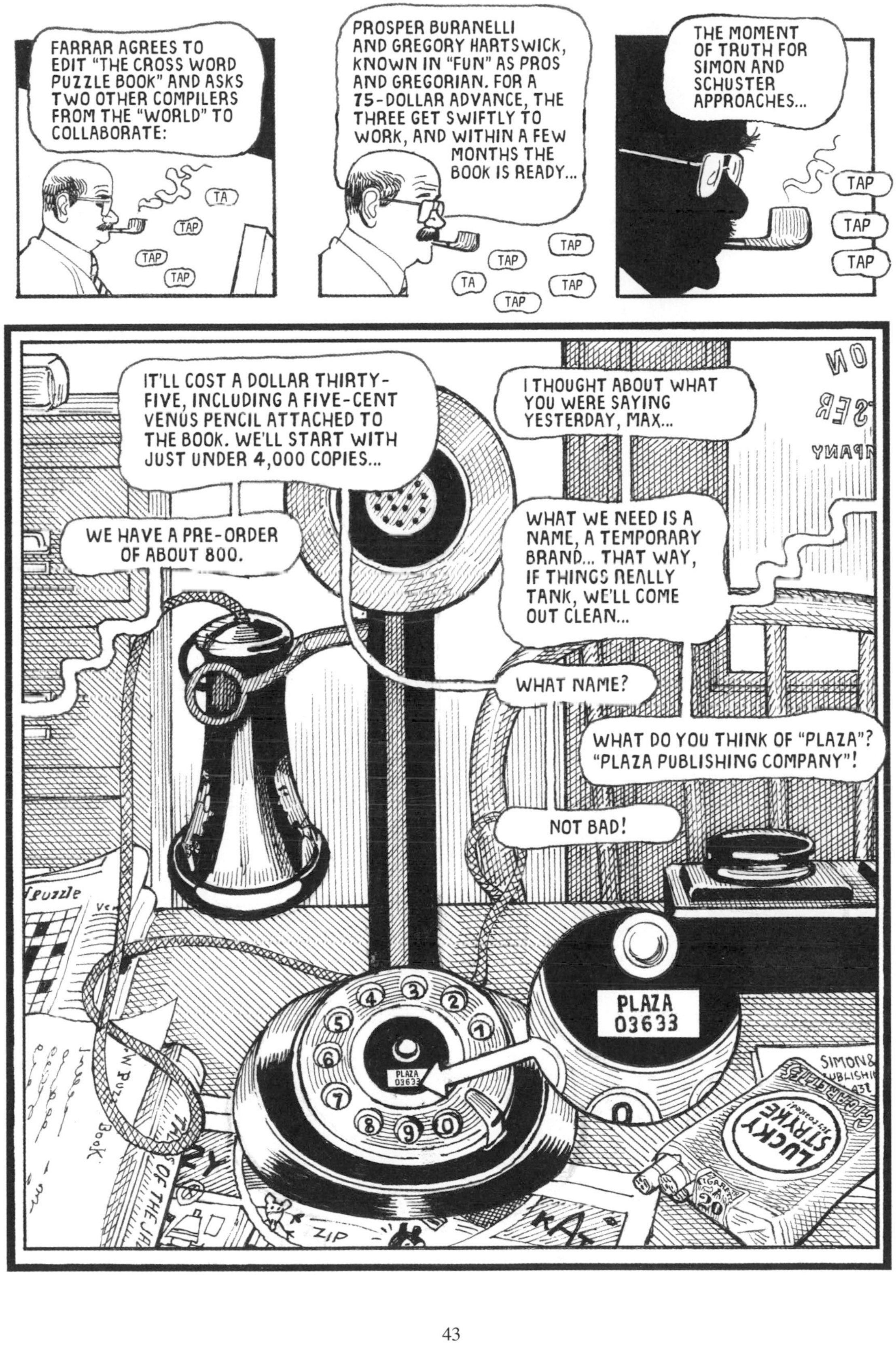
FARRAR AGREES TO EDIT "THE CROSS WORD PUZZLE BOOK" AND ASKS TWO OTHER COMPILERS FROM THE "WORLD" TO COLLABORATE:
TA
TAP
TAP
TAP
PROSPER BURANELLI AND GREGORY HARTSWICK, KNOWN IN "FUN" AS PROS AND GREGORIAN. FOR A 75-DOLLAR ADVANCE, THE THREE GET SWIFTLY TO WORK, AND WITHIN A FEW MONTHS THE BOOK IS READY...
TAP
TAP
TA
TAP
TAP
THE MOMENT OF TRUTH FOR SIMON AND SCHUSTER APPROACHES...
TAP
TAP
TAP
IT'LL COST A DOLLAR THIRTY-FIVE, INCLUDING A FIVE-CENT VENUS PENCIL ATTACHED TO THE BOOK. WE'LL START WITH JUST UNDER 4,000 COPIES...
I THOUGHT ABOUT WHAT YOU WERE SAYING YESTERDAY, MAX...
WE HAVE A PRE-ORDER OF ABOUT 800.
WHAT WE NEED IS A NAME, A TEMPORARY BRAND... THAT WAY, IF THINGS REALLY TANK, WE'LL COME OUT CLEAN...
WHAT NAME?
WHAT DO YOU THINK OF "PLAZA"? "PLAZA PUBLISHING COMPANY"!
NOT BAD!
PLAZA 03633

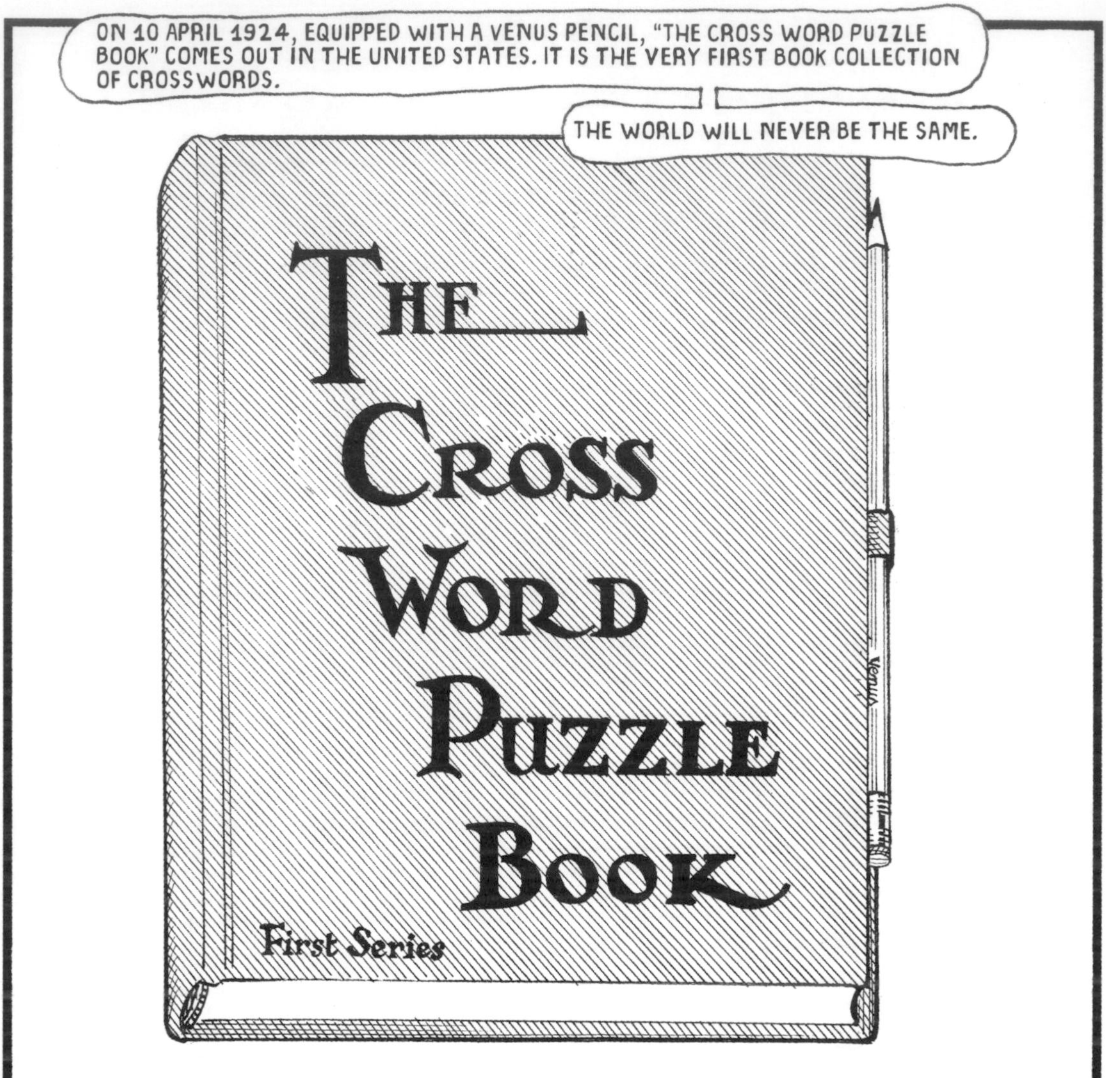
ON 10 APRIL 1924, EQUIPPED WITH A VENUS PENCIL, "THE CROSS WORD PUZZLE BOOK" COMES OUT IN THE UNITED STATES. IT IS THE VERY FIRST BOOK COLLECTION OF CROSSWORDS.
THE WORLD WILL NEVER BE THE SAME.
THE CROSS WORD PUZZLE BOOK
First Series
VENUS

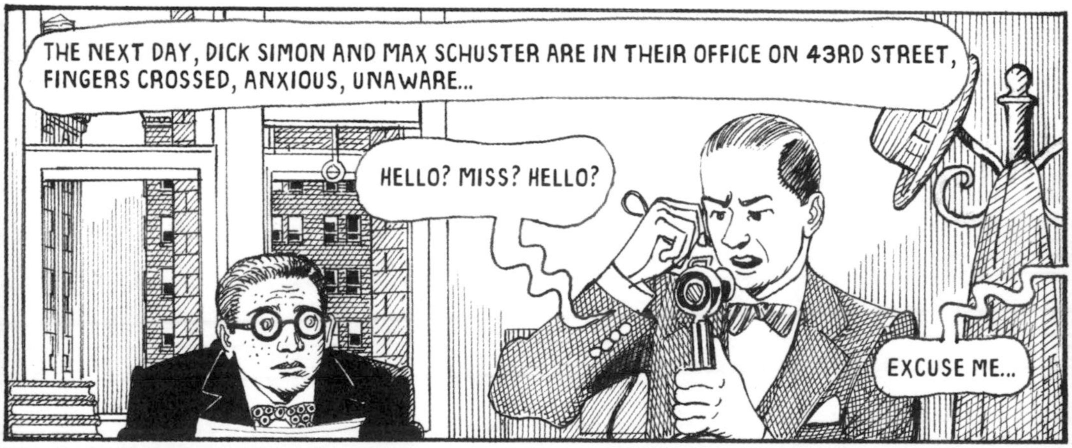
THE NEXT DAY, DICK SIMON AND MAX SCHUSTER ARE IN THEIR OFFICE ON 43RD STREET, FINGERS CROSSED, ANXIOUS, UNAWARE...
HELLO? MISS? HELLO?
EXCUSE ME...

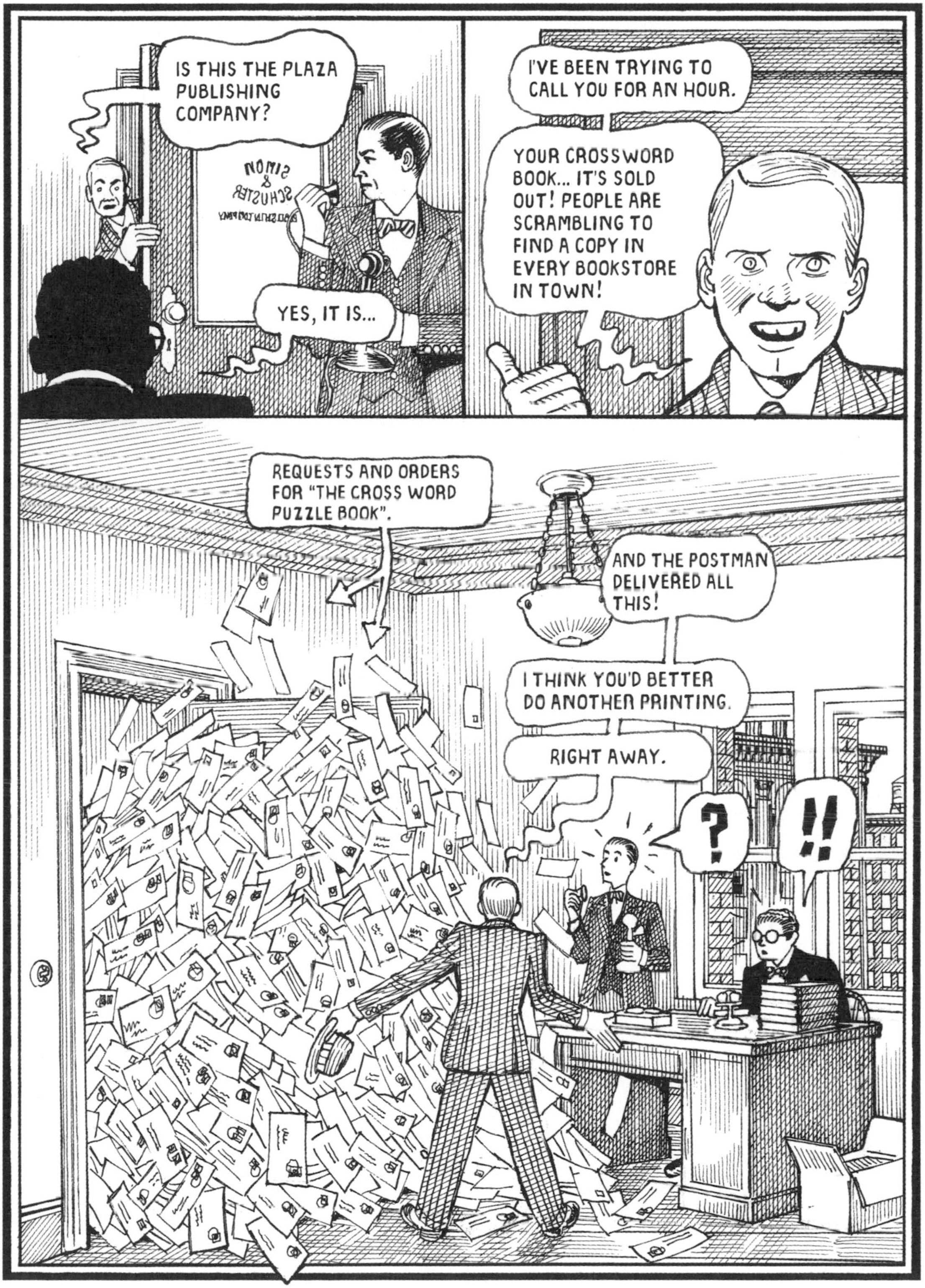
IS THIS THE PLAZA PUBLISHING COMPANY?
YES, IT IS...
I'VE BEEN TRYING TO CALL YOU FOR AN HOUR.
YOUR CROSSWORD BOOK... IT'S SOLD OUT! PEOPLE ARE SCRAMBLING TO FIND A COPY IN EVERY BOOKSTORE IN TOWN!
REQUESTS AND ORDERS FOR "THE CROSS WORD PUZZLE BOOK".
AND THE POSTMAN DELIVERED ALL THIS!
I THINK YOU'D BETTER DO ANOTHER PRINTING.
RIGHT AWAY.
?
!!

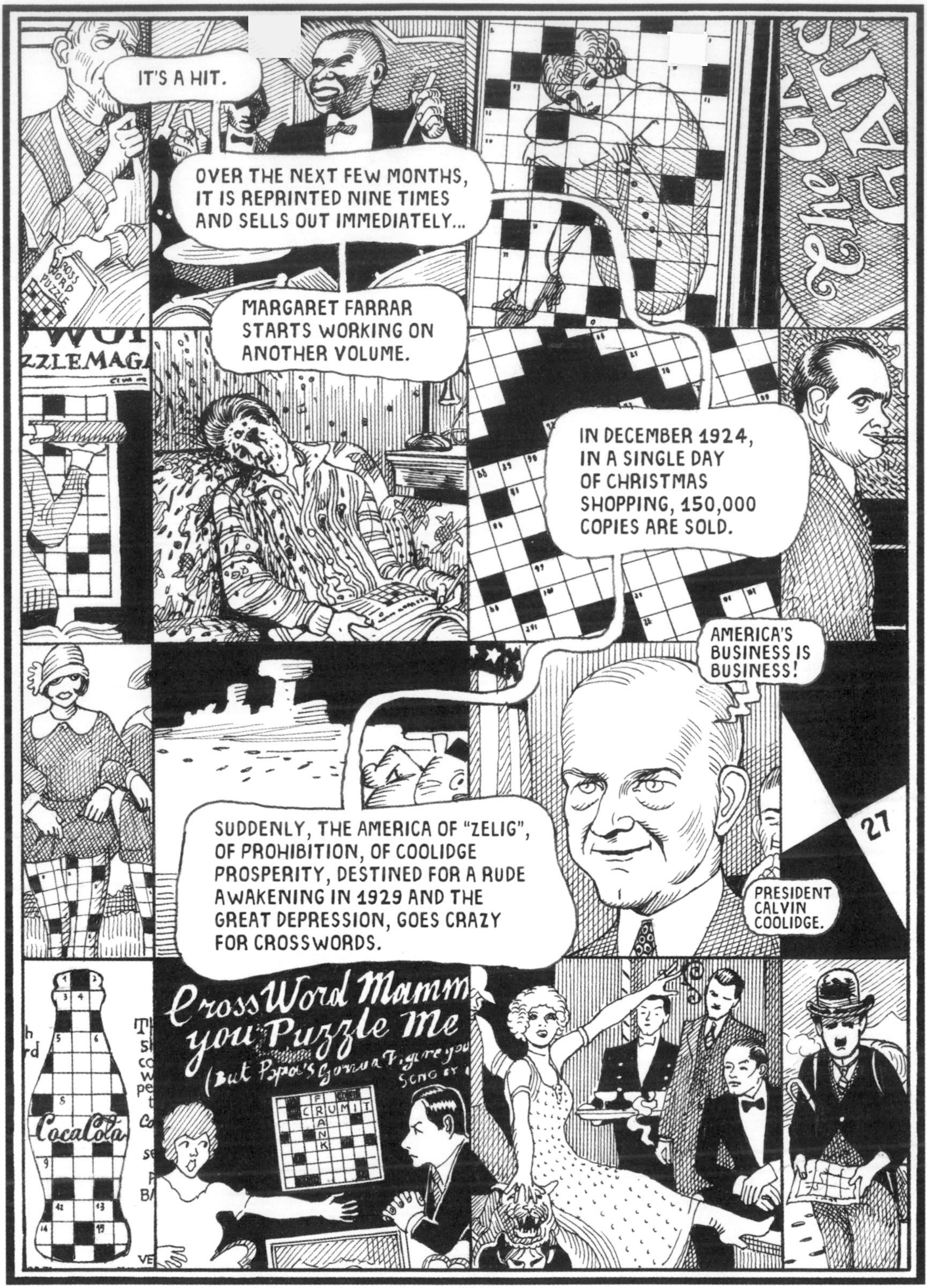
IT'S A HIT.
OVER THE NEXT FEW MONTHS, IT IS REPRINTED NINE TIMES AND SELLS OUT IMMEDIATELY...
MARGARET FARRAR STARTS WORKING ON ANOTHER VOLUME.
IN DECEMBER 1924, IN A SINGLE DAY OF CHRISTMAS SHOPPING, 150,000 COPIES ARE SOLD.
AMERICA'S BUSINESS IS BUSINESS!
PRESIDENT CALVIN COOLIDGE.
SUDDENLY, THE AMERICA OF "ZELIG", OF PROHIBITION, OF COOLIDGE PROSPERITY, DESTINED FOR A RUDE AWAKENING IN 1929 AND THE GREAT DEPRESSION, GOES CRAZY FOR CROSSWORDS.
27
CocaCola
CRUMIT
FRANK

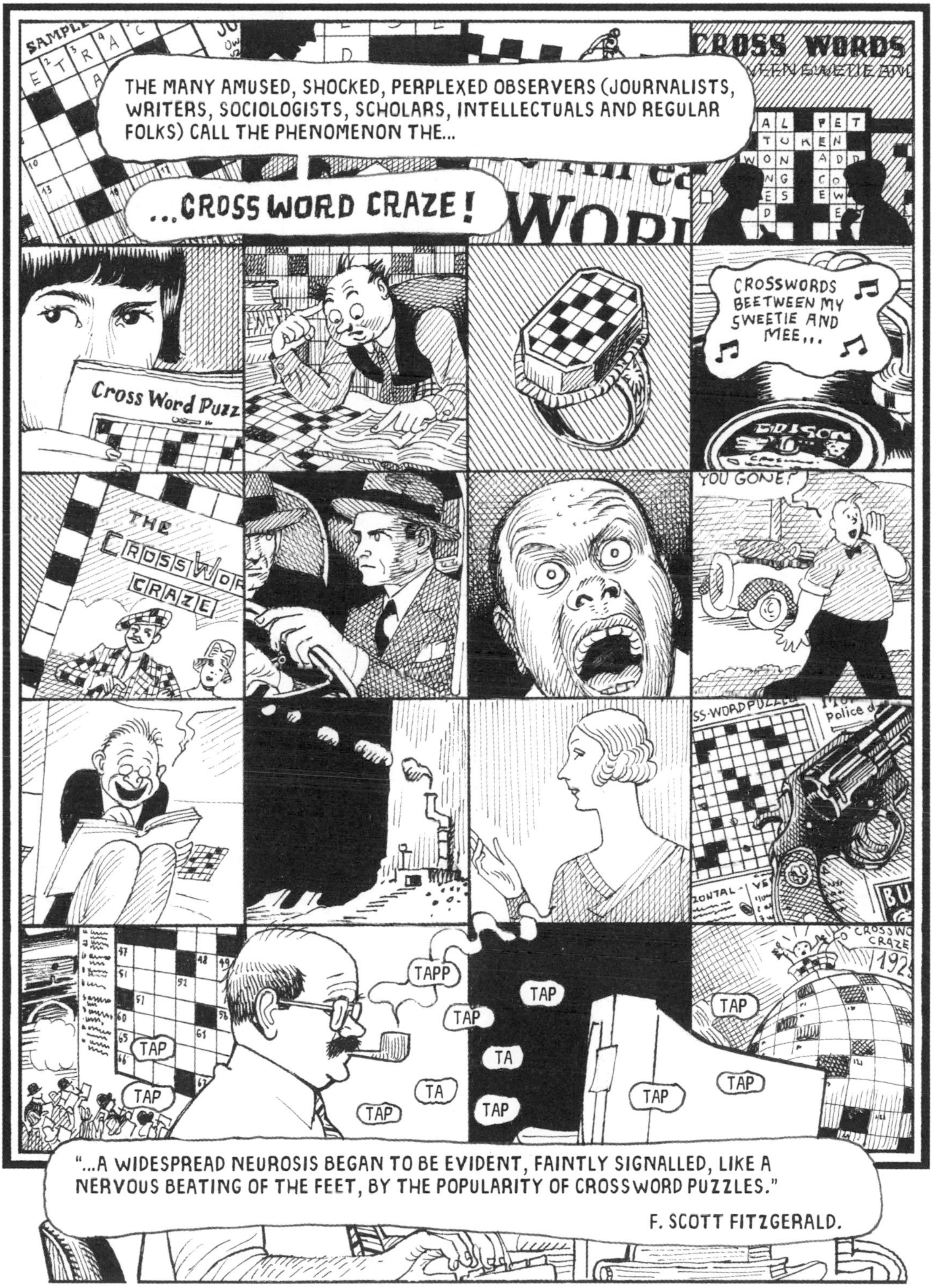
THE MANY AMUSED, SHOCKED, PERPLEXED OBSERVERS (JOURNALISTS, WRITERS, SOCIOLOGISTS, SCHOLARS, INTELLECTUALS AND REGULAR FOLKS) CALL THE PHENOMENON THE...
...CROSS WORD CRAZE!
CROSS WORDS
Cross Word Puzz
CROSSWORDS BEETWEEN MY SWEETIE AND MEE,,,
THE CROSSWORD CRAZE
YOU GONE?
Police d
TAP
TAP
TAPP
TAP
TA
TAP
TAP
TA
TAP
TAP
TAP
TAP
CROSSWO CRAZE 1925
"...A WIDESPREAD NEUROSIS BEGAN TO BE EVIDENT, FAINTLY SIGNALLED, LIKE A NERVOUS BEATING OF THE FEET, BY THE POPULARITY OF CROSSWORD PUZZLES."
F. SCOTT FITZGERALD.

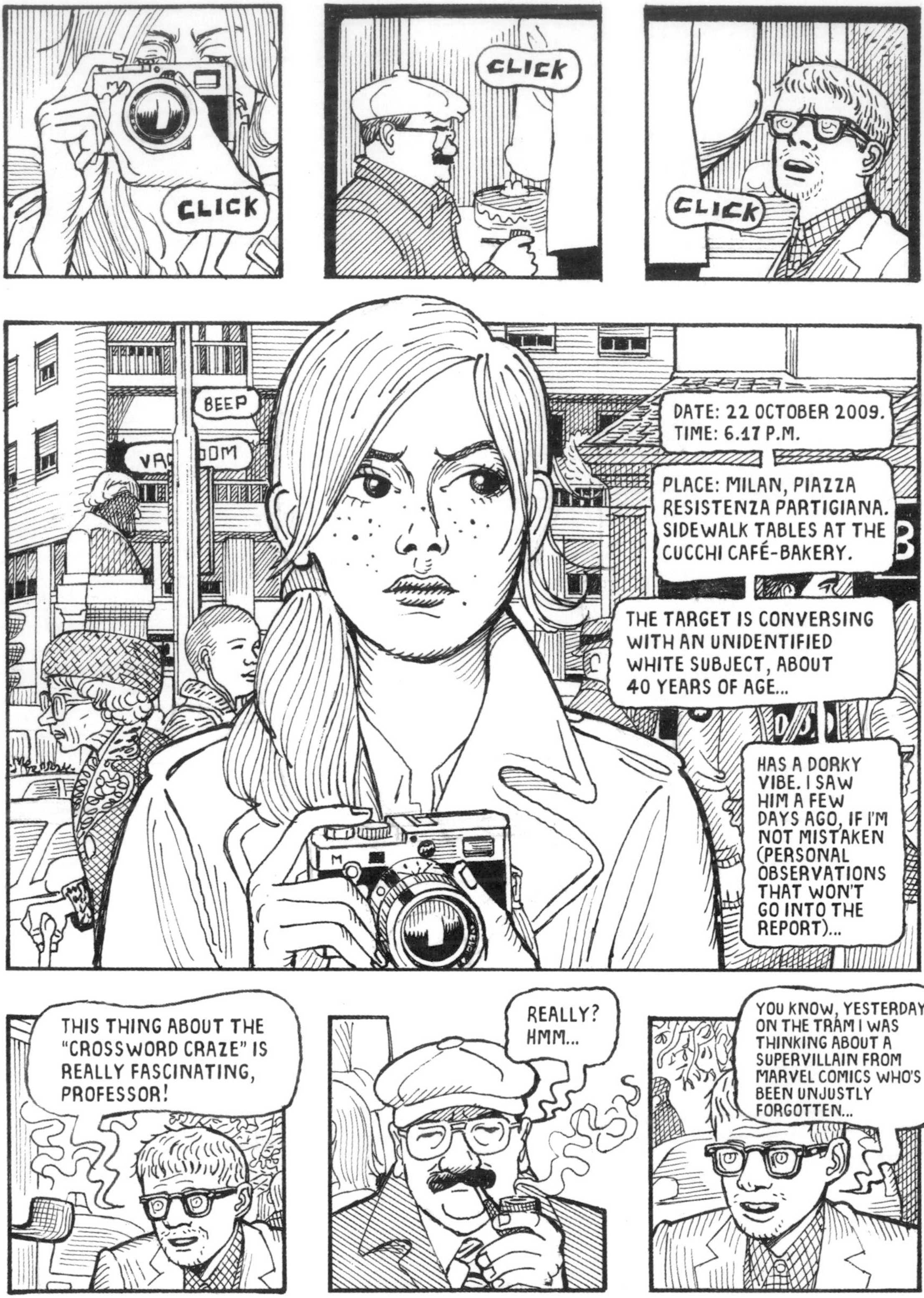
CLICK
CLICK
CLICK
BEEP
VR... OOM
DATE: 22 OCTOBER 2009.
TIME: 6.17 P.M.
PLACE: MILAN, PIAZZA RESISTENZA PARTIGIANA. SIDEWALK TABLES AT THE CUCCHI CAFÉ-BAKERY.
THE TARGET IS CONVERSING WITH AN UNIDENTIFIED WHITE SUBJECT, ABOUT 40 YEARS OF AGE...
HAS A DORKY VIBE. I SAW HIM A FEW DAYS AGO, IF I'M NOT MISTAKEN (PERSONAL OBSERVATIONS THAT WON'T GO INTO THE REPORT)...
THIS THING ABOUT THE "CROSSWORD CRAZE" IS REALLY FASCINATING, PROFESSOR!
REALLY? HMM...
YOU KNOW, YESTERDAY ON THE TRAM I WAS THINKING ABOUT A SUPERVILLAIN FROM MARVEL COMICS WHO'S BEEN UNJUSTLY FORGOTTEN...

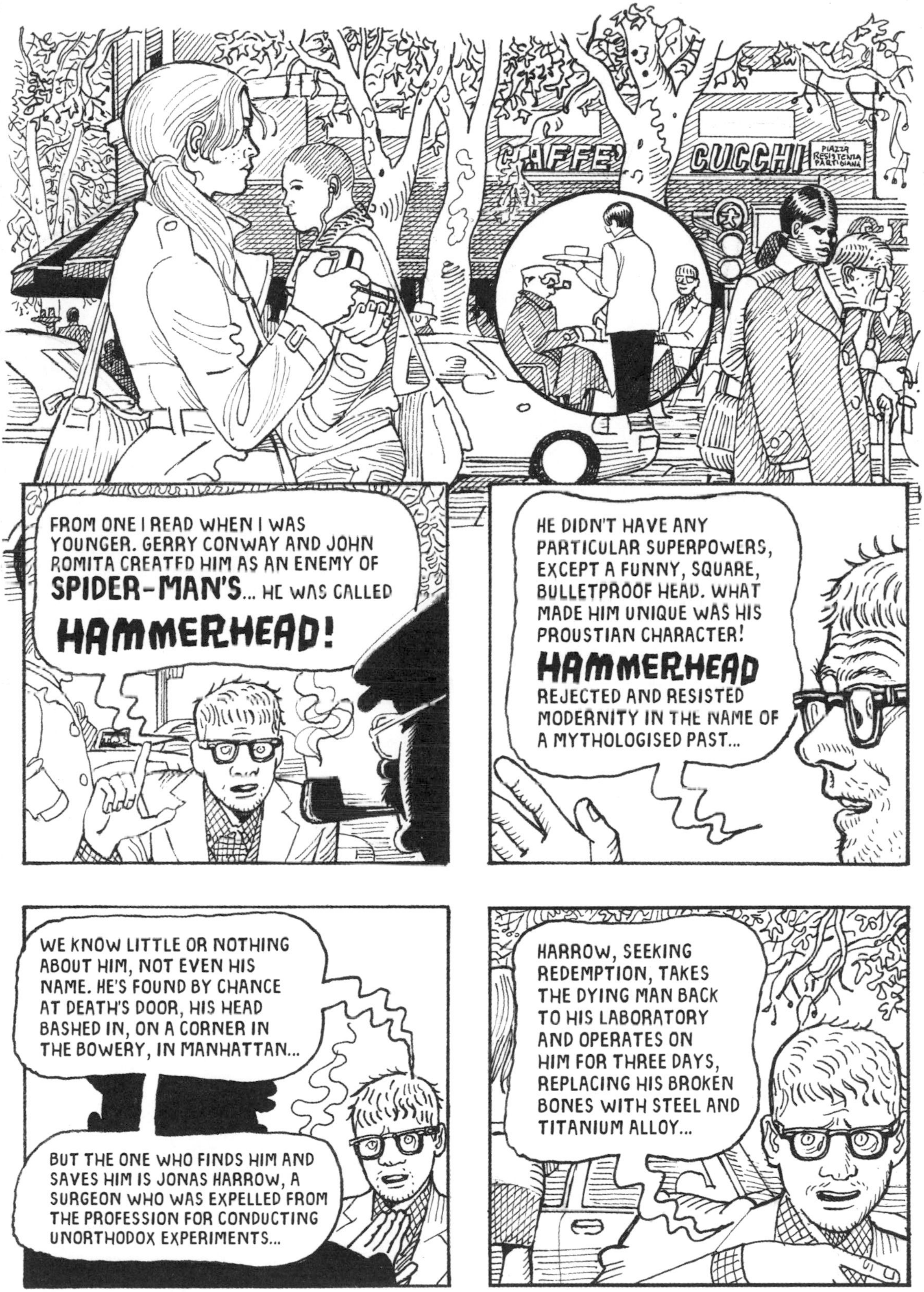
CAFFE' CUCCHI
PIAZZA RESISTENZA PARTIGIANA
FROM ONE I READ WHEN I WAS YOUNGER. GERRY CONWAY AND JOHN ROMITA CREATED HIM AS AN ENEMY OF SPIDER-MAN'S... HE WAS CALLED HAMMERHEAD!
HE DIDN'T HAVE ANY PARTICULAR SUPERPOWERS, EXCEPT A FUNNY, SQUARE, BULLETPROOF HEAD. WHAT MADE HIM UNIQUE WAS HIS PROUSTIAN CHARACTER! HAMMERHEAD REJECTED AND RESISTED MODERNITY IN THE NAME OF A MYTHOLOGISED PAST...
WE KNOW LITTLE OR NOTHING ABOUT HIM, NOT EVEN HIS NAME. HE'S FOUND BY CHANCE AT DEATH'S DOOR, HIS HEAD BASHED IN, ON A CORNER IN THE BOWERY, IN MANHATTAN...
BUT THE ONE WHO FINDS HIM AND SAVES HIM IS JONAS HARROW, A SURGEON WHO WAS EXPELLED FROM THE PROFESSION FOR CONDUCTING UNORTHODOX EXPERIMENTS...
HARROW, SEEKING REDEMPTION, TAKES THE DYING MAN BACK TO HIS LABORATORY AND OPERATES ON HIM FOR THREE DAYS, REPLACING HIS BROKEN BONES WITH STEEL AND TITANIUM ALLOY...

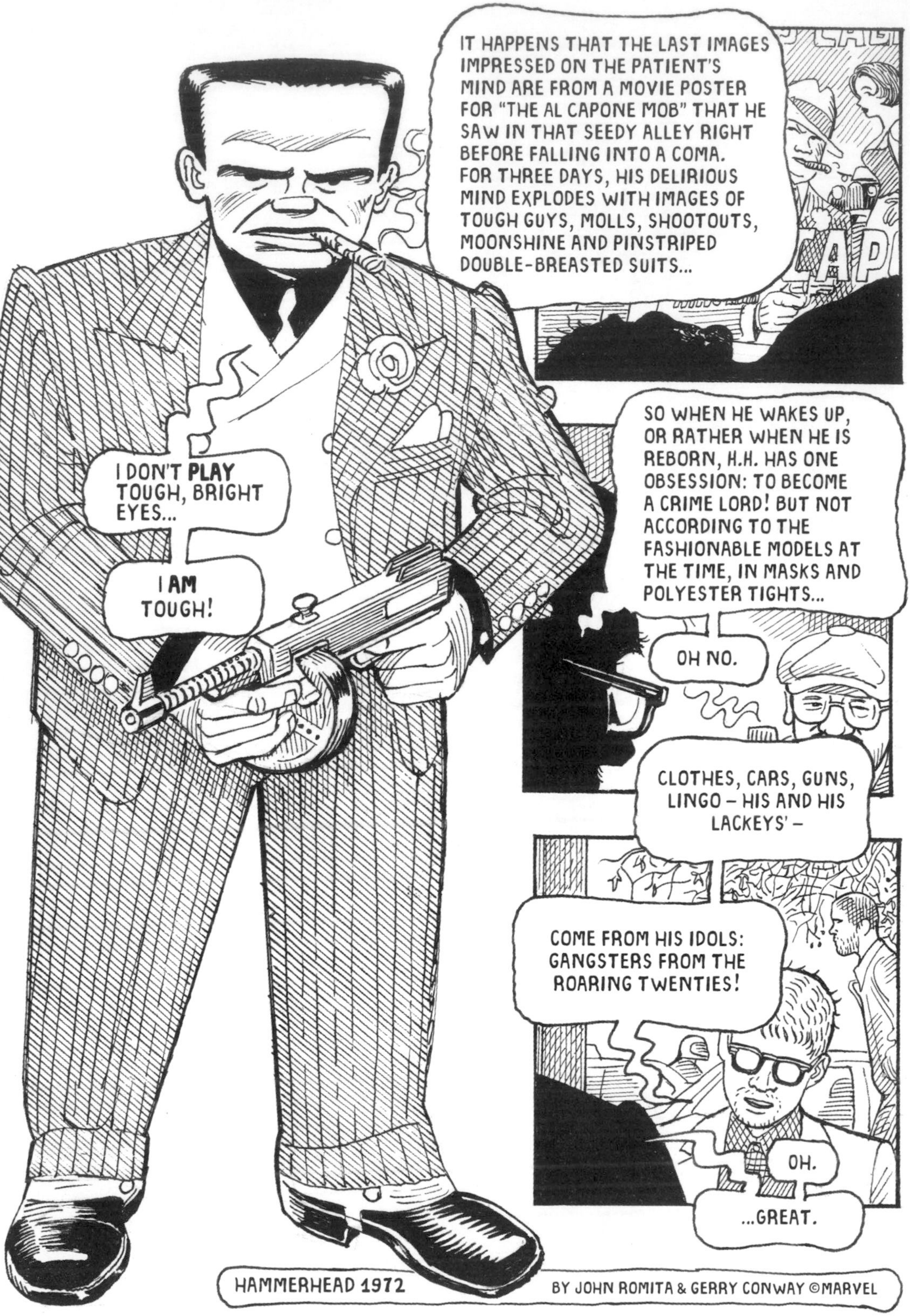
IT HAPPENS THAT THE LAST IMAGES IMPRESSED ON THE PATIENT'S MIND ARE FROM A MOVIE POSTER FOR "THE AL CAPONE MOB" THAT HE SAW IN THAT SEEDY ALLEY RIGHT BEFORE FALLING INTO A COMA. FOR THREE DAYS, HIS DELIRIOUS MIND EXPLODES WITH IMAGES OF TOUGH GUYS, MOLLS, SHOOTOUTS, MOONSHINE AND PINSTRIPED DOUBLE-BREASTED SUITS...
I DON'T **PLAY** TOUGH, BRIGHT EYES...
I **AM** TOUGH!
SO WHEN HE WAKES UP, OR RATHER WHEN HE IS REBORN, H.H. HAS ONE OBSESSION: TO BECOME A CRIME LORD! BUT NOT ACCORDING TO THE FASHIONABLE MODELS AT THE TIME, IN MASKS AND POLYESTER TIGHTS...
OH NO.
CLOTHES, CARS, GUNS, LINGO – HIS AND HIS LACKEYS' –
COME FROM HIS IDOLS: GANGSTERS FROM THE ROARING TWENTIES!
OH.
...GREAT.
HAMMERHEAD 1972
BY JOHN ROMITA & GERRY CONWAY ©MARVEL

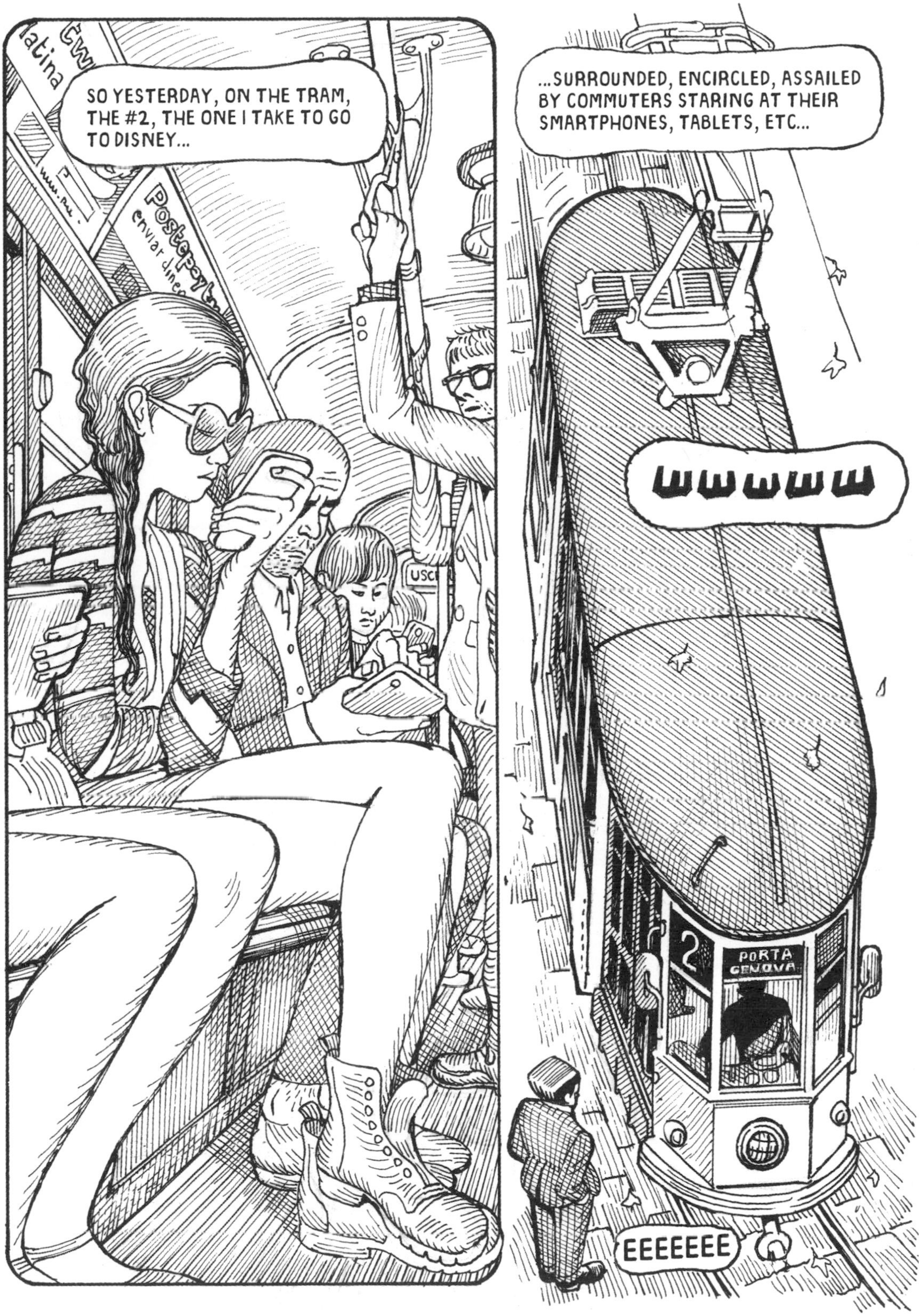
SO YESTERDAY, ON THE TRAM, THE #2, THE ONE I TAKE TO GO TO DISNEY...
...SURROUNDED, ENCIRCLED, ASSAILED BY COMMUTERS STARING AT THEIR SMARTPHONES, TABLETS, ETC...
WWWWWW
2
PORTA GENOVA
EEEEEEE

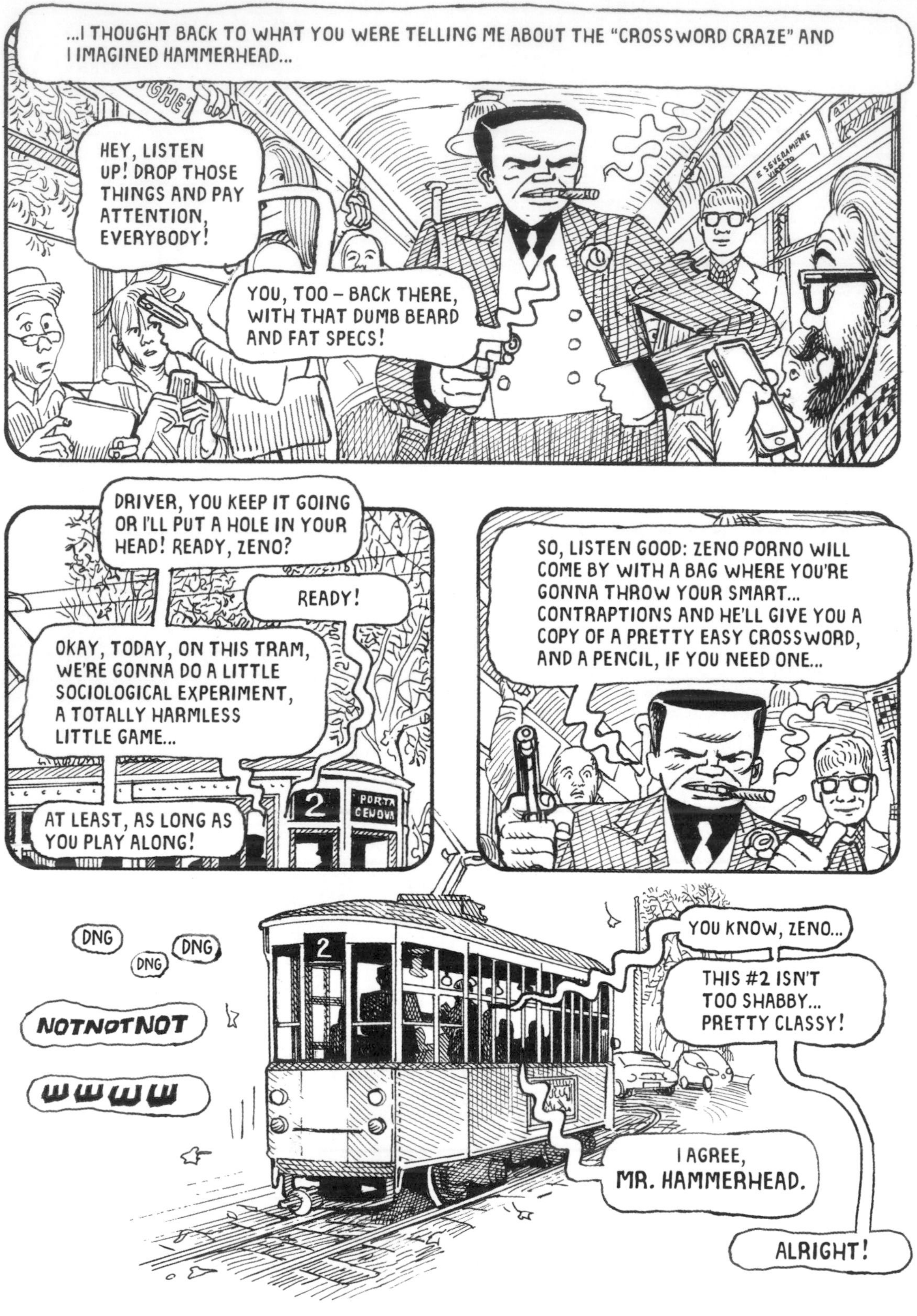
...I THOUGHT BACK TO WHAT YOU WERE TELLING ME ABOUT THE "CROSSWORD CRAZE" AND I IMAGINED HAMMERHEAD...
HEY, LISTEN UP! DROP THOSE THINGS AND PAY ATTENTION, EVERYBODY!
YOU, TOO – BACK THERE, WITH THAT DUMB BEARD AND FAT SPECS!
DRIVER, YOU KEEP IT GOING OR I'LL PUT A HOLE IN YOUR HEAD! READY, ZENO?
READY!
OKAY, TODAY, ON THIS TRAM, WE'RE GONNA DO A LITTLE SOCIOLOGICAL EXPERIMENT, A TOTALLY HARMLESS LITTLE GAME...
AT LEAST, AS LONG AS YOU PLAY ALONG!
2
PORTA GENOVA
SO, LISTEN GOOD: ZENO PORNO WILL COME BY WITH A BAG WHERE YOU'RE GONNA THROW YOUR SMART... CONTRAPTIONS AND HE'LL GIVE YOU A COPY OF A PRETTY EASY CROSSWORD, AND A PENCIL, IF YOU NEED ONE...
DNG
DNG
DNG
NOTNOTNOT
WWWW
2
YOU KNOW, ZENO...
THIS #2 ISN'T TOO SHABBY... PRETTY CLASSY!
I AGREE, MR. HAMMERHEAD.
ALRIGHT!

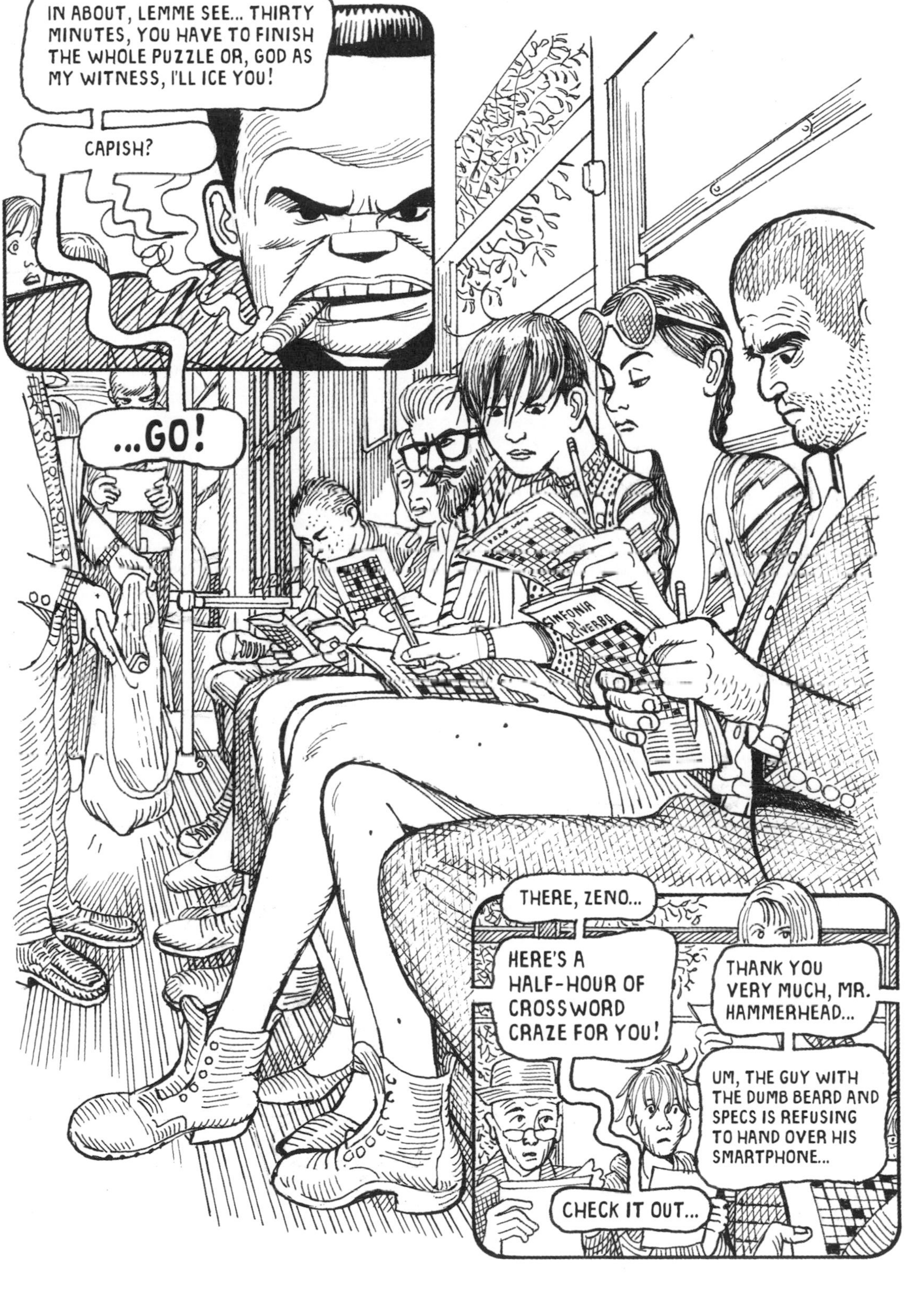
IN ABOUT, LEMME SEE... THIRTY MINUTES, YOU HAVE TO FINISH THE WHOLE PUZZLE OR, GOD AS MY WITNESS, I'LL ICE YOU!
CAPISH?
...GO!
SINFONIA DI VERBA
THERE, ZENO...
HERE'S A HALF-HOUR OF CROSSWORD CRAZE FOR YOU!
CHECK IT OUT...
THANK YOU VERY MUCH, MR. HAMMERHEAD...
UM, THE GUY WITH THE DUMB BEARD AND SPECS IS REFUSING TO HAND OVER HIS SMARTPHONE...

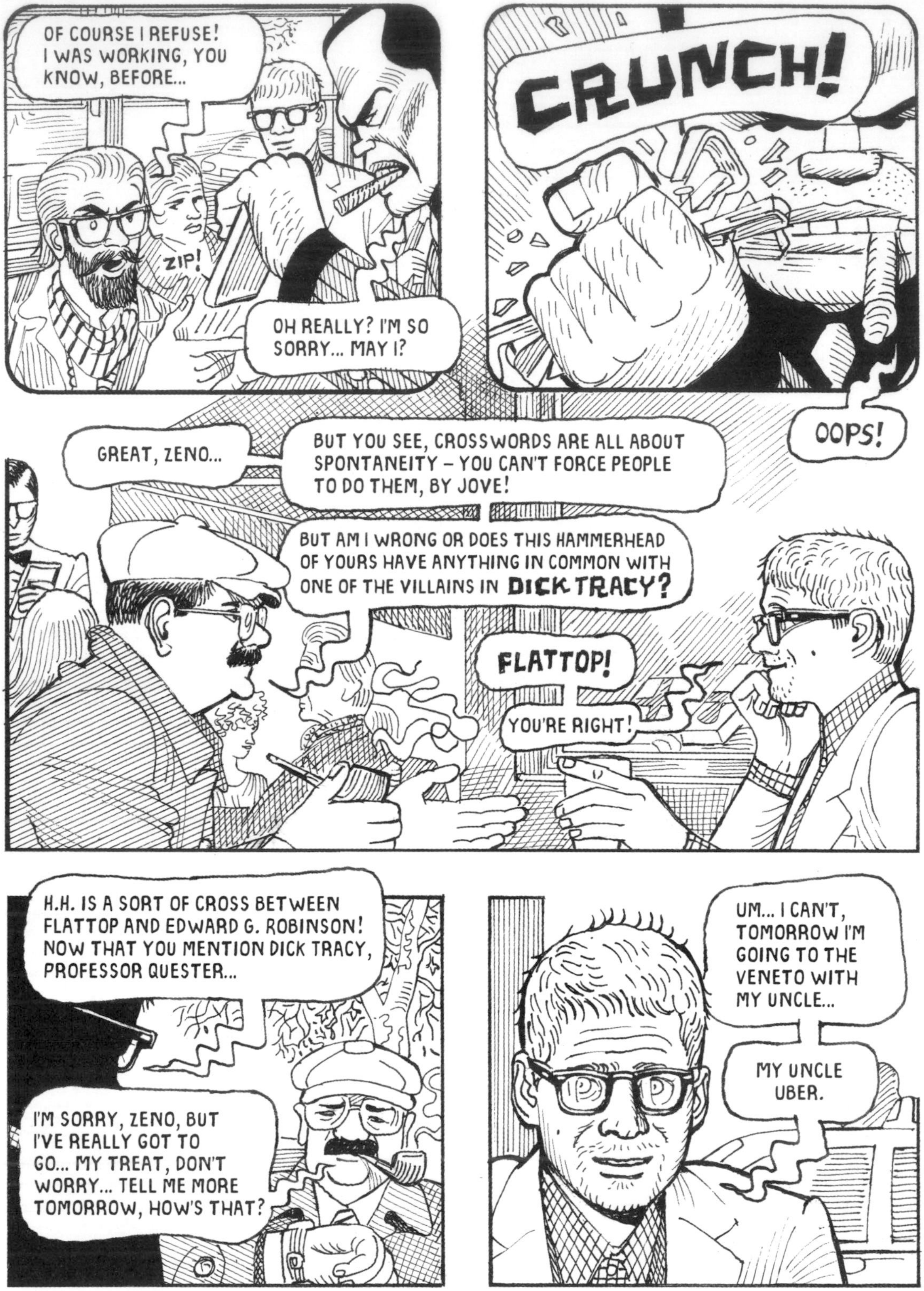
OF COURSE I REFUSE! I WAS WORKING, YOU KNOW, BEFORE...
ZIP!
OH REALLY? I'M SO SORRY... MAY I?
CRUNCH!
OOPS!
GREAT, ZENO...
BUT YOU SEE, CROSSWORDS ARE ALL ABOUT SPONTANEITY – YOU CAN'T FORCE PEOPLE TO DO THEM, BY JOVE!
BUT AM I WRONG OR DOES THIS HAMMERHEAD OF YOURS HAVE ANYTHING IN COMMON WITH ONE OF THE VILLAINS IN DICK TRACY?
FLATTOP!
YOU'RE RIGHT!
H.H. IS A SORT OF CROSS BETWEEN FLATTOP AND EDWARD G. ROBINSON! NOW THAT YOU MENTION DICK TRACY, PROFESSOR QUESTER...
I'M SORRY, ZENO, BUT I'VE REALLY GOT TO GO... MY TREAT, DON'T WORRY... TELL ME MORE TOMORROW, HOW'S THAT?
UM... I CAN'T, TOMORROW I'M GOING TO THE VENETO WITH MY UNCLE...
MY UNCLE UBER.

How Green was my Valley

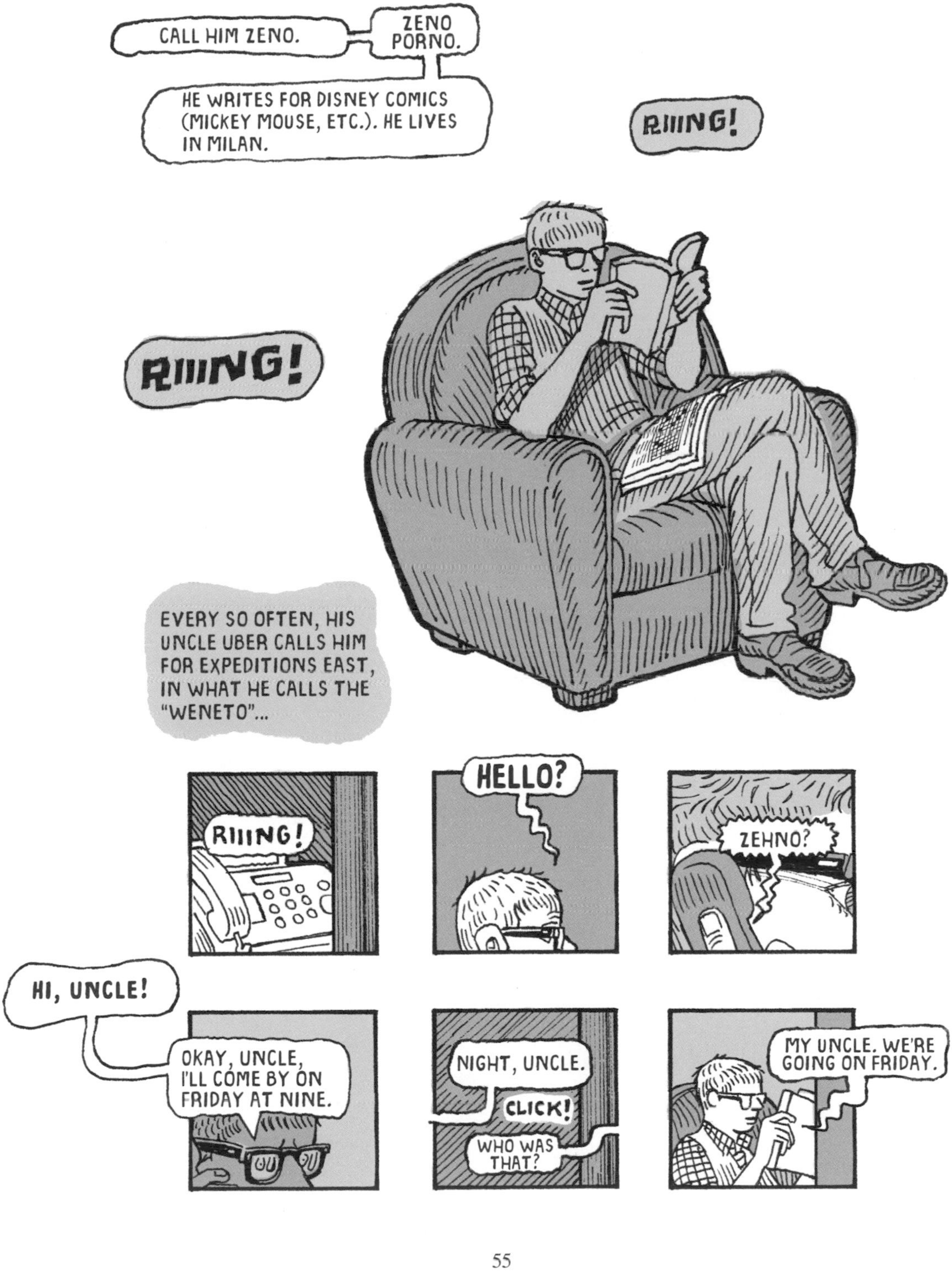

CALL HIM ZENO.
ZENO PORNO.
HE WRITES FOR DISNEY COMICS (MICKEY MOUSE, ETC.). HE LIVES IN MILAN.
RIIING!
RIIING!
EVERY SO OFTEN, HIS UNCLE UBER CALLS HIM FOR EXPEDITIONS EAST, IN WHAT HE CALLS THE "WENETO"...
RIIING!
HELLO?
ZEHNO?
HI, UNCLE!
OKAY, UNCLE, I'LL COME BY ON FRIDAY AT NINE.
NIGHT, UNCLE.
CLICK!
WHO WAS THAT?
MY UNCLE. WE'RE GOING ON FRIDAY.

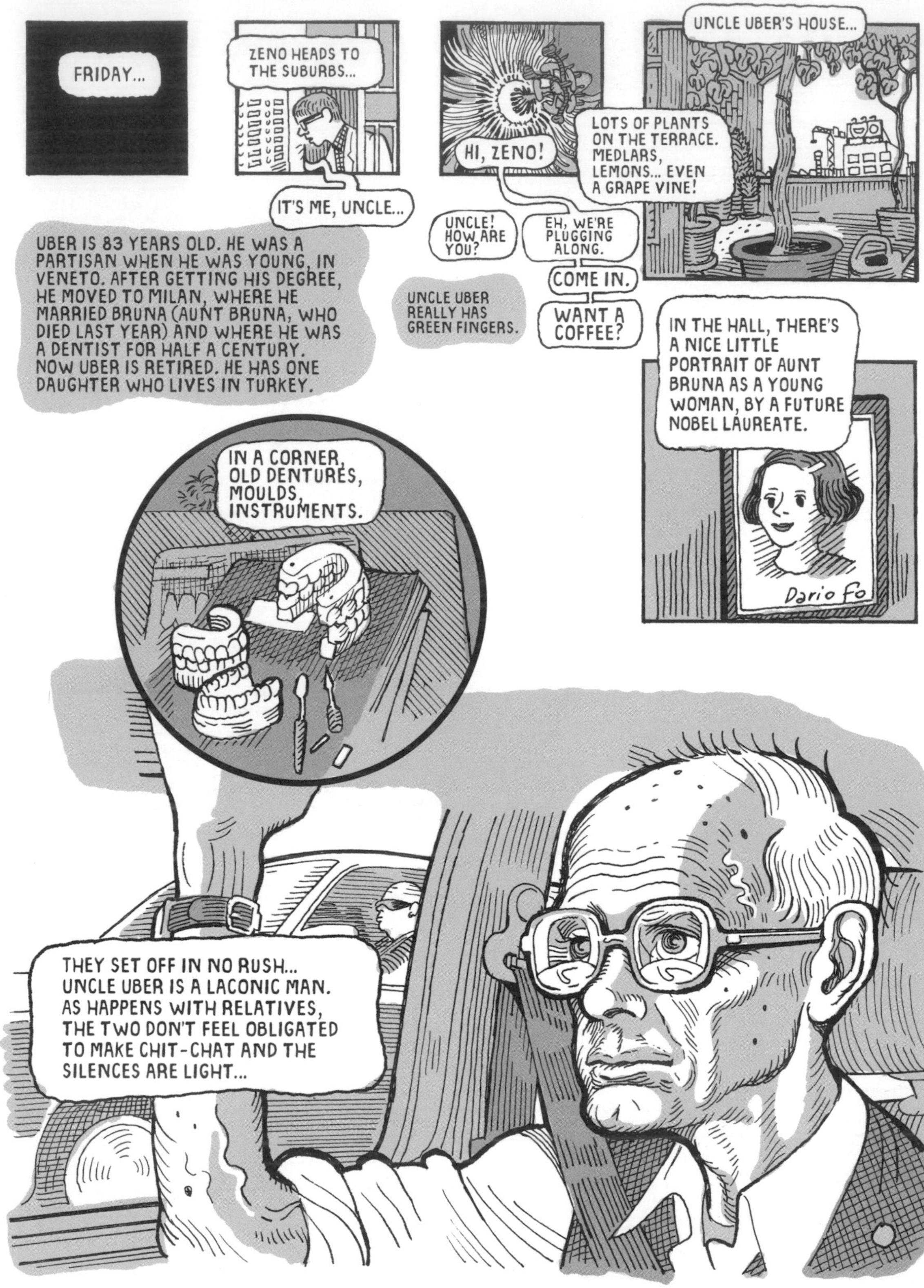

FRIDAY...
ZENO HEADS TO THE SUBURBS...
IT'S ME, UNCLE...
HI, ZENO!
UNCLE! HOW ARE YOU?
EH, WE'RE PLUGGING ALONG.
COME IN.
WANT A COFFEE?
UNCLE UBER'S HOUSE...
LOTS OF PLANTS ON THE TERRACE. MEDLARS, LEMONS... EVEN A GRAPE VINE!
UBER IS 83 YEARS OLD. HE WAS A PARTISAN WHEN HE WAS YOUNG, IN VENETO. AFTER GETTING HIS DEGREE, HE MOVED TO MILAN, WHERE HE MARRIED BRUNA (AUNT BRUNA, WHO DIED LAST YEAR) AND WHERE HE WAS A DENTIST FOR HALF A CENTURY. NOW UBER IS RETIRED. HE HAS ONE DAUGHTER WHO LIVES IN TURKEY.
UNCLE UBER REALLY HAS GREEN FINGERS.
IN THE HALL, THERE'S A NICE LITTLE PORTRAIT OF AUNT BRUNA AS A YOUNG WOMAN, BY A FUTURE NOBEL LAUREATE.
Dario Fo
IN A CORNER, OLD DENTURES, MOULDS, INSTRUMENTS.
THEY SET OFF IN NO RUSH... UNCLE UBER IS A LACONIC MAN. AS HAPPENS WITH RELATIVES, THE TWO DON'T FEEL OBLIGATED TO MAKE CHIT-CHAT AND THE SILENCES ARE LIGHT...

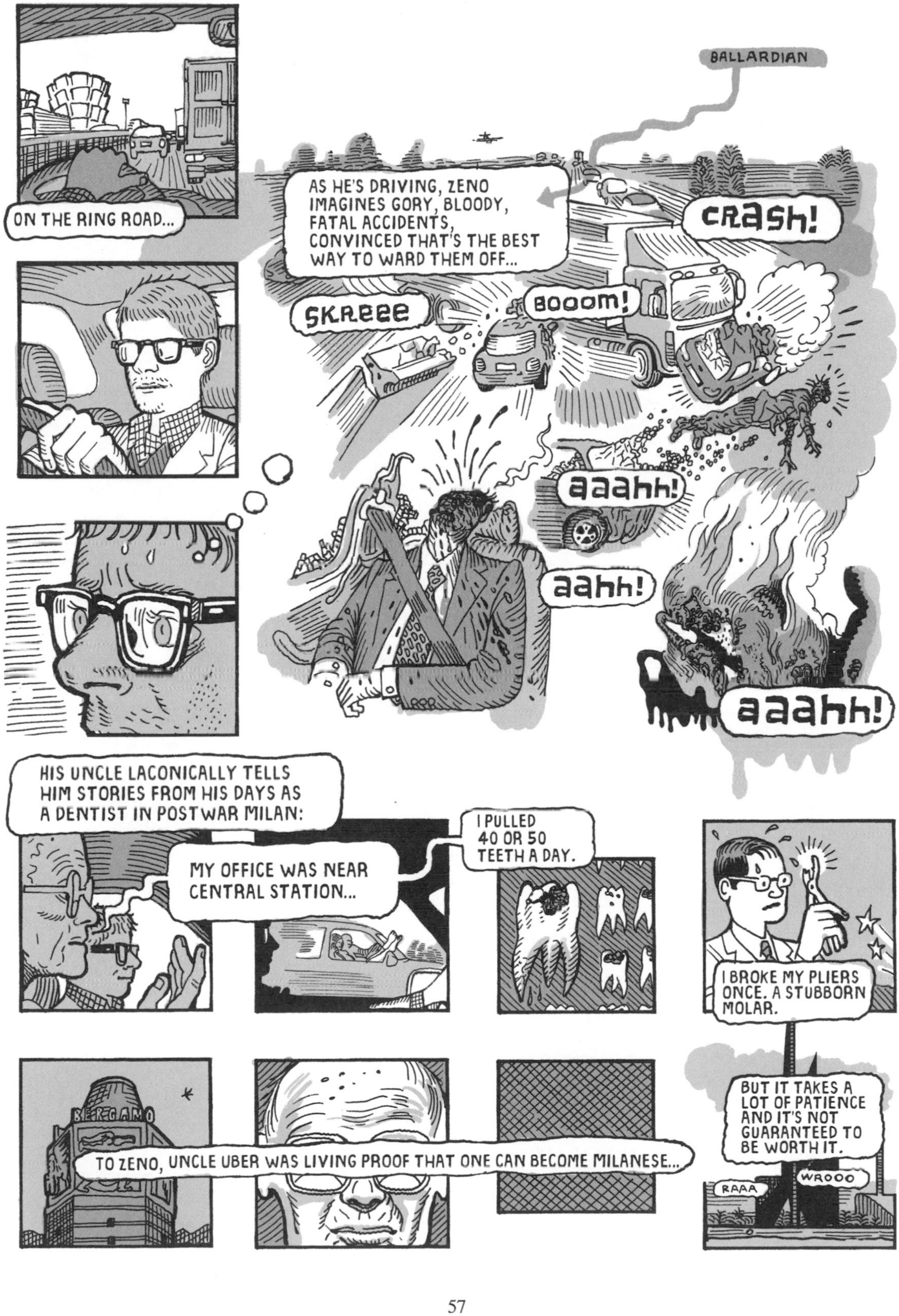

ON THE RING ROAD...
BALLARDIAN
AS HE'S DRIVING, ZENO IMAGINES GORY, BLOODY, FATAL ACCIDENTS, CONVINCED THAT'S THE BEST WAY TO WARD THEM OFF...
CRASH!
SKREEE
BOOOM!
aaahh!
aahh!
aaahh!
HIS UNCLE LACONICALLY TELLS HIM STORIES FROM HIS DAYS AS A DENTIST IN POSTWAR MILAN:
MY OFFICE WAS NEAR CENTRAL STATION...
I PULLED 40 OR 50 TEETH A DAY.
I BROKE MY PLIERS ONCE. A STUBBORN MOLAR.
BERGAMO
TO ZENO, UNCLE UBER WAS LIVING PROOF THAT ONE CAN BECOME MILANESE...
BUT IT TAKES A LOT OF PATIENCE AND IT'S NOT GUARANTEED TO BE WORTH IT.
RAAA
WROOO

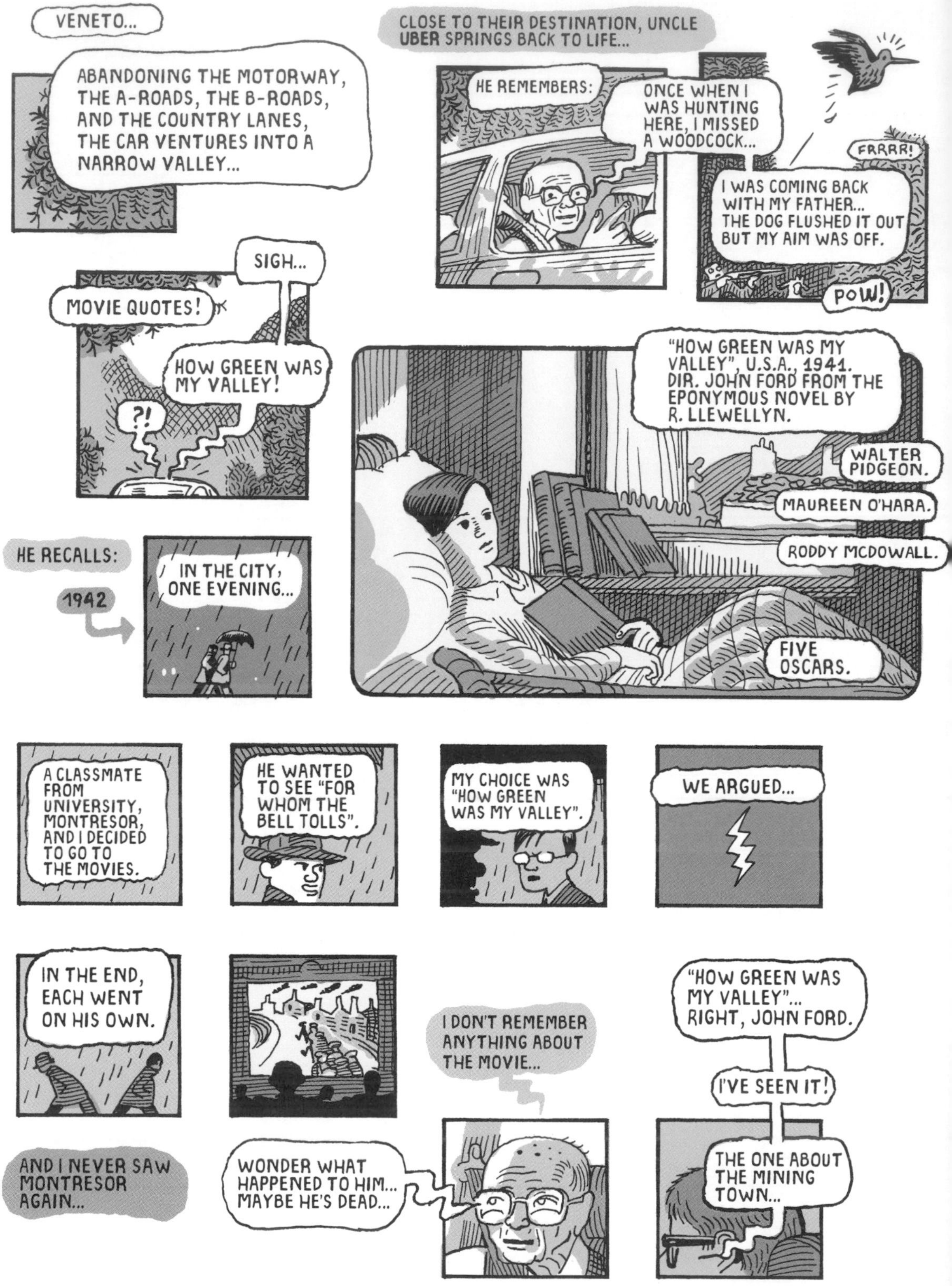
VENETO...
ABANDONING THE MOTORWAY, THE A-ROADS, THE B-ROADS, AND THE COUNTRY LANES, THE CAR VENTURES INTO A NARROW VALLEY...
SIGH...
MOVIE QUOTES!
HOW GREEN WAS MY VALLEY!
?!
CLOSE TO THEIR DESTINATION, UNCLE UBER SPRINGS BACK TO LIFE...
HE REMEMBERS:
ONCE WHEN I WAS HUNTING HERE, I MISSED A WOODCOCK...
FRRRR!
I WAS COMING BACK WITH MY FATHER... THE DOG FLUSHED IT OUT BUT MY AIM WAS OFF.
POW!
HE RECALLS:
1942
IN THE CITY, ONE EVENING...
"HOW GREEN WAS MY VALLEY", U.S.A., 1941. DIR. JOHN FORD FROM THE EPONYMOUS NOVEL BY R. LLEWELLYN.
WALTER PIDGEON.
MAUREEN O'HARA.
RODDY MCDOWALL.
FIVE OSCARS.
A CLASSMATE FROM UNIVERSITY, MONTRESOR, AND I DECIDED TO GO TO THE MOVIES.
HE WANTED TO SEE "FOR WHOM THE BELL TOLLS".
MY CHOICE WAS "HOW GREEN WAS MY VALLEY".
WE ARGUED...
IN THE END, EACH WENT ON HIS OWN.
AND I NEVER SAW MONTRESOR AGAIN...
I DON'T REMEMBER ANYTHING ABOUT THE MOVIE...
WONDER WHAT HAPPENED TO HIM... MAYBE HE'S DEAD...
"HOW GREEN WAS MY VALLEY"... RIGHT, JOHN FORD.
I'VE SEEN IT!
THE ONE ABOUT THE MINING TOWN...

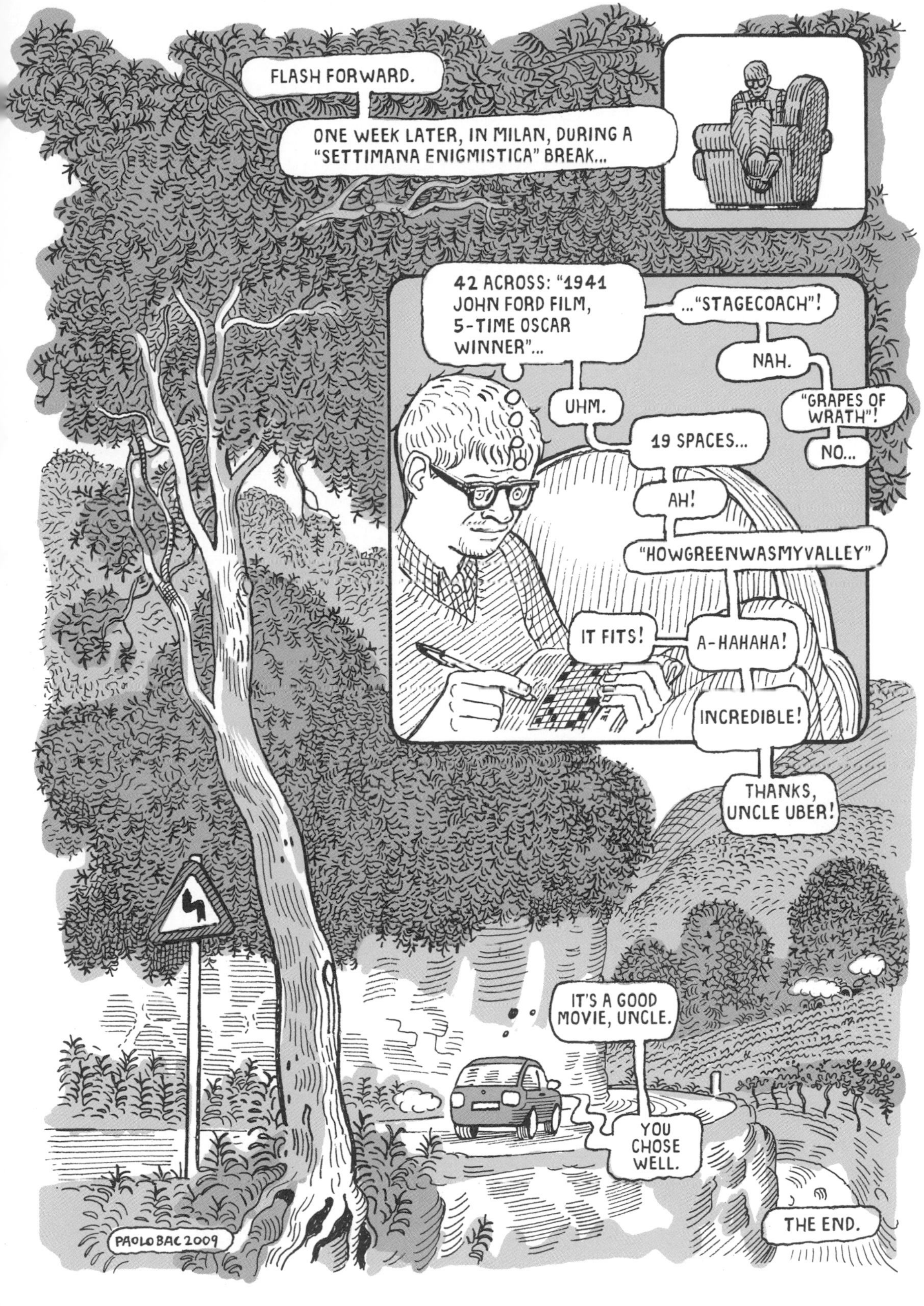
FLASH FORWARD.
ONE WEEK LATER, IN MILAN, DURING A "SETTIMANA ENIGMISTICA" BREAK...
42 ACROSS: "1941 JOHN FORD FILM, 5-TIME OSCAR WINNER"...
..."STAGECOACH"!
NAH.
"GRAPES OF WRATH"!
NO...
UHM.
19 SPACES...
AH!
"HOWGREENWASMYVALLEY"
IT FITS!
A-HAHAHA!
INCREDIBLE!
THANKS, UNCLE UBER!
IT'S A GOOD MOVIE, UNCLE.
YOU CHOSE WELL.
THE END.
PAOLO BAC 2009

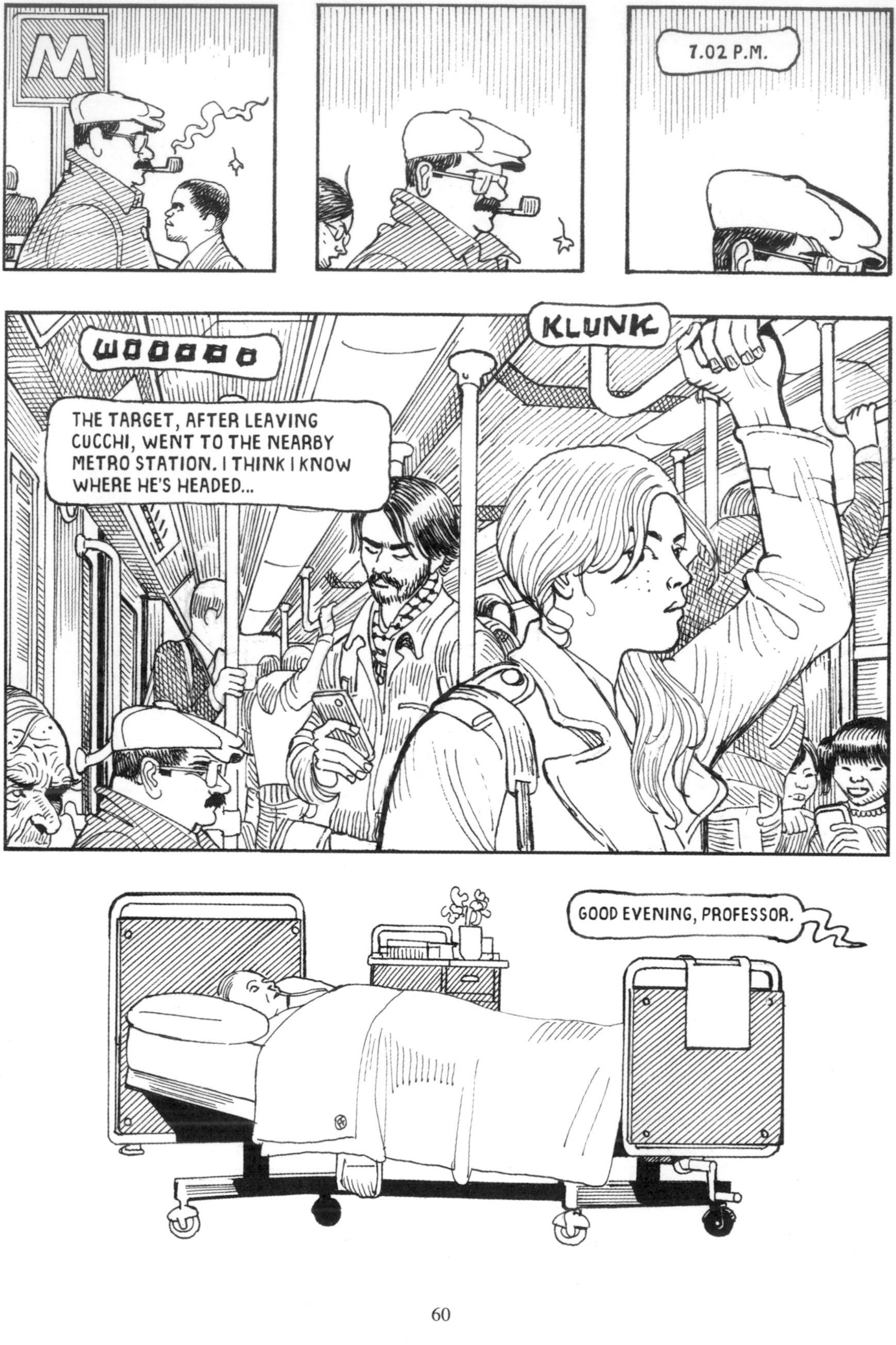
M
7.02 P.M.
WOOOOO
KLUNK
THE TARGET, AFTER LEAVING CUCCHI, WENT TO THE NEARBY METRO STATION. I THINK I KNOW WHERE HE'S HEADED...
GOOD EVENING, PROFESSOR.

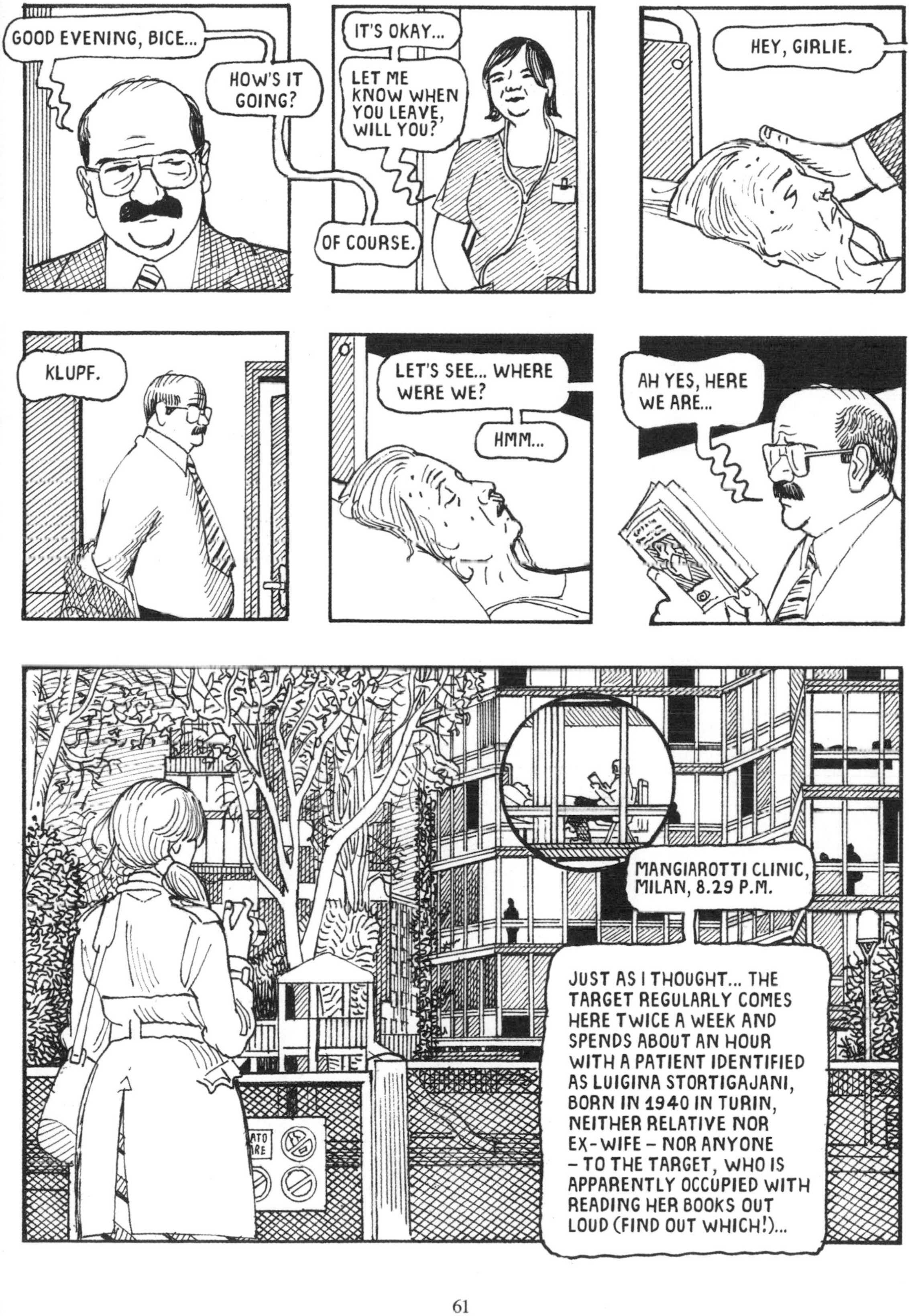
GOOD EVENING, BICE...
HOW'S IT GOING?
OF COURSE.
IT'S OKAY...
LET ME KNOW WHEN YOU LEAVE, WILL YOU?
HEY, GIRLIE.
KLUPF.
LET'S SEE... WHERE WERE WE?
HMM...
AH YES, HERE WE ARE...
MANGIAROTTI CLINIC, MILAN, 8.29 P.M.
JUST AS I THOUGHT... THE TARGET REGULARLY COMES HERE TWICE A WEEK AND SPENDS ABOUT AN HOUR WITH A PATIENT IDENTIFIED AS LUIGINA STORTIGAJANI, BORN IN 1940 IN TURIN, NEITHER RELATIVE NOR EX-WIFE – NOR ANYONE – TO THE TARGET, WHO IS APPARENTLY OCCUPIED WITH READING HER BOOKS OUT LOUD (FIND OUT WHICH!)...

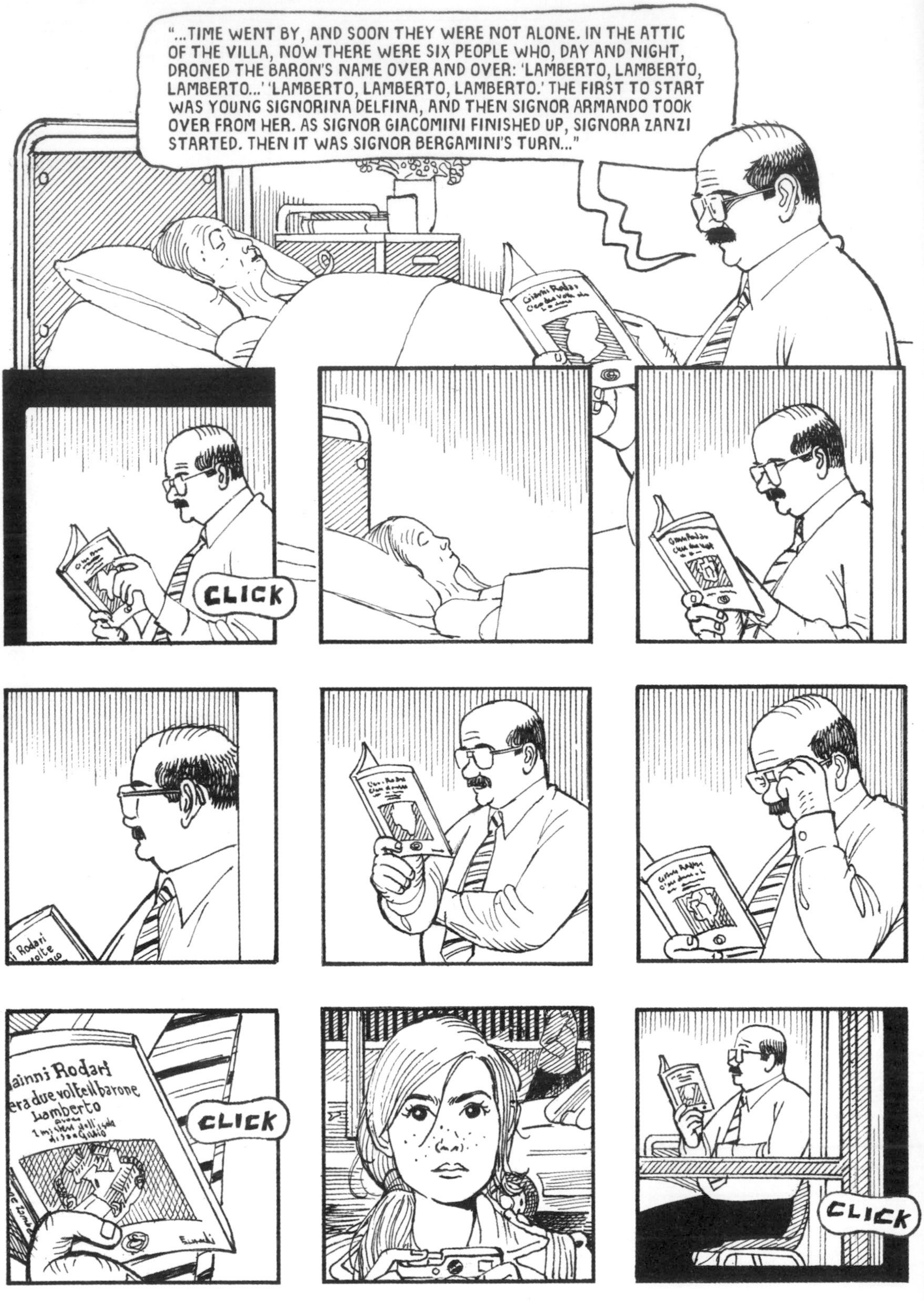
"...TIME WENT BY, AND SOON THEY WERE NOT ALONE. IN THE ATTIC OF THE VILLA, NOW THERE WERE SIX PEOPLE WHO, DAY AND NIGHT, DRONED THE BARON'S NAME OVER AND OVER: 'LAMBERTO, LAMBERTO, LAMBERTO...' 'LAMBERTO, LAMBERTO, LAMBERTO.' THE FIRST TO START WAS YOUNG SIGNORINA DELFINA, AND THEN SIGNOR ARMANDO TOOK OVER FROM HER. AS SIGNOR GIACOMINI FINISHED UP, SIGNORA ZANZI STARTED. THEN IT WAS SIGNOR BERGAMINI'S TURN..."
CLICK
ianni Rodari
era due volteilbarone
Lamberto
CLICK
CLICK

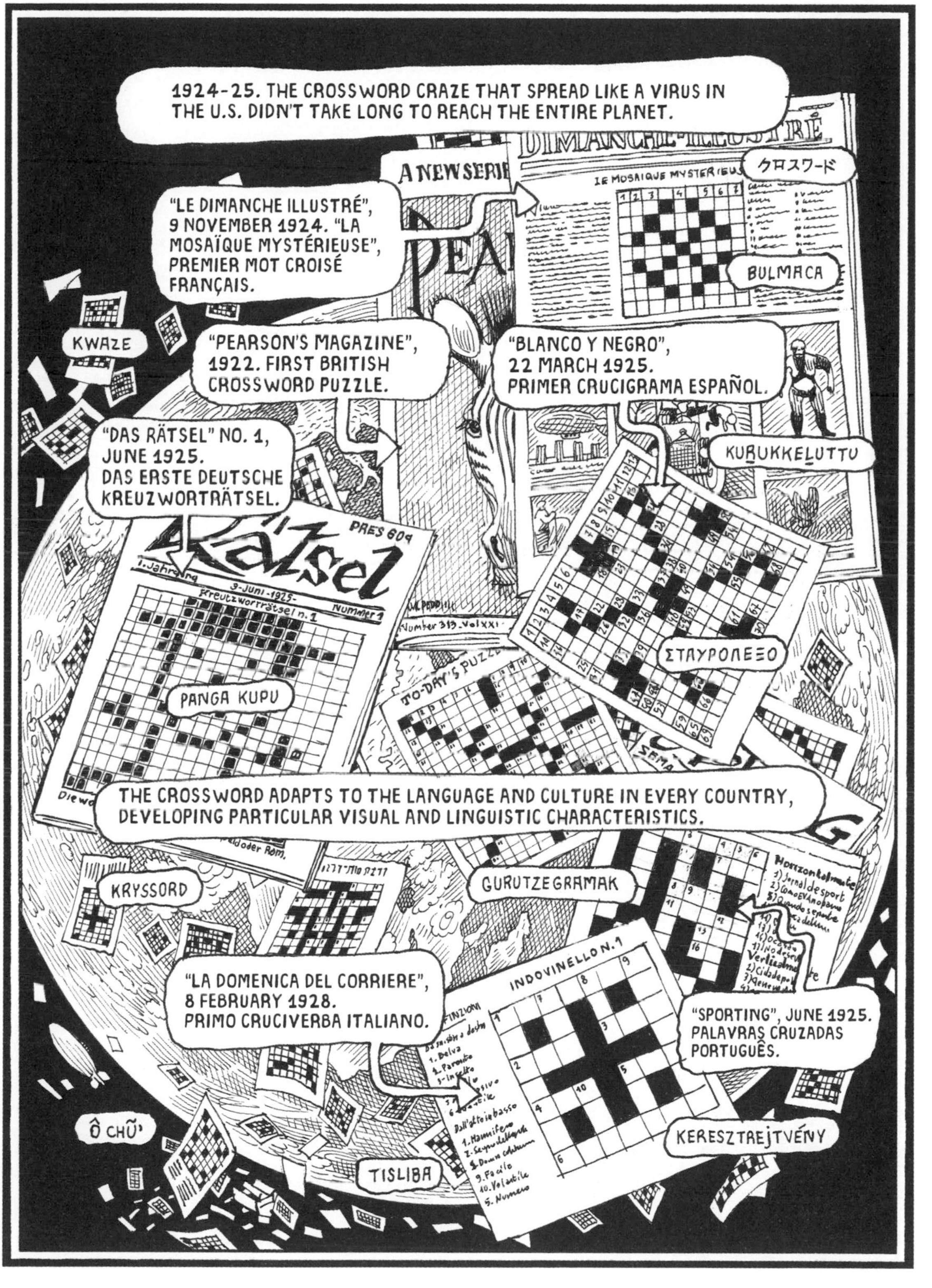

1924-25. THE CROSSWORD CRAZE THAT SPREAD LIKE A VIRUS IN THE U.S. DIDN'T TAKE LONG TO REACH THE ENTIRE PLANET.
"LE DIMANCHE ILLUSTRÉ", 9 NOVEMBER 1924. "LA MOSAÏQUE MYSTÉRIEUSE", PREMIER MOT CROISÉ FRANÇAIS.
クロスワード
BULMACA
KWAZE
"PEARSON'S MAGAZINE", 1922. FIRST BRITISH CROSSWORD PUZZLE.
"BLANCO Y NEGRO", 22 MARCH 1925. PRIMER CRUCIGRAMA ESPAÑOL.
"DAS RÄTSEL" NO. 1, JUNE 1925. DAS ERSTE DEUTSCHE KREUZWORTRÄTSEL.
KURUKKELUTTU
Rätsel
ΣΤΑΥΡΟΛΕΞΟ
PANGA KUPU
THE CROSSWORD ADAPTS TO THE LANGUAGE AND CULTURE IN EVERY COUNTRY, DEVELOPING PARTICULAR VISUAL AND LINGUISTIC CHARACTERISTICS.
KRYSSORD
GURUTZEGRAMAK
"LA DOMENICA DEL CORRIERE", 8 FEBRUARY 1928. PRIMO CRUCIVERBA ITALIANO.
INDOVINELLO N. 1
"SPORTING", JUNE 1925. PALAVRAS CRUZADAS PORTUGUÊS.
Ô CHỮ
TISLIBA
KERESZTREJTVÉNY

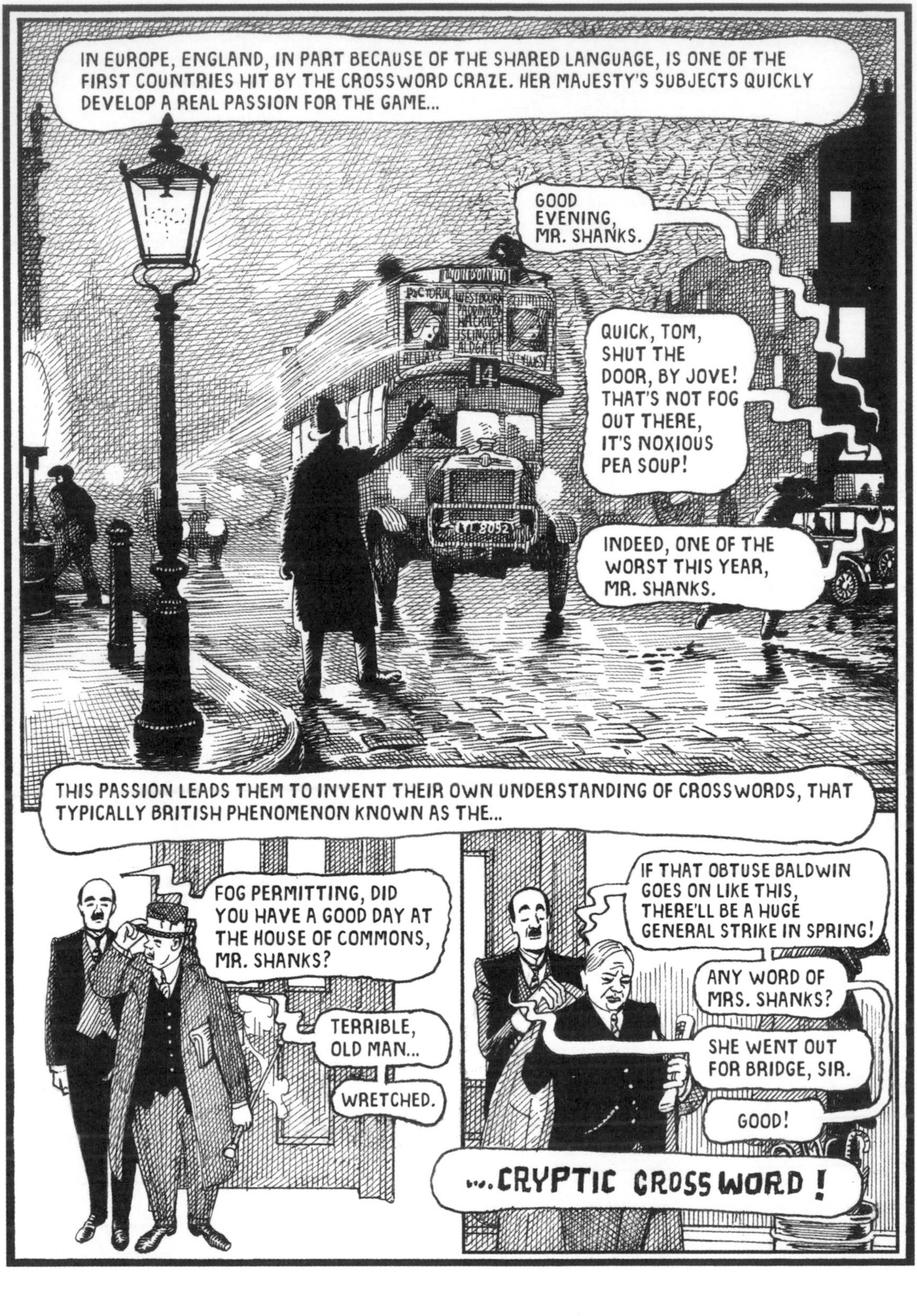

IN EUROPE, ENGLAND, IN PART BECAUSE OF THE SHARED LANGUAGE, IS ONE OF THE FIRST COUNTRIES HIT BY THE CROSSWORD CRAZE. HER MAJESTY'S SUBJECTS QUICKLY DEVELOP A REAL PASSION FOR THE GAME...
GOOD EVENING, MR. SHANKS.
QUICK, TOM, SHUT THE DOOR, BY JOVE! THAT'S NOT FOG OUT THERE, IT'S NOXIOUS PEA SOUP!
INDEED, ONE OF THE WORST THIS YEAR, MR. SHANKS.
14
THIS PASSION LEADS THEM TO INVENT THEIR OWN UNDERSTANDING OF CROSSWORDS, THAT TYPICALLY BRITISH PHENOMENON KNOWN AS THE...
FOG PERMITTING, DID YOU HAVE A GOOD DAY AT THE HOUSE OF COMMONS, MR. SHANKS?
TERRIBLE, OLD MAN...
WRETCHED.
IF THAT OBTUSE BALDWIN GOES ON LIKE THIS, THERE'LL BE A HUGE GENERAL STRIKE IN SPRING!
ANY WORD OF MRS. SHANKS?
SHE WENT OUT FOR BRIDGE, SIR.
GOOD!
....CRYPTIC CROSSWORD!

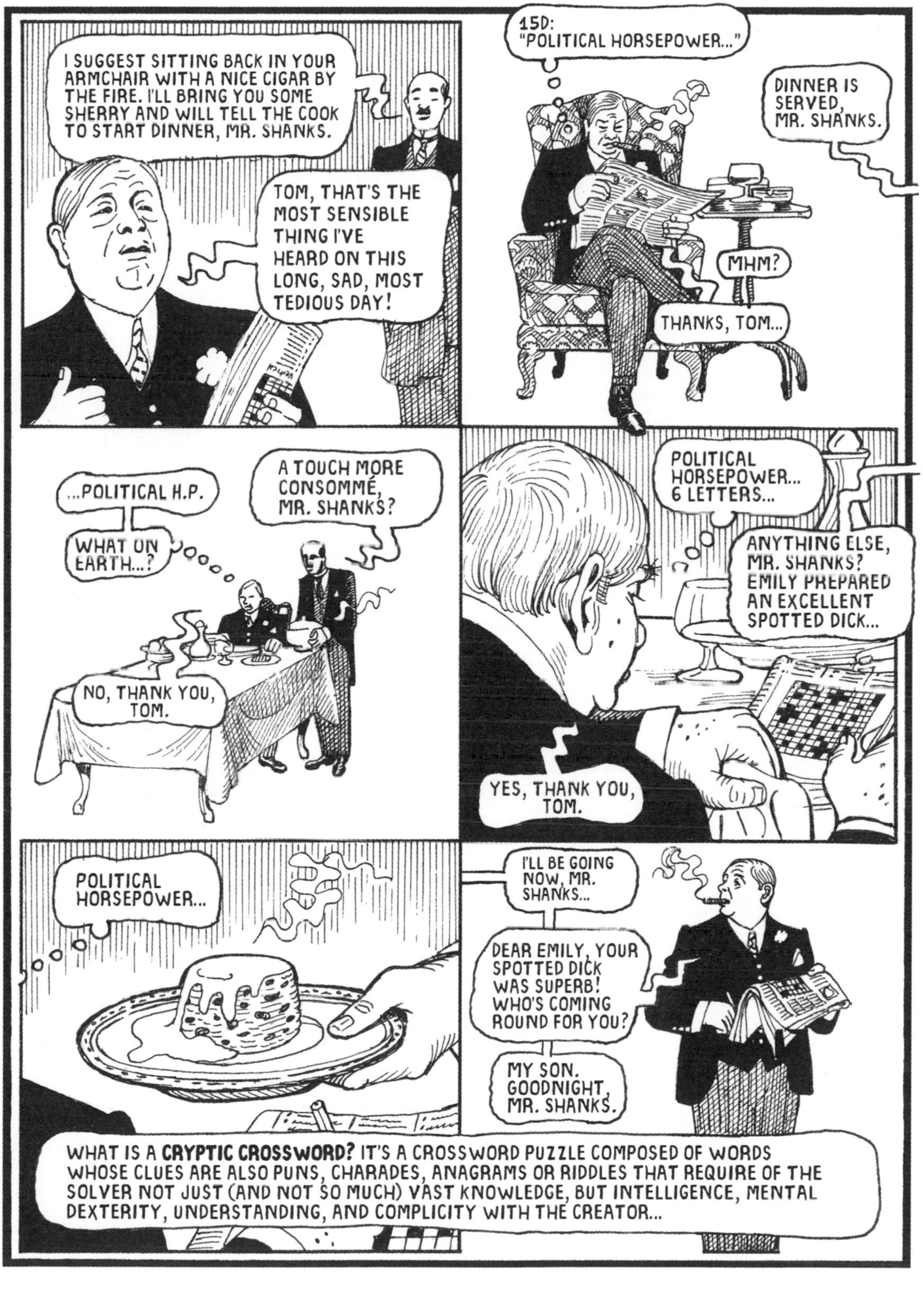
I SUGGEST SITTING BACK IN YOUR ARMCHAIR WITH A NICE CIGAR BY THE FIRE. I'LL BRING YOU SOME SHERRY AND WILL TELL THE COOK TO START DINNER, MR. SHANKS.
TOM, THAT'S THE MOST SENSIBLE THING I'VE HEARD ON THIS LONG, SAD, MOST TEDIOUS DAY!
15D: "POLITICAL HORSEPOWER..."
DINNER IS SERVED, MR. SHANKS.
MHM?
THANKS, TOM...
...POLITICAL H.P.
WHAT ON EARTH...?
A TOUCH MORE CONSOMMÉ, MR. SHANKS?
NO, THANK YOU, TOM.
POLITICAL HORSEPOWER... 6 LETTERS...
ANYTHING ELSE, MR. SHANKS? EMILY PREPARED AN EXCELLENT SPOTTED DICK...
YES, THANK YOU, TOM.
POLITICAL HORSEPOWER...
I'LL BE GOING NOW, MR. SHANKS...
DEAR EMILY, YOUR SPOTTED DICK WAS SUPERB! WHO'S COMING ROUND FOR YOU?
MY SON. GOODNIGHT, MR. SHANKS.
WHAT IS A CRYPTIC CROSSWORD? IT'S A CROSSWORD PUZZLE COMPOSED OF WORDS WHOSE CLUES ARE ALSO PUNS, CHARADES, ANAGRAMS OR RIDDLES THAT REQUIRE OF THE SOLVER NOT JUST (AND NOT SO MUCH) VAST KNOWLEDGE, BUT INTELLIGENCE, MENTAL DEXTERITY, UNDERSTANDING, AND COMPLICITY WITH THE CREATOR...

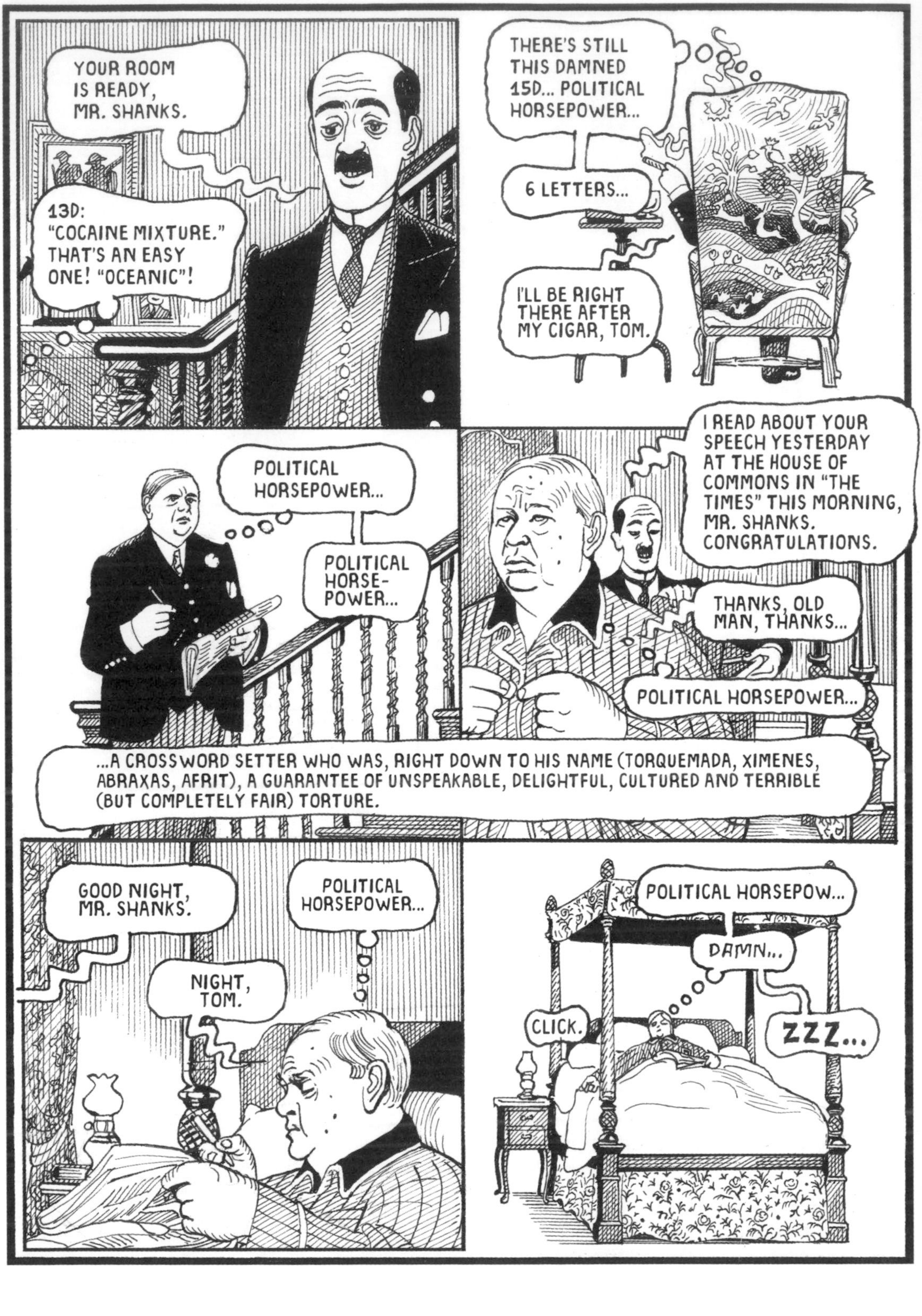
YOUR ROOM IS READY, MR. SHANKS.
13D: "COCAINE MIXTURE." THAT'S AN EASY ONE! "OCEANIC"!
THERE'S STILL THIS DAMNED 15D... POLITICAL HORSEPOWER...
6 LETTERS...
I'LL BE RIGHT THERE AFTER MY CIGAR, TOM.
POLITICAL HORSEPOWER...
POLITICAL HORSE-POWER...
I READ ABOUT YOUR SPEECH YESTERDAY AT THE HOUSE OF COMMONS IN "THE TIMES" THIS MORNING, MR. SHANKS. CONGRATULATIONS.
THANKS, OLD MAN, THANKS...
POLITICAL HORSEPOWER...
...A CROSSWORD SETTER WHO WAS, RIGHT DOWN TO HIS NAME (TORQUEMADA, XIMENES, ABRAXAS, AFRIT), A GUARANTEE OF UNSPEAKABLE, DELIGHTFUL, CULTURED AND TERRIBLE (BUT COMPLETELY FAIR) TORTURE.
GOOD NIGHT, MR. SHANKS.
POLITICAL HORSEPOWER...
NIGHT, TOM.
POLITICAL HORSEPOW...
DAMN...
CLICK.
ZZZ...

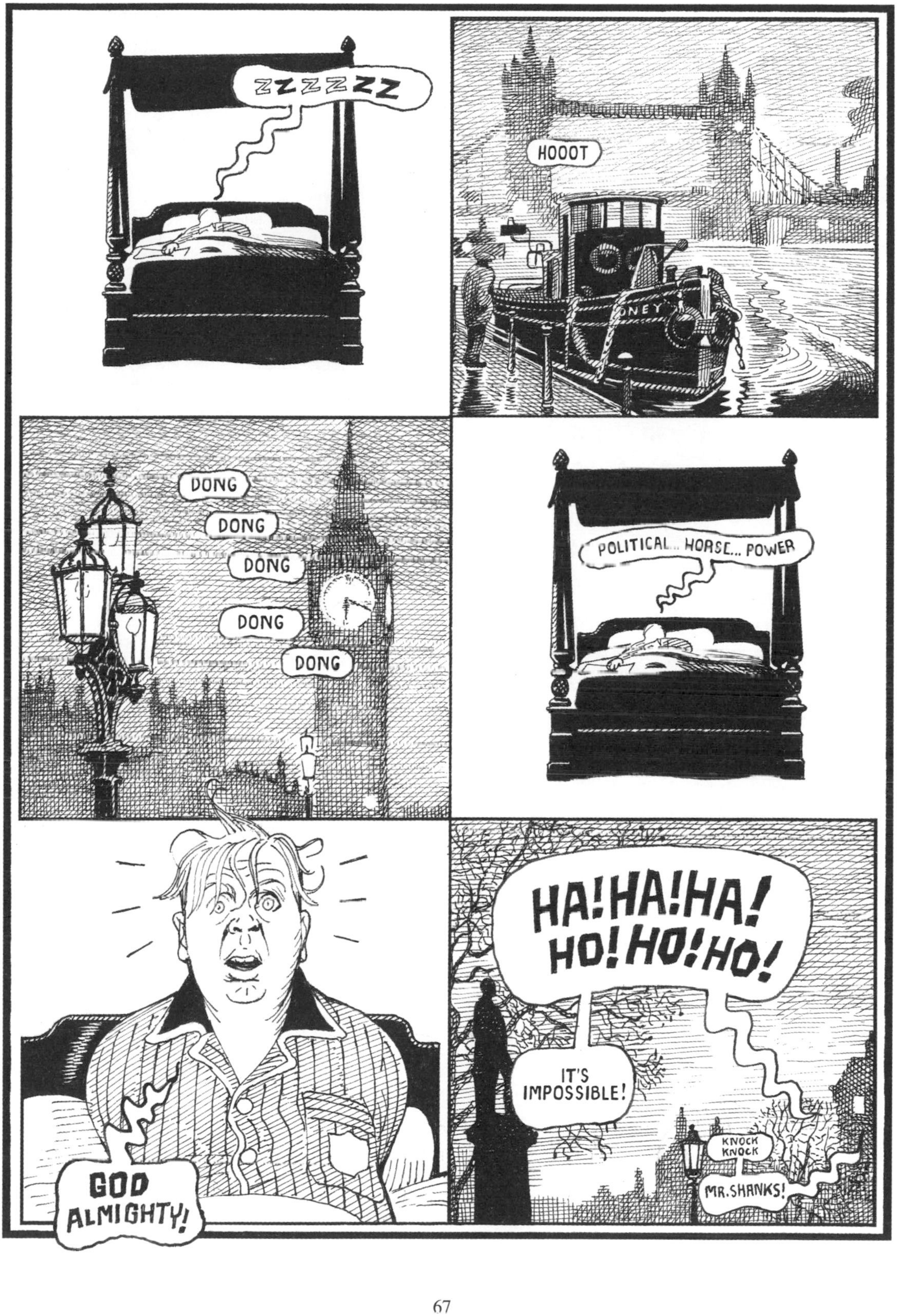
ZZZZZZ
HOOOT
ONEY
DONG
DONG
DONG
DONG
DONG
POLITICAL... HORSE... POWER
GOD ALMIGHTY!
HA!HA!HA! HO!HO!HO!
IT'S IMPOSSIBLE!
KNOCK KNOCK
MR. SHANKS!

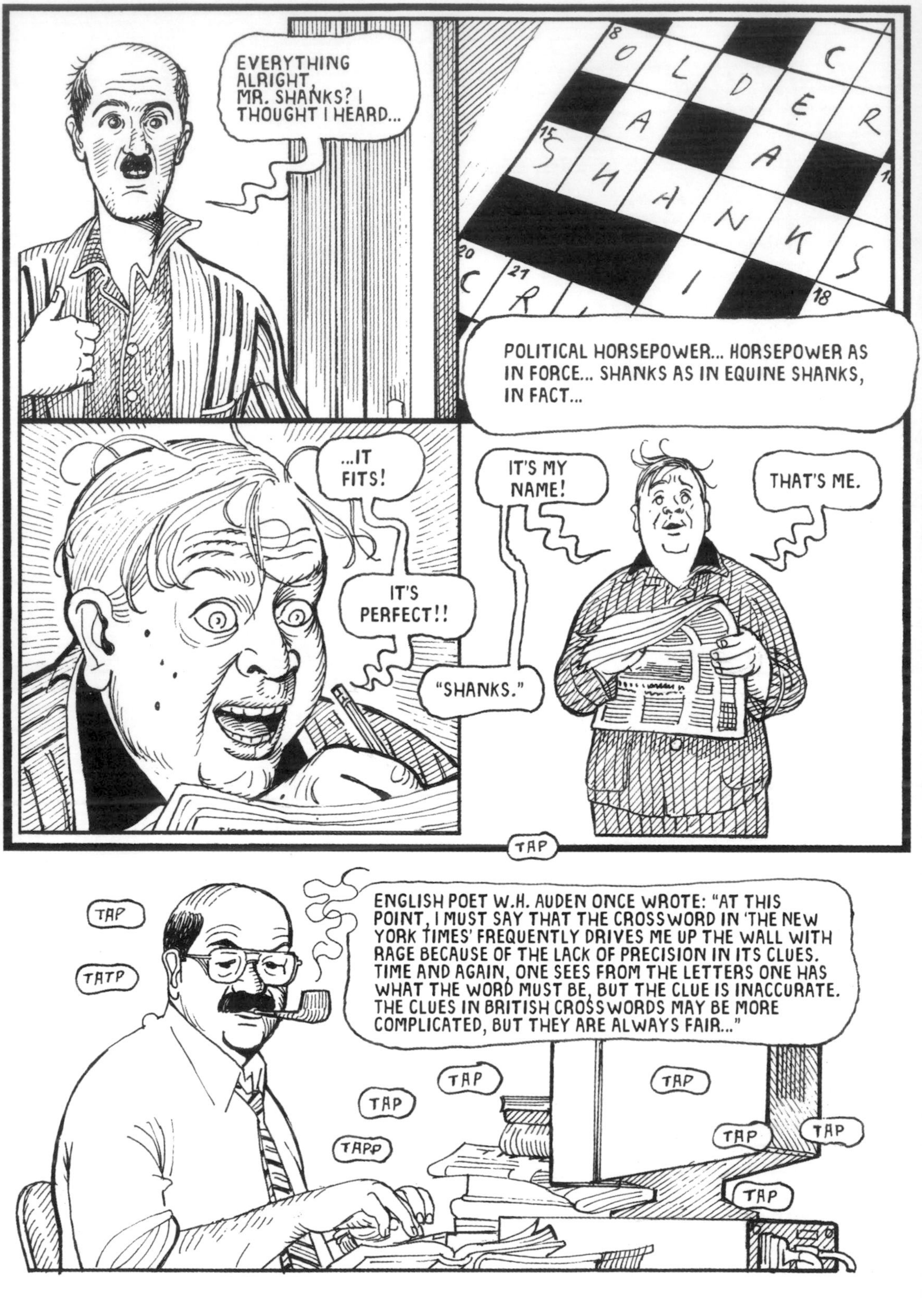
EVERYTHING ALRIGHT, MR. SHANKS? I THOUGHT I HEARD...
POLITICAL HORSEPOWER... HORSEPOWER AS IN FORCE... SHANKS AS IN EQUINE SHANKS, IN FACT...
...IT FITS!
IT'S PERFECT!!
"SHANKS."
IT'S MY NAME!
THAT'S ME.
TAP
TAP
TATP
ENGLISH POET W.H. AUDEN ONCE WROTE: "AT THIS POINT, I MUST SAY THAT THE CROSSWORD IN 'THE NEW YORK TIMES' FREQUENTLY DRIVES ME UP THE WALL WITH RAGE BECAUSE OF THE LACK OF PRECISION IN ITS CLUES. TIME AND AGAIN, ONE SEES FROM THE LETTERS ONE HAS WHAT THE WORD MUST BE, BUT THE CLUE IS INACCURATE. THE CLUES IN BRITISH CROSSWORDS MAY BE MORE COMPLICATED, BUT THEY ARE ALWAYS FAIR..."
TAP
TAP
TAP
TAPP
TAP
TAP
TAP

the NEXT one

A SHORT STORY WITH AN OUTDATED, UNFUNNY JOKE.

TEN THOUSAND, SEVEN HUNDRED AND EIGHTY-NINTH

WHEN, AFTER LUNCH, HIS COUSIN NANCY INVITED HIM TO THE "HEALTH TRAIL" THAT INCLUDED AN ART EXHIBITION, ZENO PORNO MADE HIS   MISTAKE (THE   HAD BEEN LEAVING MILAN FOR OLD VENETO WITH HIS UNCLE UBER).

TEN THOUSAND, SEVEN HUNDRED AND EIGHTY-EIGHTH

WANT TO?

JUST TO GET OUT OF THE HOUSE.

IT'S A NICE DAY.

WHY NOT? OKAY, LET'S GO.

sentiero dell'arte

HOW'S UNCLE UBER?

HE'S GOOD!

NANCY

ZENO

NANCY BELONGS TO THE RICH SIDE OF THE FAMILY. SHE STUDIED IN THE U.S. AND TEACHES ENGLISH AT A MIDDLE SCHOOL. UNCLE ITALO'S PROBLEMATIC   DAUGHTER.

FAVOURITE

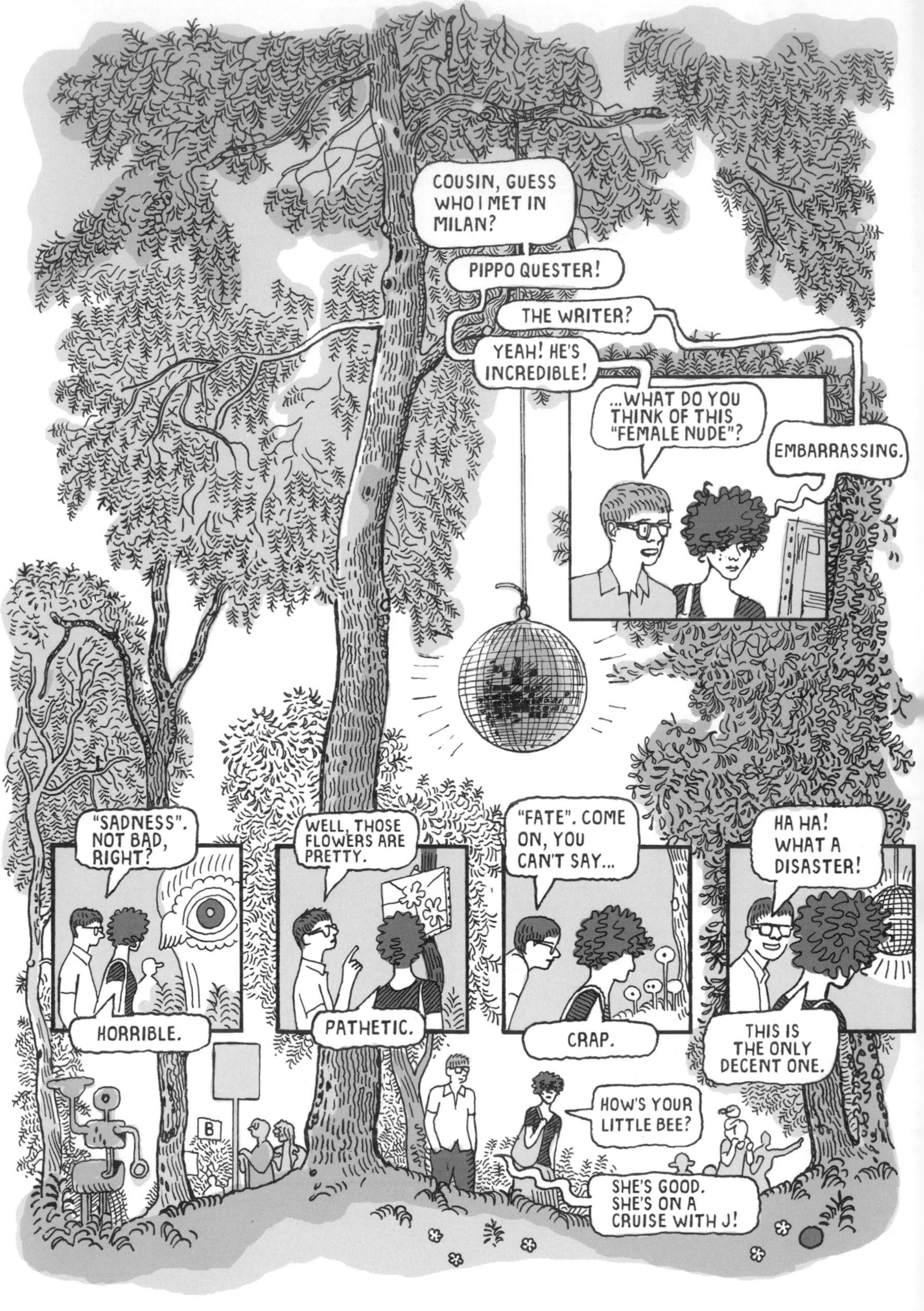
COUSIN, GUESS WHO I MET IN MILAN?
PIPPO QUESTER!
THE WRITER?
YEAH! HE'S INCREDIBLE!
...WHAT DO YOU THINK OF THIS "FEMALE NUDE"?
EMBARRASSING.
"SADNESS". NOT BAD, RIGHT?
HORRIBLE.
WELL, THOSE FLOWERS ARE PRETTY.
PATHETIC.
"FATE". COME ON, YOU CAN'T SAY...
CRAP.
HA HA! WHAT A DISASTER!
THIS IS THE ONLY DECENT ONE.
B
HOW'S YOUR LITTLE BEE?
SHE'S GOOD. SHE'S ON A CRUISE WITH J!

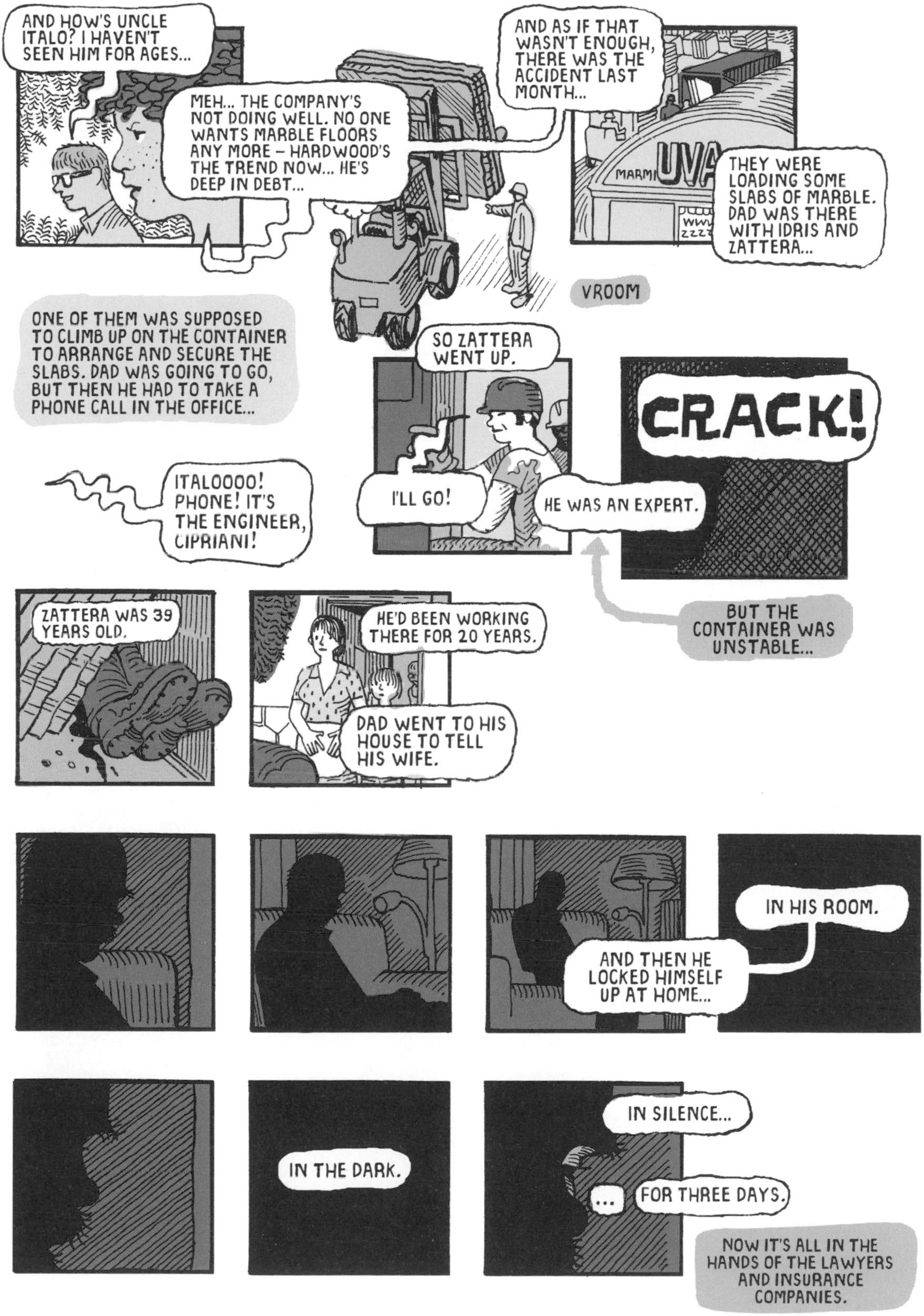
AND HOW'S UNCLE ITALO? I HAVEN'T SEEN HIM FOR AGES...
MEH... THE COMPANY'S NOT DOING WELL. NO ONE WANTS MARBLE FLOORS ANY MORE – HARDWOOD'S THE TREND NOW... HE'S DEEP IN DEBT...
AND AS IF THAT WASN'T ENOUGH, THERE WAS THE ACCIDENT LAST MONTH...
MARMI UVA
THEY WERE LOADING SOME SLABS OF MARBLE. DAD WAS THERE WITH IDRIS AND ZATTERA...
VROOM
ONE OF THEM WAS SUPPOSED TO CLIMB UP ON THE CONTAINER TO ARRANGE AND SECURE THE SLABS. DAD WAS GOING TO GO, BUT THEN HE HAD TO TAKE A PHONE CALL IN THE OFFICE...
ITALOOOO! PHONE! IT'S THE ENGINEER, CIPRIANI!
SO ZATTERA WENT UP.
I'LL GO!
HE WAS AN EXPERT.
CRACK!
BUT THE CONTAINER WAS UNSTABLE...
ZATTERA WAS 39 YEARS OLD.
HE'D BEEN WORKING THERE FOR 20 YEARS.
DAD WENT TO HIS HOUSE TO TELL HIS WIFE.
AND THEN HE LOCKED HIMSELF UP AT HOME...
IN HIS ROOM.
IN THE DARK.
IN SILENCE...
...
FOR THREE DAYS.
NOW IT'S ALL IN THE HANDS OF THE LAWYERS AND INSURANCE COMPANIES.

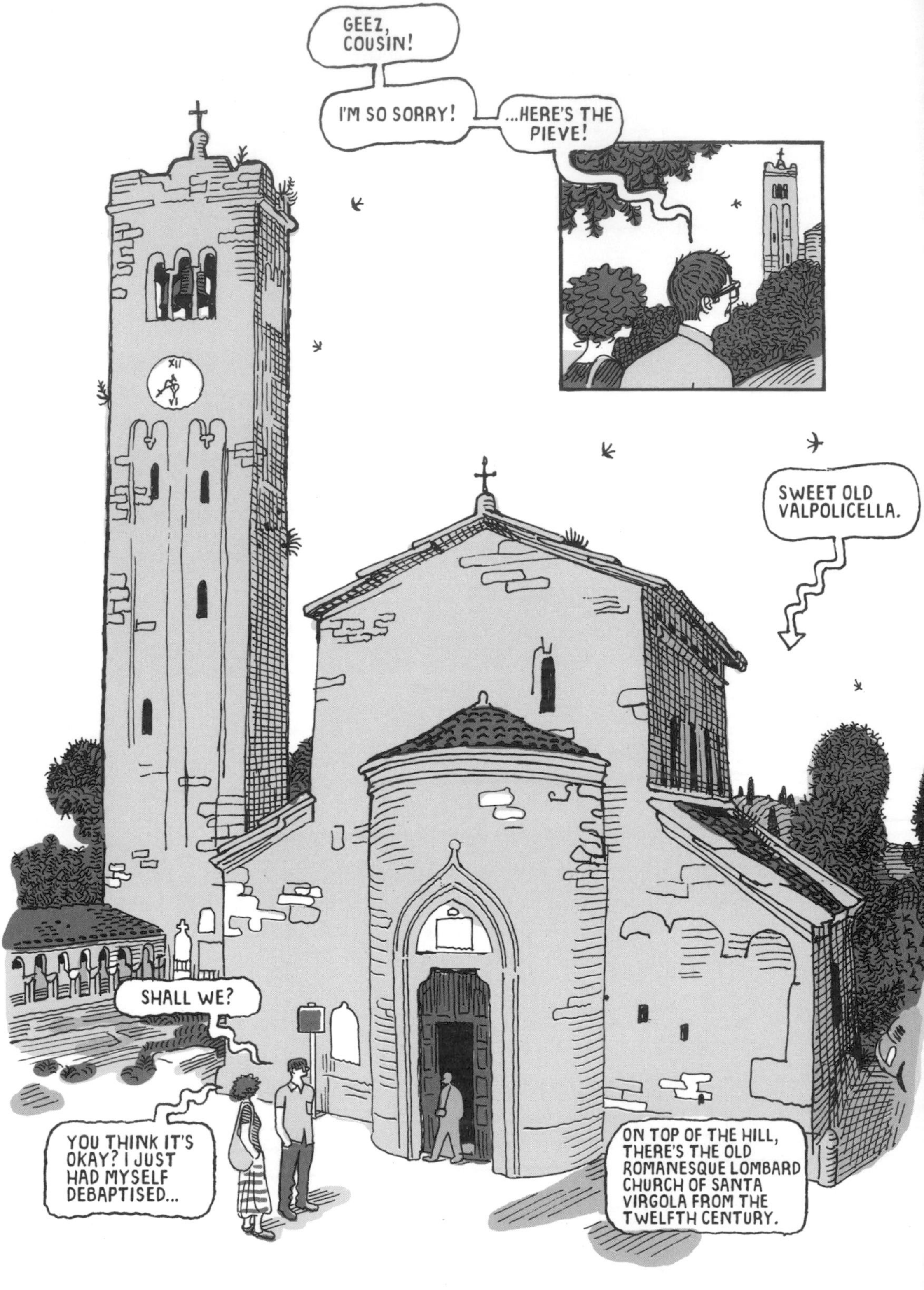
GEEZ, COUSIN!
I'M SO SORRY!
...HERE'S THE PIEVE!
SWEET OLD VALPOLICELLA.
SHALL WE?
YOU THINK IT'S OKAY? I JUST HAD MYSELF DEBAPTISED...
ON TOP OF THE HILL, THERE'S THE OLD ROMANESQUE LOMBARD CHURCH OF SANTA VIRGOLA FROM THE TWELFTH CENTURY.

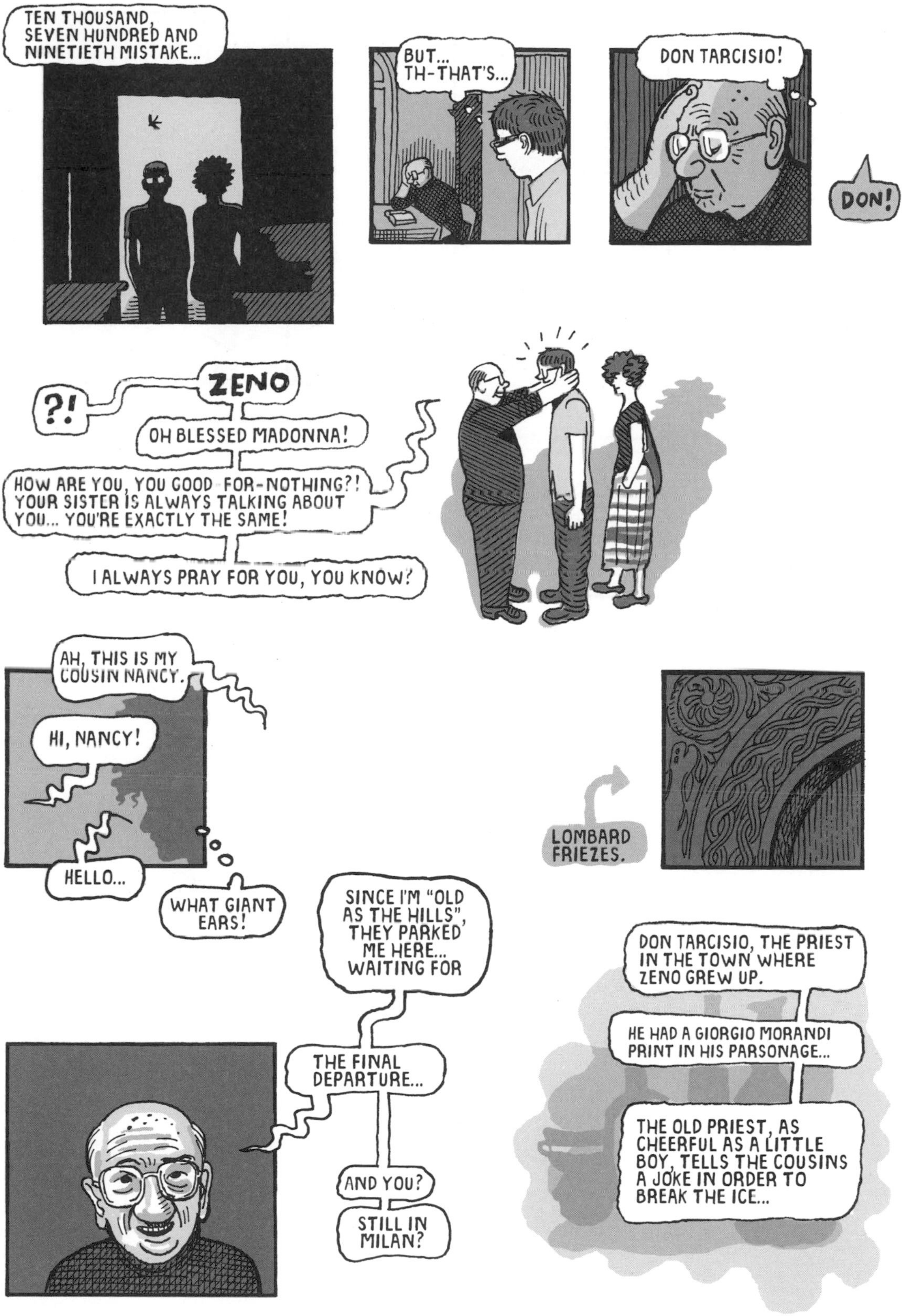
TEN THOUSAND, SEVEN HUNDRED AND NINETIETH MISTAKE...
BUT... TH-THAT'S...
DON TARCISIO!
DON!
?!
ZENO
OH BLESSED MADONNA!
HOW ARE YOU, YOU GOOD-FOR-NOTHING?! YOUR SISTER IS ALWAYS TALKING ABOUT YOU... YOU'RE EXACTLY THE SAME!
I ALWAYS PRAY FOR YOU, YOU KNOW?
AH, THIS IS MY COUSIN NANCY.
HI, NANCY!
HELLO...
WHAT GIANT EARS!
LOMBARD FRIEZES.
SINCE I'M "OLD AS THE HILLS", THEY PARKED ME HERE... WAITING FOR
THE FINAL DEPARTURE...
AND YOU?
STILL IN MILAN?
DON TARCISIO, THE PRIEST IN THE TOWN WHERE ZENO GREW UP.
HE HAD A GIORGIO MORANDI PRINT IN HIS PARSONAGE...
THE OLD PRIEST, AS CHEERFUL AS A LITTLE BOY, TELLS THE COUSINS A JOKE IN ORDER TO BREAK THE ICE...

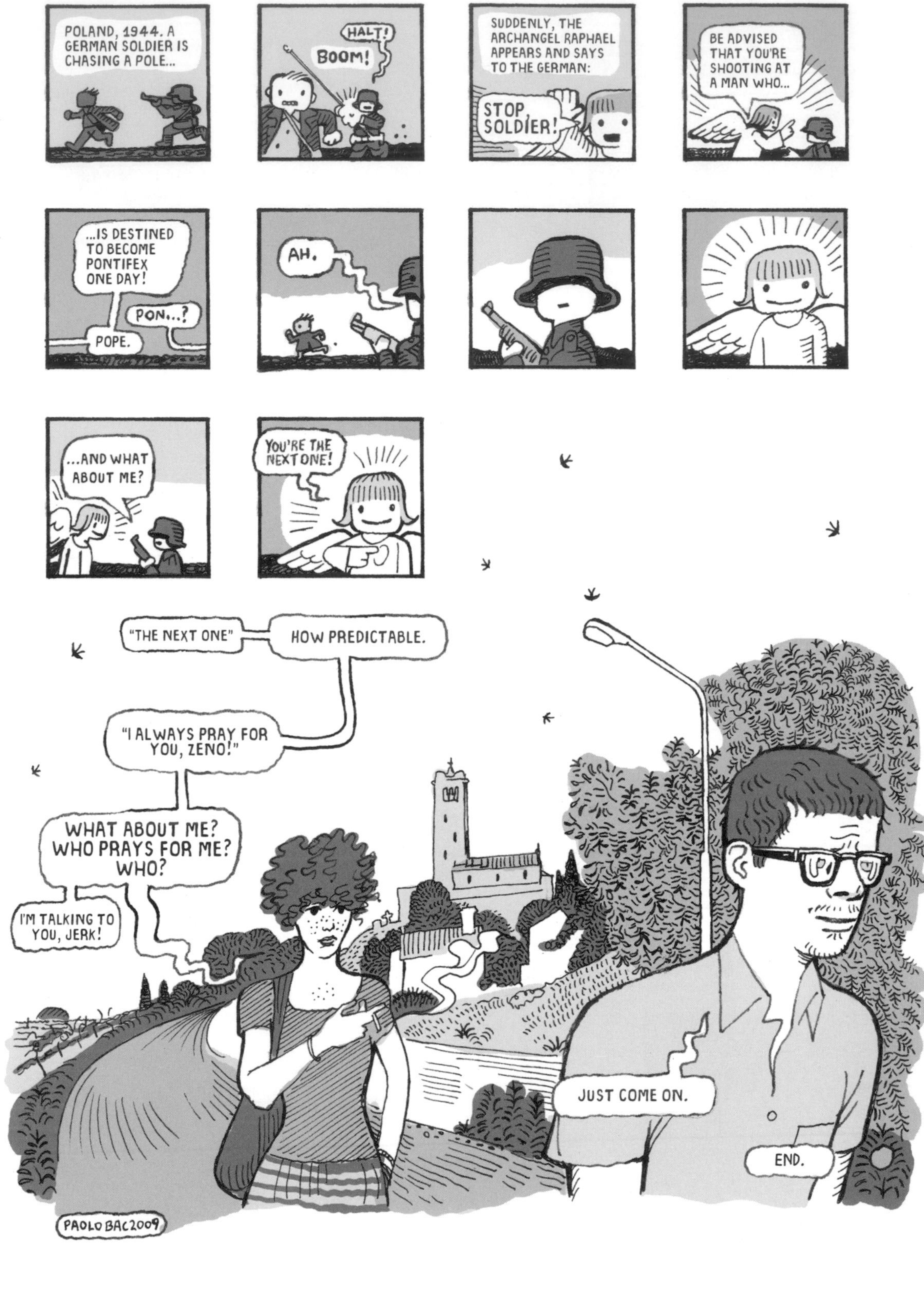

POLAND, 1944. A GERMAN SOLDIER IS CHASING A POLE...
HALT!
BOOM!
SUDDENLY, THE ARCHANGEL RAPHAEL APPEARS AND SAYS TO THE GERMAN:
STOP, SOLDIER!
BE ADVISED THAT YOU'RE SHOOTING AT A MAN WHO...
...IS DESTINED TO BECOME PONTIFEX ONE DAY!
PON...?
POPE.
AH.
...AND WHAT ABOUT ME?
YOU'RE THE NEXT ONE!
"THE NEXT ONE"
HOW PREDICTABLE.
"I ALWAYS PRAY FOR YOU, ZENO!"
WHAT ABOUT ME? WHO PRAYS FOR ME? WHO?
I'M TALKING TO YOU, JERK!
JUST COME ON.
END.
PAOLO BAC 2009

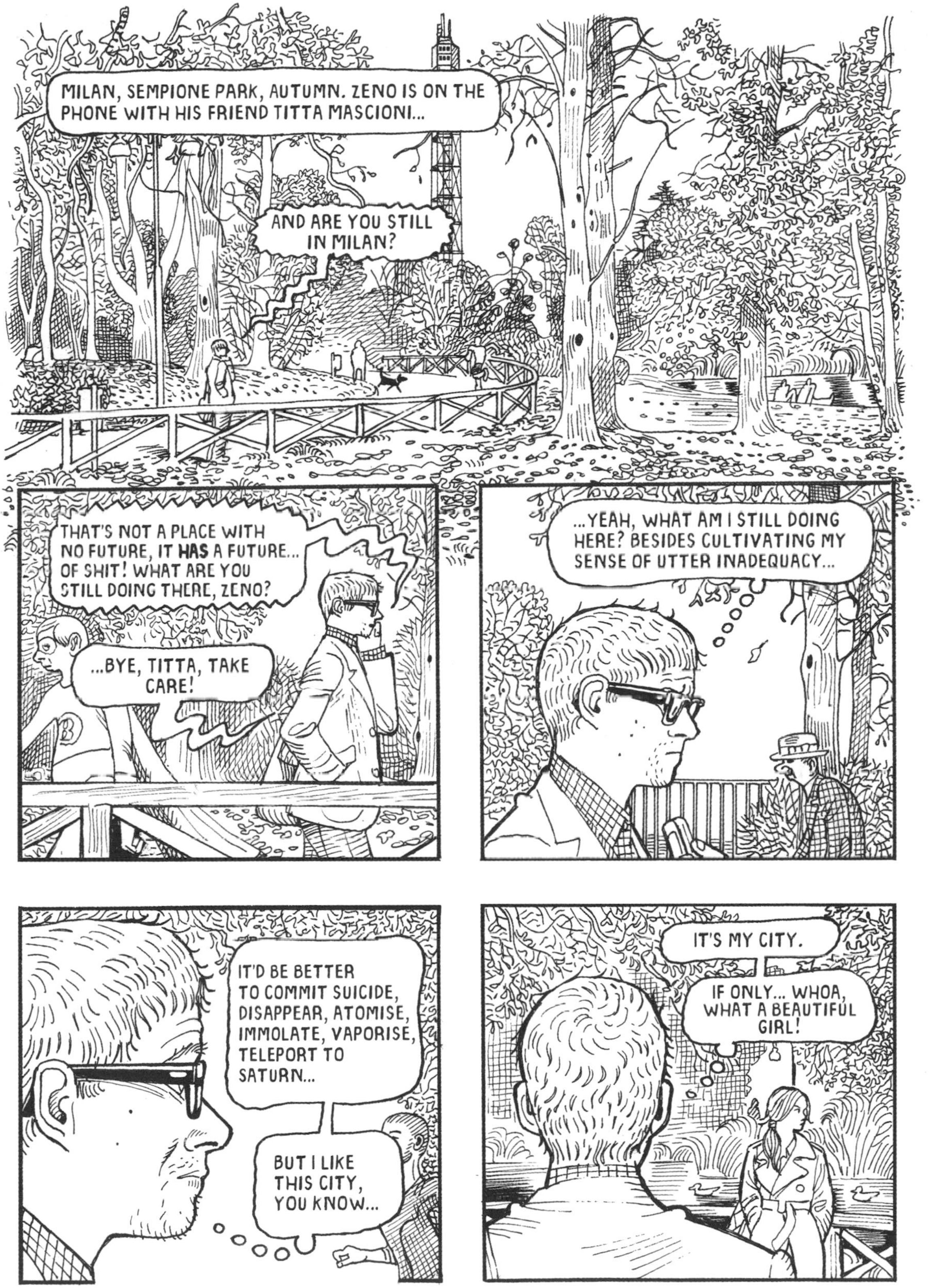
MILAN, SEMPIONE PARK, AUTUMN. ZENO IS ON THE PHONE WITH HIS FRIEND TITTA MASCIONI...
AND ARE YOU STILL IN MILAN?
THAT'S NOT A PLACE WITH NO FUTURE, IT HAS A FUTURE... OF SHIT! WHAT ARE YOU STILL DOING THERE, ZENO?
...BYE, TITTA, TAKE CARE!
...YEAH, WHAT AM I STILL DOING HERE? BESIDES CULTIVATING MY SENSE OF UTTER INADEQUACY...
IT'D BE BETTER TO COMMIT SUICIDE, DISAPPEAR, ATOMISE, IMMOLATE, VAPORISE, TELEPORT TO SATURN...
BUT I LIKE THIS CITY, YOU KNOW...
IT'S MY CITY.
IF ONLY... WHOA, WHAT A BEAUTIFUL GIRL!

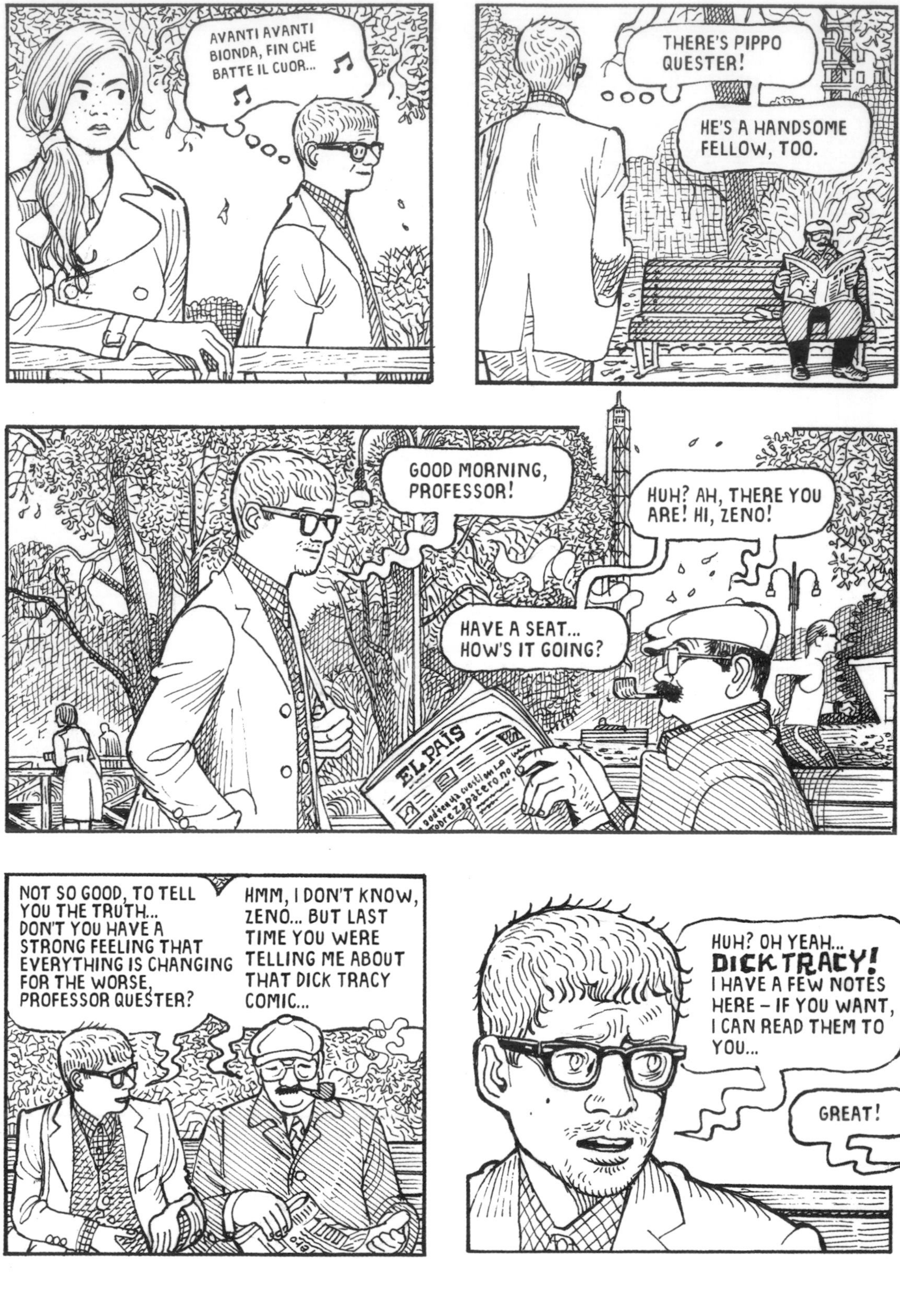
AVANTI AVANTI BIONDA, FIN CHE BATTE IL CUOR...
THERE'S PIPPO QUESTER!
HE'S A HANDSOME FELLOW, TOO.
GOOD MORNING, PROFESSOR!
HUH? AH, THERE YOU ARE! HI, ZENO!
HAVE A SEAT... HOW'S IT GOING?
EL PAÍS
NOT SO GOOD, TO TELL YOU THE TRUTH... DON'T YOU HAVE A STRONG FEELING THAT EVERYTHING IS CHANGING FOR THE WORSE, PROFESSOR QUESTER?
HMM, I DON'T KNOW, ZENO... BUT LAST TIME YOU WERE TELLING ME ABOUT THAT DICK TRACY COMIC...
HUH? OH YEAH... DICK TRACY! I HAVE A FEW NOTES HERE – IF YOU WANT, I CAN READ THEM TO YOU...
GREAT!

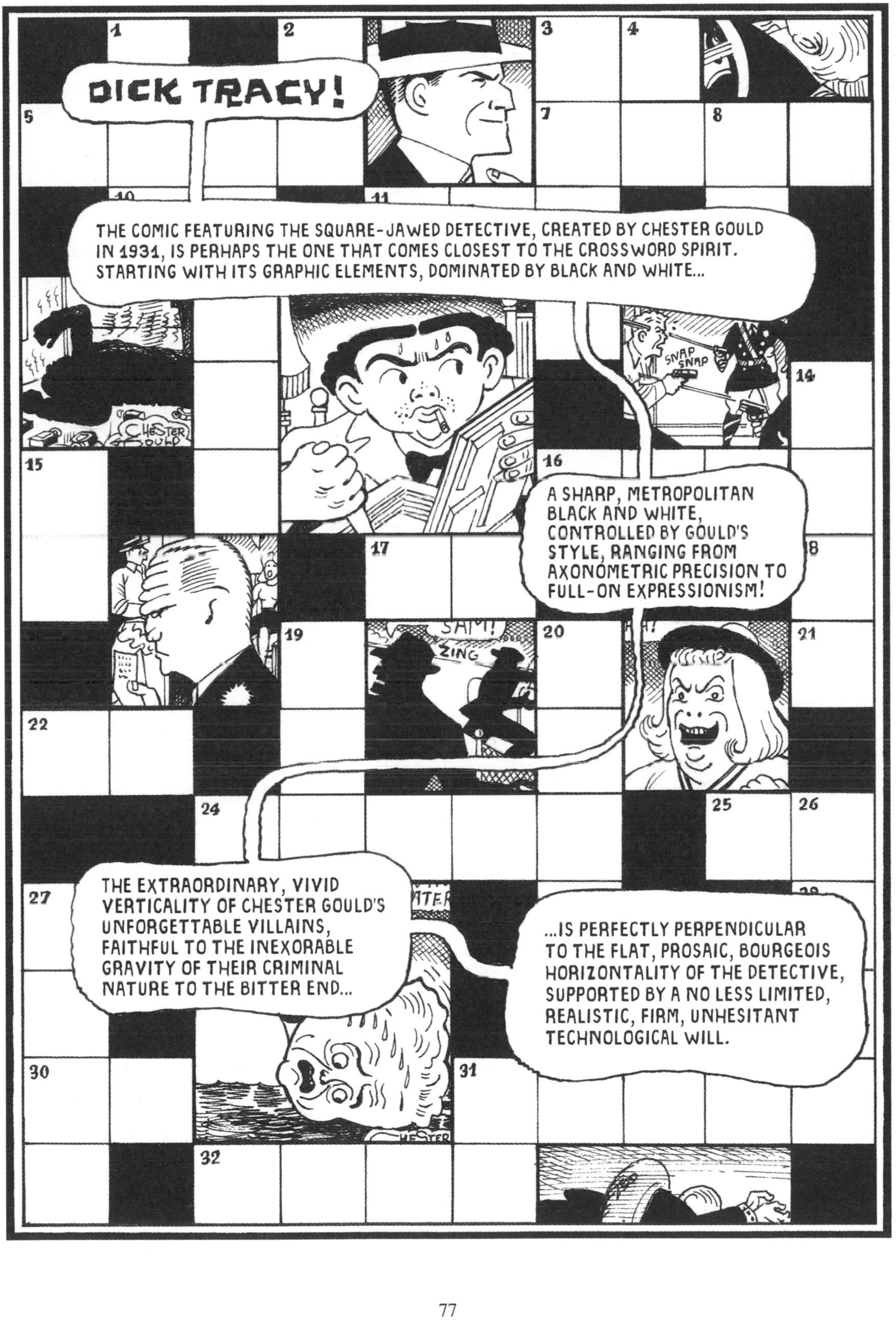
DICK TRACY!
THE COMIC FEATURING THE SQUARE-JAWED DETECTIVE, CREATED BY CHESTER GOULD IN 1931, IS PERHAPS THE ONE THAT COMES CLOSEST TO THE CROSSWORD SPIRIT. STARTING WITH ITS GRAPHIC ELEMENTS, DOMINATED BY BLACK AND WHITE...
A SHARP, METROPOLITAN BLACK AND WHITE, CONTROLLED BY GOULD'S STYLE, RANGING FROM AXONOMETRIC PRECISION TO FULL-ON EXPRESSIONISM!
THE EXTRAORDINARY, VIVID VERTICALITY OF CHESTER GOULD'S UNFORGETTABLE VILLAINS, FAITHFUL TO THE INEXORABLE GRAVITY OF THEIR CRIMINAL NATURE TO THE BITTER END...
...IS PERFECTLY PERPENDICULAR TO THE FLAT, PROSAIC, BOURGEOIS HORIZONTALITY OF THE DETECTIVE, SUPPORTED BY A NO LESS LIMITED, REALISTIC, FIRM, UNHESITANT TECHNOLOGICAL WILL.

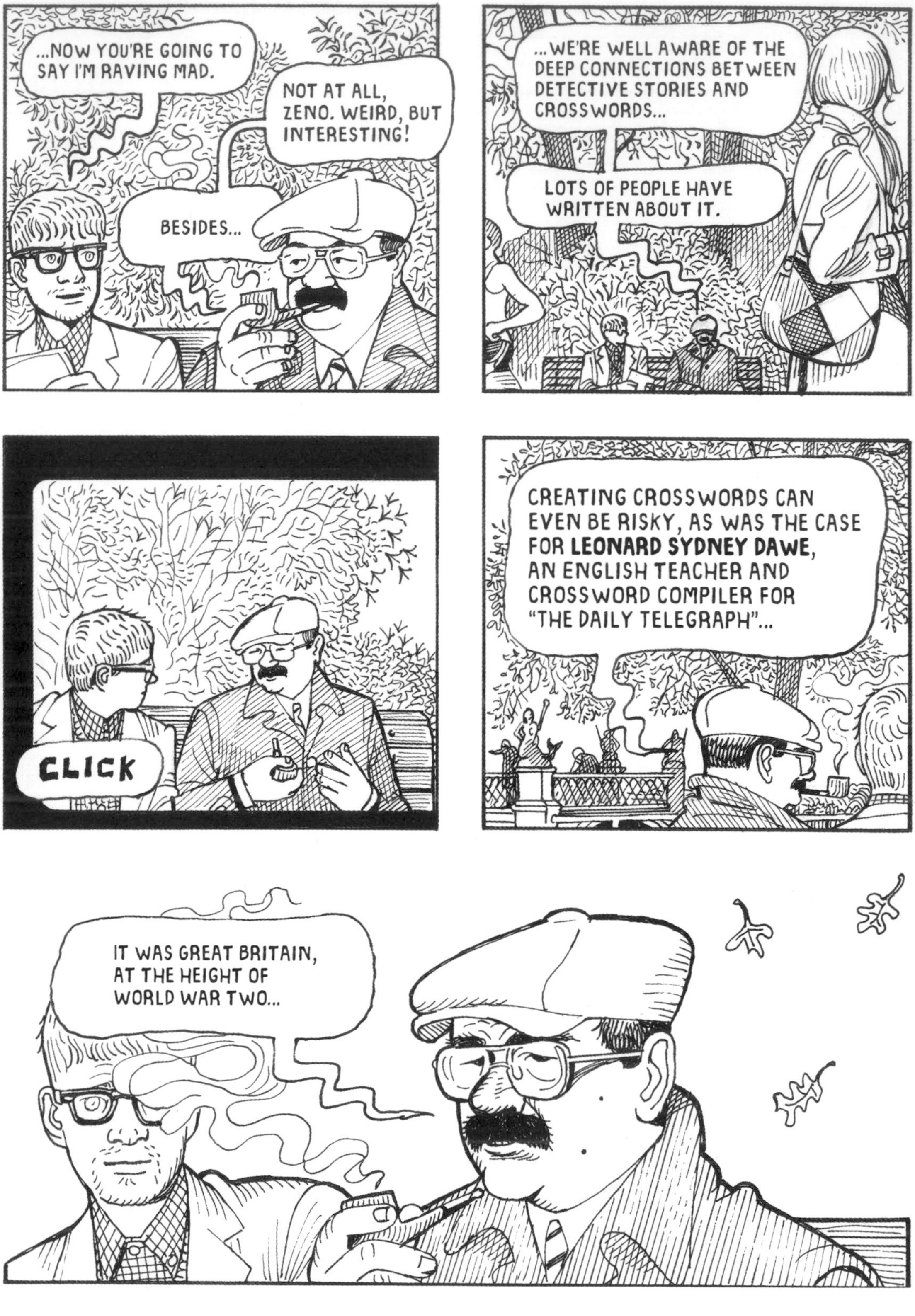
...NOW YOU'RE GOING TO SAY I'M RAVING MAD.
NOT AT ALL, ZENO. WEIRD, BUT INTERESTING!
BESIDES...
...WE'RE WELL AWARE OF THE DEEP CONNECTIONS BETWEEN DETECTIVE STORIES AND CROSSWORDS...
LOTS OF PEOPLE HAVE WRITTEN ABOUT IT.
CLICK
CREATING CROSSWORDS CAN EVEN BE RISKY, AS WAS THE CASE FOR **LEONARD SYDNEY DAWE**, AN ENGLISH TEACHER AND CROSSWORD COMPILER FOR "THE DAILY TELEGRAPH"...
IT WAS GREAT BRITAIN, AT THE HEIGHT OF WORLD WAR TWO...

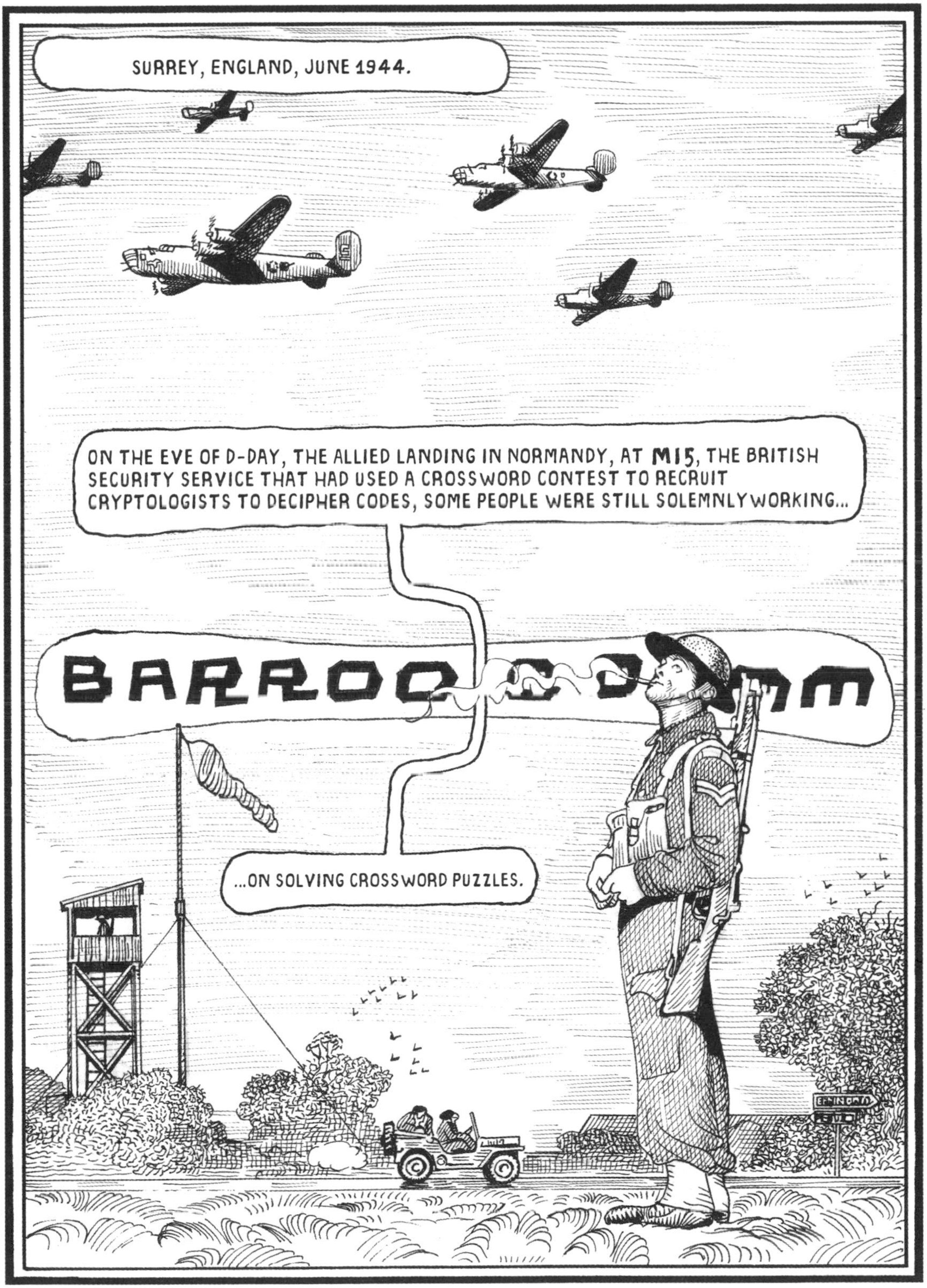
SURREY, ENGLAND, JUNE 1944.
ON THE EVE OF D-DAY, THE ALLIED LANDING IN NORMANDY, AT MI5, THE BRITISH SECURITY SERVICE THAT HAD USED A CROSSWORD CONTEST TO RECRUIT CRYPTOLOGISTS TO DECIPHER CODES, SOME PEOPLE WERE STILL SOLEMNLY WORKING...
BARROOOOOMM
...ON SOLVING CROSSWORD PUZZLES.

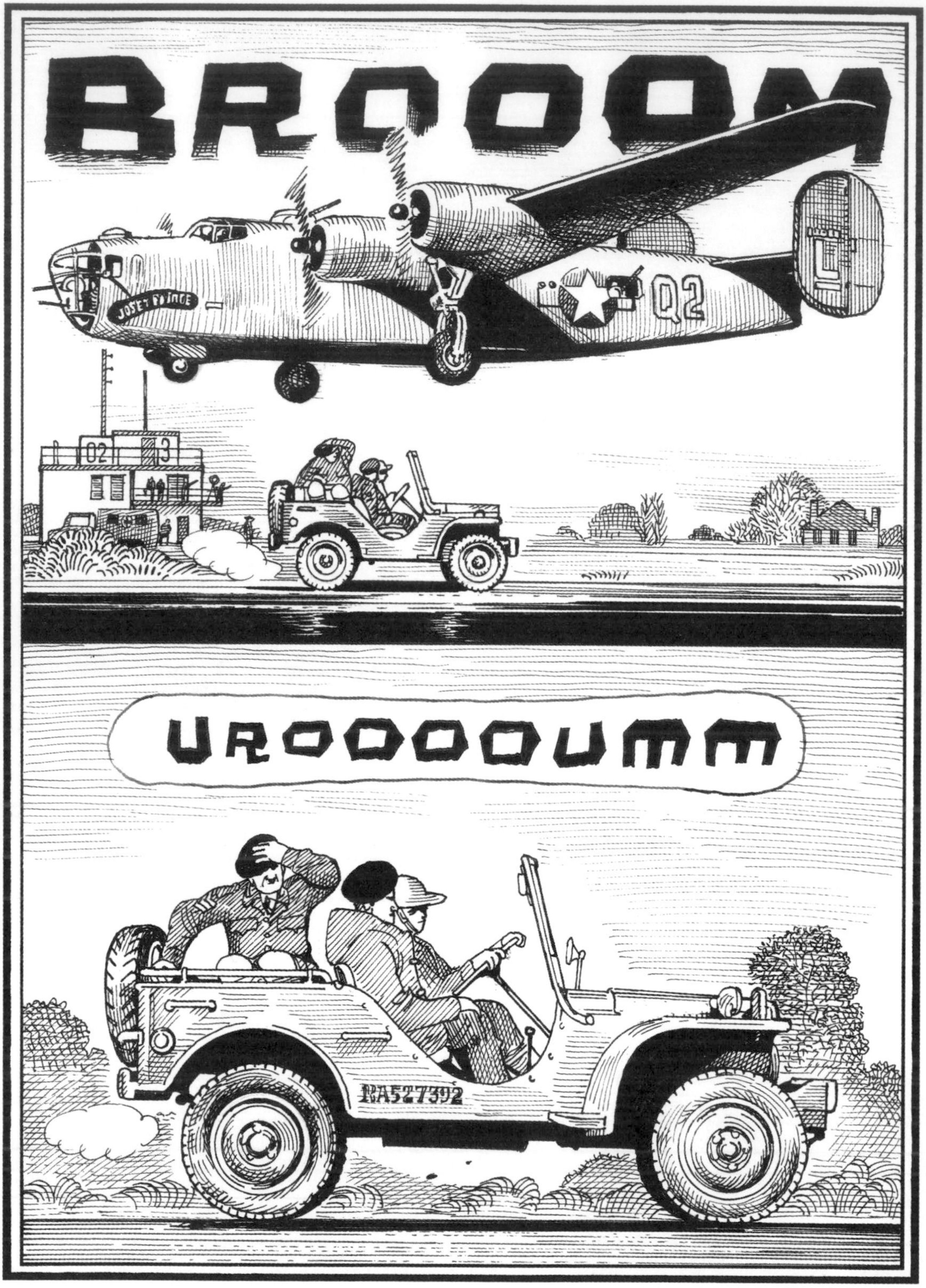
BROOOM
Q2
Q2 3
UROOOOUMM
RA527392

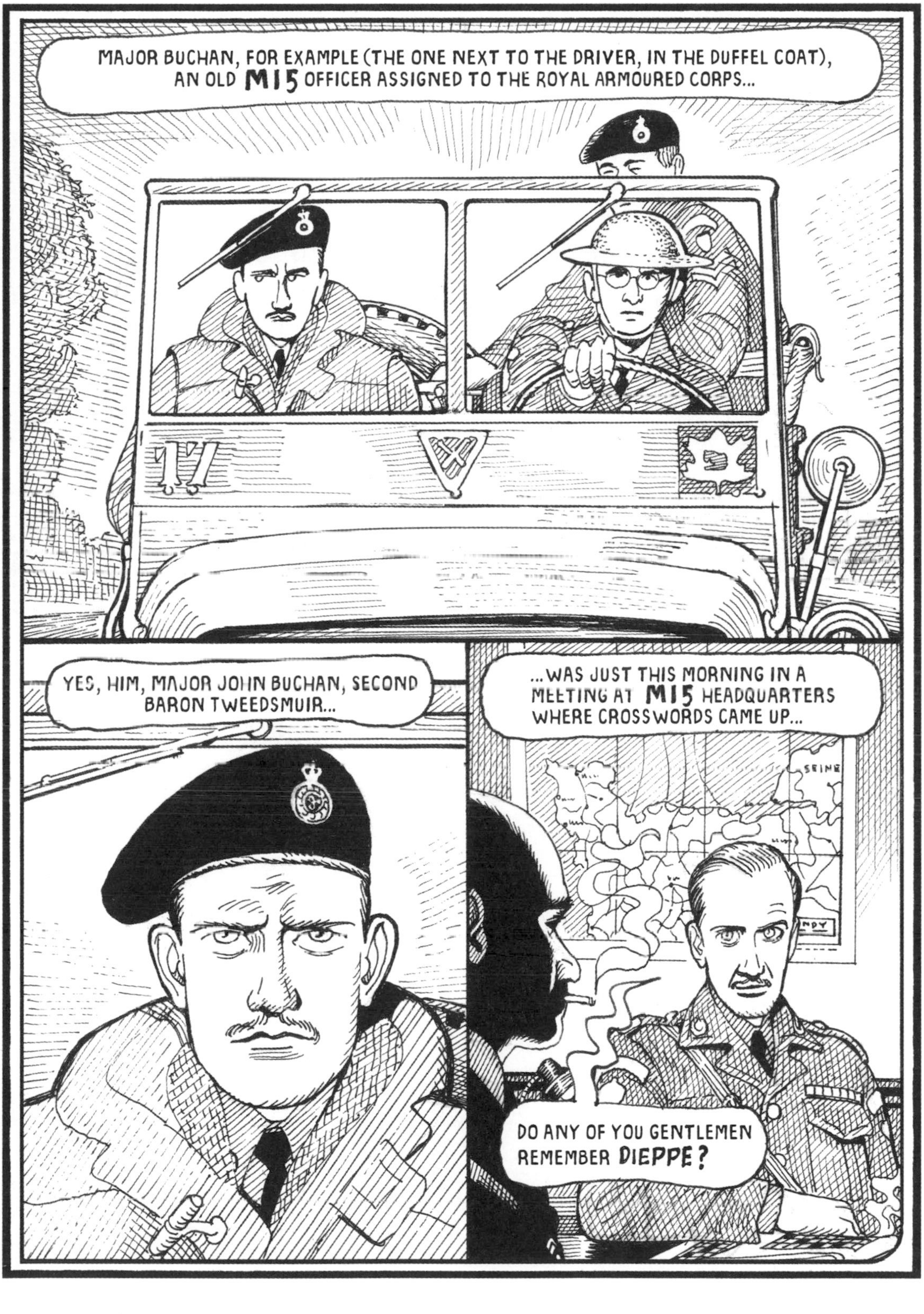
MAJOR BUCHAN, FOR EXAMPLE (THE ONE NEXT TO THE DRIVER, IN THE DUFFEL COAT), AN OLD MI5 OFFICER ASSIGNED TO THE ROYAL ARMOURED CORPS...
YES, HIM, MAJOR JOHN BUCHAN, SECOND BARON TWEEDSMUIR...
...WAS JUST THIS MORNING IN A MEETING AT MI5 HEADQUARTERS WHERE CROSSWORDS CAME UP...
SEINE
DO ANY OF YOU GENTLEMEN REMEMBER DIEPPE?

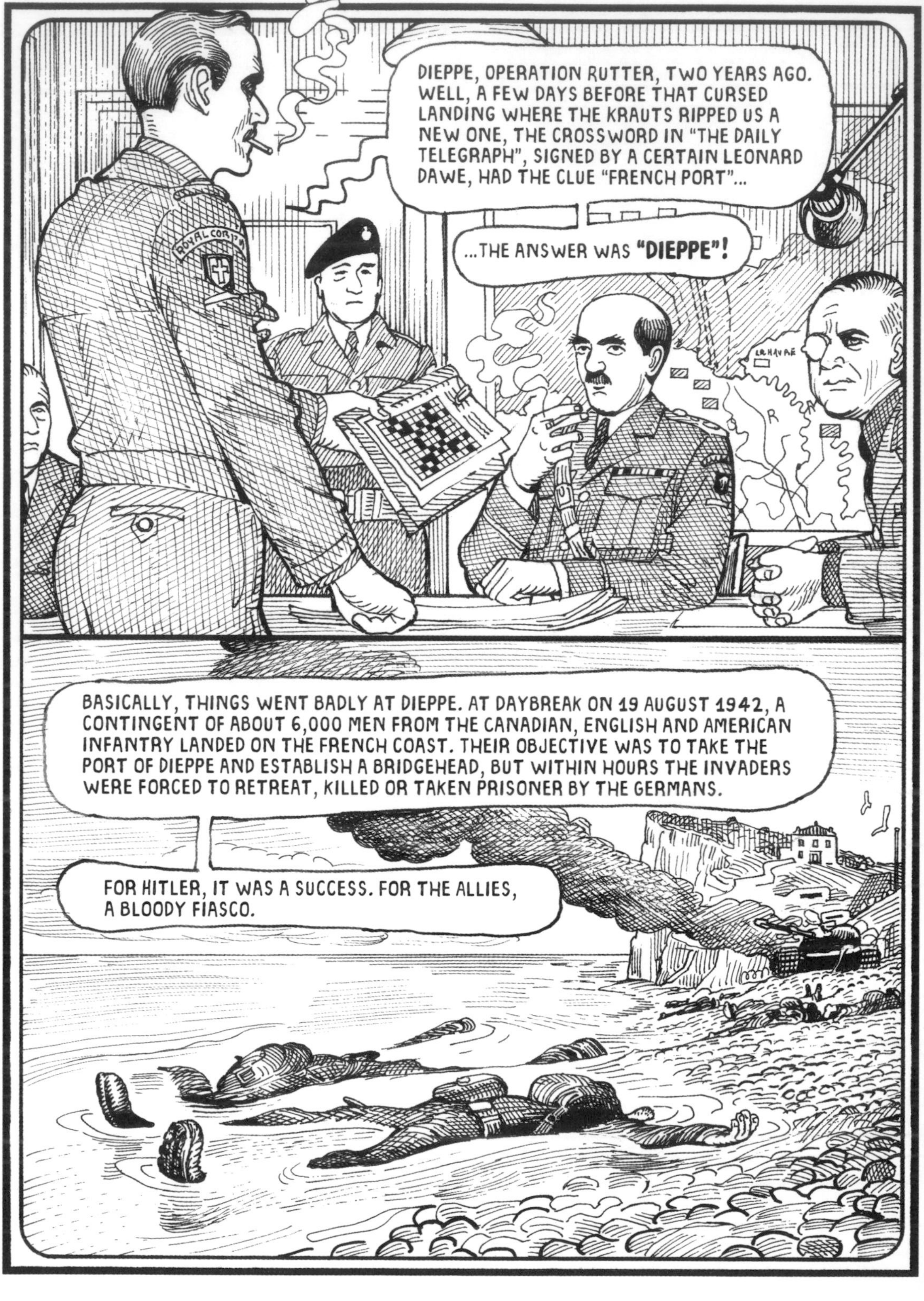
DIEPPE, OPERATION RUTTER, TWO YEARS AGO. WELL, A FEW DAYS BEFORE THAT CURSED LANDING WHERE THE KRAUTS RIPPED US A NEW ONE, THE CROSSWORD IN "THE DAILY TELEGRAPH", SIGNED BY A CERTAIN LEONARD DAWE, HAD THE CLUE "FRENCH PORT"...
...THE ANSWER WAS **"DIEPPE"**!
BASICALLY, THINGS WENT BADLY AT DIEPPE. AT DAYBREAK ON 19 AUGUST 1942, A CONTINGENT OF ABOUT 6,000 MEN FROM THE CANADIAN, ENGLISH AND AMERICAN INFANTRY LANDED ON THE FRENCH COAST. THEIR OBJECTIVE WAS TO TAKE THE PORT OF DIEPPE AND ESTABLISH A BRIDGEHEAD, BUT WITHIN HOURS THE INVADERS WERE FORCED TO RETREAT, KILLED OR TAKEN PRISONER BY THE GERMANS.
FOR HITLER, IT WAS A SUCCESS. FOR THE ALLIES, A BLOODY FIASCO.

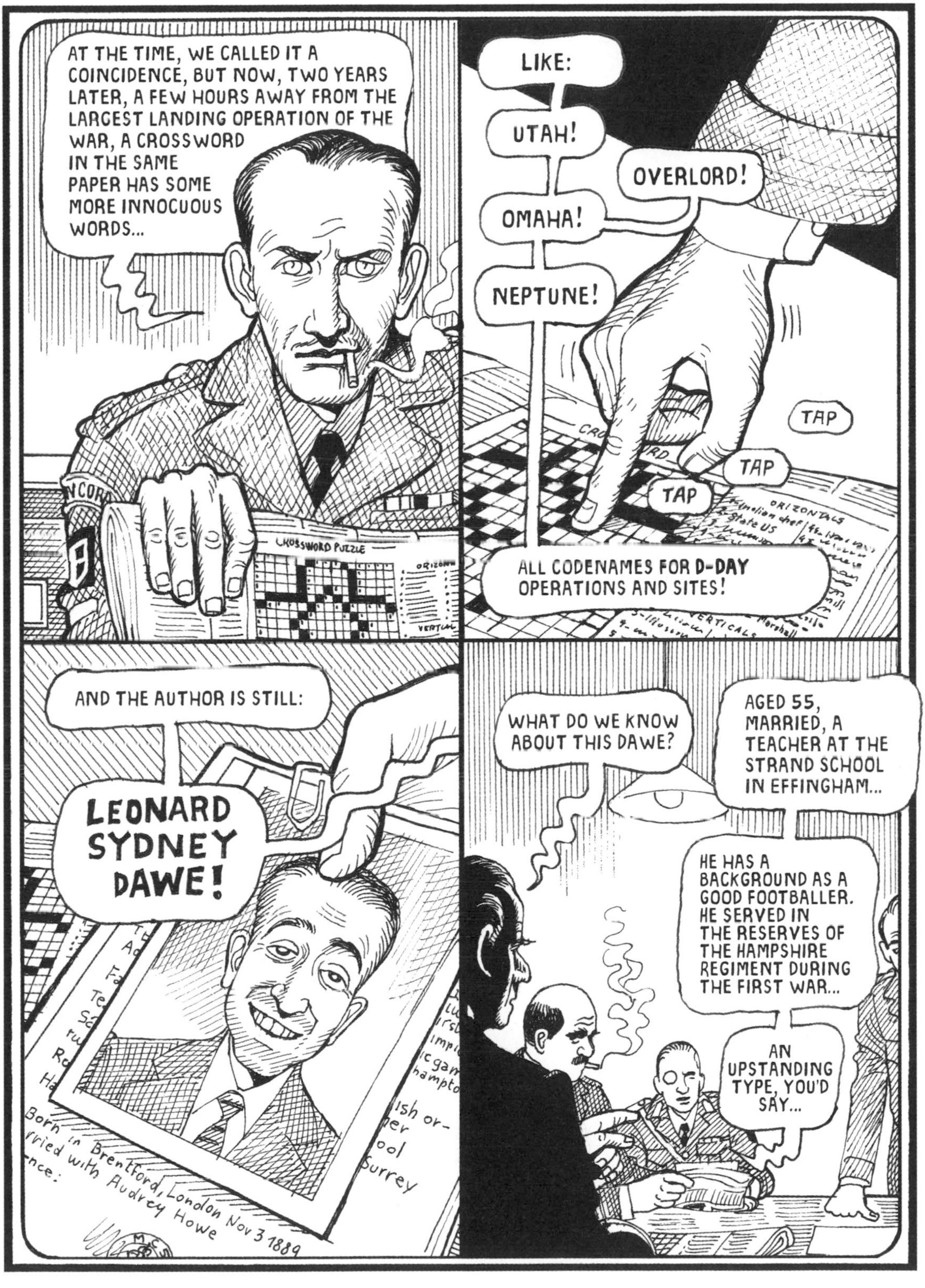

AT THE TIME, WE CALLED IT A COINCIDENCE, BUT NOW, TWO YEARS LATER, A FEW HOURS AWAY FROM THE LARGEST LANDING OPERATION OF THE WAR, A CROSSWORD IN THE SAME PAPER HAS SOME MORE INNOCUOUS WORDS...
CROSSWORD PUZZLE
LIKE:
UTAH!
OVERLORD!
OMAHA!
NEPTUNE!
TAP
TAP
TAP
ALL CODENAMES FOR D-DAY OPERATIONS AND SITES!
AND THE AUTHOR IS STILL:
LEONARD SYDNEY DAWE!
Born in Brentford, London Nov 3 1889
Audrey Howe
Surrey
WHAT DO WE KNOW ABOUT THIS DAWE?
AGED 55, MARRIED, A TEACHER AT THE STRAND SCHOOL IN EFFINGHAM...
HE HAS A BACKGROUND AS A GOOD FOOTBALLER. HE SERVED IN THE RESERVES OF THE HAMPSHIRE REGIMENT DURING THE FIRST WAR...
AN UPSTANDING TYPE, YOU'D SAY...

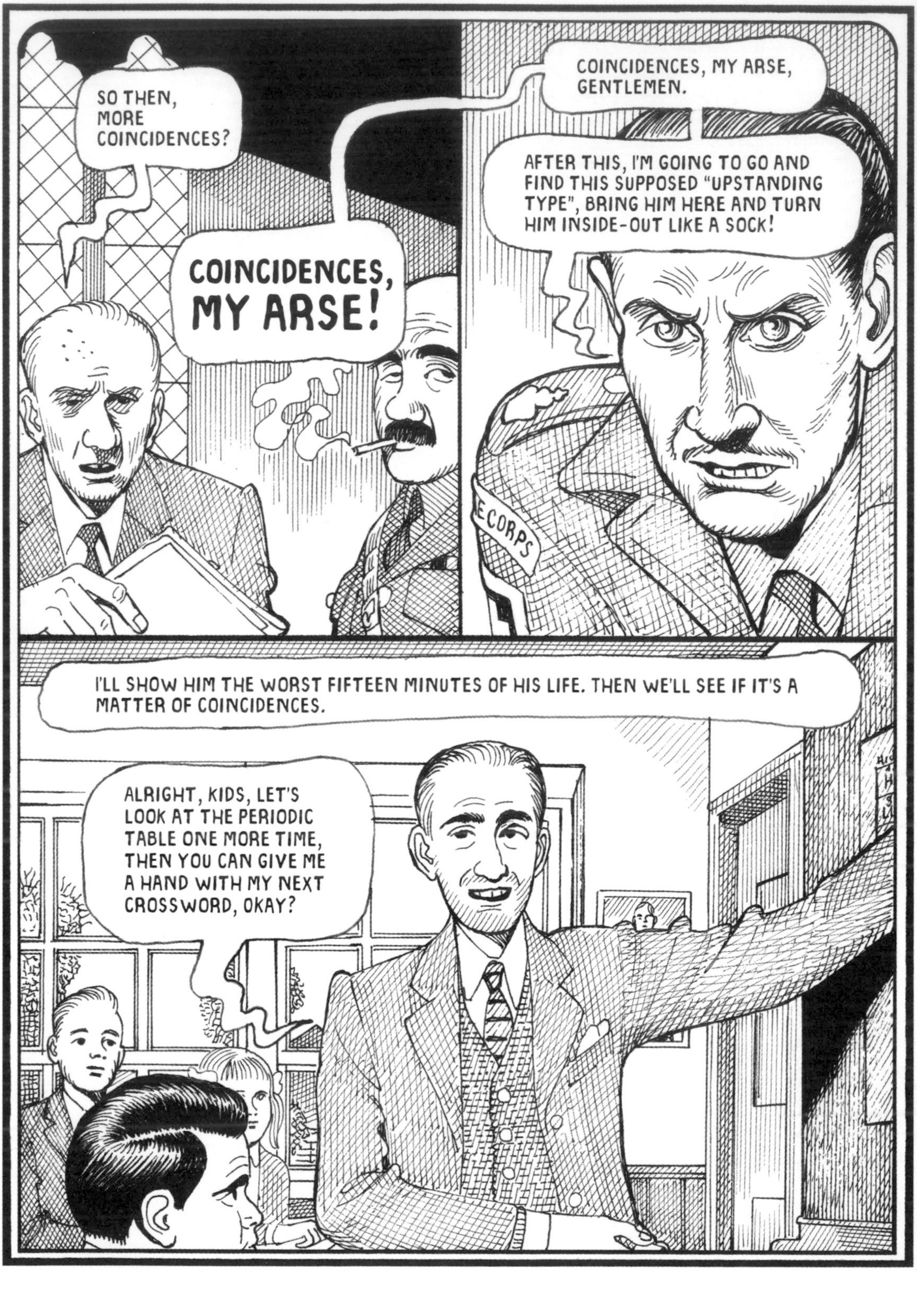
SO THEN, MORE COINCIDENCES?
COINCIDENCES, MY ARSE!
COINCIDENCES, MY ARSE, GENTLEMEN.
AFTER THIS, I'M GOING TO GO AND FIND THIS SUPPOSED "UPSTANDING TYPE", BRING HIM HERE AND TURN HIM INSIDE-OUT LIKE A SOCK!
E CORPS
I'LL SHOW HIM THE WORST FIFTEEN MINUTES OF HIS LIFE. THEN WE'LL SEE IF IT'S A MATTER OF COINCIDENCES.
ALRIGHT, KIDS, LET'S LOOK AT THE PERIODIC TABLE ONE MORE TIME, THEN YOU CAN GIVE ME A HAND WITH MY NEXT CROSSWORD, OKAY?

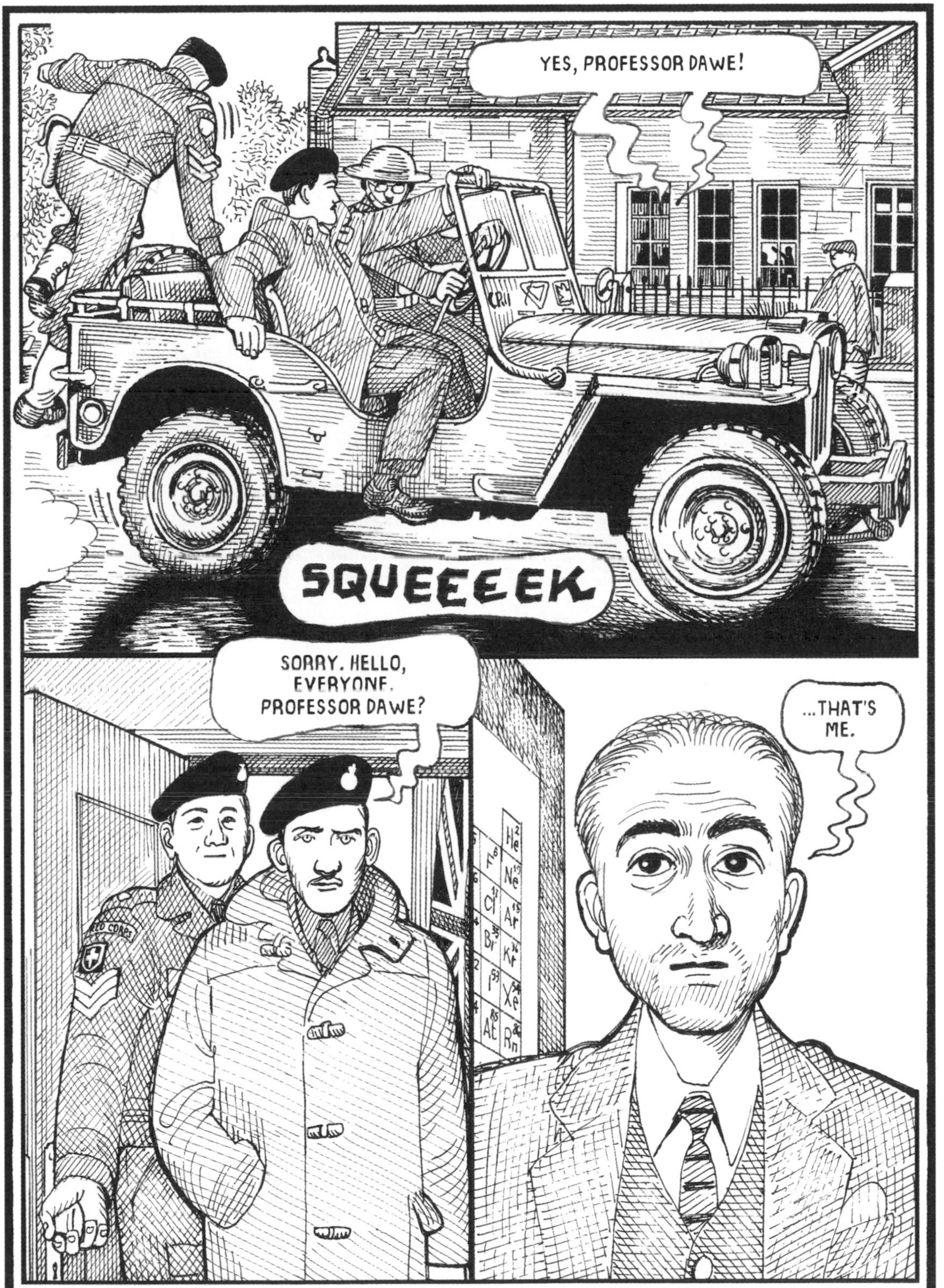
YES, PROFESSOR DAWE!
SQUEEEEK
SORRY. HELLO, EVERYONE. PROFESSOR DAWE?
...THAT'S ME.

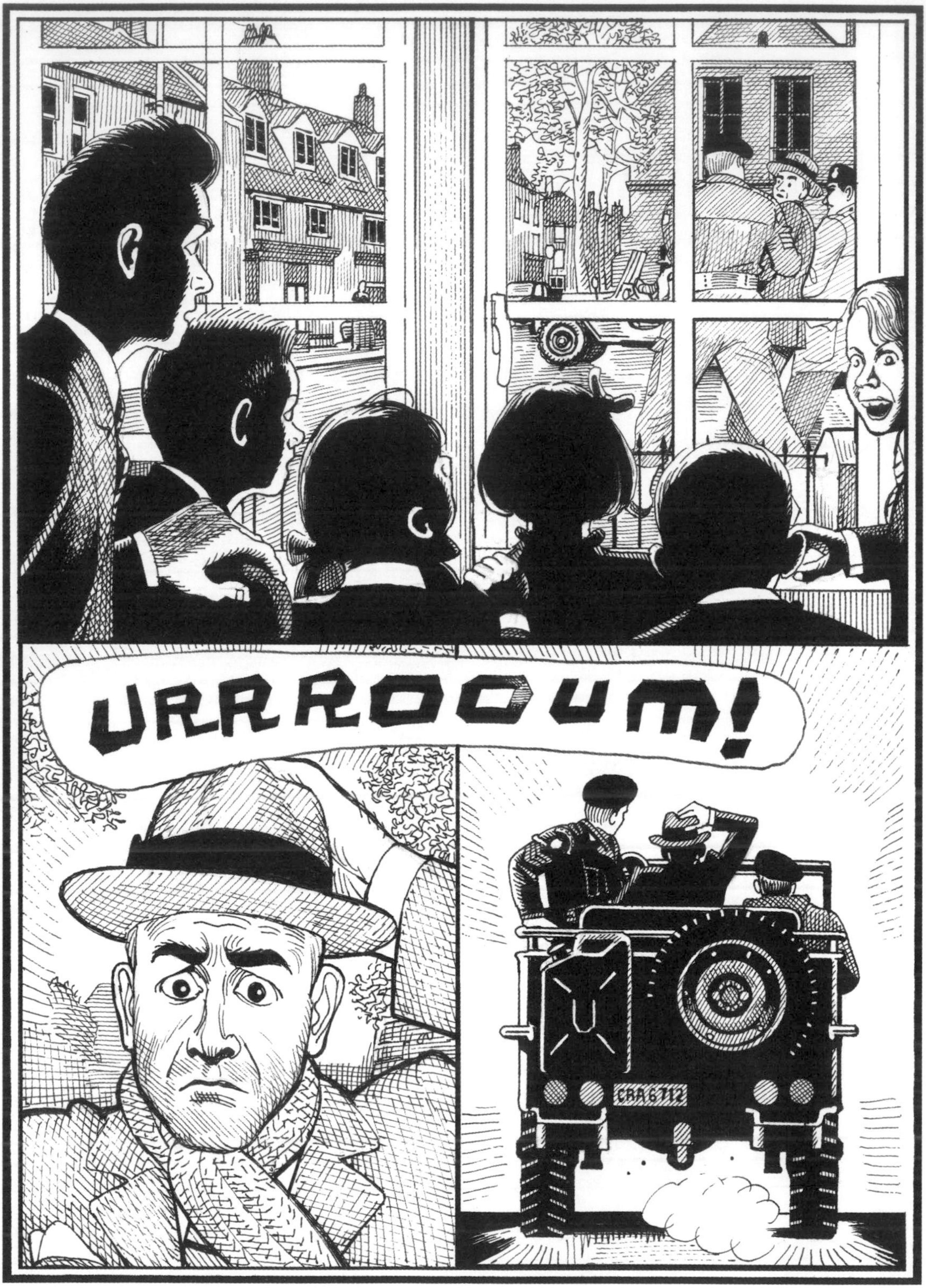
URRROOUM!
CRA 6712

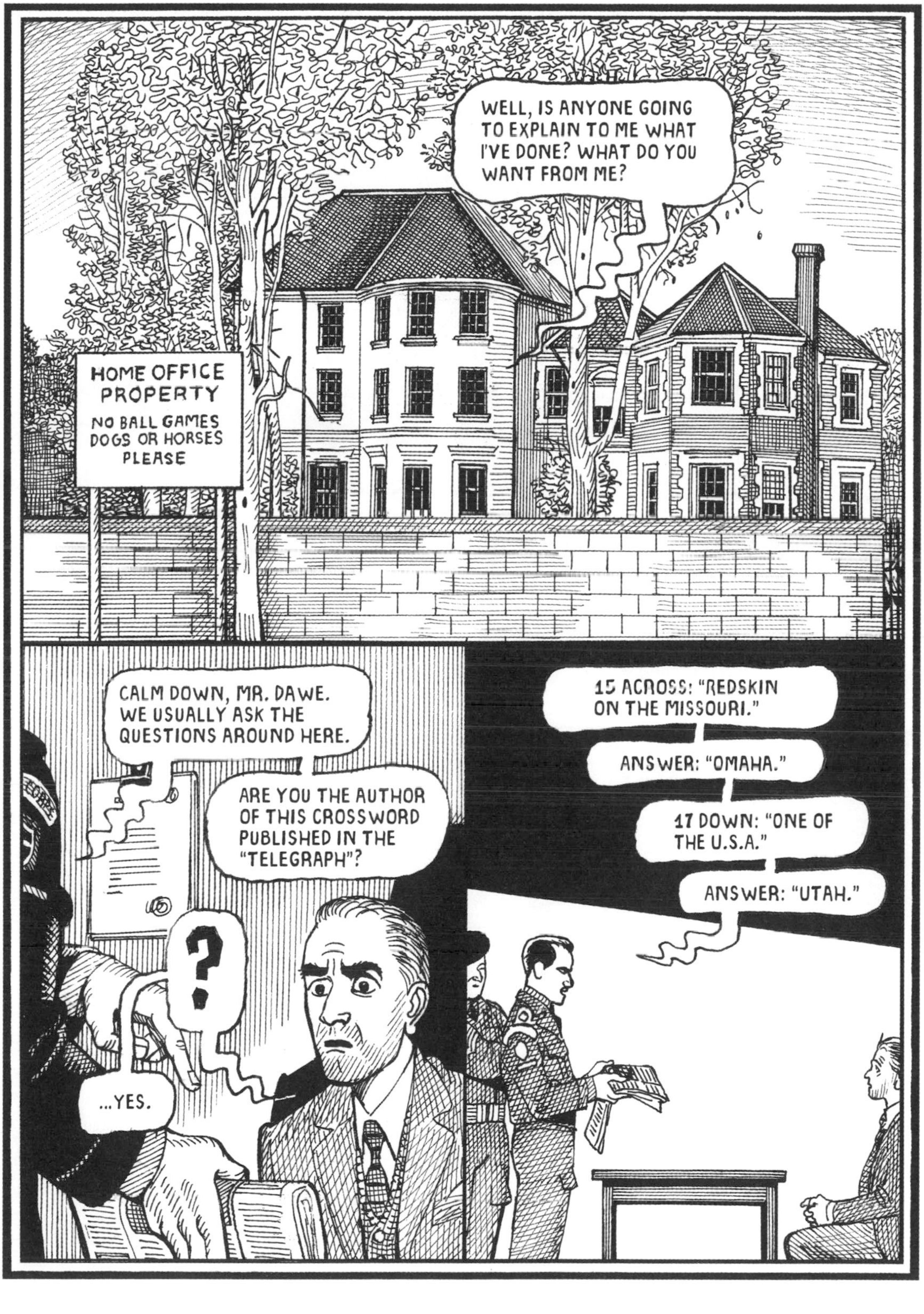

WELL, IS ANYONE GOING TO EXPLAIN TO ME WHAT I'VE DONE? WHAT DO YOU WANT FROM ME?
HOME OFFICE PROPERTY
NO BALL GAMES DOGS OR HORSES PLEASE
CALM DOWN, MR. DAWE. WE USUALLY ASK THE QUESTIONS AROUND HERE.
ARE YOU THE AUTHOR OF THIS CROSSWORD PUBLISHED IN THE "TELEGRAPH"?
?
...YES.
15 ACROSS: "REDSKIN ON THE MISSOURI."
ANSWER: "OMAHA."
17 DOWN: "ONE OF THE U.S.A."
ANSWER: "UTAH."

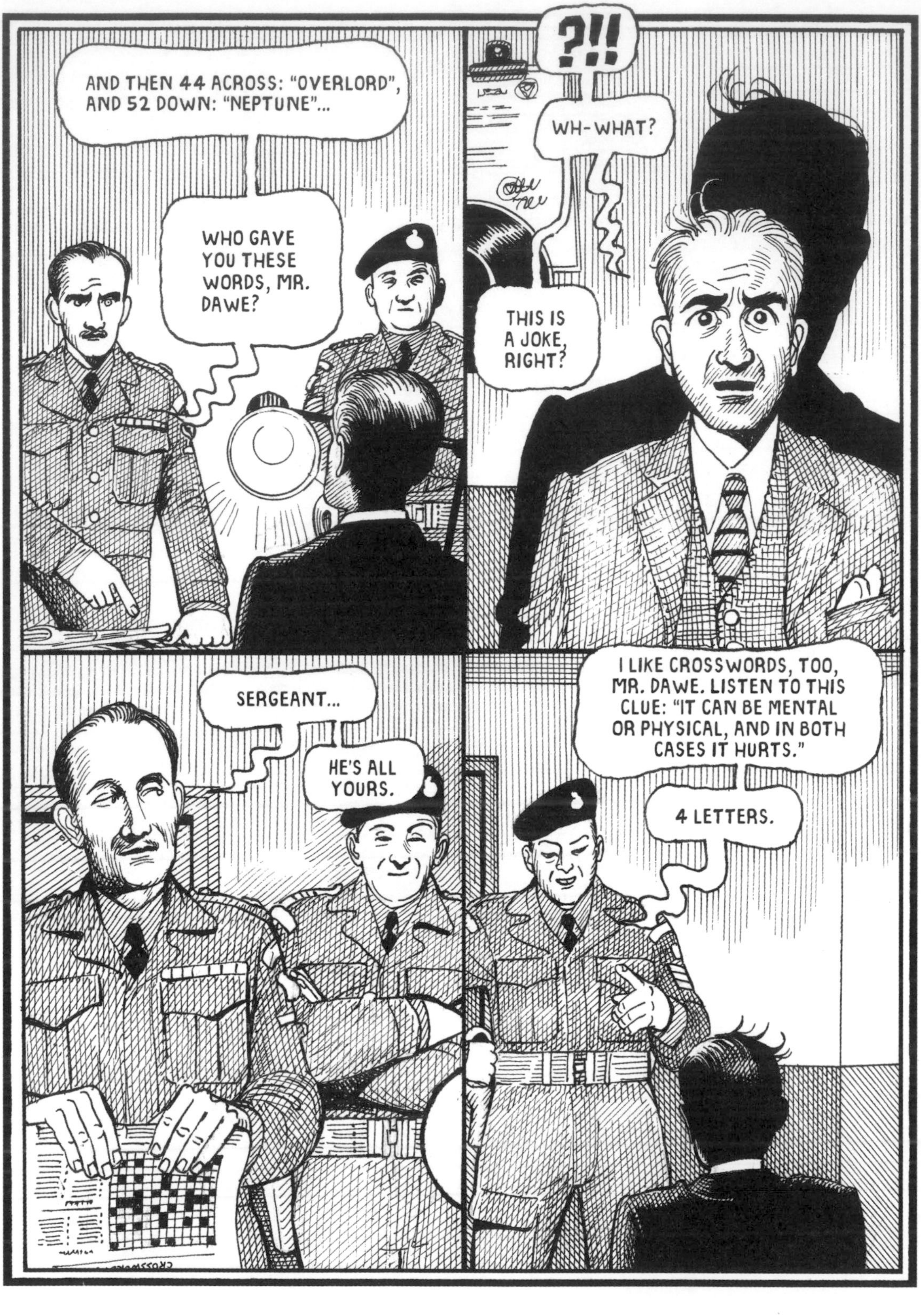
AND THEN 44 ACROSS: "OVERLORD", AND 52 DOWN: "NEPTUNE"...
WHO GAVE YOU THESE WORDS, MR. DAWE?
?!!
WH-WHAT?
THIS IS A JOKE, RIGHT?
SERGEANT...
HE'S ALL YOURS.
I LIKE CROSSWORDS, TOO, MR. DAWE. LISTEN TO THIS CLUE: "IT CAN BE MENTAL OR PHYSICAL, AND IN BOTH CASES IT HURTS."
4 LETTERS.

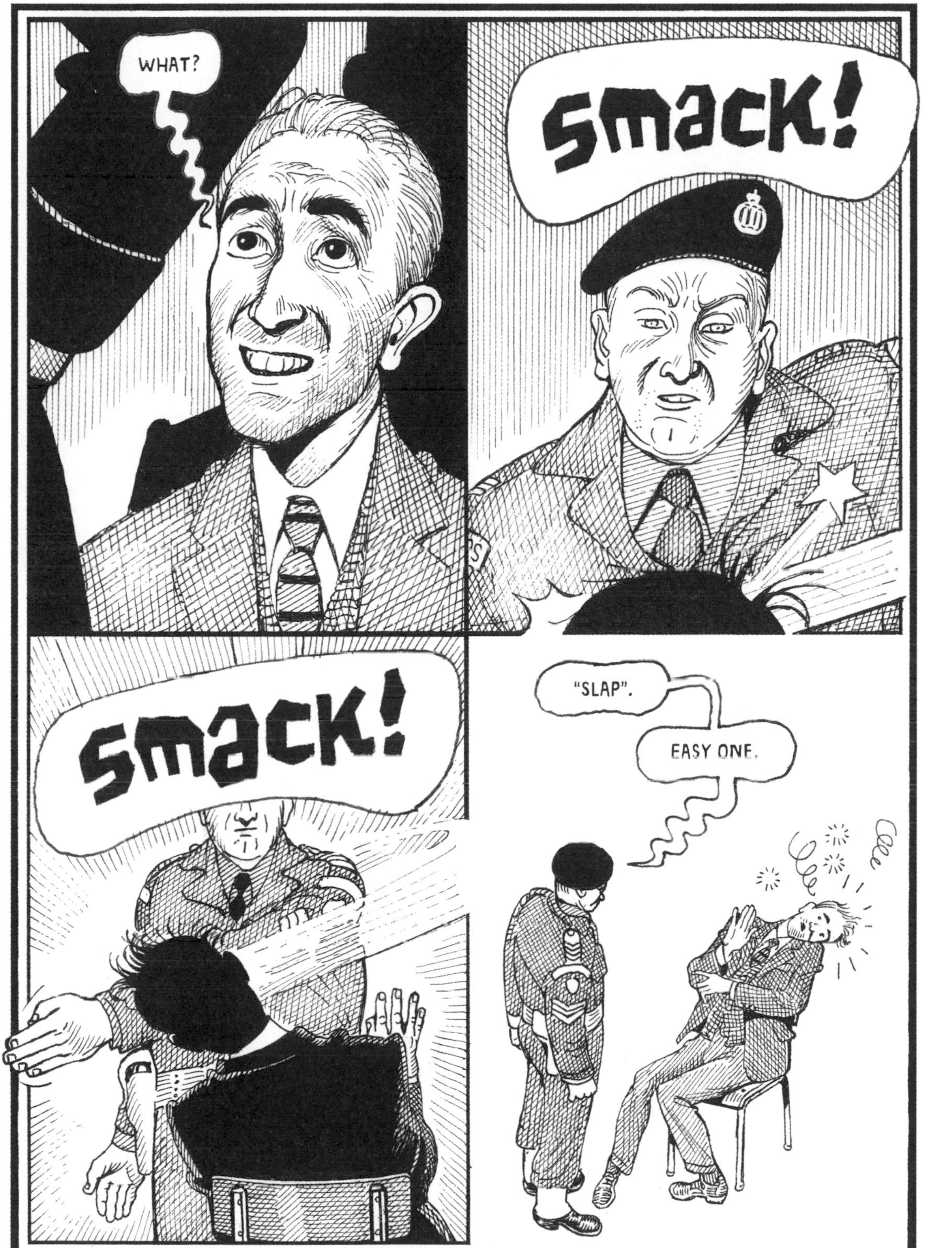
WHAT?
SMACK!
SMACK!
"SLAP".
EASY ONE.

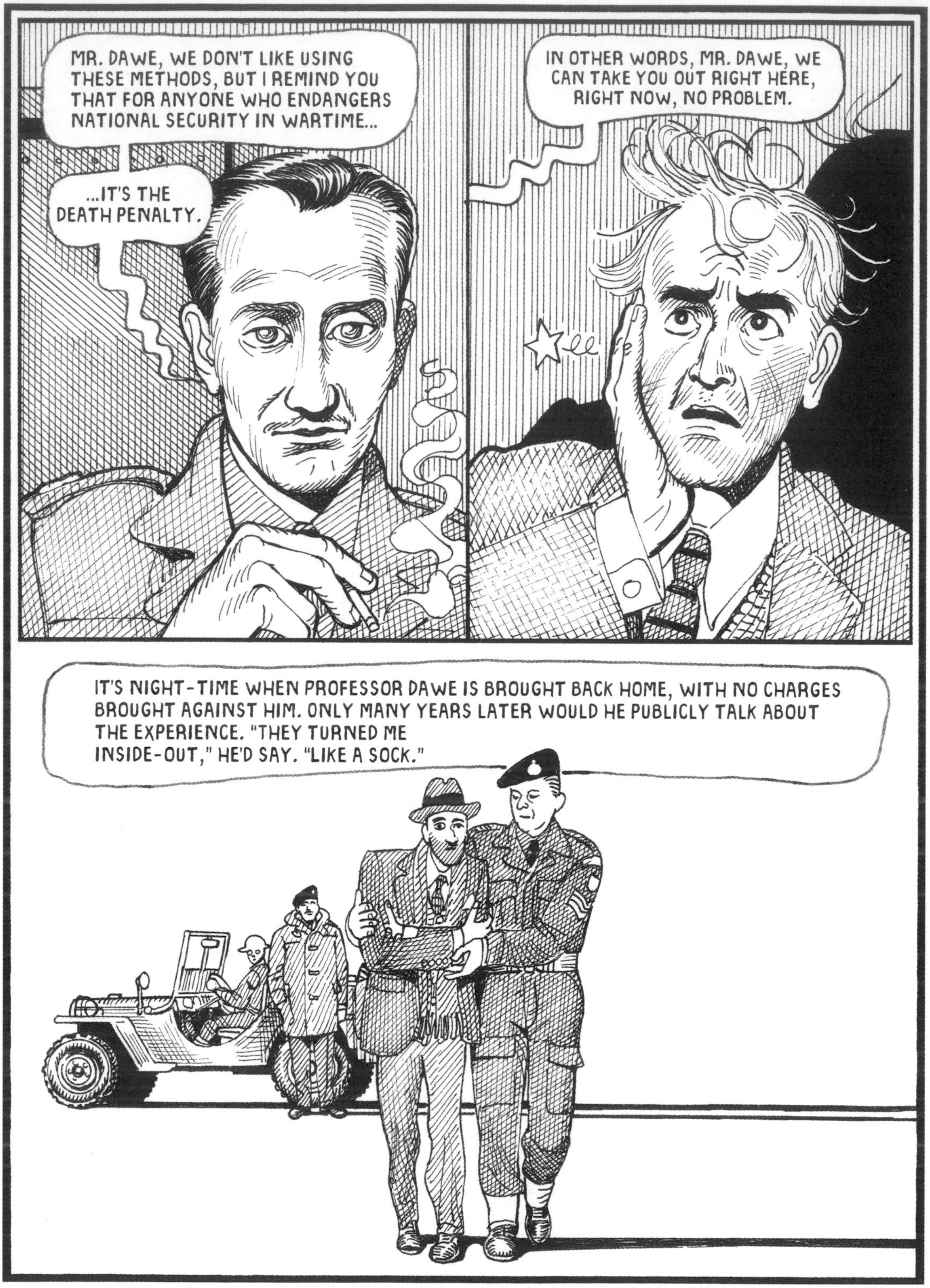
MR. DAWE, WE DON'T LIKE USING THESE METHODS, BUT I REMIND YOU THAT FOR ANYONE WHO ENDANGERS NATIONAL SECURITY IN WARTIME...
...IT'S THE DEATH PENALTY.
IN OTHER WORDS, MR. DAWE, WE CAN TAKE YOU OUT RIGHT HERE, RIGHT NOW, NO PROBLEM.
IT'S NIGHT-TIME WHEN PROFESSOR DAWE IS BROUGHT BACK HOME, WITH NO CHARGES BROUGHT AGAINST HIM. ONLY MANY YEARS LATER WOULD HE PUBLICLY TALK ABOUT THE EXPERIENCE. "THEY TURNED ME INSIDE-OUT," HE'D SAY. "LIKE A SOCK."

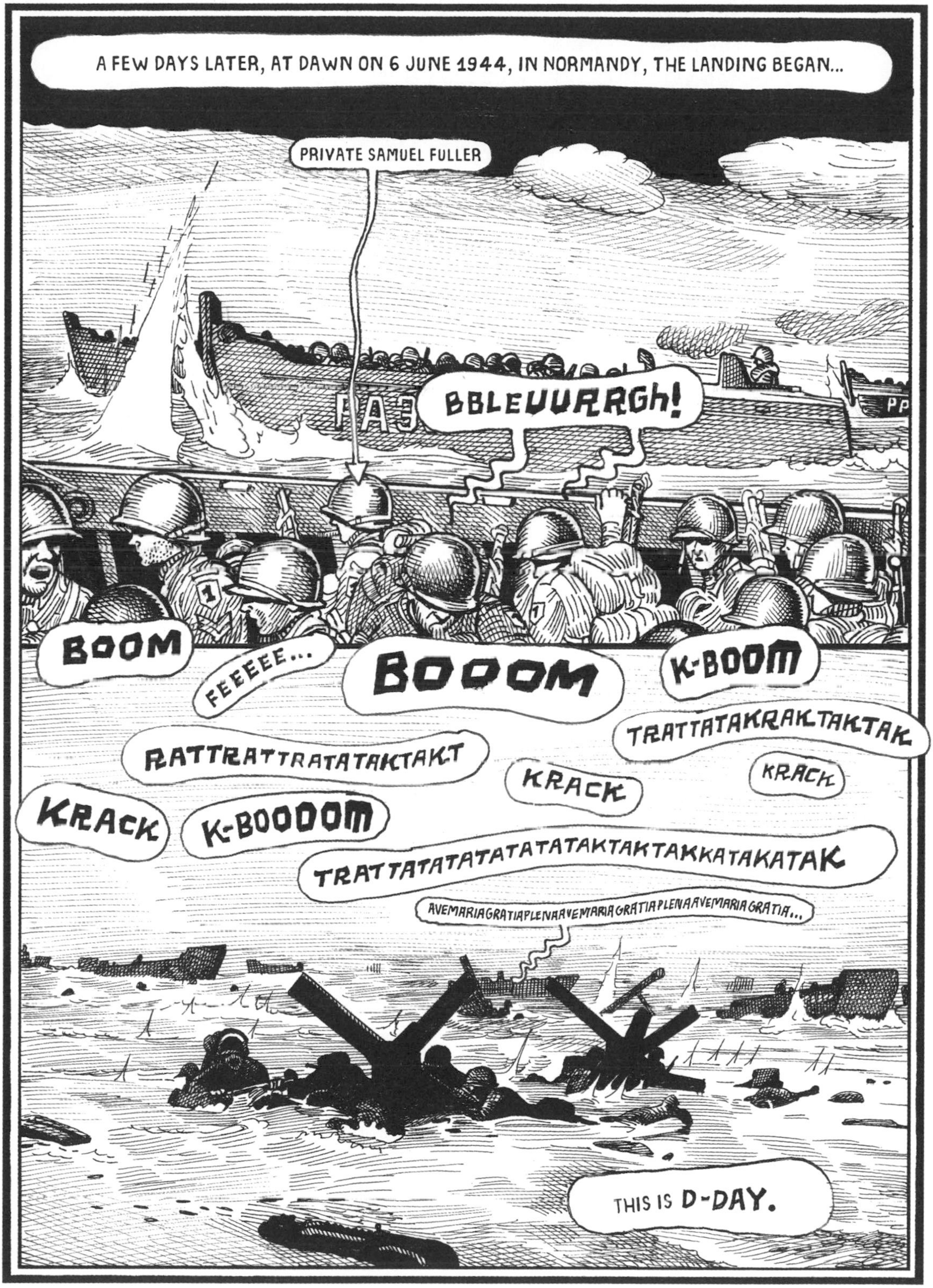

A FEW DAYS LATER, AT DAWN ON 6 JUNE 1944, IN NORMANDY, THE LANDING BEGAN...
PRIVATE SAMUEL FULLER
BBLEUURRGh!
BOOM
FEEEEE...
BOOOM
K-BOOM
TRATTATAKRAKTAKTAK
RATTRATTRATATAKTAKT
KRACK
KRACK
KRACK
K-BOOOOM
TRATTATATATATATATAKTAKTAKKATAKATAK
AVEMARIAGRATIAPLENAAVEMARIAGRATIAPLENAAVEMARIAGRATIA...
THIS IS D-DAY.

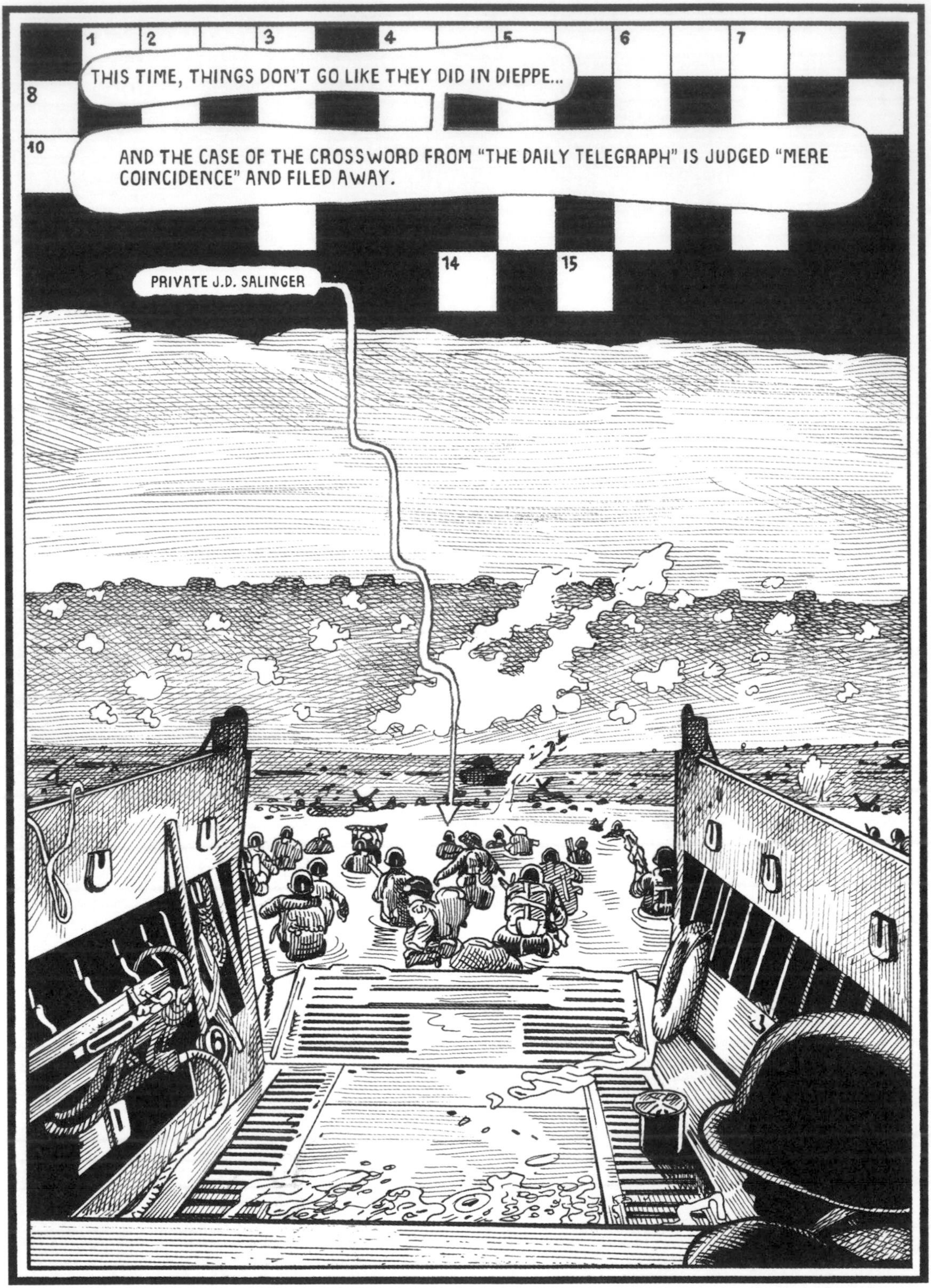
1
2
3
4
5
6
7
8
10
THIS TIME, THINGS DON'T GO LIKE THEY DID IN DIEPPE...
AND THE CASE OF THE CROSSWORD FROM "THE DAILY TELEGRAPH" IS JUDGED "MERE COINCIDENCE" AND FILED AWAY.
14
15
PRIVATE J.D. SALINGER

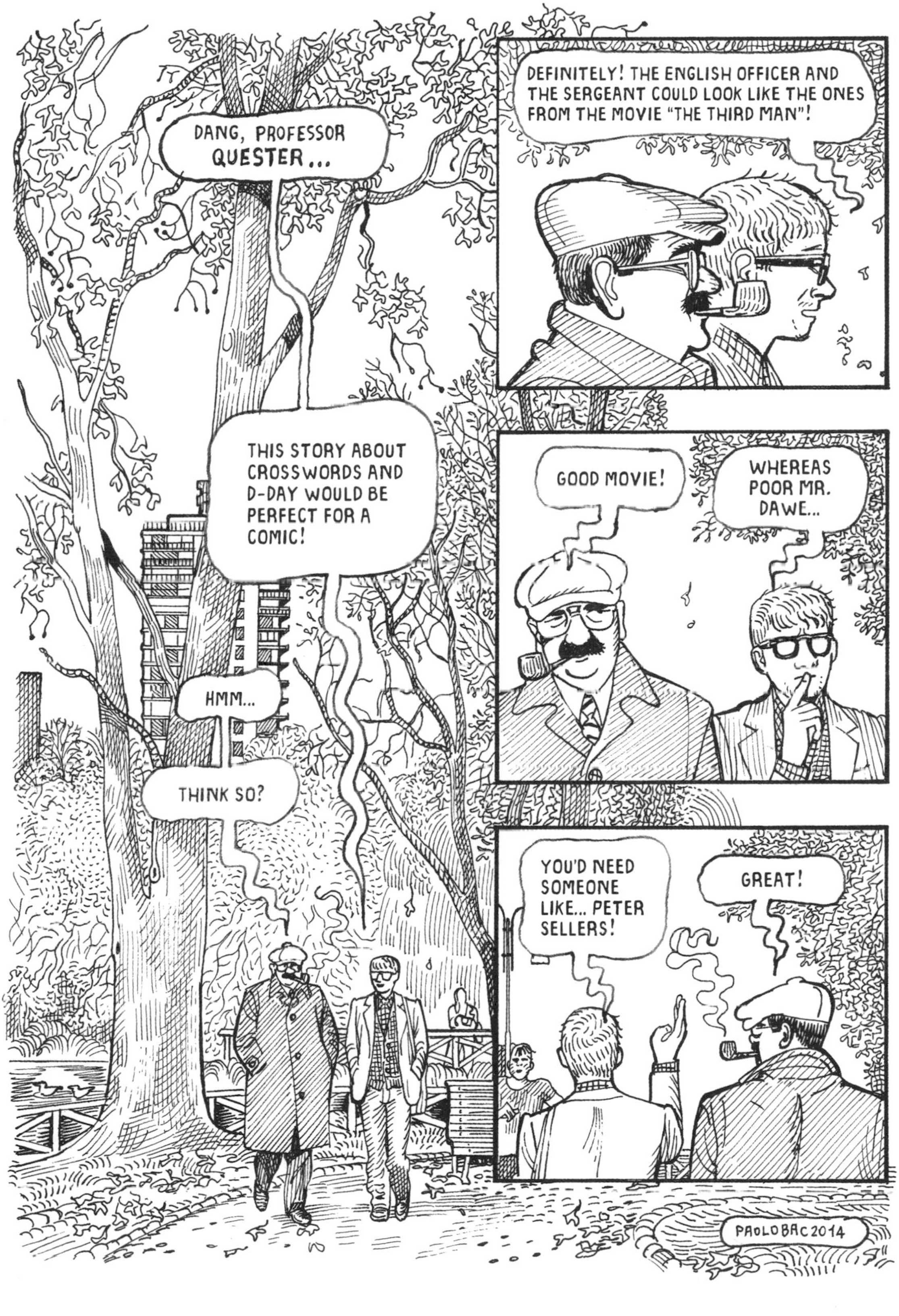
DANG, PROFESSOR QUESTER...
THIS STORY ABOUT CROSSWORDS AND D-DAY WOULD BE PERFECT FOR A COMIC!
HMM...
THINK SO?
DEFINITELY! THE ENGLISH OFFICER AND THE SERGEANT COULD LOOK LIKE THE ONES FROM THE MOVIE "THE THIRD MAN"!
GOOD MOVIE!
WHEREAS POOR MR. DAWE...
YOU'D NEED SOMEONE LIKE... PETER SELLERS!
GREAT!
PAOLOBAC2014

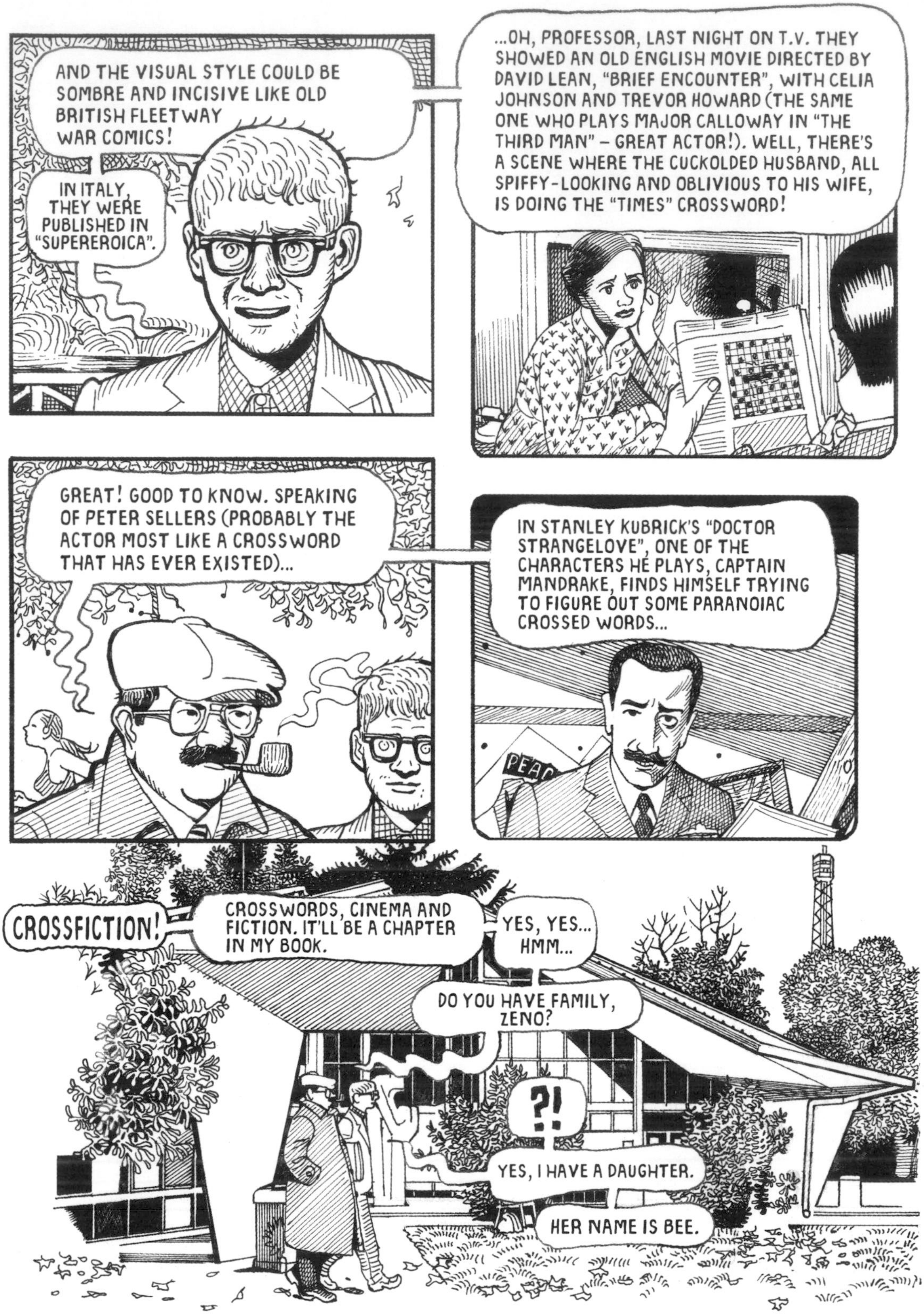
AND THE VISUAL STYLE COULD BE SOMBRE AND INCISIVE LIKE OLD BRITISH FLEETWAY WAR COMICS!
IN ITALY, THEY WERE PUBLISHED IN "SUPEREROICA".
...OH, PROFESSOR, LAST NIGHT ON T.V. THEY SHOWED AN OLD ENGLISH MOVIE DIRECTED BY DAVID LEAN, "BRIEF ENCOUNTER", WITH CELIA JOHNSON AND TREVOR HOWARD (THE SAME ONE WHO PLAYS MAJOR CALLOWAY IN "THE THIRD MAN" – GREAT ACTOR!). WELL, THERE'S A SCENE WHERE THE CUCKOLDED HUSBAND, ALL SPIFFY-LOOKING AND OBLIVIOUS TO HIS WIFE, IS DOING THE "TIMES" CROSSWORD!
GREAT! GOOD TO KNOW. SPEAKING OF PETER SELLERS (PROBABLY THE ACTOR MOST LIKE A CROSSWORD THAT HAS EVER EXISTED)...
IN STANLEY KUBRICK'S "DOCTOR STRANGELOVE", ONE OF THE CHARACTERS HE PLAYS, CAPTAIN MANDRAKE, FINDS HIMSELF TRYING TO FIGURE OUT SOME PARANOIAC CROSSED WORDS...
CROSSFICTION!
CROSSWORDS, CINEMA AND FICTION. IT'LL BE A CHAPTER IN MY BOOK.
YES, YES... HMM...
DO YOU HAVE FAMILY, ZENO?
?!
YES, I HAVE A DAUGHTER.
HER NAME IS BEE.

MARYA HOIA HUTTA

WHICH MEANS "THE DEAD DOG" IN URDU (I THINK)

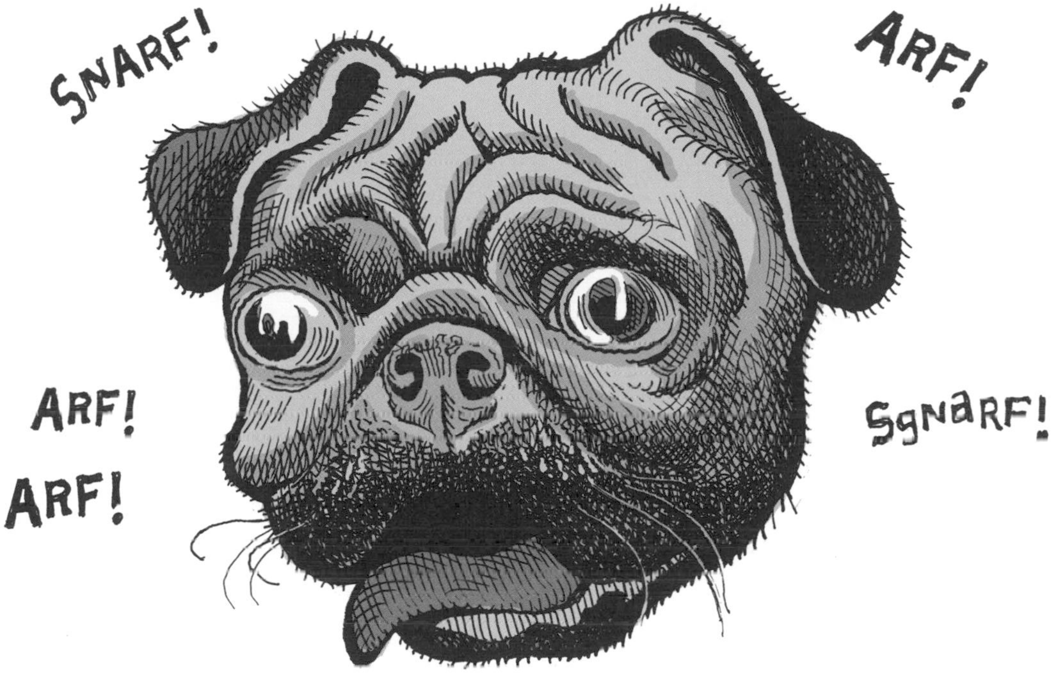
SNARF!
ARF!
ARF!
ARF!
SgNaRF!

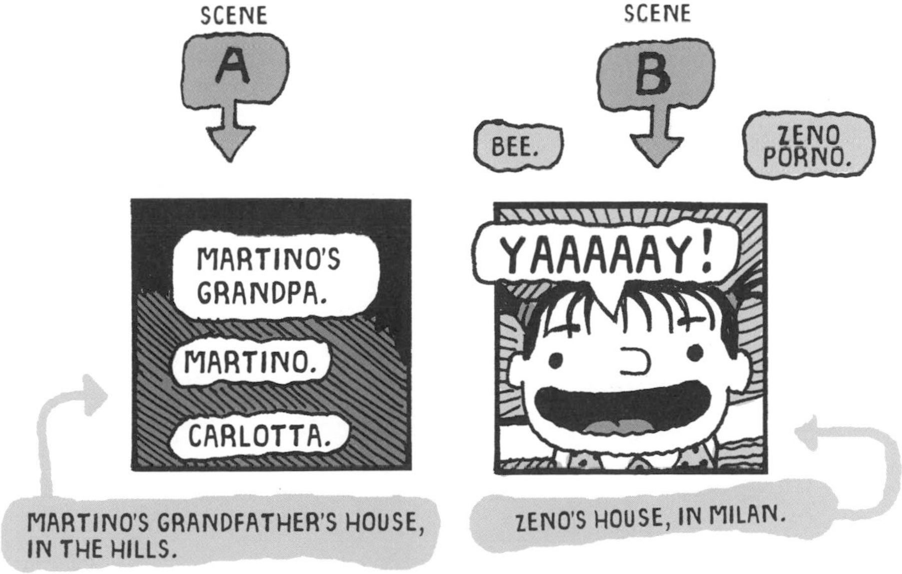
SCENE
A
SCENE
B
BEE.
ZENO PORNO.
MARTINO'S GRANDPA.
MARTINO.
CARLOTTA.
YAAAAAY!
MARTINO'S GRANDFATHER'S HOUSE, IN THE HILLS.
ZENO'S HOUSE, IN MILAN.

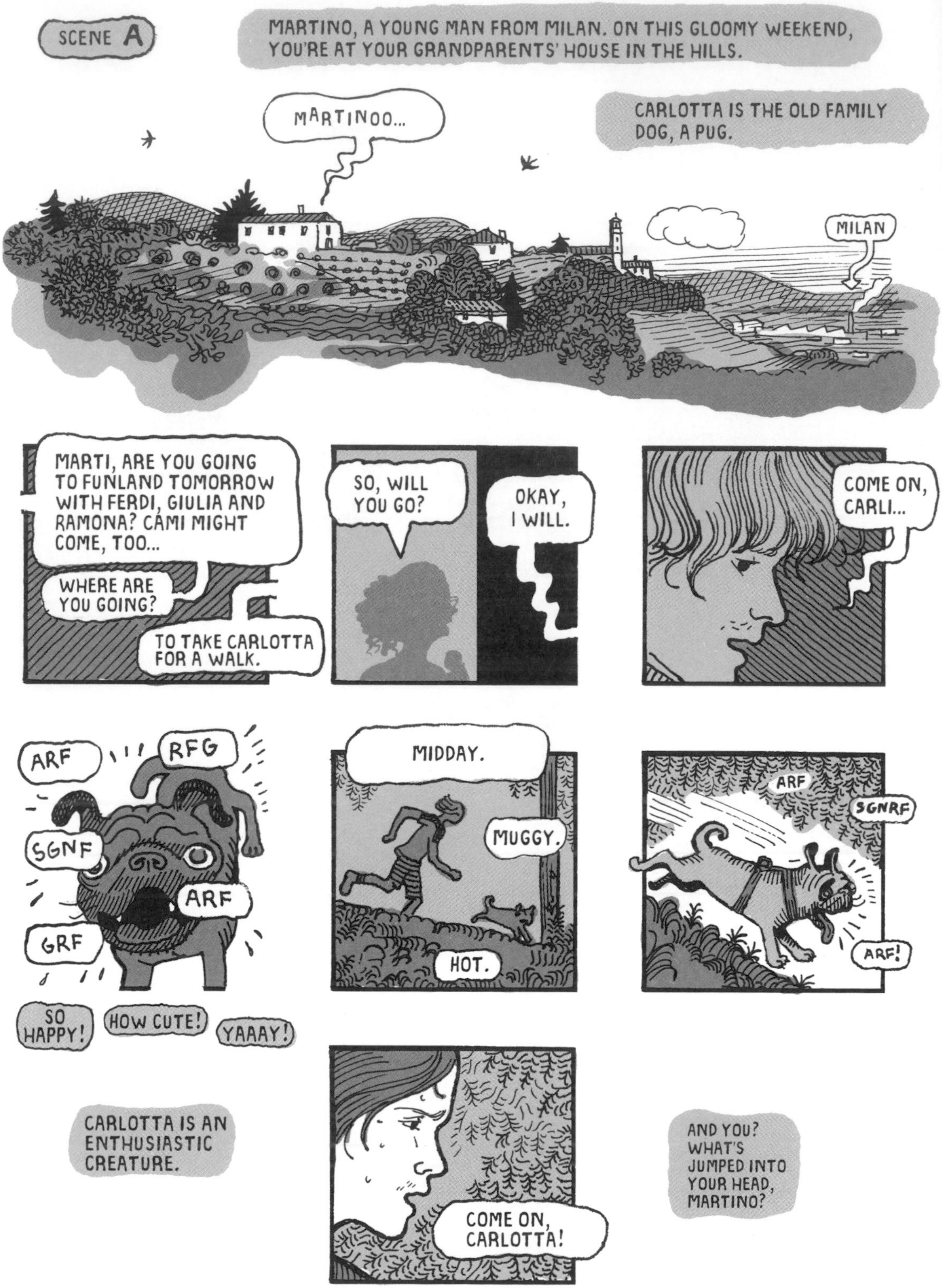
SCENE A
MARTINO, A YOUNG MAN FROM MILAN. ON THIS GLOOMY WEEKEND, YOU'RE AT YOUR GRANDPARENTS' HOUSE IN THE HILLS.
MARTINOO...
CARLOTTA IS THE OLD FAMILY DOG, A PUG.
MILAN
MARTI, ARE YOU GOING TO FUNLAND TOMORROW WITH FERDI, GIULIA AND RAMONA? CAMI MIGHT COME, TOO...
WHERE ARE YOU GOING?
TO TAKE CARLOTTA FOR A WALK.
SO, WILL YOU GO?
OKAY, I WILL.
COME ON, CARLI...
ARF
RFG
SGNF
ARF
GRF
SO HAPPY!
HOW CUTE!
YAAAY!
MIDDAY.
MUGGY.
HOT.
ARF
SGNRF
ARF!
CARLOTTA IS AN ENTHUSIASTIC CREATURE.
COME ON, CARLOTTA!
AND YOU? WHAT'S JUMPED INTO YOUR HEAD, MARTINO?

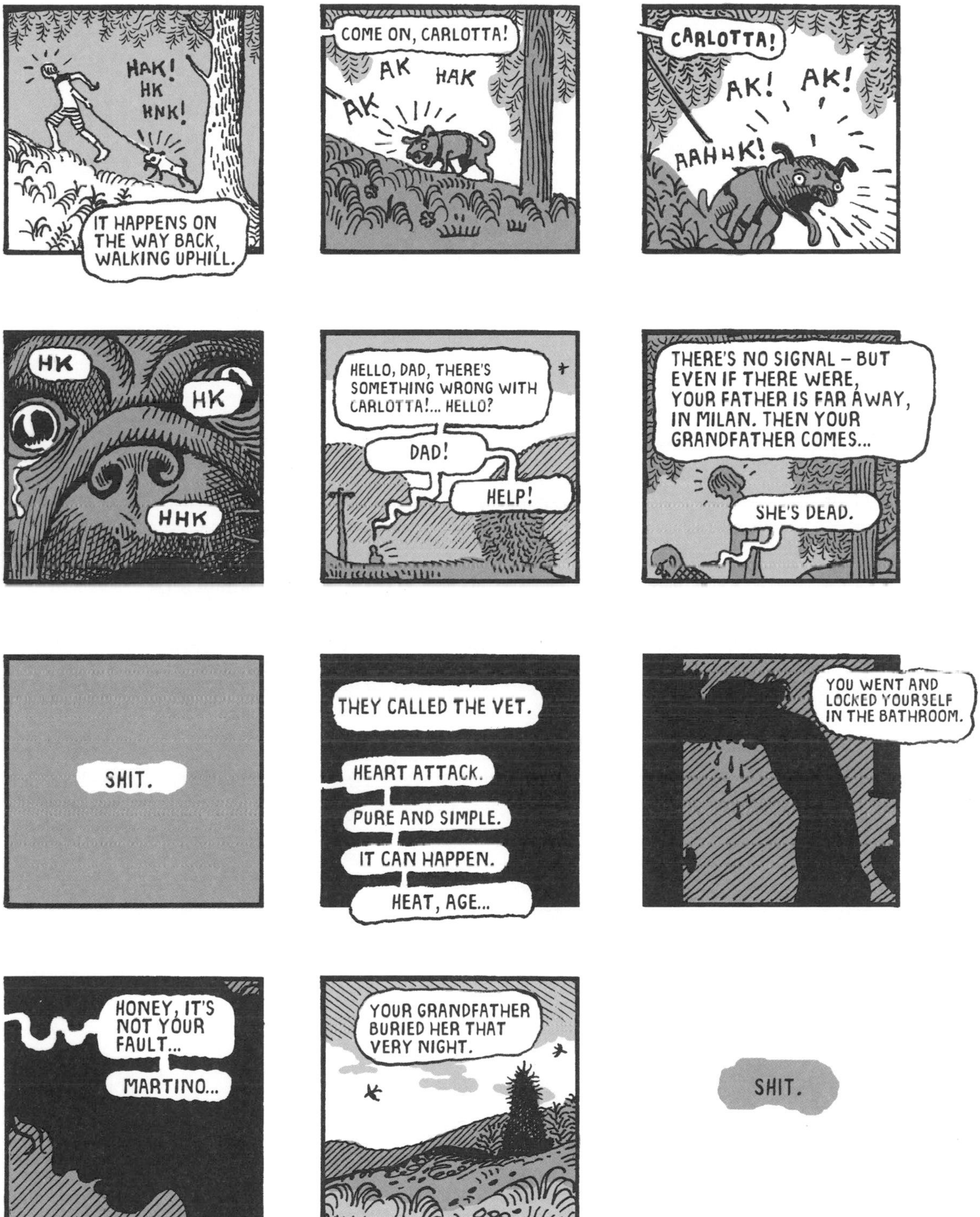
HAK! HK HNK!
IT HAPPENS ON THE WAY BACK, WALKING UPHILL.
COME ON, CARLOTTA!
AK AK HAK
CARLOTTA!
AK! AK! AAHHK!
HK
HK
HHK
HELLO, DAD, THERE'S SOMETHING WRONG WITH CARLOTTA!... HELLO?
DAD!
HELP!
THERE'S NO SIGNAL – BUT EVEN IF THERE WERE, YOUR FATHER IS FAR AWAY, IN MILAN. THEN YOUR GRANDFATHER COMES...
SHE'S DEAD.
SHIT.
THEY CALLED THE VET.
HEART ATTACK.
PURE AND SIMPLE.
IT CAN HAPPEN.
HEAT, AGE...
YOU WENT AND LOCKED YOURSELF IN THE BATHROOM.
HONEY, IT'S NOT YOUR FAULT...
MARTINO...
YOUR GRANDFATHER BURIED HER THAT VERY NIGHT.
SHIT.

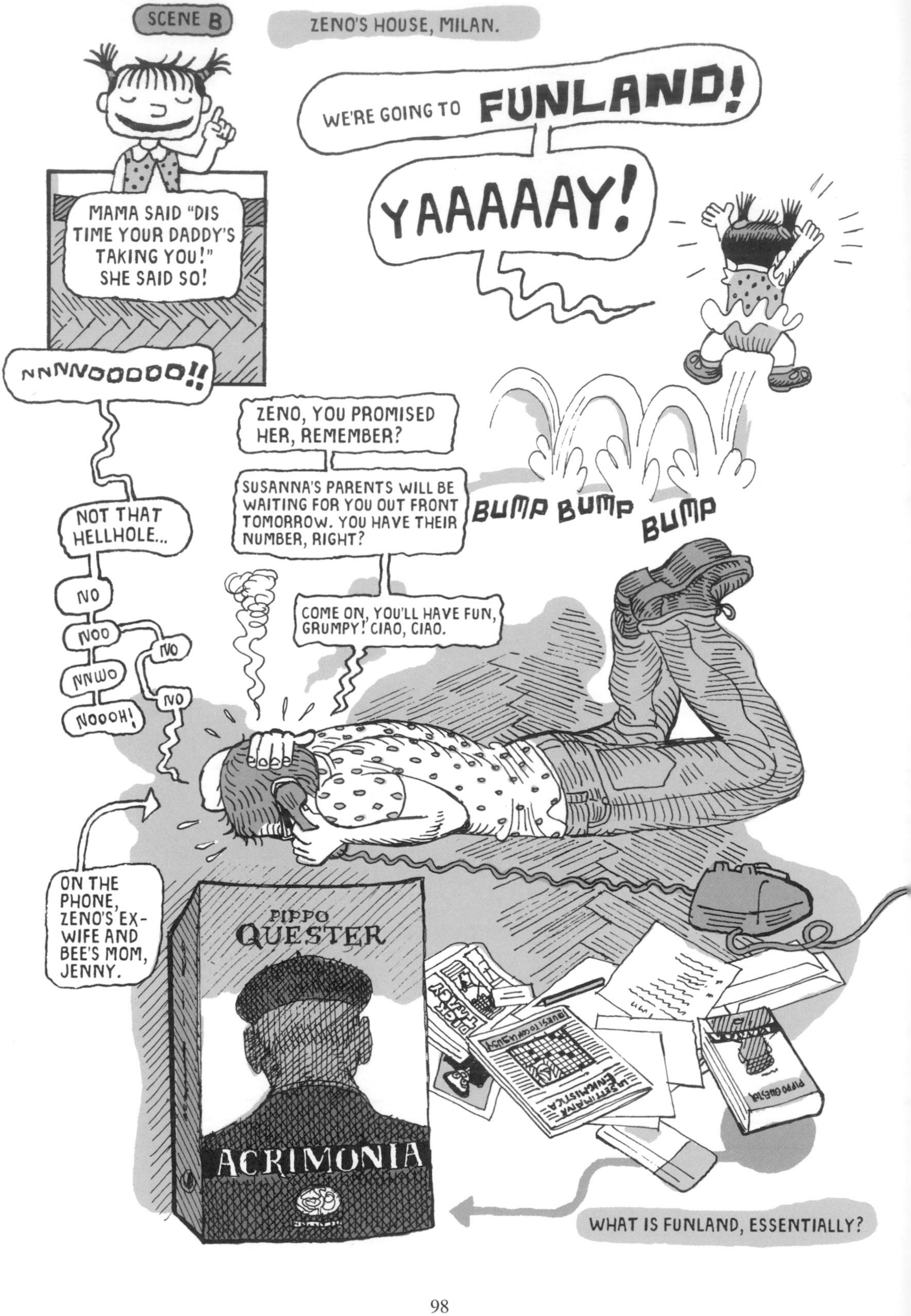
SCENE B
ZENO'S HOUSE, MILAN.
MAMA SAID "DIS TIME YOUR DADDY'S TAKING YOU!" SHE SAID SO!
WE'RE GOING TO FUNLAND!
YAAAAAY!
NNNNOOOOO!!
NOT THAT HELLHOLE...
NO
NOO
NNWO
NOOOH!
NO
NO
ZENO, YOU PROMISED HER, REMEMBER?
SUSANNA'S PARENTS WILL BE WAITING FOR YOU OUT FRONT TOMORROW. YOU HAVE THEIR NUMBER, RIGHT?
COME ON, YOU'LL HAVE FUN, GRUMPY! CIAO, CIAO.
BUMP BUMP BUMP
ON THE PHONE, ZENO'S EX-WIFE AND BEE'S MOM, JENNY.
PIPPO QUESTER
ACRIMONIA
WHAT IS FUNLAND, ESSENTIALLY?

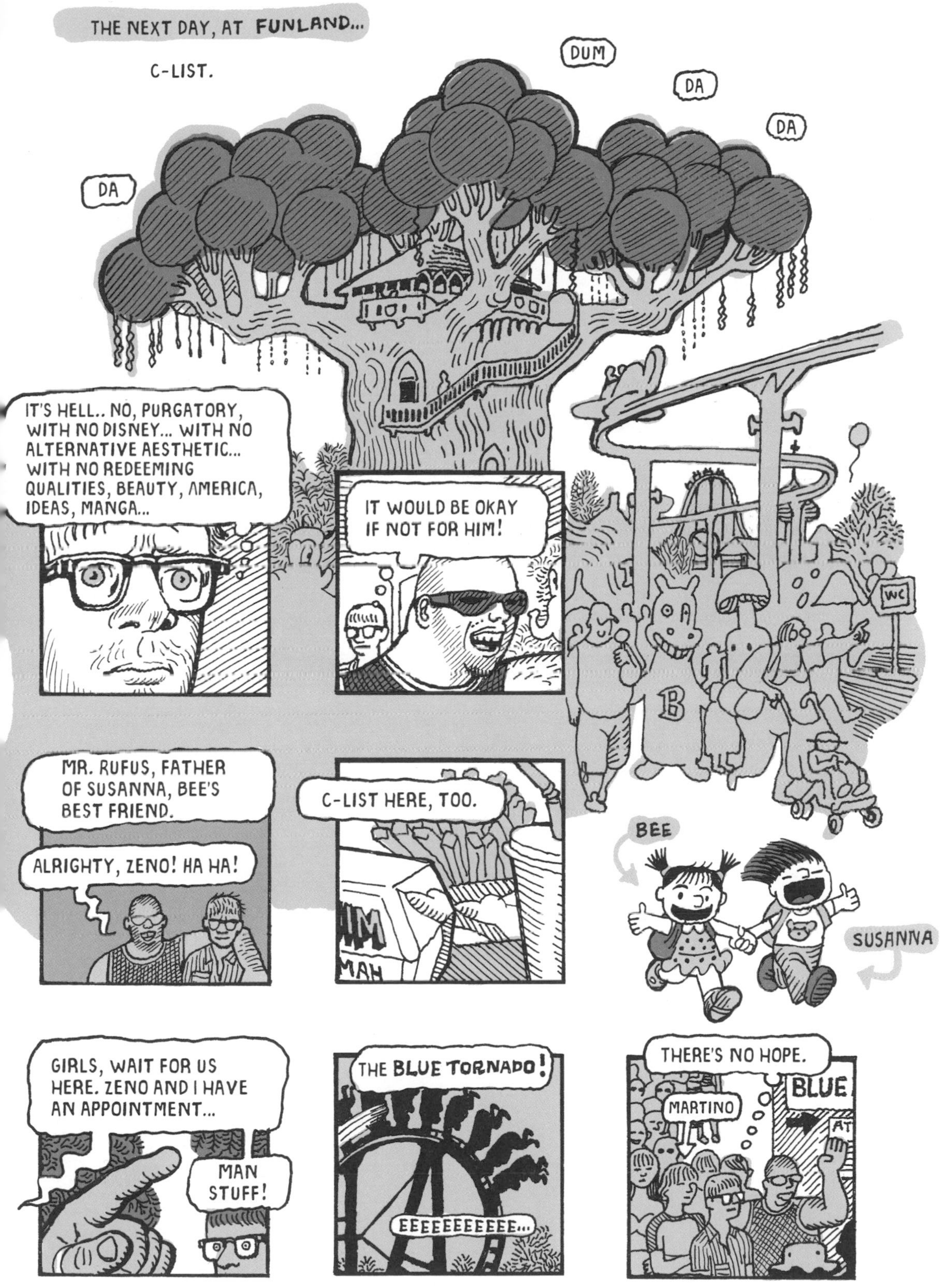
THE NEXT DAY, AT FUNLAND...
C-LIST.
DUM
DA
DA
DA
DA
IT'S HELL.. NO, PURGATORY, WITH NO DISNEY... WITH NO ALTERNATIVE AESTHETIC... WITH NO REDEEMING QUALITIES, BEAUTY, AMERICA, IDEAS, MANGA...
IT WOULD BE OKAY IF NOT FOR HIM!
MR. RUFUS, FATHER OF SUSANNA, BEE'S BEST FRIEND.
ALRIGHTY, ZENO! HA HA!
C-LIST HERE, TOO.
BEE
SUSANNA
GIRLS, WAIT FOR US HERE. ZENO AND I HAVE AN APPOINTMENT...
MAN STUFF!
THE BLUE TORNADO!
EEEEEEEEEEE...
THERE'S NO HOPE.
MARTINO
BLUE

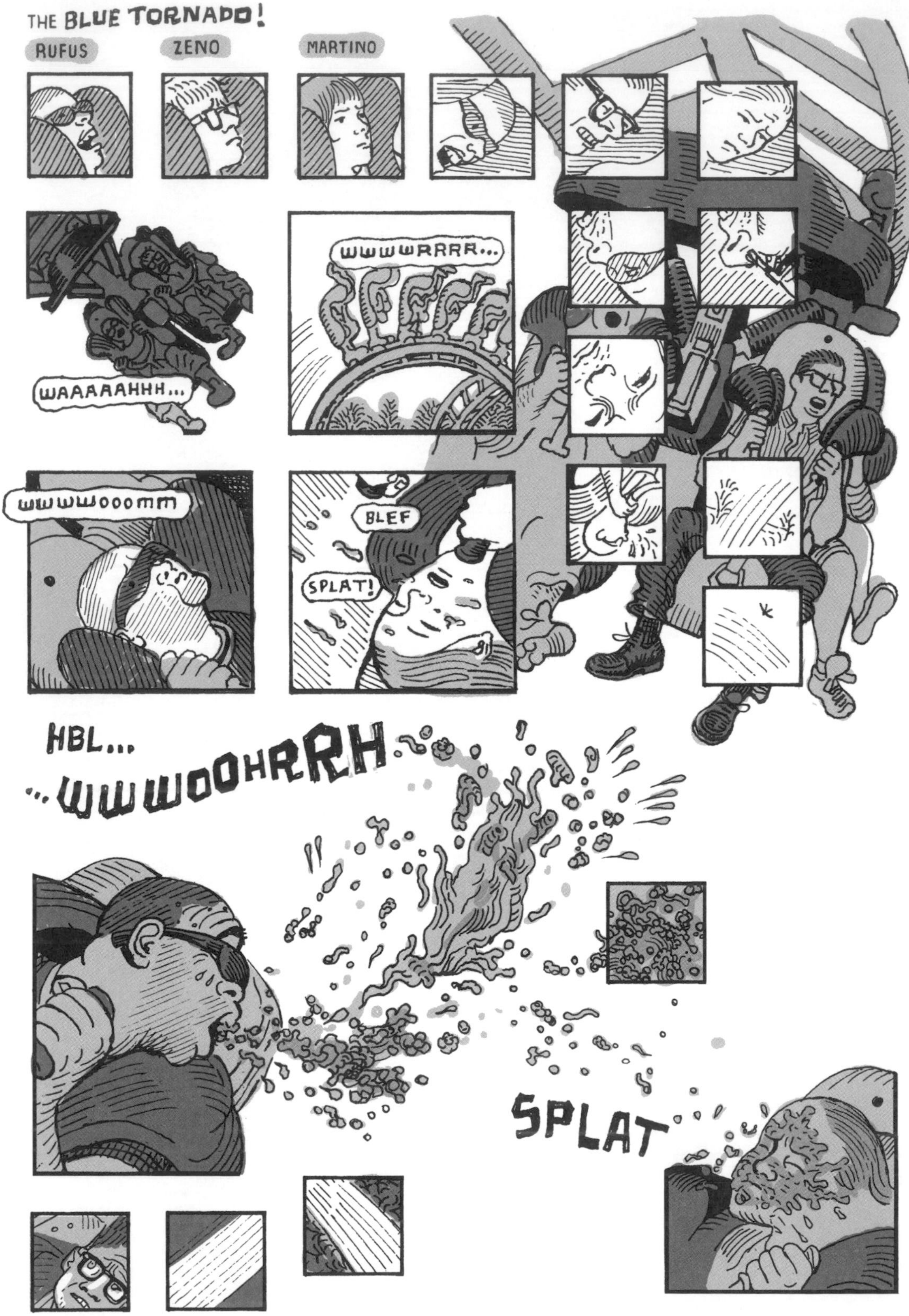
THE BLUE TORNADO!
RUFUS
ZENO
MARTINO
WAAAAAHHH...
WWWWRRRR...
WWWWOOOMM
BLEF
SPLAT!
HBL...
...WWWOOHRRRH
SPLAT

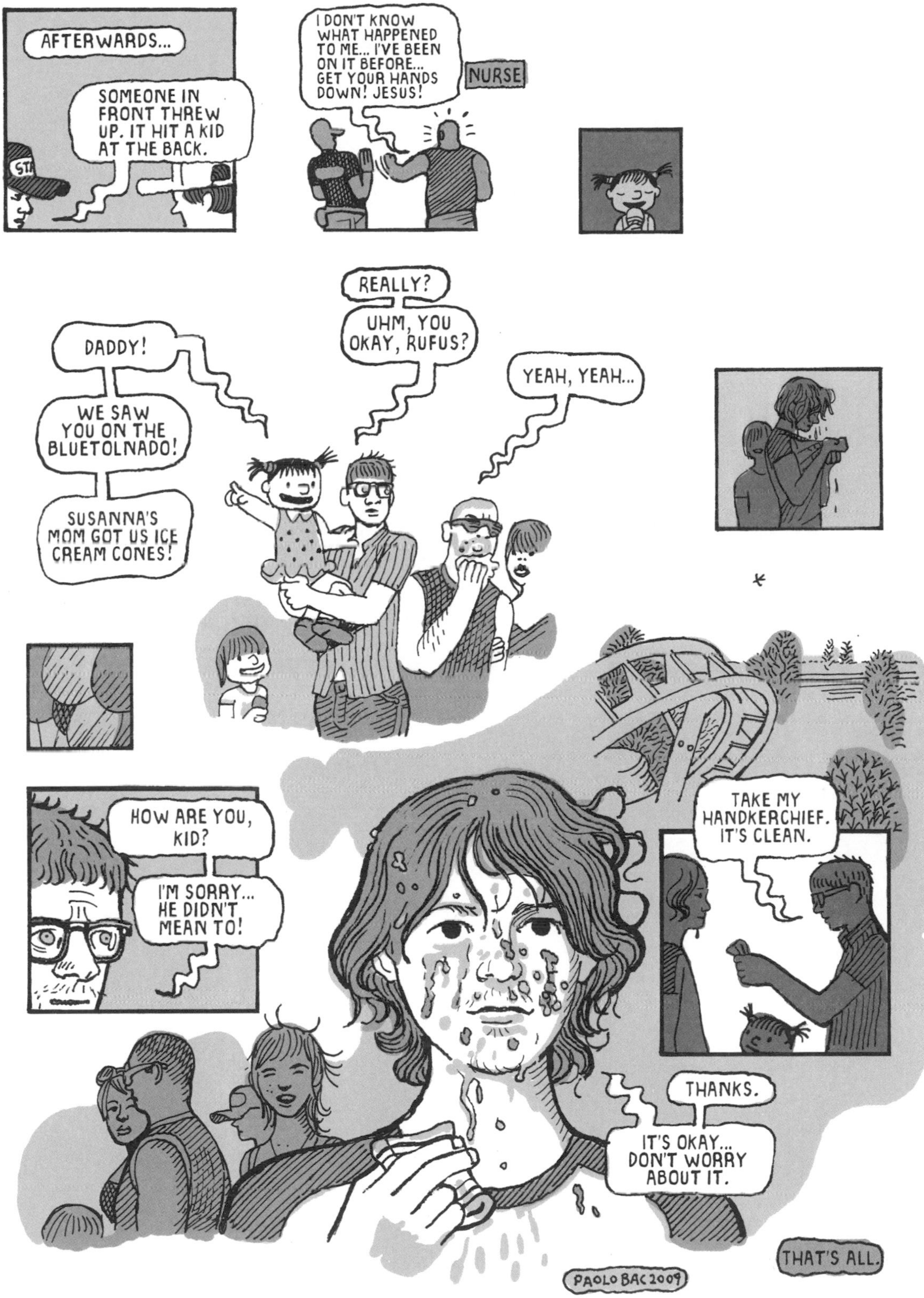
AFTERWARDS...
SOMEONE IN FRONT THREW UP. IT HIT A KID AT THE BACK.
I DON'T KNOW WHAT HAPPENED TO ME... I'VE BEEN ON IT BEFORE... GET YOUR HANDS DOWN! JESUS!
NURSE
DADDY!
WE SAW YOU ON THE BLUETOLNADO!
SUSANNA'S MOM GOT US ICE CREAM CONES!
REALLY?
UHM, YOU OKAY, RUFUS?
YEAH, YEAH...
HOW ARE YOU, KID?
I'M SORRY... HE DIDN'T MEAN TO!
TAKE MY HANDKERCHIEF. IT'S CLEAN.
THANKS.
IT'S OKAY... DON'T WORRY ABOUT IT.
THAT'S ALL.
PAOLO BAC 2009

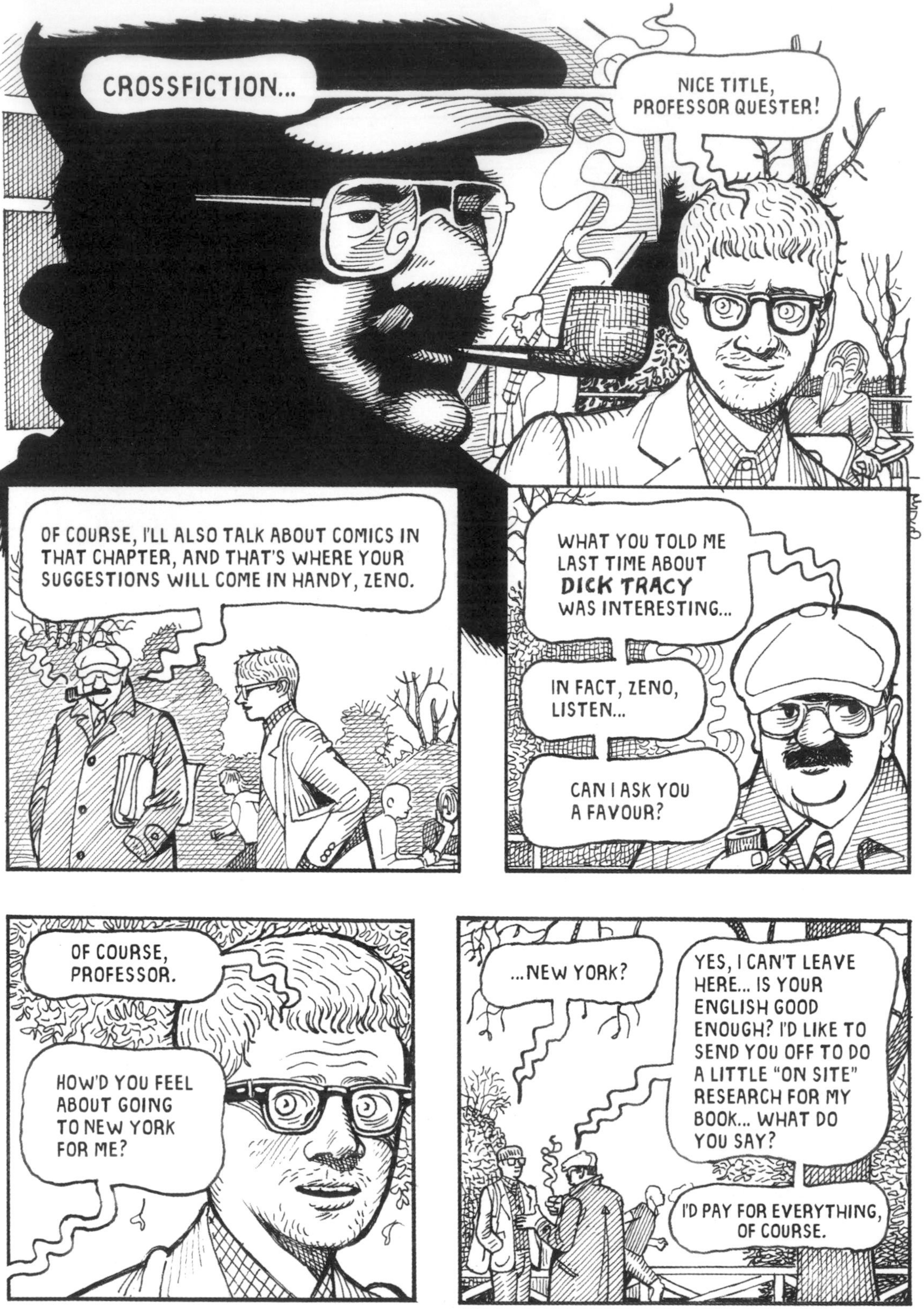
CROSSFICTION...
NICE TITLE, PROFESSOR QUESTER!
OF COURSE, I'LL ALSO TALK ABOUT COMICS IN THAT CHAPTER, AND THAT'S WHERE YOUR SUGGESTIONS WILL COME IN HANDY, ZENO.
WHAT YOU TOLD ME LAST TIME ABOUT DICK TRACY WAS INTERESTING...
IN FACT, ZENO, LISTEN...
CAN I ASK YOU A FAVOUR?
OF COURSE, PROFESSOR.
HOW'D YOU FEEL ABOUT GOING TO NEW YORK FOR ME?
...NEW YORK?
YES, I CAN'T LEAVE HERE... IS YOUR ENGLISH GOOD ENOUGH? I'D LIKE TO SEND YOU OFF TO DO A LITTLE "ON SITE" RESEARCH FOR MY BOOK... WHAT DO YOU SAY?
I'D PAY FOR EVERYTHING, OF COURSE.

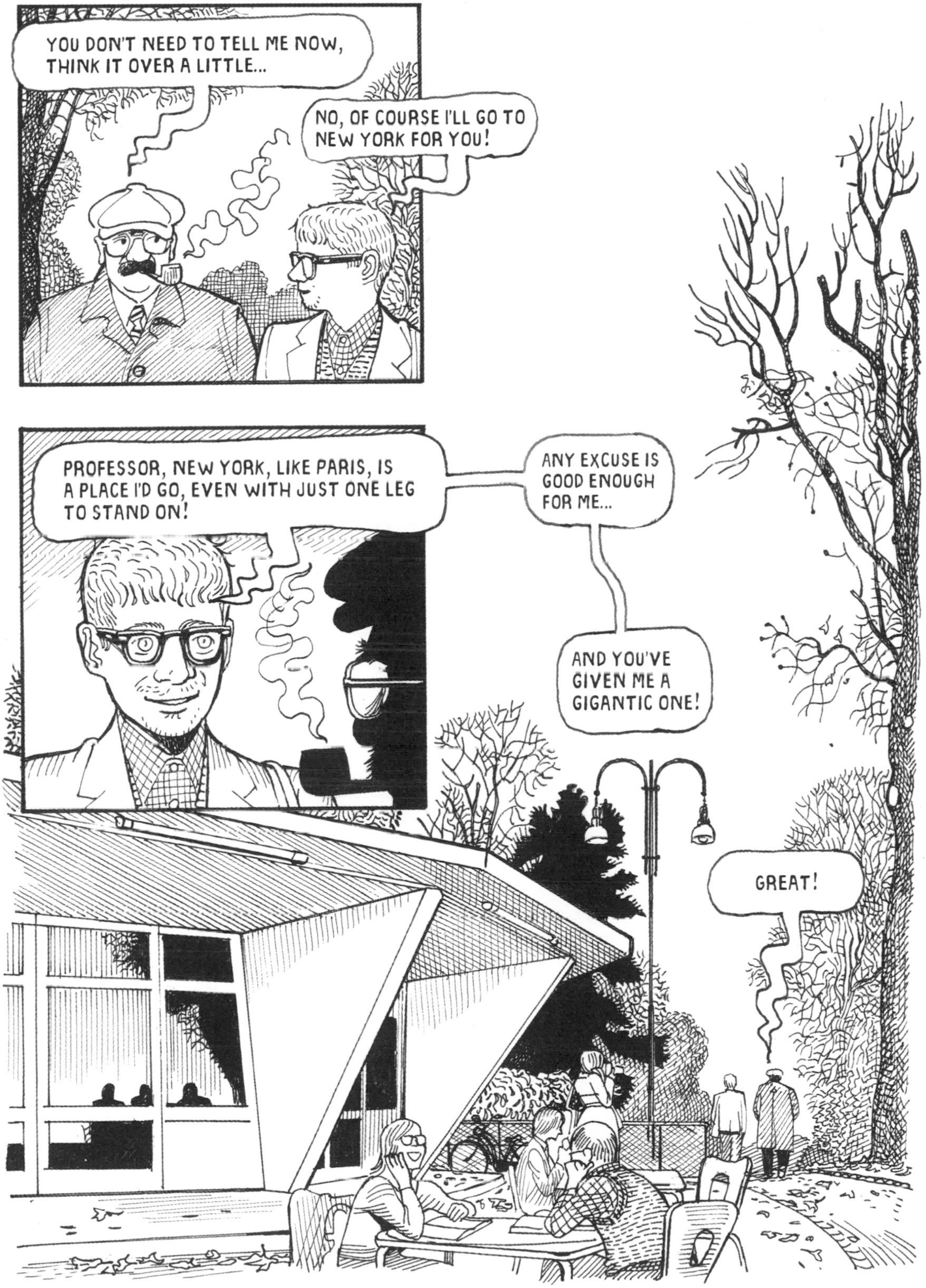
YOU DON'T NEED TO TELL ME NOW, THINK IT OVER A LITTLE...
NO, OF COURSE I'LL GO TO NEW YORK FOR YOU!
PROFESSOR, NEW YORK, LIKE PARIS, IS A PLACE I'D GO, EVEN WITH JUST ONE LEG TO STAND ON!
ANY EXCUSE IS GOOD ENOUGH FOR ME...
AND YOU'VE GIVEN ME A GIGANTIC ONE!
GREAT!

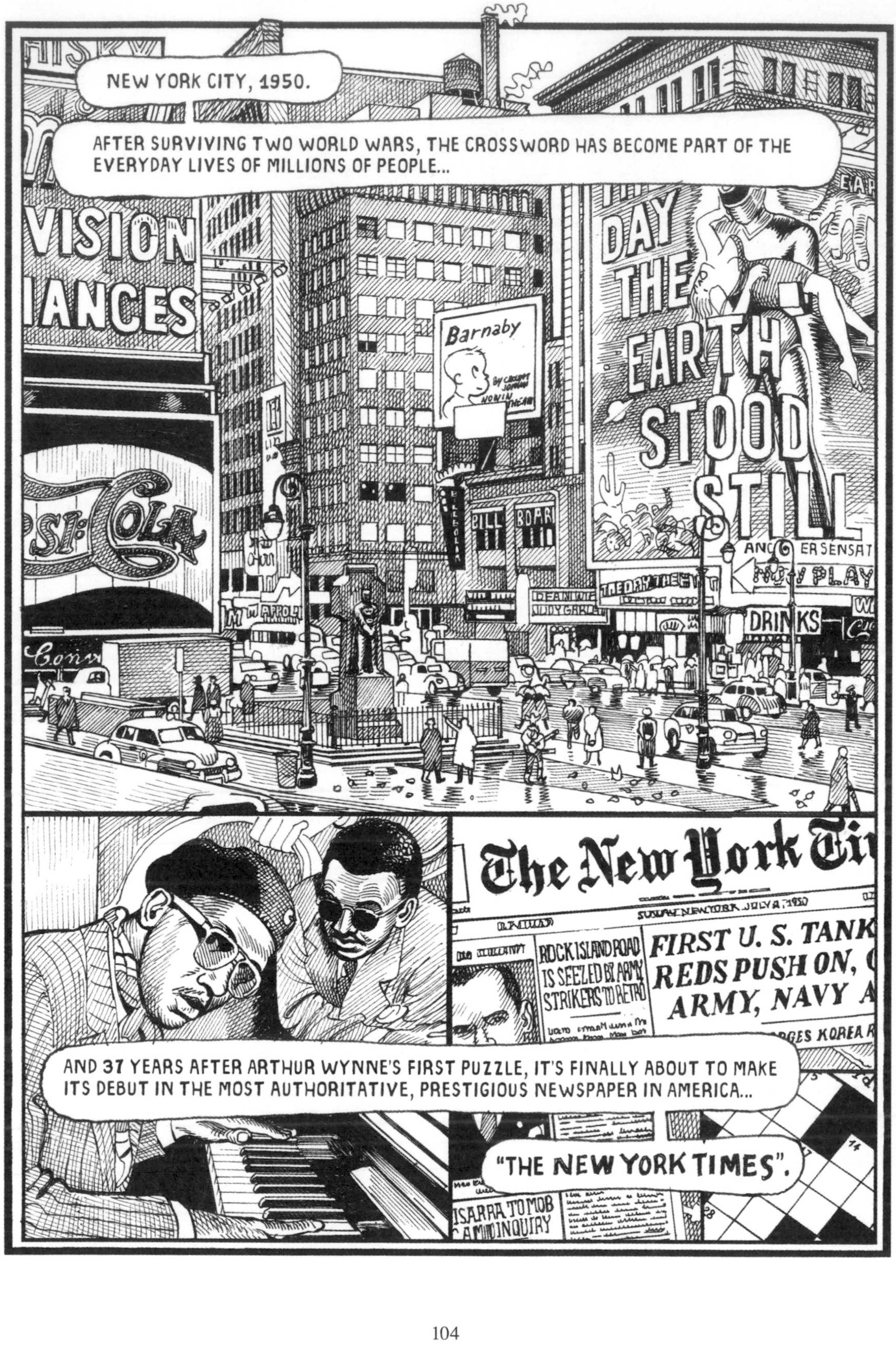
NEW YORK CITY, 1950.
AFTER SURVIVING TWO WORLD WARS, THE CROSSWORD HAS BECOME PART OF THE EVERYDAY LIVES OF MILLIONS OF PEOPLE...
VISION
IANCES
DAY THE EARTH STOOD STILL
Barnaby
DRINKS
The New York Ti
FIRST U. S. TANK
REDS PUSH ON,
ARMY, NAVY A
ROCK ISLAND ROAD IS SEEZED BY ARMY
AND 37 YEARS AFTER ARTHUR WYNNE'S FIRST PUZZLE, IT'S FINALLY ABOUT TO MAKE ITS DEBUT IN THE MOST AUTHORITATIVE, PRESTIGIOUS NEWSPAPER IN AMERICA...
"THE NEW YORK TIMES".

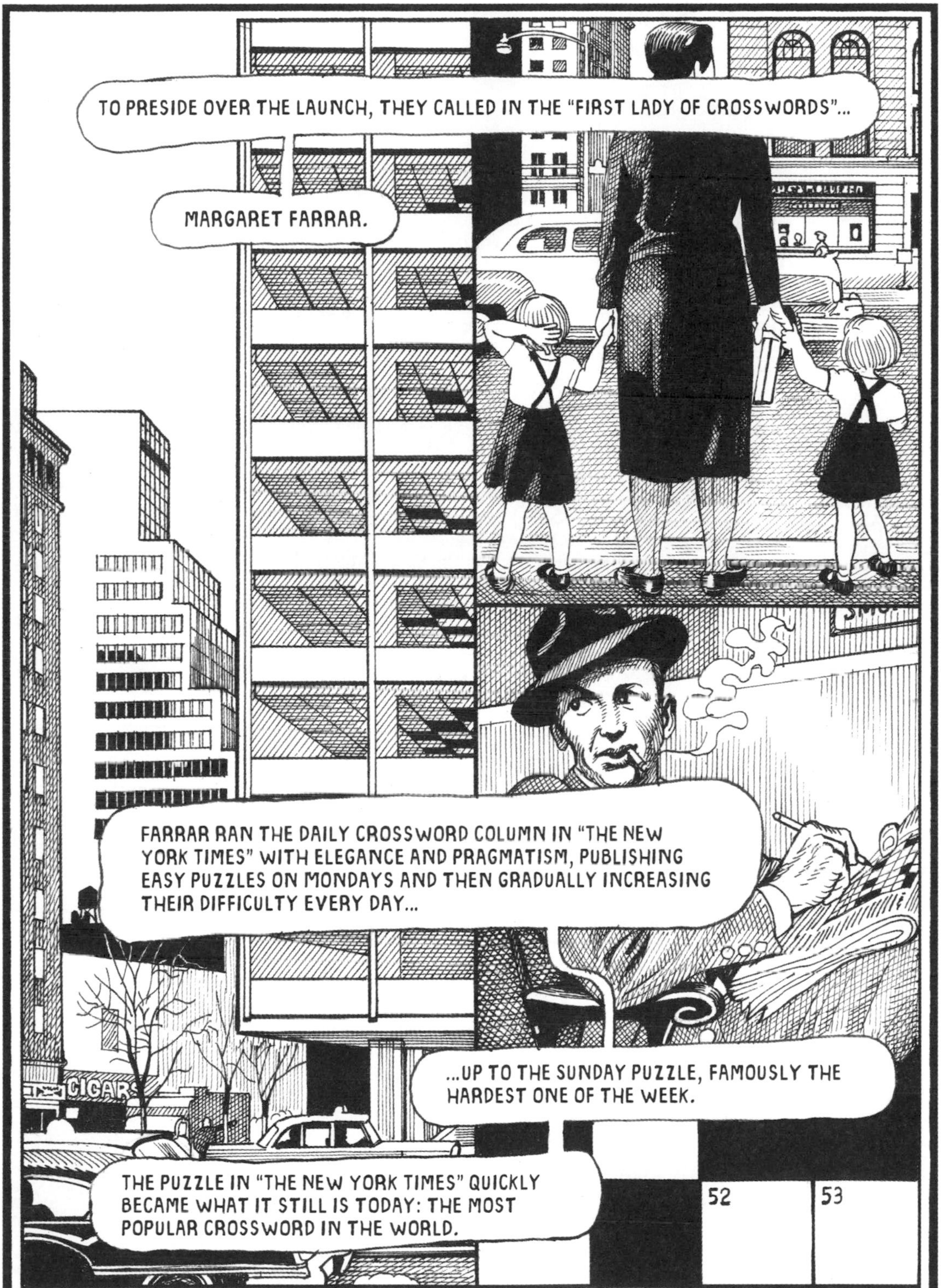
TO PRESIDE OVER THE LAUNCH, THEY CALLED IN THE "FIRST LADY OF CROSSWORDS"...
MARGARET FARRAR.
FARRAR RAN THE DAILY CROSSWORD COLUMN IN "THE NEW YORK TIMES" WITH ELEGANCE AND PRAGMATISM, PUBLISHING EASY PUZZLES ON MONDAYS AND THEN GRADUALLY INCREASING THEIR DIFFICULTY EVERY DAY...
...UP TO THE SUNDAY PUZZLE, FAMOUSLY THE HARDEST ONE OF THE WEEK.
THE PUZZLE IN "THE NEW YORK TIMES" QUICKLY BECAME WHAT IT STILL IS TODAY: THE MOST POPULAR CROSSWORD IN THE WORLD.
CIGARS
52
53

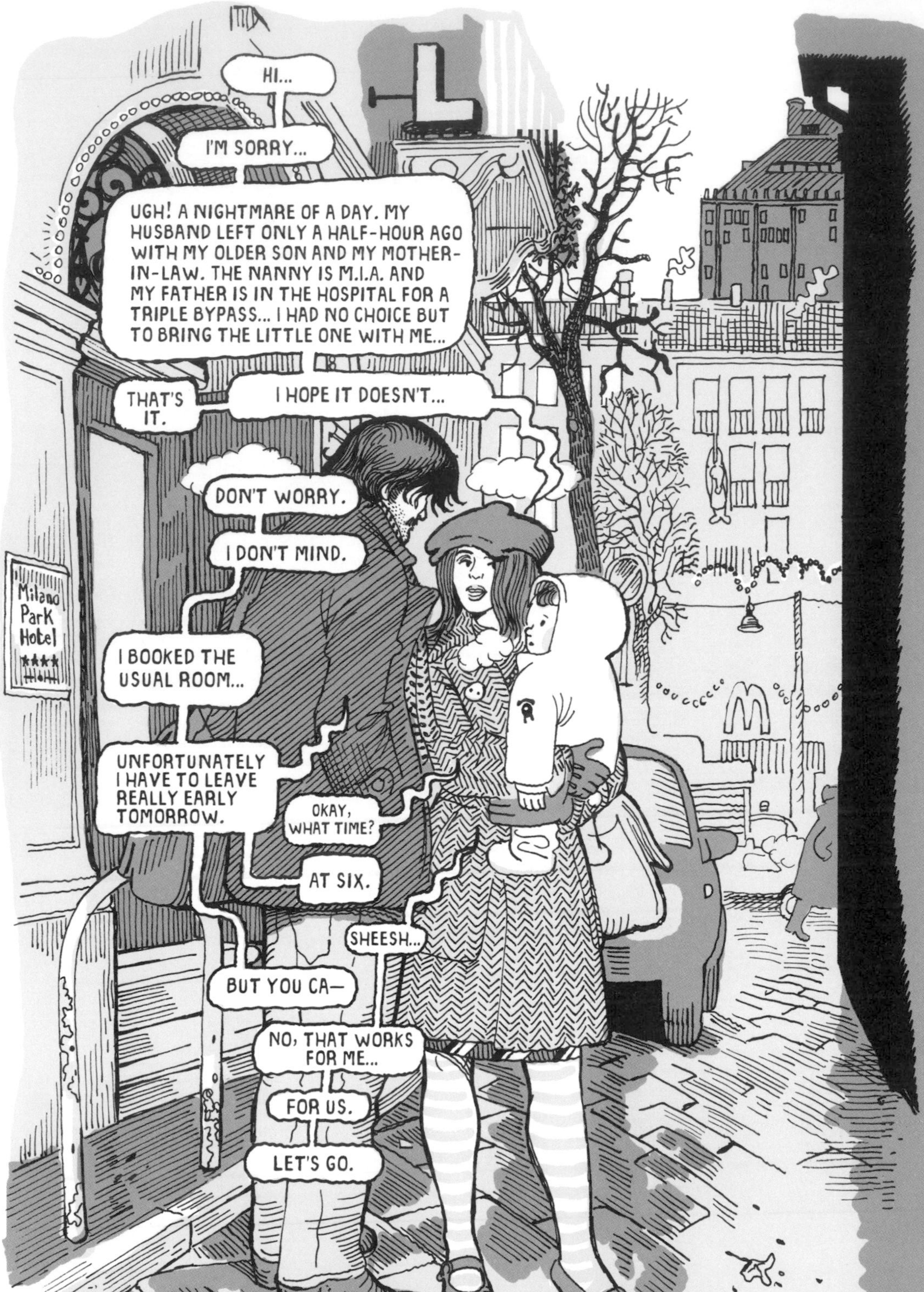
HI...
I'M SORRY...
UGH! A NIGHTMARE OF A DAY. MY HUSBAND LEFT ONLY A HALF-HOUR AGO WITH MY OLDER SON AND MY MOTHER-IN-LAW. THE NANNY IS M.I.A. AND MY FATHER IS IN THE HOSPITAL FOR A TRIPLE BYPASS... I HAD NO CHOICE BUT TO BRING THE LITTLE ONE WITH ME...
THAT'S IT.
I HOPE IT DOESN'T...
DON'T WORRY.
I DON'T MIND.
Milano Park Hotel
I BOOKED THE USUAL ROOM...
UNFORTUNATELY I HAVE TO LEAVE REALLY EARLY TOMORROW.
OKAY, WHAT TIME?
AT SIX.
SHEESH...
BUT YOU CA—
NO, THAT WORKS FOR ME...
FOR US.
LET'S GO.

THE HOW AND WHEN

HERE ARE YOUR I.D.'S... UH, IF YOU'D LIKE, WE HAVE A COT FOR THE BABY.
NO, THANKS.
WWWW
KLUNK!
48

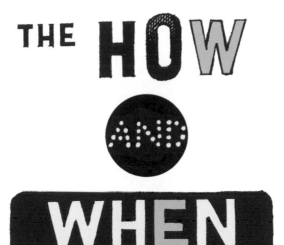

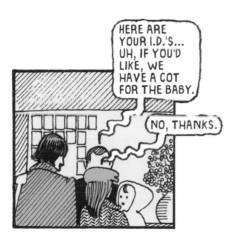

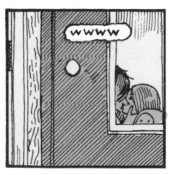

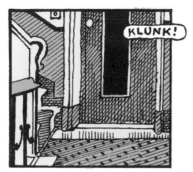

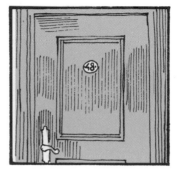

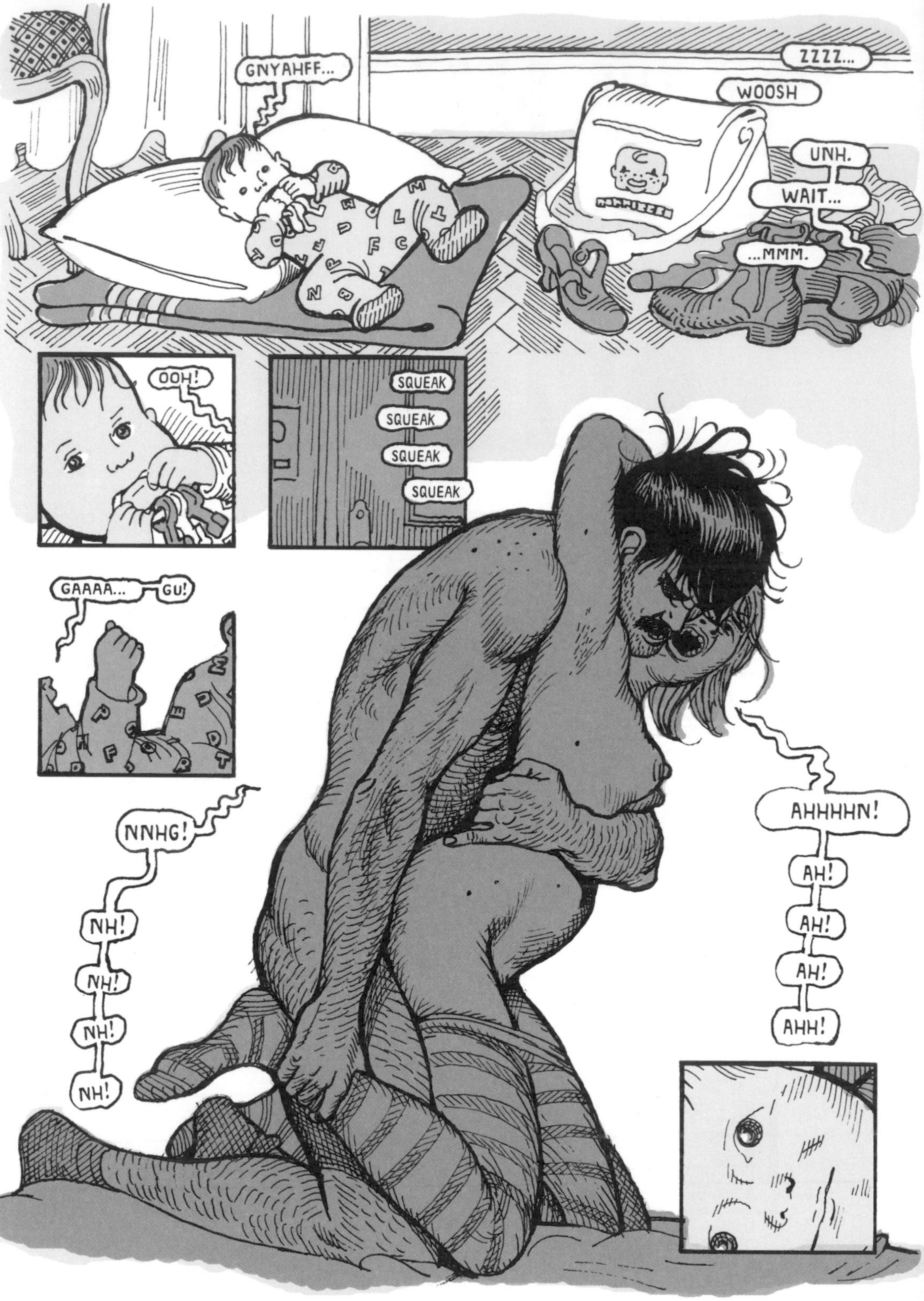
GNYAHFF...
ZZZZ...
WOOSH
UNH.
WAIT...
...MMM.
OOH!
SQUEAK
SQUEAK
SQUEAK
SQUEAK
GAAAA... GU!
NNHG!
NH!
NH!
NH!
NH!
AHHHHN!
AH!
AH!
AH!
AHH!

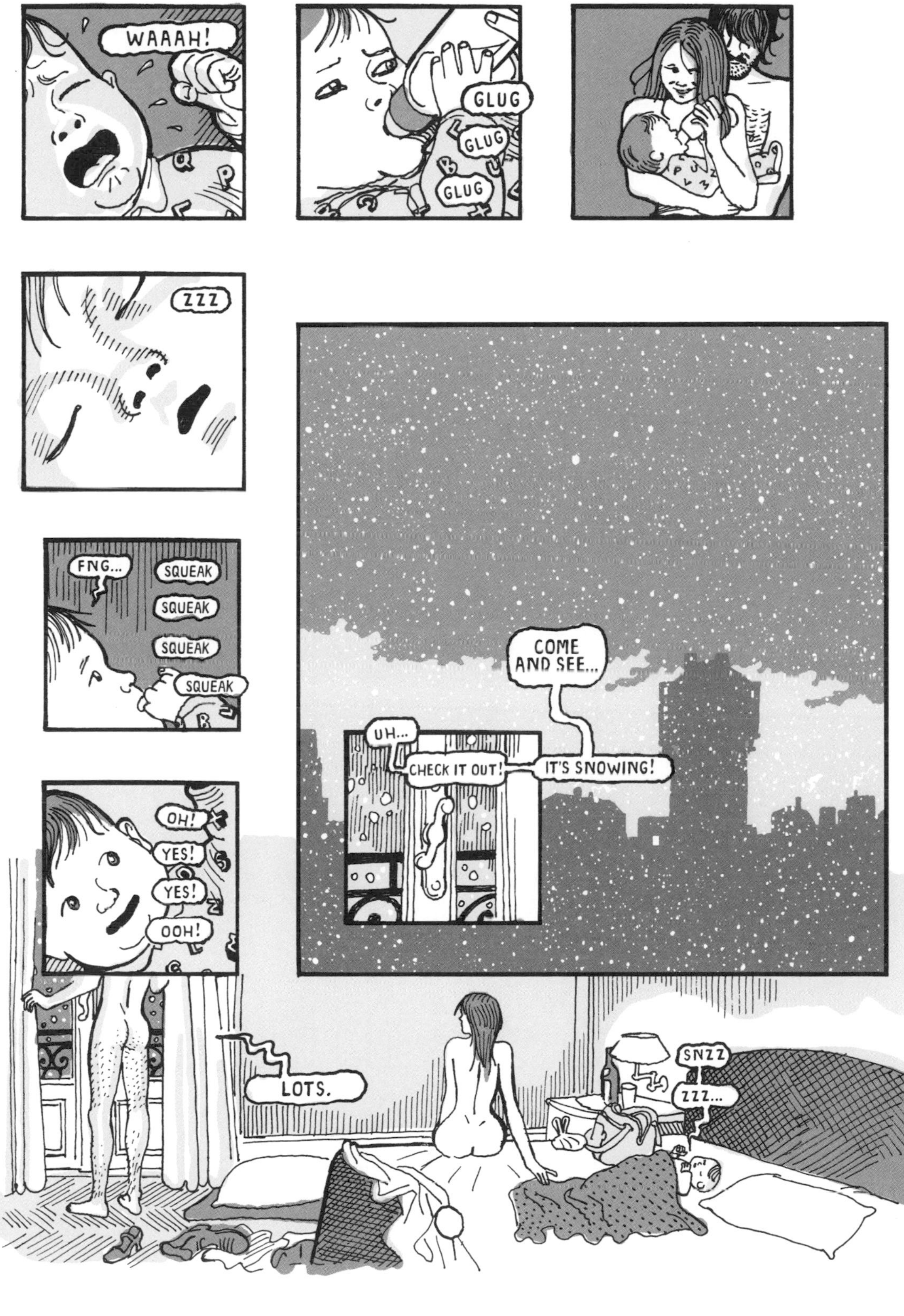

WAAAH!
GLUG
GLUG
GLUG
ZZZ
FNG...
SQUEAK
SQUEAK
SQUEAK
SQUEAK
OH!
YES!
YES!
OOH!
UH...
CHECK IT OUT!
IT'S SNOWING!
COME AND SEE...
LOTS.
SNZZ
ZZZ...

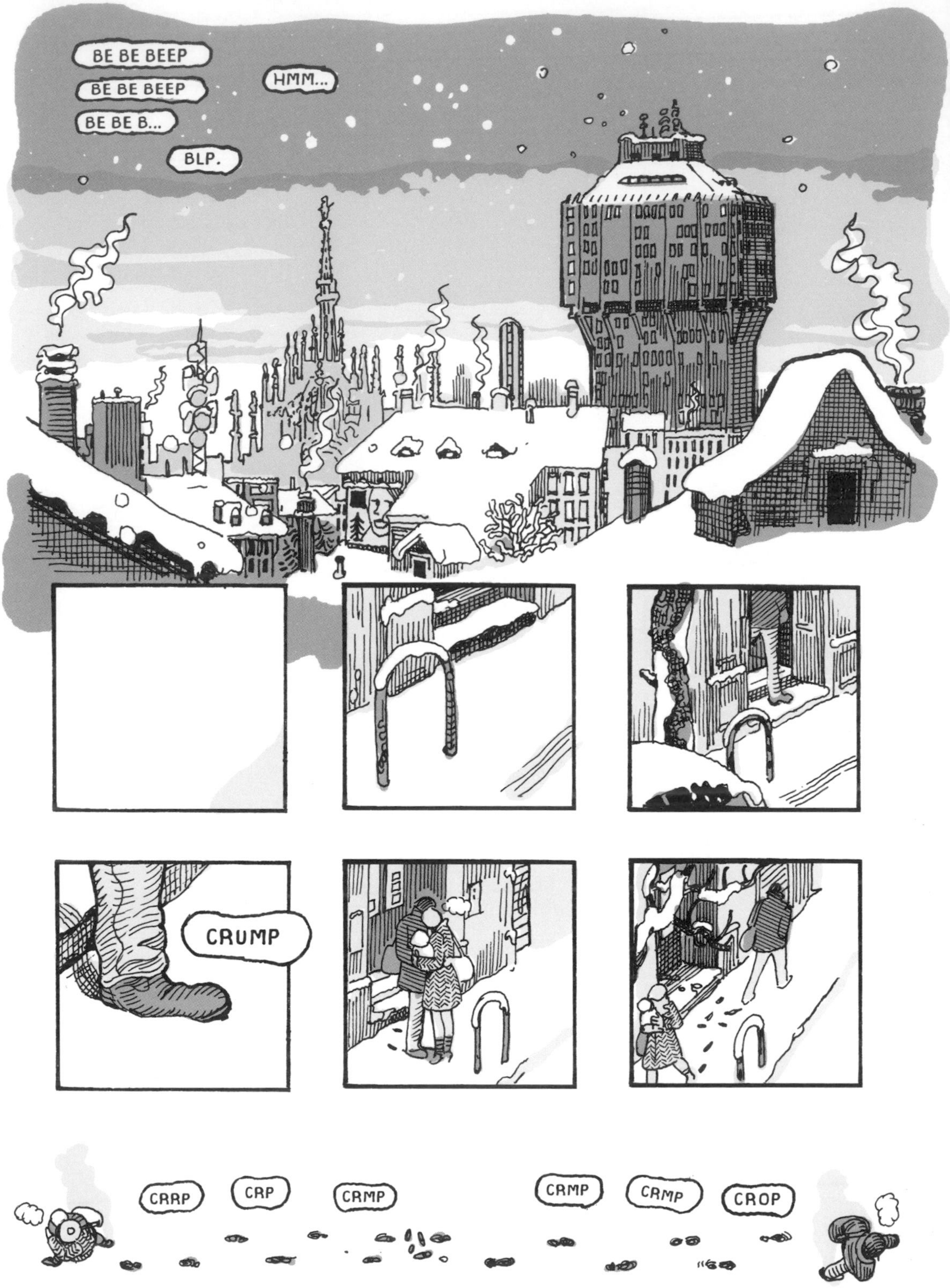
BE BE BEEP
BE BE BEEP
BE BE B...
BLP.
HMM...
CRUMP
CRRP
CRP
CRMP
CRMP
CRMP
CROP

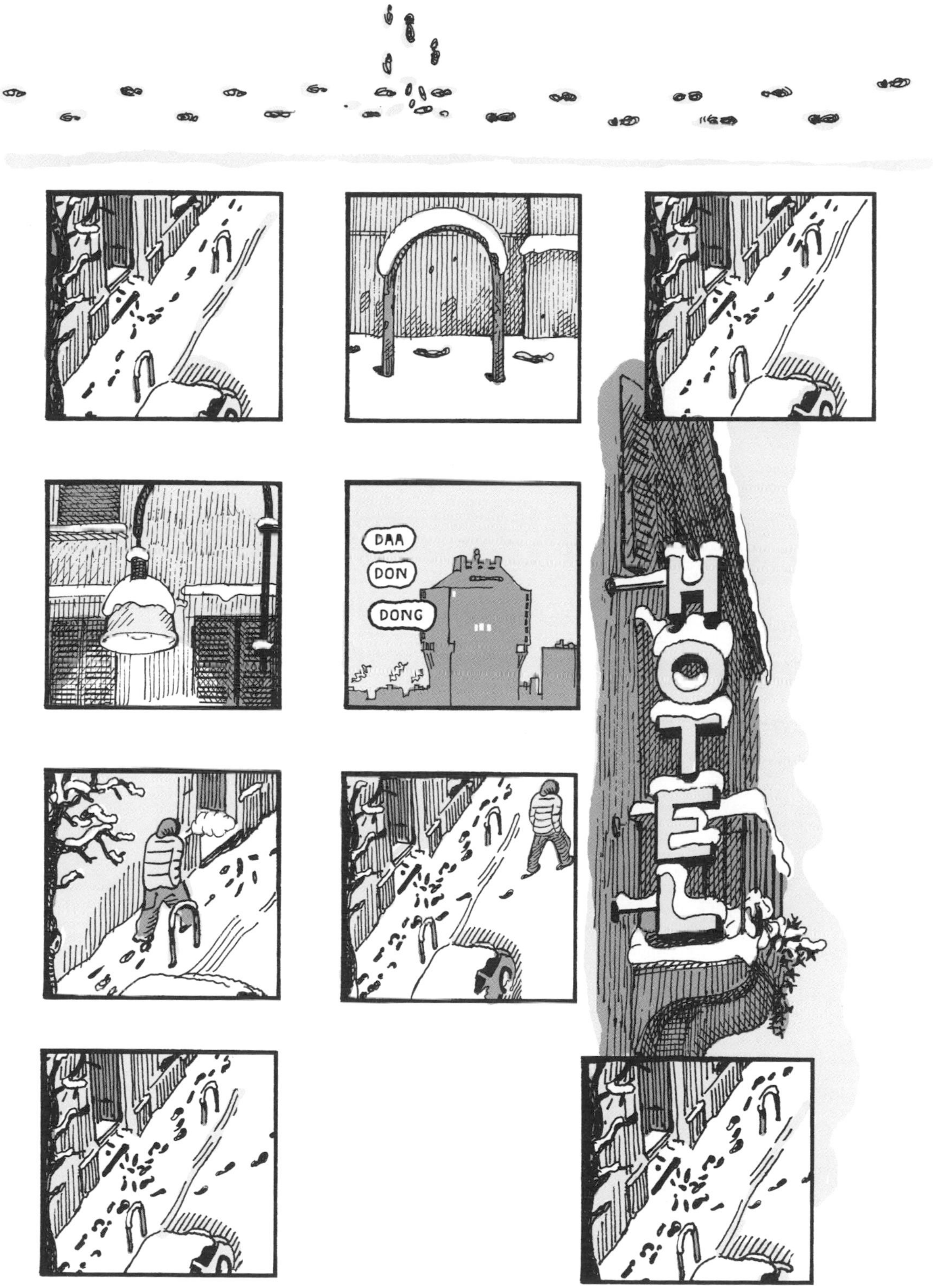
DAA
DON
DONG
HOTEL

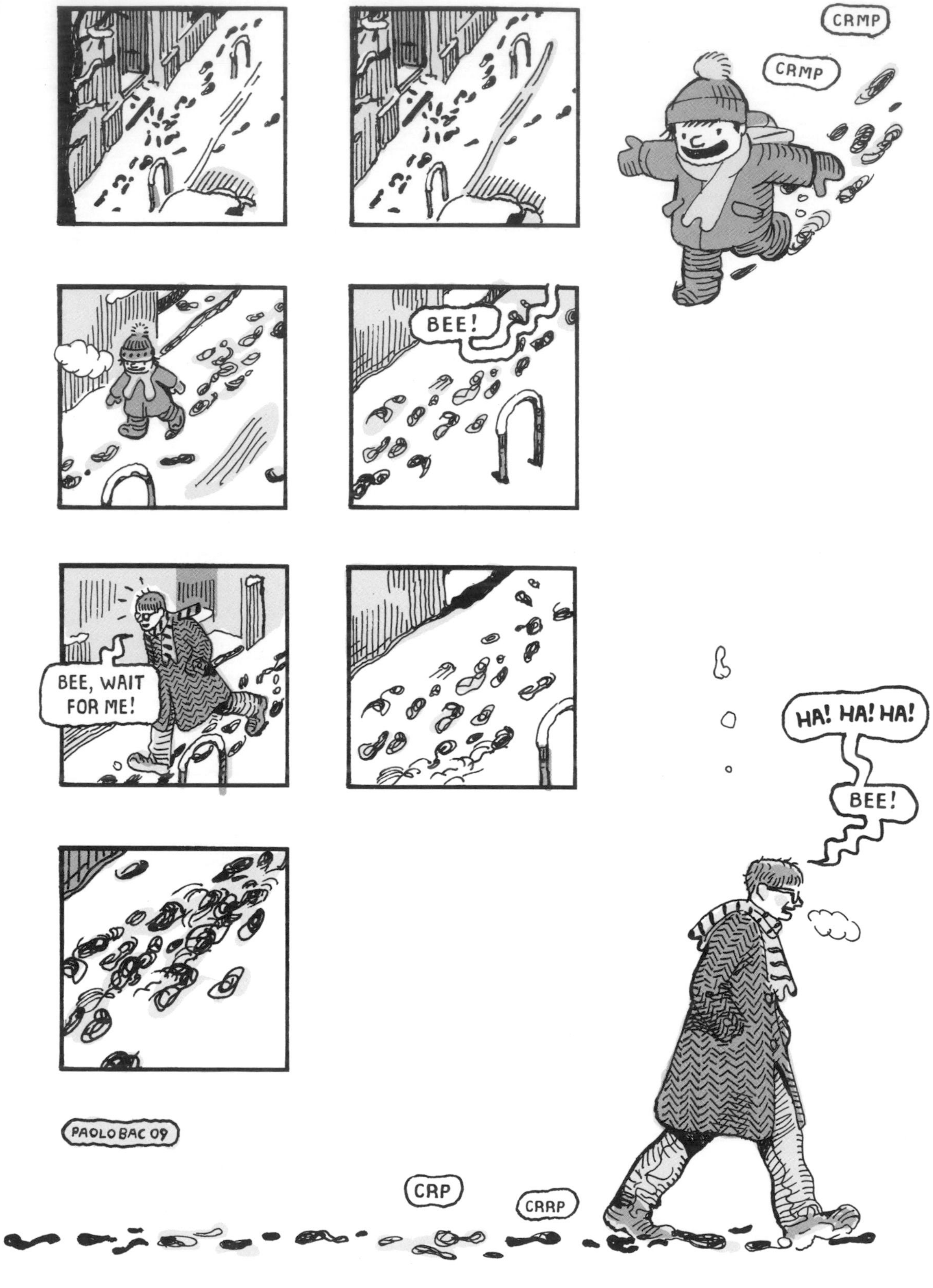
CRMP
CRMP
BEE!
BEE, WAIT FOR ME!
HA! HA! HA!
BEE!
PAOLOBAC 09
CRP
CRRP

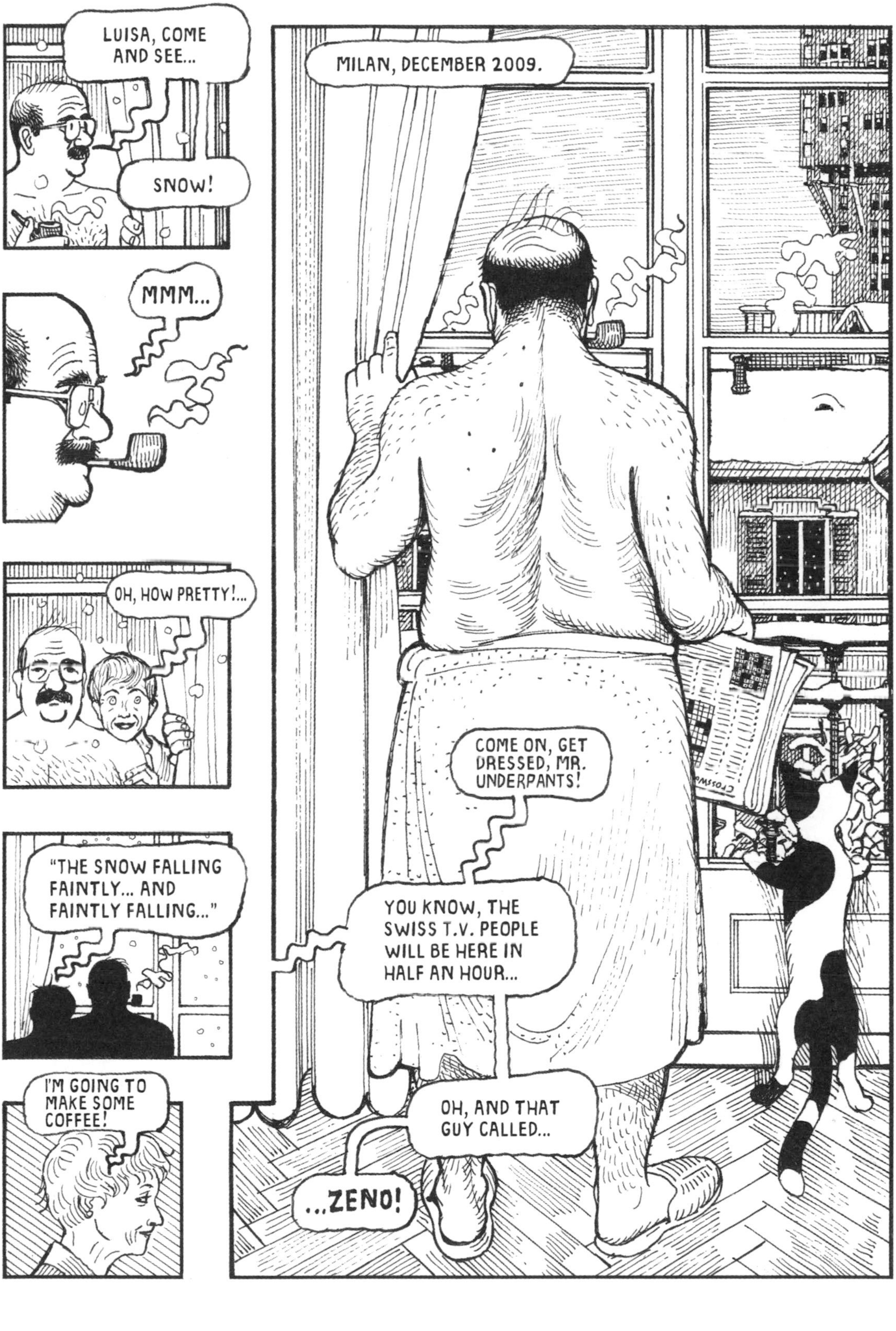
LUISA, COME AND SEE...
SNOW!
MMM...
OH, HOW PRETTY!...
"THE SNOW FALLING FAINTLY... AND FAINTLY FALLING..."
I'M GOING TO MAKE SOME COFFEE!
MILAN, DECEMBER 2009.
COME ON, GET DRESSED, MR. UNDERPANTS!
YOU KNOW, THE SWISS T.V. PEOPLE WILL BE HERE IN HALF AN HOUR...
OH, AND THAT GUY CALLED...
...ZENO!

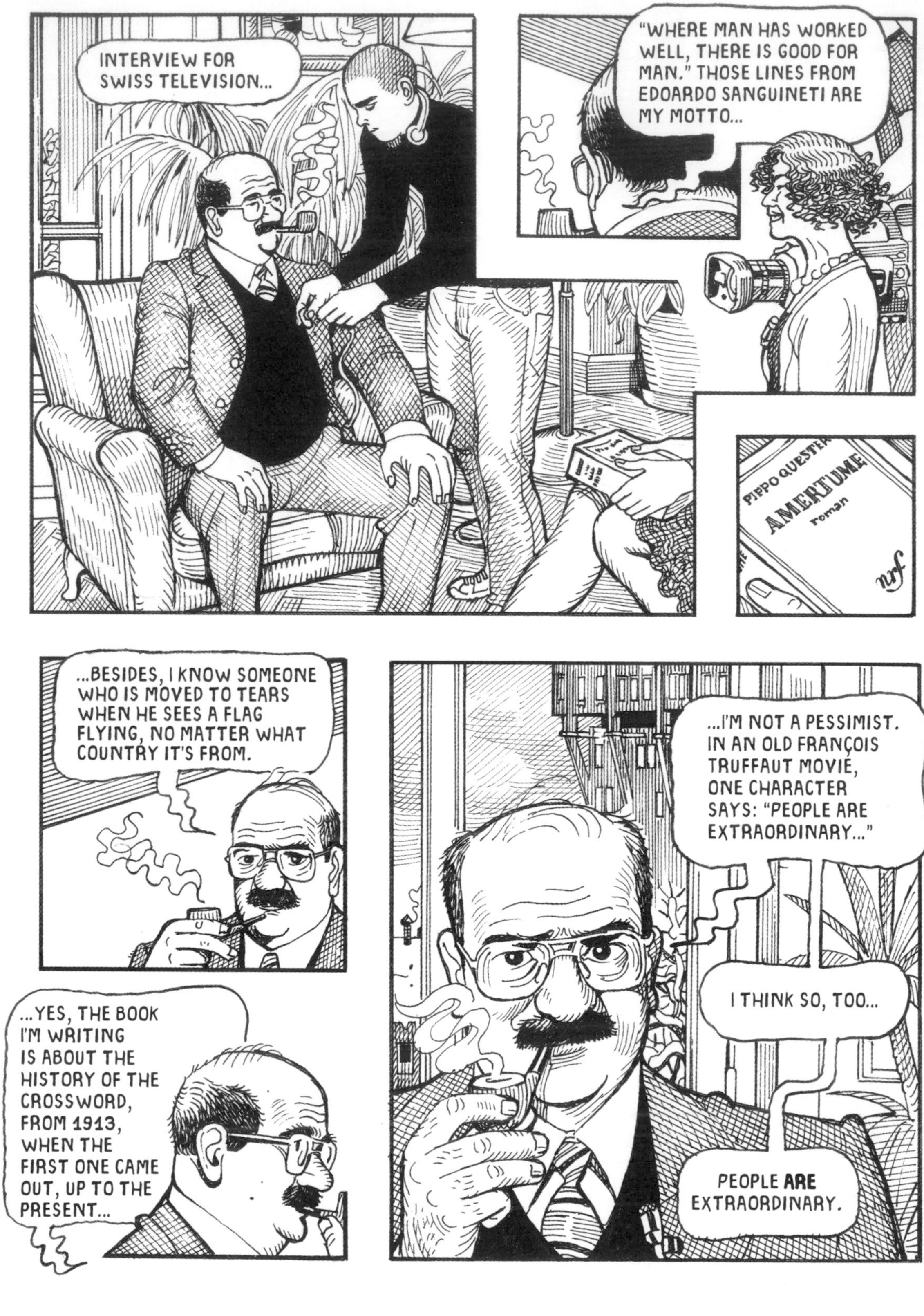
INTERVIEW FOR SWISS TELEVISION...
"WHERE MAN HAS WORKED WELL, THERE IS GOOD FOR MAN." THOSE LINES FROM EDOARDO SANGUINETI ARE MY MOTTO...
PIPPO QUESTER
AMERTUME
roman
nrf
...BESIDES, I KNOW SOMEONE WHO IS MOVED TO TEARS WHEN HE SEES A FLAG FLYING, NO MATTER WHAT COUNTRY IT'S FROM.
...YES, THE BOOK I'M WRITING IS ABOUT THE HISTORY OF THE CROSSWORD, FROM 1913, WHEN THE FIRST ONE CAME OUT, UP TO THE PRESENT...
...I'M NOT A PESSIMIST. IN AN OLD FRANÇOIS TRUFFAUT MOVIE, ONE CHARACTER SAYS: "PEOPLE ARE EXTRAORDINARY..."
I THINK SO, TOO...
PEOPLE **ARE** EXTRAORDINARY.

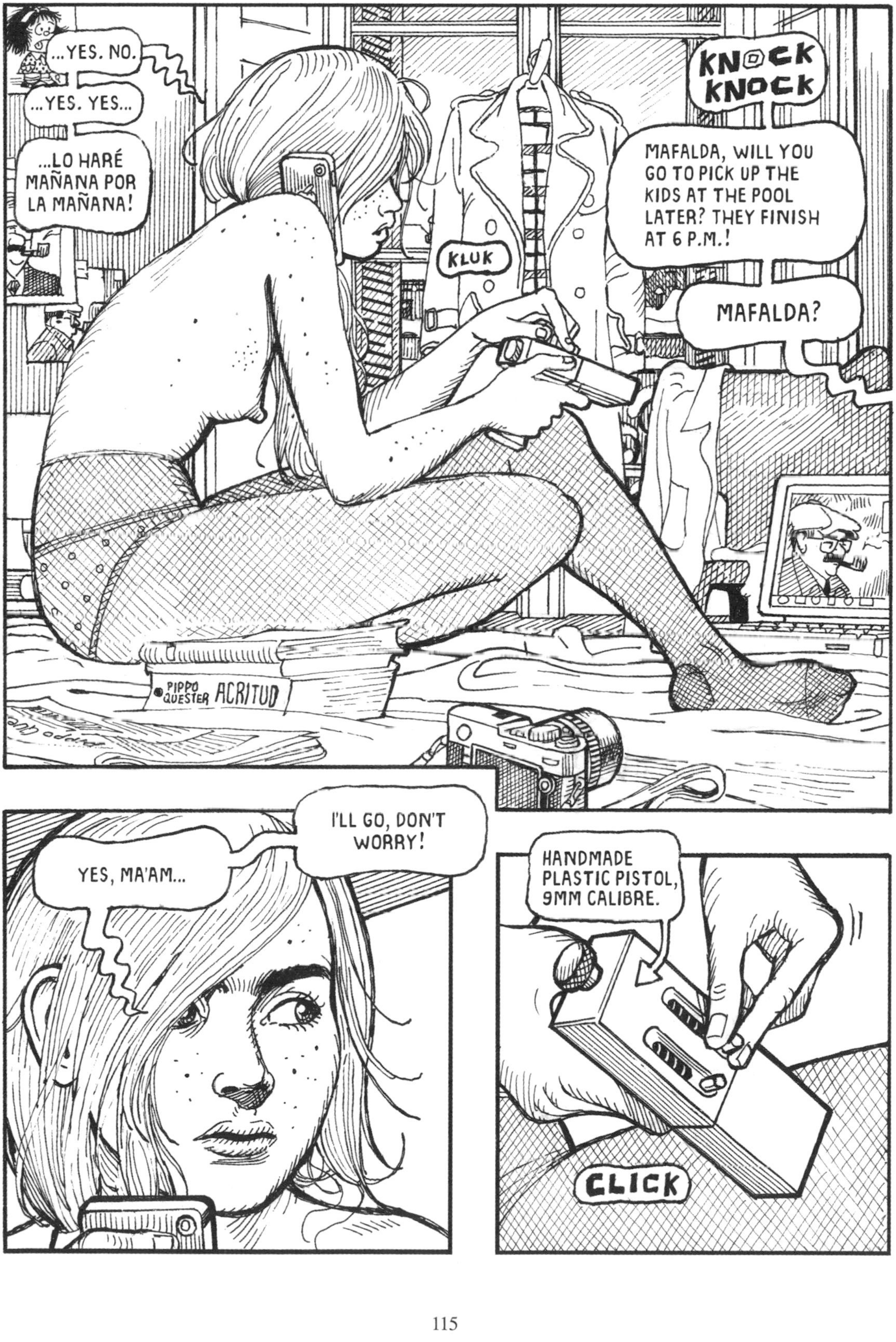
...YES. NO.
...YES. YES...
...LO HARÉ MAÑANA POR LA MAÑANA!
KNOCK KNOCK
MAFALDA, WILL YOU GO TO PICK UP THE KIDS AT THE POOL LATER? THEY FINISH AT 6 P.M.!
KLUK
MAFALDA?
PIPPO QUESTER ACRITUD
YES, MA'AM...
I'LL GO, DON'T WORRY!
HANDMADE PLASTIC PISTOL, 9MM CALIBRE.
CLICK

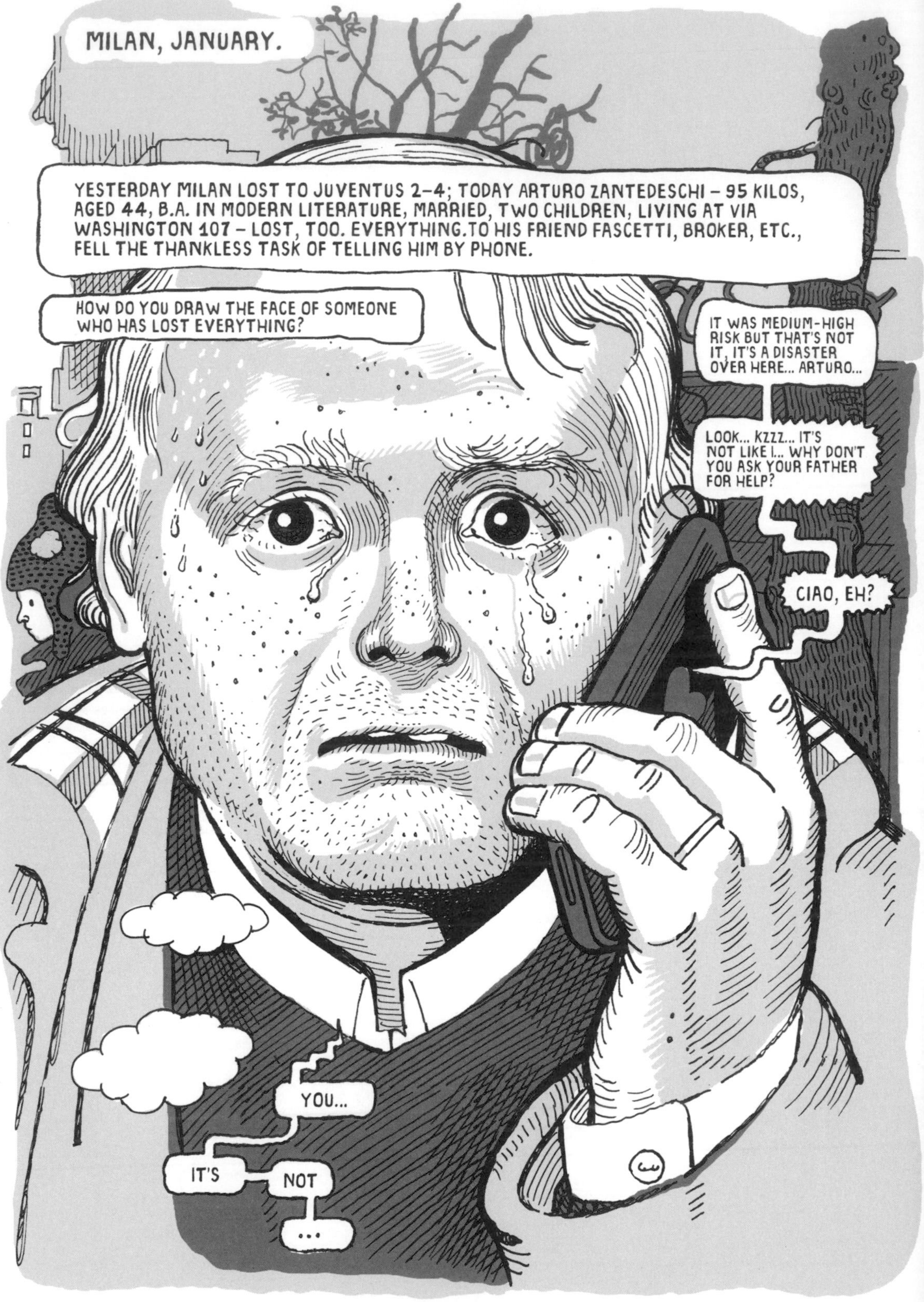
MILAN, JANUARY.
YESTERDAY MILAN LOST TO JUVENTUS 2–4; TODAY ARTURO ZANTEDESCHI – 95 KILOS, AGED 44, B.A. IN MODERN LITERATURE, MARRIED, TWO CHILDREN, LIVING AT VIA WASHINGTON 107 – LOST, TOO. EVERYTHING. TO HIS FRIEND FASCETTI, BROKER, ETC., FELL THE THANKLESS TASK OF TELLING HIM BY PHONE.
HOW DO YOU DRAW THE FACE OF SOMEONE WHO HAS LOST EVERYTHING?
IT WAS MEDIUM-HIGH RISK BUT THAT'S NOT IT, IT'S A DISASTER OVER HERE... ARTURO...
LOOK... KZZZ... IT'S NOT LIKE I... WHY DON'T YOU ASK YOUR FATHER FOR HELP?
CIAO, EH?
YOU...
IT'S
NOT
...

NEGRONI SBAGLIATO

PIDSTUPIDSTUPIDSTUPIDS

STUPID.
BIP
VROO
BEEEP
STUPID.
STUPID.
SNIF
STUPID!
STUPID
STUPID
STUPID!
ARTURO!
STUPID HERE, OUTSIDE BAR BASSO, WHERE ARTURO IS MEETING ZENO.
HI, ZENO.

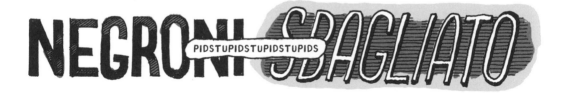

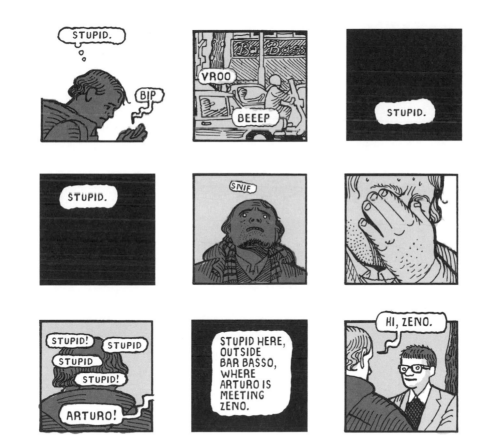

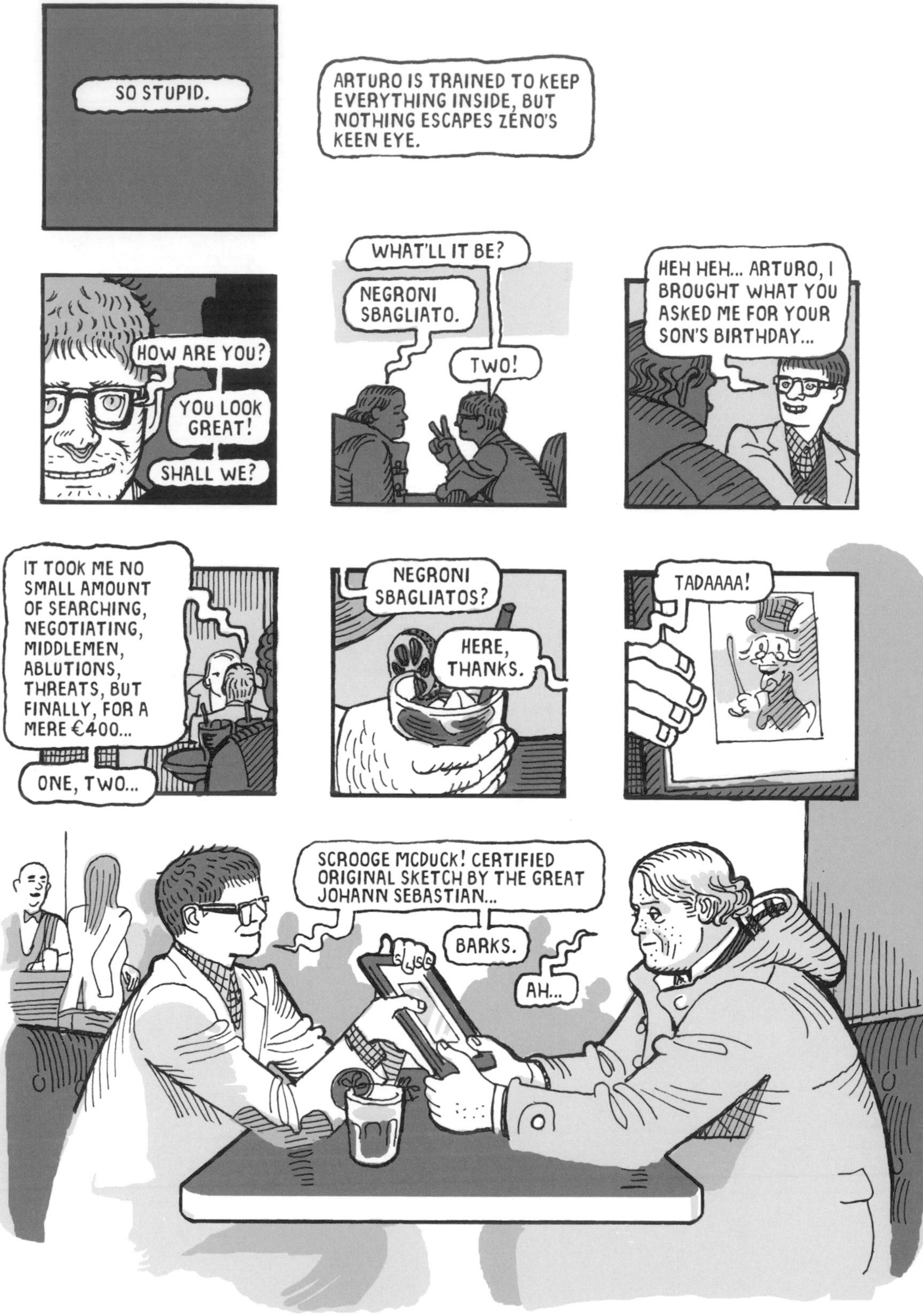
SO STUPID.
ARTURO IS TRAINED TO KEEP EVERYTHING INSIDE, BUT NOTHING ESCAPES ZENO'S KEEN EYE.
HOW ARE YOU?
YOU LOOK GREAT!
SHALL WE?
WHAT'LL IT BE?
NEGRONI SBAGLIATO.
TWO!
HEH HEH... ARTURO, I BROUGHT WHAT YOU ASKED ME FOR YOUR SON'S BIRTHDAY...
IT TOOK ME NO SMALL AMOUNT OF SEARCHING, NEGOTIATING, MIDDLEMEN, ABLUTIONS, THREATS, BUT FINALLY, FOR A MERE €400...
ONE, TWO...
NEGRONI SBAGLIATOS?
HERE, THANKS.
TADAAAA!
SCROOGE MCDUCK! CERTIFIED ORIGINAL SKETCH BY THE GREAT JOHANN SEBASTIAN...
BARKS.
AH...

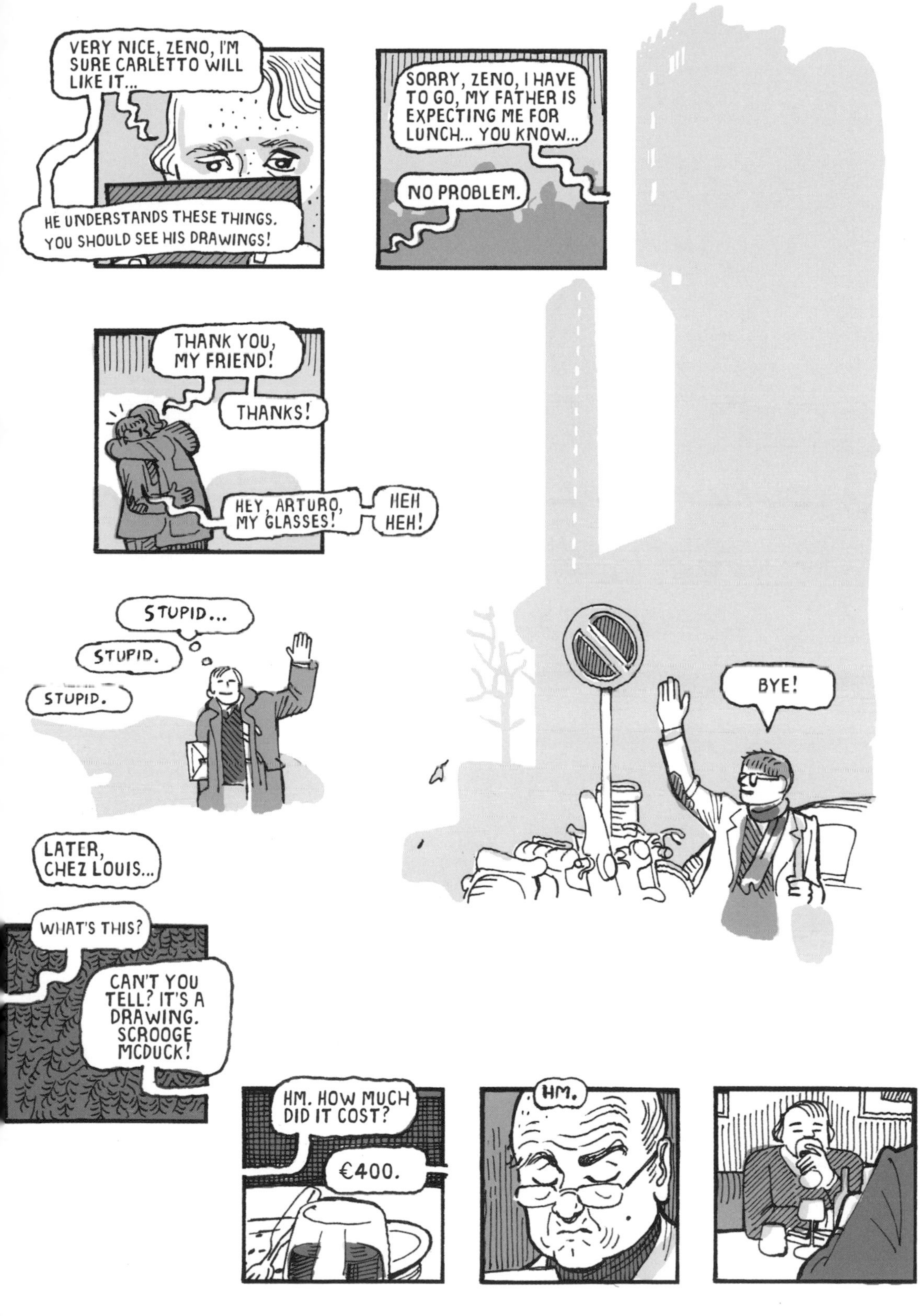
VERY NICE, ZENO, I'M SURE CARLETTO WILL LIKE IT...
HE UNDERSTANDS THESE THINGS. YOU SHOULD SEE HIS DRAWINGS!
SORRY, ZENO, I HAVE TO GO, MY FATHER IS EXPECTING ME FOR LUNCH... YOU KNOW...
NO PROBLEM.
THANK YOU, MY FRIEND!
THANKS!
HEY, ARTURO, MY GLASSES!
HEH HEH!
STUPID...
STUPID.
STUPID.
BYE!
LATER, CHEZ LOUIS...
WHAT'S THIS?
CAN'T YOU TELL? IT'S A DRAWING. SCROOGE MCDUCK!
HM. HOW MUCH DID IT COST?
€400.
HM.

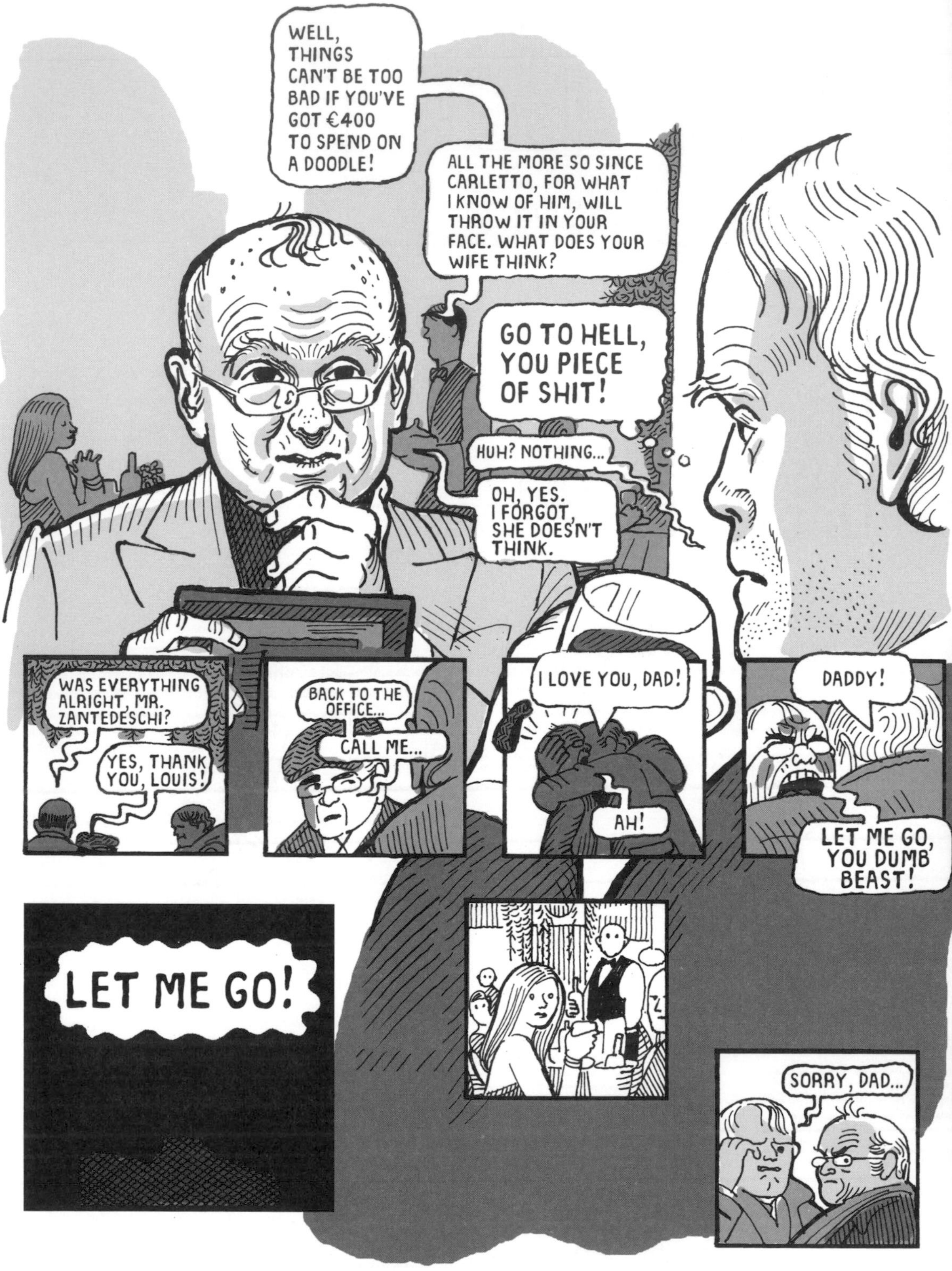
WELL, THINGS CAN'T BE TOO BAD IF YOU'VE GOT €400 TO SPEND ON A DOODLE!
ALL THE MORE SO SINCE CARLETTO, FOR WHAT I KNOW OF HIM, WILL THROW IT IN YOUR FACE. WHAT DOES YOUR WIFE THINK?
GO TO HELL, YOU PIECE OF SHIT!
HUH? NOTHING...
OH, YES. I FORGOT, SHE DOESN'T THINK.
WAS EVERYTHING ALRIGHT, MR. ZANTEDESCHI?
YES, THANK YOU, LOUIS!
BACK TO THE OFFICE...
CALL ME...
I LOVE YOU, DAD!
AH!
DADDY!
LET ME GO, YOU DUMB BEAST!
LET ME GO!
SORRY, DAD...

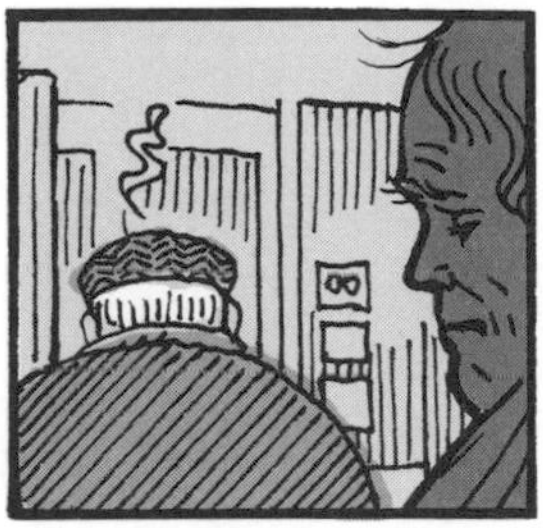

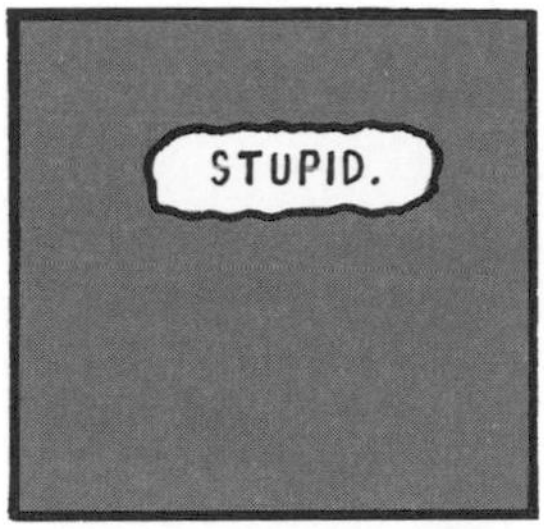
STUPID.

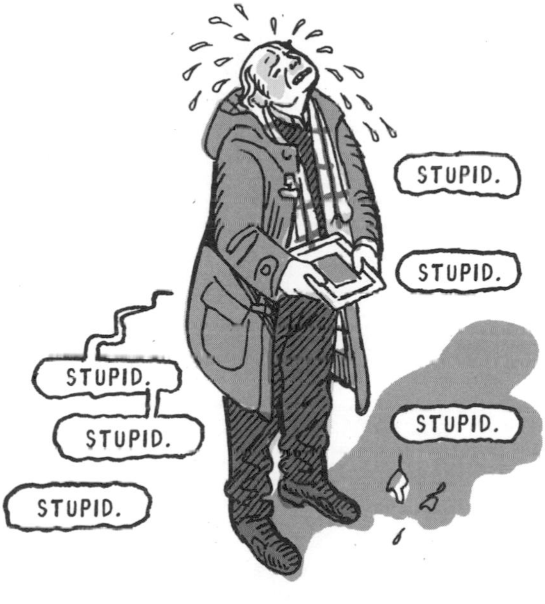
STUPID.
STUPID.
STUPID.
STUPID.
STUPID.
STUPID.

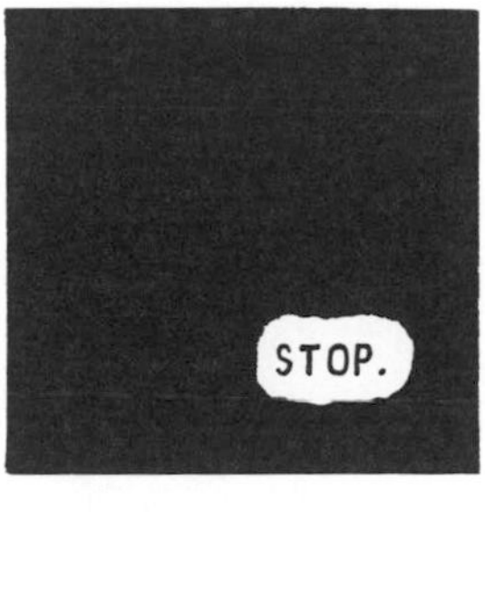
STOP.

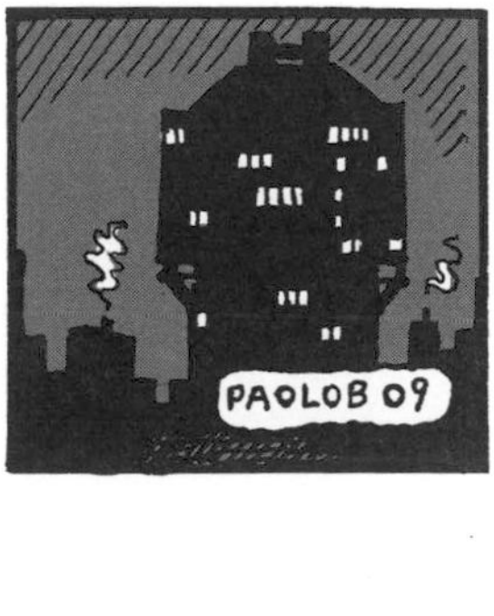
PAOLOB 09

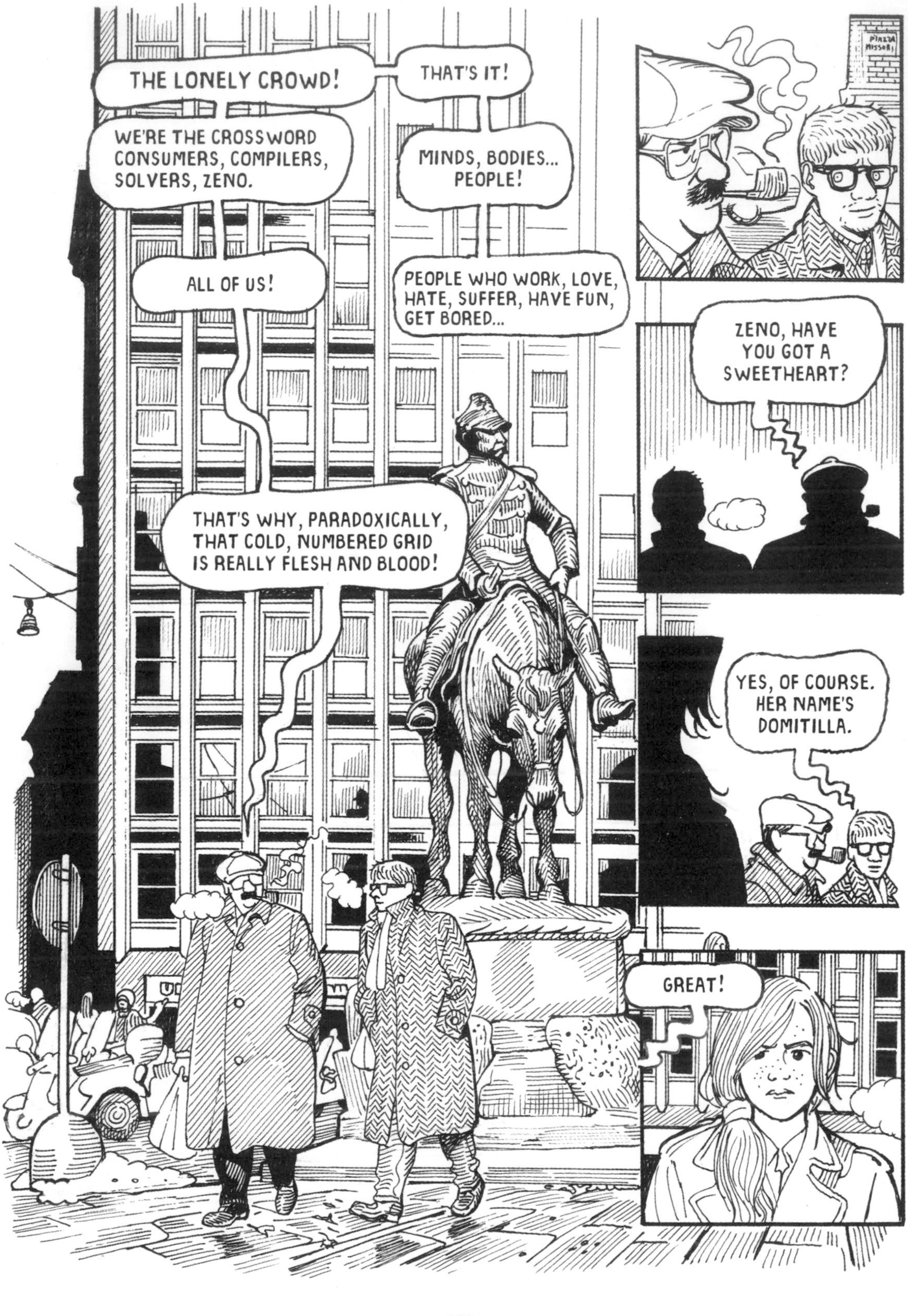
THE LONELY CROWD!
THAT'S IT!
WE'RE THE CROSSWORD CONSUMERS, COMPILERS, SOLVERS, ZENO.
MINDS, BODIES... PEOPLE!
ALL OF US!
PEOPLE WHO WORK, LOVE, HATE, SUFFER, HAVE FUN, GET BORED...
THAT'S WHY, PARADOXICALLY, THAT COLD, NUMBERED GRID IS REALLY FLESH AND BLOOD!
PIAZZA MISSORI
ZENO, HAVE YOU GOT A SWEETHEART?
YES, OF COURSE. HER NAME'S DOMITILLA.
GREAT!

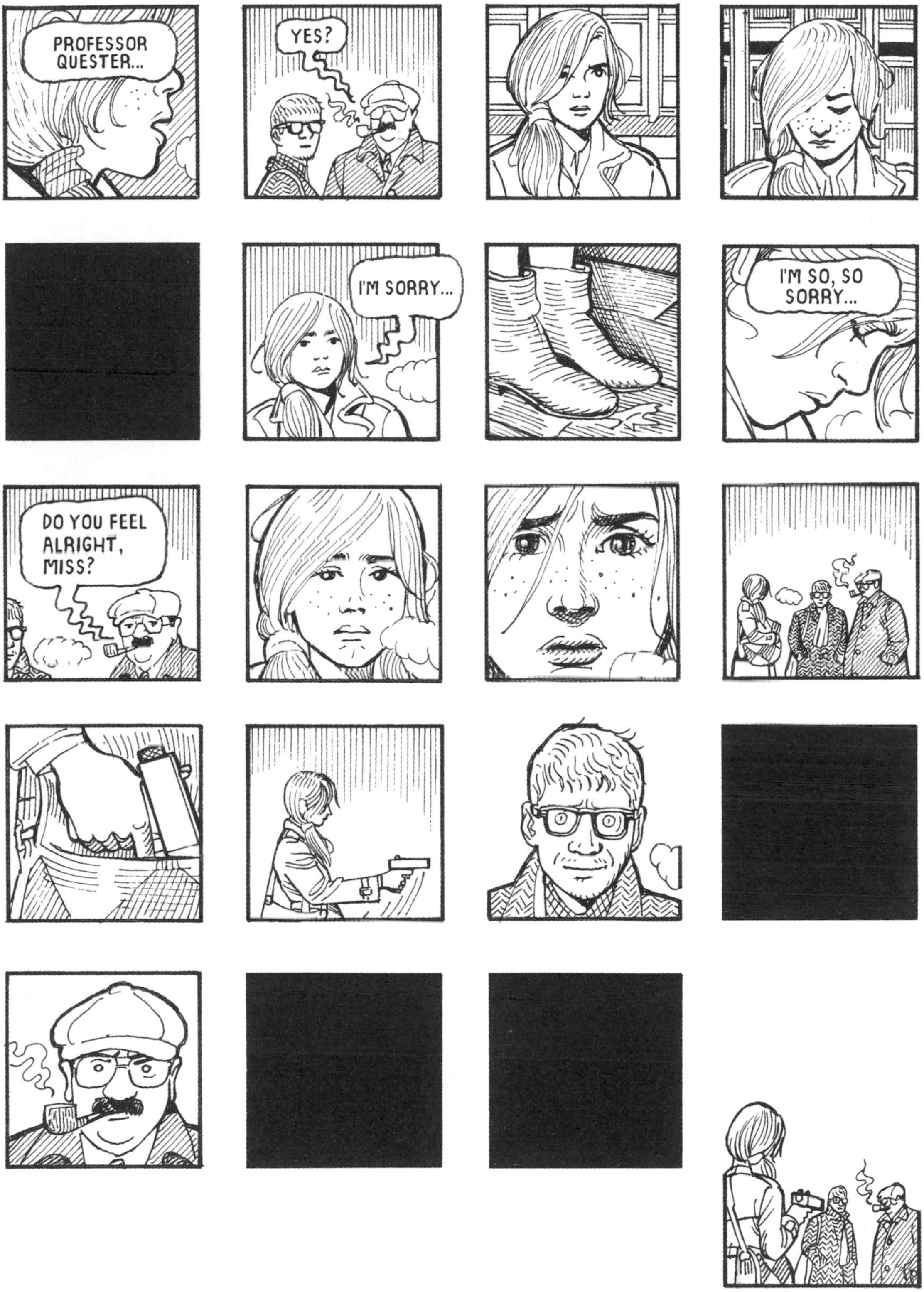
PROFESSOR QUESTER...
YES?
I'M SORRY...
I'M SO, SO SORRY...
DO YOU FEEL ALRIGHT, MISS?

PLASTIC PISTOL BUILT AND USED BY "MITCH" MALKOVICH IN THE MOVIE "IN THE LINE OF FIRE" (U.S.A., 1993, DIR. WOLFGANG PETERSEN) WITH CLINT EASTWOOD, JOHN MALKOVICH, RENE RUSSO...

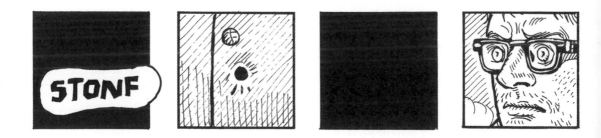

STONF

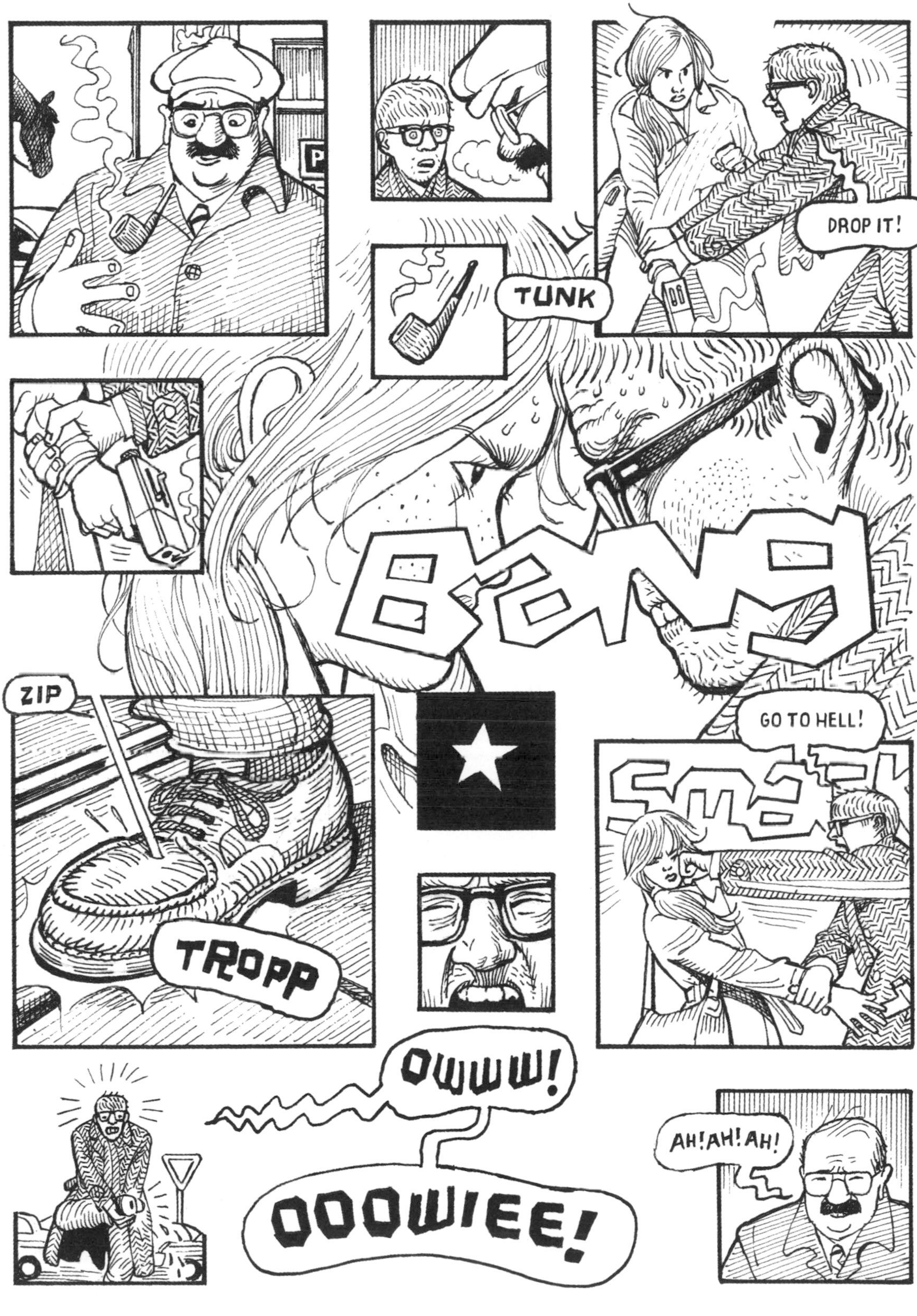
TUNK
DROP IT!
BANG
ZIP
TROPP
GO TO HELL!
OWWW!
OOOWIEE!
AH!AH!AH!

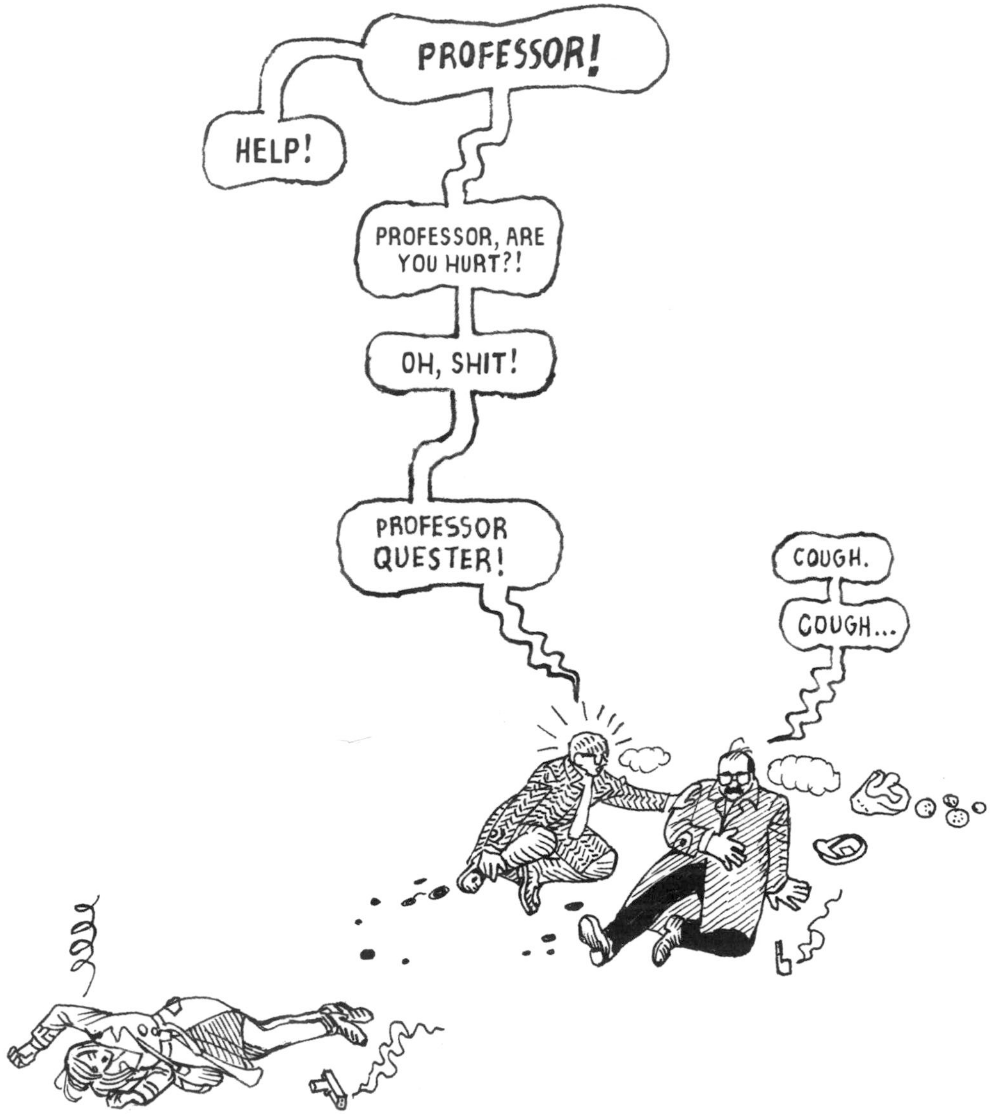
PROFESSOR!
HELP!
PROFESSOR, ARE YOU HURT?!
OH, SHIT!
PROFESSOR QUESTER!
COUGH.
COUGH...

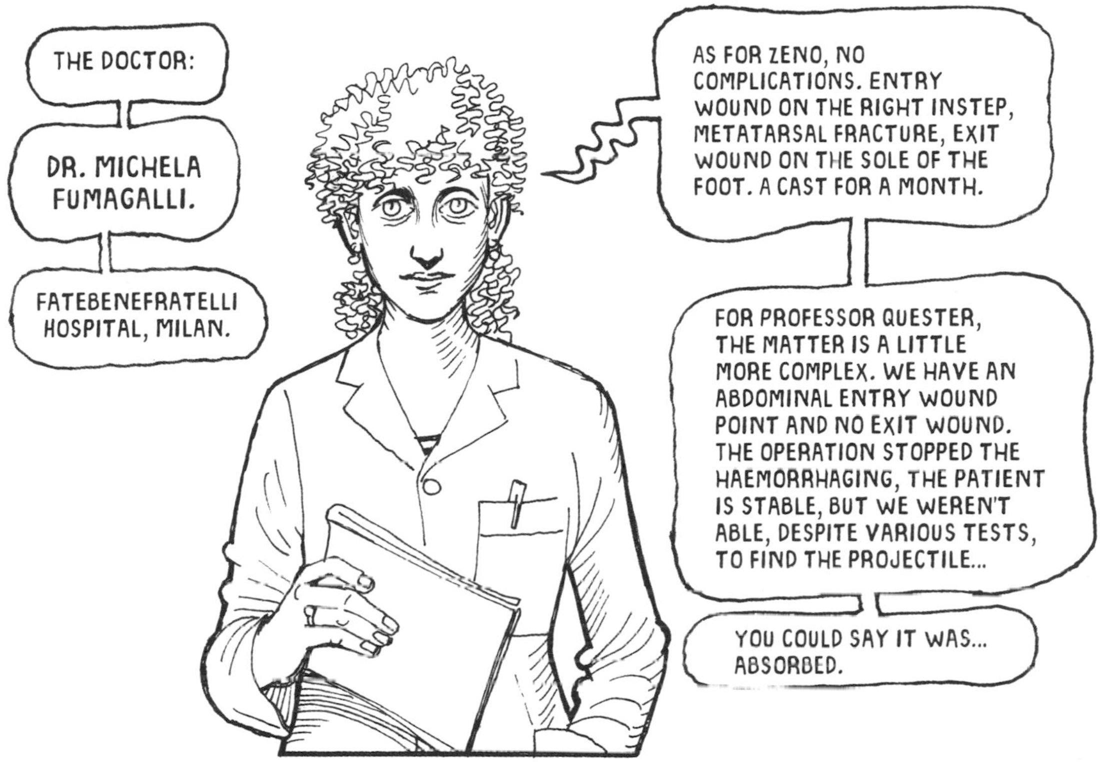
THE DOCTOR:
DR. MICHELA FUMAGALLI.
FATEBENEFRATELLI HOSPITAL, MILAN.
AS FOR ZENO, NO COMPLICATIONS. ENTRY WOUND ON THE RIGHT INSTEP, METATARSAL FRACTURE, EXIT WOUND ON THE SOLE OF THE FOOT. A CAST FOR A MONTH.
FOR PROFESSOR QUESTER, THE MATTER IS A LITTLE MORE COMPLEX. WE HAVE AN ABDOMINAL ENTRY WOUND POINT AND NO EXIT WOUND. THE OPERATION STOPPED THE HAEMORRHAGING, THE PATIENT IS STABLE, BUT WE WEREN'T ABLE, DESPITE VARIOUS TESTS, TO FIND THE PROJECTILE...
YOU COULD SAY IT WAS... ABSORBED.

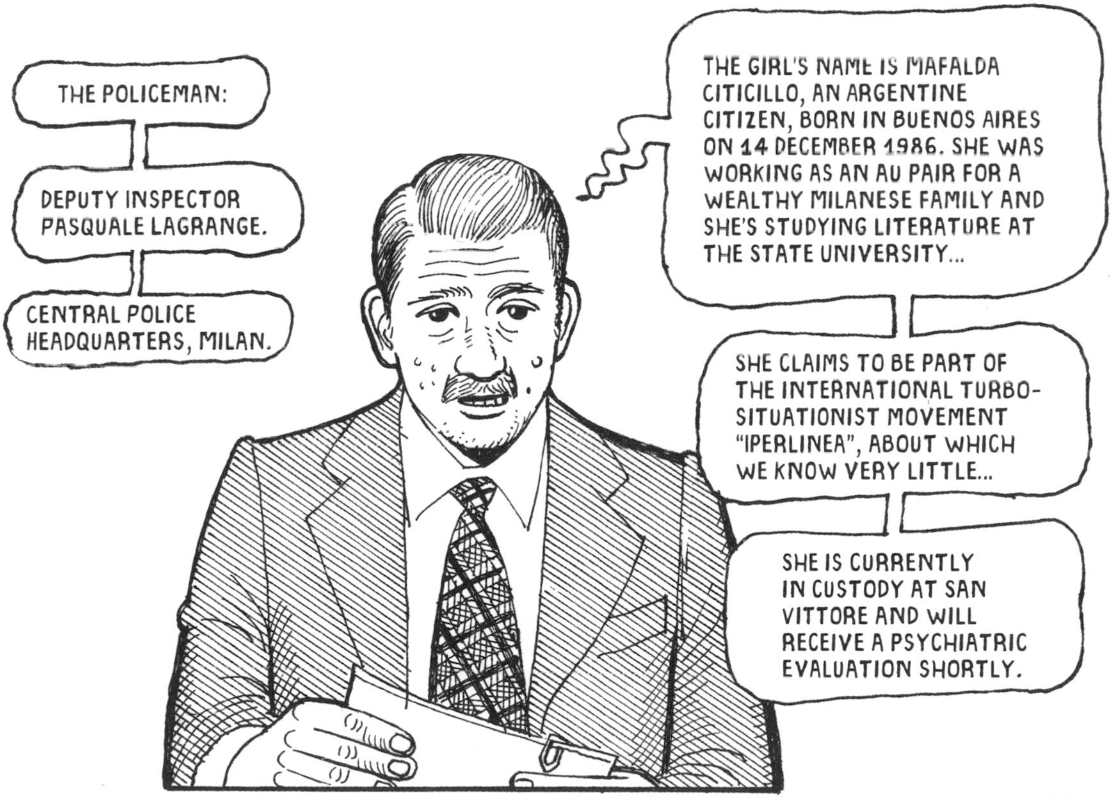
THE POLICEMAN:
DEPUTY INSPECTOR PASQUALE LAGRANGE.
CENTRAL POLICE HEADQUARTERS, MILAN.
THE GIRL'S NAME IS MAFALDA CITICILLO, AN ARGENTINE CITIZEN, BORN IN BUENOS AIRES ON 14 DECEMBER 1986. SHE WAS WORKING AS AN AU PAIR FOR A WEALTHY MILANESE FAMILY AND SHE'S STUDYING LITERATURE AT THE STATE UNIVERSITY...
SHE CLAIMS TO BE PART OF THE INTERNATIONAL TURBO-SITUATIONIST MOVEMENT "IPERLINEA", ABOUT WHICH WE KNOW VERY LITTLE...
SHE IS CURRENTLY IN CUSTODY AT SAN VITTORE AND WILL RECEIVE A PSYCHIATRIC EVALUATION SHORTLY.

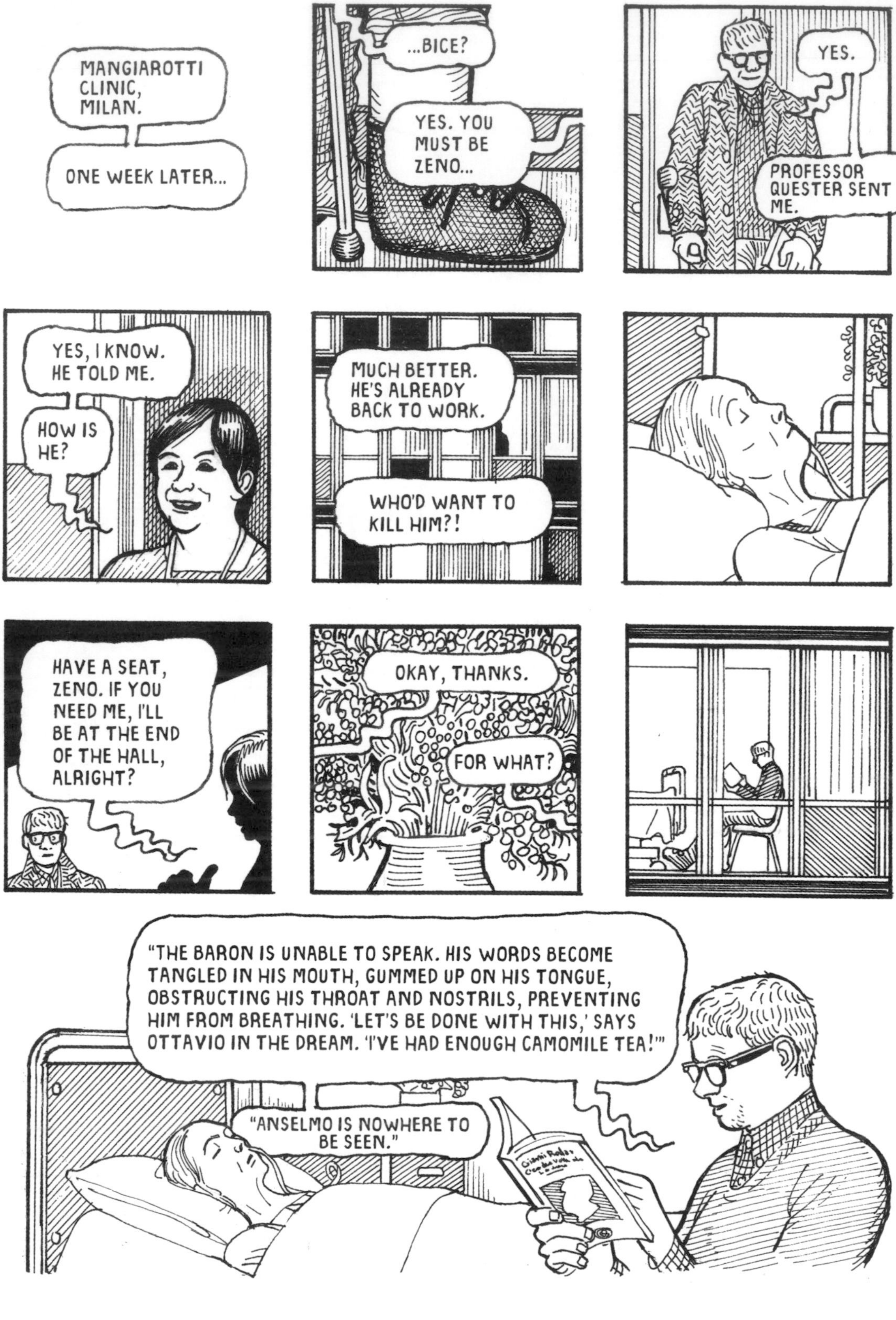
MANGIAROTTI CLINIC, MILAN.
ONE WEEK LATER...
...BICE?
YES. YOU MUST BE ZENO...
YES.
PROFESSOR QUESTER SENT ME.
YES, I KNOW. HE TOLD ME.
HOW IS HE?
MUCH BETTER. HE'S ALREADY BACK TO WORK.
WHO'D WANT TO KILL HIM?!
HAVE A SEAT, ZENO. IF YOU NEED ME, I'LL BE AT THE END OF THE HALL, ALRIGHT?
OKAY, THANKS.
FOR WHAT?
"THE BARON IS UNABLE TO SPEAK. HIS WORDS BECOME TANGLED IN HIS MOUTH, GUMMED UP ON HIS TONGUE, OBSTRUCTING HIS THROAT AND NOSTRILS, PREVENTING HIM FROM BREATHING. 'LET'S BE DONE WITH THIS,' SAYS OTTAVIO IN THE DREAM. 'I'VE HAD ENOUGH CAMOMILE TEA!'"
"ANSELMO IS NOWHERE TO BE SEEN."

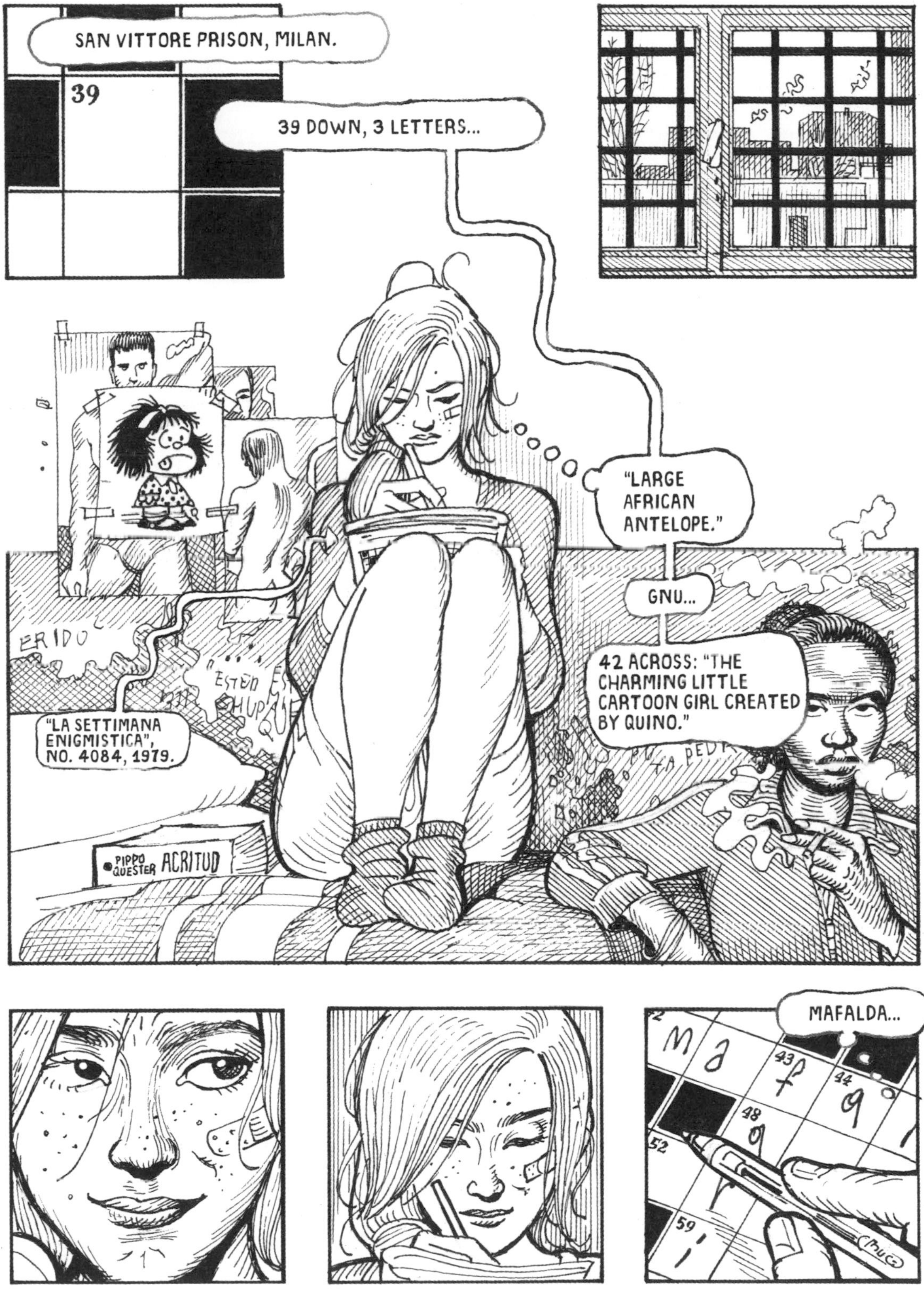
SAN VITTORE PRISON, MILAN.
39
39 DOWN, 3 LETTERS...
"LARGE AFRICAN ANTELOPE."
GNU...
42 ACROSS: "THE CHARMING LITTLE CARTOON GIRL CREATED BY QUINO."
"LA SETTIMANA ENIGMISTICA", NO. 4084, 1979.
PIPPO QUESTER ACRITUD
MAFALDA...

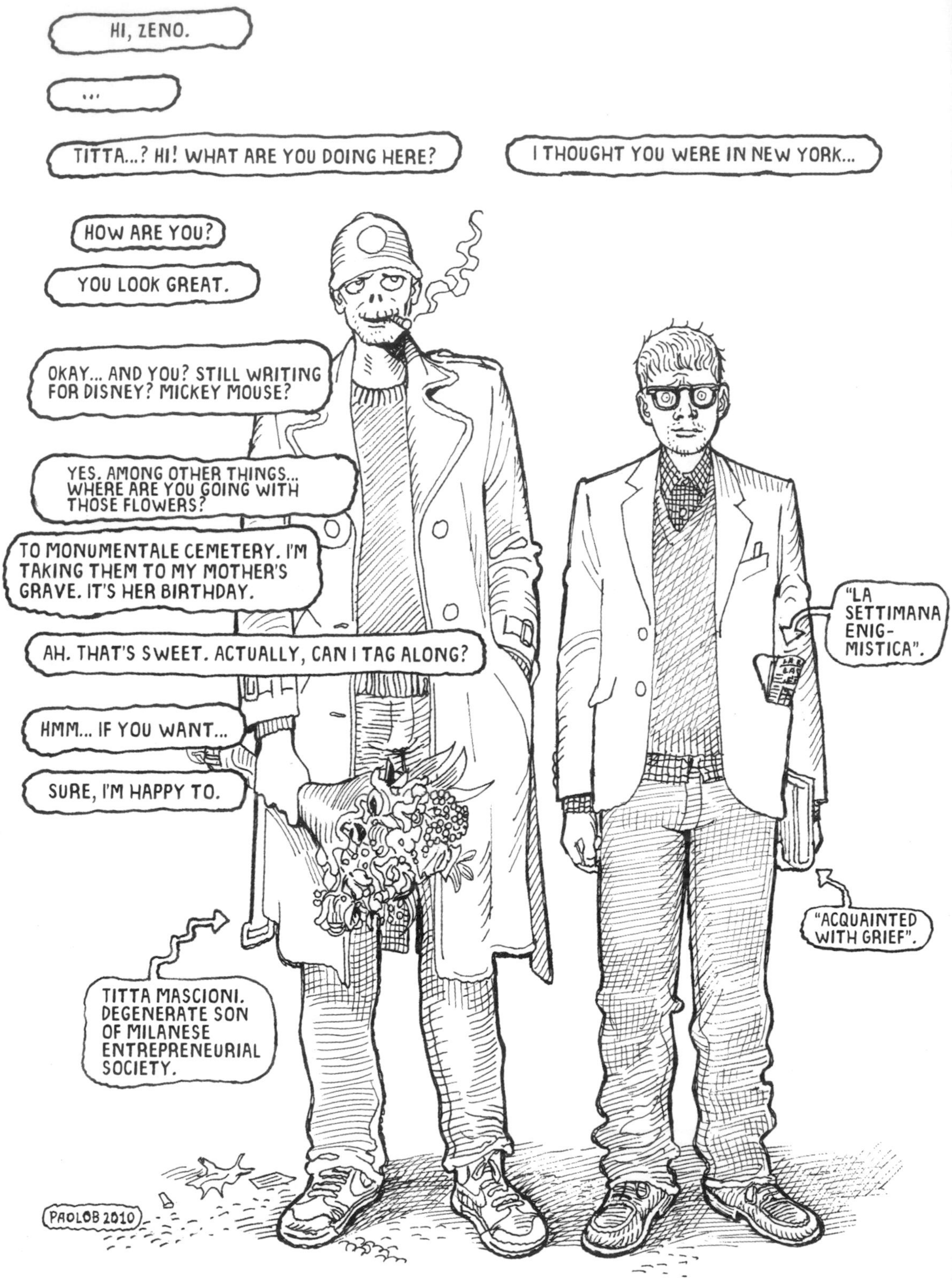
HI, ZENO.
...
TITTA...? HI! WHAT ARE YOU DOING HERE?
I THOUGHT YOU WERE IN NEW YORK...
HOW ARE YOU?
YOU LOOK GREAT.
OKAY... AND YOU? STILL WRITING FOR DISNEY? MICKEY MOUSE?
YES. AMONG OTHER THINGS... WHERE ARE YOU GOING WITH THOSE FLOWERS?
TO MONUMENTALE CEMETERY. I'M TAKING THEM TO MY MOTHER'S GRAVE. IT'S HER BIRTHDAY.
AH. THAT'S SWEET. ACTUALLY, CAN I TAG ALONG?
HMM... IF YOU WANT...
SURE, I'M HAPPY TO.
"LA SETTIMANA ENIG-MISTICA".
"ACQUAINTED WITH GRIEF".
TITTA MASCIONI. DEGENERATE SON OF MILANESE ENTREPRENEURIAL SOCIETY.
PAOLOB 2010

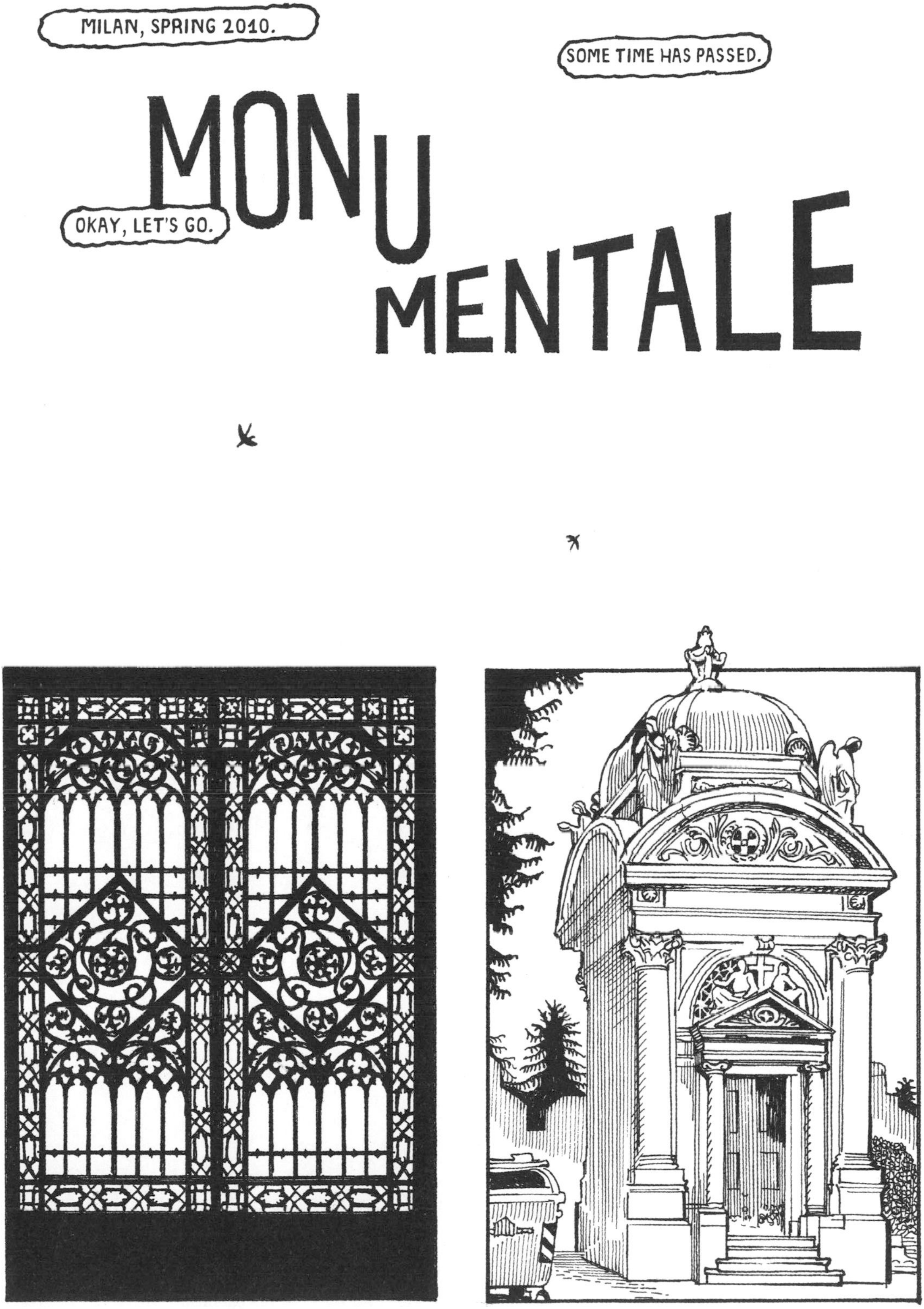
MILAN, SPRING 2010.
SOME TIME HAS PASSED.
MONUMENTALE
OKAY, LET'S GO.

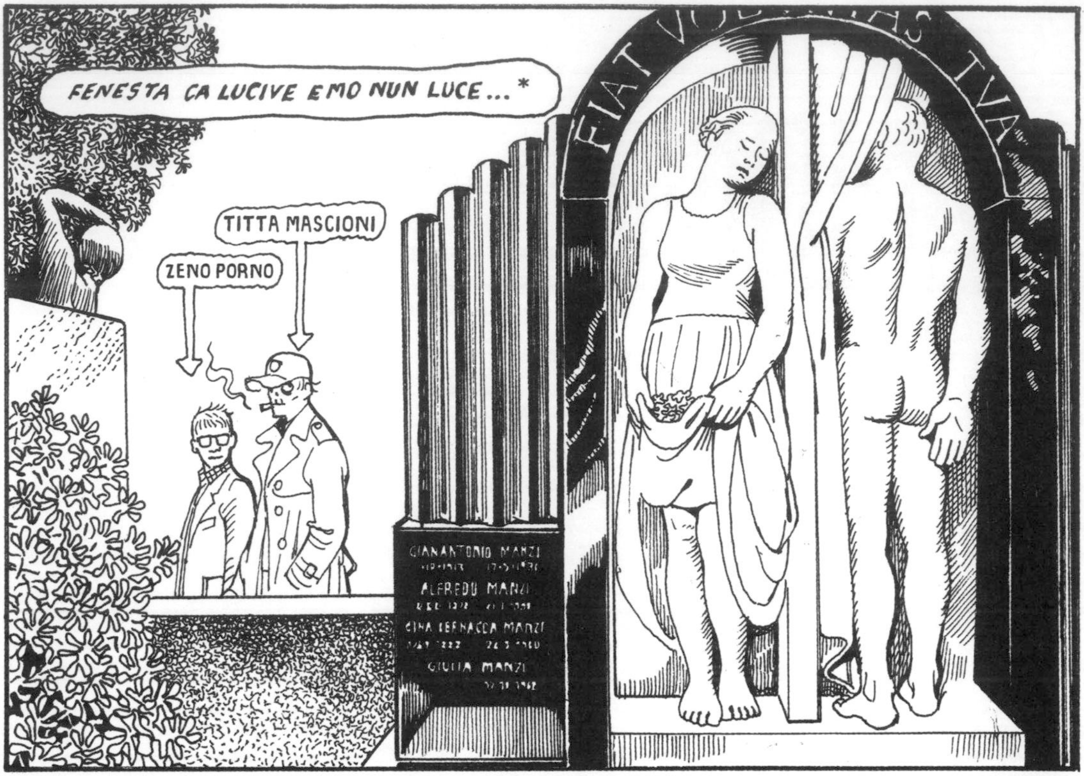
FENESTA CA LUCIVE E MO NUN LUCE...*
TITTA MASCIONI
ZENO PORNO
GIANANTONIO MANZI
ALFREDO MANZI
GIULIA MANZI

* FROM THE NEAPOLITAN SONG "FENESTA CA LUCIVE": "THE WINDOW THAT SHONE AND NOW IS DARK..."

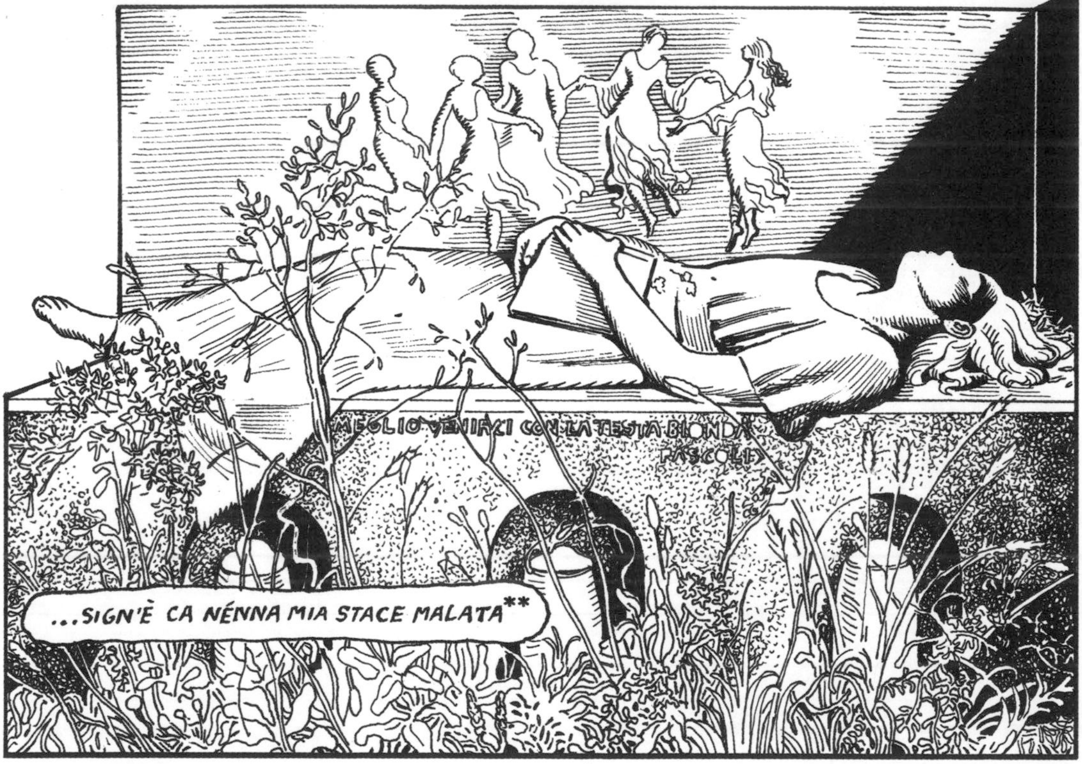
MEGLIO VENIRCI CON LA TESTA BIONDA
PASCOLI
...SIGN'È CA NÉNNA MIA STACE MALATA**

** "...A SIGN THAT MY DARLING IS ILL."

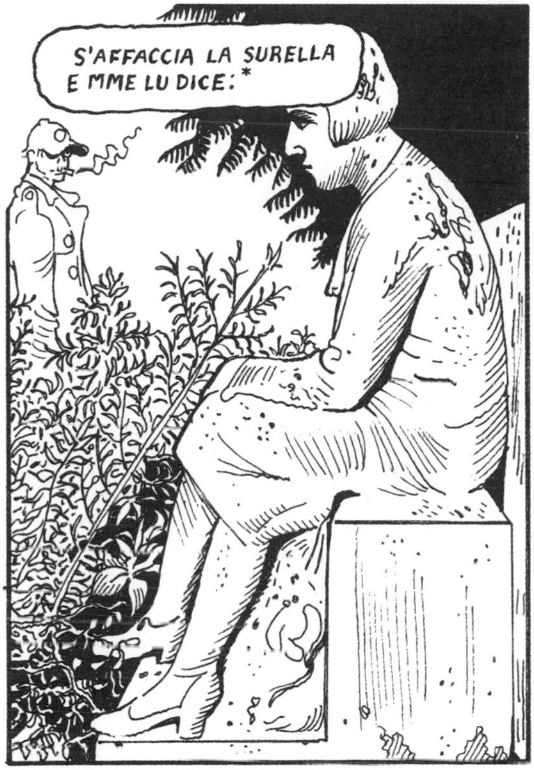
S'AFFACCIA LA SURELLA E MME LU DICE:*

* "HER SISTER COMES OUT AND TELLS ME:"

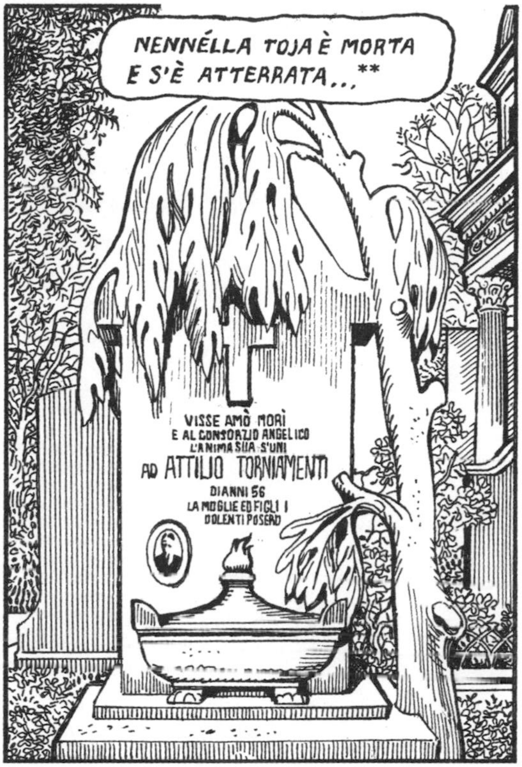
NENNÉLLA TOJA È MORTA E S'È ATTERRATA...**
VISSE AMÒ MORÌ
E AL CONSORZIO ANGELICO
L'ANIMA SUA S'UNÌ
AD ATTILIO TORNIAMENTI
DIANNI 56
LA MOGLIE ED FIGLI I
DOLENTI POSERO

** "YOUR DARLING GIRL IS DEAD AND GONE..."

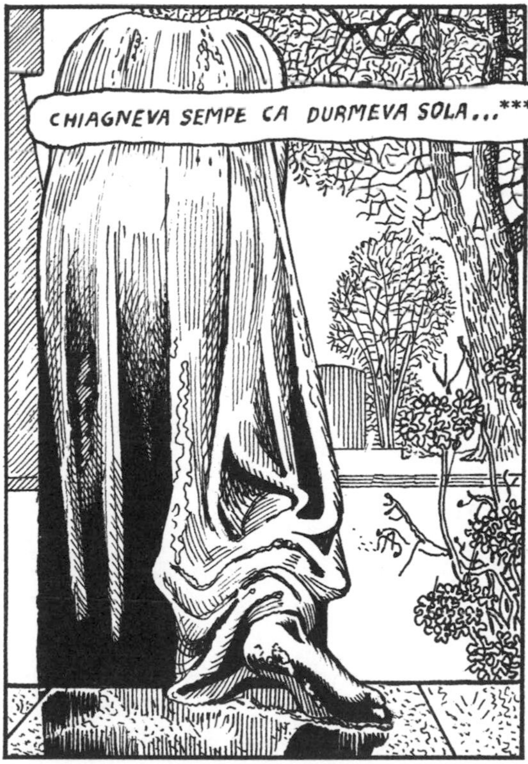
CHIAGNEVA SEMPE CA DURMEVA SOLA...***

*** "SHE ALWAYS CRIED BECAUSE SHE SLEPT ALONE..."

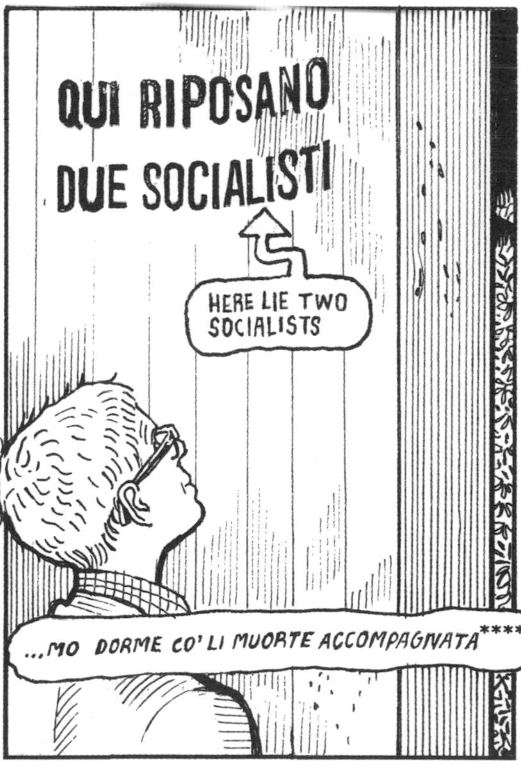
QUI RIPOSANO DUE SOCIALISTI
HERE LIE TWO SOCIALISTS
...MO DORME CO' LI MUORTE ACCOMPAGNATA****

**** "...NOW SHE SLEEPS NEXT TO THE DEAD."

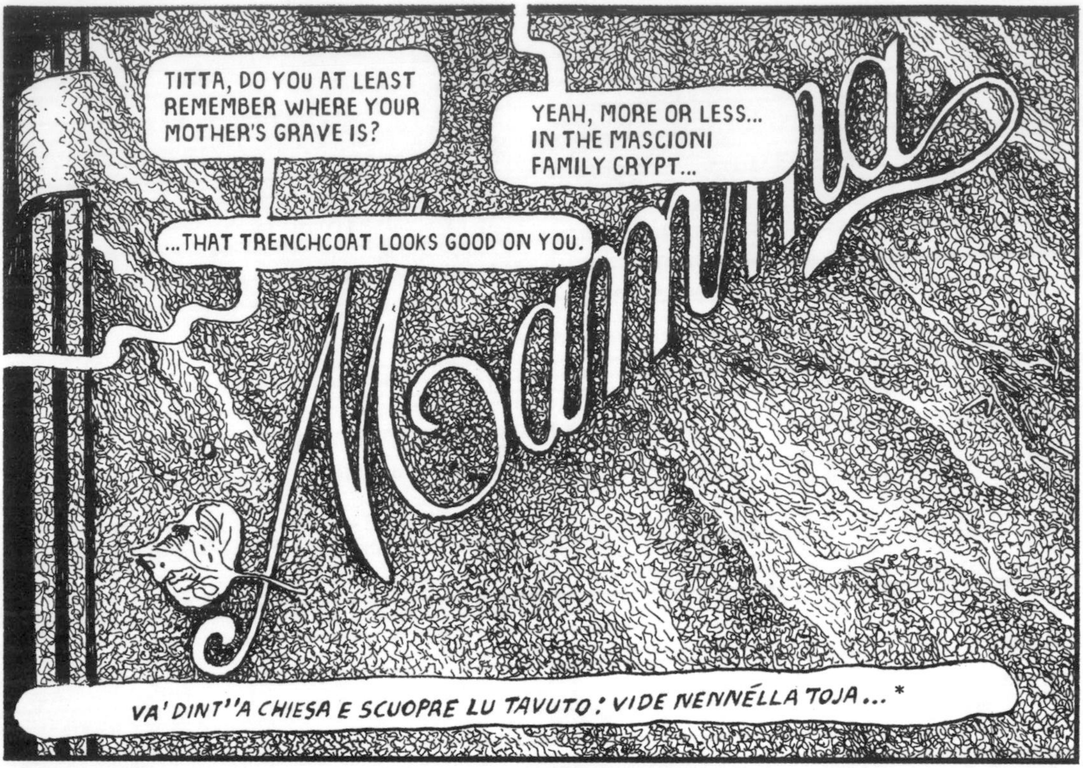
TITTA, DO YOU AT LEAST REMEMBER WHERE YOUR MOTHER'S GRAVE IS?
YEAH, MORE OR LESS... IN THE MASCIONI FAMILY CRYPT...
...THAT TRENCHCOAT LOOKS GOOD ON YOU.
Mamma
VA' DINT''A CHIESA E SCUOPRE LU TAVUTO: VIDE NENNÉLLA TOJA... *

* "GO IN THE CHURCH AND LOOK AT THE TOMB: LOOK AT WHAT YOUR DARLING HAS BECOME..."

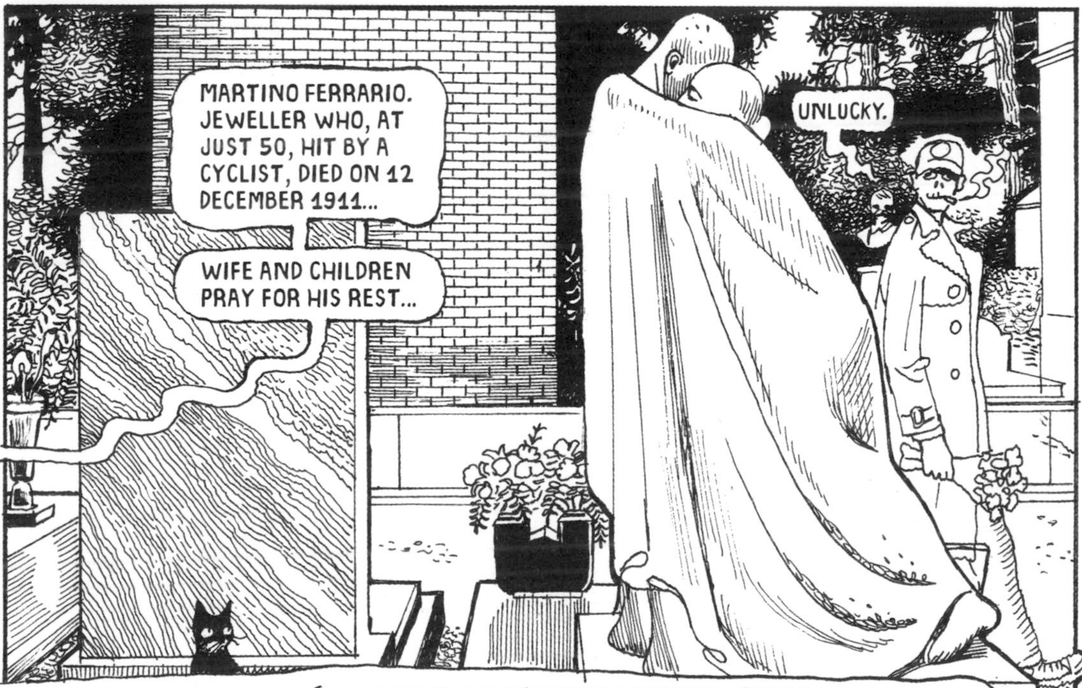
MARTINO FERRARIO. JEWELLER WHO, AT JUST 50, HIT BY A CYCLIST, DIED ON 12 DECEMBER 1911...
WIFE AND CHILDREN PRAY FOR HIS REST...
UNLUCKY.
...DA CHELLA VOCCA CA N'ASCÉANO SCIURE, MO N'ESCENO LI VIERME... OH! CHE PIATATE! **

** "FROM THAT MOUTH, WHERE FLOWERS BLOOMED, NOW COME WORMS... OH, MERCY!"

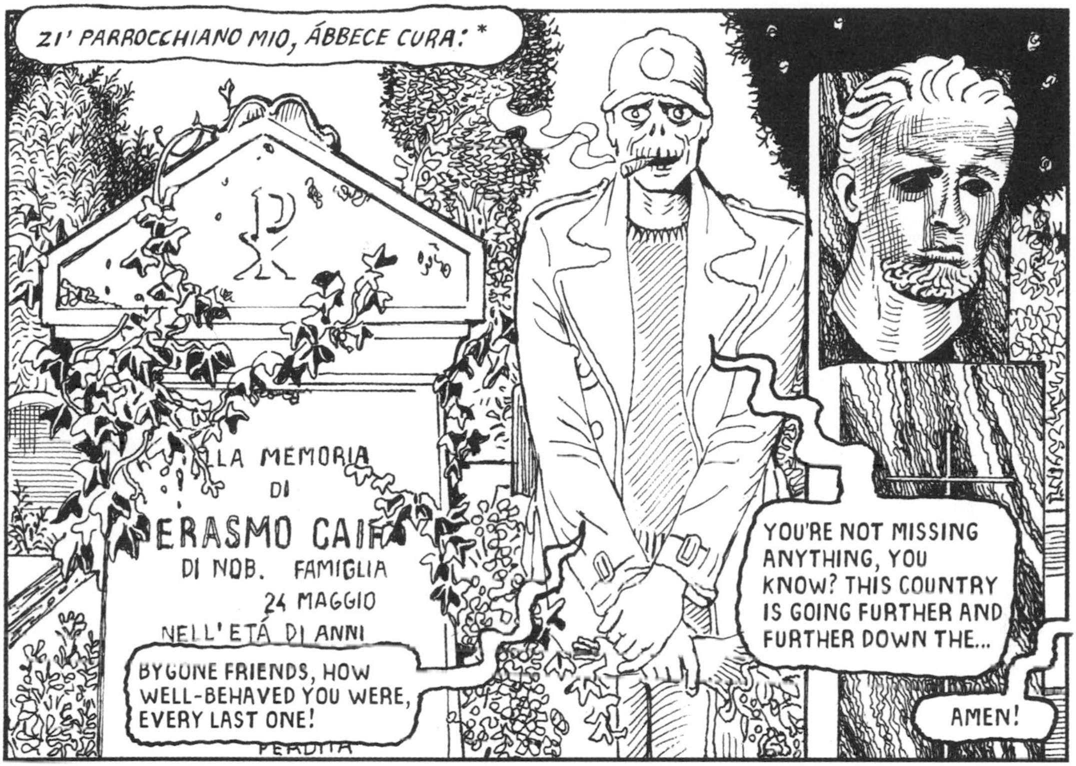
ZI' PARROCCHIANO MIO, ÁBBECE CURA: *
LLA MEMORIA
DI
ERASMO CAIF
DI NOB. FAMIGLIA
24 MAGGIO
NELL'ETÁ DI ANNI
BYGONE FRIENDS, HOW WELL-BEHAVED YOU WERE, EVERY LAST ONE!
YOU'RE NOT MISSING ANYTHING, YOU KNOW? THIS COUNTRY IS GOING FURTHER AND FURTHER DOWN THE...
AMEN!

* "MY DEAR PRIEST, WATCH OVER HER:"

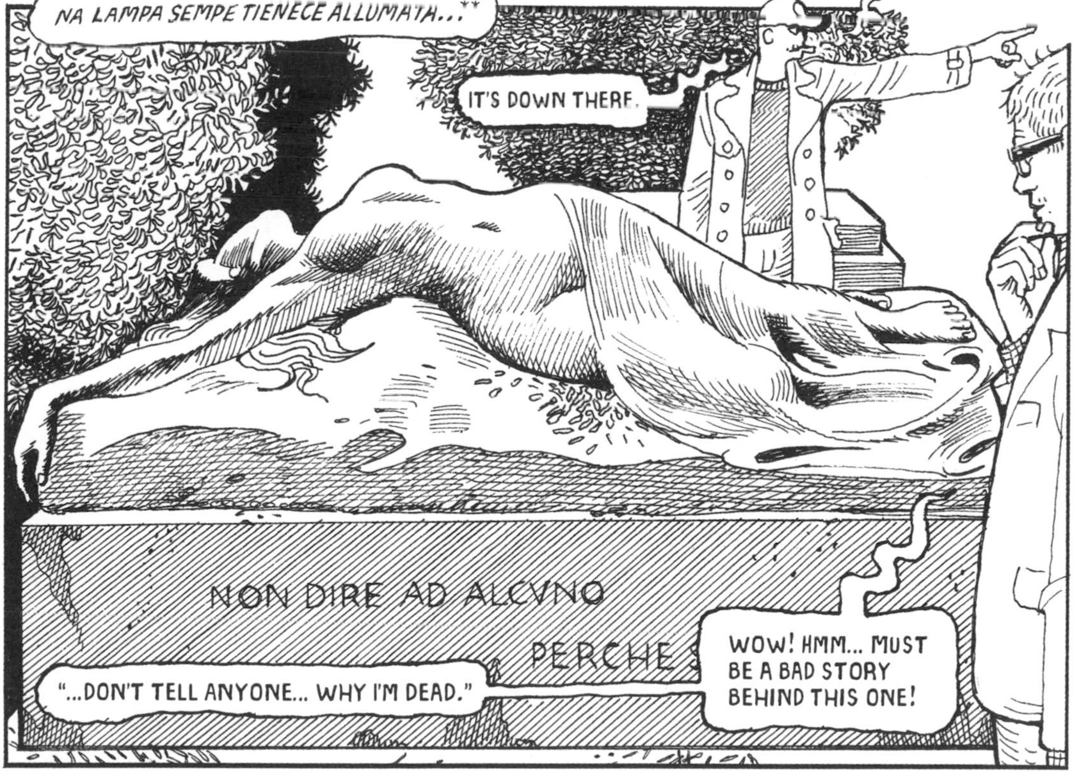
NA LAMPA SEMPE TIENECE ALLUMATA...**
IT'S DOWN THERE.
NON DIRE AD ALCVNO
PERCHE
"...DON'T TELL ANYONE... WHY I'M DEAD."
WOW! HMM... MUST BE A BAD STORY BEHIND THIS ONE!

** "KEEP A LITTLE LAMP ALWAYS LIT FOR HER..."

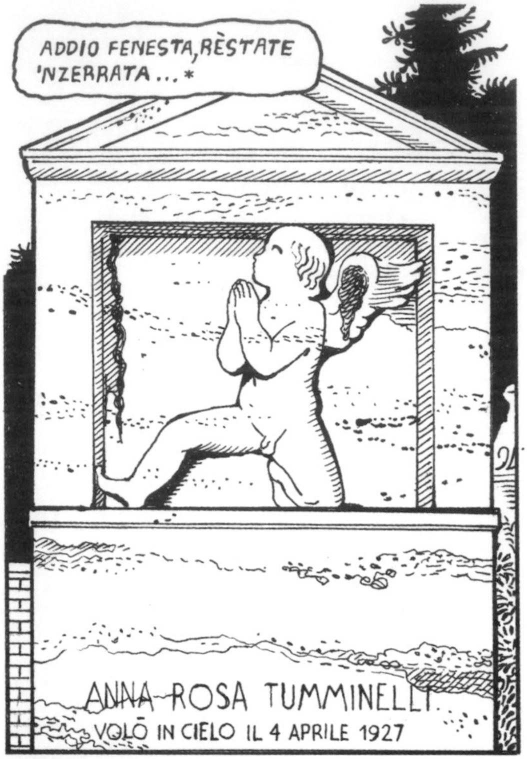
ADDIO FENESTA, RÈSTATE 'NZERRATA... *
ANNA-ROSA TUMMINELLI
VOLÒ IN CIELO IL 4 APRILE 1927

* "FAREWELL, WINDOW, STAY CLOSED..."

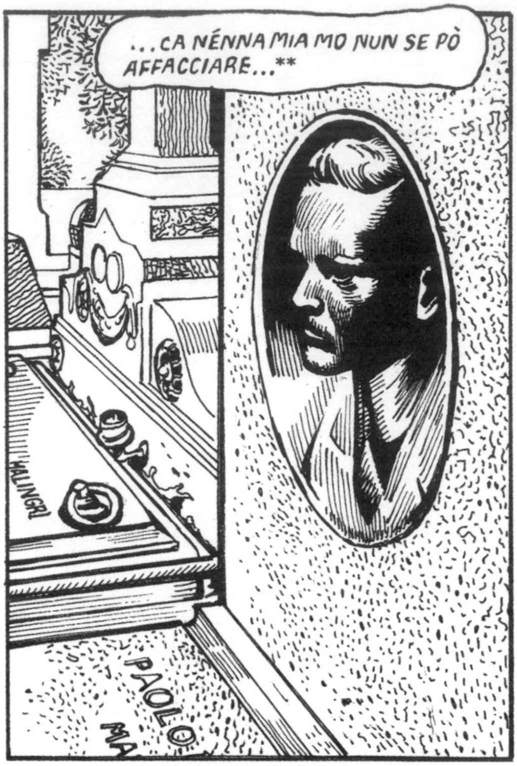
...CA NÉNNA MIA MO NUN SE PÒ AFFACCIARE... **
PAOLO
MA

** "...SINCE MY LOVE CAN'T LOOK OUT ANY MORE..."

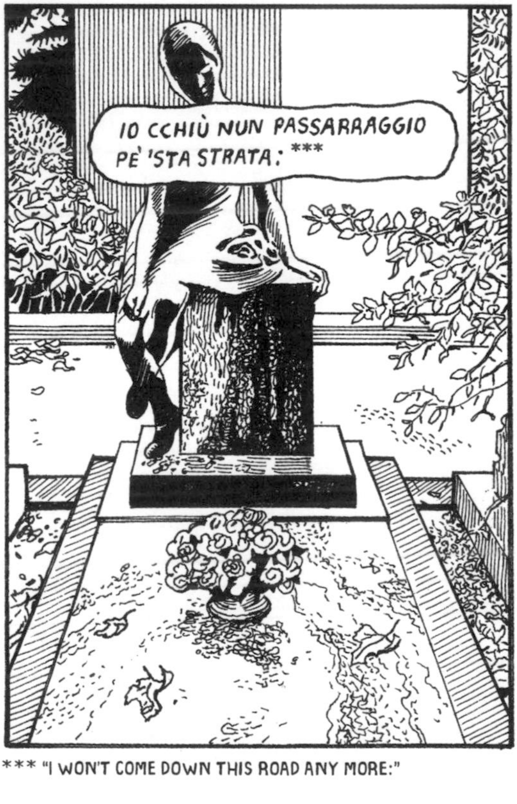
IO CCHIÙ NUN PASSARRAGGIO PÈ 'STA STRATA: ***

*** "I WON'T COME DOWN THIS ROAD ANY MORE:"

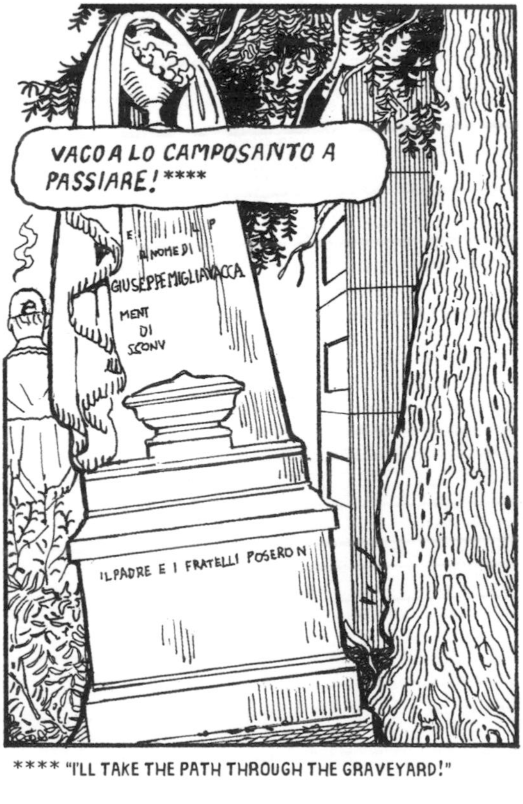
VACO A LO CAMPOSANTO A PASSIARE! ****
A NOME DI
GIUSEPPE MIGLIAVACCA
MENT
DI
SCONV
IL PADRE E I FRATELLI POSERO N

**** "I'LL TAKE THE PATH THROUGH THE GRAVEYARD!"

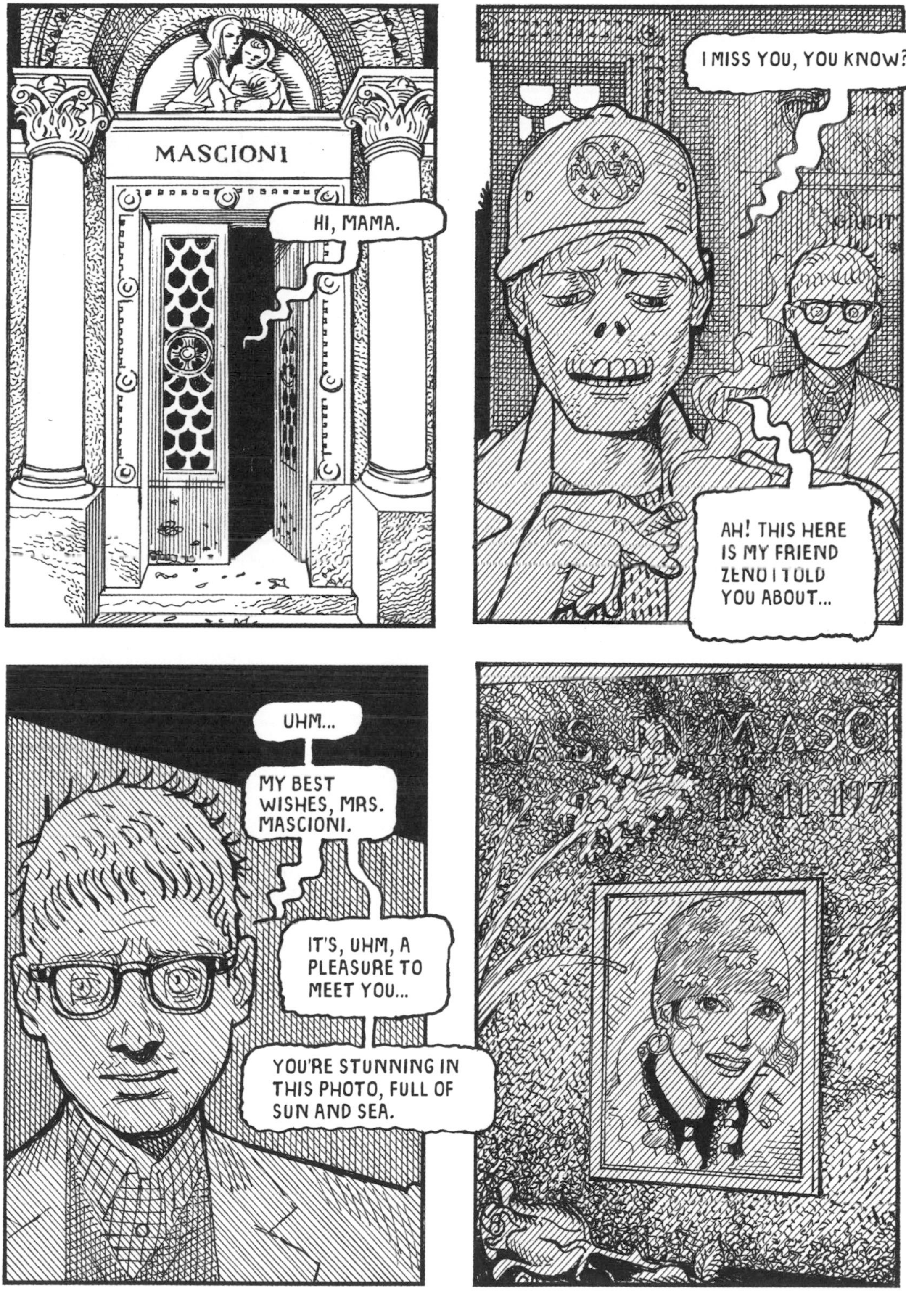
MASCIONI
HI, MAMA.
I MISS YOU, YOU KNOW?
AH! THIS HERE IS MY FRIEND ZENO I TOLD YOU ABOUT...
UHM...
MY BEST WISHES, MRS. MASCIONI.
IT'S, UHM, A PLEASURE TO MEET YOU...
YOU'RE STUNNING IN THIS PHOTO, FULL OF SUN AND SEA.

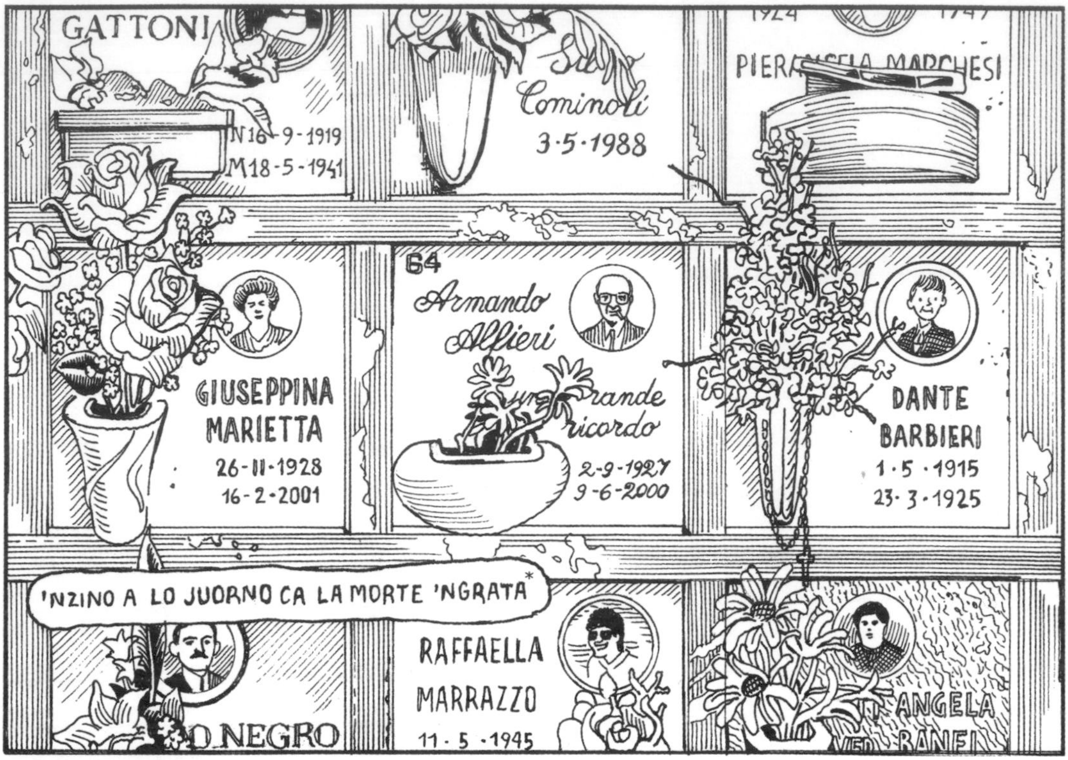
GATTONI
N16-9-1919
M18-5-1941
Cominoli
3·5·1988
64
Armando
Alfieri
2-9-1927
9-6-2000
GIUSEPPINA
MARIETTA
26-11-1928
16-2-2001
DANTE
BARBIERI
1·5·1915
23·3·1925
'NZINO A LO JUORNO CA LA MORTE 'NGRATA*
RAFFAELLA
MARRAZZO
11·5·1945
ANGELA

* "UNTIL THE DAY WHEN THANKLESS DEATH..."

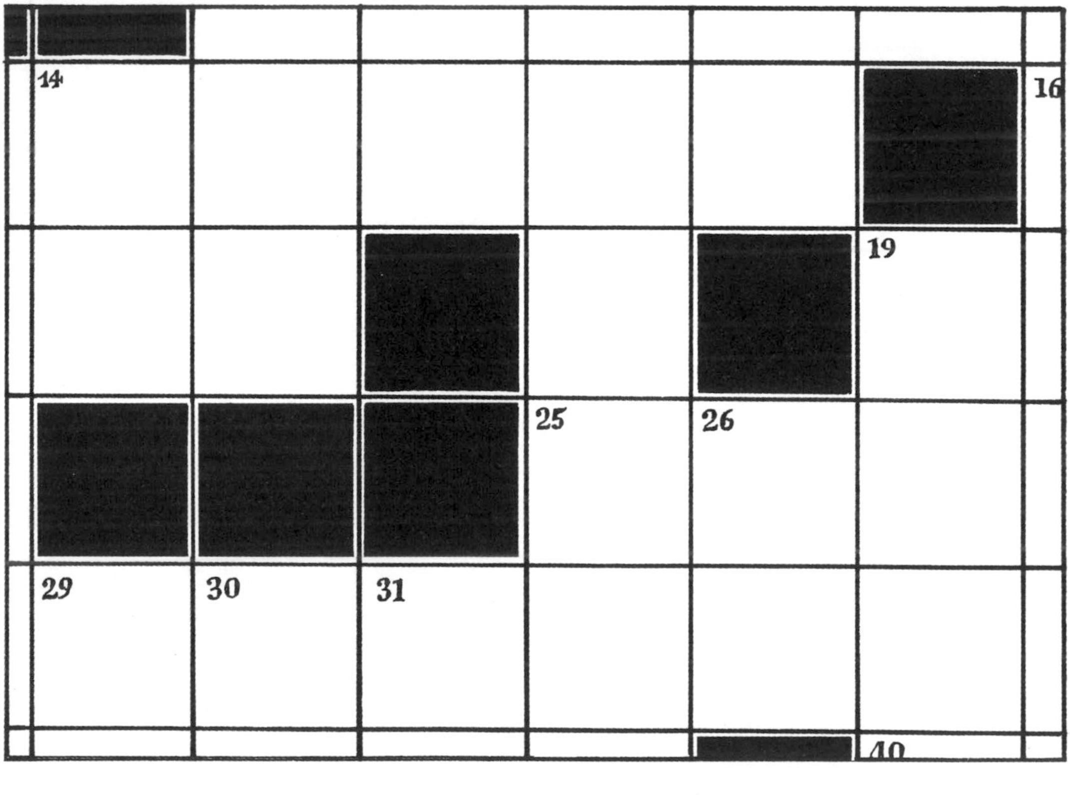
14
16
19
25
26
29
30
31
40

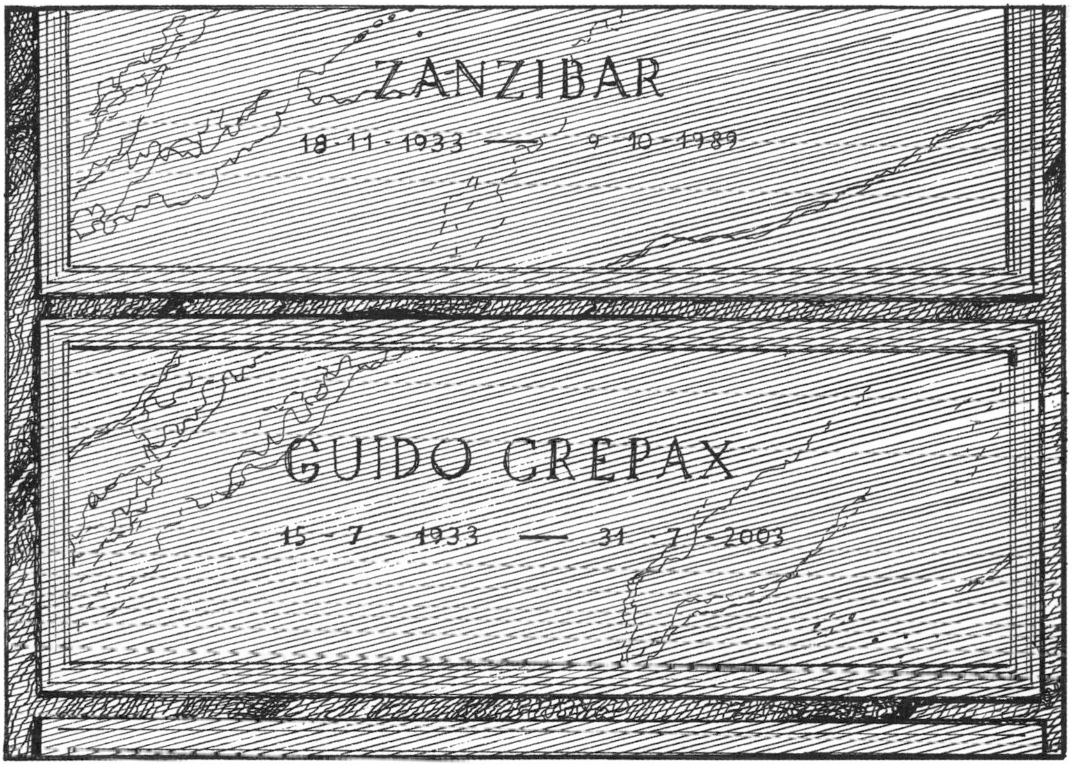

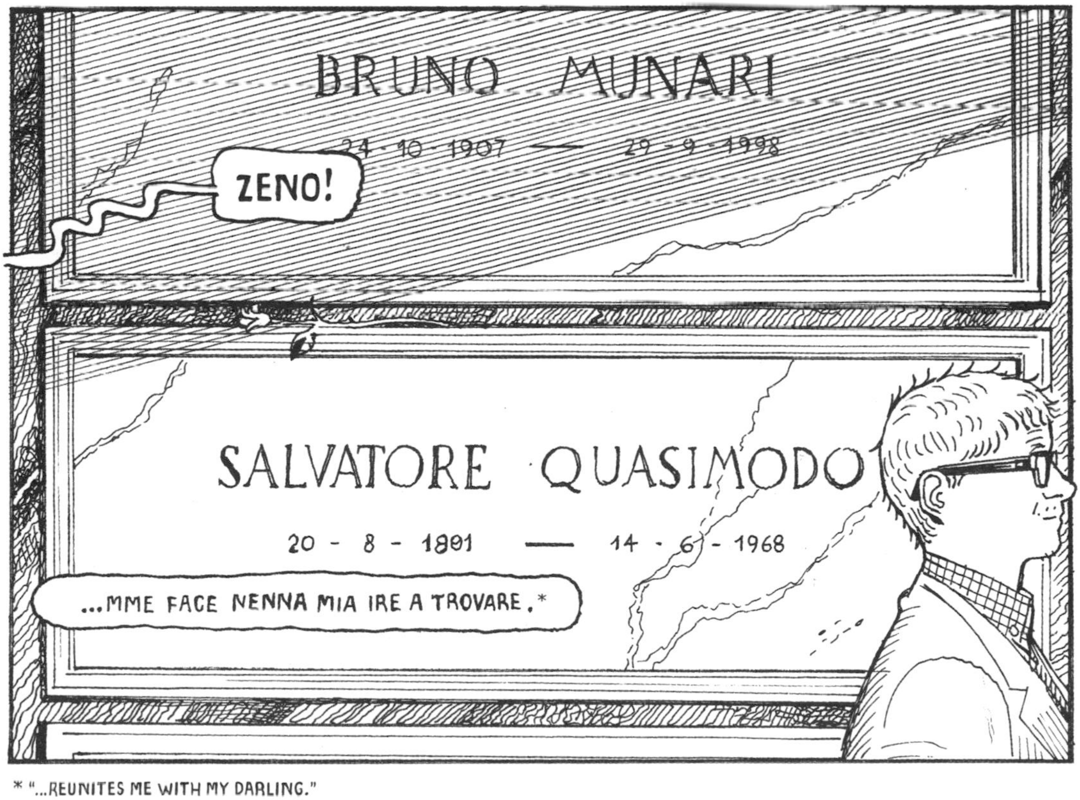

* "...REUNITES ME WITH MY DARLING."

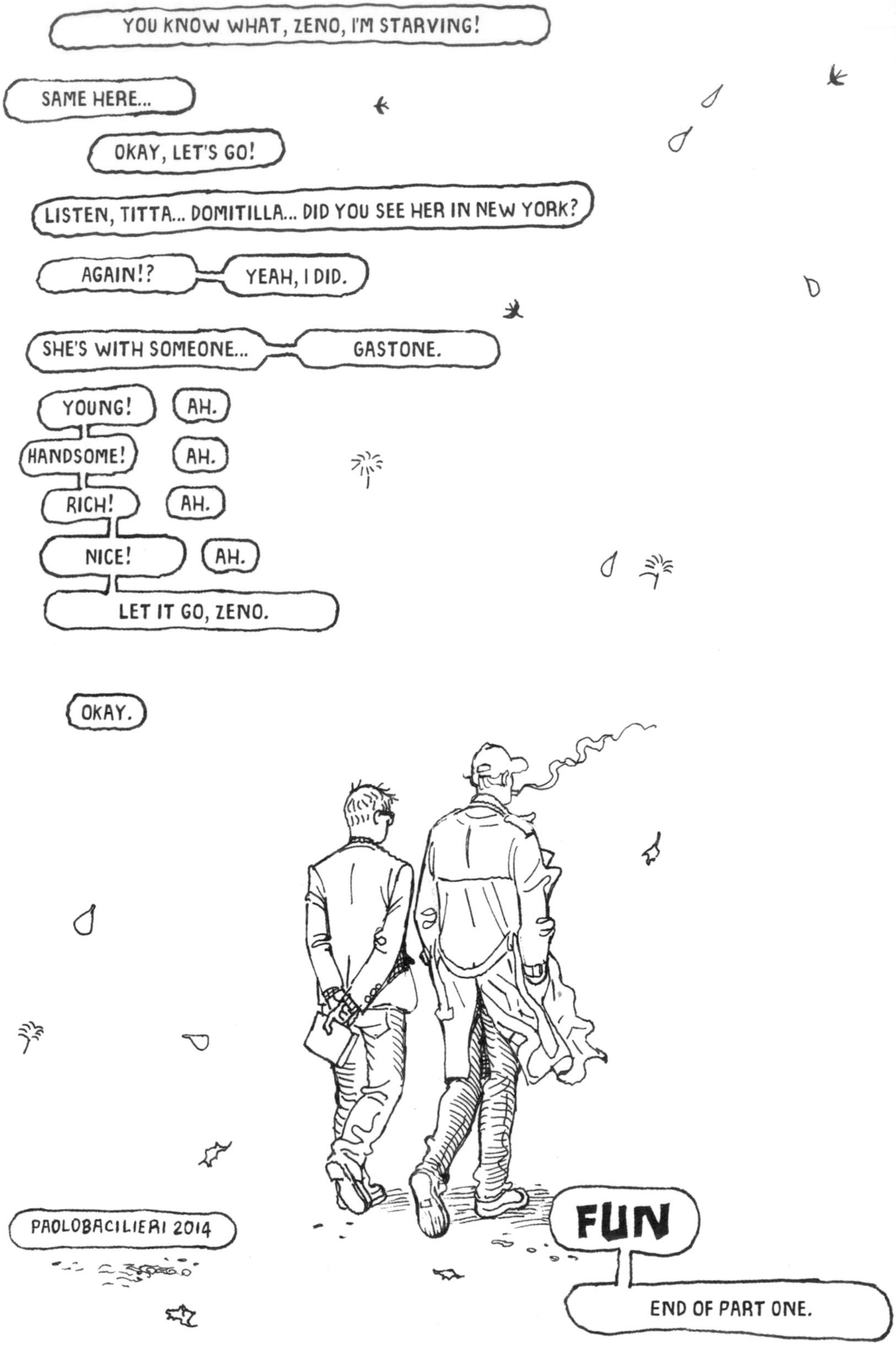

YOU KNOW WHAT, ZENO, I'M STARVING!
SAME HERE...
OKAY, LET'S GO!
LISTEN, TITTA... DOMITILLA... DID YOU SEE HER IN NEW YORK?
AGAIN!?
YEAH, I DID.
SHE'S WITH SOMEONE...
GASTONE.
YOUNG!
AH.
HANDSOME!
AH.
RICH!
AH.
NICE!
AH.
LET IT GO, ZENO.
OKAY.
PAOLOBACILIERI 2014
FUN
END OF PART ONE.

More FUN

ILI-HS

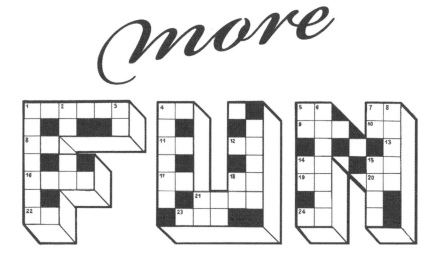

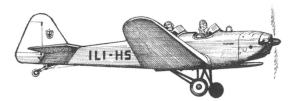

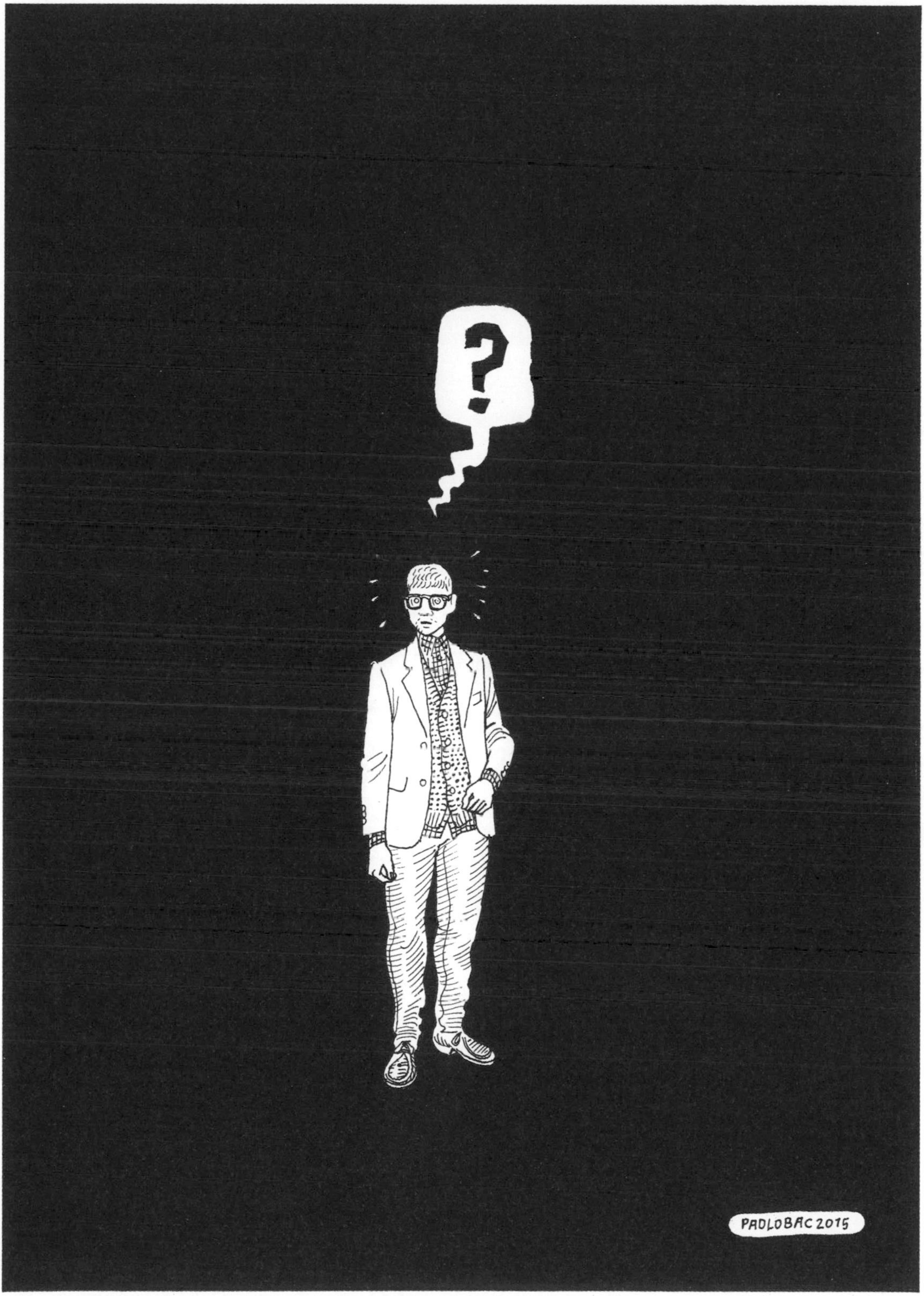
?
PAOLOBAC 2015

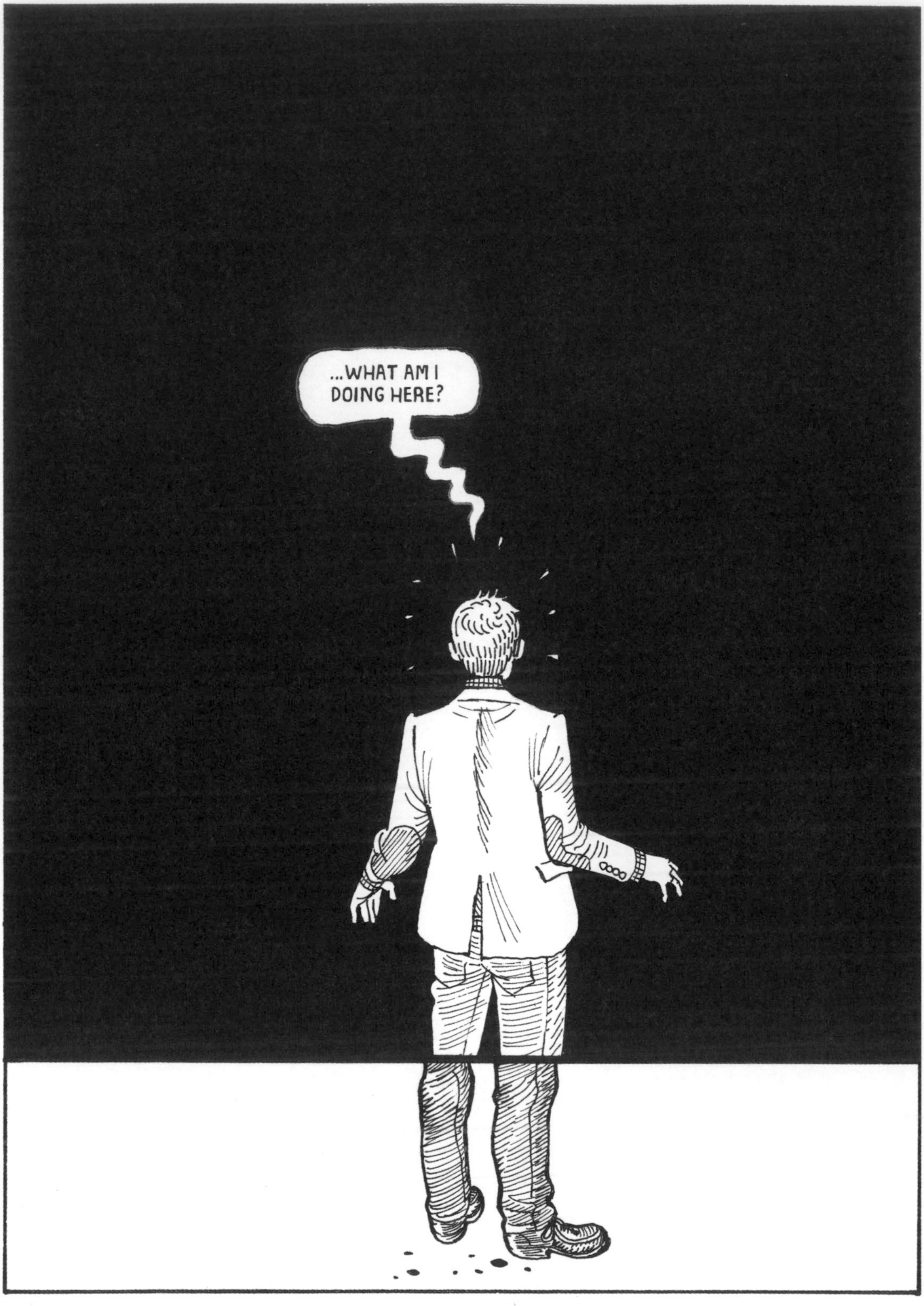
...WHAT AM I DOING HERE?

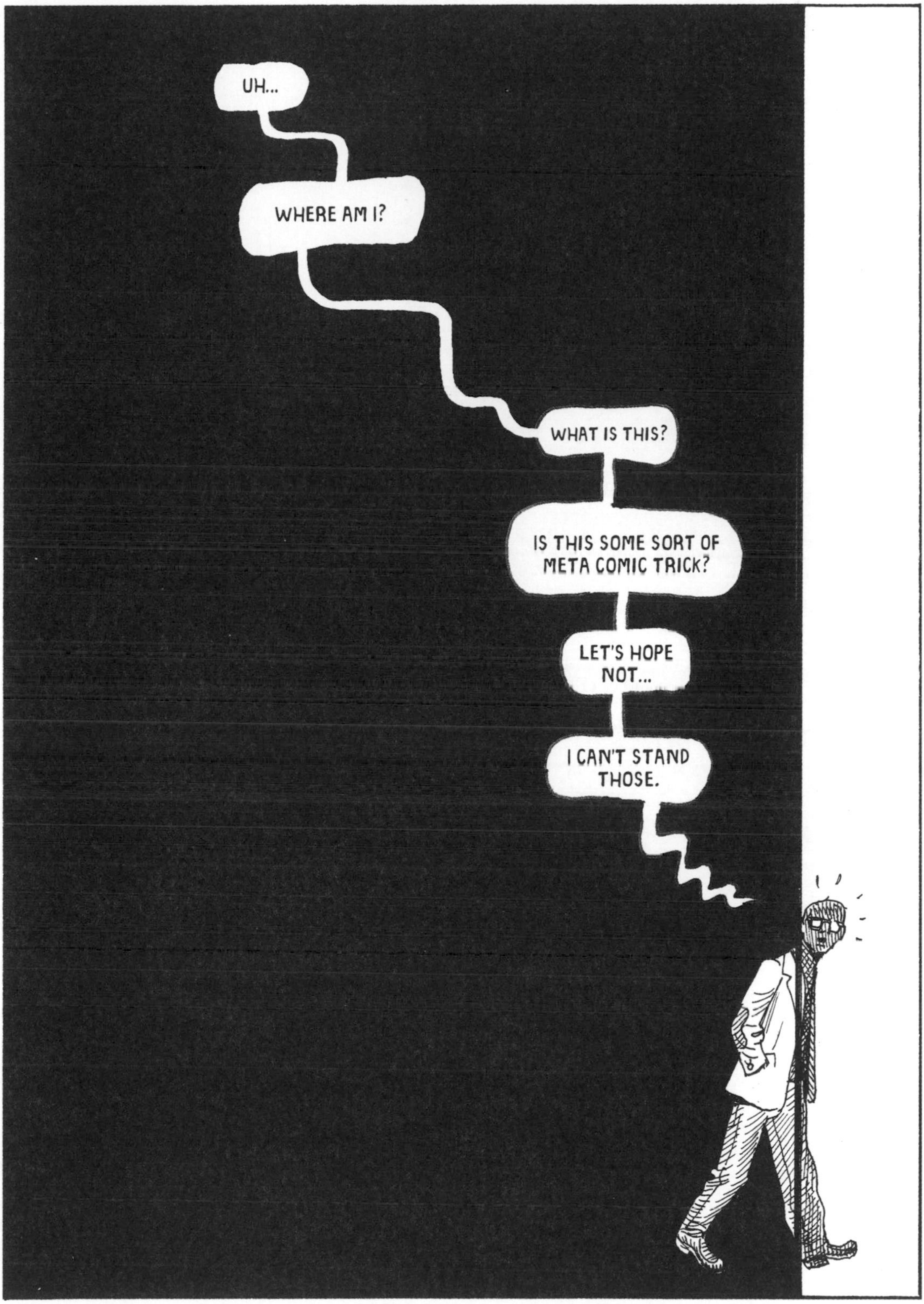
UH...
WHERE AM I?
WHAT IS THIS?
IS THIS SOME SORT OF META COMIC TRICK?
LET'S HOPE NOT...
I CAN'T STAND THOSE.

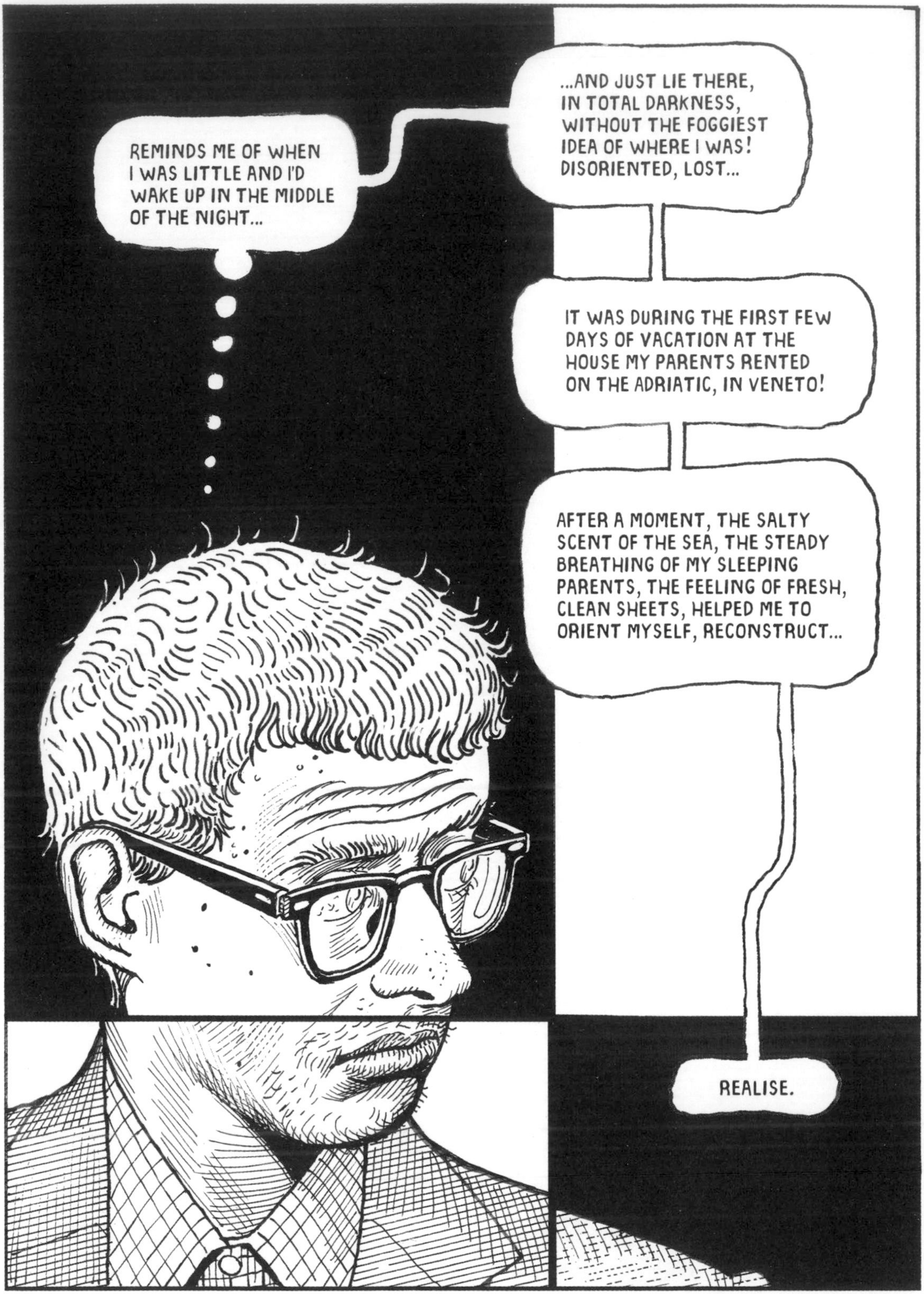
REMINDS ME OF WHEN I WAS LITTLE AND I'D WAKE UP IN THE MIDDLE OF THE NIGHT...
...AND JUST LIE THERE, IN TOTAL DARKNESS, WITHOUT THE FOGGIEST IDEA OF WHERE I WAS! DISORIENTED, LOST...
IT WAS DURING THE FIRST FEW DAYS OF VACATION AT THE HOUSE MY PARENTS RENTED ON THE ADRIATIC, IN VENETO!
AFTER A MOMENT, THE SALTY SCENT OF THE SEA, THE STEADY BREATHING OF MY SLEEPING PARENTS, THE FEELING OF FRESH, CLEAN SHEETS, HELPED ME TO ORIENT MYSELF, RECONSTRUCT...
REALISE.

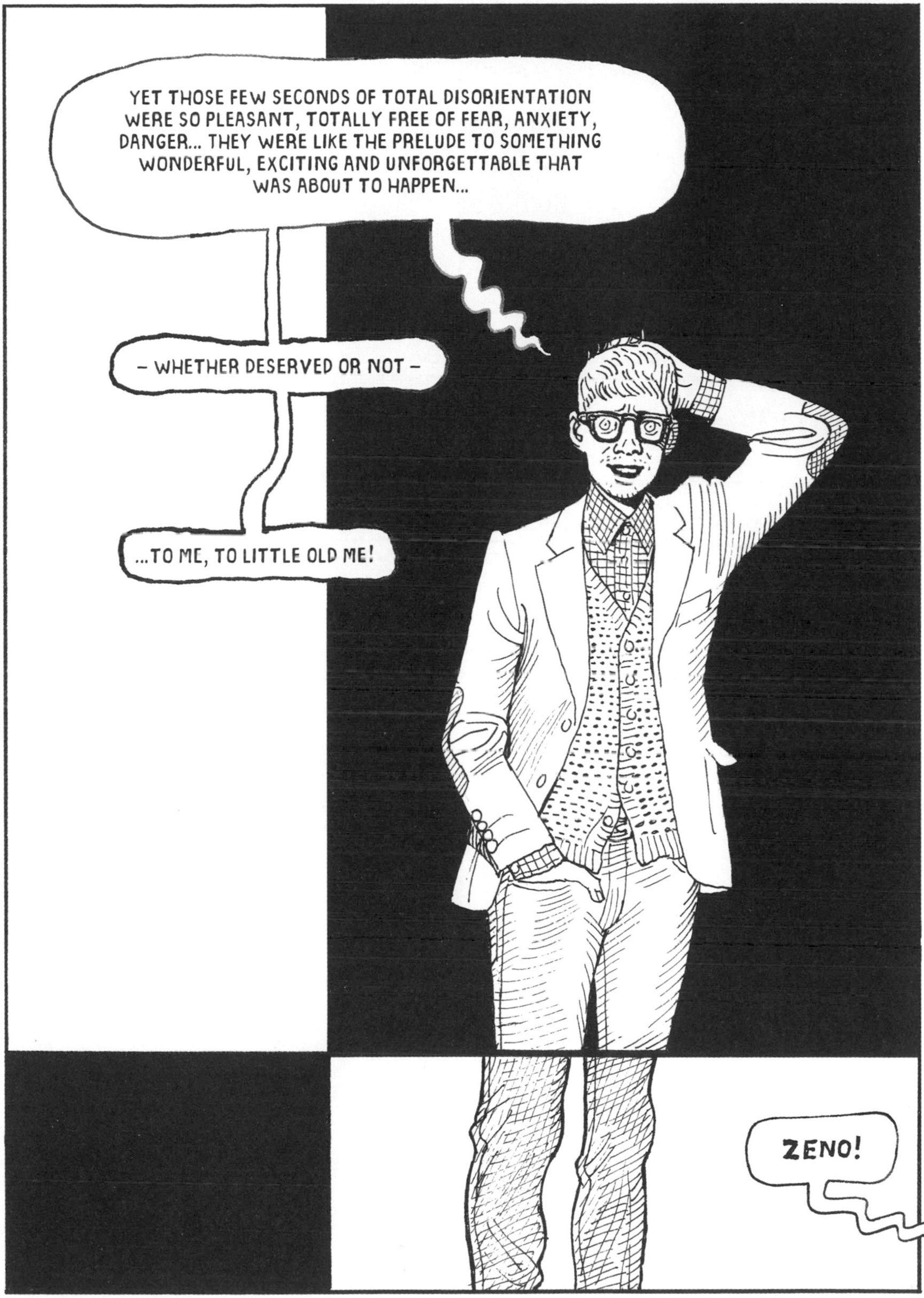

YET THOSE FEW SECONDS OF TOTAL DISORIENTATION WERE SO PLEASANT, TOTALLY FREE OF FEAR, ANXIETY, DANGER... THEY WERE LIKE THE PRELUDE TO SOMETHING WONDERFUL, EXCITING AND UNFORGETTABLE THAT WAS ABOUT TO HAPPEN...
– WHETHER DESERVED OR NOT –
...TO ME, TO LITTLE OLD ME!
ZENO!

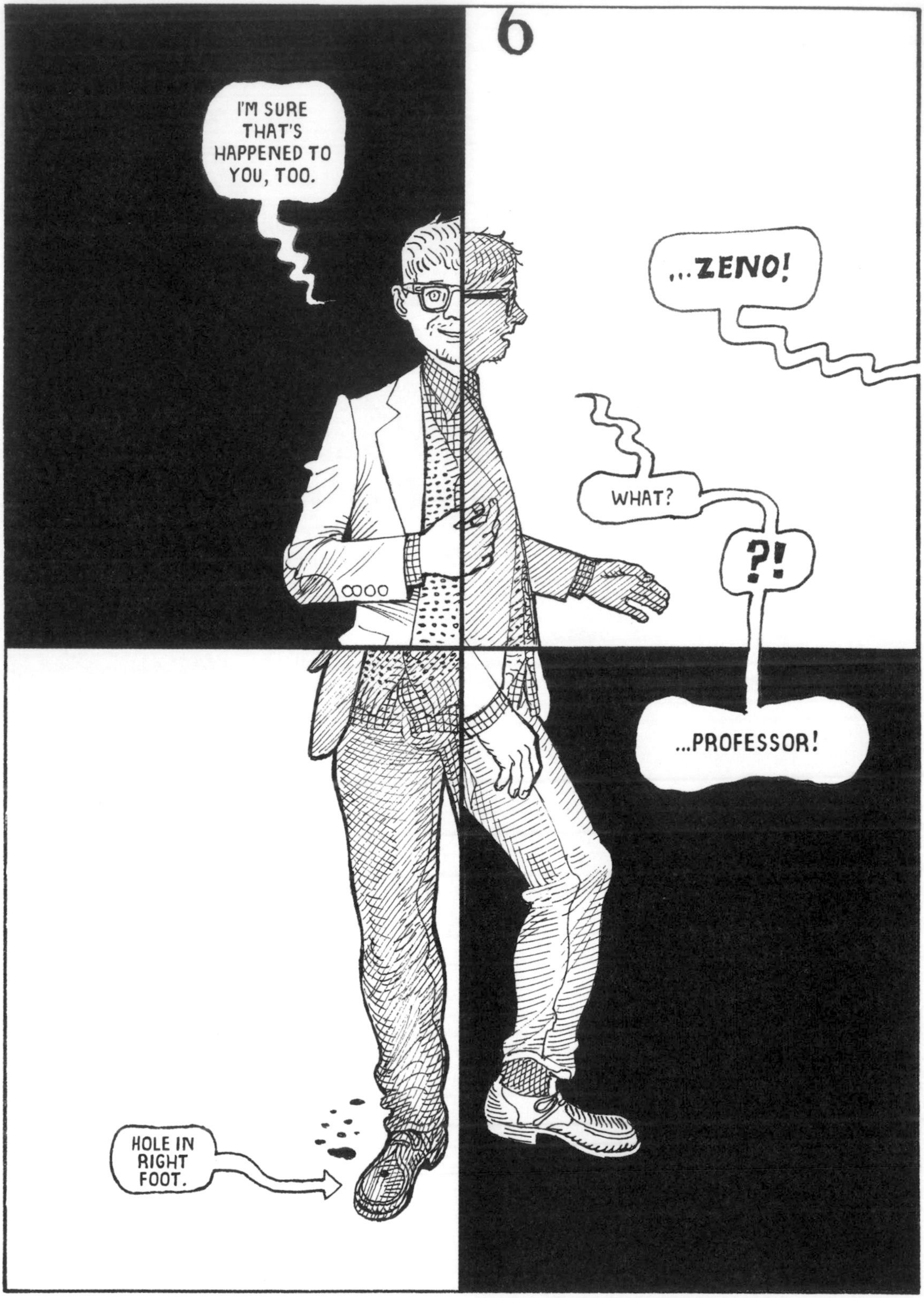
6
I'M SURE THAT'S HAPPENED TO YOU, TOO.
...ZENO!
WHAT?
?!
...PROFESSOR!
HOLE IN RIGHT FOOT.

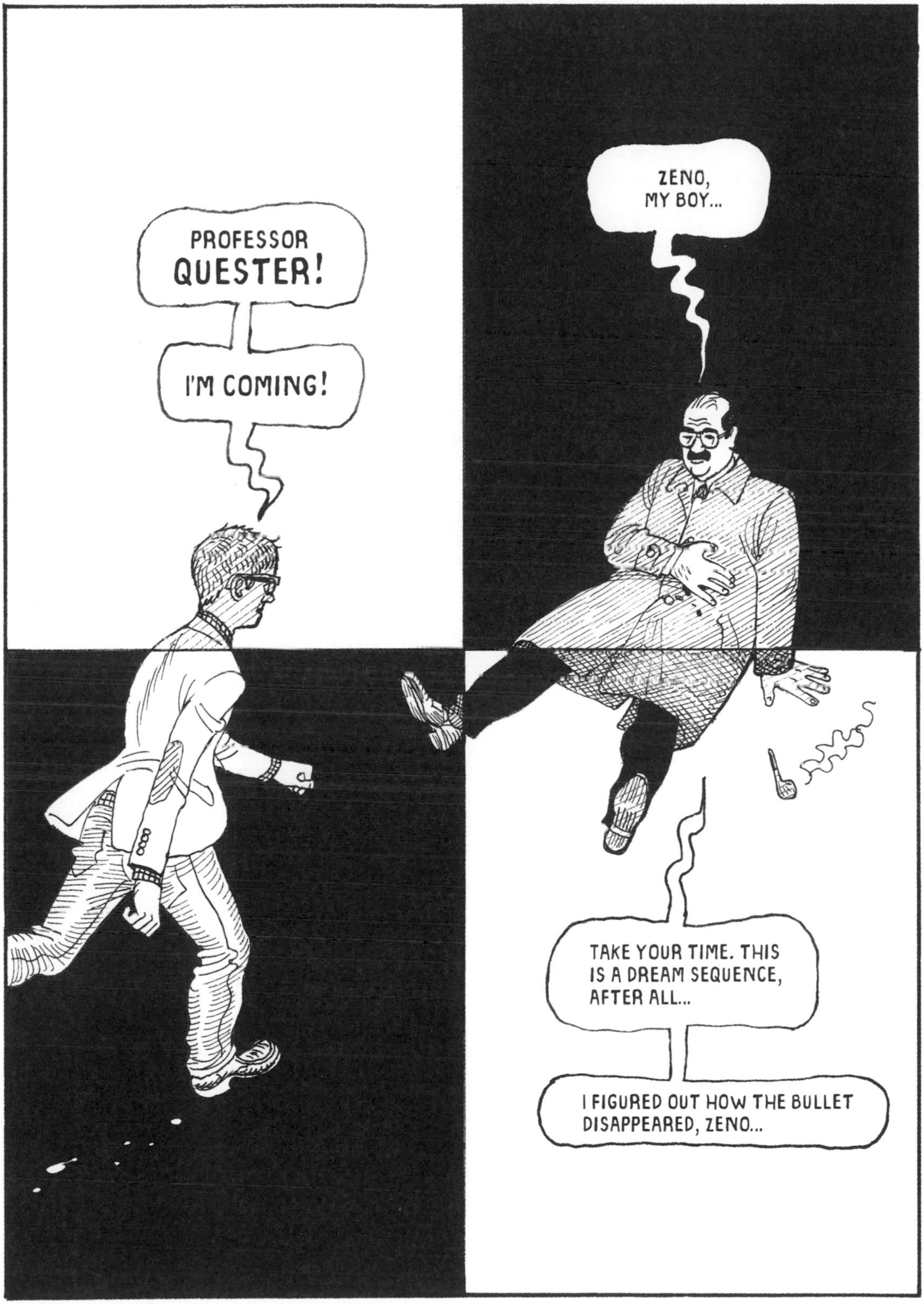
PROFESSOR QUESTER!
I'M COMING!
ZENO, MY BOY...
TAKE YOUR TIME. THIS IS A DREAM SEQUENCE, AFTER ALL...
I FIGURED OUT HOW THE BULLET DISAPPEARED, ZENO...

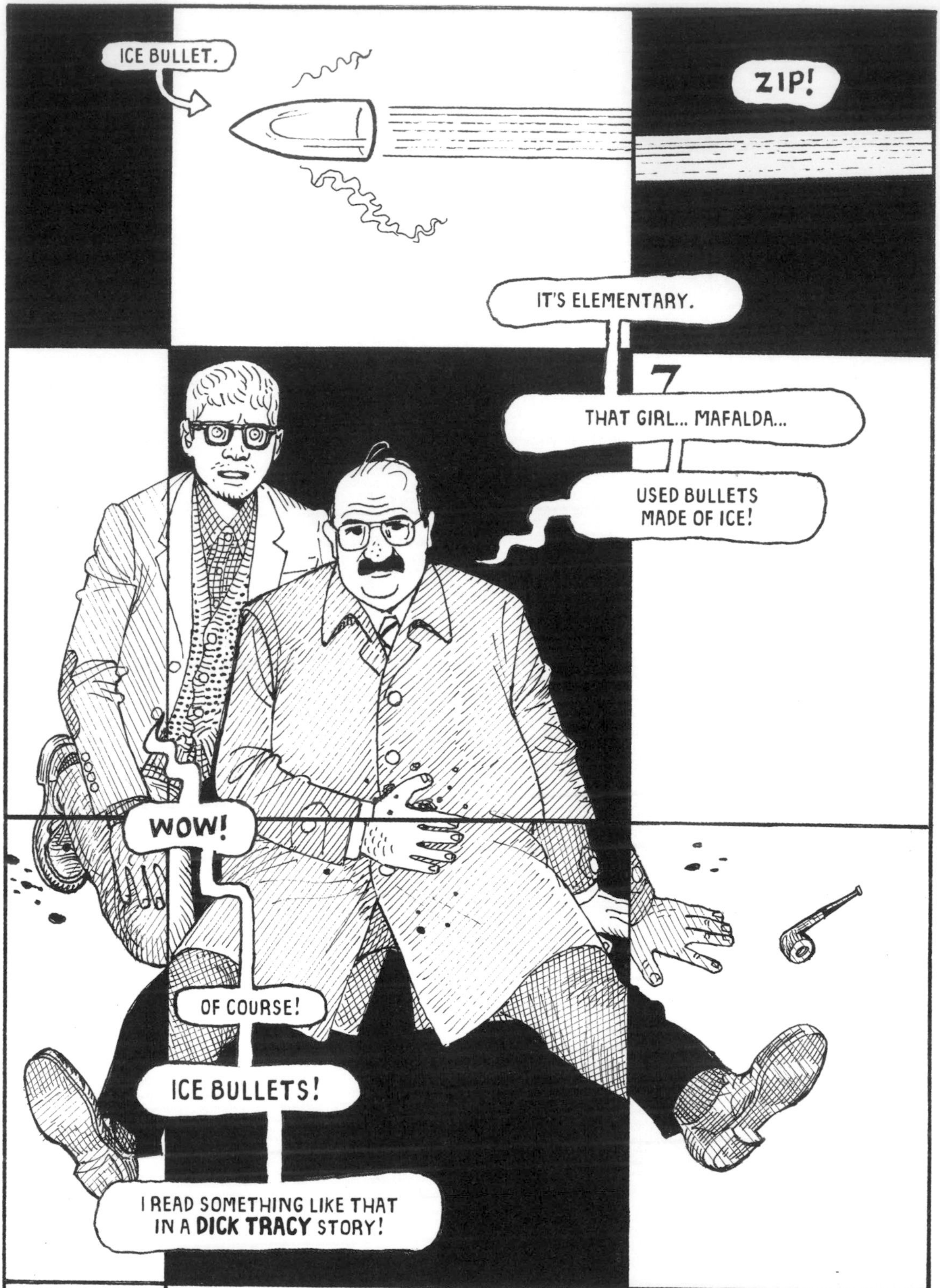
ICE BULLET.
ZIP!
IT'S ELEMENTARY.
7
THAT GIRL... MAFALDA...
USED BULLETS MADE OF ICE!
WOW!
OF COURSE!
ICE BULLETS!
I READ SOMETHING LIKE THAT IN A DICK TRACY STORY!

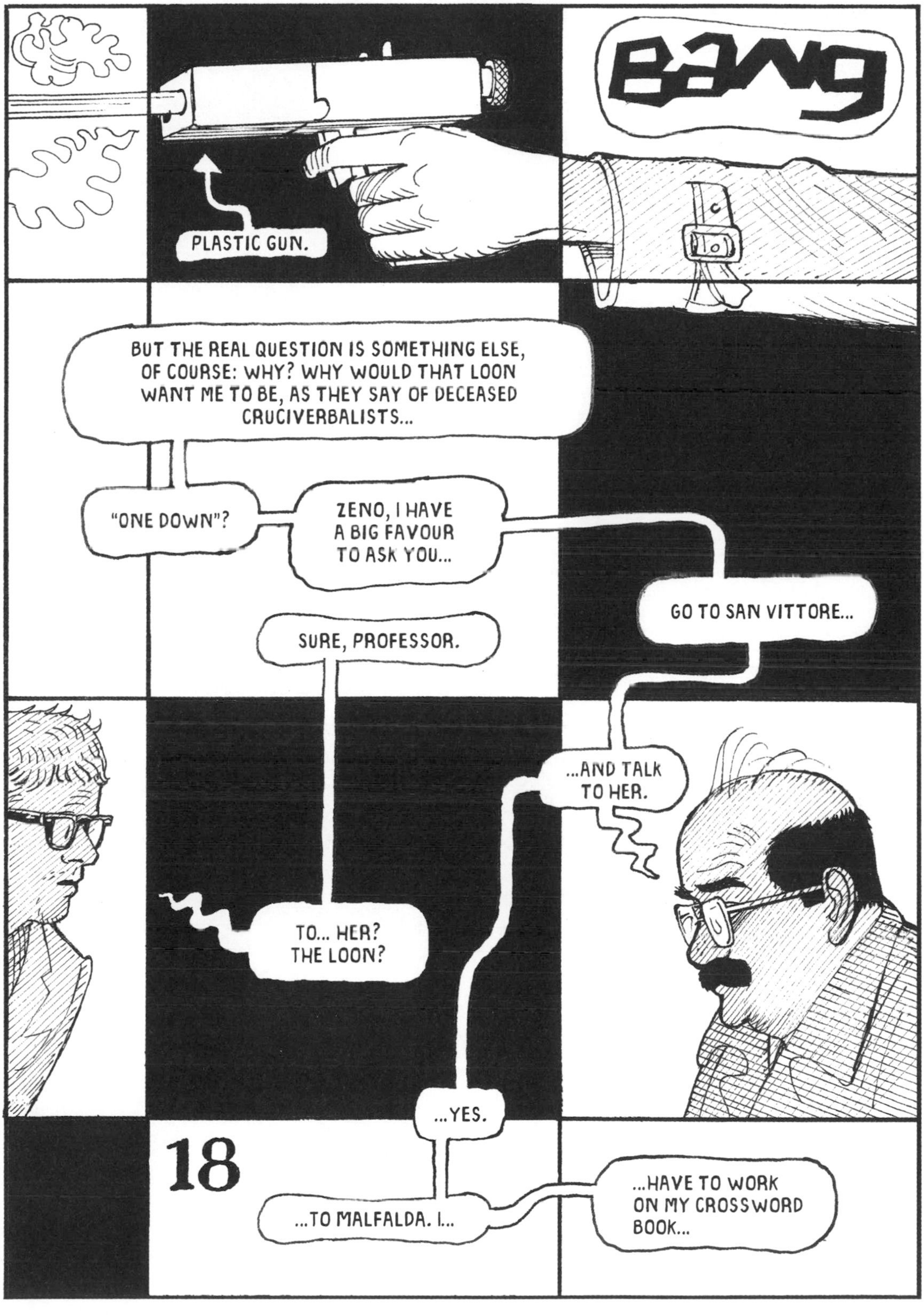
BANG
PLASTIC GUN.
BUT THE REAL QUESTION IS SOMETHING ELSE, OF COURSE: WHY? WHY WOULD THAT LOON WANT ME TO BE, AS THEY SAY OF DECEASED CRUCIVERBALISTS...
"ONE DOWN"?
ZENO, I HAVE A BIG FAVOUR TO ASK YOU...
GO TO SAN VITTORE...
SURE, PROFESSOR.
...AND TALK TO HER.
TO... HER? THE LOON?
...YES.
18
...TO MALFALDA. I...
...HAVE TO WORK ON MY CROSSWORD BOOK...

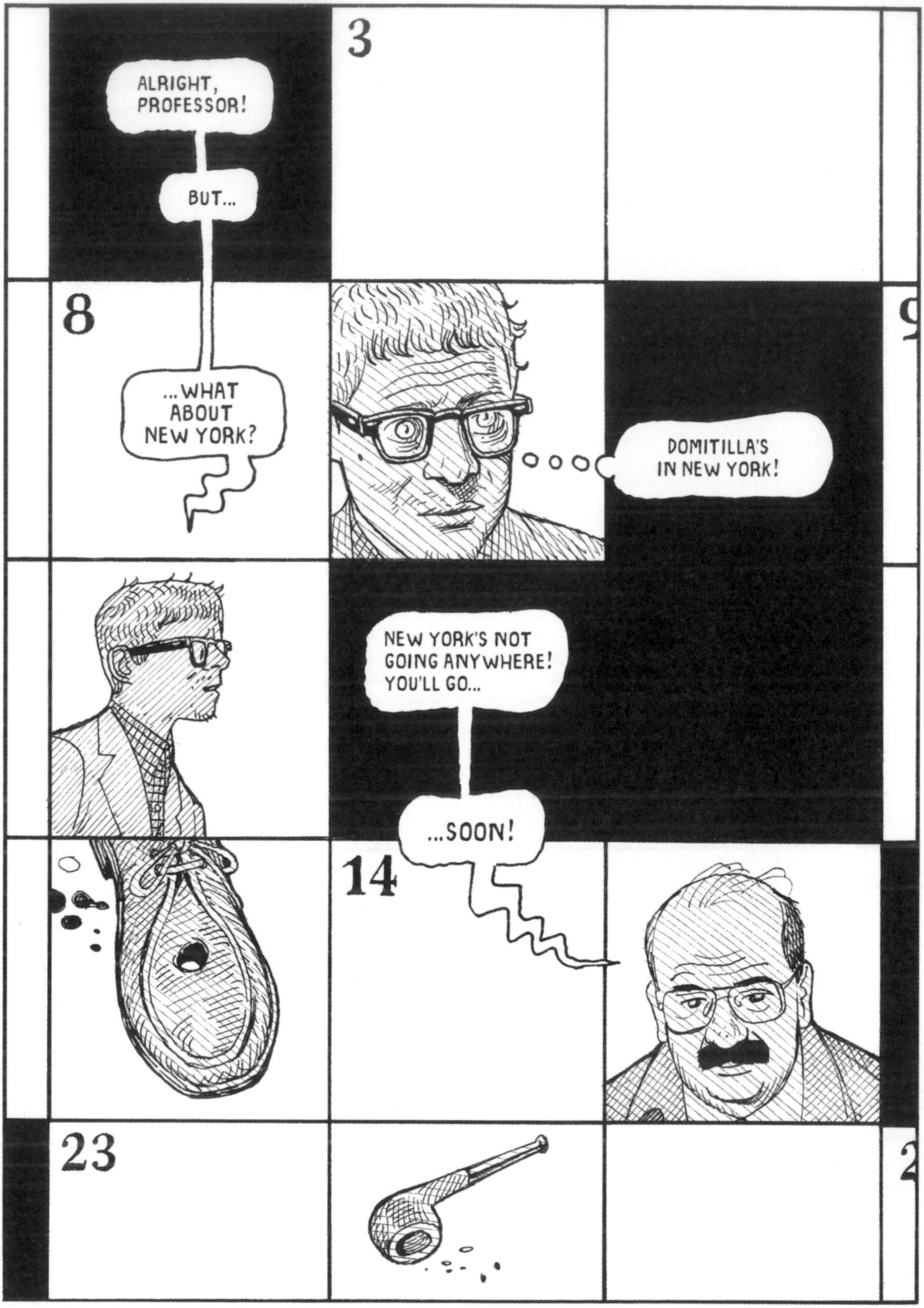
3
ALRIGHT, PROFESSOR!
BUT...
8
...WHAT ABOUT NEW YORK?
DOMITILLA'S IN NEW YORK!
NEW YORK'S NOT GOING ANYWHERE! YOU'LL GO...
...SOON!
14
23

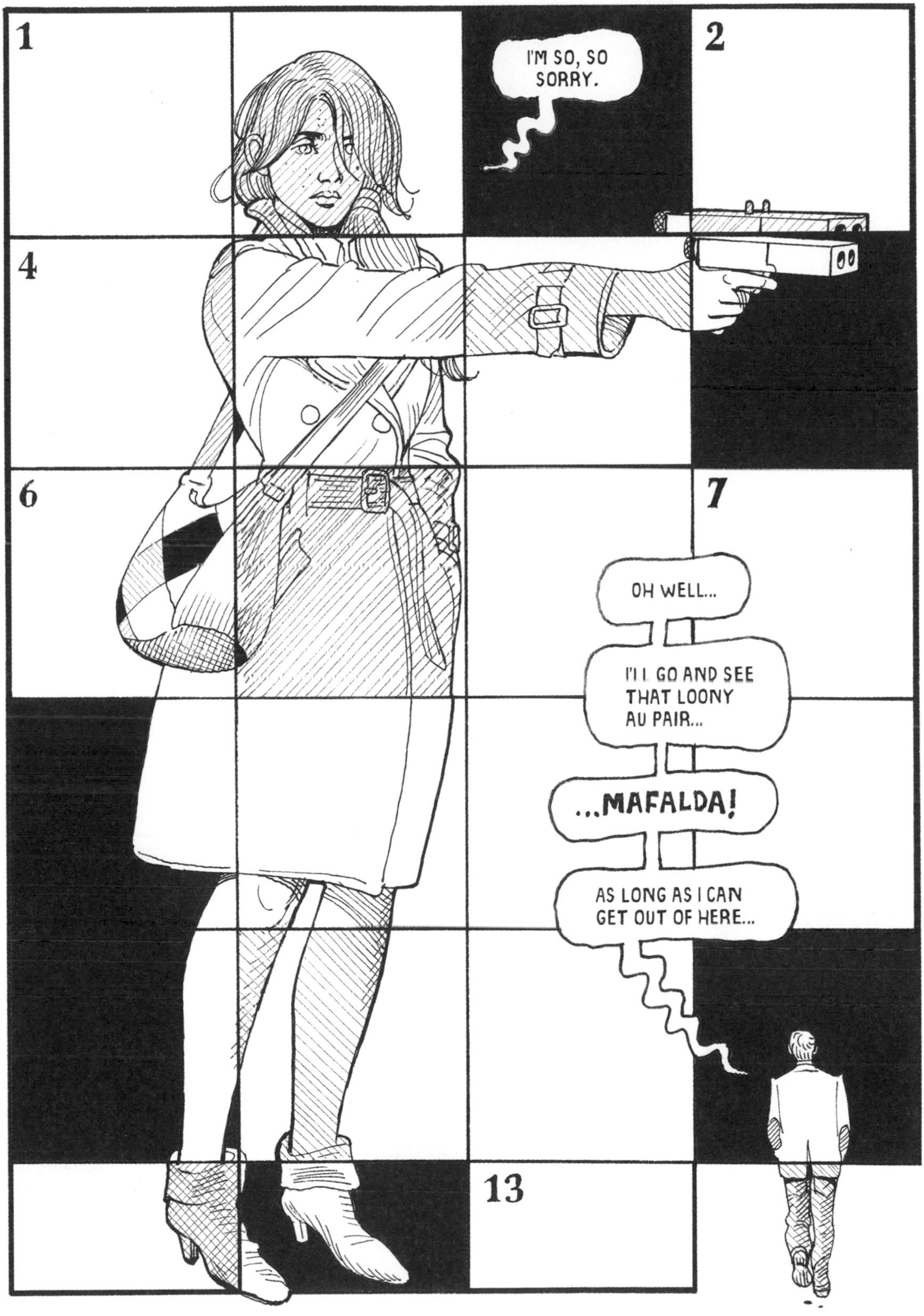
1
2
I'M SO, SO SORRY.
4
6
7
OH WELL...
I'LL GO AND SEE THAT LOONY AU PAIR...
...MAFALDA!
AS LONG AS I CAN GET OUT OF HERE...
13

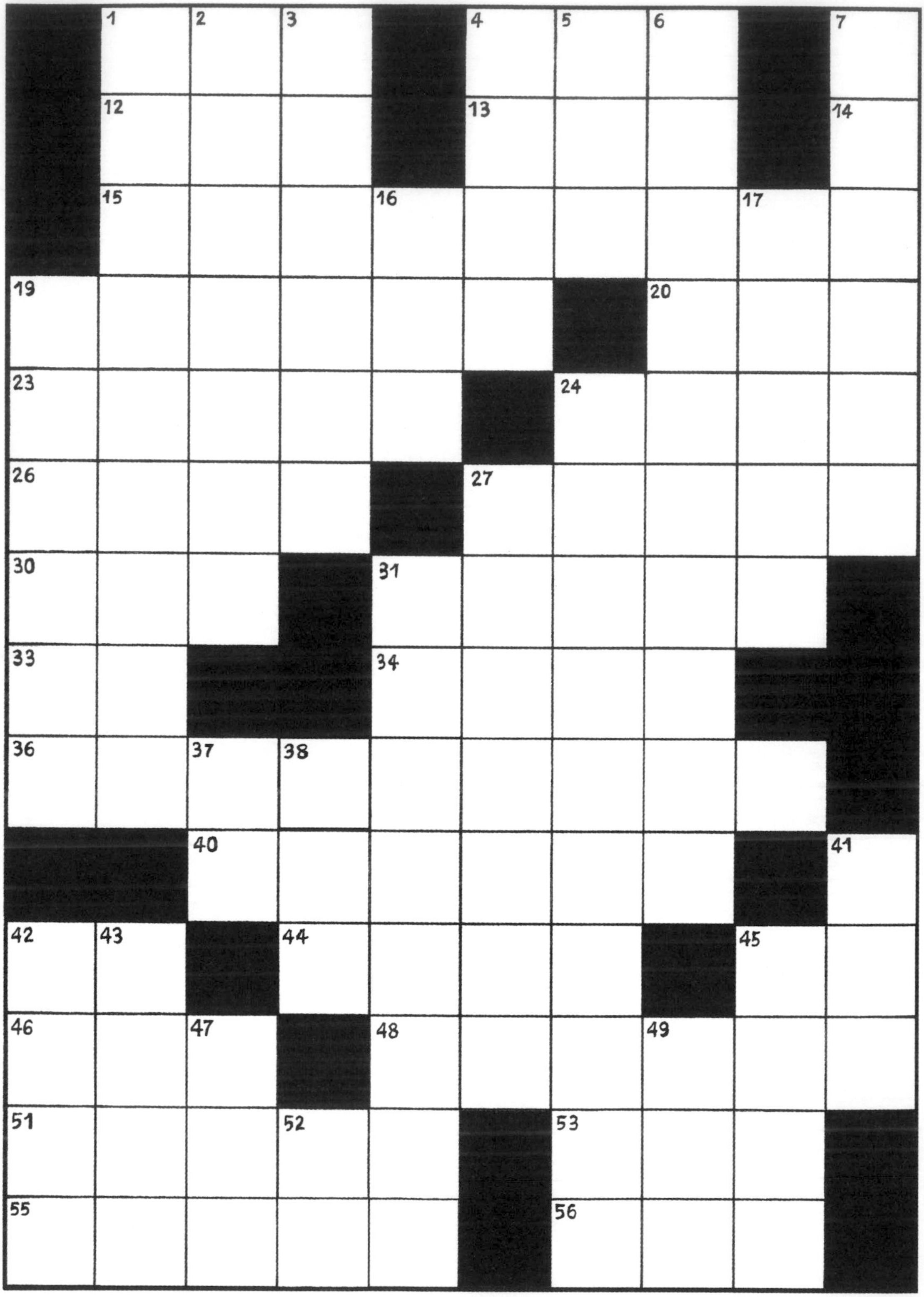

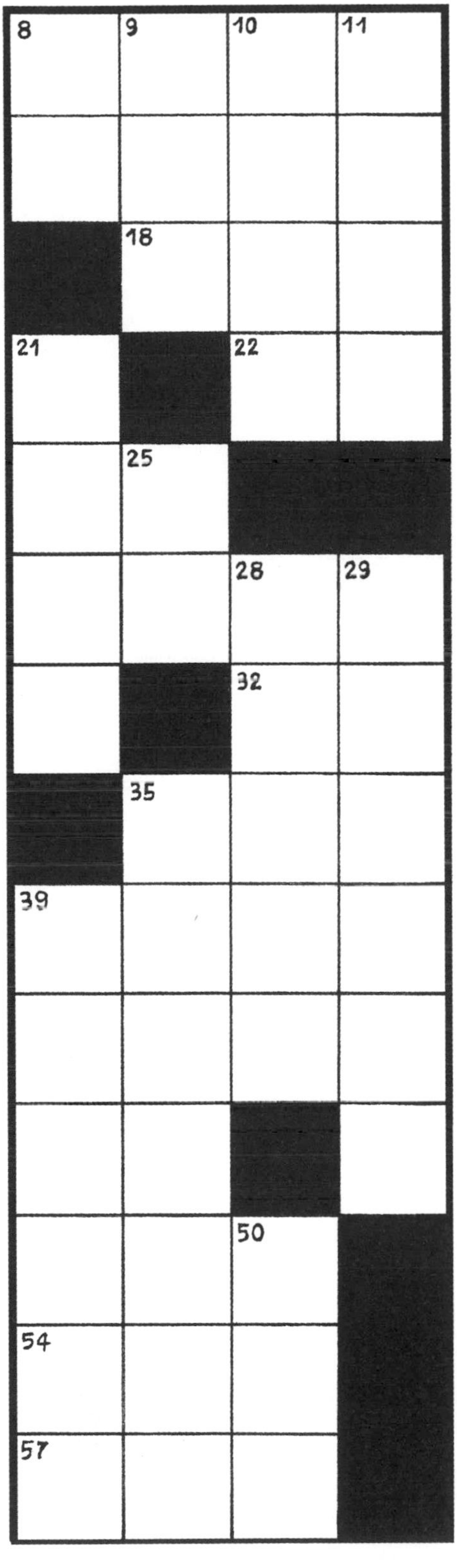
8
9
10
11
18
21
22
25
28
29
32
35
39
50
54
57

PAOLO BACILIERI

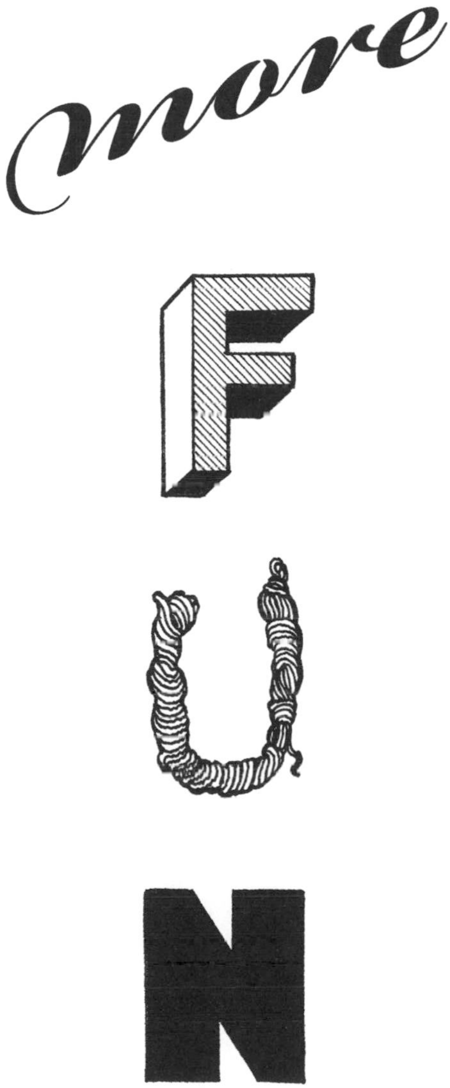
more
FUN

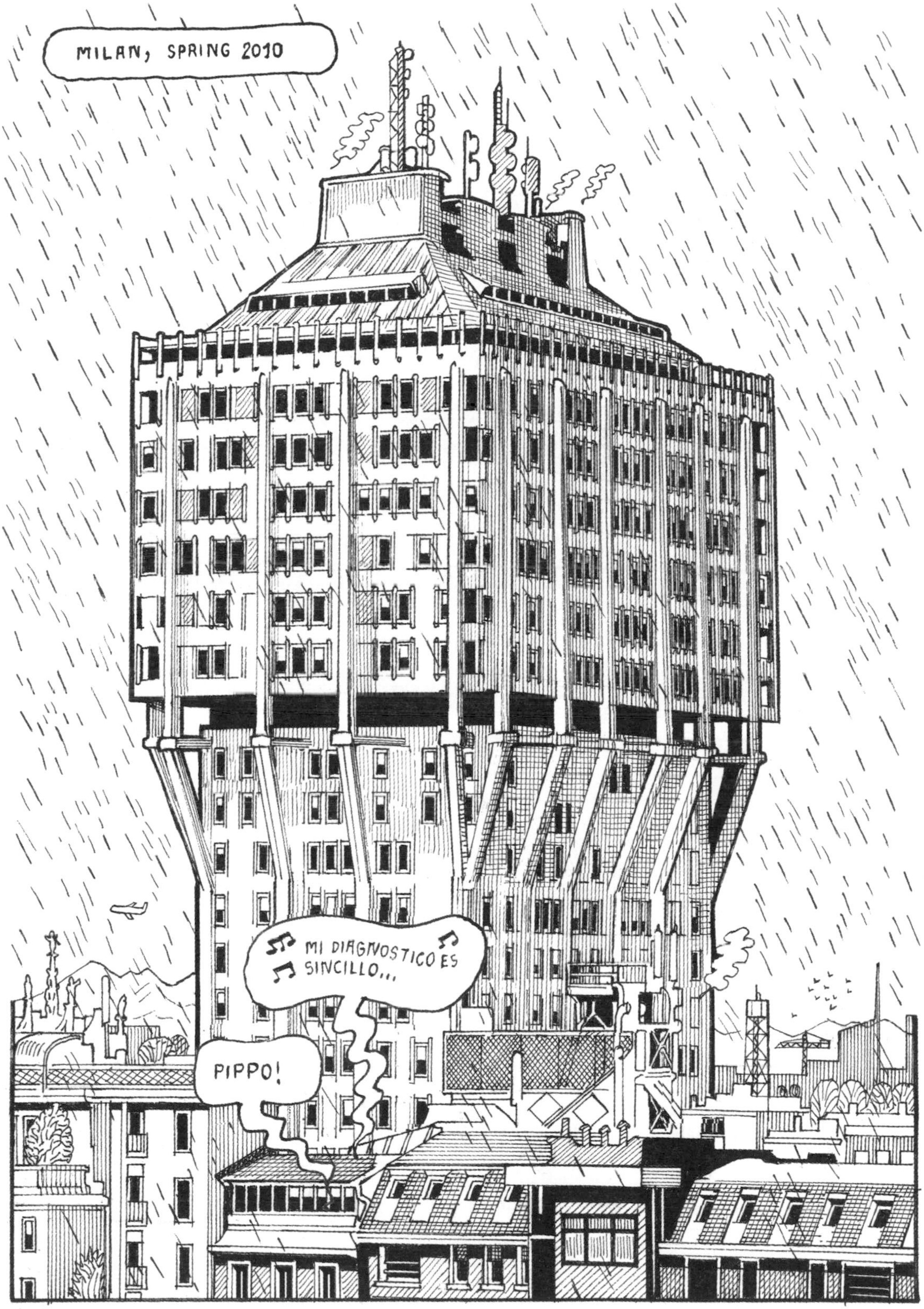
MILAN, SPRING 2010
MI DIAGNOSTICO ES SINCILLO...
PIPPO!

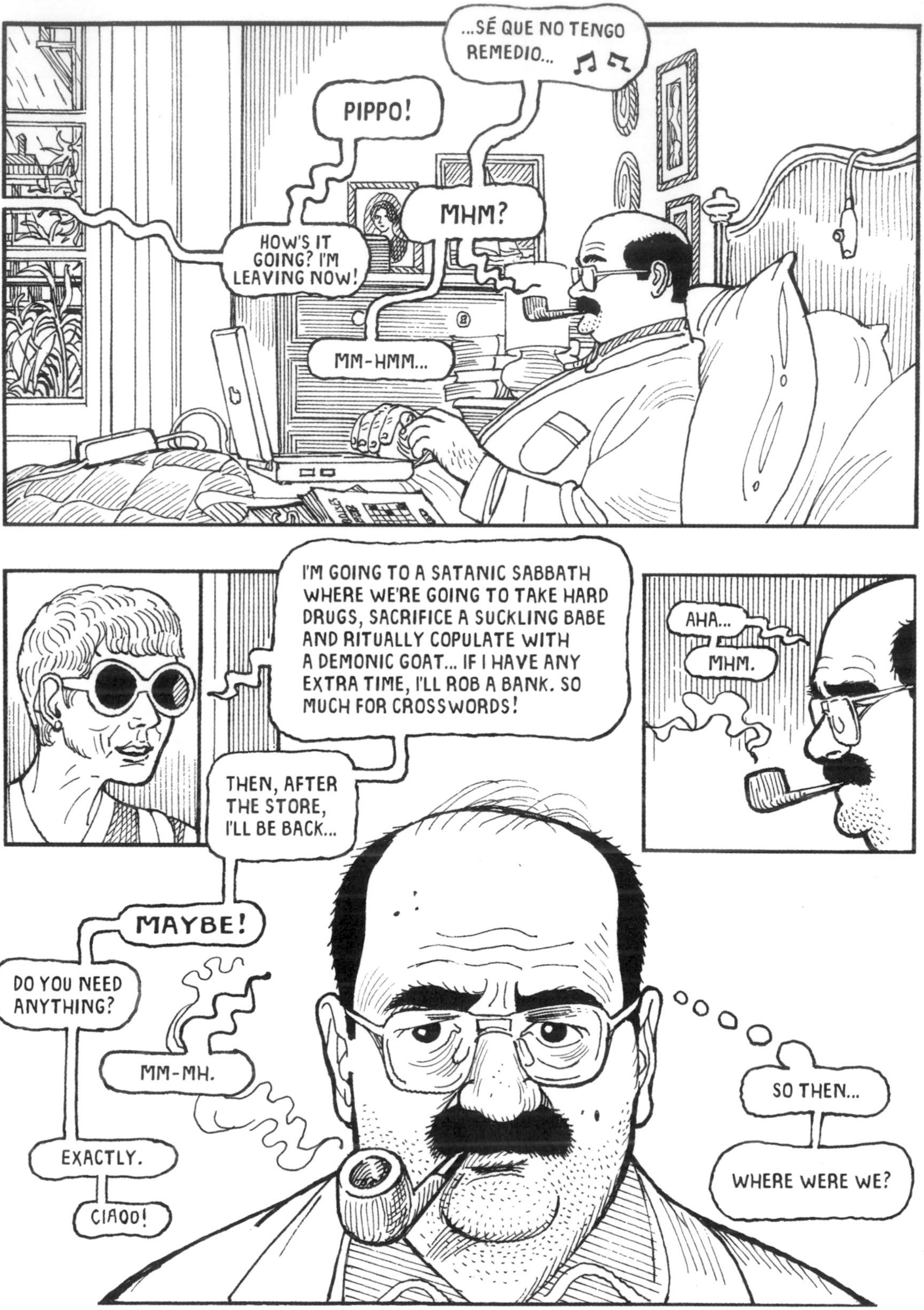
HOW'S IT GOING? I'M LEAVING NOW!
PIPPO!
MHM?
...SÉ QUE NO TENGO REMEDIO...
MM-HMM...
I'M GOING TO A SATANIC SABBATH WHERE WE'RE GOING TO TAKE HARD DRUGS, SACRIFICE A SUCKLING BABE AND RITUALLY COPULATE WITH A DEMONIC GOAT... IF I HAVE ANY EXTRA TIME, I'LL ROB A BANK. SO MUCH FOR CROSSWORDS!
AHA...
MHM.
THEN, AFTER THE STORE, I'LL BE BACK...
MAYBE!
DO YOU NEED ANYTHING?
MM-MH.
EXACTLY.
CIAOO!
SO THEN...
WHERE WERE WE?

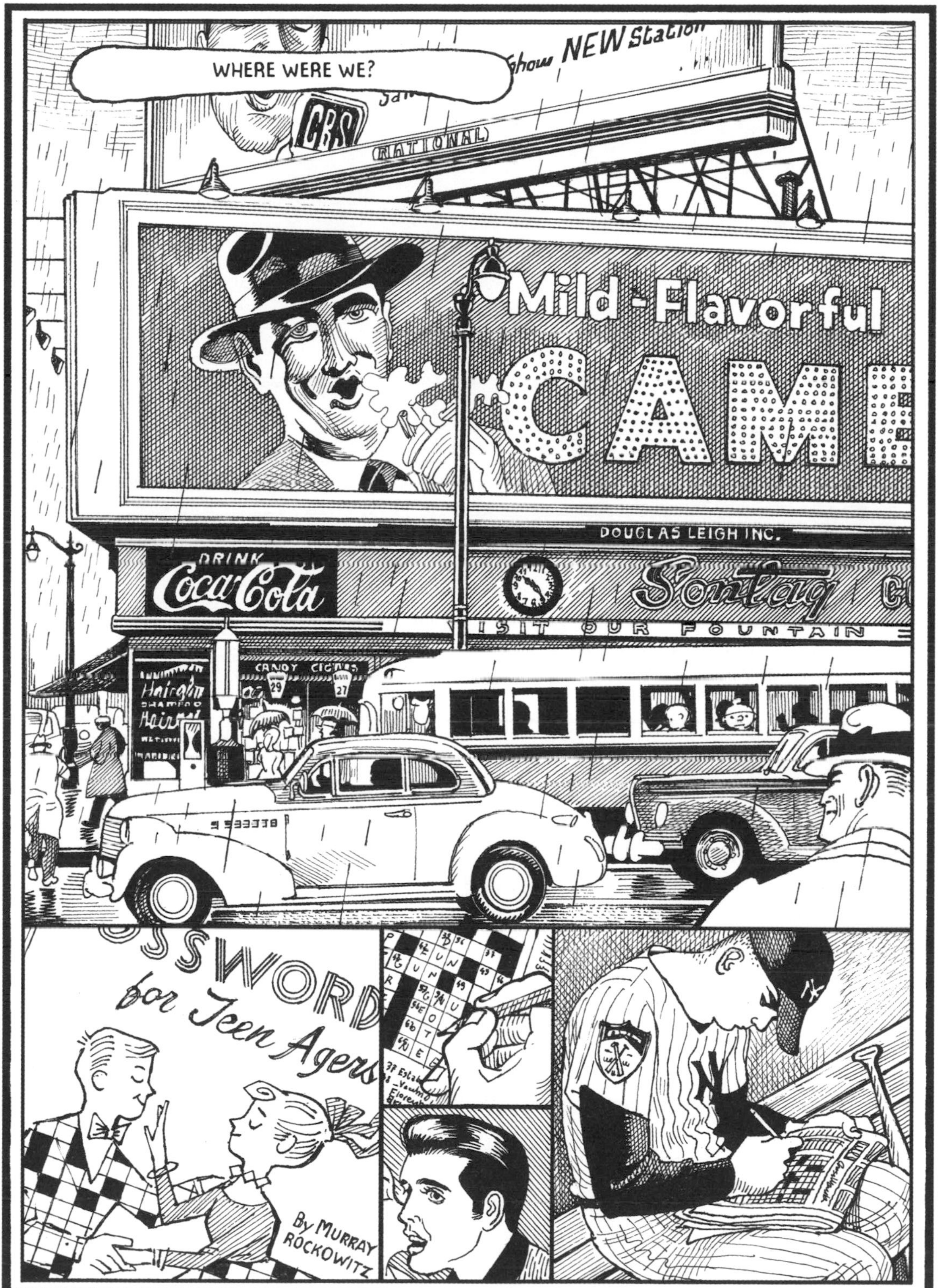

WHERE WERE WE?
Show NEW Station
CBS
NATIONAL
Mild-Flavorful
CAM
DOUGLAS LEIGH INC.
DRINK
Coca-Cola
Sontag
VISIT OUR FOUNTAIN
CANDY CIGARS
SSWORD
for Teen Agers
By MURRAY ROCKOWITZ

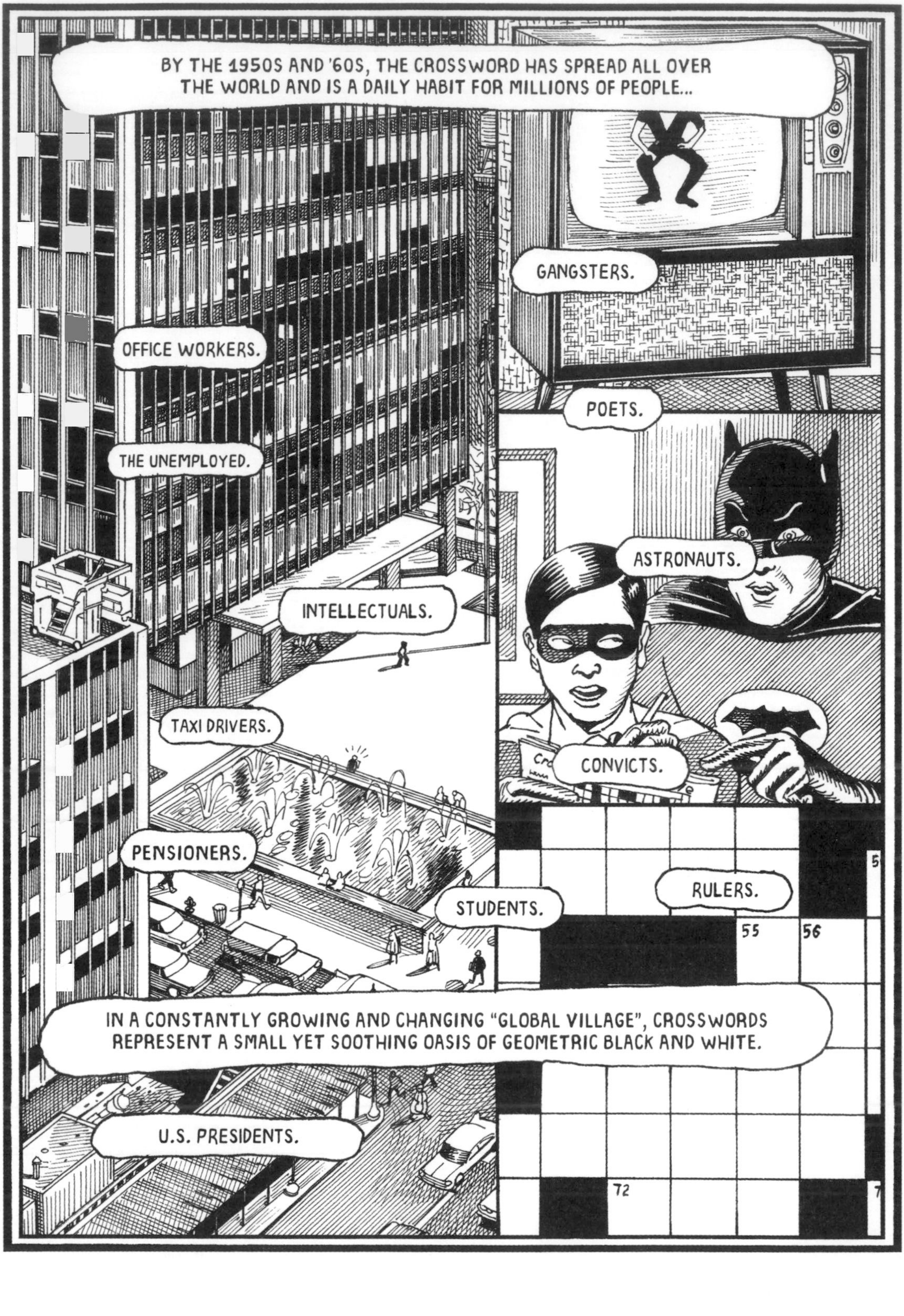

BY THE 1950S AND '60S, THE CROSSWORD HAS SPREAD ALL OVER THE WORLD AND IS A DAILY HABIT FOR MILLIONS OF PEOPLE...
OFFICE WORKERS.
THE UNEMPLOYED.
GANGSTERS.
POETS.
ASTRONAUTS.
INTELLECTUALS.
TAXI DRIVERS.
CONVICTS.
PENSIONERS.
RULERS.
STUDENTS.
55
56
IN A CONSTANTLY GROWING AND CHANGING "GLOBAL VILLAGE", CROSSWORDS REPRESENT A SMALL YET SOOTHING OASIS OF GEOMETRIC BLACK AND WHITE.
U.S. PRESIDENTS.
72

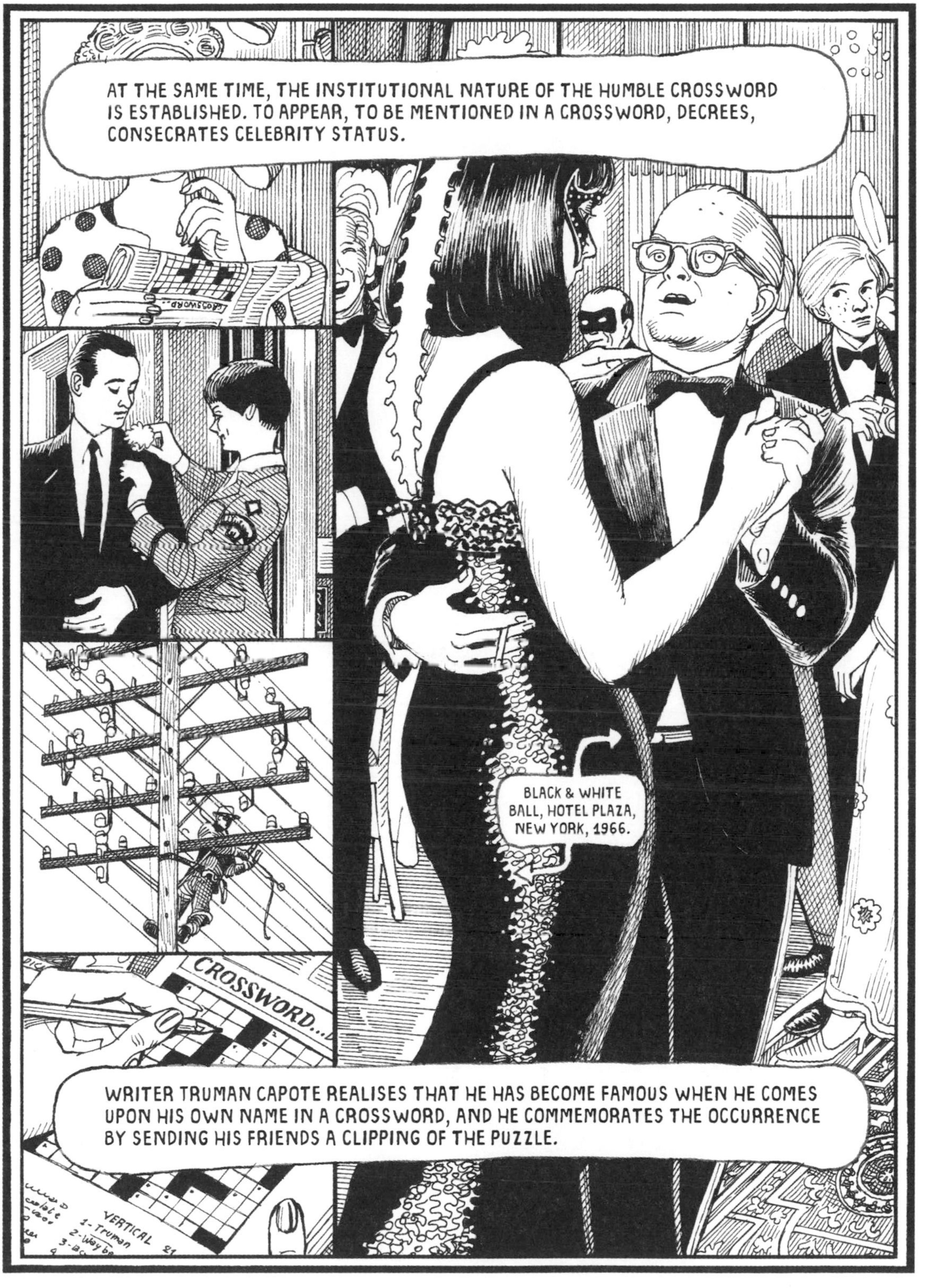
AT THE SAME TIME, THE INSTITUTIONAL NATURE OF THE HUMBLE CROSSWORD IS ESTABLISHED. TO APPEAR, TO BE MENTIONED IN A CROSSWORD, DECREES, CONSECRATES CELEBRITY STATUS.
BLACK & WHITE BALL, HOTEL PLAZA, NEW YORK, 1966.
CROSSWORD...
WRITER TRUMAN CAPOTE REALISES THAT HE HAS BECOME FAMOUS WHEN HE COMES UPON HIS OWN NAME IN A CROSSWORD, AND HE COMMEMORATES THE OCCURRENCE BY SENDING HIS FRIENDS A CLIPPING OF THE PUZZLE.
VERTICAL
1- Truman

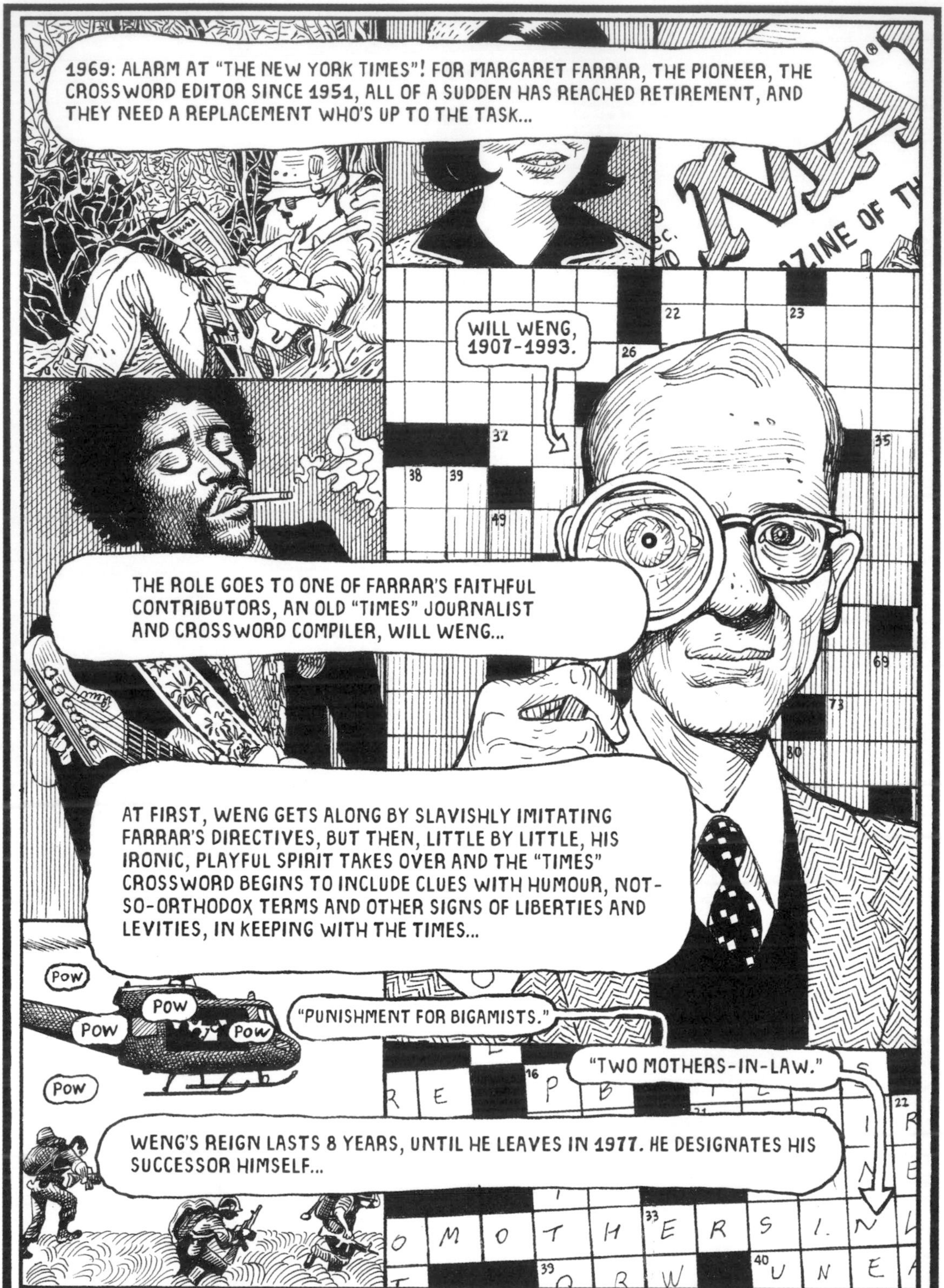
1969: ALARM AT "THE NEW YORK TIMES"! FOR MARGARET FARRAR, THE PIONEER, THE CROSSWORD EDITOR SINCE 1951, ALL OF A SUDDEN HAS REACHED RETIREMENT, AND THEY NEED A REPLACEMENT WHO'S UP TO THE TASK...
WILL WENG, 1907-1993.
THE ROLE GOES TO ONE OF FARRAR'S FAITHFUL CONTRIBUTORS, AN OLD "TIMES" JOURNALIST AND CROSSWORD COMPILER, WILL WENG...
AT FIRST, WENG GETS ALONG BY SLAVISHLY IMITATING FARRAR'S DIRECTIVES, BUT THEN, LITTLE BY LITTLE, HIS IRONIC, PLAYFUL SPIRIT TAKES OVER AND THE "TIMES" CROSSWORD BEGINS TO INCLUDE CLUES WITH HUMOUR, NOT-SO-ORTHODOX TERMS AND OTHER SIGNS OF LIBERTIES AND LEVITIES, IN KEEPING WITH THE TIMES...
POW
POW
POW
POW
POW
"PUNISHMENT FOR BIGAMISTS."
"TWO MOTHERS-IN-LAW."
WENG'S REIGN LASTS 8 YEARS, UNTIL HE LEAVES IN 1977. HE DESIGNATES HIS SUCCESSOR HIMSELF...

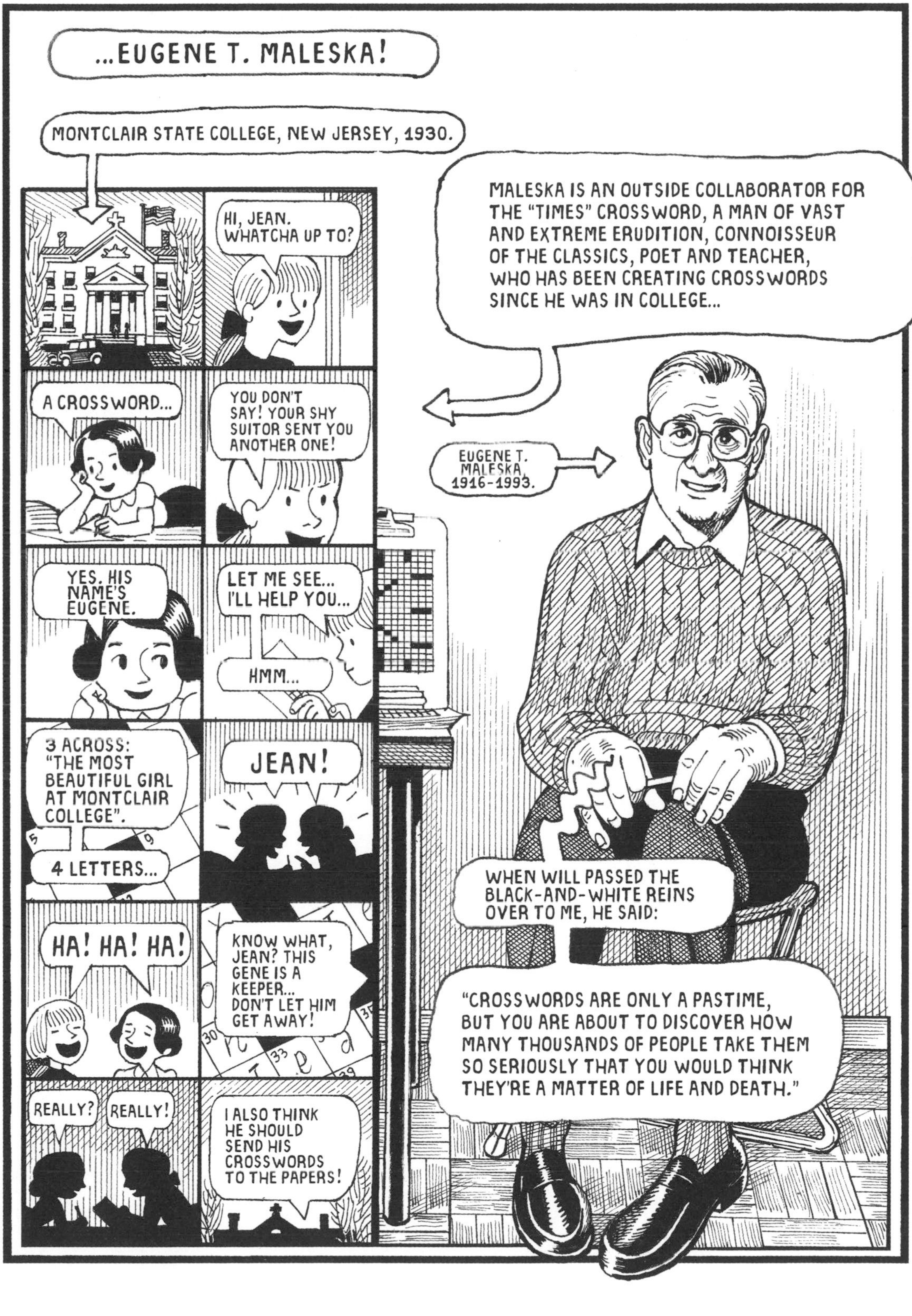
...EUGENE T. MALESKA!
MONTCLAIR STATE COLLEGE, NEW JERSEY, 1930.
HI, JEAN. WHATCHA UP TO?
A CROSSWORD...
YOU DON'T SAY! YOUR SHY SUITOR SENT YOU ANOTHER ONE!
YES. HIS NAME'S EUGENE.
LET ME SEE... I'LL HELP YOU...
HMM...
3 ACROSS: "THE MOST BEAUTIFUL GIRL AT MONTCLAIR COLLEGE".
4 LETTERS...
JEAN!
HA! HA! HA!
KNOW WHAT, JEAN? THIS GENE IS A KEEPER... DON'T LET HIM GET AWAY!
REALLY?
REALLY!
I ALSO THINK HE SHOULD SEND HIS CROSSWORDS TO THE PAPERS!
MALESKA IS AN OUTSIDE COLLABORATOR FOR THE "TIMES" CROSSWORD, A MAN OF VAST AND EXTREME ERUDITION, CONNOISSEUR OF THE CLASSICS, POET AND TEACHER, WHO HAS BEEN CREATING CROSSWORDS SINCE HE WAS IN COLLEGE...
EUGENE T. MALESKA, 1916-1993.
WHEN WILL PASSED THE BLACK-AND-WHITE REINS OVER TO ME, HE SAID:
"CROSSWORDS ARE ONLY A PASTIME, BUT YOU ARE ABOUT TO DISCOVER HOW MANY THOUSANDS OF PEOPLE TAKE THEM SO SERIOUSLY THAT YOU WOULD THINK THEY'RE A MATTER OF LIFE AND DEATH."

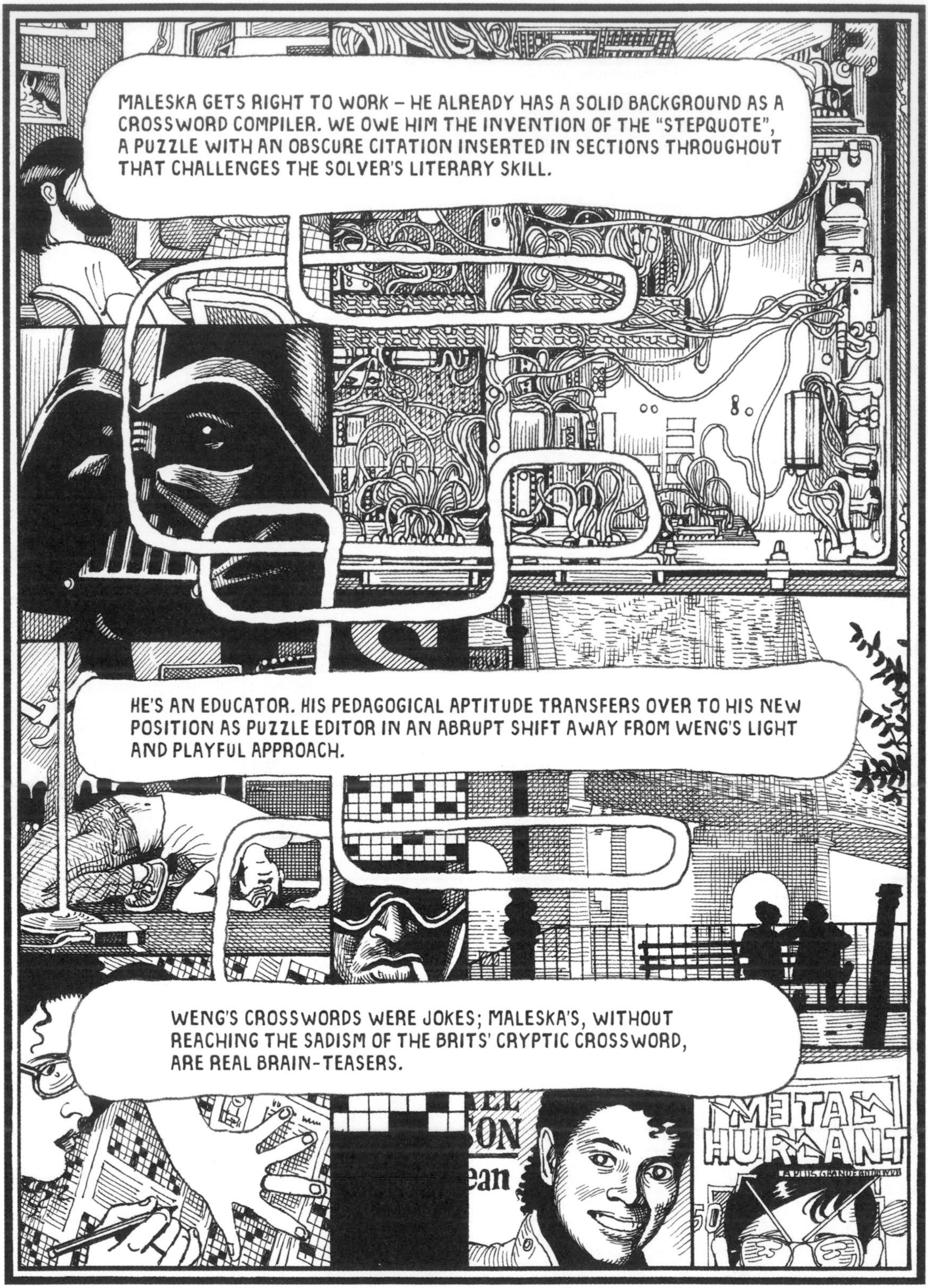
MALESKA GETS RIGHT TO WORK – HE ALREADY HAS A SOLID BACKGROUND AS A CROSSWORD COMPILER. WE OWE HIM THE INVENTION OF THE "STEPQUOTE", A PUZZLE WITH AN OBSCURE CITATION INSERTED IN SECTIONS THROUGHOUT THAT CHALLENGES THE SOLVER'S LITERARY SKILL.
HE'S AN EDUCATOR. HIS PEDAGOGICAL APTITUDE TRANSFERS OVER TO HIS NEW POSITION AS PUZZLE EDITOR IN AN ABRUPT SHIFT AWAY FROM WENG'S LIGHT AND PLAYFUL APPROACH.
WENG'S CROSSWORDS WERE JOKES; MALESKA'S, WITHOUT REACHING THE SADISM OF THE BRITS' CRYPTIC CROSSWORD, ARE REAL BRAIN-TEASERS.
METAL HURLANT

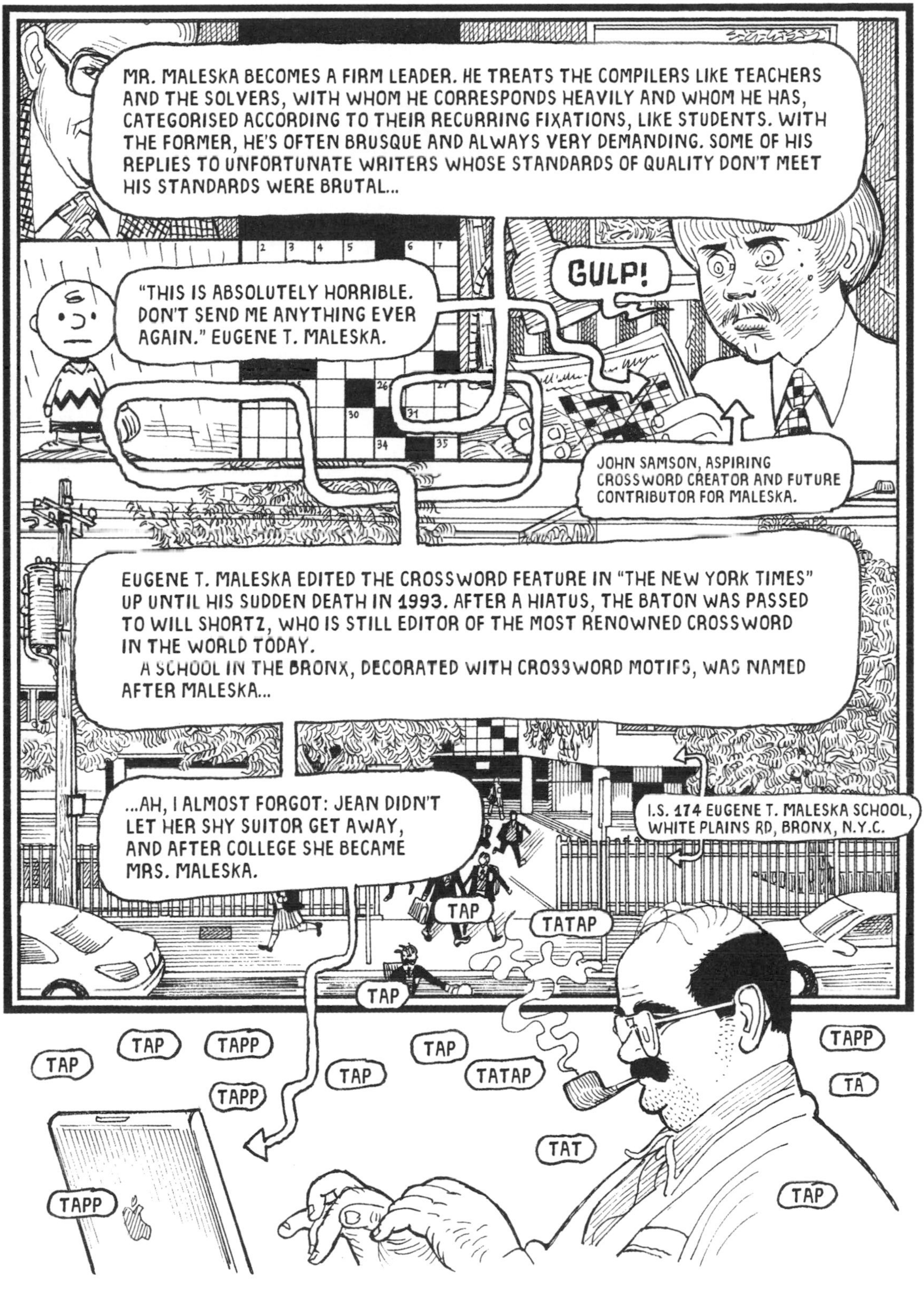
MR. MALESKA BECOMES A FIRM LEADER. HE TREATS THE COMPILERS LIKE TEACHERS AND THE SOLVERS, WITH WHOM HE CORRESPONDS HEAVILY AND WHOM HE HAS, CATEGORISED ACCORDING TO THEIR RECURRING FIXATIONS, LIKE STUDENTS. WITH THE FORMER, HE'S OFTEN BRUSQUE AND ALWAYS VERY DEMANDING. SOME OF HIS REPLIES TO UNFORTUNATE WRITERS WHOSE STANDARDS OF QUALITY DON'T MEET HIS STANDARDS WERE BRUTAL...
"THIS IS ABSOLUTELY HORRIBLE. DON'T SEND ME ANYTHING EVER AGAIN." EUGENE T. MALESKA.
GULP!
JOHN SAMSON, ASPIRING CROSSWORD CREATOR AND FUTURE CONTRIBUTOR FOR MALESKA.
EUGENE T. MALESKA EDITED THE CROSSWORD FEATURE IN "THE NEW YORK TIMES" UP UNTIL HIS SUDDEN DEATH IN 1993. AFTER A HIATUS, THE BATON WAS PASSED TO WILL SHORTZ, WHO IS STILL EDITOR OF THE MOST RENOWNED CROSSWORD IN THE WORLD TODAY.
A SCHOOL IN THE BRONX, DECORATED WITH CROSSWORD MOTIFS, WAS NAMED AFTER MALESKA...
...AH, I ALMOST FORGOT: JEAN DIDN'T LET HER SHY SUITOR GET AWAY, AND AFTER COLLEGE SHE BECAME MRS. MALESKA.
I.S. 174 EUGENE T. MALESKA SCHOOL, WHITE PLAINS RD, BRONX, N.Y.C.
TAP
TATAP
TAP
TAP
TAP
TAPP
TAPP
TAP
TAP
TATAP
TAPP
TA
TAT
TAPP
TAP

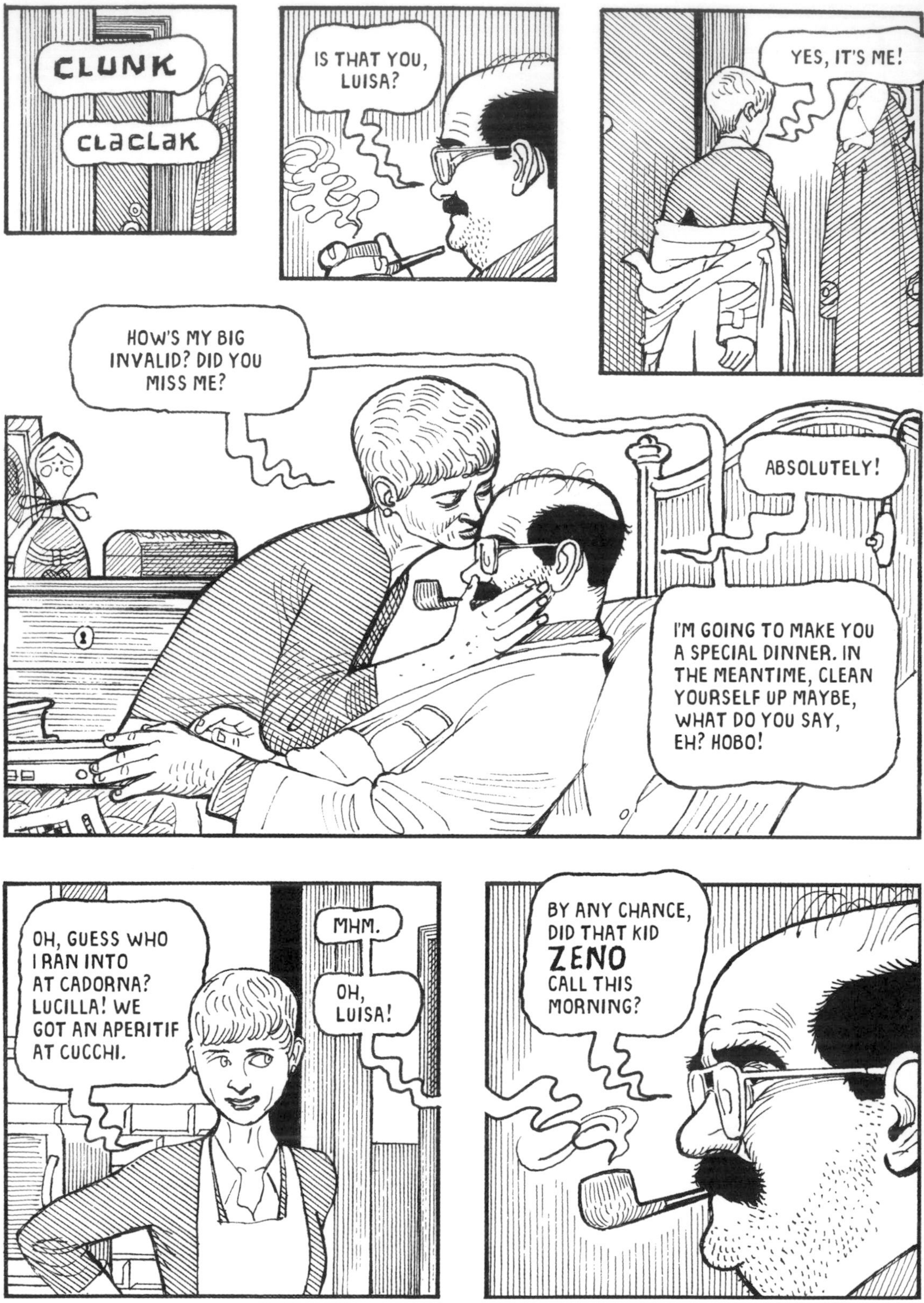
CLUNK
CLACLAK
IS THAT YOU, LUISA?
YES, IT'S ME!
HOW'S MY BIG INVALID? DID YOU MISS ME?
ABSOLUTELY!
I'M GOING TO MAKE YOU A SPECIAL DINNER. IN THE MEANTIME, CLEAN YOURSELF UP MAYBE, WHAT DO YOU SAY, EH? HOBO!
OH, GUESS WHO I RAN INTO AT CADORNA? LUCILLA! WE GOT AN APERITIF AT CUCCHI.
MHM.
OH, LUISA!
BY ANY CHANCE, DID THAT KID ZENO CALL THIS MORNING?

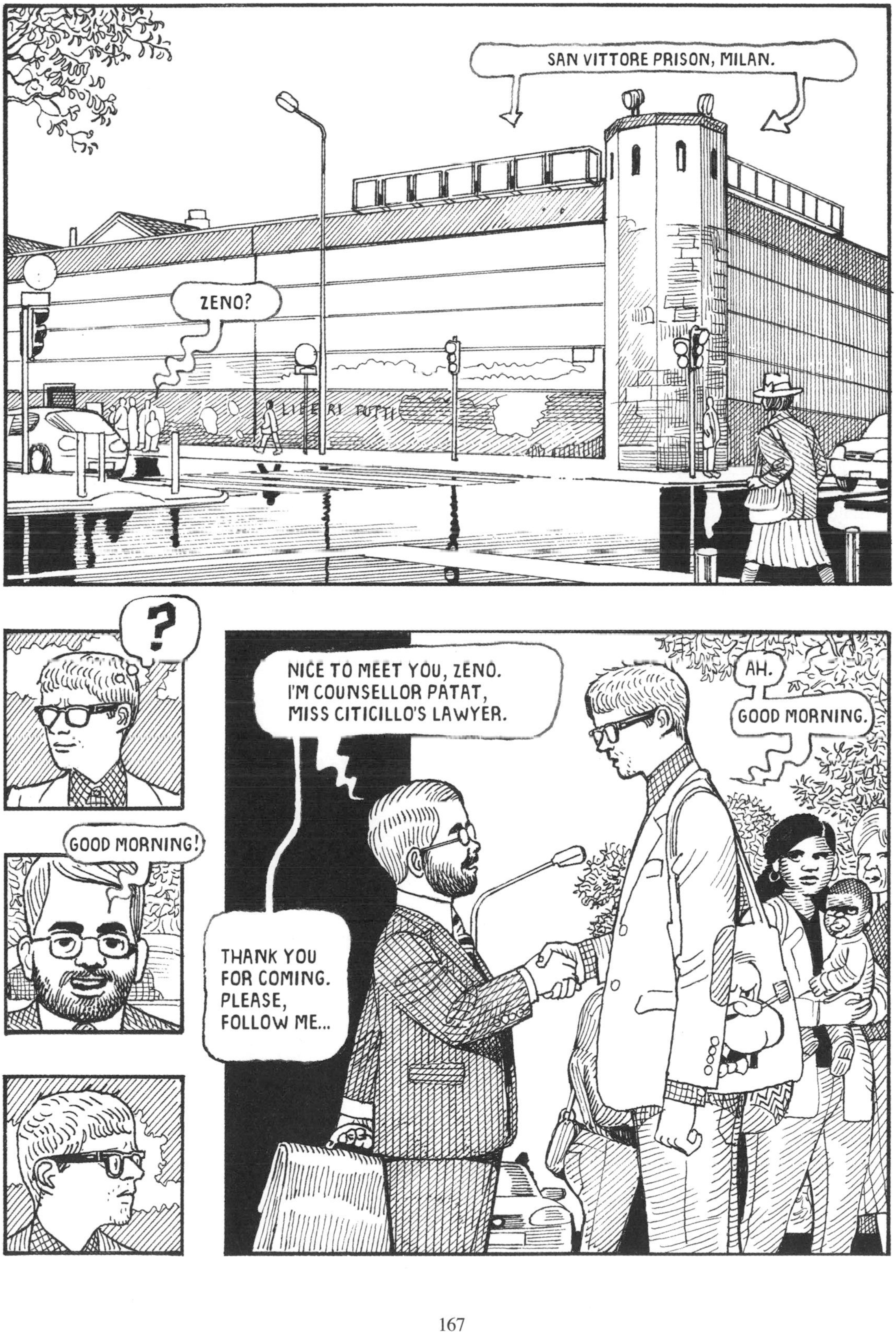
SAN VITTORE PRISON, MILAN.
ZENO?
?
GOOD MORNING!
NICE TO MEET YOU, ZENO. I'M COUNSELLOR PATAT, MISS CITICILLO'S LAWYER.
AH.
GOOD MORNING.
THANK YOU FOR COMING. PLEASE, FOLLOW ME...

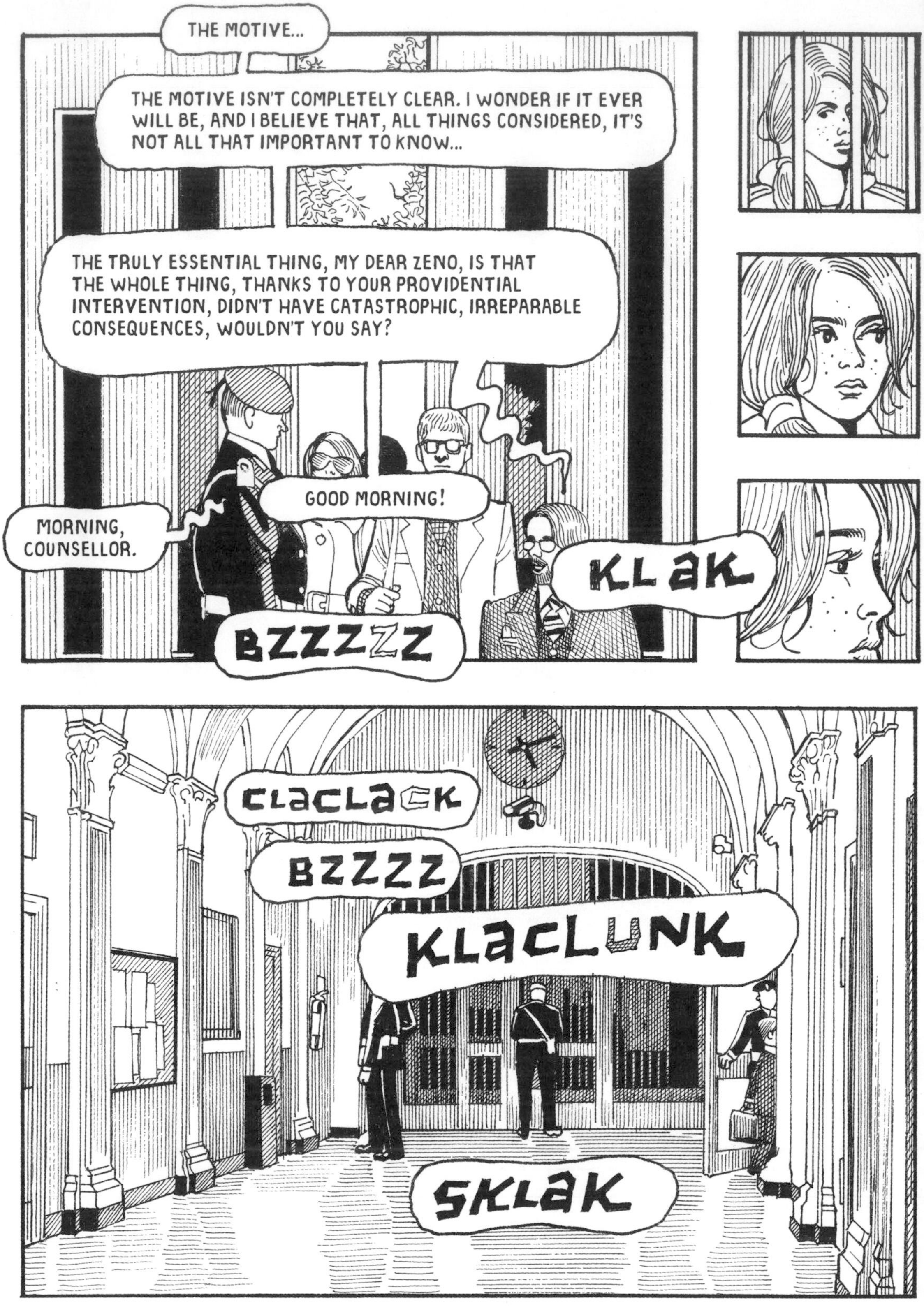
THE MOTIVE...
THE MOTIVE ISN'T COMPLETELY CLEAR. I WONDER IF IT EVER WILL BE, AND I BELIEVE THAT, ALL THINGS CONSIDERED, IT'S NOT ALL THAT IMPORTANT TO KNOW...
THE TRULY ESSENTIAL THING, MY DEAR ZENO, IS THAT THE WHOLE THING, THANKS TO YOUR PROVIDENTIAL INTERVENTION, DIDN'T HAVE CATASTROPHIC, IRREPARABLE CONSEQUENCES, WOULDN'T YOU SAY?
GOOD MORNING!
MORNING, COUNSELLOR.
BZZZZZ
KLAK
CLACLACK
BZZZZ
KLACLUNK
SKLAK

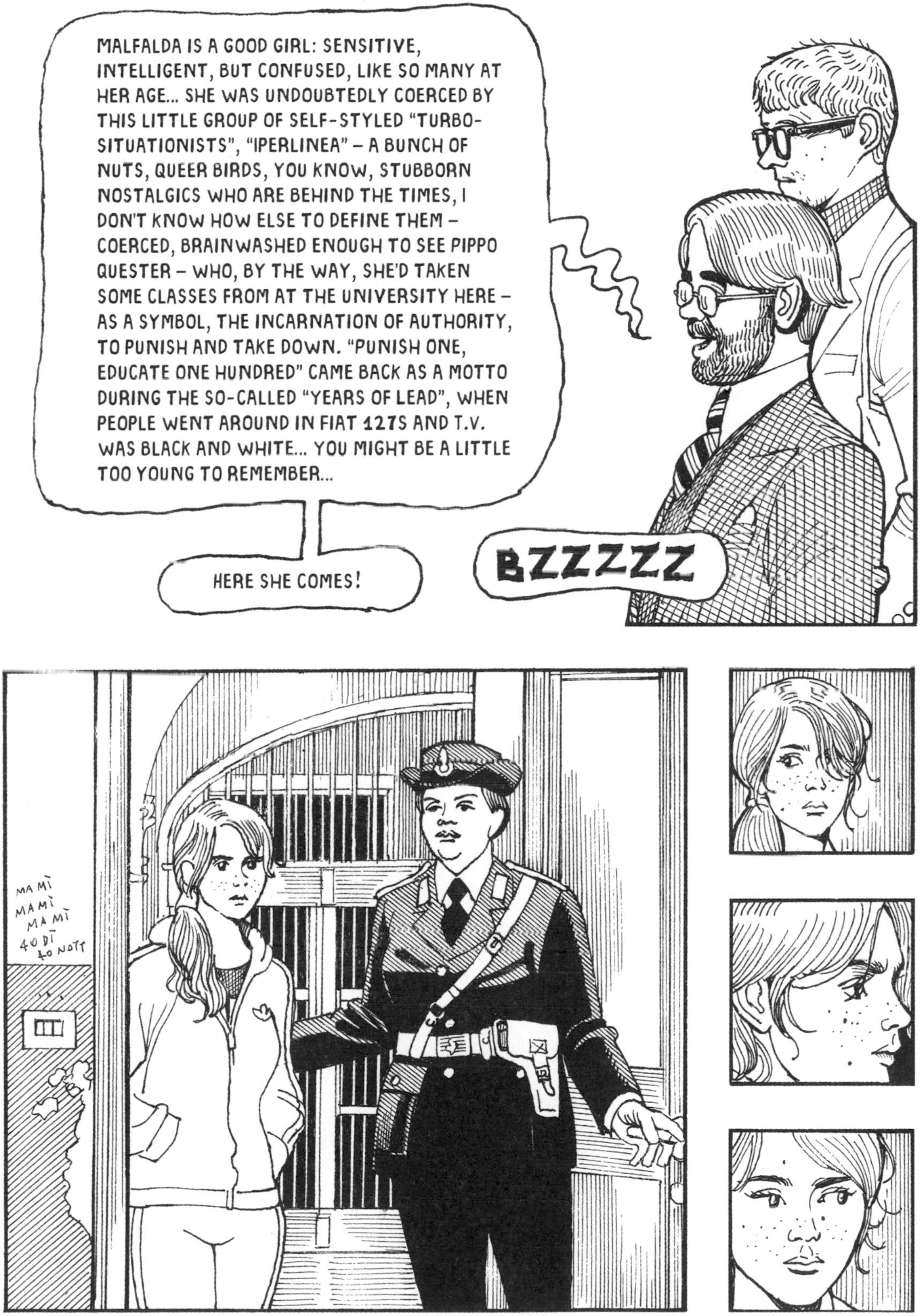
MALFALDA IS A GOOD GIRL: SENSITIVE, INTELLIGENT, BUT CONFUSED, LIKE SO MANY AT HER AGE... SHE WAS UNDOUBTEDLY COERCED BY THIS LITTLE GROUP OF SELF-STYLED "TURBO-SITUATIONISTS", "IPERLINEA" – A BUNCH OF NUTS, QUEER BIRDS, YOU KNOW, STUBBORN NOSTALGICS WHO ARE BEHIND THE TIMES, I DON'T KNOW HOW ELSE TO DEFINE THEM – COERCED, BRAINWASHED ENOUGH TO SEE PIPPO QUESTER – WHO, BY THE WAY, SHE'D TAKEN SOME CLASSES FROM AT THE UNIVERSITY HERE – AS A SYMBOL, THE INCARNATION OF AUTHORITY, TO PUNISH AND TAKE DOWN. "PUNISH ONE, EDUCATE ONE HUNDRED" CAME BACK AS A MOTTO DURING THE SO-CALLED "YEARS OF LEAD", WHEN PEOPLE WENT AROUND IN FIAT 127S AND T.V. WAS BLACK AND WHITE... YOU MIGHT BE A LITTLE TOO YOUNG TO REMEMBER...
HERE SHE COMES!
BZZZZZ
MA MÌ
MA MÌ
MA MÌ
40 DÌ
40 NOTT

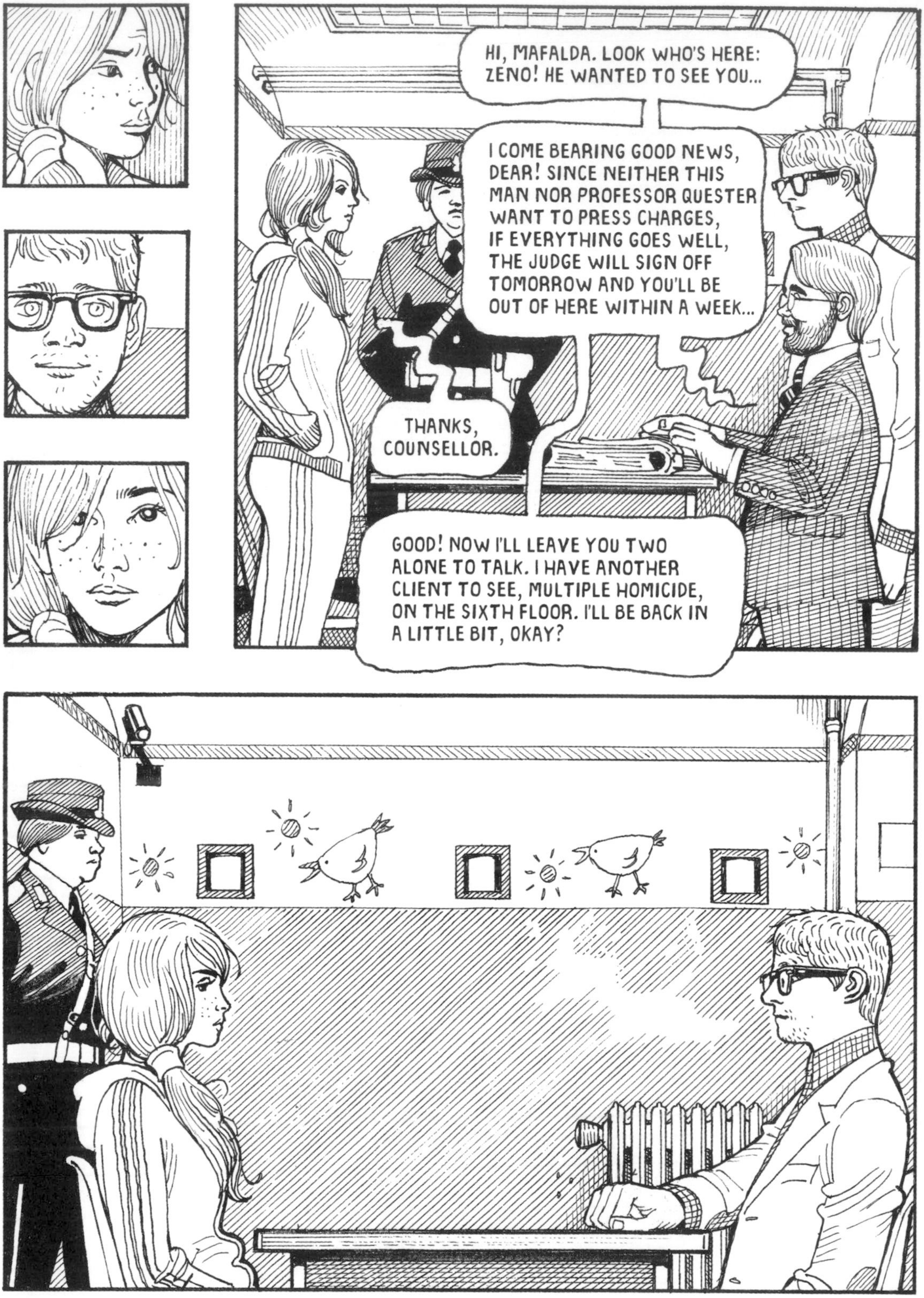
HI, MAFALDA. LOOK WHO'S HERE: ZENO! HE WANTED TO SEE YOU...
I COME BEARING GOOD NEWS, DEAR! SINCE NEITHER THIS MAN NOR PROFESSOR QUESTER WANT TO PRESS CHARGES, IF EVERYTHING GOES WELL, THE JUDGE WILL SIGN OFF TOMORROW AND YOU'LL BE OUT OF HERE WITHIN A WEEK...
THANKS, COUNSELLOR.
GOOD! NOW I'LL LEAVE YOU TWO ALONE TO TALK. I HAVE ANOTHER CLIENT TO SEE, MULTIPLE HOMICIDE, ON THE SIXTH FLOOR. I'LL BE BACK IN A LITTLE BIT, OKAY?

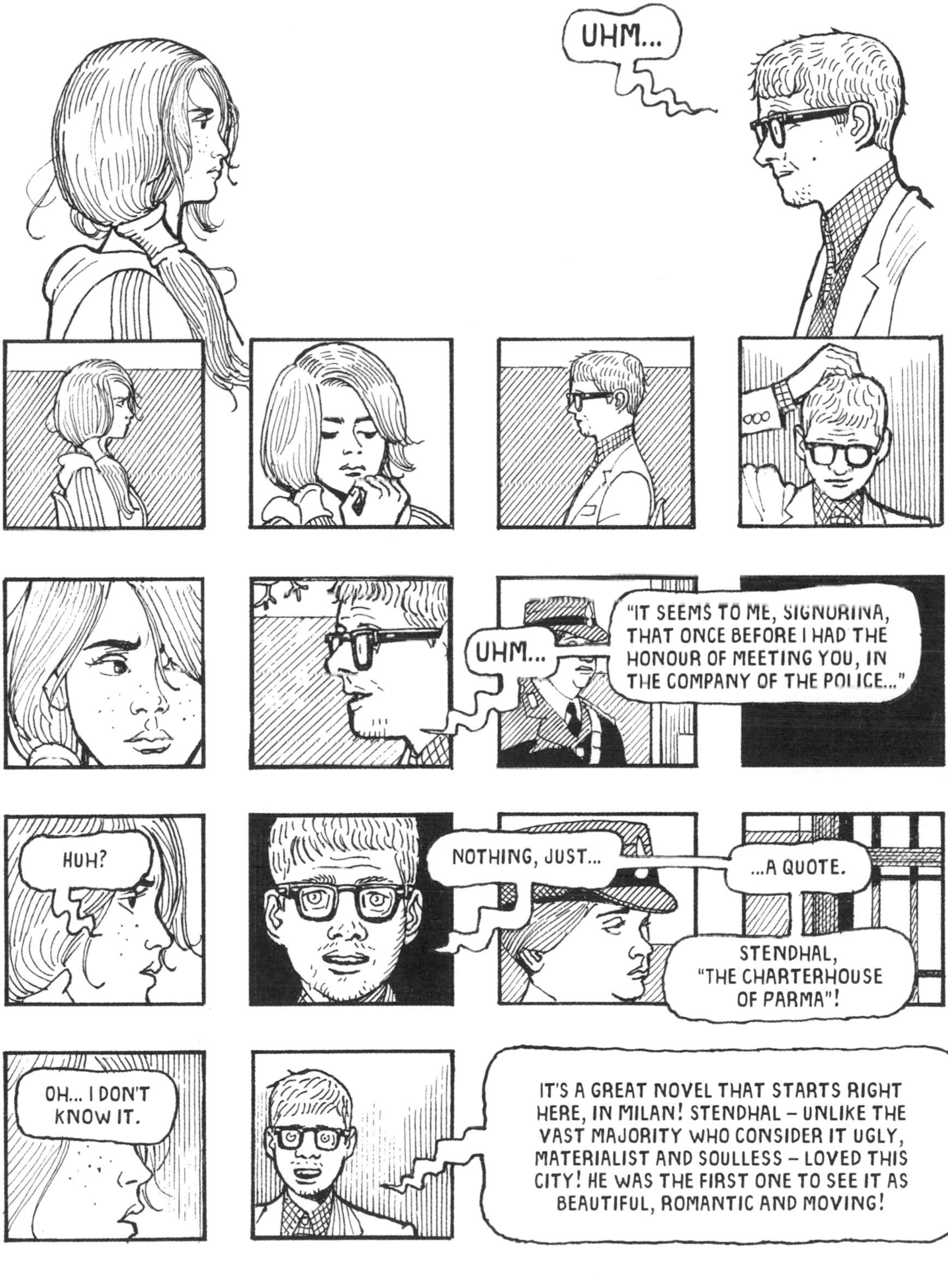

UHM...
UHM...
"IT SEEMS TO ME, SIGNORINA, THAT ONCE BEFORE I HAD THE HONOUR OF MEETING YOU, IN THE COMPANY OF THE POLICE..."
HUH?
NOTHING, JUST...
...A QUOTE.
STENDHAL, "THE CHARTERHOUSE OF PARMA"!
OH... I DON'T KNOW IT.
IT'S A GREAT NOVEL THAT STARTS RIGHT HERE, IN MILAN! STENDHAL – UNLIKE THE VAST MAJORITY WHO CONSIDER IT UGLY, MATERIALIST AND SOULLESS – LOVED THIS CITY! HE WAS THE FIRST ONE TO SEE IT AS BEAUTIFUL, ROMANTIC AND MOVING!

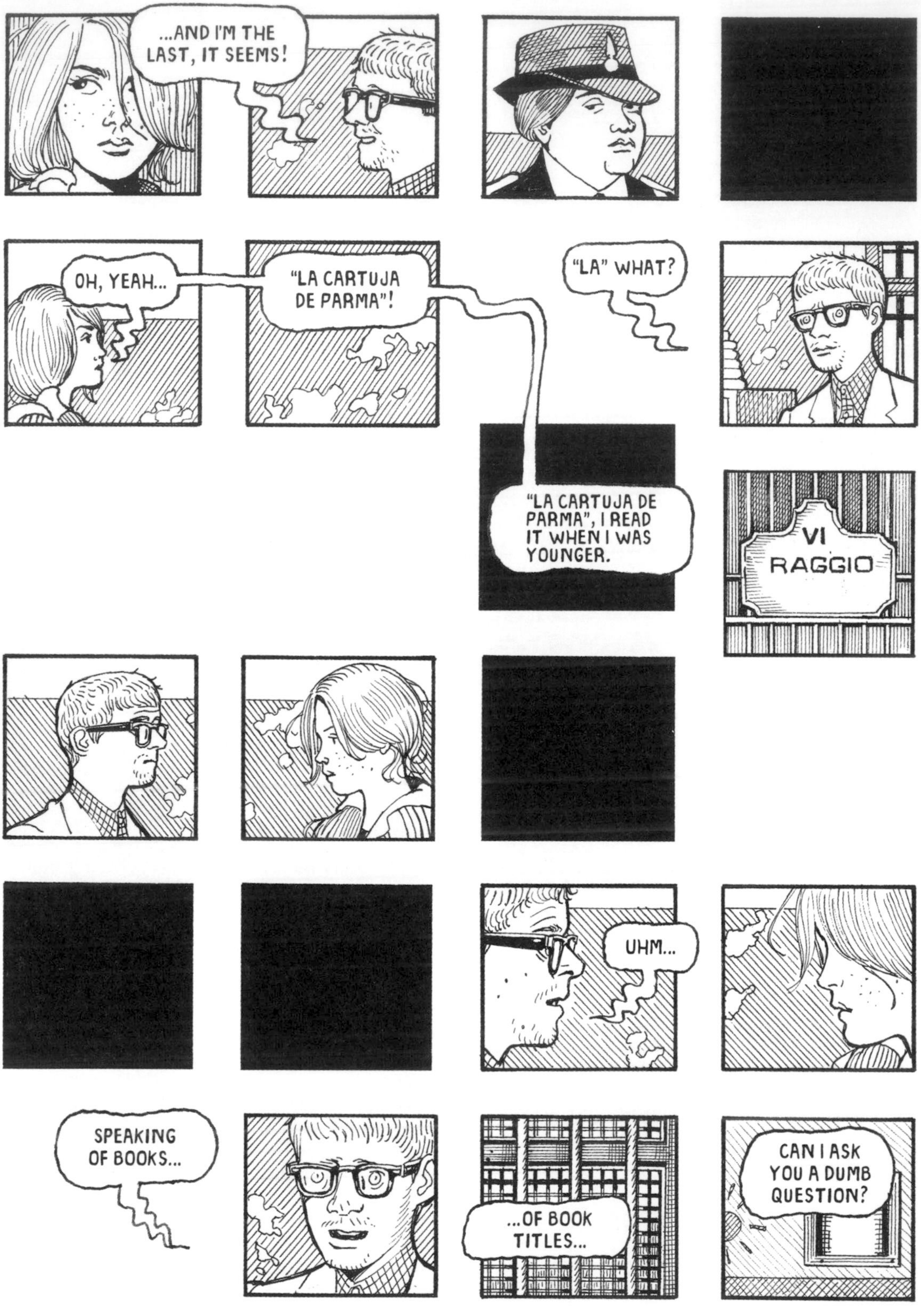
...AND I'M THE LAST, IT SEEMS!
OH, YEAH...
"LA CARTUJA DE PARMA"!
"LA" WHAT?
"LA CARTUJA DE PARMA", I READ IT WHEN I WAS YOUNGER.
VI RAGGIO
UHM...
SPEAKING OF BOOKS...
...OF BOOK TITLES...
CAN I ASK YOU A DUMB QUESTION?

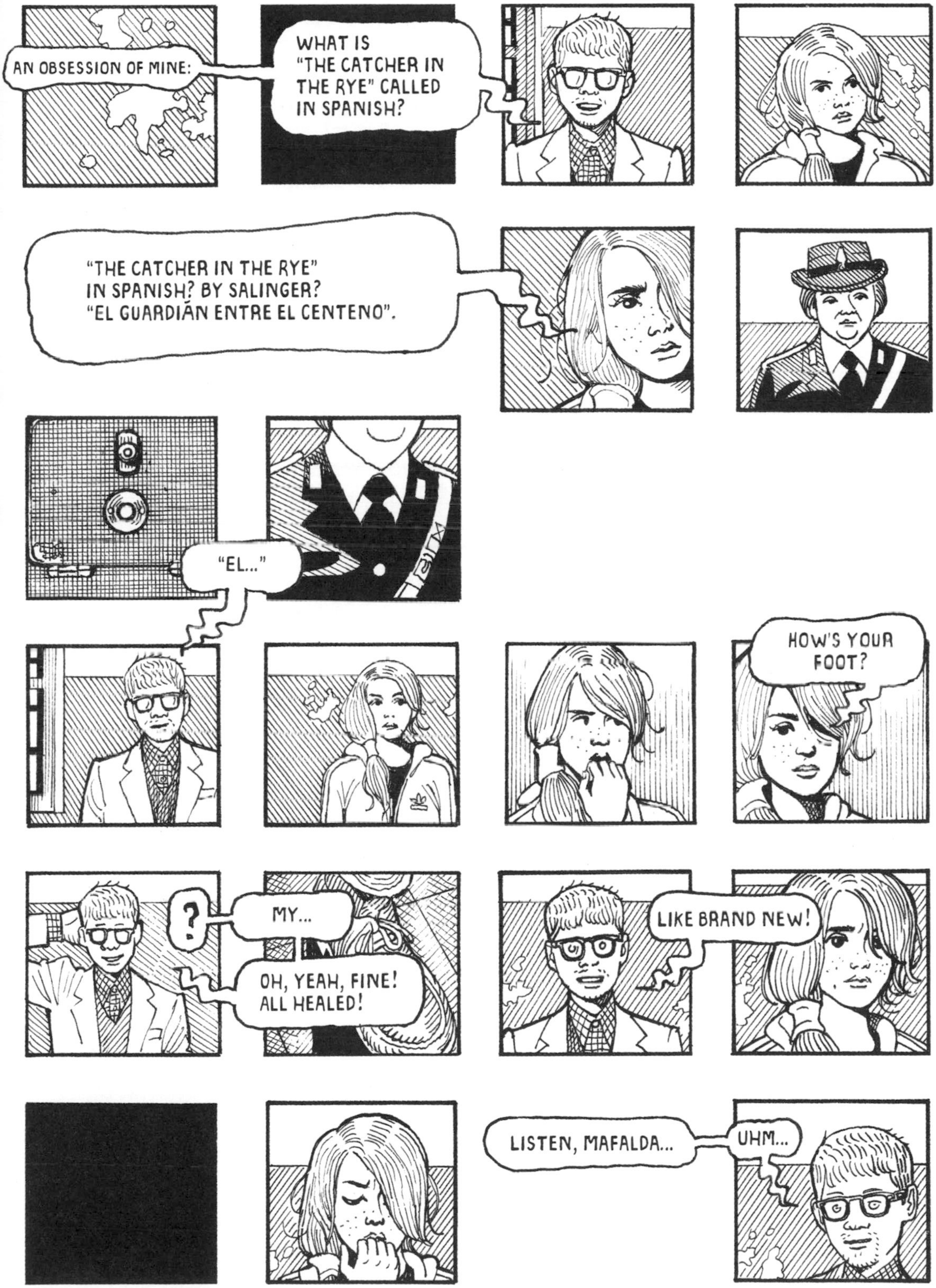
AN OBSESSION OF MINE:
WHAT IS "THE CATCHER IN THE RYE" CALLED IN SPANISH?
"THE CATCHER IN THE RYE" IN SPANISH? BY SALINGER? "EL GUARDIÁN ENTRE EL CENTENO".
"EL..."
HOW'S YOUR FOOT?
?
MY...
OH, YEAH, FINE! ALL HEALED!
LIKE BRAND NEW!
LISTEN, MAFALDA...
UHM...

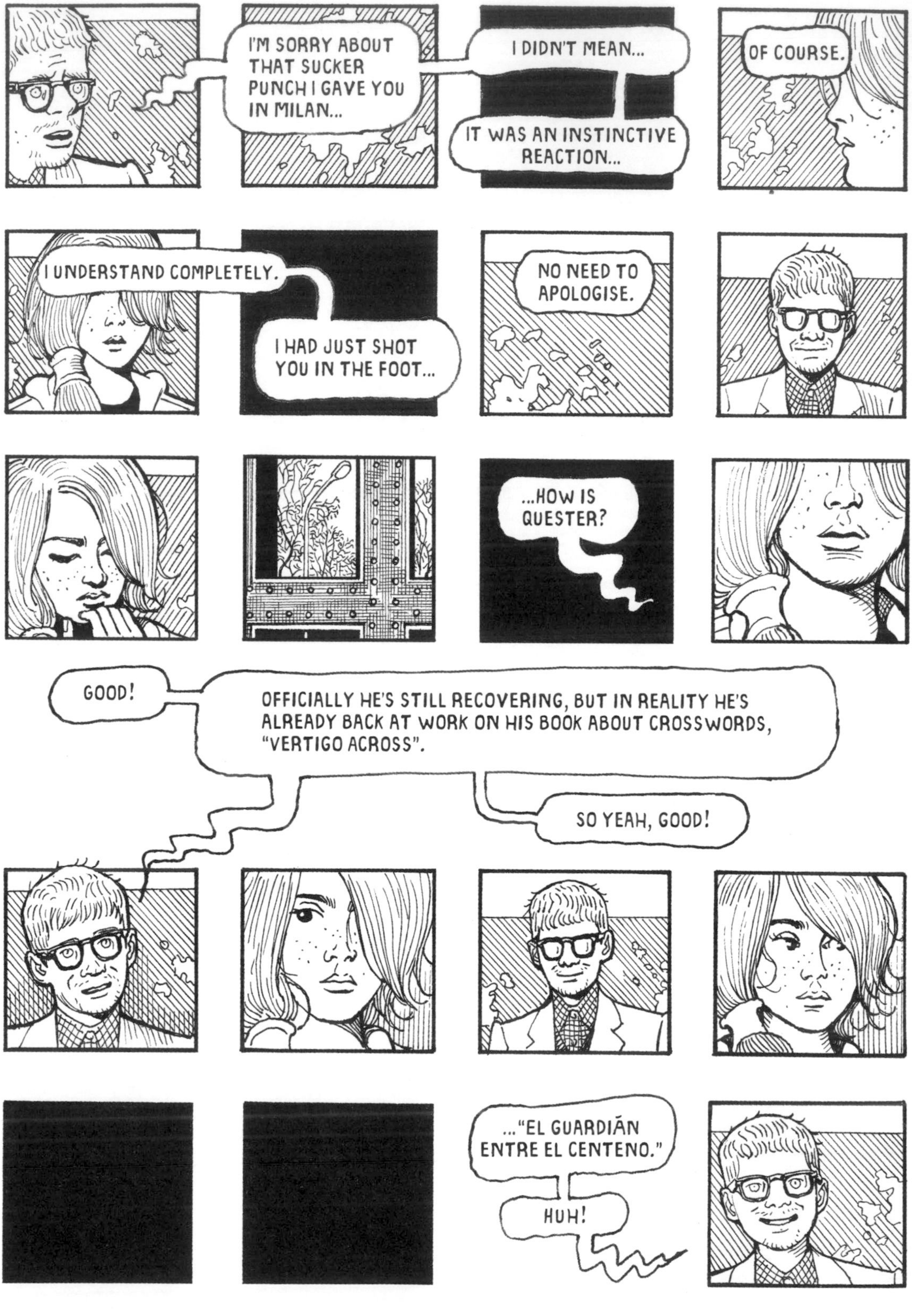
I'M SORRY ABOUT THAT SUCKER PUNCH I GAVE YOU IN MILAN...
I DIDN'T MEAN...
IT WAS AN INSTINCTIVE REACTION...
OF COURSE.
I UNDERSTAND COMPLETELY.
I HAD JUST SHOT YOU IN THE FOOT...
NO NEED TO APOLOGISE.
...HOW IS QUESTER?
GOOD!
OFFICIALLY HE'S STILL RECOVERING, BUT IN REALITY HE'S ALREADY BACK AT WORK ON HIS BOOK ABOUT CROSSWORDS, "VERTIGO ACROSS".
SO YEAH, GOOD!
..."EL GUARDIÁN ENTRE EL CENTENO."
HUH!

the CATCHER in the RYE

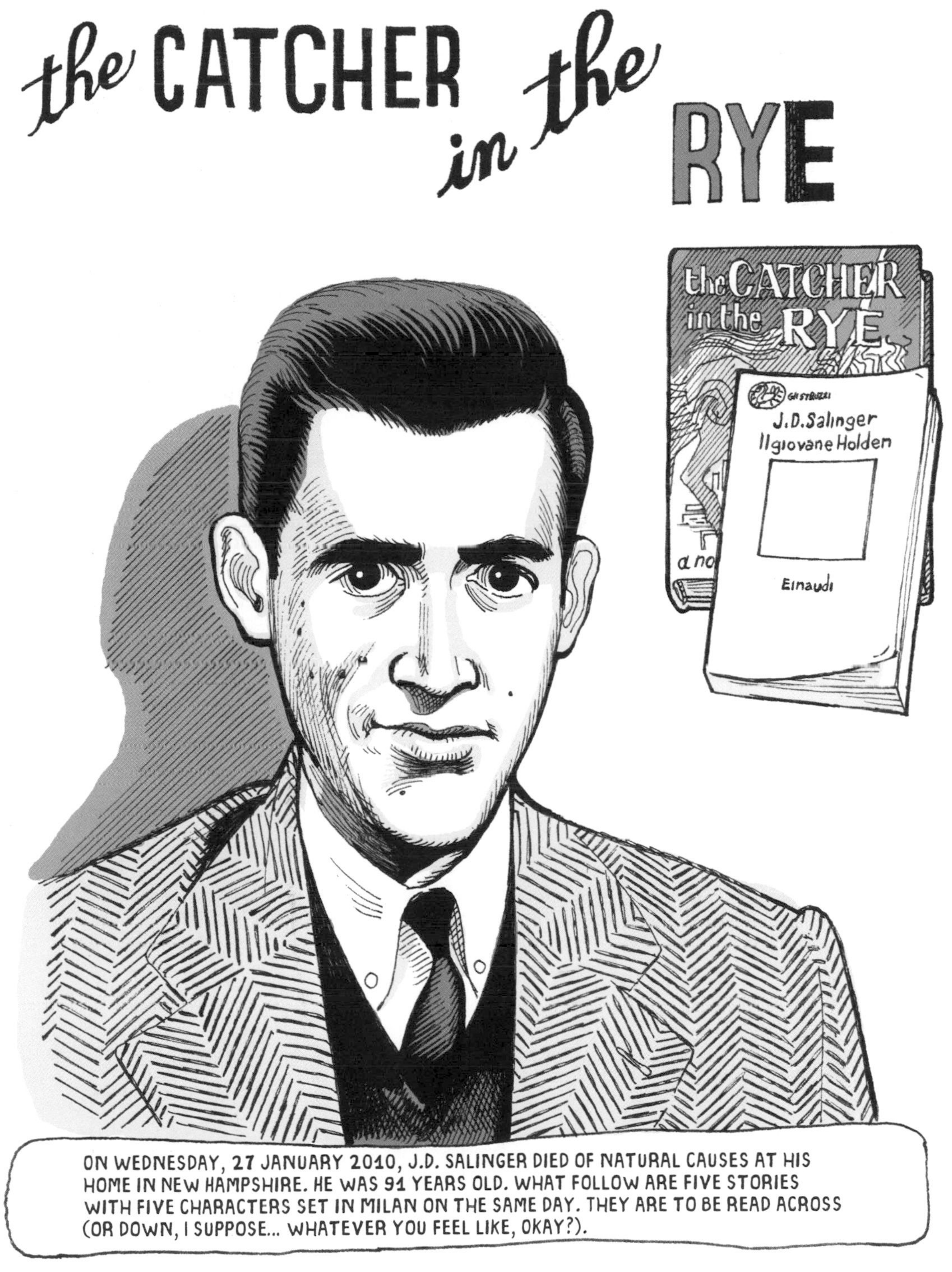
the CATCHER in the RYE
J.D. Salinger
Il giovane Holden
Einaudi
ON WEDNESDAY, 27 JANUARY 2010, J.D. SALINGER DIED OF NATURAL CAUSES AT HIS HOME IN NEW HAMPSHIRE. HE WAS 91 YEARS OLD. WHAT FOLLOW ARE FIVE STORIES WITH FIVE CHARACTERS SET IN MILAN ON THE SAME DAY. THEY ARE TO BE READ ACROSS (OR DOWN, I SUPPOSE... WHATEVER YOU FEEL LIKE, OKAY?).

CAPTAIN BISCOTTI, MILANESE SUPERHERO.

ZENO PORNO, DISNEY WRITER, ETC.

NELLA POGGI, ART RESTORER.

ARTÚ, NELLA'S DOG.

STREETLIGHT IN FRONT OF SAN VITTORE.

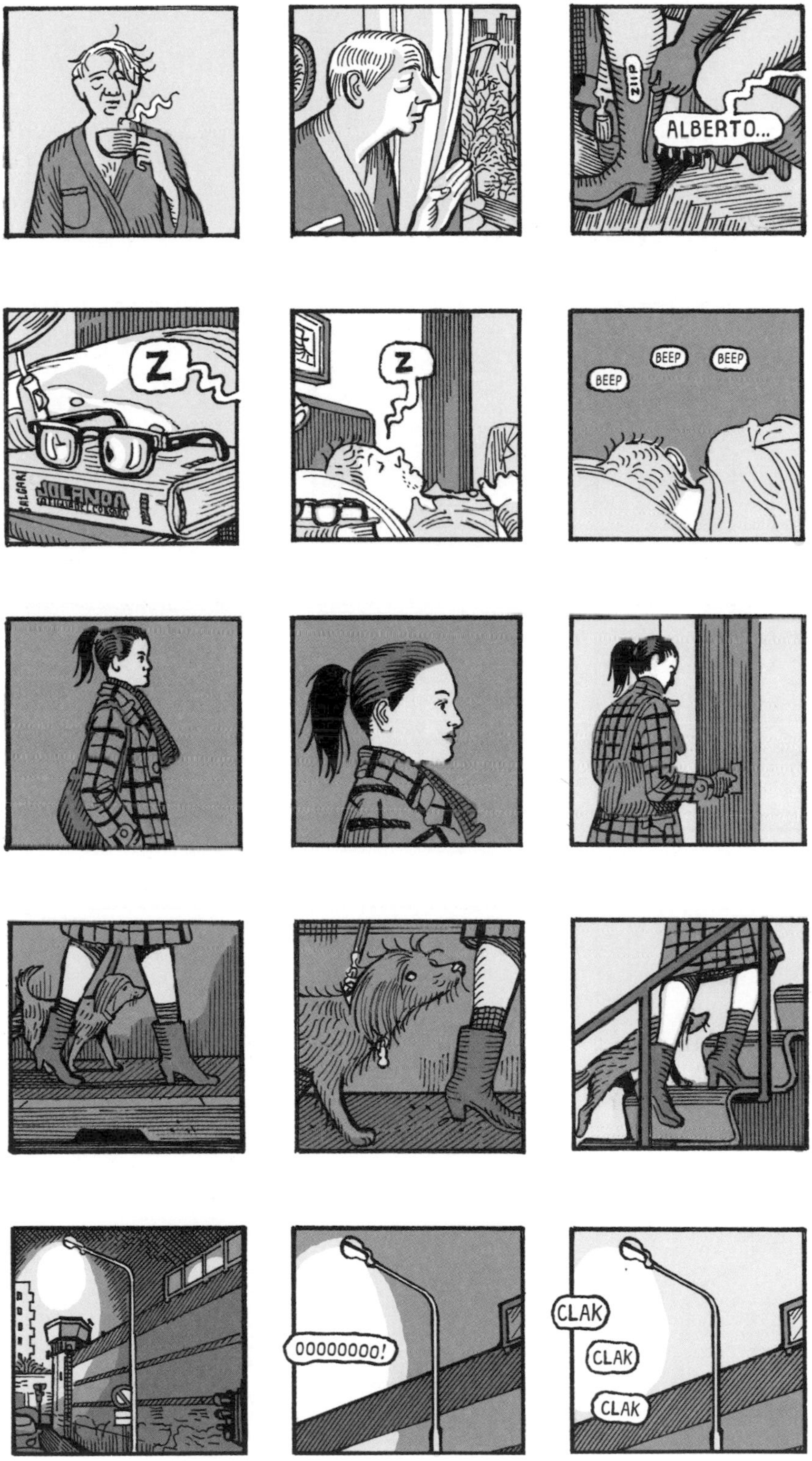
ZIIP
ALBERTO...
Z
Z
BEEP
BEEP
BEEP
OOOOOOOO!
CLAK
CLAK
CLAK

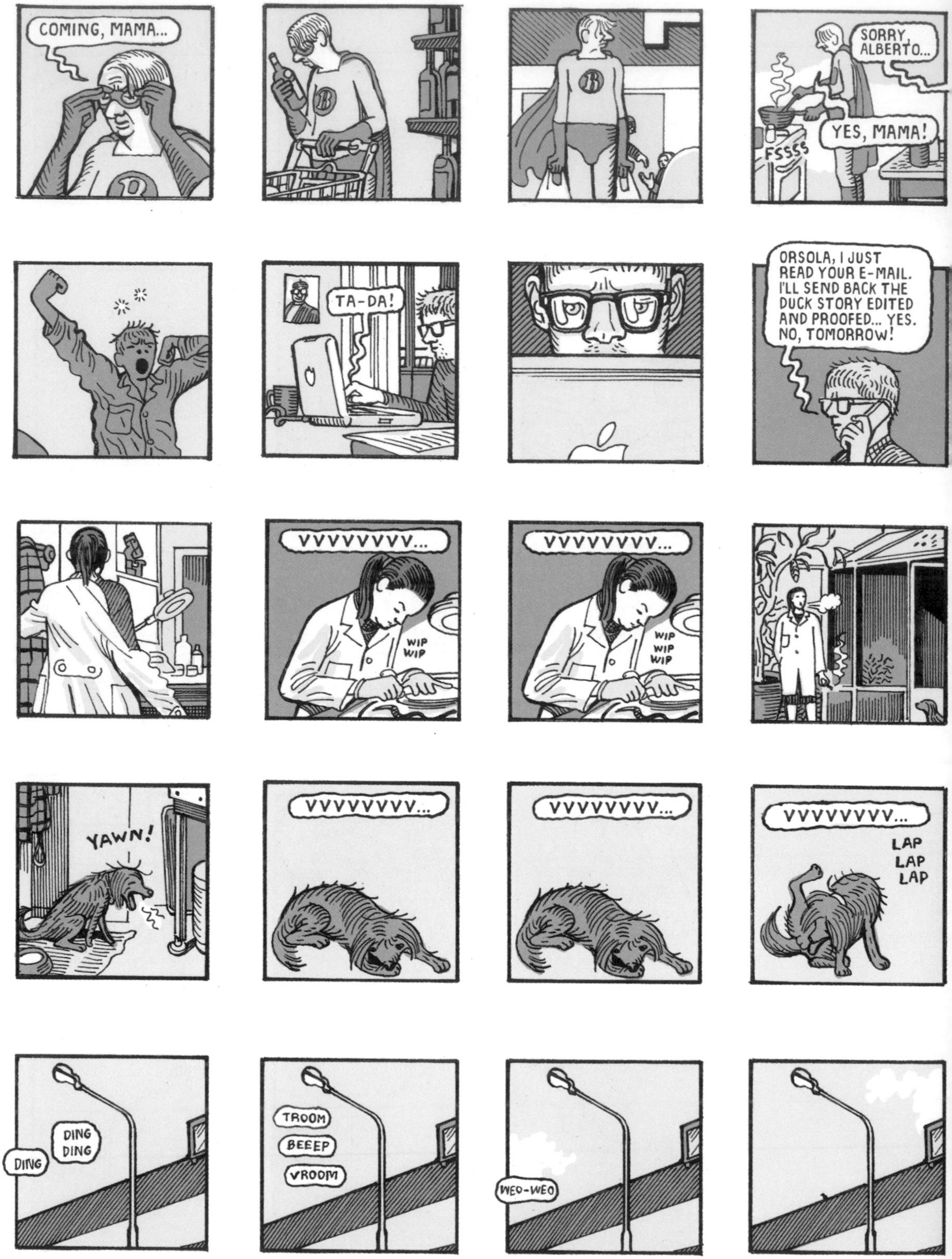
COMING, MAMA...
SORRY, ALBERTO...
YES, MAMA!
FSSSS
TA-DA!
ORSOLA, I JUST READ YOUR E-MAIL. I'LL SEND BACK THE DUCK STORY EDITED AND PROOFED... YES. NO, TOMORROW!
VVVVVVVV...
WIP WIP
VVVVVVVV...
WIP WIP WIP
YAWN!
VVVVVVVV...
VVVVVVVV...
VVVVVVVV...
LAP LAP LAP
DING DING
DING
TROOM
BEEEP
VROOM
WEO-WEO

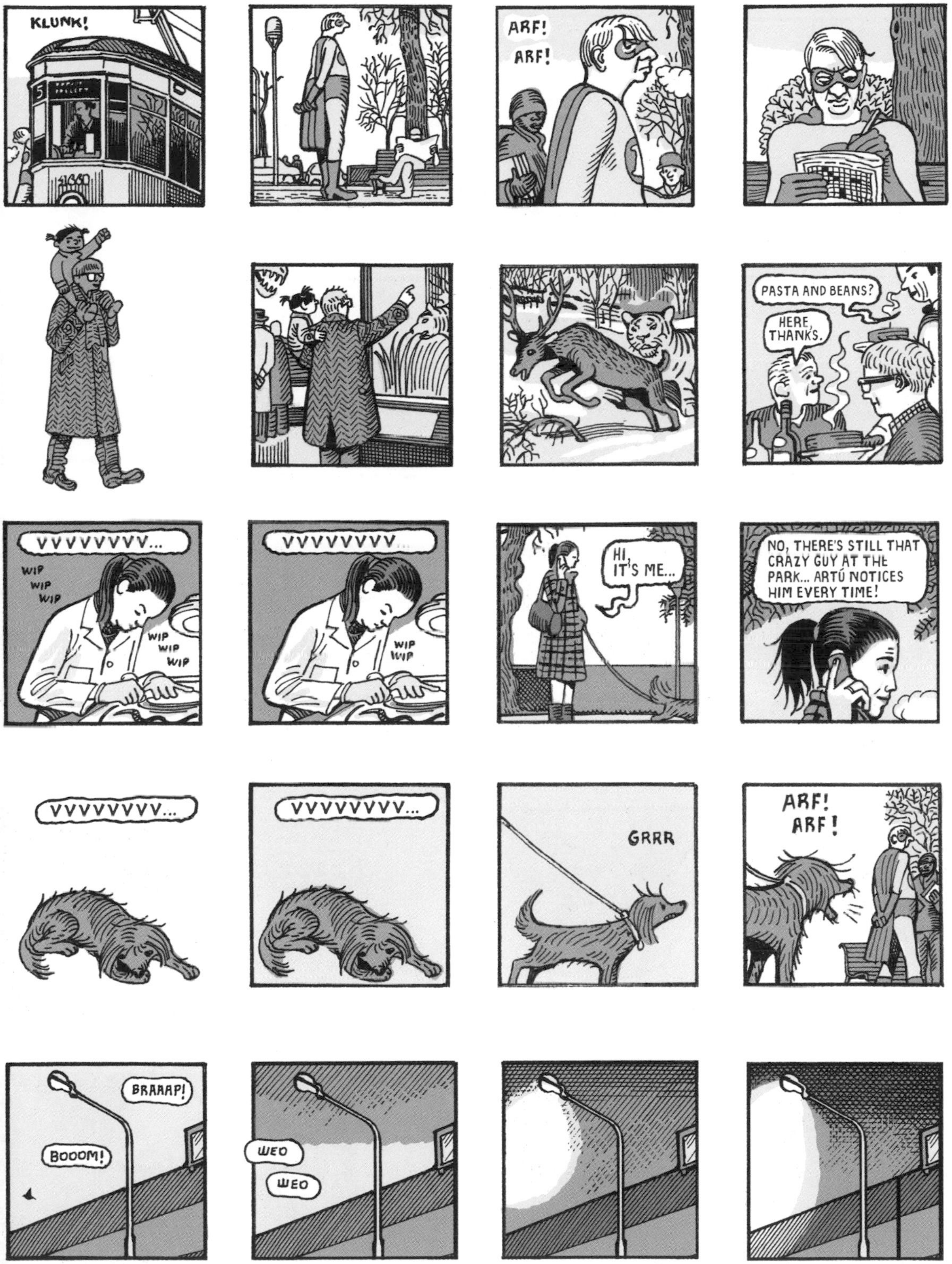
KLUNK!
ARF!
ARF!
PASTA AND BEANS?
HERE, THANKS.
VVVVVVVV...
WIP
WIP
WIP
WIP
WIP
WIP
VVVVVVVV...
WIP
WIP
HI, IT'S ME...
NO, THERE'S STILL THAT CRAZY GUY AT THE PARK... ARTÚ NOTICES HIM EVERY TIME!
VVVVVVVV...
VVVVVVVV...
GRRR
ARF!
ARF!
BRAAAP!
BOOOM!
WEO
WEO

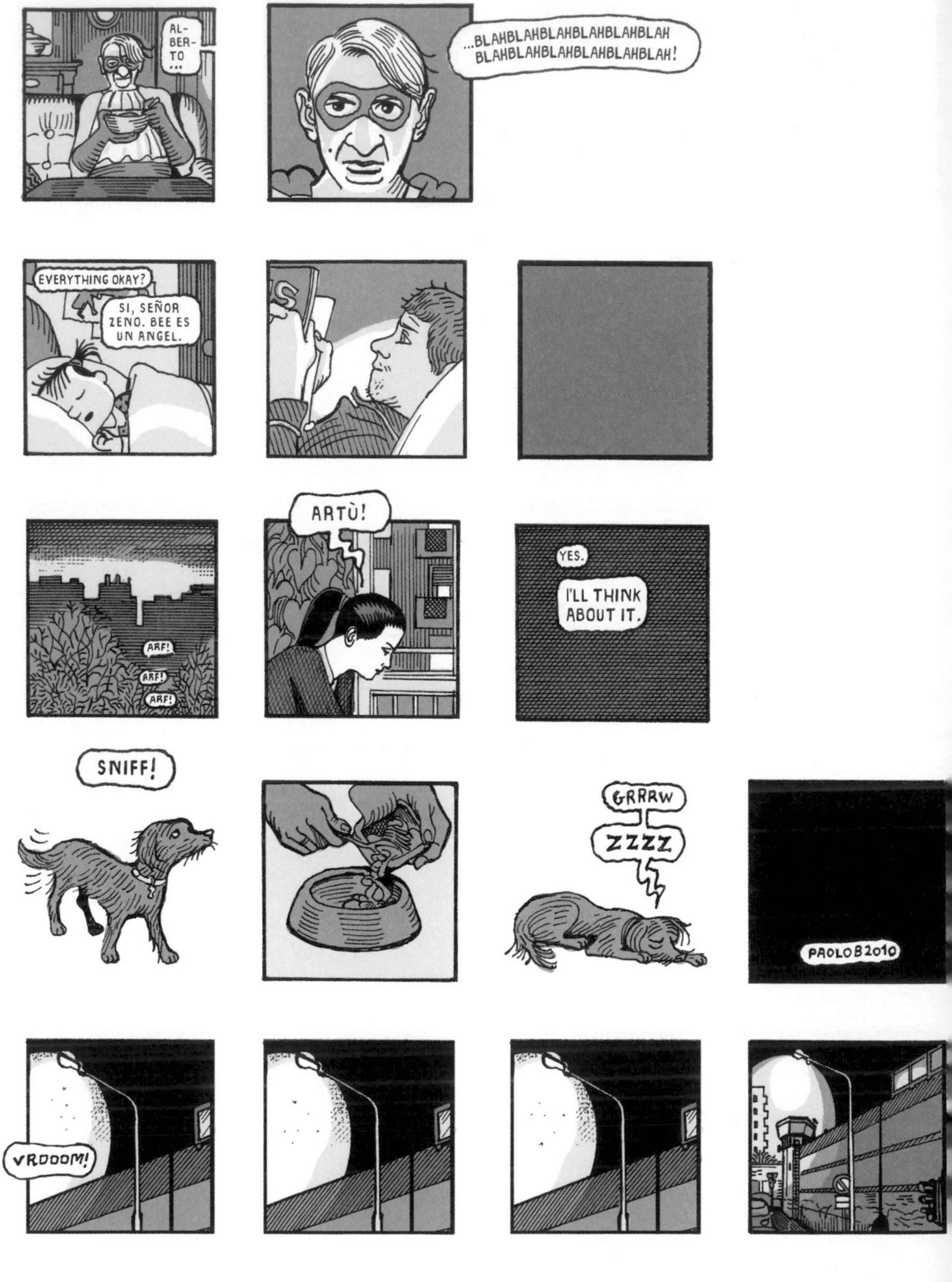
AL-
BER-
TO
...
...BLAHBLAHBLAHBLAHBLAHBLAH
BLAHBLAHBLAHBLAHBLAHBLAH!
EVERYTHING OKAY?
SI, SEÑOR ZENO. BEE ES UN ANGEL.
ARF!
ARF!
ARF!
ARTÙ!
YES.
I'LL THINK ABOUT IT.
SNIFF!
GRRRW
ZZZZ
PAOLOB2010
VROOOM!

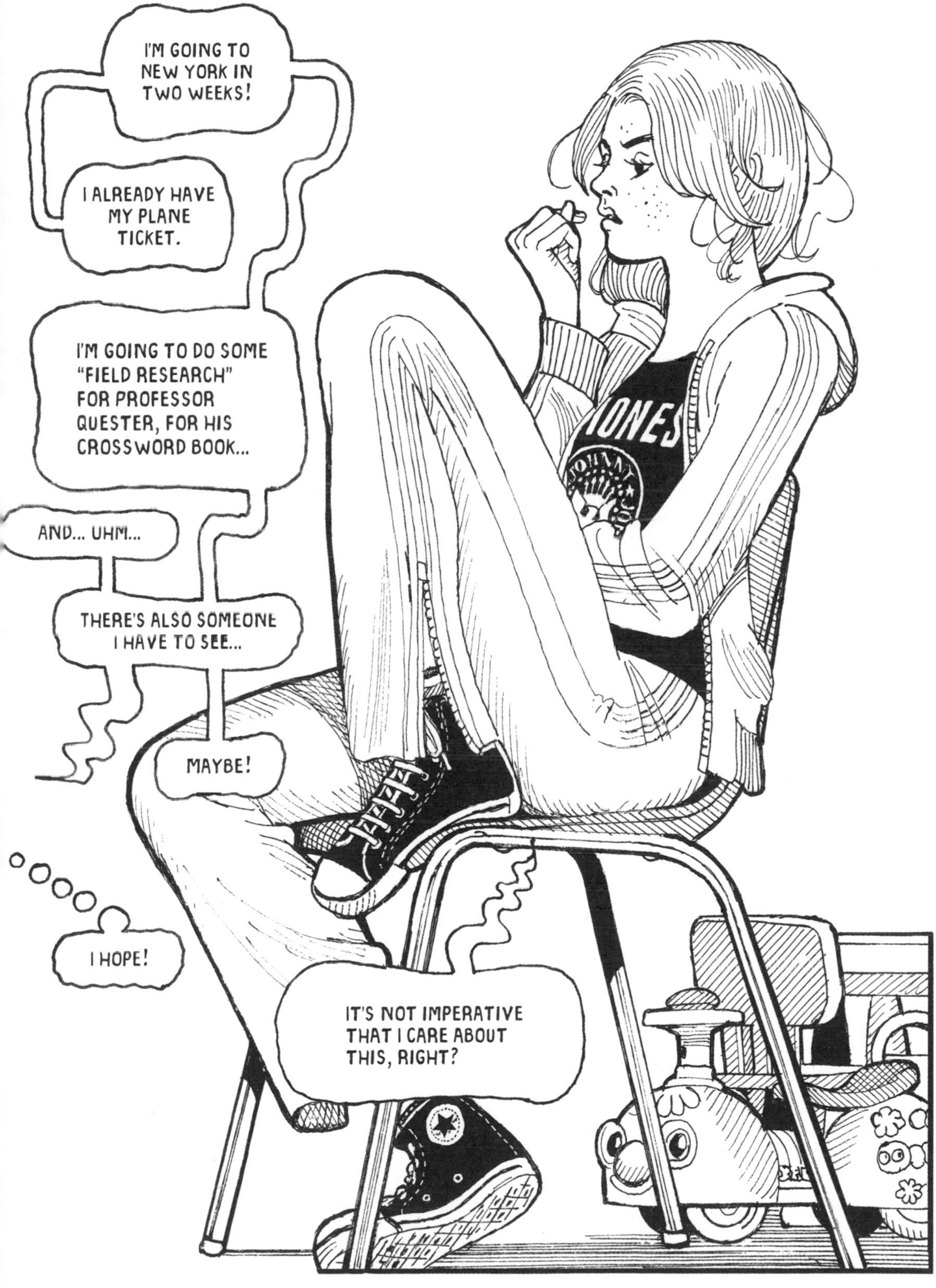
I'M GOING TO NEW YORK IN TWO WEEKS!
I ALREADY HAVE MY PLANE TICKET.
I'M GOING TO DO SOME "FIELD RESEARCH" FOR PROFESSOR QUESTER, FOR HIS CROSSWORD BOOK...
AND... UHM...
THERE'S ALSO SOMEONE I HAVE TO SEE...
MAYBE!
I HOPE!
IT'S NOT IMPERATIVE THAT I CARE ABOUT THIS, RIGHT?
RAMONES
JOHNNY

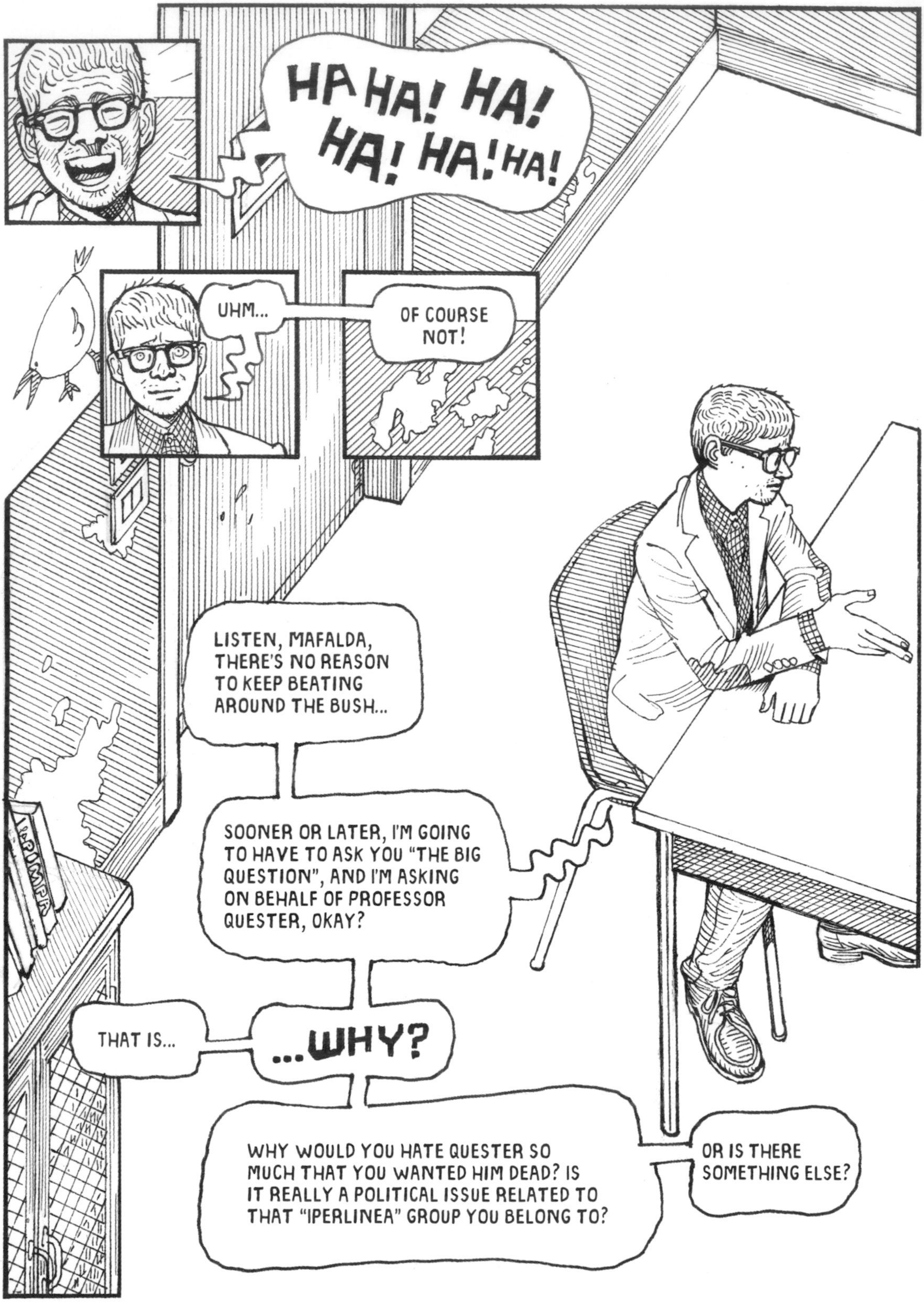
HA HA! HA!
HA! HA! HA!
UHM...
OF COURSE NOT!
LISTEN, MAFALDA, THERE'S NO REASON TO KEEP BEATING AROUND THE BUSH...
SOONER OR LATER, I'M GOING TO HAVE TO ASK YOU "THE BIG QUESTION", AND I'M ASKING ON BEHALF OF PROFESSOR QUESTER, OKAY?
THAT IS...
...WHY?
WHY WOULD YOU HATE QUESTER SO MUCH THAT YOU WANTED HIM DEAD? IS IT REALLY A POLITICAL ISSUE RELATED TO THAT "IPERLINEA" GROUP YOU BELONG TO?
OR IS THERE SOMETHING ELSE?

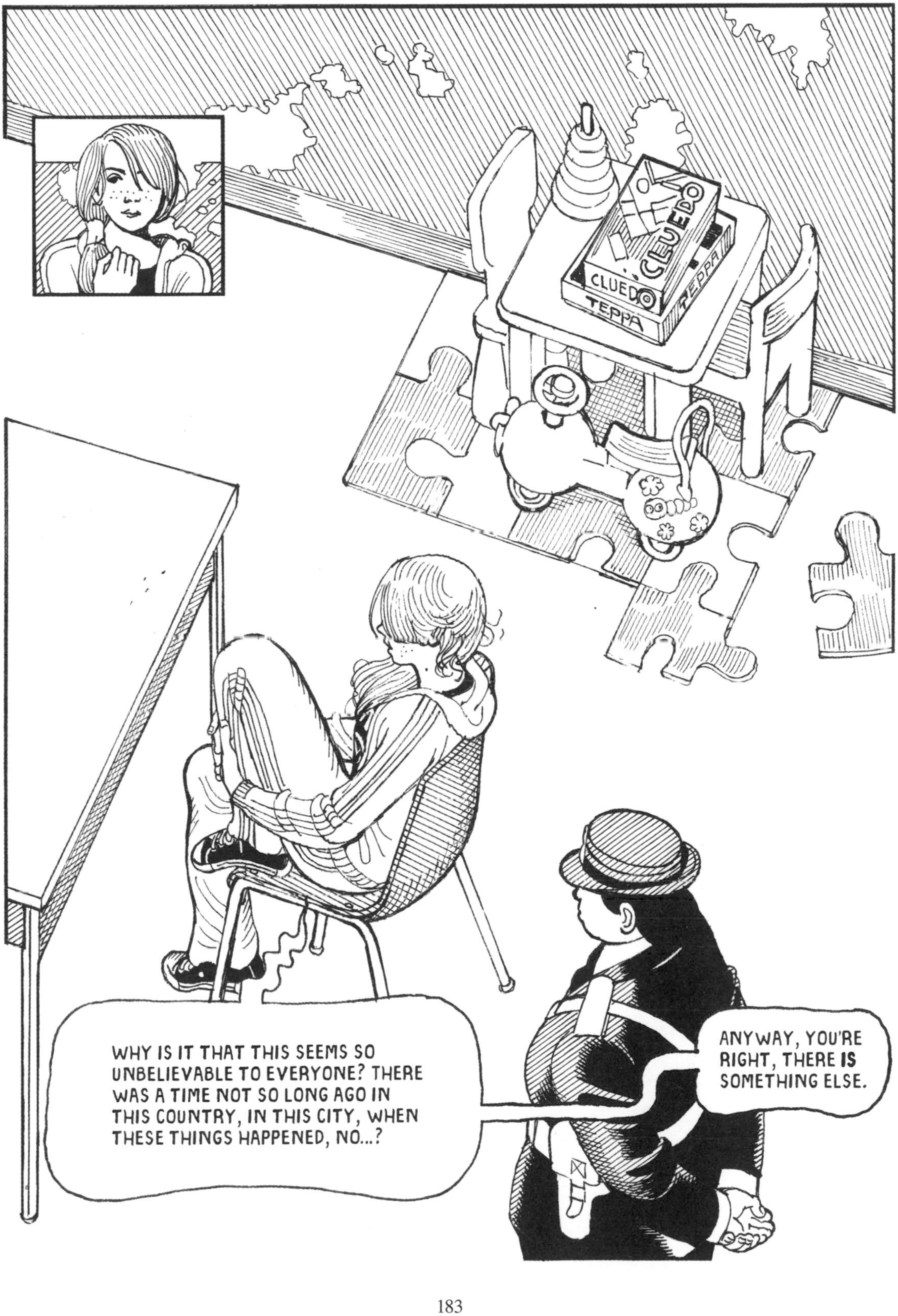
CLUEDO
TEPPA
CLUEDO
TEPPA
WHY IS IT THAT THIS SEEMS SO UNBELIEVABLE TO EVERYONE? THERE WAS A TIME NOT SO LONG AGO IN THIS COUNTRY, IN THIS CITY, WHEN THESE THINGS HAPPENED, NO...?
ANYWAY, YOU'RE RIGHT, THERE **IS** SOMETHING ELSE.

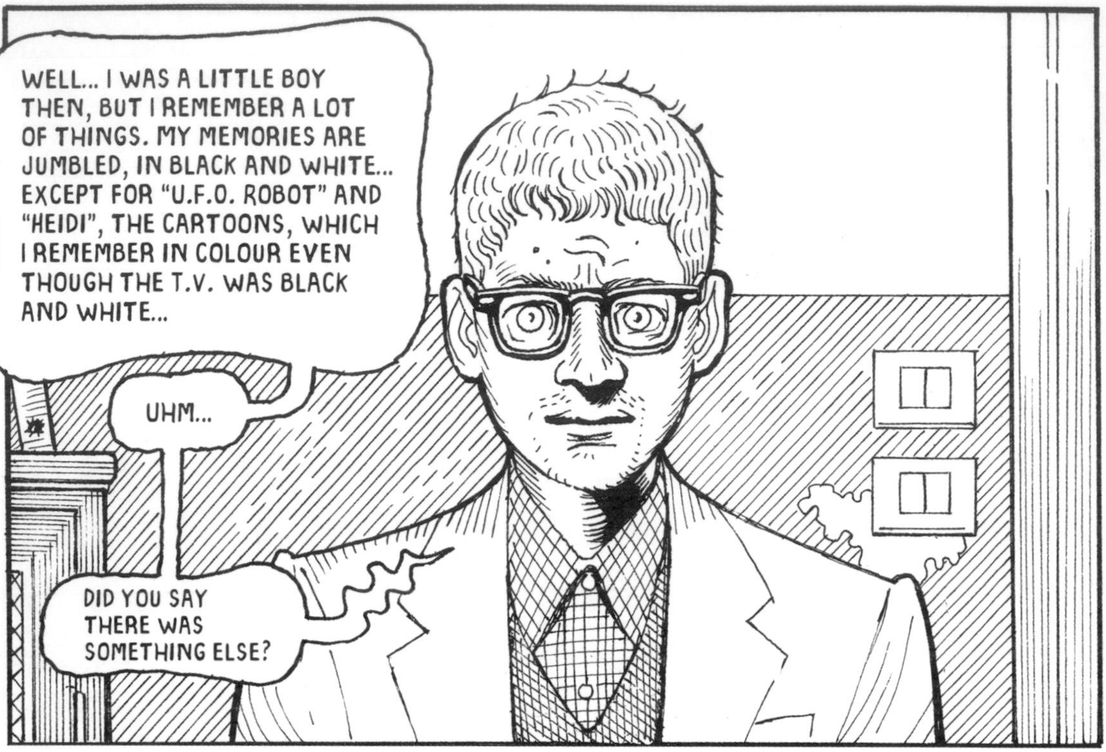
WELL... I WAS A LITTLE BOY THEN, BUT I REMEMBER A LOT OF THINGS. MY MEMORIES ARE JUMBLED, IN BLACK AND WHITE... EXCEPT FOR "U.F.O. ROBOT" AND "HEIDI", THE CARTOONS, WHICH I REMEMBER IN COLOUR EVEN THOUGH THE T.V. WAS BLACK AND WHITE...
UHM...
DID YOU SAY THERE WAS SOMETHING ELSE?

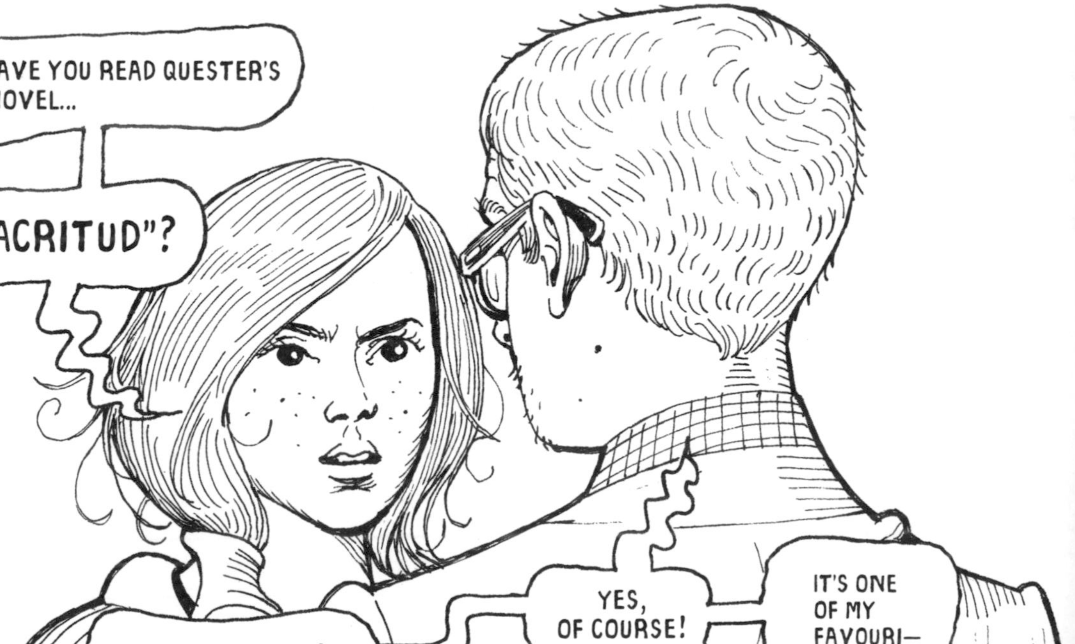
HAVE YOU READ QUESTER'S NOVEL...
"ACRITUD"?
"ACRIMONY"!
YES, OF COURSE!
IT'S ONE OF MY FAVOURI—

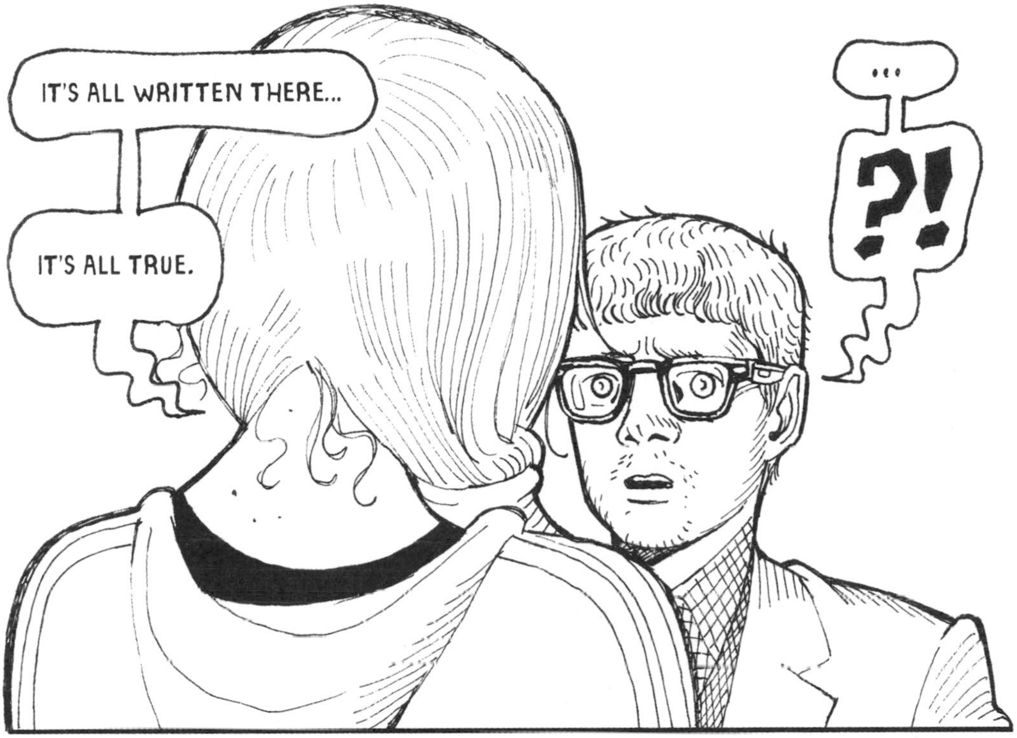
IT'S ALL WRITTEN THERE...
IT'S ALL TRUE.
...
?!

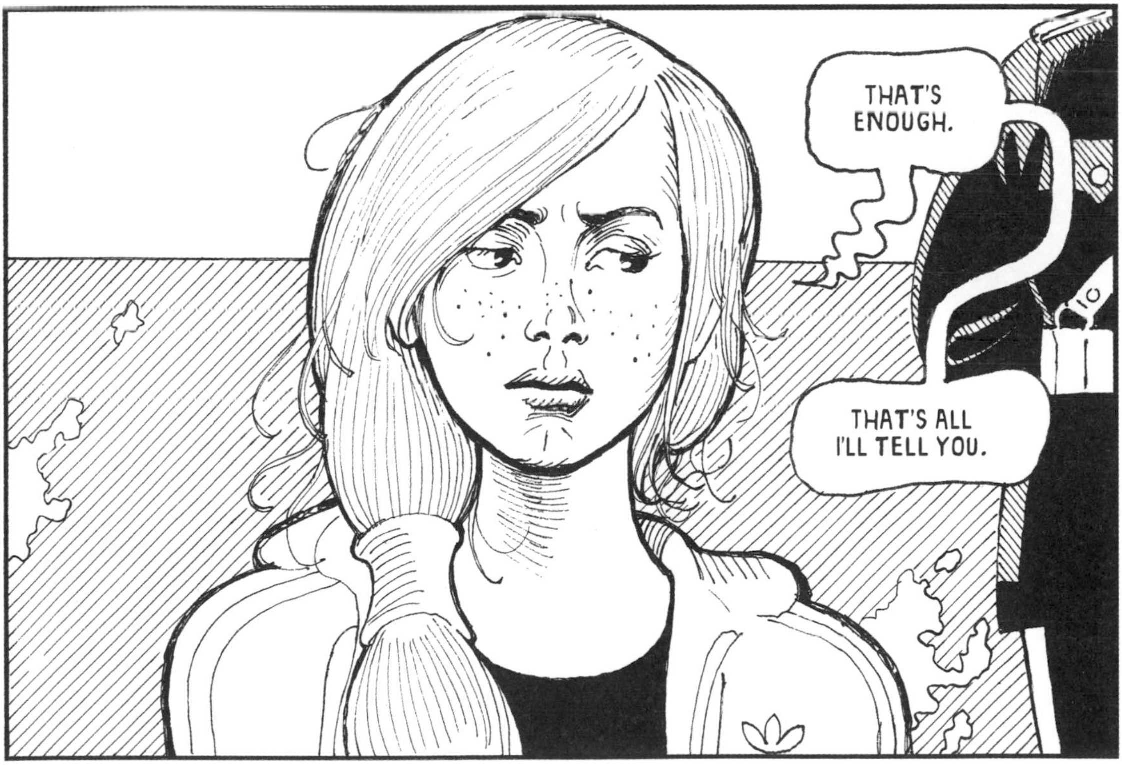
THAT'S ENOUGH.
THAT'S ALL I'LL TELL YOU.

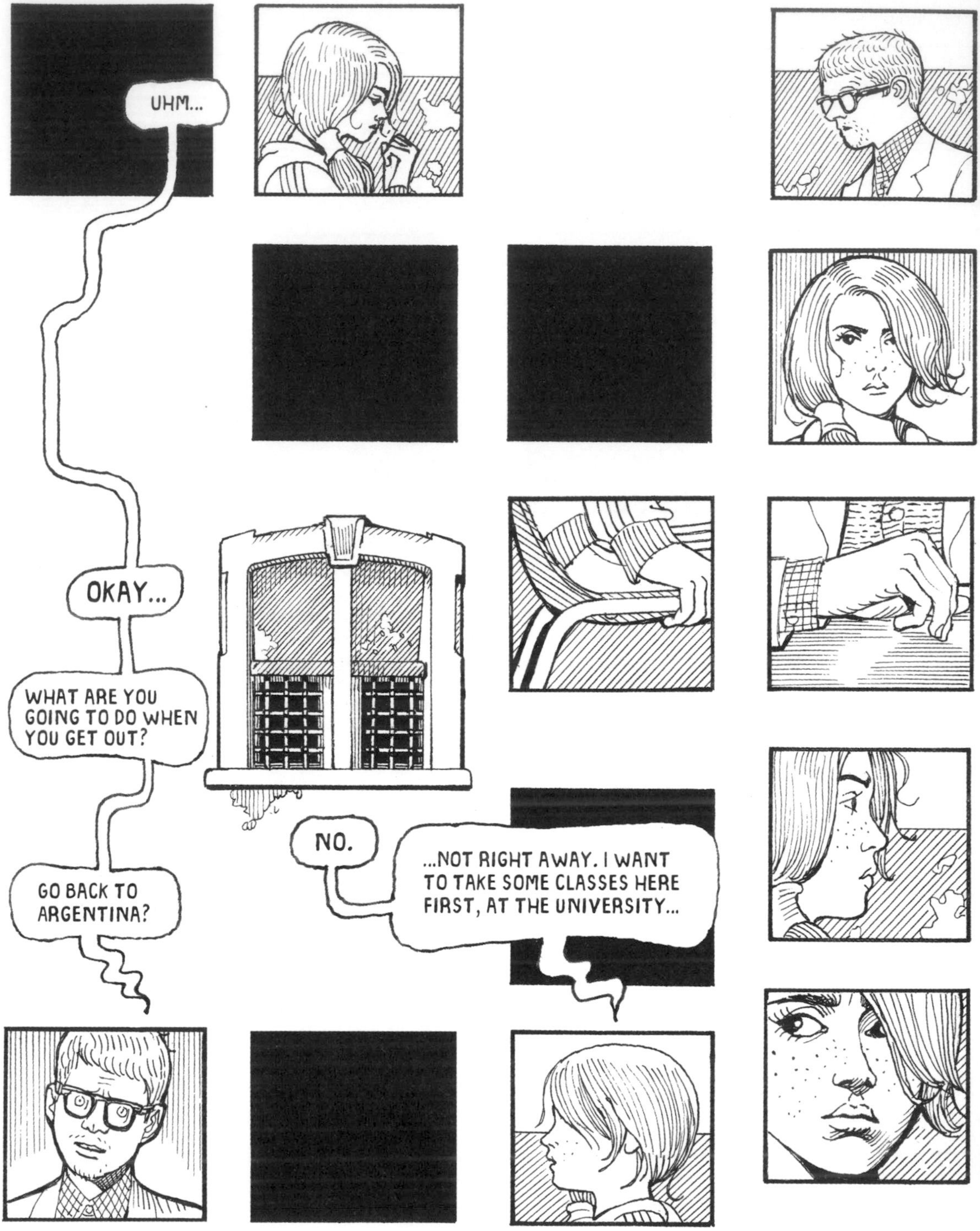
UHM...
OKAY...
WHAT ARE YOU GOING TO DO WHEN YOU GET OUT?
GO BACK TO ARGENTINA?
NO.
...NOT RIGHT AWAY. I WANT TO TAKE SOME CLASSES HERE FIRST, AT THE UNIVERSITY...

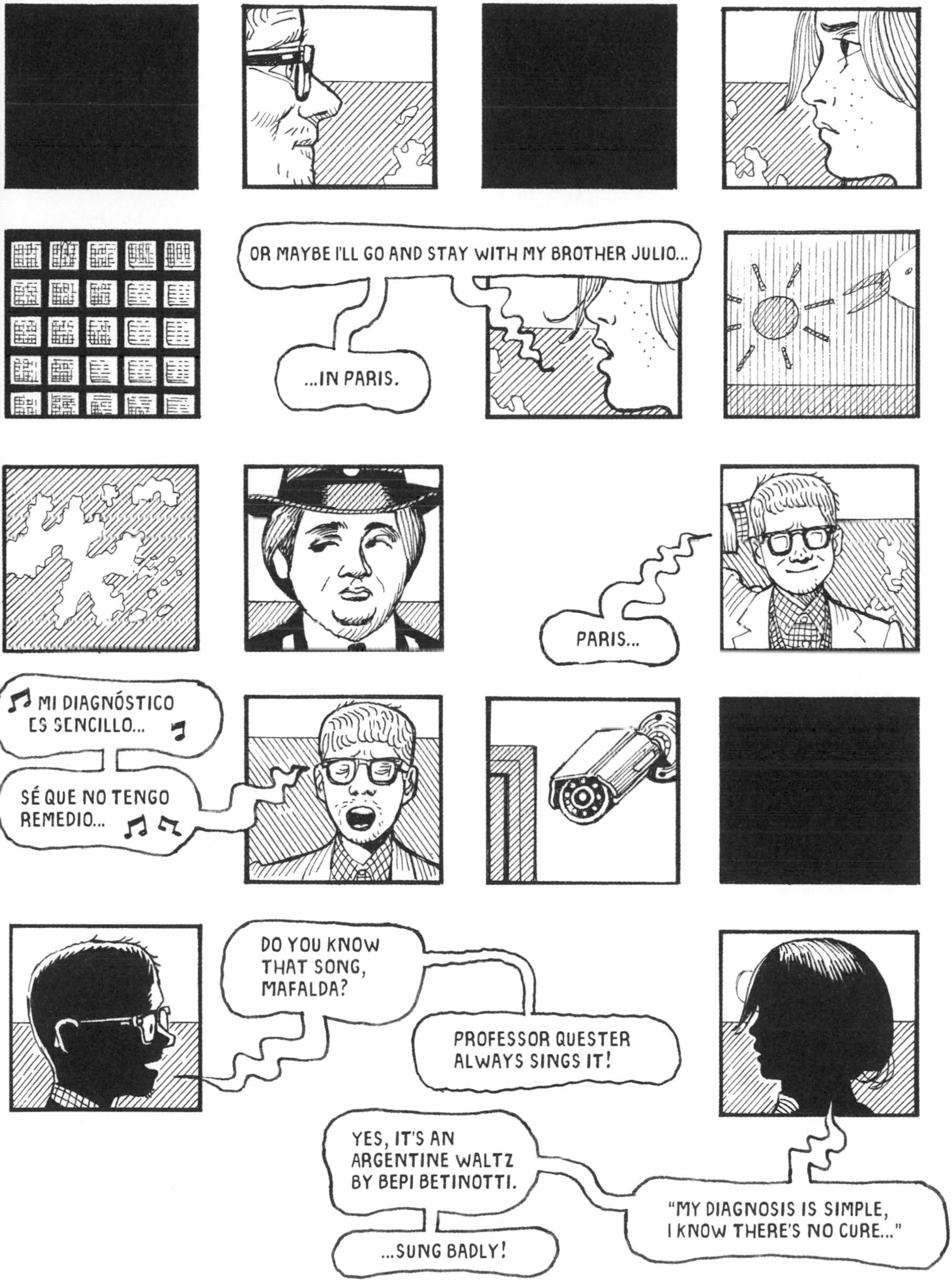
OR MAYBE I'LL GO AND STAY WITH MY BROTHER JULIO...
...IN PARIS.
PARIS...
MI DIAGNÓSTICO ES SENCILLO...
SÉ QUE NO TENGO REMEDIO...
DO YOU KNOW THAT SONG, MAFALDA?
PROFESSOR QUESTER ALWAYS SINGS IT!
YES, IT'S AN ARGENTINE WALTZ BY BEPI BETINOTTI.
...SUNG BADLY!
"MY DIAGNOSIS IS SIMPLE, I KNOW THERE'S NO CURE..."

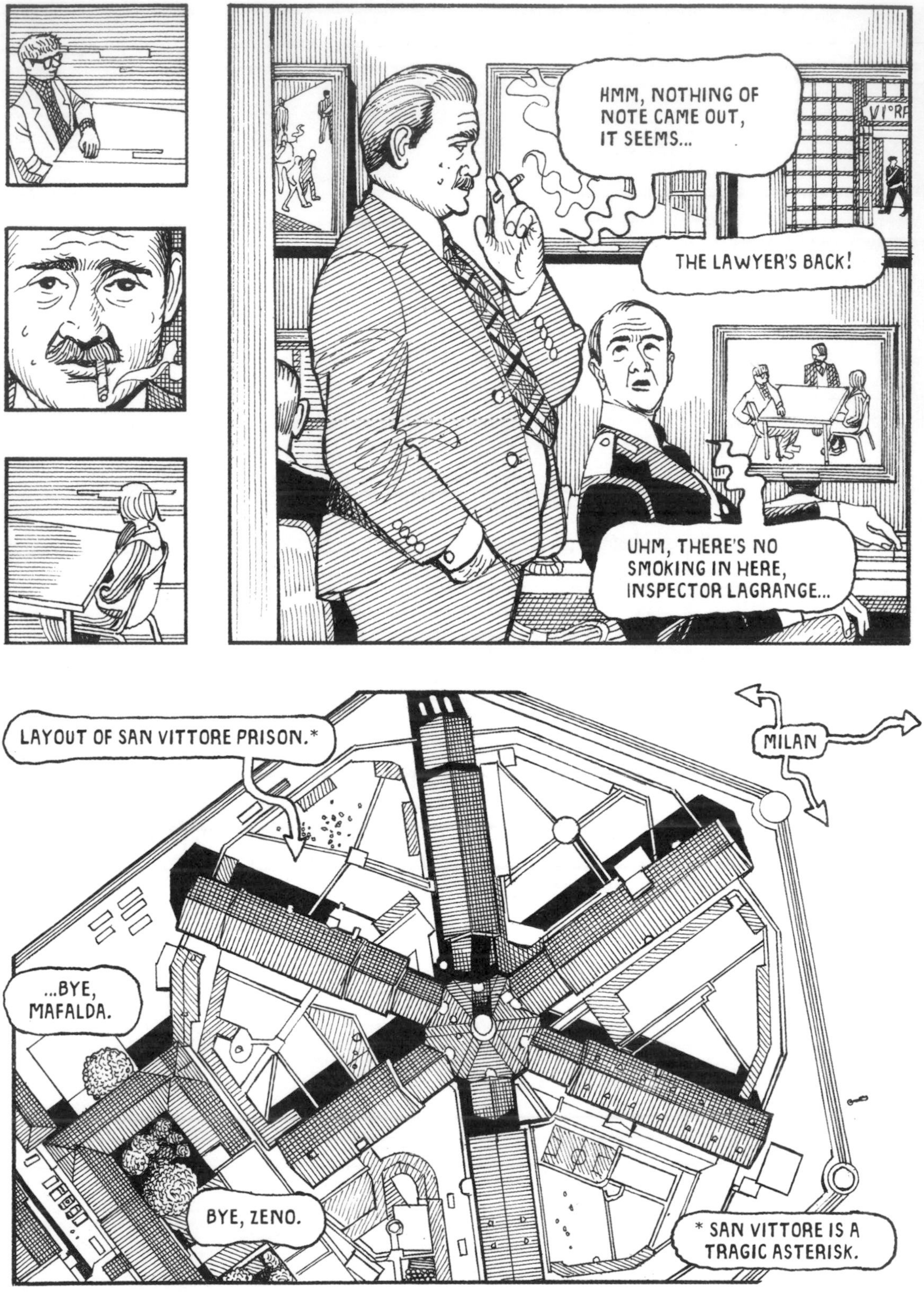

HMM, NOTHING OF NOTE CAME OUT, IT SEEMS...
THE LAWYER'S BACK!
UHM, THERE'S NO SMOKING IN HERE, INSPECTOR LAGRANGE...
LAYOUT OF SAN VITTORE PRISON.*
MILAN
...BYE, MAFALDA.
BYE, ZENO.
* SAN VITTORE IS A TRAGIC ASTERISK.

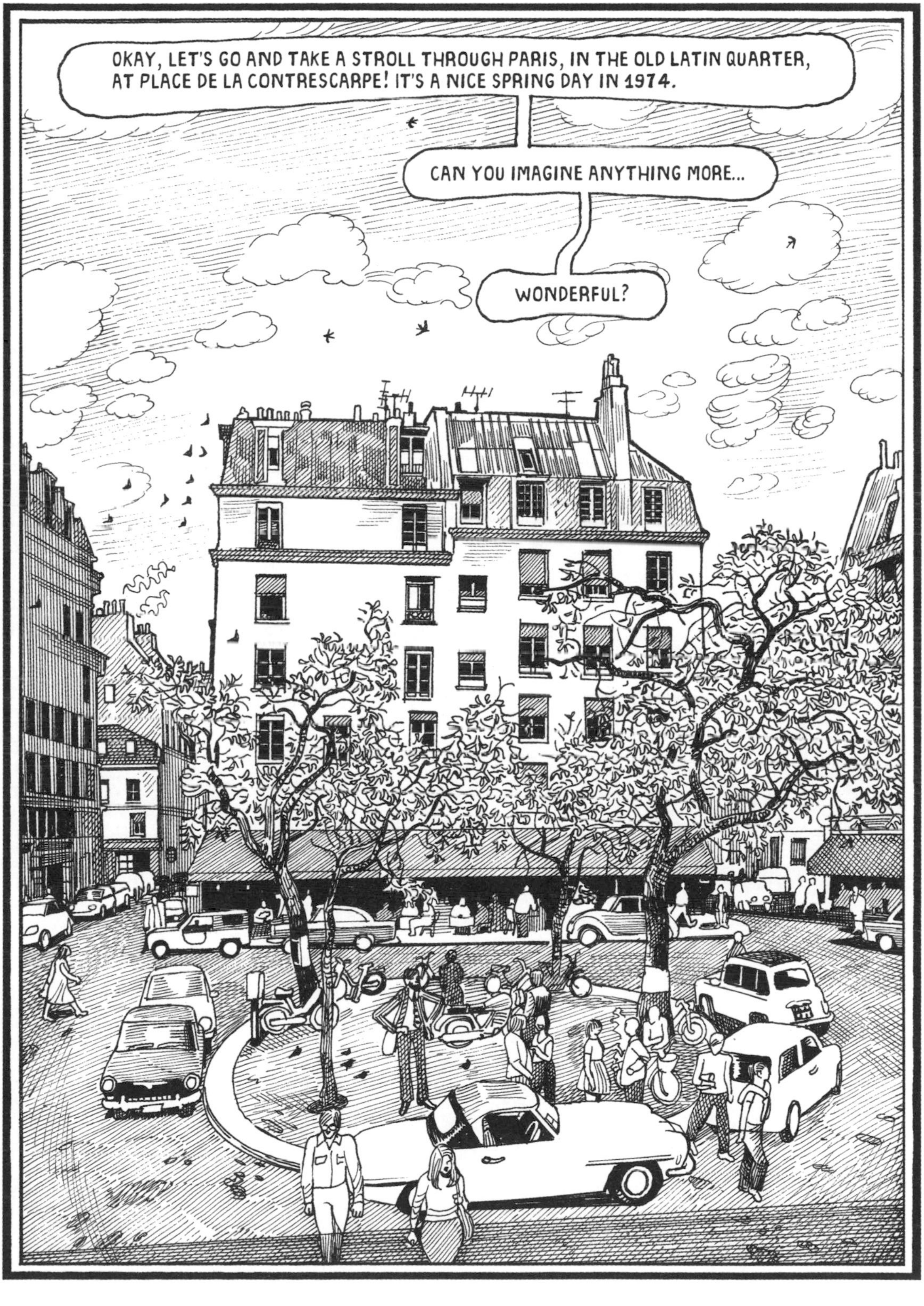
OKAY, LET'S GO AND TAKE A STROLL THROUGH PARIS, IN THE OLD LATIN QUARTER, AT PLACE DE LA CONTRESCARPE! IT'S A NICE SPRING DAY IN 1974.
CAN YOU IMAGINE ANYTHING MORE...
WONDERFUL?

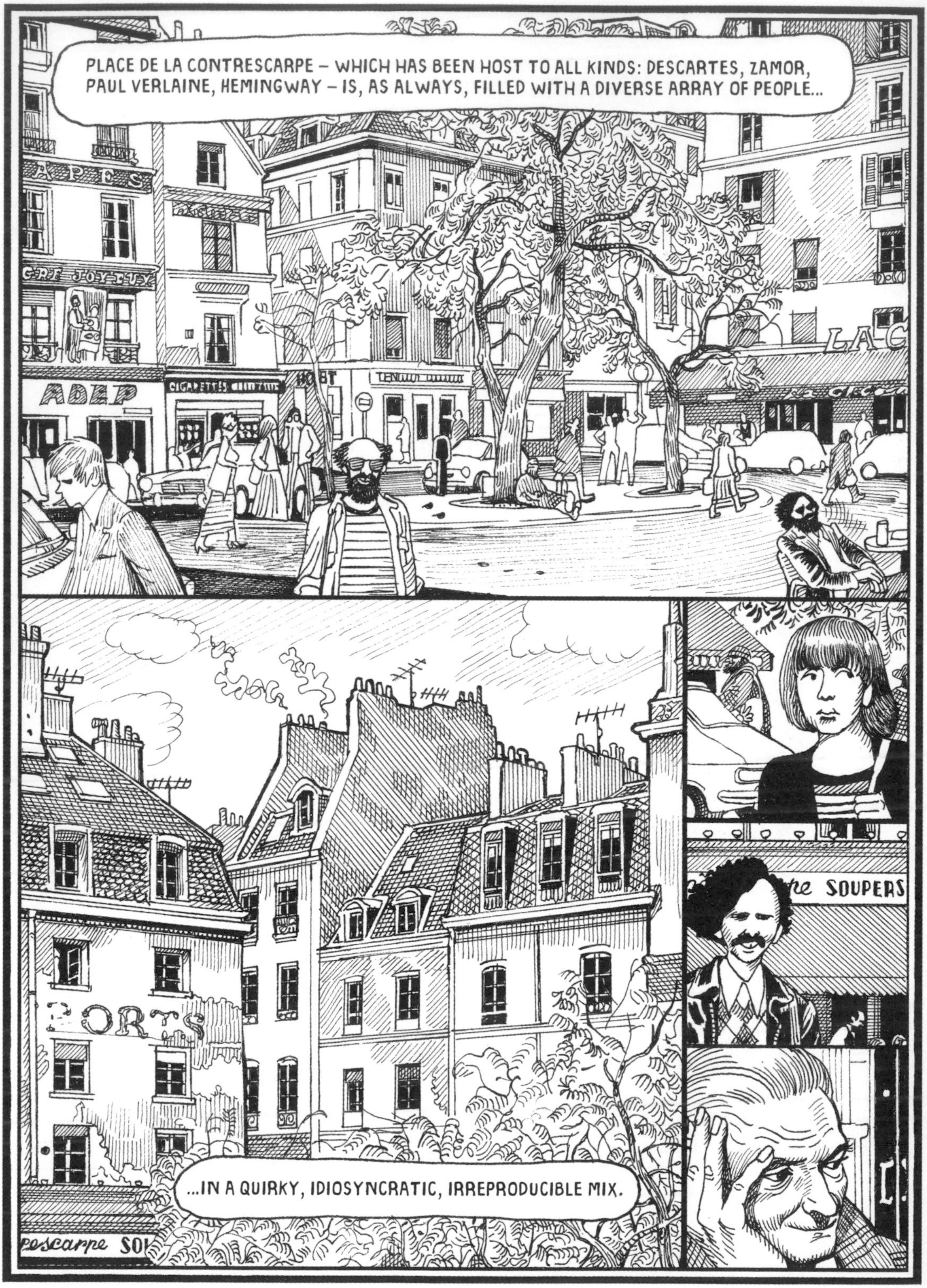
PLACE DE LA CONTRESCARPE – WHICH HAS BEEN HOST TO ALL KINDS: DESCARTES, ZAMOR, PAUL VERLAINE, HEMINGWAY – IS, AS ALWAYS, FILLED WITH A DIVERSE ARRAY OF PEOPLE...
CIGARETTES
...IN A QUIRKY, IDIOSYNCRATIC, IRREPRODUCIBLE MIX.
SOUPERS

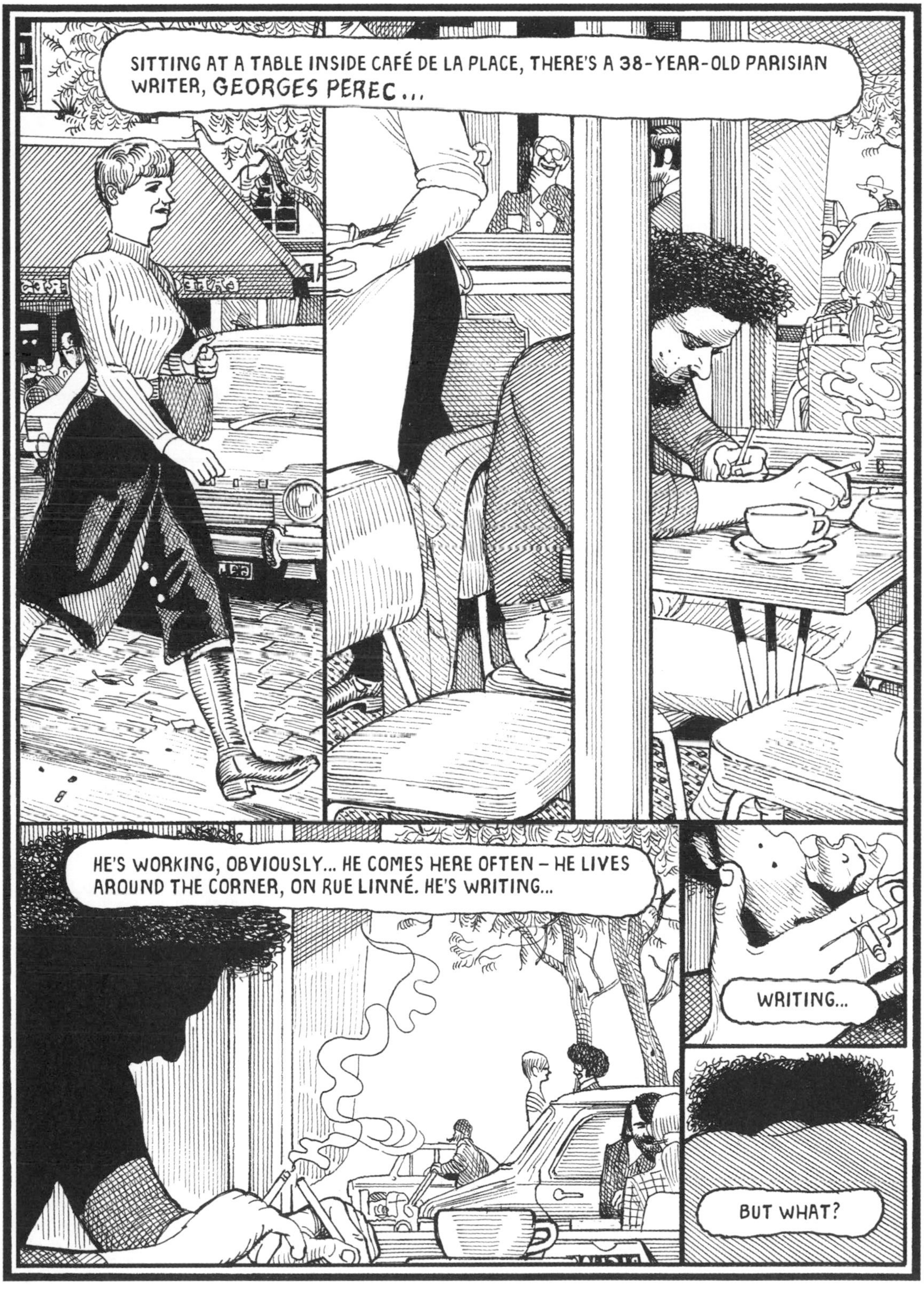
SITTING AT A TABLE INSIDE CAFÉ DE LA PLACE, THERE'S A 38-YEAR-OLD PARISIAN WRITER, GEORGES PEREC...
HE'S WORKING, OBVIOUSLY... HE COMES HERE OFTEN – HE LIVES AROUND THE CORNER, ON RUE LINNÉ. HE'S WRITING...
WRITING...
BUT WHAT?

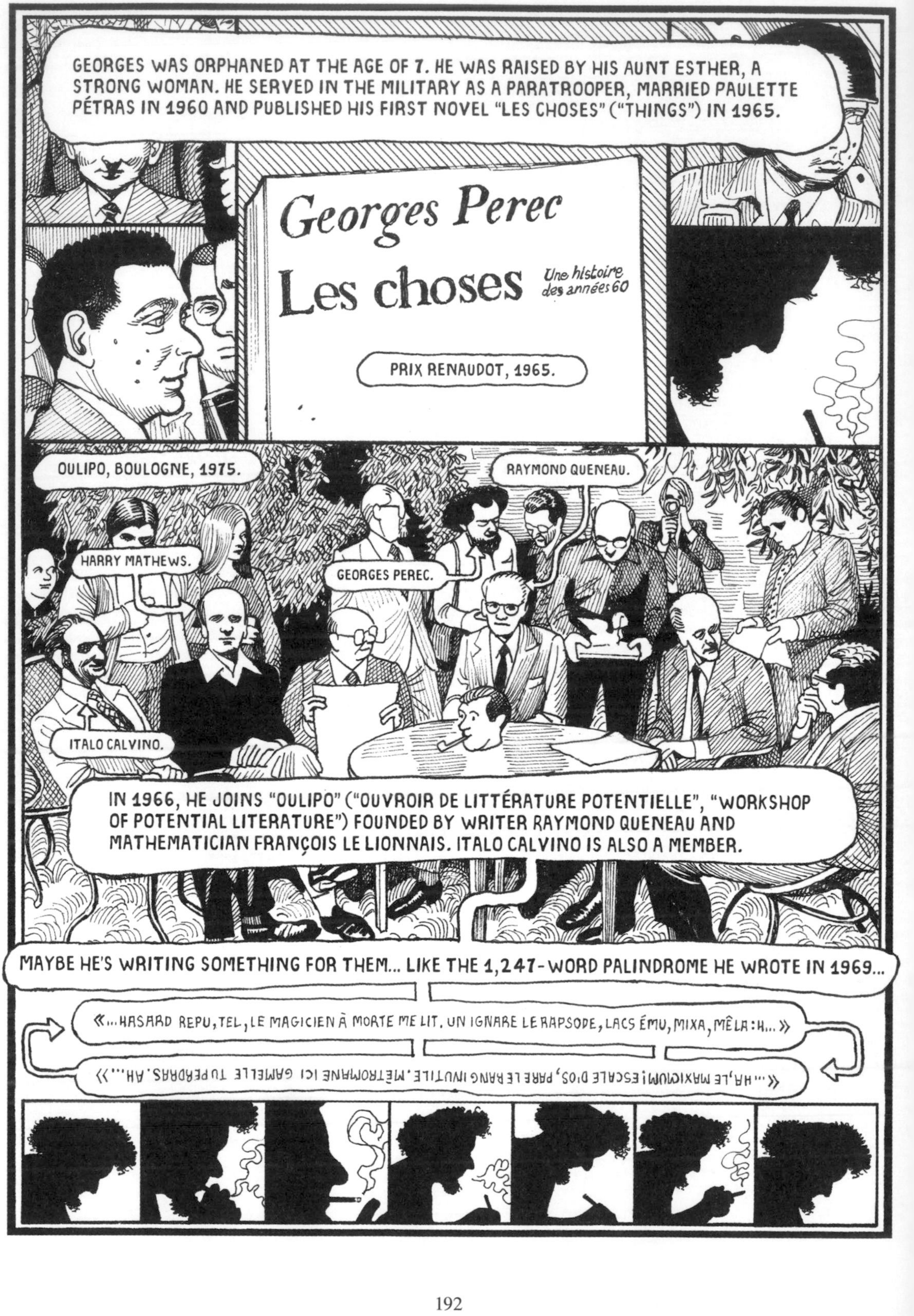

GEORGES WAS ORPHANED AT THE AGE OF 7. HE WAS RAISED BY HIS AUNT ESTHER, A STRONG WOMAN. HE SERVED IN THE MILITARY AS A PARATROOPER, MARRIED PAULETTE PÉTRAS IN 1960 AND PUBLISHED HIS FIRST NOVEL "LES CHOSES" ("THINGS") IN 1965.
Georges Perec
Les choses
Une histoire des années 60
PRIX RENAUDOT, 1965.
OULIPO, BOULOGNE, 1975.
RAYMOND QUENEAU.
HARRY MATHEWS.
GEORGES PEREC.
ITALO CALVINO.
IN 1966, HE JOINS "OULIPO" ("OUVROIR DE LITTÉRATURE POTENTIELLE", "WORKSHOP OF POTENTIAL LITERATURE") FOUNDED BY WRITER RAYMOND QUENEAU AND MATHEMATICIAN FRANÇOIS LE LIONNAIS. ITALO CALVINO IS ALSO A MEMBER.
MAYBE HE'S WRITING SOMETHING FOR THEM... LIKE THE 1,247-WORD PALINDROME HE WROTE IN 1969...
«...HASARD REPU, TEL, LE MAGICIEN À MORTE ME LIT. UN IGNARE LE RAPSODE, LACS ÉMU, MIXA, MÊLA: H...»
«...HA, LE MAXIMUM! ESCALE D'IOS, PARE LE RANG INUTILE. MÉTROMANE ICI GAMELLE TU PERDRAS. AH...»

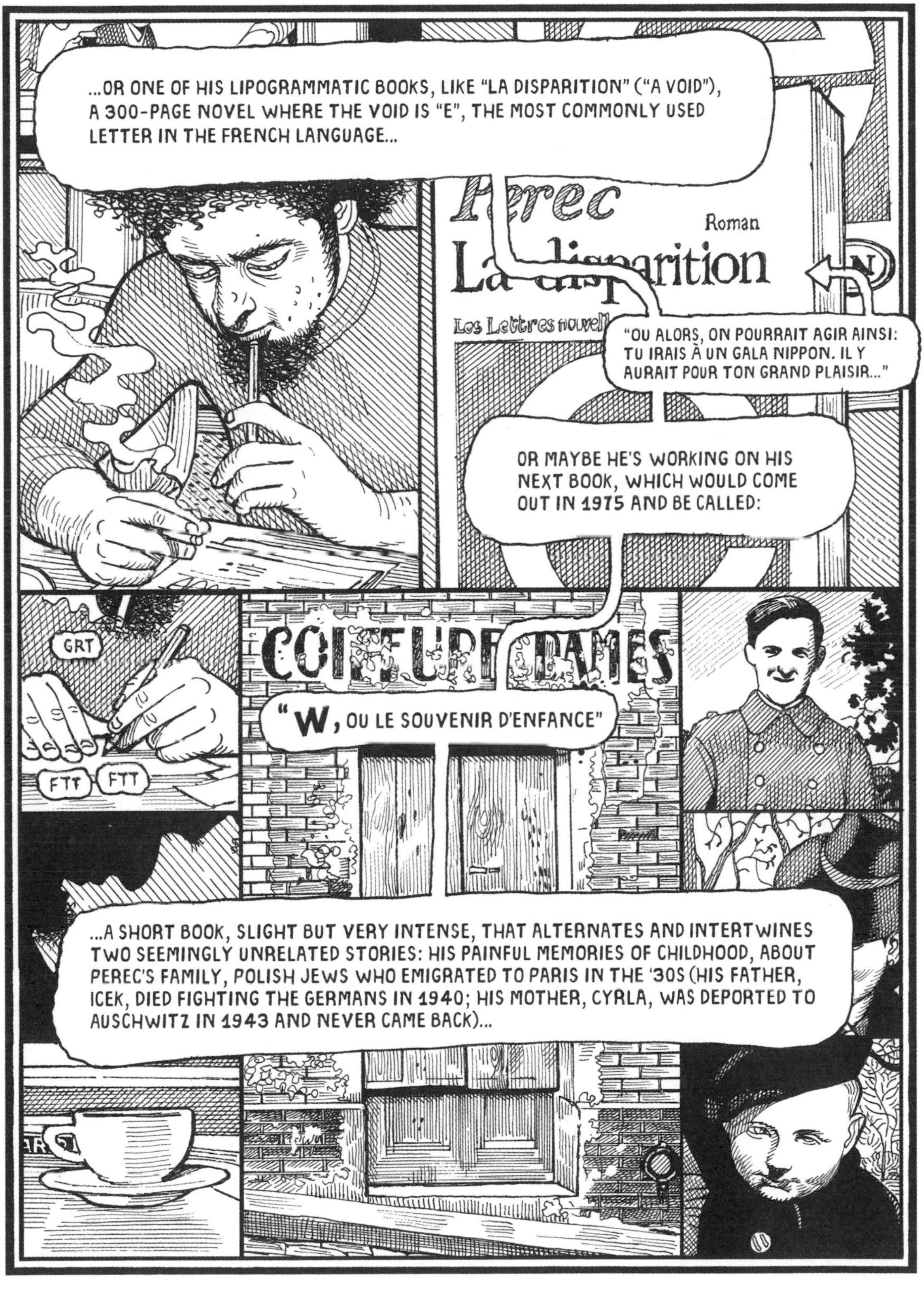
...OR ONE OF HIS LIPOGRAMMATIC BOOKS, LIKE "LA DISPARITION" ("A VOID"), A 300-PAGE NOVEL WHERE THE VOID IS "E", THE MOST COMMONLY USED LETTER IN THE FRENCH LANGUAGE...
Perec
Roman
La disparition
Les Lettres nouvell
"OU ALORS, ON POURRAIT AGIR AINSI: TU IRAIS À UN GALA NIPPON. IL Y AURAIT POUR TON GRAND PLAISIR..."
OR MAYBE HE'S WORKING ON HIS NEXT BOOK, WHICH WOULD COME OUT IN 1975 AND BE CALLED:
GRT
FTT FTT
"W, OU LE SOUVENIR D'ENFANCE"
...A SHORT BOOK, SLIGHT BUT VERY INTENSE, THAT ALTERNATES AND INTERTWINES TWO SEEMINGLY UNRELATED STORIES: HIS PAINFUL MEMORIES OF CHILDHOOD, ABOUT PEREC'S FAMILY, POLISH JEWS WHO EMIGRATED TO PARIS IN THE '30S (HIS FATHER, ICEK, DIED FIGHTING THE GERMANS IN 1940; HIS MOTHER, CYRLA, WAS DEPORTED TO AUSCHWITZ IN 1943 AND NEVER CAME BACK)...

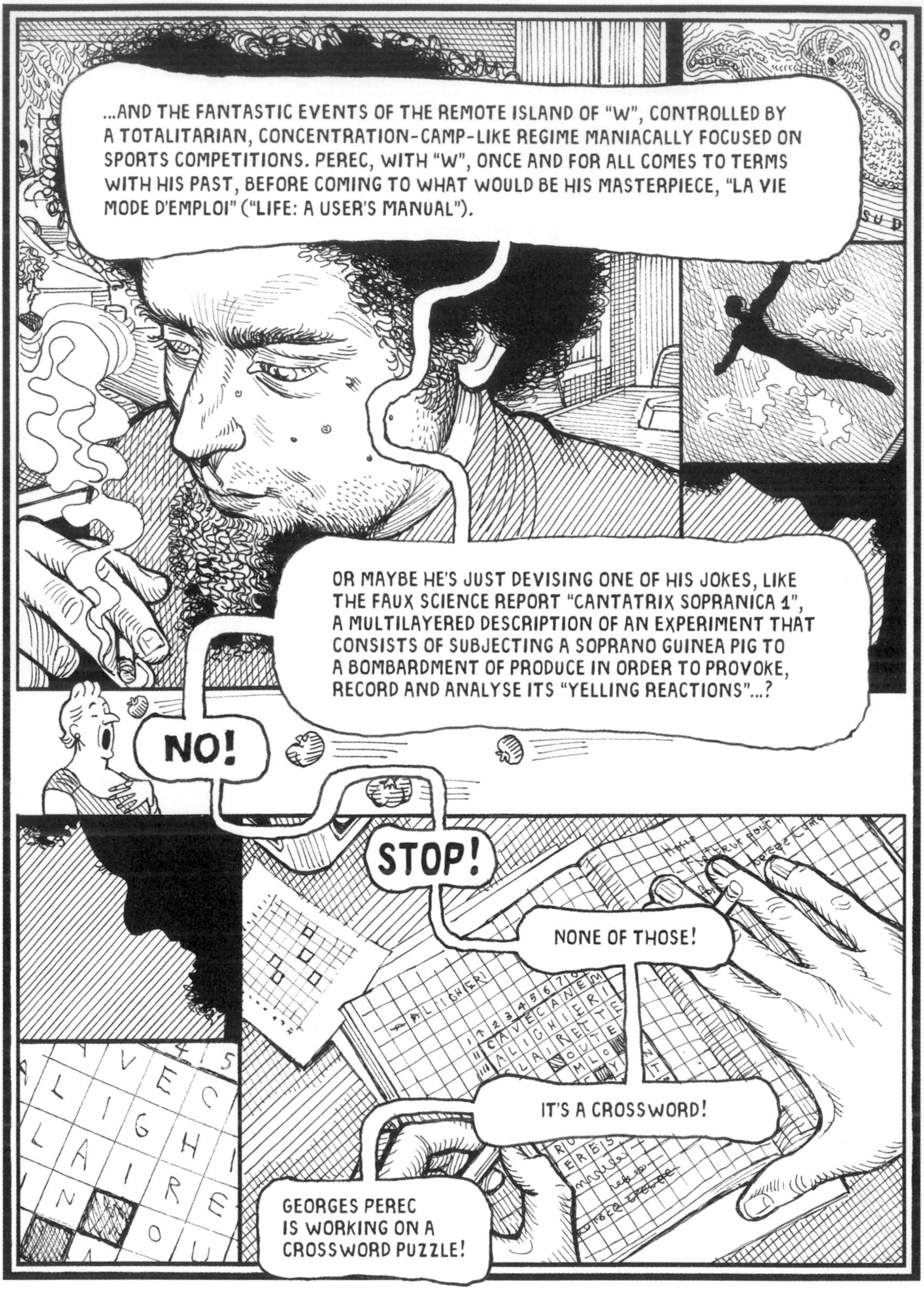
...AND THE FANTASTIC EVENTS OF THE REMOTE ISLAND OF "W", CONTROLLED BY A TOTALITARIAN, CONCENTRATION-CAMP-LIKE REGIME MANIACALLY FOCUSED ON SPORTS COMPETITIONS. PEREC, WITH "W", ONCE AND FOR ALL COMES TO TERMS WITH HIS PAST, BEFORE COMING TO WHAT WOULD BE HIS MASTERPIECE, "LA VIE MODE D'EMPLOI" ("LIFE: A USER'S MANUAL").
OR MAYBE HE'S JUST DEVISING ONE OF HIS JOKES, LIKE THE FAUX SCIENCE REPORT "CANTATRIX SOPRANICA 1", A MULTILAYERED DESCRIPTION OF AN EXPERIMENT THAT CONSISTS OF SUBJECTING A SOPRANO GUINEA PIG TO A BOMBARDMENT OF PRODUCE IN ORDER TO PROVOKE, RECORD AND ANALYSE ITS "YELLING REACTIONS"...?
NO!
STOP!
NONE OF THOSE!
IT'S A CROSSWORD!
GEORGES PEREC IS WORKING ON A CROSSWORD PUZZLE!

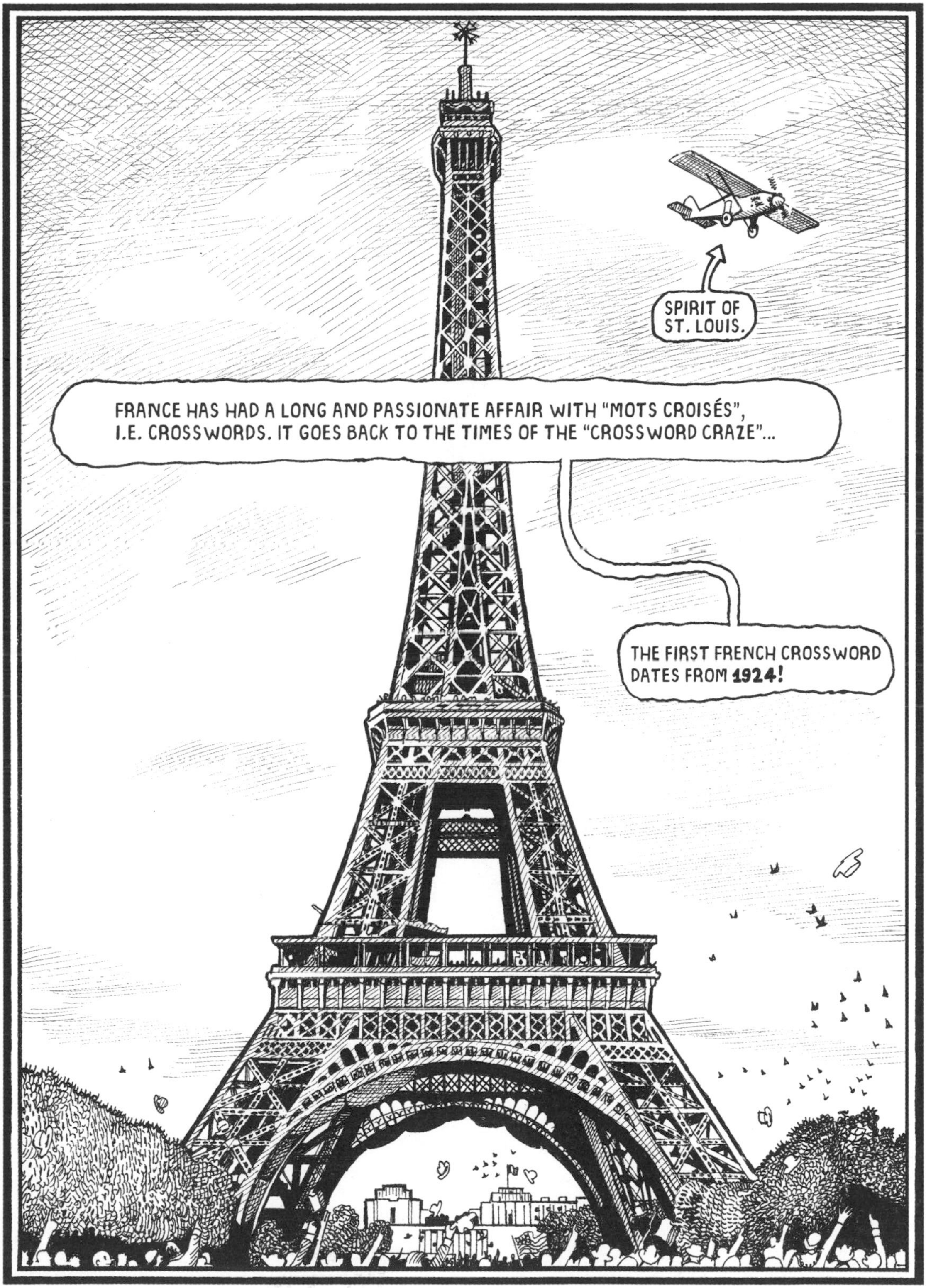
SPIRIT OF ST. LOUIS.
FRANCE HAS HAD A LONG AND PASSIONATE AFFAIR WITH "MOTS CROISÉS", I.E. CROSSWORDS. IT GOES BACK TO THE TIMES OF THE "CROSSWORD CRAZE"...
THE FIRST FRENCH CROSSWORD DATES FROM 1924!

THE HOME OF THE "MOT D'ESPRIT", WHICH HAD BEEN PRACTISING THE ART OF THE APHORISM FOR CENTURIES, INSTANTLY FALLS IN LOVE WITH THE NEW AMERICAN GAME — AND JUST LIKE ACROSS THE CHANNEL, THEY IMMEDIATELY, NATURALLY, ADAPT ITS FORM AND CONTENT TO THEIR OWN CHARACTER, THEIR OWN CULTURE...

PLUS, MANY "CLASSIC" FRENCH APHORISMS ARE ALREADY PERFECT CROSSWORD CLUES...

EGOTIST:
A MAN WHO NEVER THINKS OF ME.

EUGÈNE LABICHE.

MUSIC:
NOISE THAT THINKS.

VICTOR HUGO.

MAN:
SOMEONE SENTENCED TO DEATH.

JULES RENARD.

IMBECILES:
EVERYONE WHO DOESN'T THINK LIKE US.

GUSTAVE FLAUBERT.

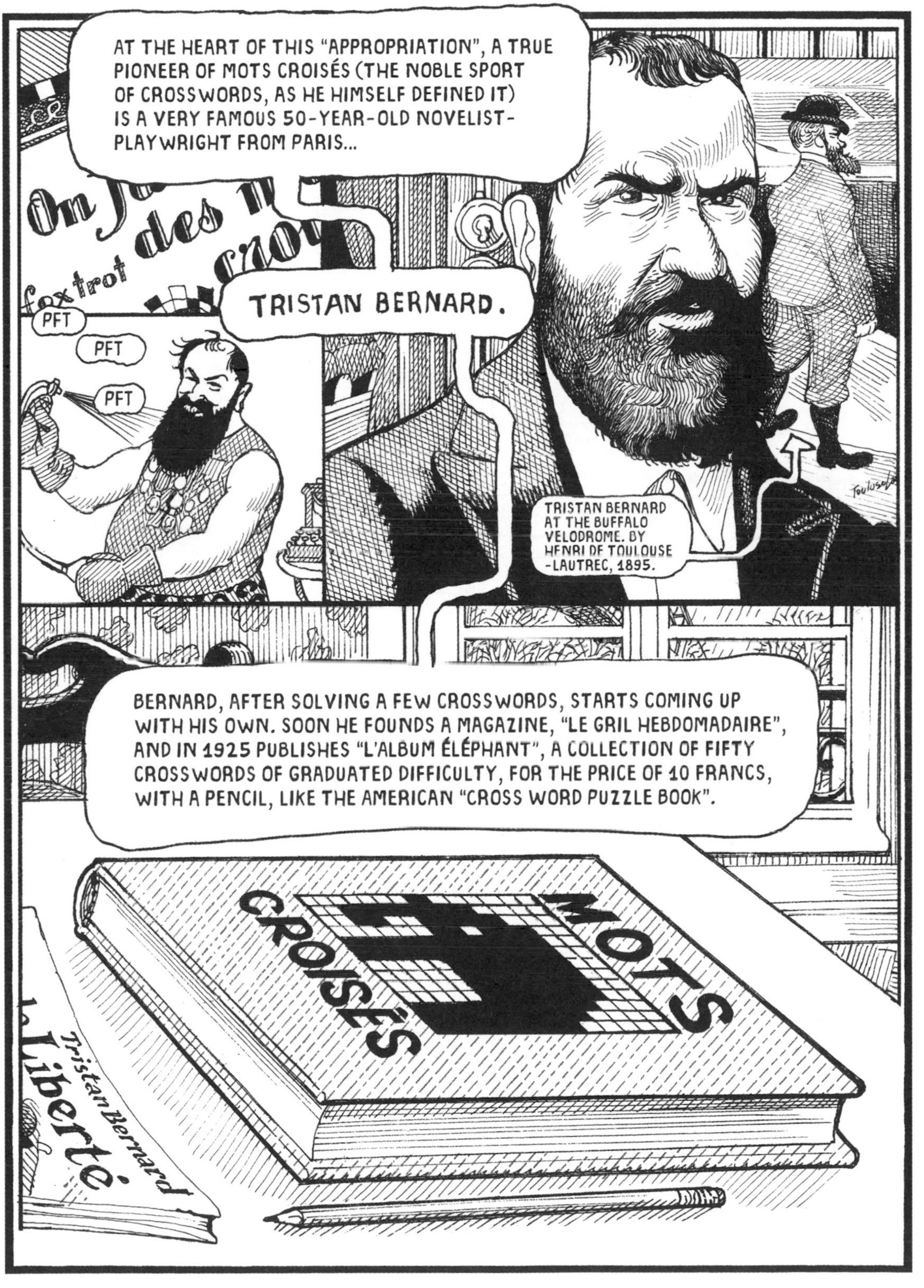
AT THE HEART OF THIS "APPROPRIATION", A TRUE PIONEER OF MOTS CROISÉS (THE NOBLE SPORT OF CROSSWORDS, AS HE HIMSELF DEFINED IT) IS A VERY FAMOUS 50-YEAR-OLD NOVELIST-PLAYWRIGHT FROM PARIS...
TRISTAN BERNARD.
fox trot
PFT
PFT
PFT
TRISTAN BERNARD AT THE BUFFALO VELODROME. BY HENRI DE TOULOUSE-LAUTREC, 1895.
BERNARD, AFTER SOLVING A FEW CROSSWORDS, STARTS COMING UP WITH HIS OWN. SOON HE FOUNDS A MAGAZINE, "LE GRIL HEBDOMADAIRE", AND IN 1925 PUBLISHES "L'ALBUM ÉLÉPHANT", A COLLECTION OF FIFTY CROSSWORDS OF GRADUATED DIFFICULTY, FOR THE PRICE OF 10 FRANCS, WITH A PENCIL, LIKE THE AMERICAN "CROSS WORD PUZZLE BOOK".
MOTS CROISÉS
Tristan Bernard
Liberté

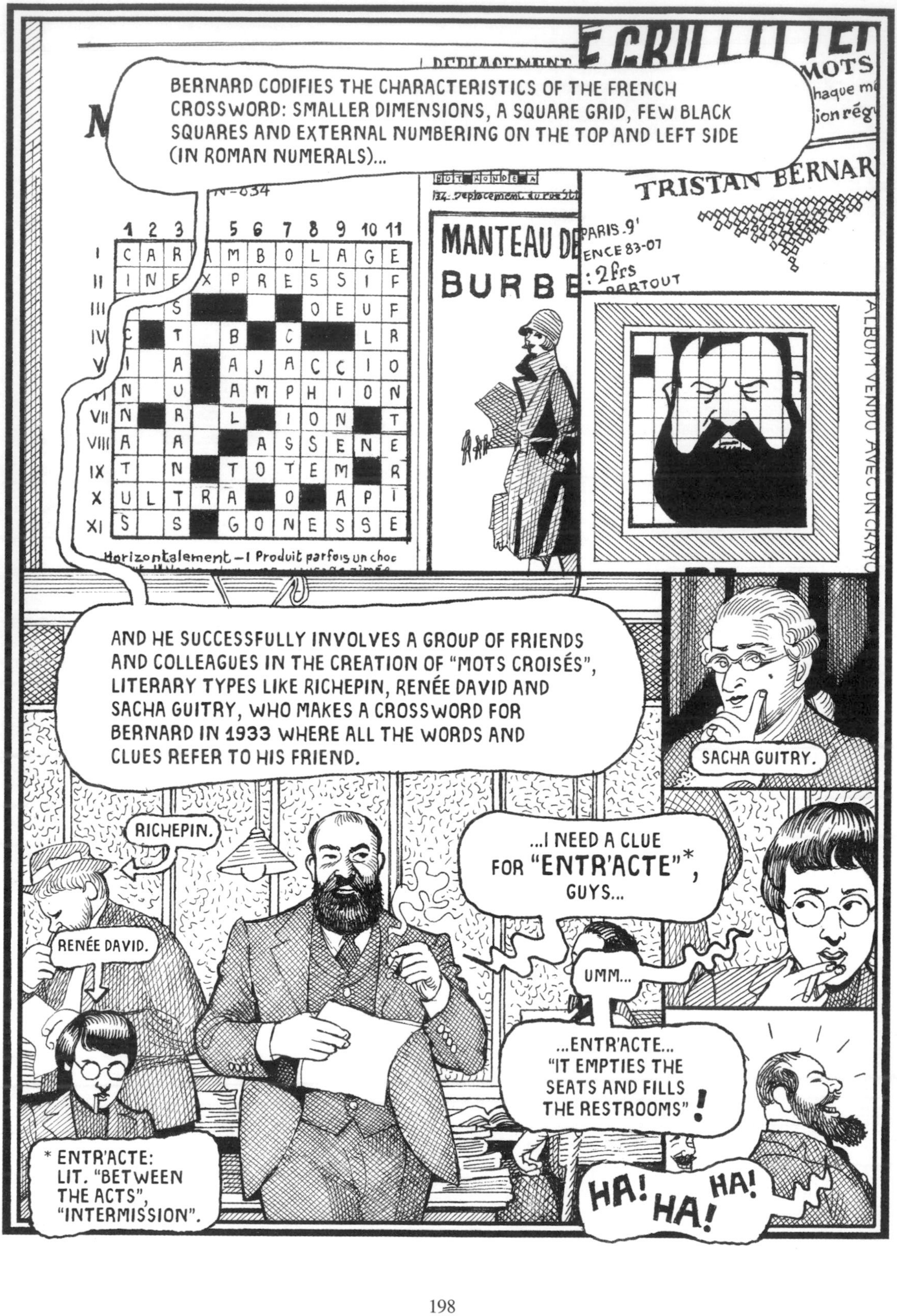
BERNARD CODIFIES THE CHARACTERISTICS OF THE FRENCH CROSSWORD: SMALLER DIMENSIONS, A SQUARE GRID, FEW BLACK SQUARES AND EXTERNAL NUMBERING ON THE TOP AND LEFT SIDE (IN ROMAN NUMERALS)...
MANTEAU DE
BURBE
TRISTAN BERNAR
Horizontalement – I Produit parfois un choc
AND HE SUCCESSFULLY INVOLVES A GROUP OF FRIENDS AND COLLEAGUES IN THE CREATION OF "MOTS CROISÉS", LITERARY TYPES LIKE RICHEPIN, RENÉE DAVID AND SACHA GUITRY, WHO MAKES A CROSSWORD FOR BERNARD IN 1933 WHERE ALL THE WORDS AND CLUES REFER TO HIS FRIEND.
SACHA GUITRY.
RICHEPIN.
...I NEED A CLUE FOR "ENTR'ACTE"*, GUYS...
RENÉE DAVID.
UMM...
...ENTR'ACTE... "IT EMPTIES THE SEATS AND FILLS THE RESTROOMS"!
* ENTR'ACTE: LIT. "BETWEEN THE ACTS", "INTERMISSION".
HA! HA! HA!

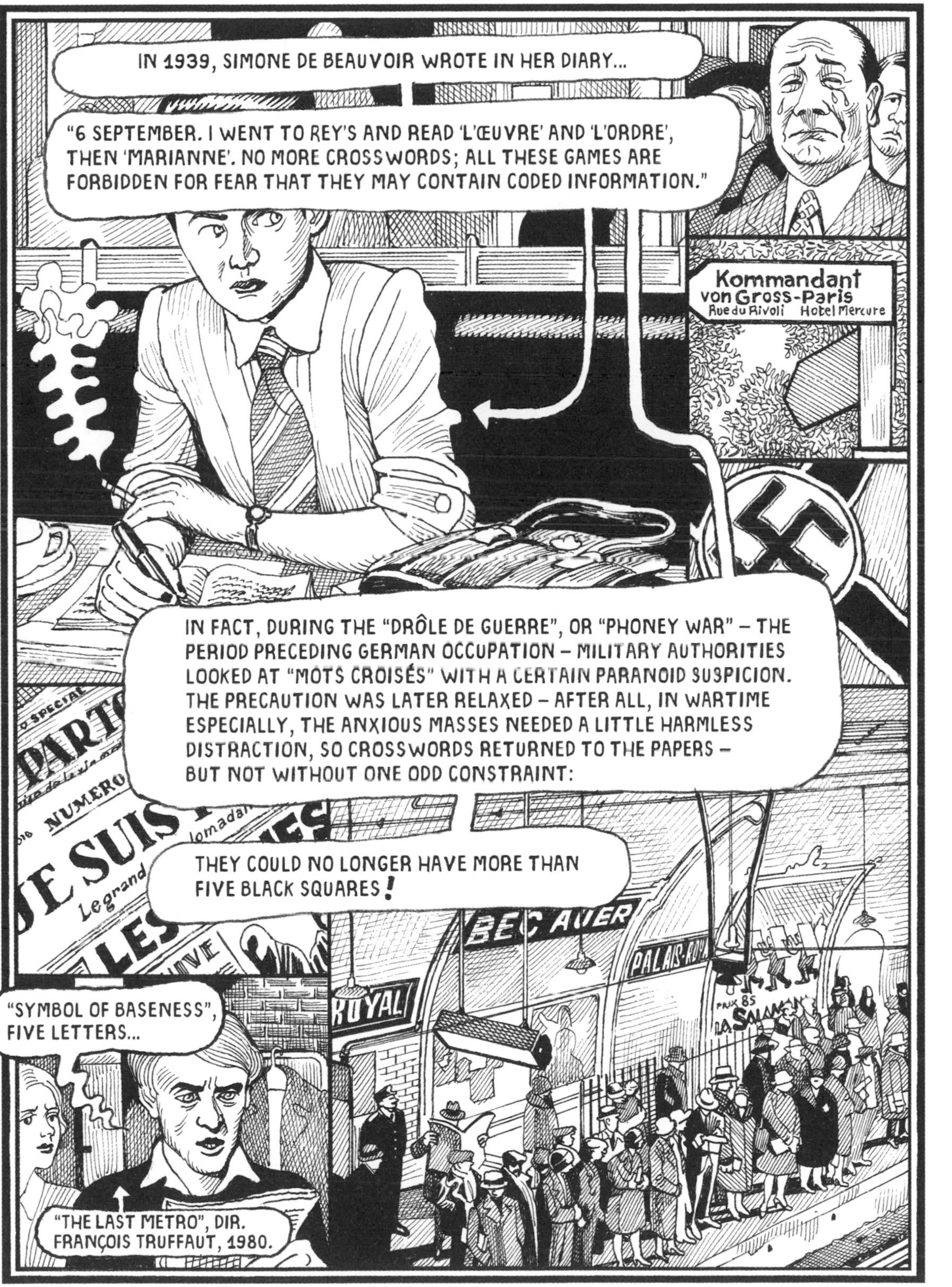
IN 1939, SIMONE DE BEAUVOIR WROTE IN HER DIARY...
"6 SEPTEMBER. I WENT TO REY'S AND READ 'L'ŒUVRE' AND 'L'ORDRE', THEN 'MARIANNE'. NO MORE CROSSWORDS; ALL THESE GAMES ARE FORBIDDEN FOR FEAR THAT THEY MAY CONTAIN CODED INFORMATION."
Kommandant von Gross-Paris
Rue du Rivoli Hotel Mercure
IN FACT, DURING THE "DRÔLE DE GUERRE", OR "PHONEY WAR" – THE PERIOD PRECEDING GERMAN OCCUPATION – MILITARY AUTHORITIES LOOKED AT "MOTS CROISÉS" WITH A CERTAIN PARANOID SUSPICION. THE PRECAUTION WAS LATER RELAXED – AFTER ALL, IN WARTIME ESPECIALLY, THE ANXIOUS MASSES NEEDED A LITTLE HARMLESS DISTRACTION, SO CROSSWORDS RETURNED TO THE PAPERS – BUT NOT WITHOUT ONE ODD CONSTRAINT:
THEY COULD NO LONGER HAVE MORE THAN FIVE BLACK SQUARES!
NUMERO
JE SUIS
LES
BEC AUER
ROYAL
PRIX 85
"SYMBOL OF BASENESS", FIVE LETTERS...
"THE LAST METRO", DIR. FRANÇOIS TRUFFAUT, 1980.

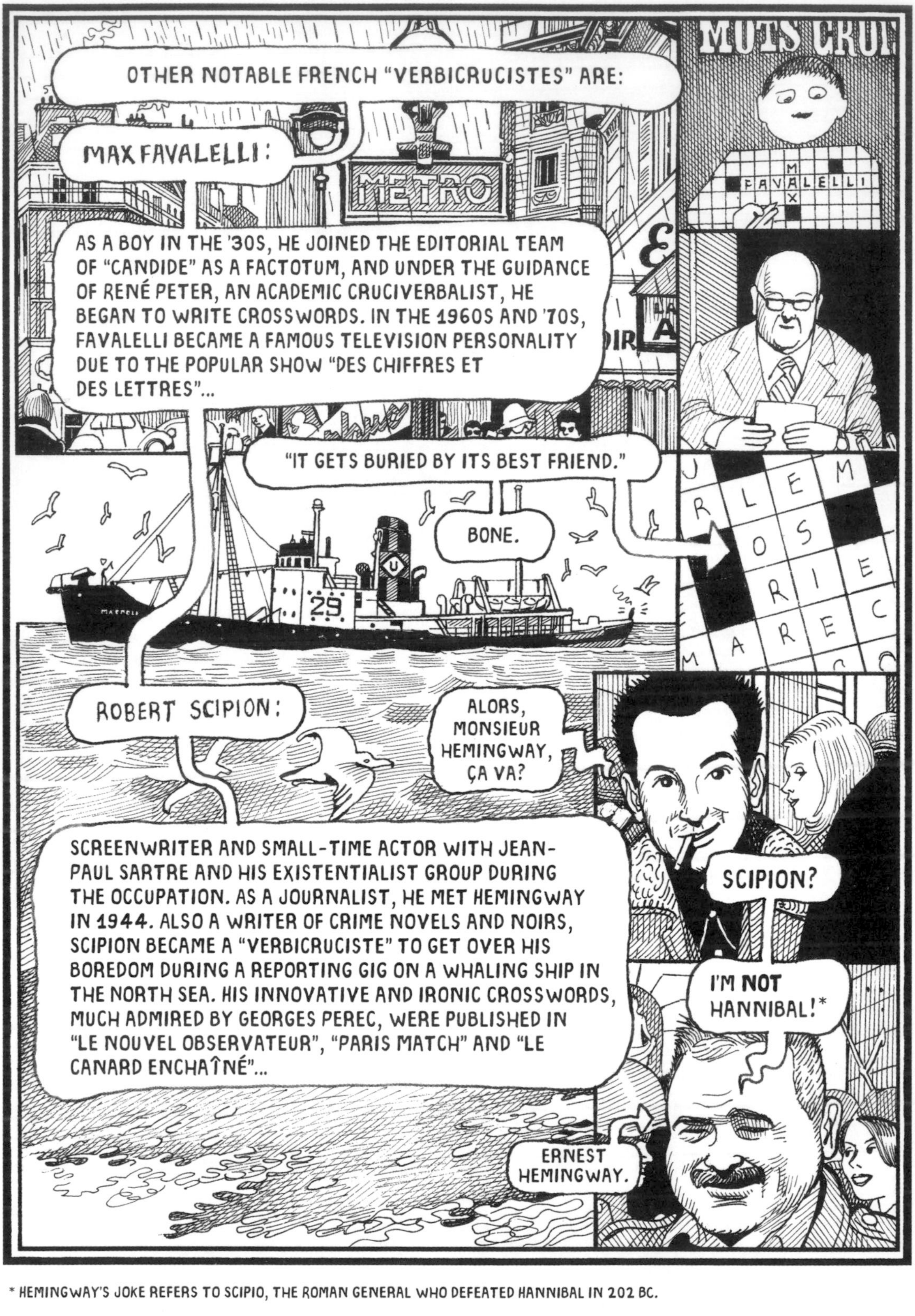
OTHER NOTABLE FRENCH "VERBICRUCISTES" ARE:
MAX FAVALELLI:
AS A BOY IN THE '30S, HE JOINED THE EDITORIAL TEAM OF "CANDIDE" AS A FACTOTUM, AND UNDER THE GUIDANCE OF RENÉ PETER, AN ACADEMIC CRUCIVERBALIST, HE BEGAN TO WRITE CROSSWORDS. IN THE 1960S AND '70S, FAVALELLI BECAME A FAMOUS TELEVISION PERSONALITY DUE TO THE POPULAR SHOW "DES CHIFFRES ET DES LETTRES"...
METRO
MOTS CROI
FAVALELLI
"IT GETS BURIED BY ITS BEST FRIEND."
BONE.
ROBERT SCIPION:
ALORS, MONSIEUR HEMINGWAY, ÇA VA?
SCREENWRITER AND SMALL-TIME ACTOR WITH JEAN-PAUL SARTRE AND HIS EXISTENTIALIST GROUP DURING THE OCCUPATION. AS A JOURNALIST, HE MET HEMINGWAY IN 1944. ALSO A WRITER OF CRIME NOVELS AND NOIRS, SCIPION BECAME A "VERBICRUCISTE" TO GET OVER HIS BOREDOM DURING A REPORTING GIG ON A WHALING SHIP IN THE NORTH SEA. HIS INNOVATIVE AND IRONIC CROSSWORDS, MUCH ADMIRED BY GEORGES PEREC, WERE PUBLISHED IN "LE NOUVEL OBSERVATEUR", "PARIS MATCH" AND "LE CANARD ENCHAÎNÉ"...
SCIPION?
I'M NOT HANNIBAL!*
ERNEST HEMINGWAY.

* HEMINGWAY'S JOKE REFERS TO SCIPIO, THE ROMAN GENERAL WHO DEFEATED HANNIBAL IN 202 BC.

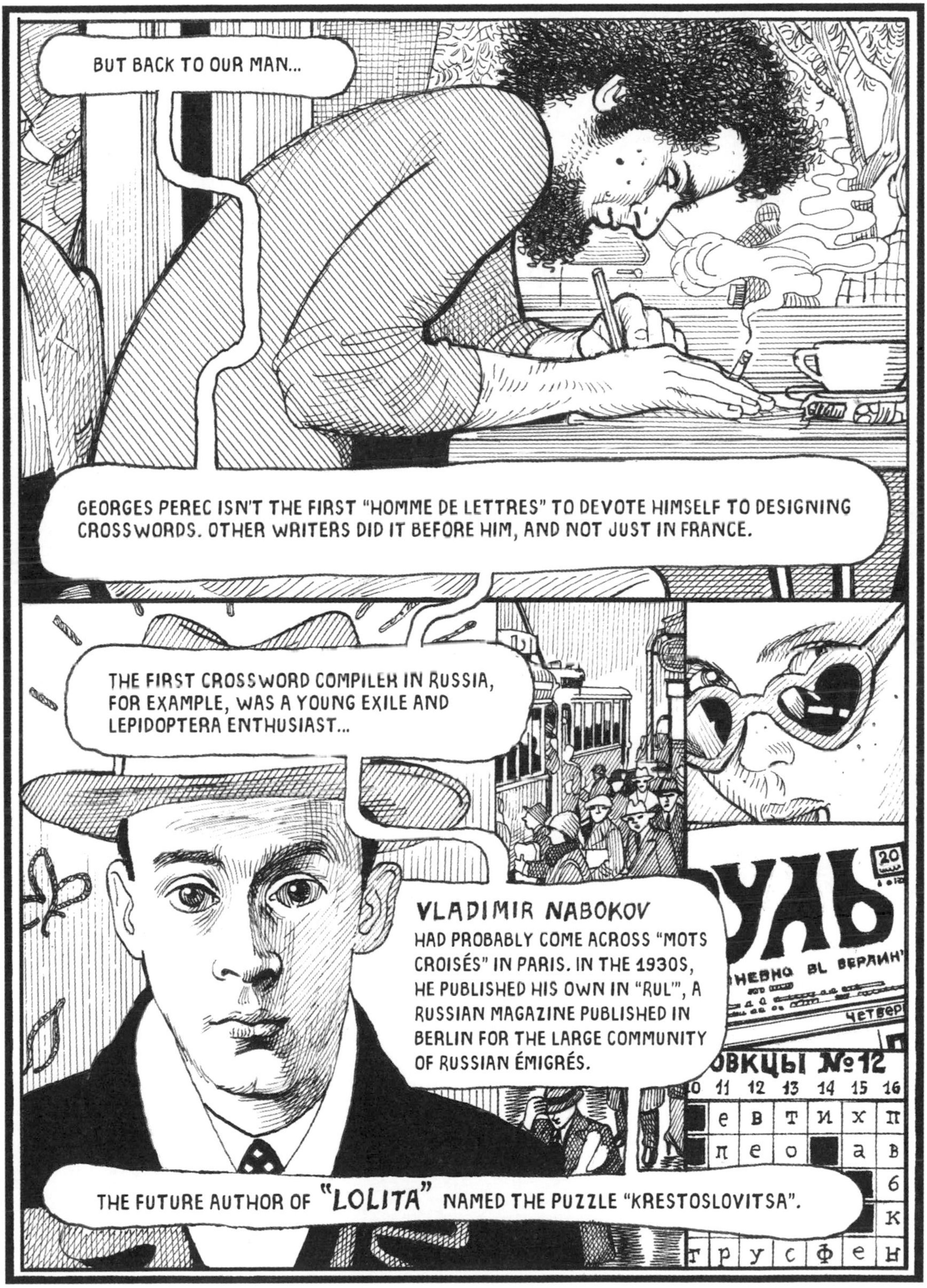
BUT BACK TO OUR MAN...
GEORGES PEREC ISN'T THE FIRST "HOMME DE LETTRES" TO DEVOTE HIMSELF TO DESIGNING CROSSWORDS. OTHER WRITERS DID IT BEFORE HIM, AND NOT JUST IN FRANCE.
THE FIRST CROSSWORD COMPILER IN RUSSIA, FOR EXAMPLE, WAS A YOUNG EXILE AND LEPIDOPTERA ENTHUSIAST...
VLADIMIR NABOKOV
HAD PROBABLY COME ACROSS "MOTS CROISÉS" IN PARIS. IN THE 1930S, HE PUBLISHED HIS OWN IN "RUL", A RUSSIAN MAGAZINE PUBLISHED IN BERLIN FOR THE LARGE COMMUNITY OF RUSSIAN ÉMIGRÉS.
THE FUTURE AUTHOR OF "LOLITA" NAMED THE PUZZLE "KRESTOSLOVITSA".

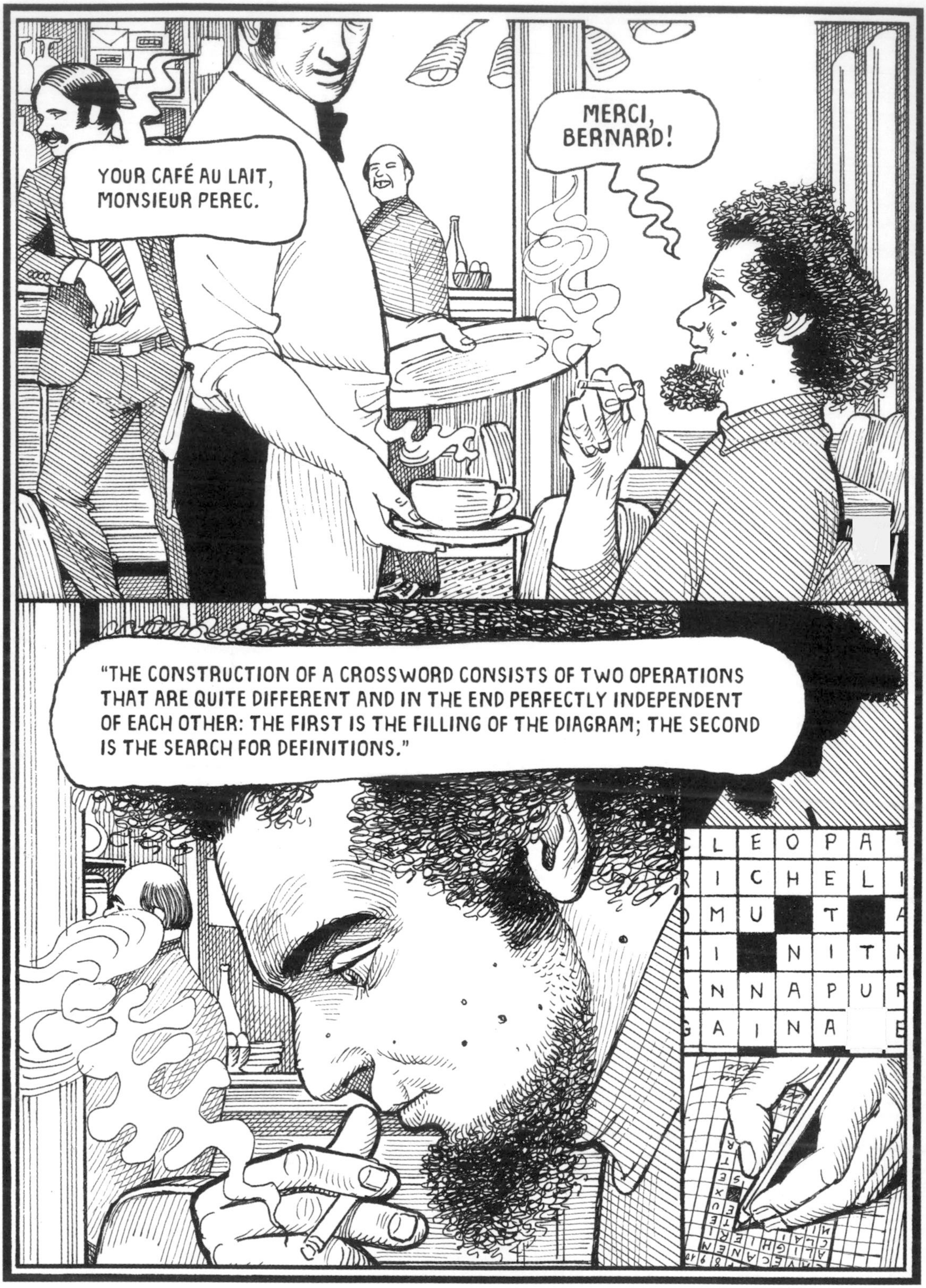
YOUR CAFÉ AU LAIT, MONSIEUR PEREC.
MERCI, BERNARD!
"THE CONSTRUCTION OF A CROSSWORD CONSISTS OF TWO OPERATIONS THAT ARE QUITE DIFFERENT AND IN THE END PERFECTLY INDEPENDENT OF EACH OTHER: THE FIRST IS THE FILLING OF THE DIAGRAM; THE SECOND IS THE SEARCH FOR DEFINITIONS."

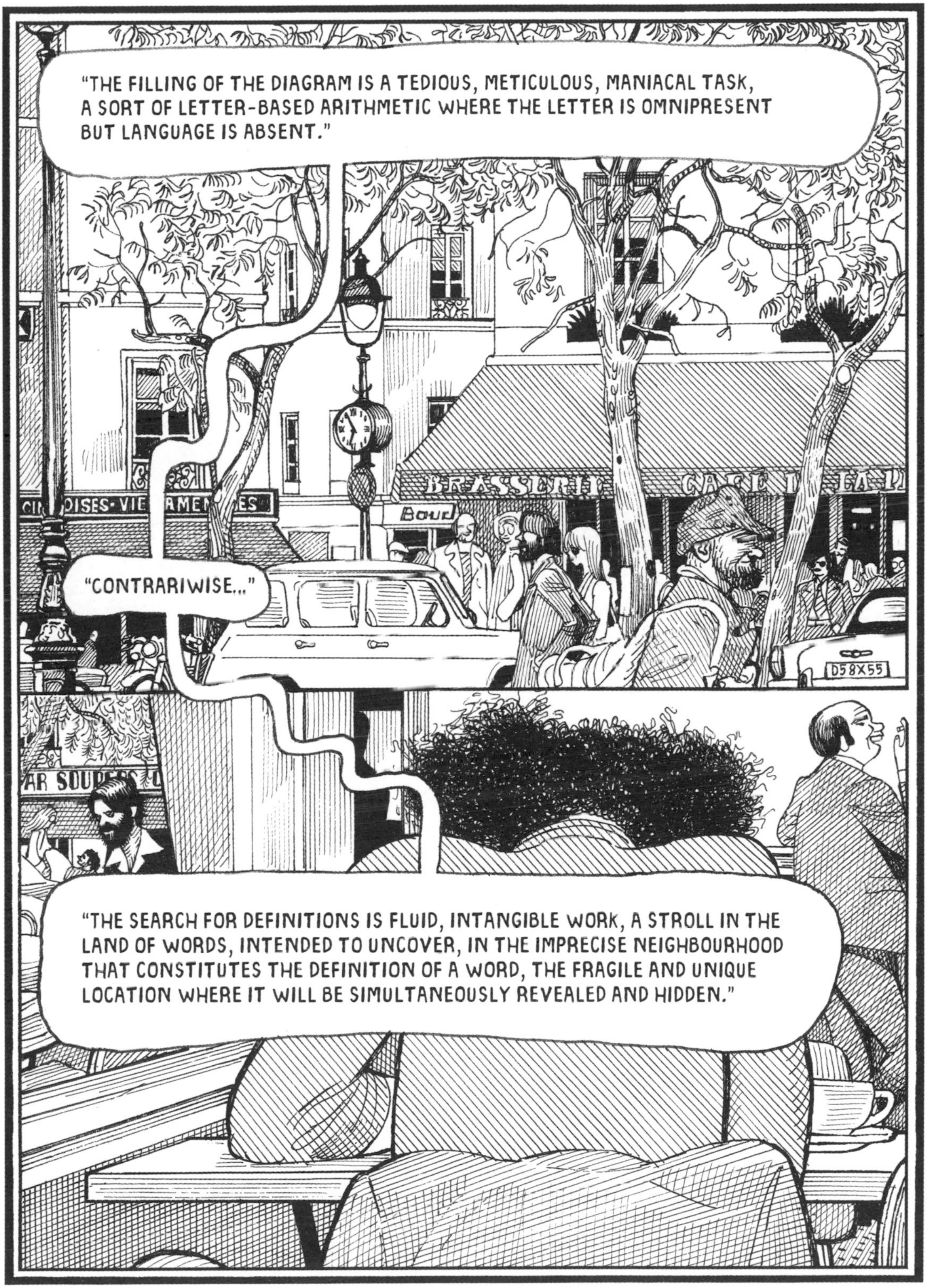
"THE FILLING OF THE DIAGRAM IS A TEDIOUS, METICULOUS, MANIACAL TASK, A SORT OF LETTER-BASED ARITHMETIC WHERE THE LETTER IS OMNIPRESENT BUT LANGUAGE IS ABSENT."
"CONTRARIWISE..."
"THE SEARCH FOR DEFINITIONS IS FLUID, INTANGIBLE WORK, A STROLL IN THE LAND OF WORDS, INTENDED TO UNCOVER, IN THE IMPRECISE NEIGHBOURHOOD THAT CONSTITUTES THE DEFINITION OF A WORD, THE FRAGILE AND UNIQUE LOCATION WHERE IT WILL BE SIMULTANEOUSLY REVEALED AND HIDDEN."

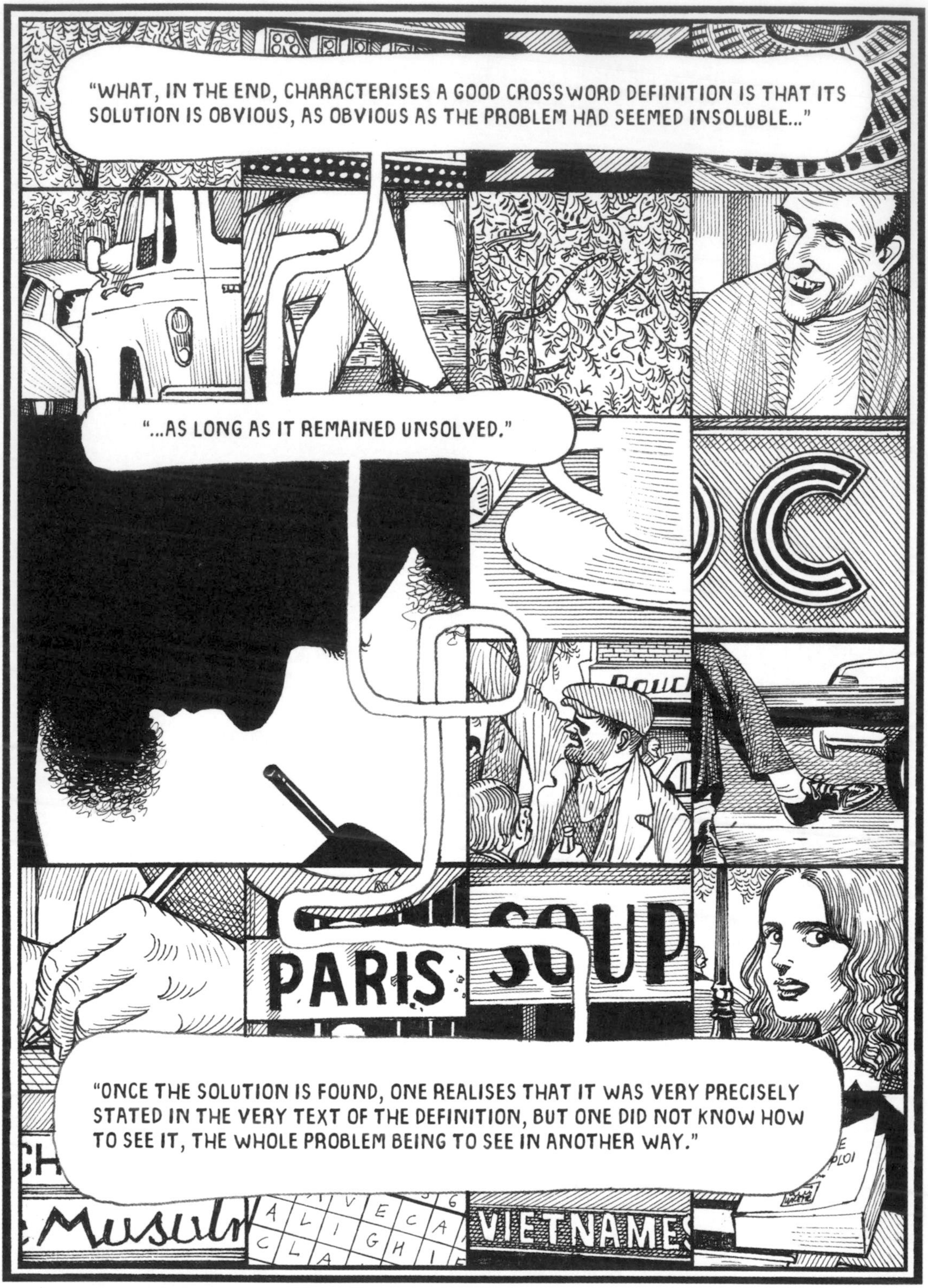
"WHAT, IN THE END, CHARACTERISES A GOOD CROSSWORD DEFINITION IS THAT ITS SOLUTION IS OBVIOUS, AS OBVIOUS AS THE PROBLEM HAD SEEMED INSOLUBLE..."
"...AS LONG AS IT REMAINED UNSOLVED."
PARIS
SOUP
"ONCE THE SOLUTION IS FOUND, ONE REALISES THAT IT WAS VERY PRECISELY STATED IN THE VERY TEXT OF THE DEFINITION, BUT ONE DID NOT KNOW HOW TO SEE IT, THE WHOLE PROBLEM BEING TO SEE IN ANOTHER WAY."

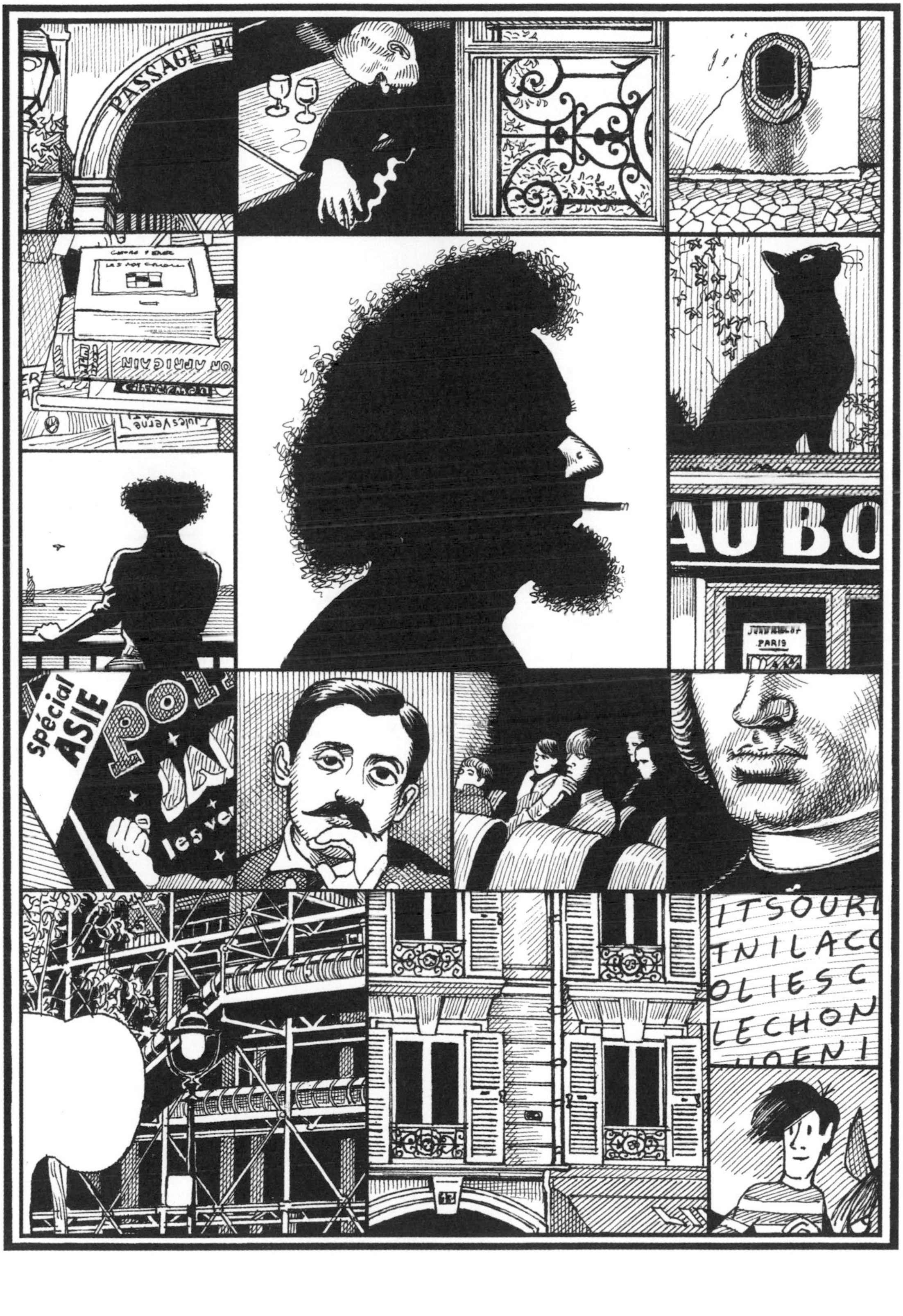

PASSAGE B
AU BO
PARIS
spécial
ASIE
les 5 ve
ITSOUR
TNILAC
OLIESC
LECHON

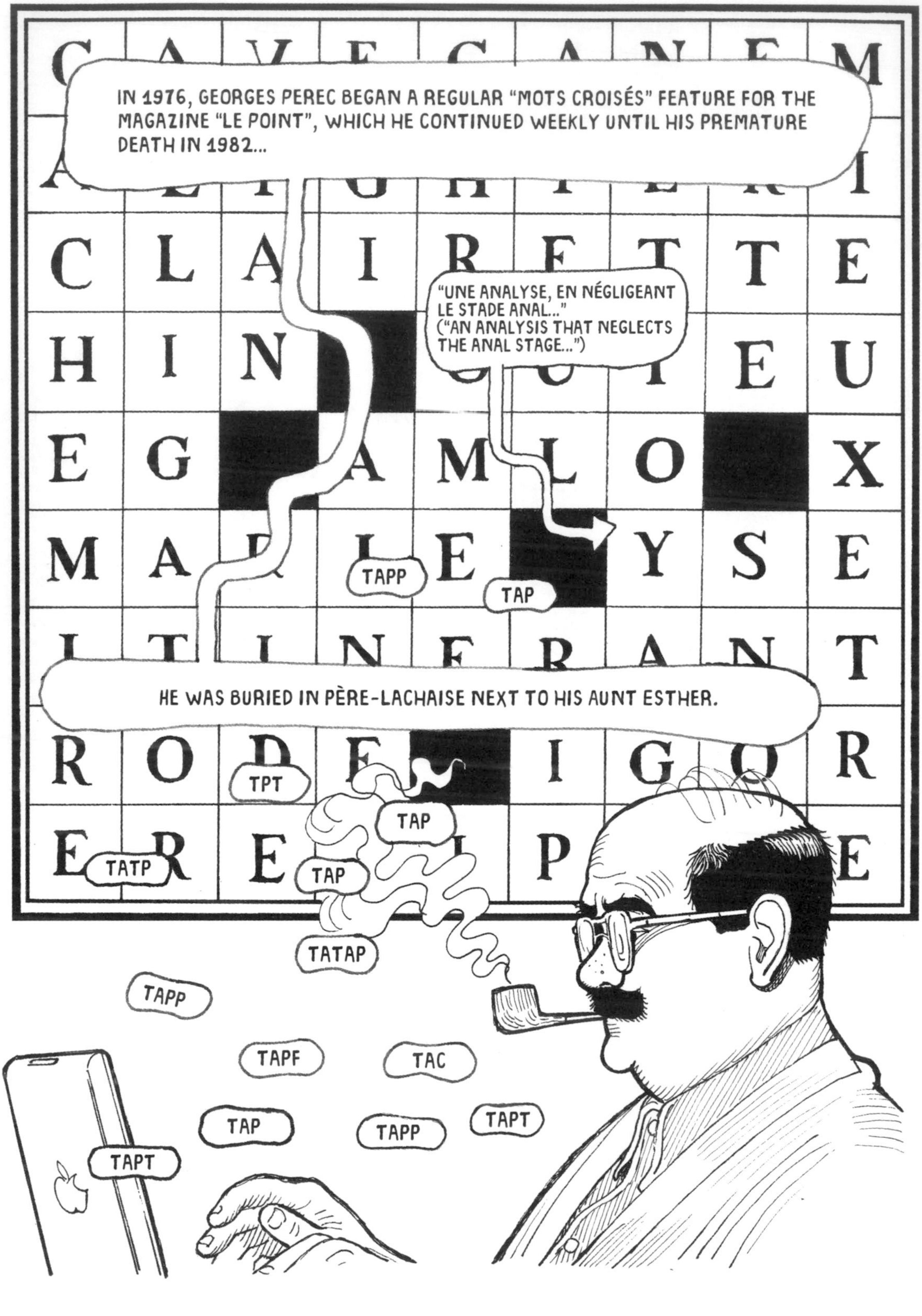
IN 1976, GEORGES PEREC BEGAN A REGULAR "MOTS CROISÉS" FEATURE FOR THE MAGAZINE "LE POINT", WHICH HE CONTINUED WEEKLY UNTIL HIS PREMATURE DEATH IN 1982...
"UNE ANALYSE, EN NÉGLIGEANT LE STADE ANAL..." ("AN ANALYSIS THAT NEGLECTS THE ANAL STAGE...")
TAPP
TAP
HE WAS BURIED IN PÈRE-LACHAISE NEXT TO HIS AUNT ESTHER.
TPT
TAP
TATP
TAP
TATAP
TAPP
TAPF
TAC
TAP
TAPP
TAPT
TAPT

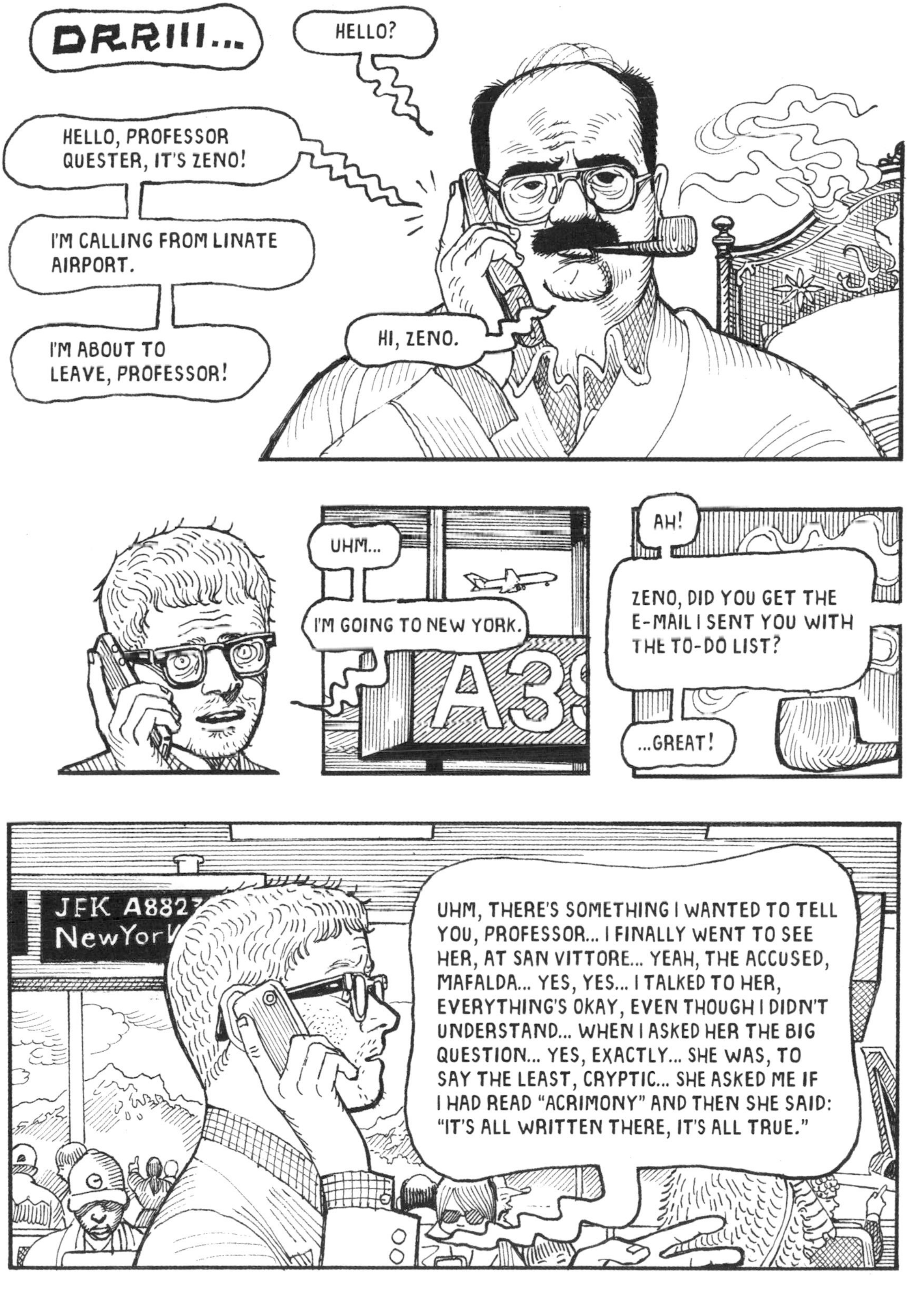
DRRIII...
HELLO?
HELLO, PROFESSOR QUESTER, IT'S ZENO!
I'M CALLING FROM LINATE AIRPORT.
I'M ABOUT TO LEAVE, PROFESSOR!
HI, ZENO.
UHM...
I'M GOING TO NEW YORK.
A39
AH!
ZENO, DID YOU GET THE E-MAIL I SENT YOU WITH THE TO-DO LIST?
...GREAT!
JFK A8823
NewYork
UHM, THERE'S SOMETHING I WANTED TO TELL YOU, PROFESSOR... I FINALLY WENT TO SEE HER, AT SAN VITTORE... YEAH, THE ACCUSED, MAFALDA... YES, YES... I TALKED TO HER, EVERYTHING'S OKAY, EVEN THOUGH I DIDN'T UNDERSTAND... WHEN I ASKED HER THE BIG QUESTION... YES, EXACTLY... SHE WAS, TO SAY THE LEAST, CRYPTIC... SHE ASKED ME IF I HAD READ "ACRIMONY" AND THEN SHE SAID: "IT'S ALL WRITTEN THERE, IT'S ALL TRUE."

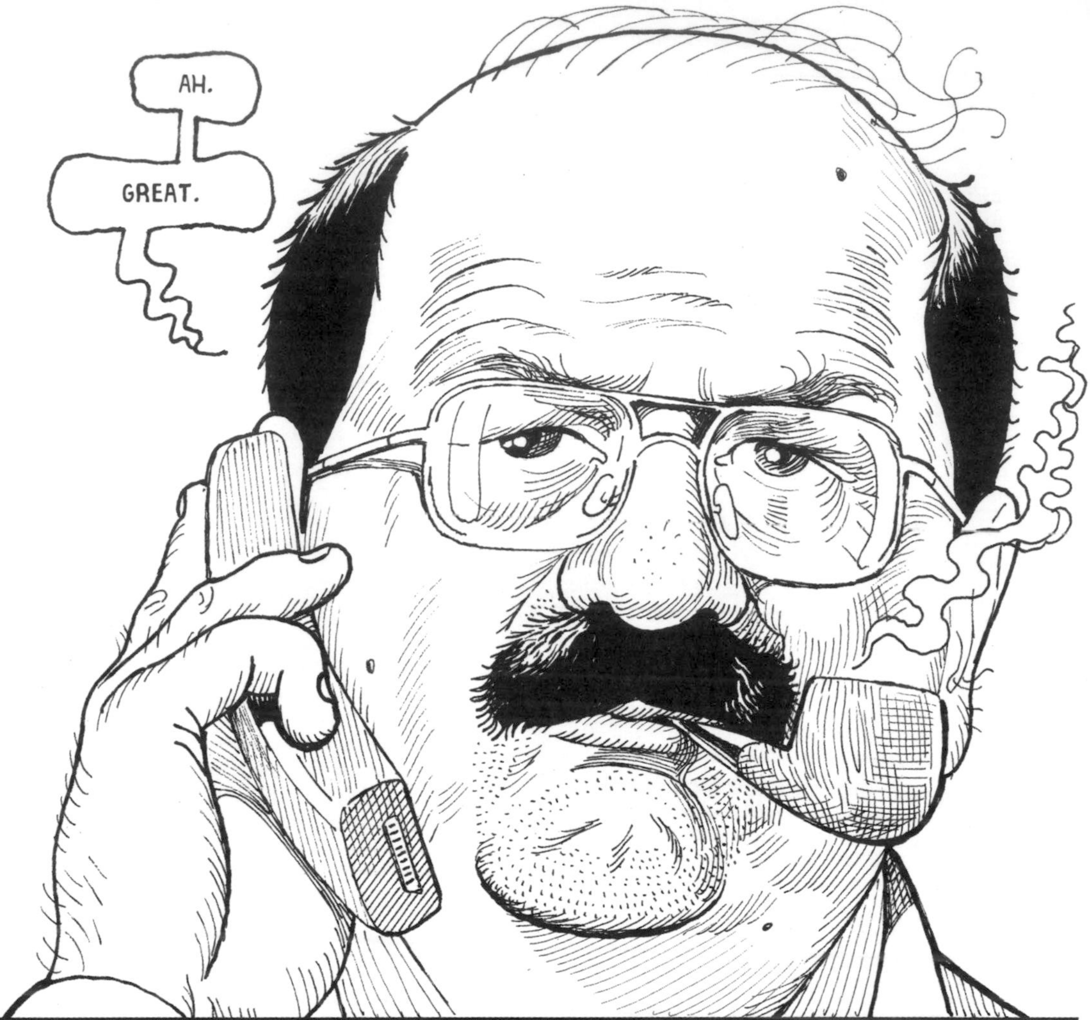
AH.
GREAT.

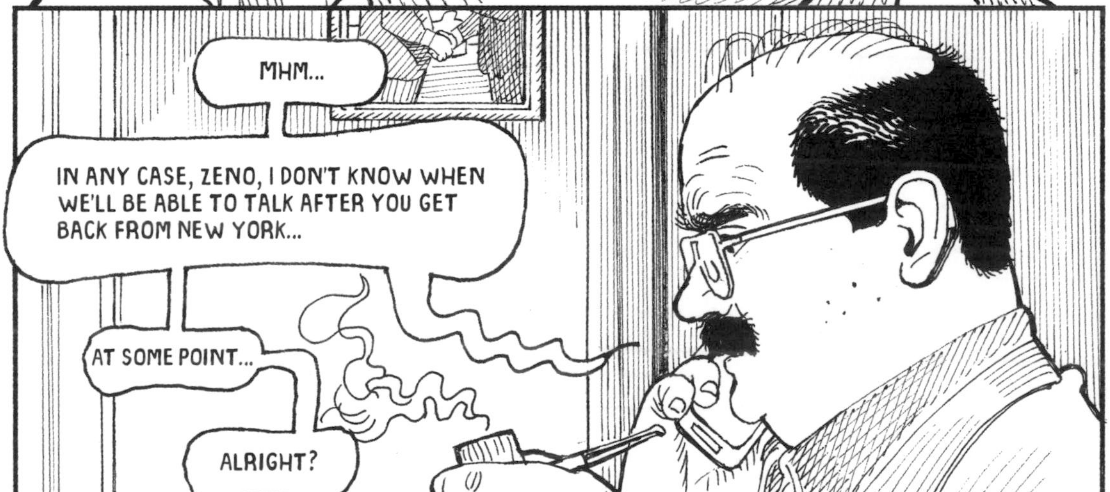
MHM...
IN ANY CASE, ZENO, I DON'T KNOW WHEN WE'LL BE ABLE TO TALK AFTER YOU GET BACK FROM NEW YORK...
AT SOME POINT...
ALRIGHT?

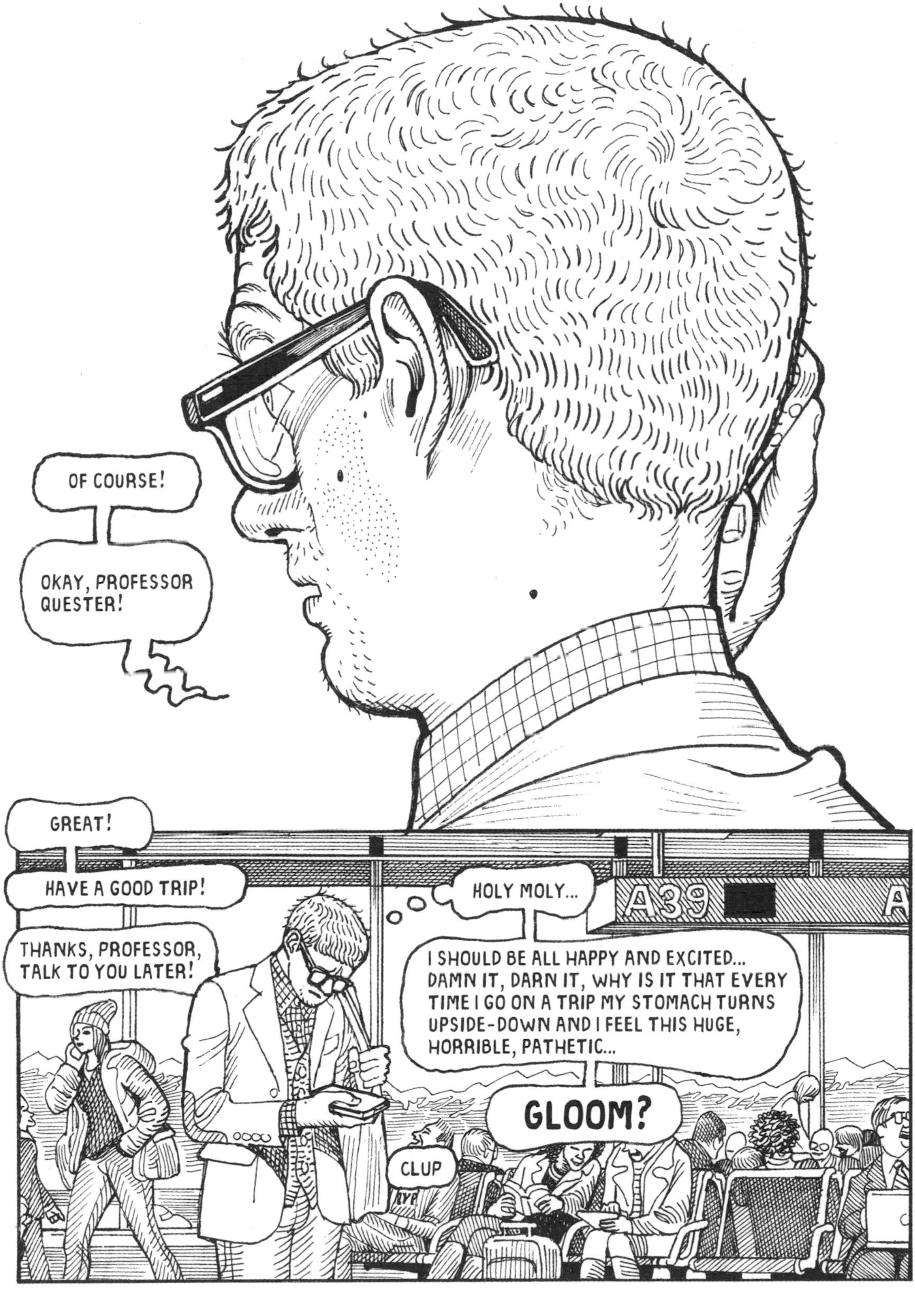
OF COURSE!
OKAY, PROFESSOR QUESTER!
GREAT!
HAVE A GOOD TRIP!
THANKS, PROFESSOR, TALK TO YOU LATER!
HOLY MOLY...
I SHOULD BE ALL HAPPY AND EXCITED... DAMN IT, DARN IT, WHY IS IT THAT EVERY TIME I GO ON A TRIP MY STOMACH TURNS UPSIDE-DOWN AND I FEEL THIS HUGE, HORRIBLE, PATHETIC...
GLOOM?
CLUP
A39

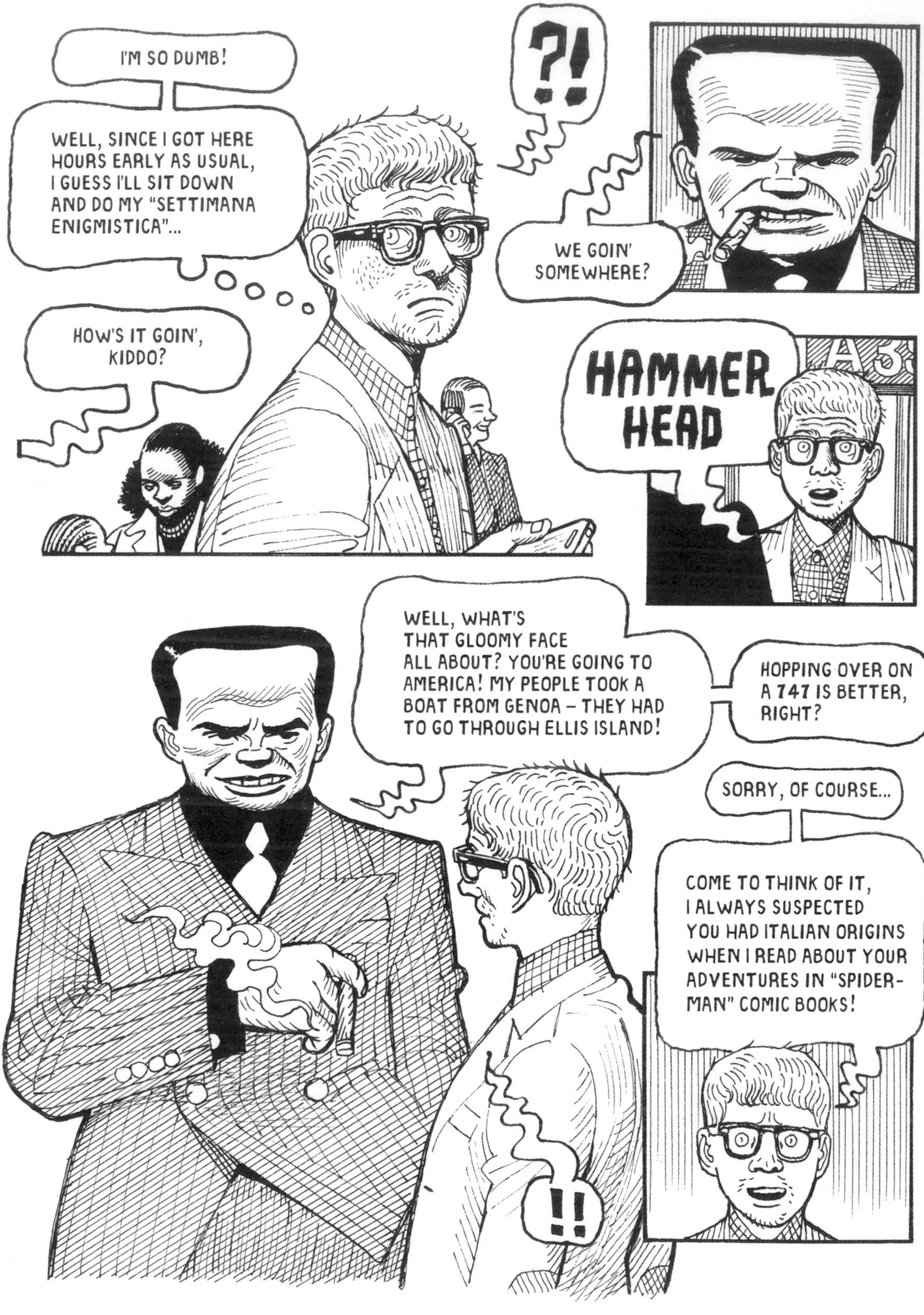
I'M SO DUMB!
WELL, SINCE I GOT HERE HOURS EARLY AS USUAL, I GUESS I'LL SIT DOWN AND DO MY "SETTIMANA ENIGMISTICA"...
HOW'S IT GOIN', KIDDO?
?!
WE GOIN' SOMEWHERE?
HAMMER HEAD
WELL, WHAT'S THAT GLOOMY FACE ALL ABOUT? YOU'RE GOING TO AMERICA! MY PEOPLE TOOK A BOAT FROM GENOA – THEY HAD TO GO THROUGH ELLIS ISLAND!
HOPPING OVER ON A 747 IS BETTER, RIGHT?
!!
SORRY, OF COURSE...
COME TO THINK OF IT, I ALWAYS SUSPECTED YOU HAD ITALIAN ORIGINS WHEN I READ ABOUT YOUR ADVENTURES IN "SPIDER-MAN" COMIC BOOKS!

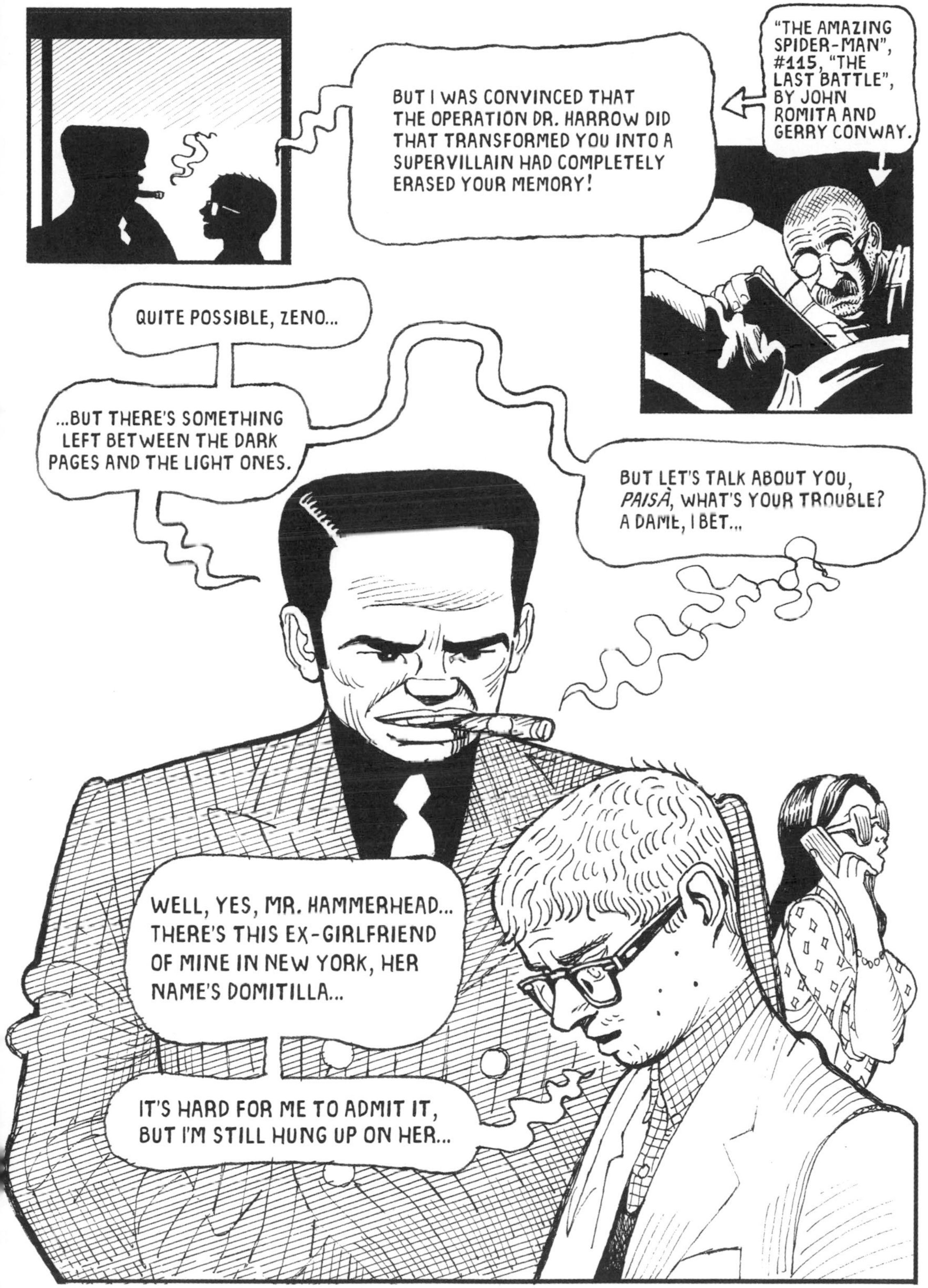
BUT I WAS CONVINCED THAT THE OPERATION DR. HARROW DID THAT TRANSFORMED YOU INTO A SUPERVILLAIN HAD COMPLETELY ERASED YOUR MEMORY!
"THE AMAZING SPIDER-MAN", #115, "THE LAST BATTLE", BY JOHN ROMITA AND GERRY CONWAY.
QUITE POSSIBLE, ZENO...
...BUT THERE'S SOMETHING LEFT BETWEEN THE DARK PAGES AND THE LIGHT ONES.
BUT LET'S TALK ABOUT YOU, *PAISÀ*, WHAT'S YOUR TROUBLE? A DAME, I BET...
WELL, YES, MR. HAMMERHEAD... THERE'S THIS EX-GIRLFRIEND OF MINE IN NEW YORK, HER NAME'S DOMITILLA...
IT'S HARD FOR ME TO ADMIT IT, BUT I'M STILL HUNG UP ON HER...

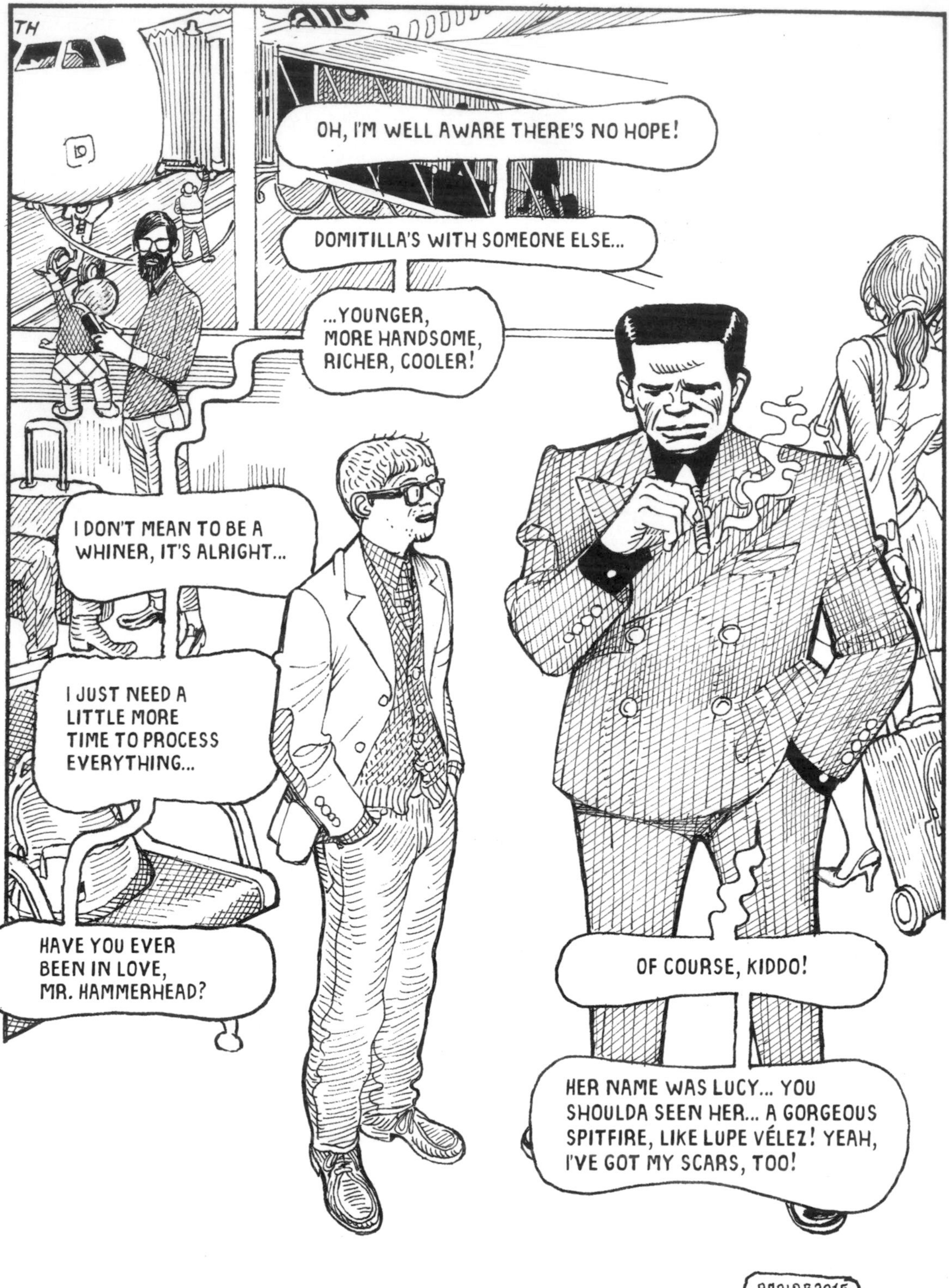
OH, I'M WELL AWARE THERE'S NO HOPE!
DOMITILLA'S WITH SOMEONE ELSE...
...YOUNGER, MORE HANDSOME, RICHER, COOLER!
I DON'T MEAN TO BE A WHINER, IT'S ALRIGHT...
I JUST NEED A LITTLE MORE TIME TO PROCESS EVERYTHING...
HAVE YOU EVER BEEN IN LOVE, MR. HAMMERHEAD?
OF COURSE, KIDDO!
HER NAME WAS LUCY... YOU SHOULDA SEEN HER... A GORGEOUS SPITFIRE, LIKE LUPE VÉLEZ! YEAH, I'VE GOT MY SCARS, TOO!
PAOLO B 2015

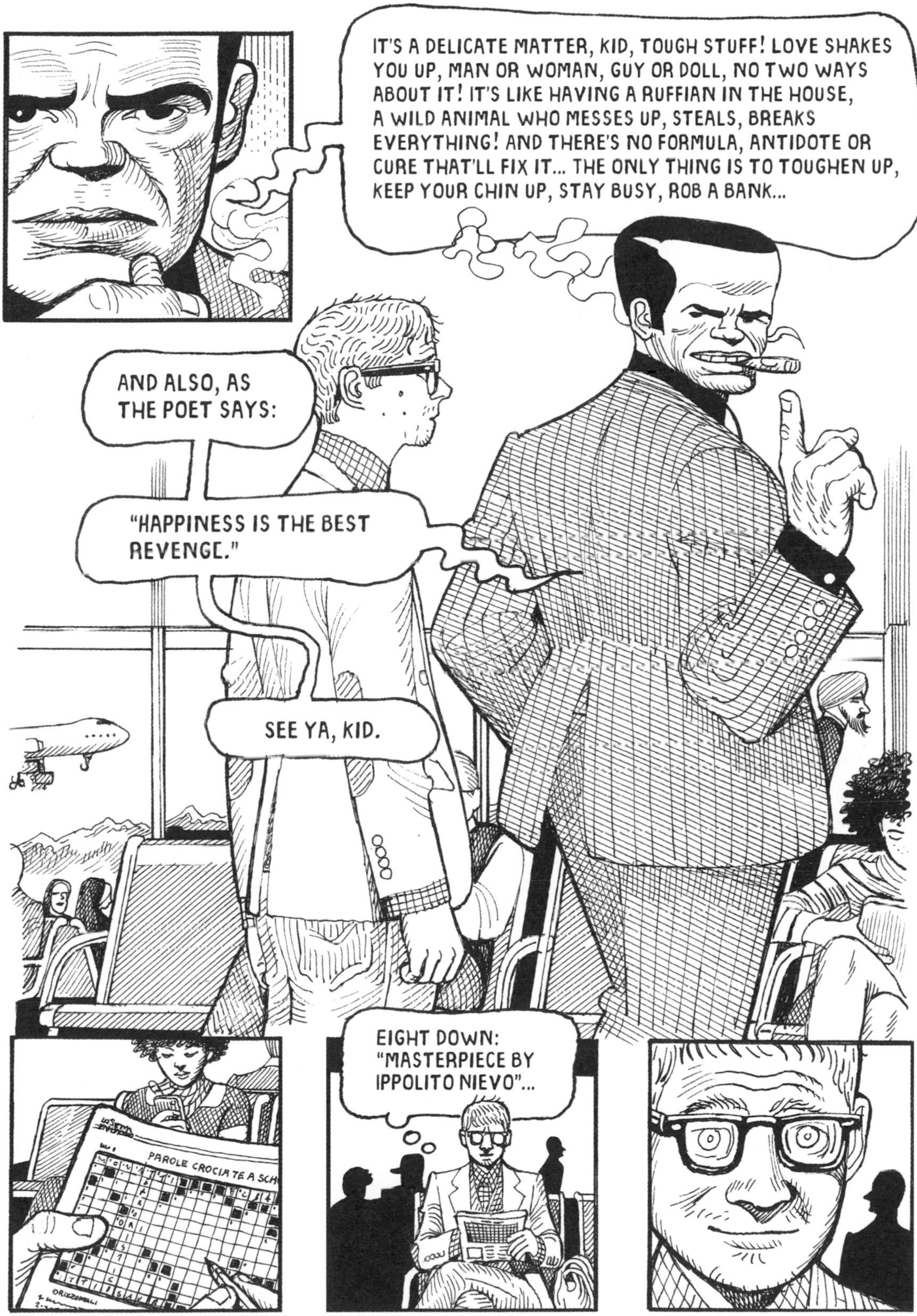
IT'S A DELICATE MATTER, KID, TOUGH STUFF! LOVE SHAKES YOU UP, MAN OR WOMAN, GUY OR DOLL, NO TWO WAYS ABOUT IT! IT'S LIKE HAVING A RUFFIAN IN THE HOUSE, A WILD ANIMAL WHO MESSES UP, STEALS, BREAKS EVERYTHING! AND THERE'S NO FORMULA, ANTIDOTE OR CURE THAT'LL FIX IT... THE ONLY THING IS TO TOUGHEN UP, KEEP YOUR CHIN UP, STAY BUSY, ROB A BANK...
AND ALSO, AS THE POET SAYS:
"HAPPINESS IS THE BEST REVENGE."
SEE YA, KID.
PAROLE CROCIATE A SCH
EIGHT DOWN: "MASTERPIECE BY IPPOLITO NIEVO"...

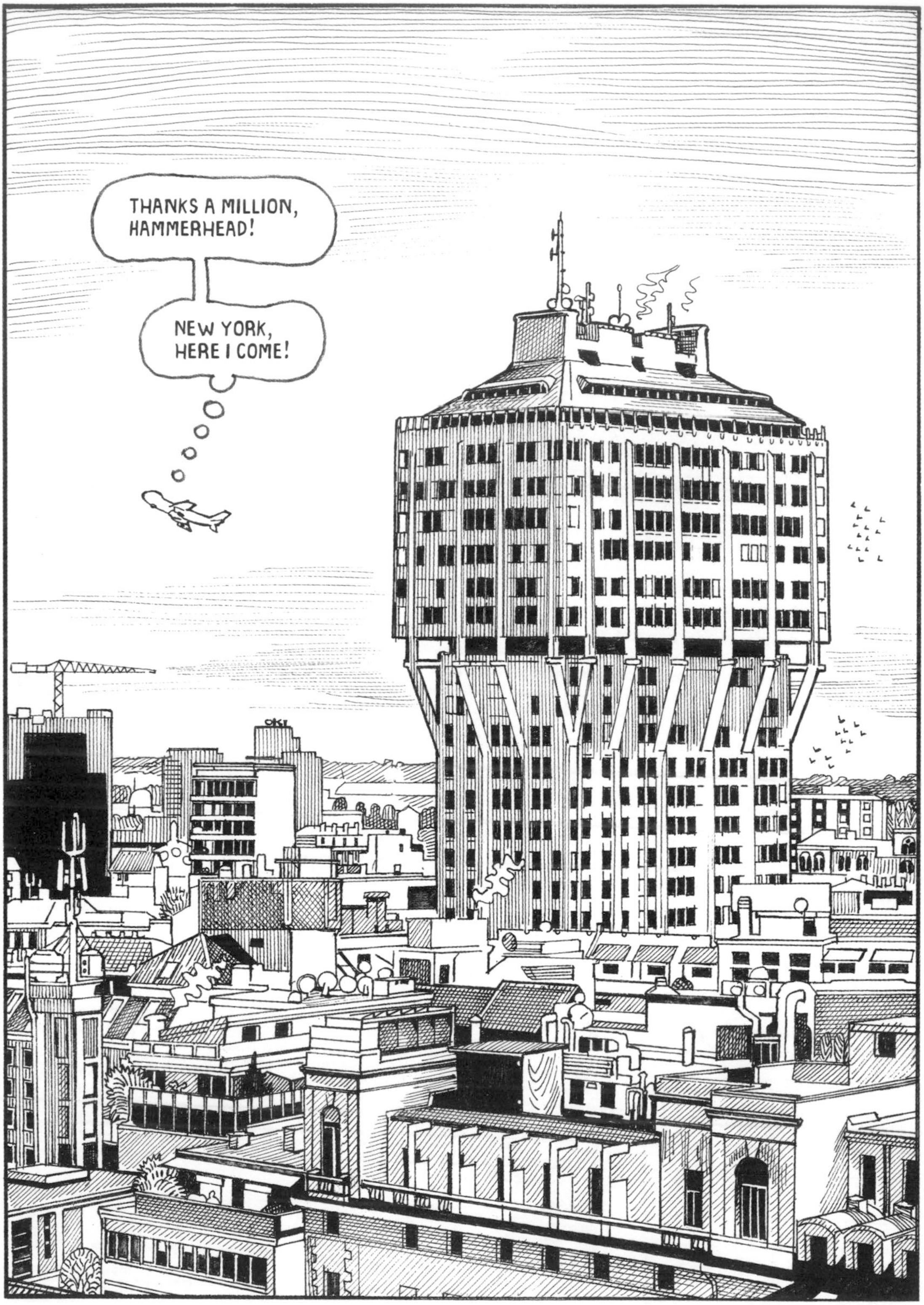
THANKS A MILLION, HAMMERHEAD!
NEW YORK, HERE I COME!
OKI

WHAT ARE YOU DOING HERE?
YOUR NAME IS MARTINO, YOU'RE FIFTEEN AND YOU'RE LYING HERE...
WAITING.
ON THE EDGE OF THE STREET TO YOUR GRANDPARENTS' HOUSE, YOU'RE WAITING...
...UN SALTINO E SONO SULLA GAMBA DI COSTEI...
UN, DUE, TRE, QUATTRO, CIN-QUE, SEI...

a RIDE

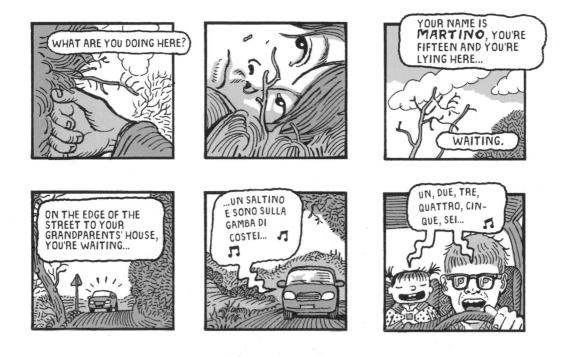

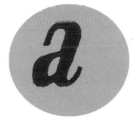

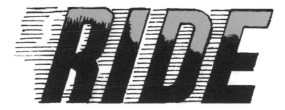

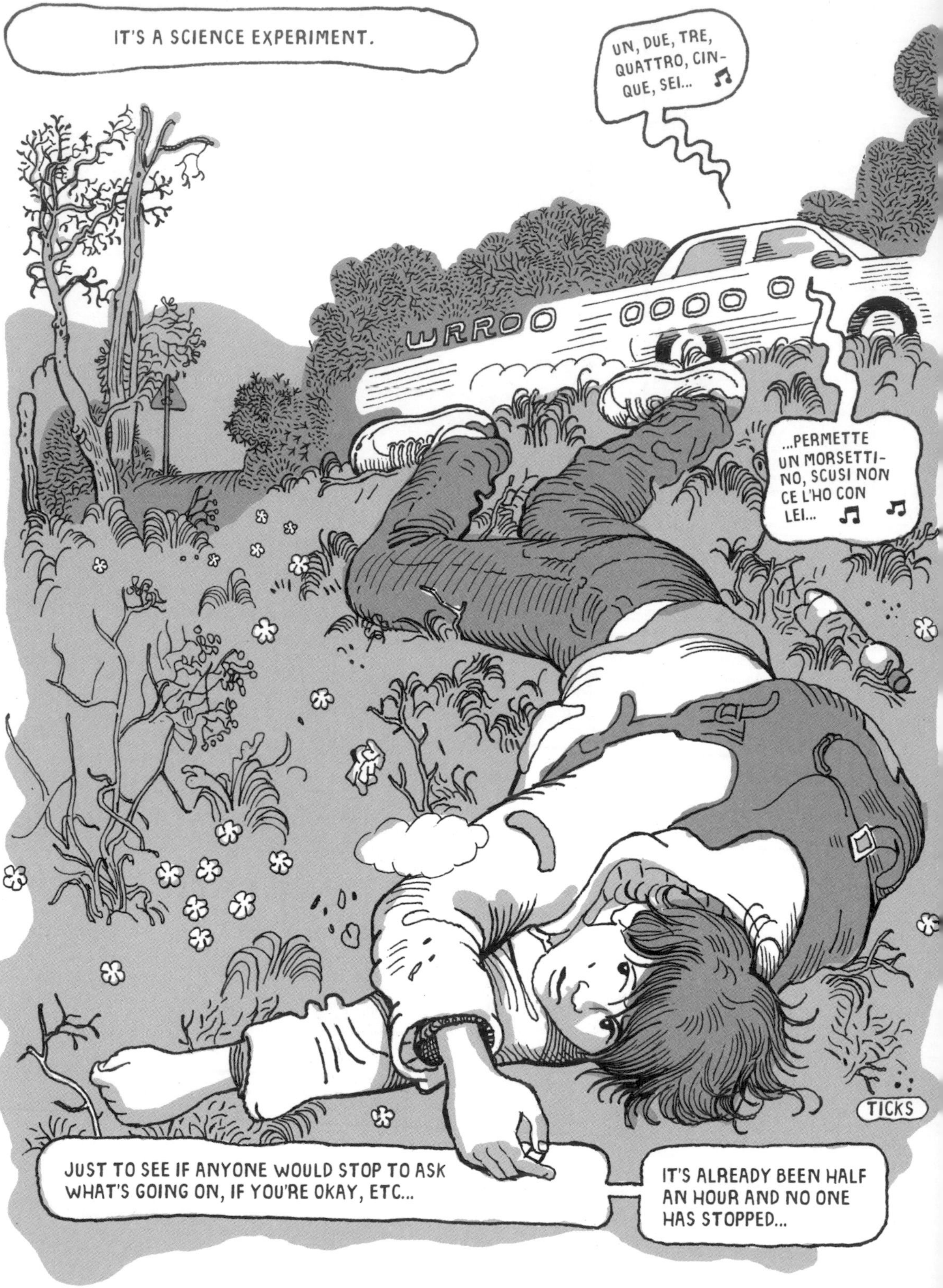
IT'S A SCIENCE EXPERIMENT.
UN, DUE, TRE, QUATTRO, CIN-QUE, SEI...
WRROO
...PERMETTE UN MORSETTI-NO, SCUSI NON CE L'HO CON LEI...
TICKS
JUST TO SEE IF ANYONE WOULD STOP TO ASK WHAT'S GOING ON, IF YOU'RE OKAY, ETC...
IT'S ALREADY BEEN HALF AN HOUR AND NO ONE HAS STOPPED...

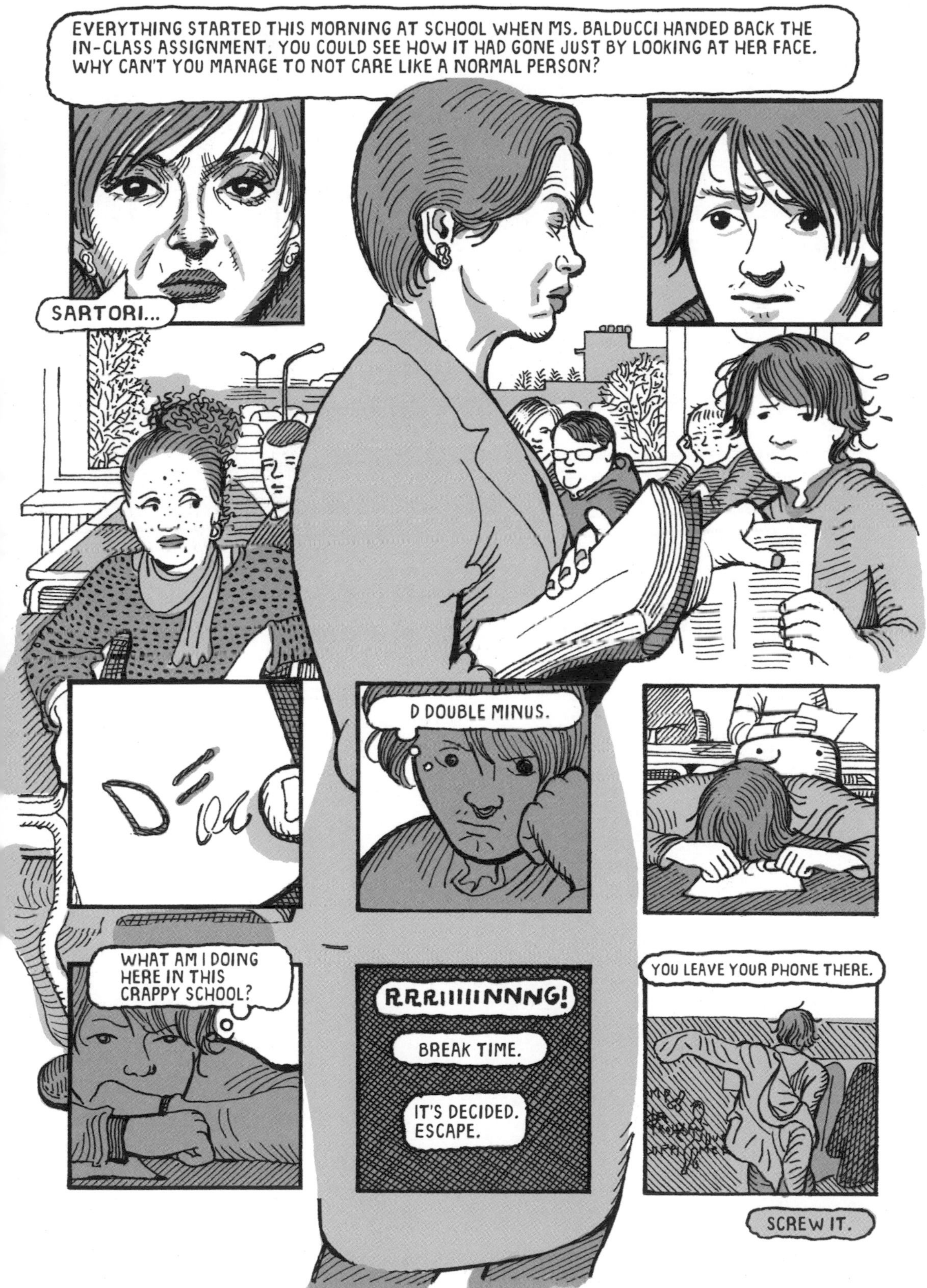
EVERYTHING STARTED THIS MORNING AT SCHOOL WHEN MS. BALDUCCI HANDED BACK THE IN-CLASS ASSIGNMENT. YOU COULD SEE HOW IT HAD GONE JUST BY LOOKING AT HER FACE. WHY CAN'T YOU MANAGE TO NOT CARE LIKE A NORMAL PERSON?
SARTORI...
D DOUBLE MINUS.
WHAT AM I DOING HERE IN THIS CRAPPY SCHOOL?
RRRIIIIIINNNG!
BREAK TIME.
IT'S DECIDED. ESCAPE.
YOU LEAVE YOUR PHONE THERE.
SCREW IT.

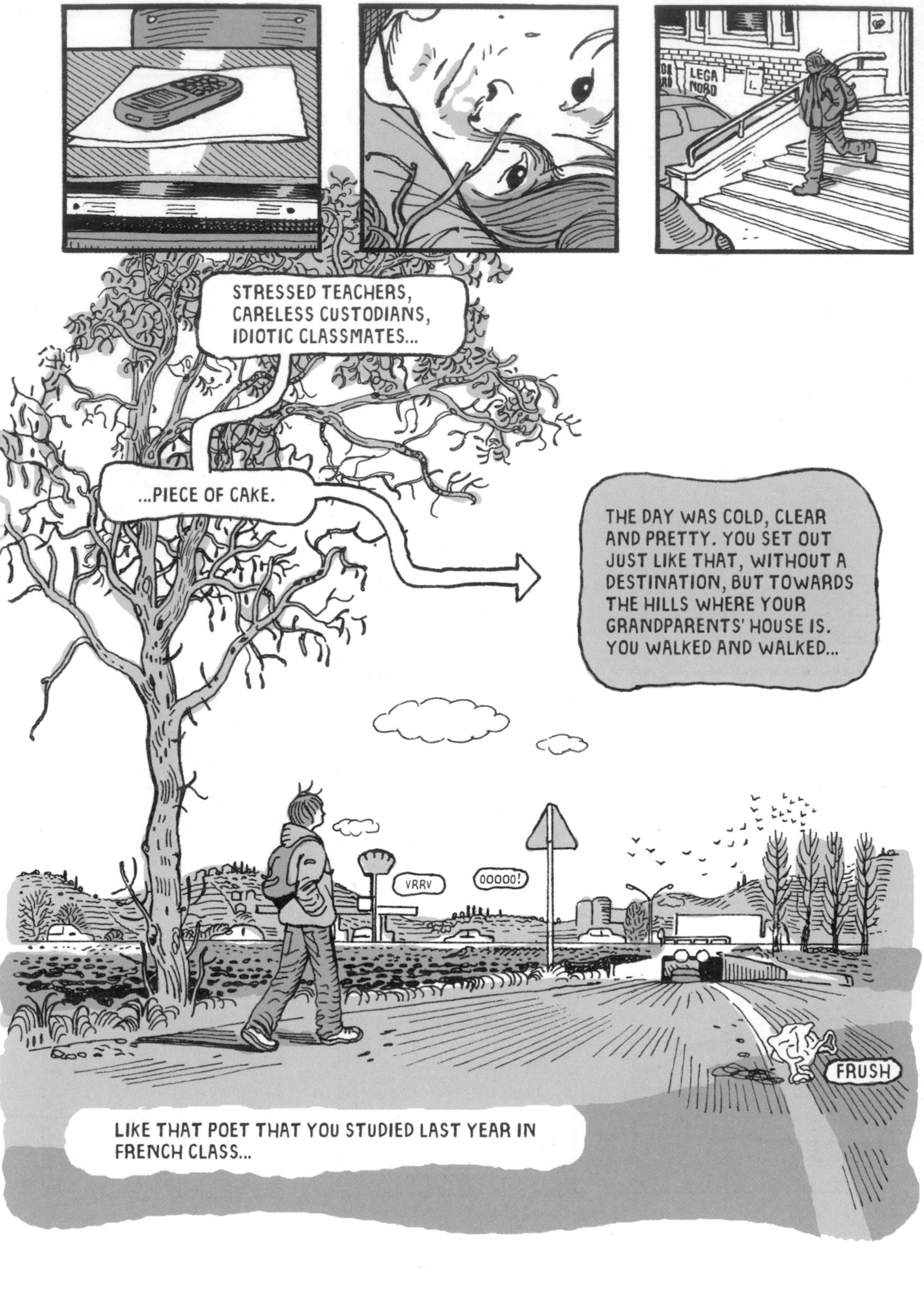
LEGA
NORD
STRESSED TEACHERS, CARELESS CUSTODIANS, IDIOTIC CLASSMATES...
...PIECE OF CAKE.
THE DAY WAS COLD, CLEAR AND PRETTY. YOU SET OUT JUST LIKE THAT, WITHOUT A DESTINATION, BUT TOWARDS THE HILLS WHERE YOUR GRANDPARENTS' HOUSE IS. YOU WALKED AND WALKED...
VRRV
OOOOO!
FRUSH
LIKE THAT POET THAT YOU STUDIED LAST YEAR IN FRENCH CLASS...

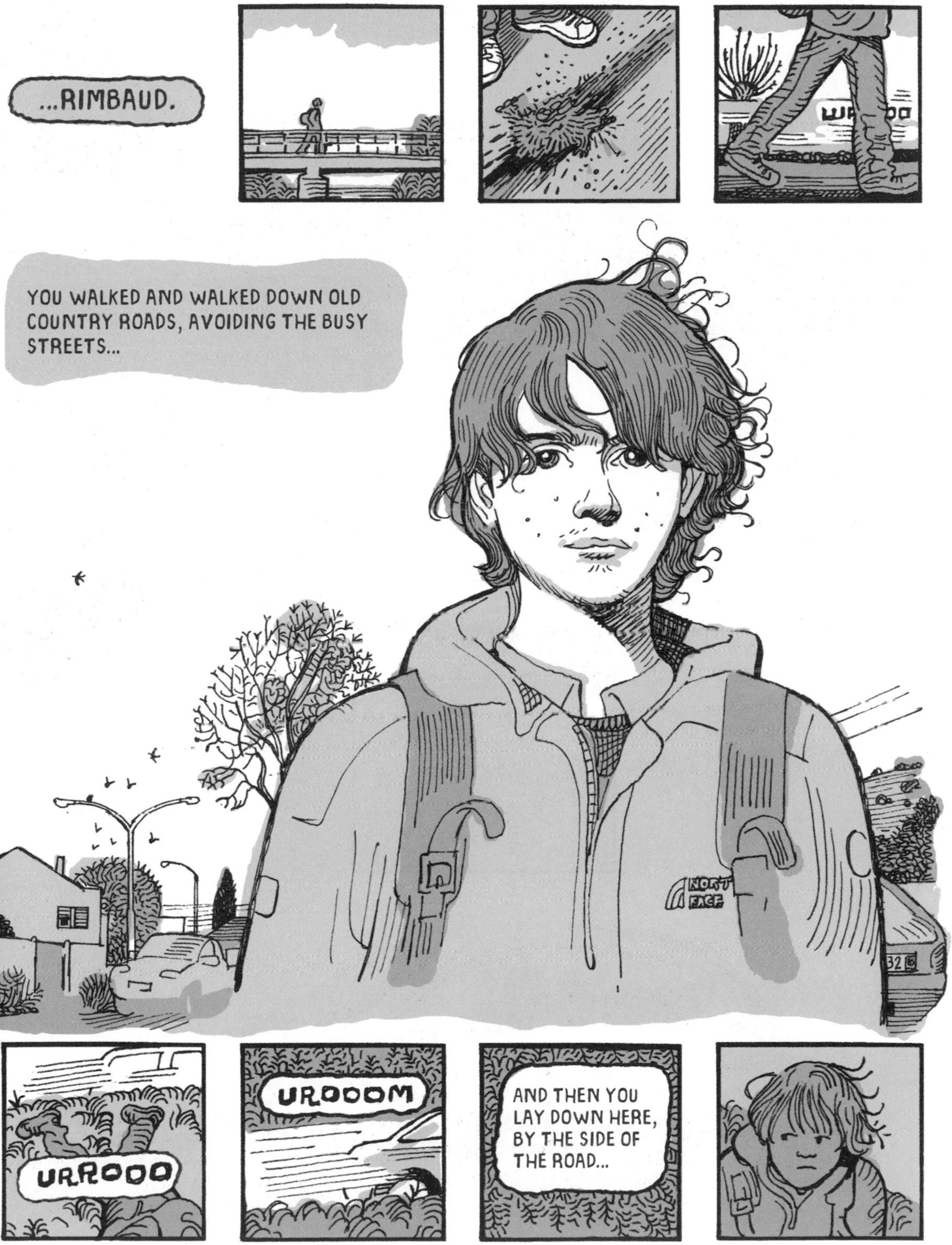
...RIMBAUD.
YOU WALKED AND WALKED DOWN OLD COUNTRY ROADS, AVOIDING THE BUSY STREETS...
URROOO
UROOOM
AND THEN YOU LAY DOWN HERE, BY THE SIDE OF THE ROAD...

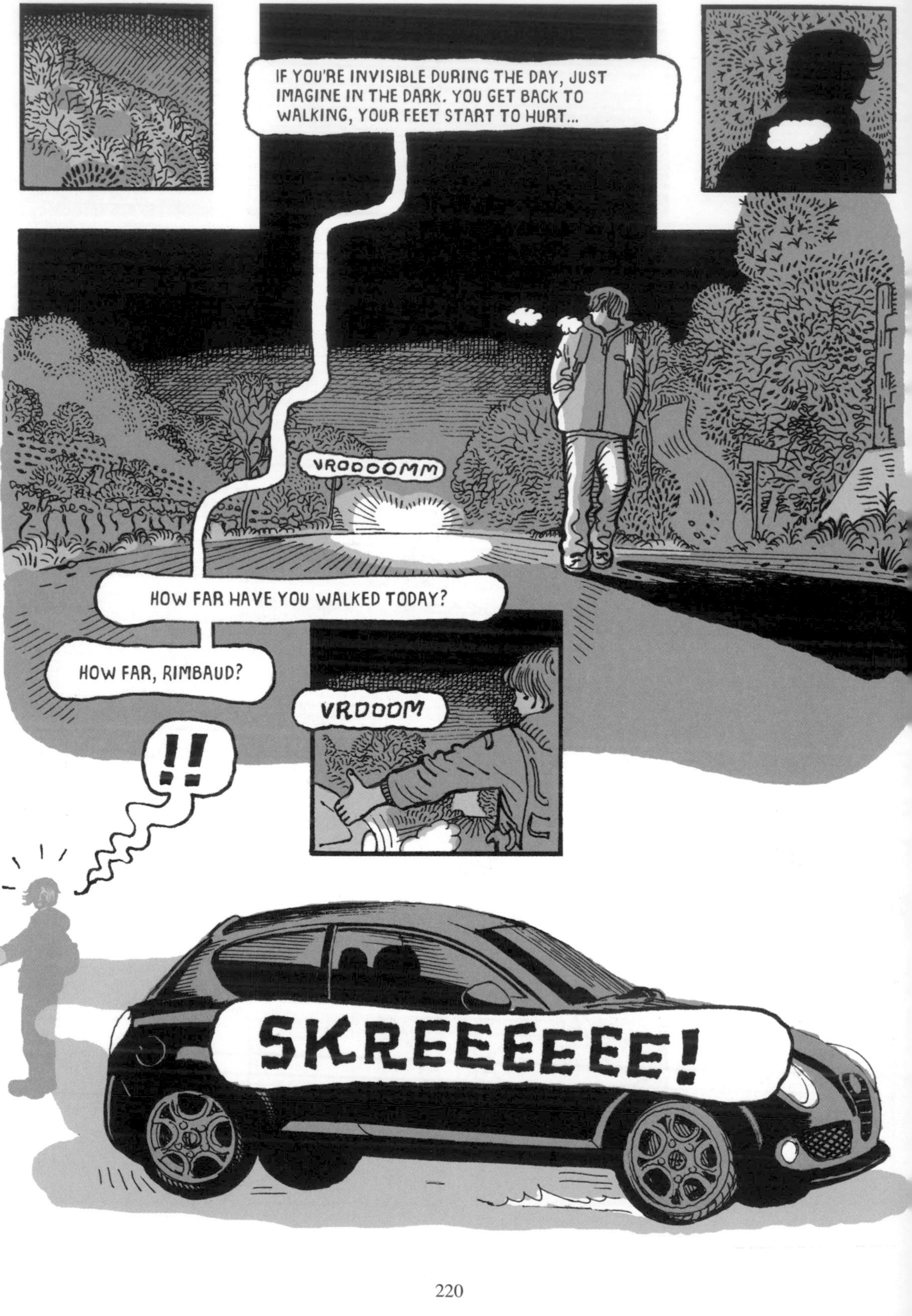
IF YOU'RE INVISIBLE DURING THE DAY, JUST IMAGINE IN THE DARK. YOU GET BACK TO WALKING, YOUR FEET START TO HURT...
VRODOOMM
HOW FAR HAVE YOU WALKED TODAY?
HOW FAR, RIMBAUD?
VRDOOM
!!
SKREEEEEE!

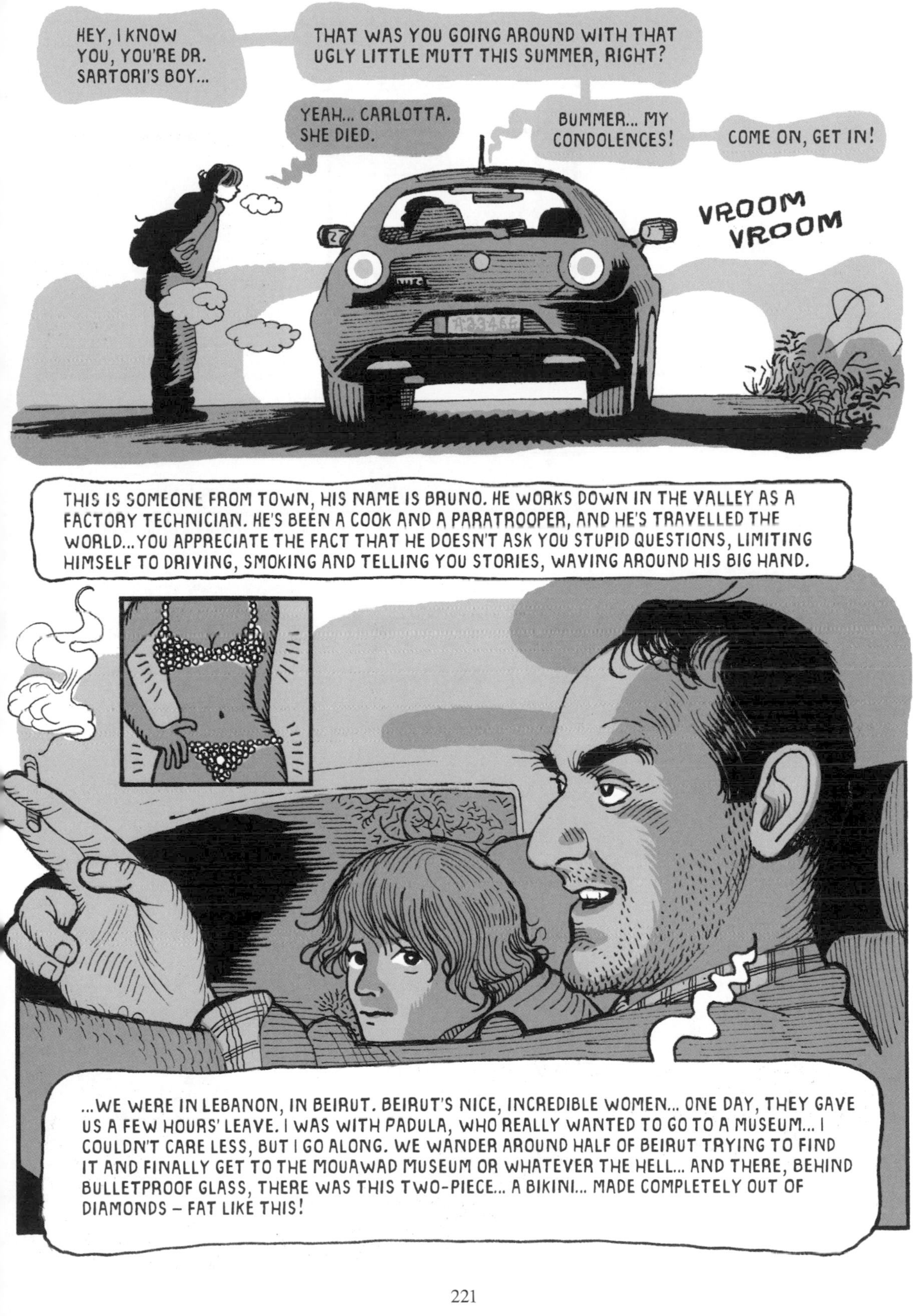
HEY, I KNOW YOU, YOU'RE DR. SARTORI'S BOY...
THAT WAS YOU GOING AROUND WITH THAT UGLY LITTLE MUTT THIS SUMMER, RIGHT?
YEAH... CARLOTTA. SHE DIED.
BUMMER... MY CONDOLENCES!
COME ON, GET IN!
VROOM VROOM
THIS IS SOMEONE FROM TOWN, HIS NAME IS BRUNO. HE WORKS DOWN IN THE VALLEY AS A FACTORY TECHNICIAN. HE'S BEEN A COOK AND A PARATROOPER, AND HE'S TRAVELLED THE WORLD... YOU APPRECIATE THE FACT THAT HE DOESN'T ASK YOU STUPID QUESTIONS, LIMITING HIMSELF TO DRIVING, SMOKING AND TELLING YOU STORIES, WAVING AROUND HIS BIG HAND.
...WE WERE IN LEBANON, IN BEIRUT. BEIRUT'S NICE, INCREDIBLE WOMEN... ONE DAY, THEY GAVE US A FEW HOURS' LEAVE. I WAS WITH PADULA, WHO REALLY WANTED TO GO TO A MUSEUM... I COULDN'T CARE LESS, BUT I GO ALONG. WE WANDER AROUND HALF OF BEIRUT TRYING TO FIND IT AND FINALLY GET TO THE MOUAWAD MUSEUM OR WHATEVER THE HELL... AND THERE, BEHIND BULLETPROOF GLASS, THERE WAS THIS TWO-PIECE... A BIKINI... MADE COMPLETELY OUT OF DIAMONDS – FAT LIKE THIS!

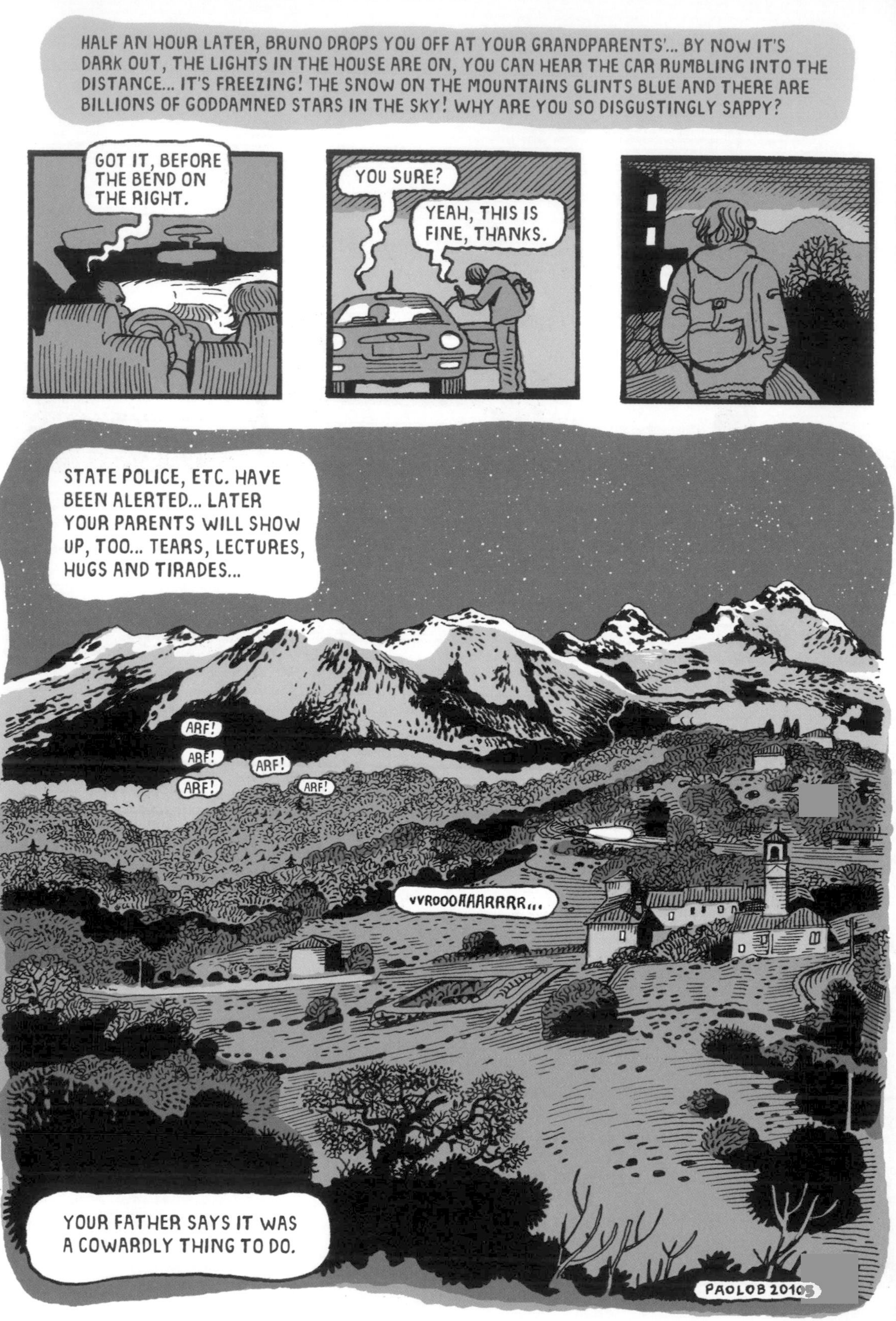
HALF AN HOUR LATER, BRUNO DROPS YOU OFF AT YOUR GRANDPARENTS'... BY NOW IT'S DARK OUT, THE LIGHTS IN THE HOUSE ARE ON, YOU CAN HEAR THE CAR RUMBLING INTO THE DISTANCE... IT'S FREEZING! THE SNOW ON THE MOUNTAINS GLINTS BLUE AND THERE ARE BILLIONS OF GODDAMNED STARS IN THE SKY! WHY ARE YOU SO DISGUSTINGLY SAPPY?
GOT IT, BEFORE THE BEND ON THE RIGHT.
YOU SURE?
YEAH, THIS IS FINE, THANKS.
STATE POLICE, ETC. HAVE BEEN ALERTED... LATER YOUR PARENTS WILL SHOW UP, TOO... TEARS, LECTURES, HUGS AND TIRADES...
ARF!
ARF!
ARF!
ARF!
ARF!
VVROOOAAARRRR...
YOUR FATHER SAYS IT WAS A COWARDLY THING TO DO.
PAOLOB 2010

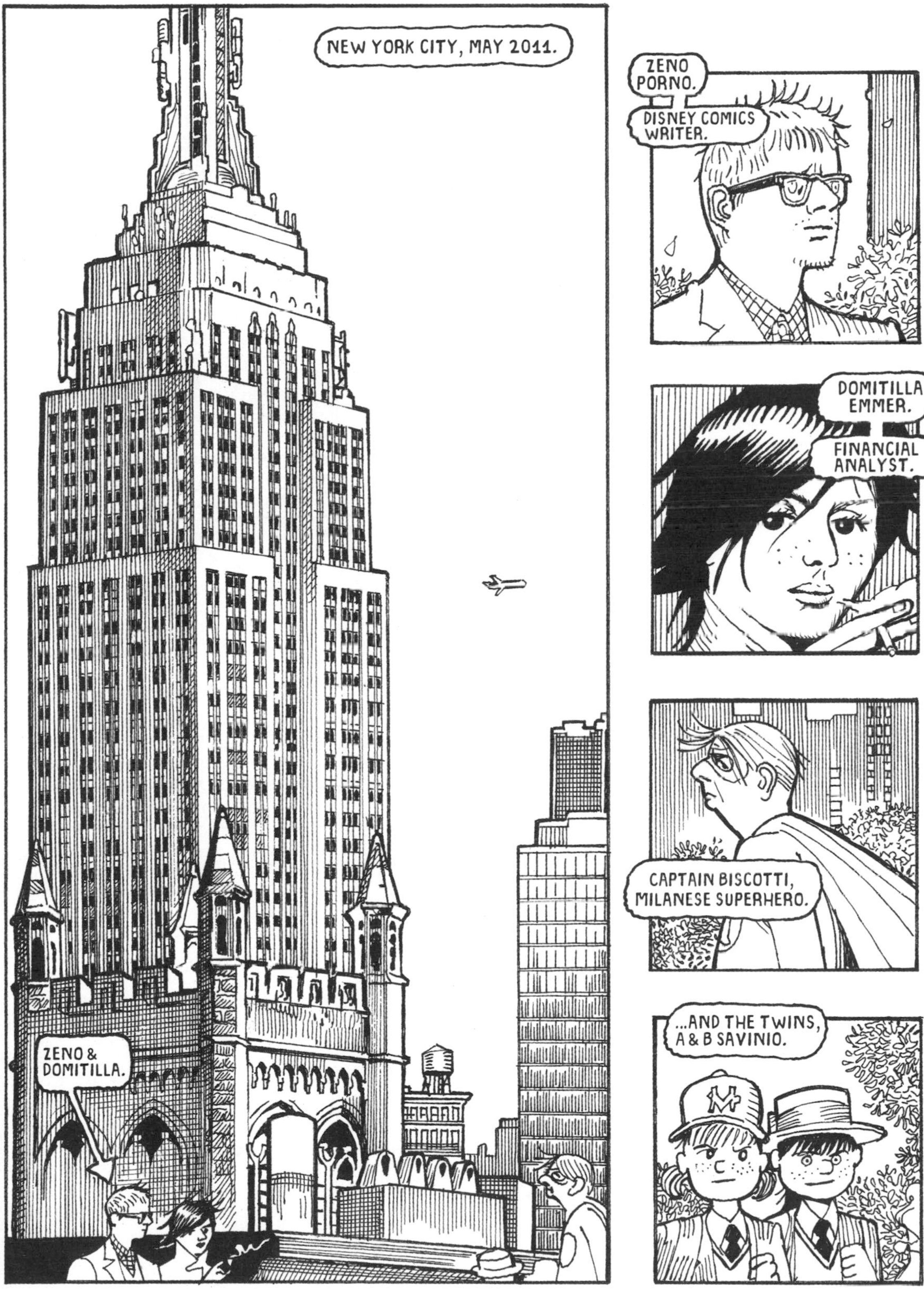
NEW YORK CITY, MAY 2011.
ZENO & DOMITILLA.
ZENO PORNO.
DISNEY COMICS WRITER.
DOMITILLA EMMER.
FINANCIAL ANALYST.
CAPTAIN BISCOTTI, MILANESE SUPERHERO.
...AND THE TWINS, A & B SAVINIO.

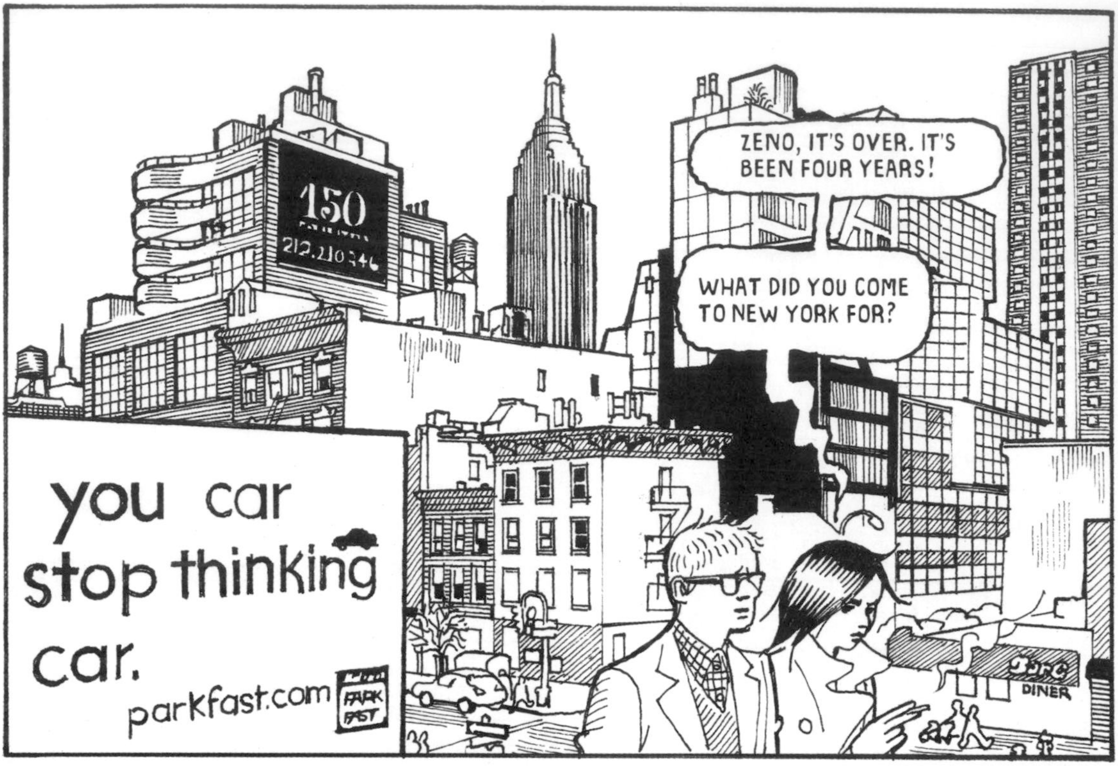
150
212.210346
you car stop thinking car.
parkfast.com
PARK FAST
DINER
ZENO, IT'S OVER. IT'S BEEN FOUR YEARS!
WHAT DID YOU COME TO NEW YORK FOR?

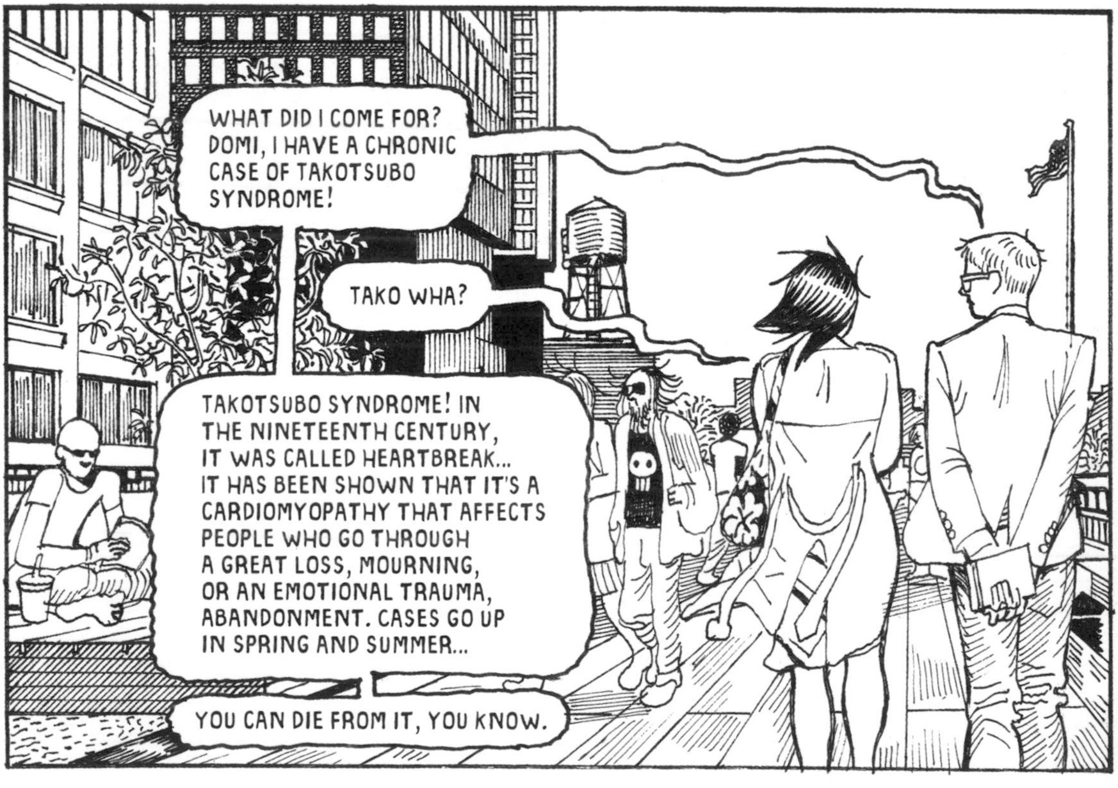
WHAT DID I COME FOR? DOMI, I HAVE A CHRONIC CASE OF TAKOTSUBO SYNDROME!
TAKO WHA?
TAKOTSUBO SYNDROME! IN THE NINETEENTH CENTURY, IT WAS CALLED HEARTBREAK... IT HAS BEEN SHOWN THAT IT'S A CARDIOMYOPATHY THAT AFFECTS PEOPLE WHO GO THROUGH A GREAT LOSS, MOURNING, OR AN EMOTIONAL TRAUMA, ABANDONMENT. CASES GO UP IN SPRING AND SUMMER...
YOU CAN DIE FROM IT, YOU KNOW.

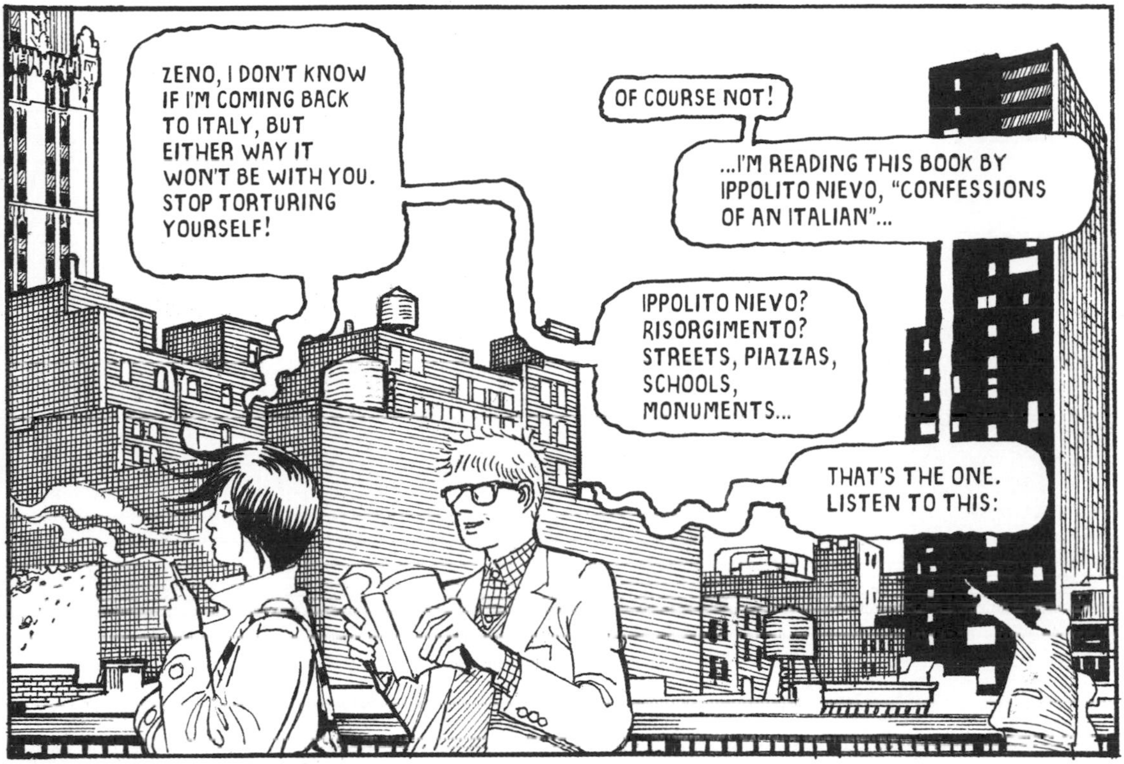
ZENO, I DON'T KNOW IF I'M COMING BACK TO ITALY, BUT EITHER WAY IT WON'T BE WITH YOU. STOP TORTURING YOURSELF!
OF COURSE NOT!
...I'M READING THIS BOOK BY IPPOLITO NIEVO, "CONFESSIONS OF AN ITALIAN"...
IPPOLITO NIEVO? RISORGIMENTO? STREETS, PIAZZAS, SCHOOLS, MONUMENTS...
THAT'S THE ONE. LISTEN TO THIS:

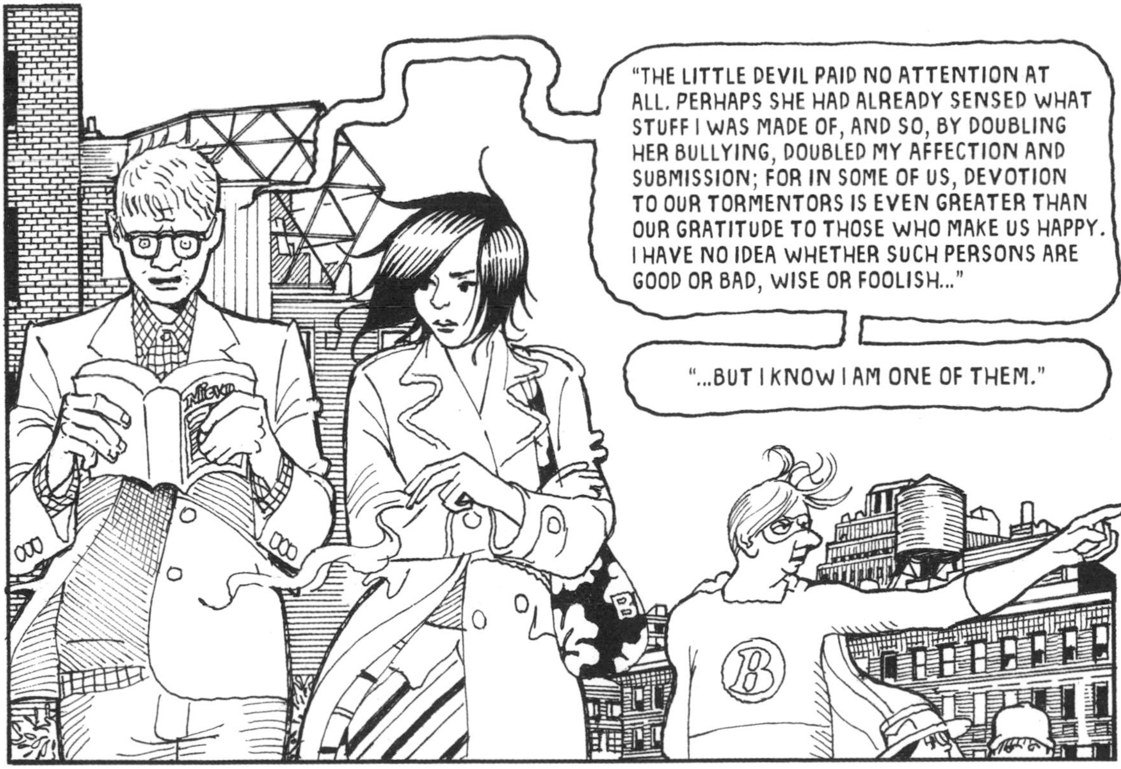
"THE LITTLE DEVIL PAID NO ATTENTION AT ALL. PERHAPS SHE HAD ALREADY SENSED WHAT STUFF I WAS MADE OF, AND SO, BY DOUBLING HER BULLYING, DOUBLED MY AFFECTION AND SUBMISSION; FOR IN SOME OF US, DEVOTION TO OUR TORMENTORS IS EVEN GREATER THAN OUR GRATITUDE TO THOSE WHO MAKE US HAPPY. I HAVE NO IDEA WHETHER SUCH PERSONS ARE GOOD OR BAD, WISE OR FOOLISH..."
"...BUT I KNOW I AM ONE OF THEM."
NIEVO

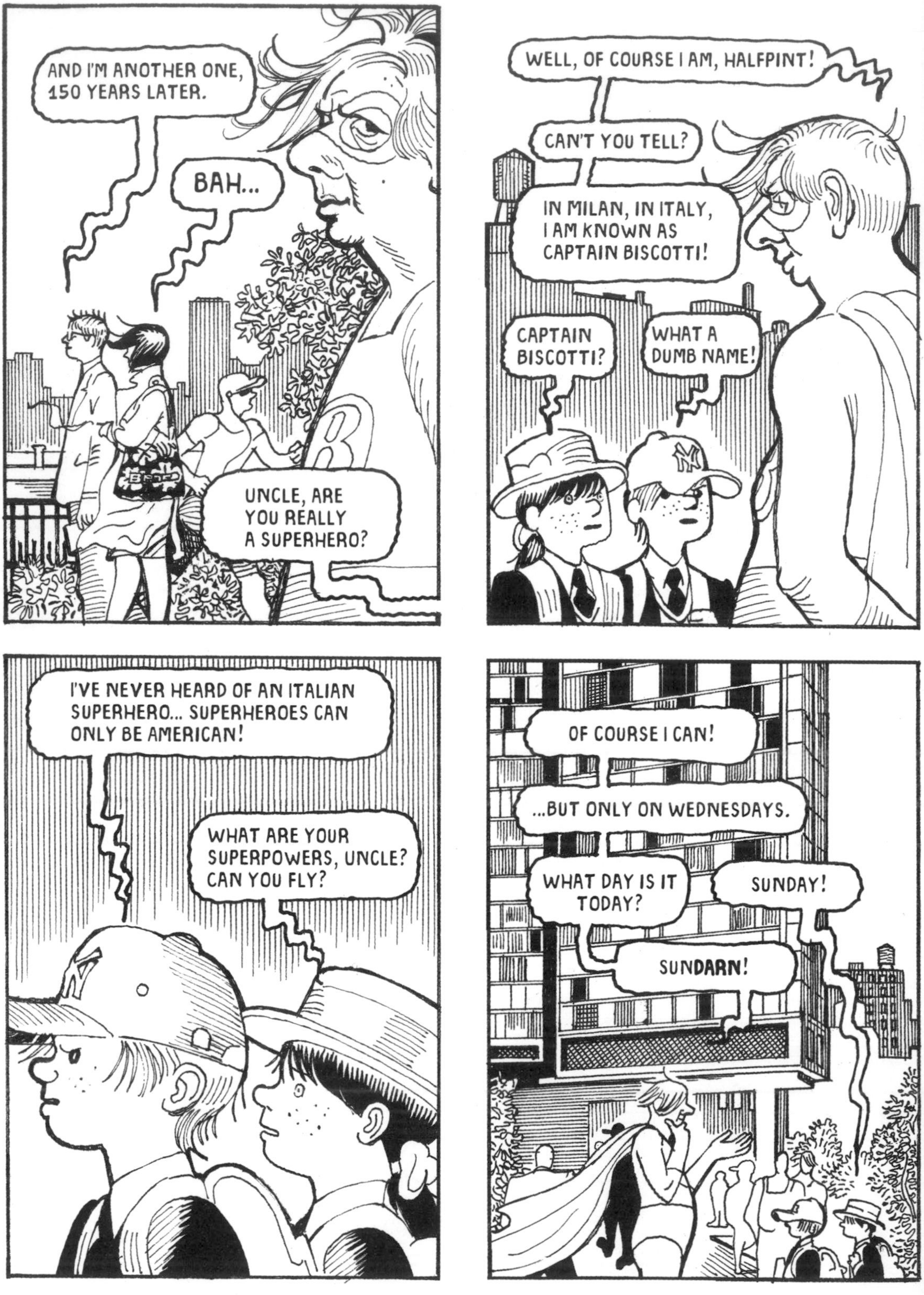
AND I'M ANOTHER ONE, 150 YEARS LATER.
BAH...
UNCLE, ARE YOU REALLY A SUPERHERO?
WELL, OF COURSE I AM, HALFPINT!
CAN'T YOU TELL?
IN MILAN, IN ITALY, I AM KNOWN AS CAPTAIN BISCOTTI!
CAPTAIN BISCOTTI?
WHAT A DUMB NAME!
I'VE NEVER HEARD OF AN ITALIAN SUPERHERO... SUPERHEROES CAN ONLY BE AMERICAN!
WHAT ARE YOUR SUPERPOWERS, UNCLE? CAN YOU FLY?
OF COURSE I CAN!
...BUT ONLY ON WEDNESDAYS.
WHAT DAY IS IT TODAY?
SUNDAY!
SUNDARN!

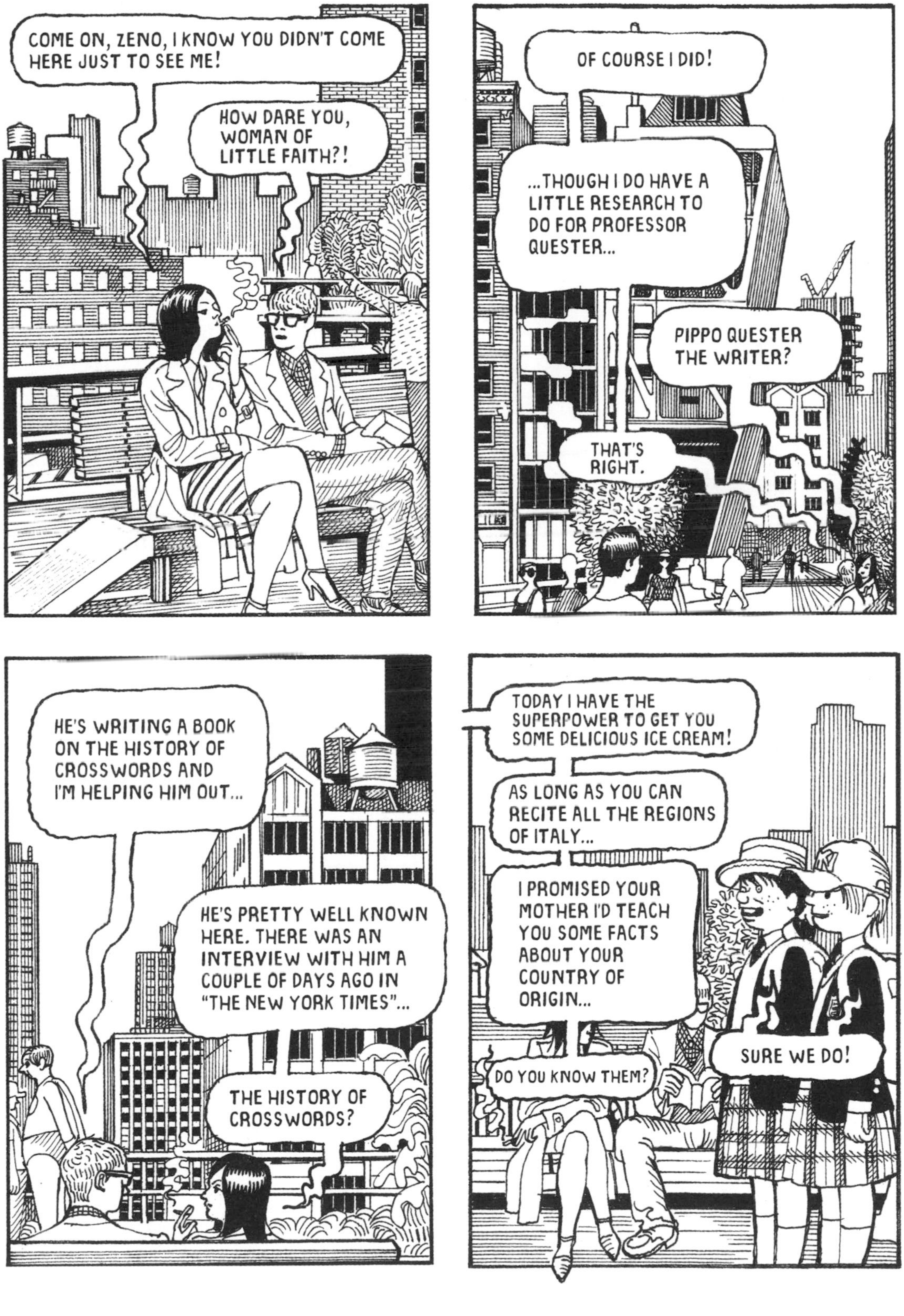
COME ON, ZENO, I KNOW YOU DIDN'T COME HERE JUST TO SEE ME!
HOW DARE YOU, WOMAN OF LITTLE FAITH?!
OF COURSE I DID!
...THOUGH I DO HAVE A LITTLE RESEARCH TO DO FOR PROFESSOR QUESTER...
PIPPO QUESTER THE WRITER?
THAT'S RIGHT.
HE'S WRITING A BOOK ON THE HISTORY OF CROSSWORDS AND I'M HELPING HIM OUT...
HE'S PRETTY WELL KNOWN HERE. THERE WAS AN INTERVIEW WITH HIM A COUPLE OF DAYS AGO IN "THE NEW YORK TIMES"...
THE HISTORY OF CROSSWORDS?
TODAY I HAVE THE SUPERPOWER TO GET YOU SOME DELICIOUS ICE CREAM!
AS LONG AS YOU CAN RECITE ALL THE REGIONS OF ITALY...
I PROMISED YOUR MOTHER I'D TEACH YOU SOME FACTS ABOUT YOUR COUNTRY OF ORIGIN...
DO YOU KNOW THEM?
SURE WE DO!

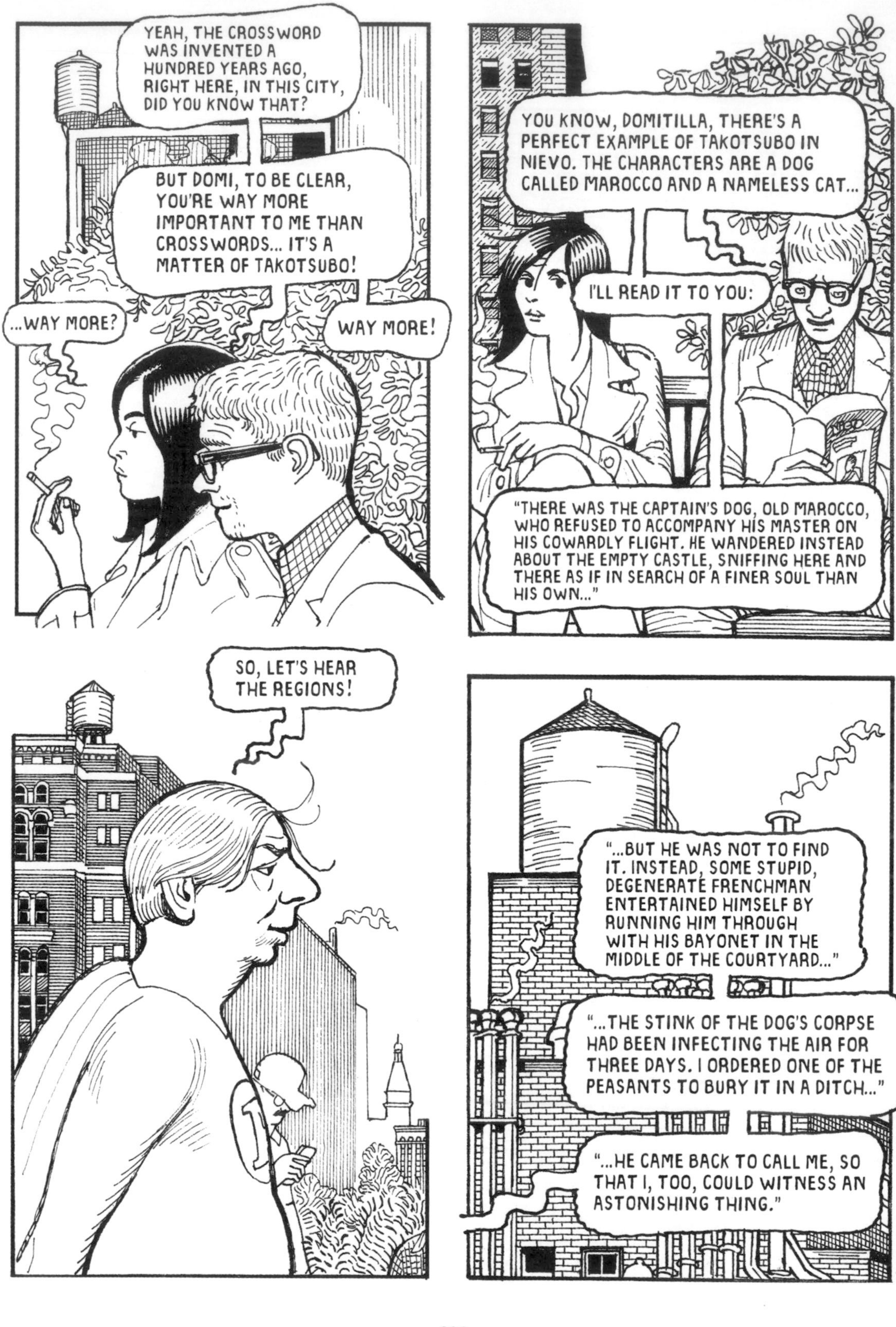
YEAH, THE CROSSWORD WAS INVENTED A HUNDRED YEARS AGO, RIGHT HERE, IN THIS CITY, DID YOU KNOW THAT?
BUT DOMI, TO BE CLEAR, YOU'RE WAY MORE IMPORTANT TO ME THAN CROSSWORDS... IT'S A MATTER OF TAKOTSUBO!
...WAY MORE?
WAY MORE!
YOU KNOW, DOMITILLA, THERE'S A PERFECT EXAMPLE OF TAKOTSUBO IN NIEVO. THE CHARACTERS ARE A DOG CALLED MAROCCO AND A NAMELESS CAT...
I'LL READ IT TO YOU:
"THERE WAS THE CAPTAIN'S DOG, OLD MAROCCO, WHO REFUSED TO ACCOMPANY HIS MASTER ON HIS COWARDLY FLIGHT. HE WANDERED INSTEAD ABOUT THE EMPTY CASTLE, SNIFFING HERE AND THERE AS IF IN SEARCH OF A FINER SOUL THAN HIS OWN..."
SO, LET'S HEAR THE REGIONS!
"...BUT HE WAS NOT TO FIND IT. INSTEAD, SOME STUPID, DEGENERATE FRENCHMAN ENTERTAINED HIMSELF BY RUNNING HIM THROUGH WITH HIS BAYONET IN THE MIDDLE OF THE COURTYARD..."
"...THE STINK OF THE DOG'S CORPSE HAD BEEN INFECTING THE AIR FOR THREE DAYS. I ORDERED ONE OF THE PEASANTS TO BURY IT IN A DITCH..."
"...HE CAME BACK TO CALL ME, SO THAT I, TOO, COULD WITNESS AN ASTONISHING THING."

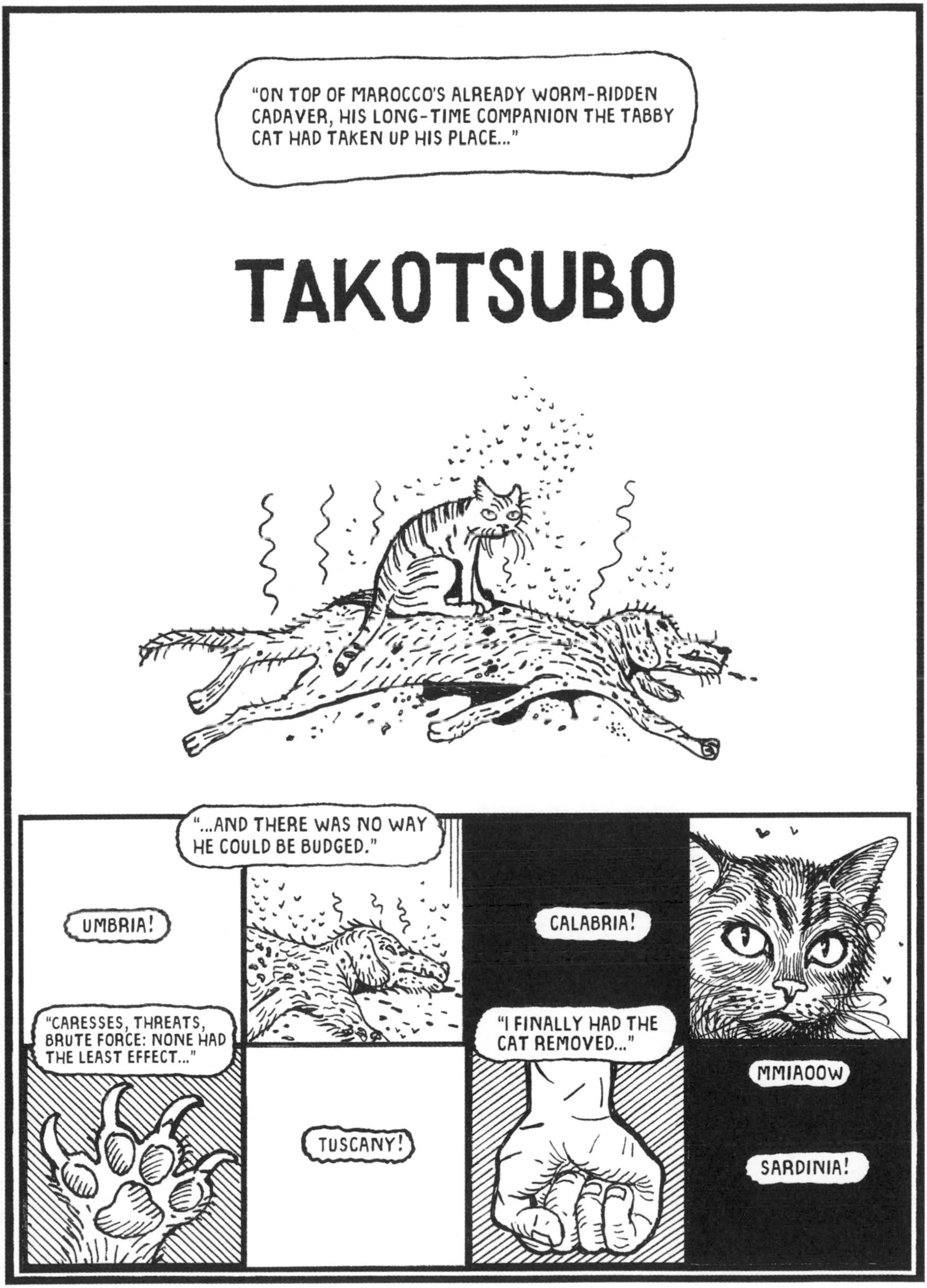
"ON TOP OF MAROCCO'S ALREADY WORM-RIDDEN CADAVER, HIS LONG-TIME COMPANION THE TABBY CAT HAD TAKEN UP HIS PLACE..."
TAKOTSUBO
"...AND THERE WAS NO WAY HE COULD BE BUDGED."
UMBRIA!
CALABRIA!
"CARESSES, THREATS, BRUTE FORCE: NONE HAD THE LEAST EFFECT..."
TUSCANY!
"I FINALLY HAD THE CAT REMOVED..."
MMIAOOW
SARDINIA!

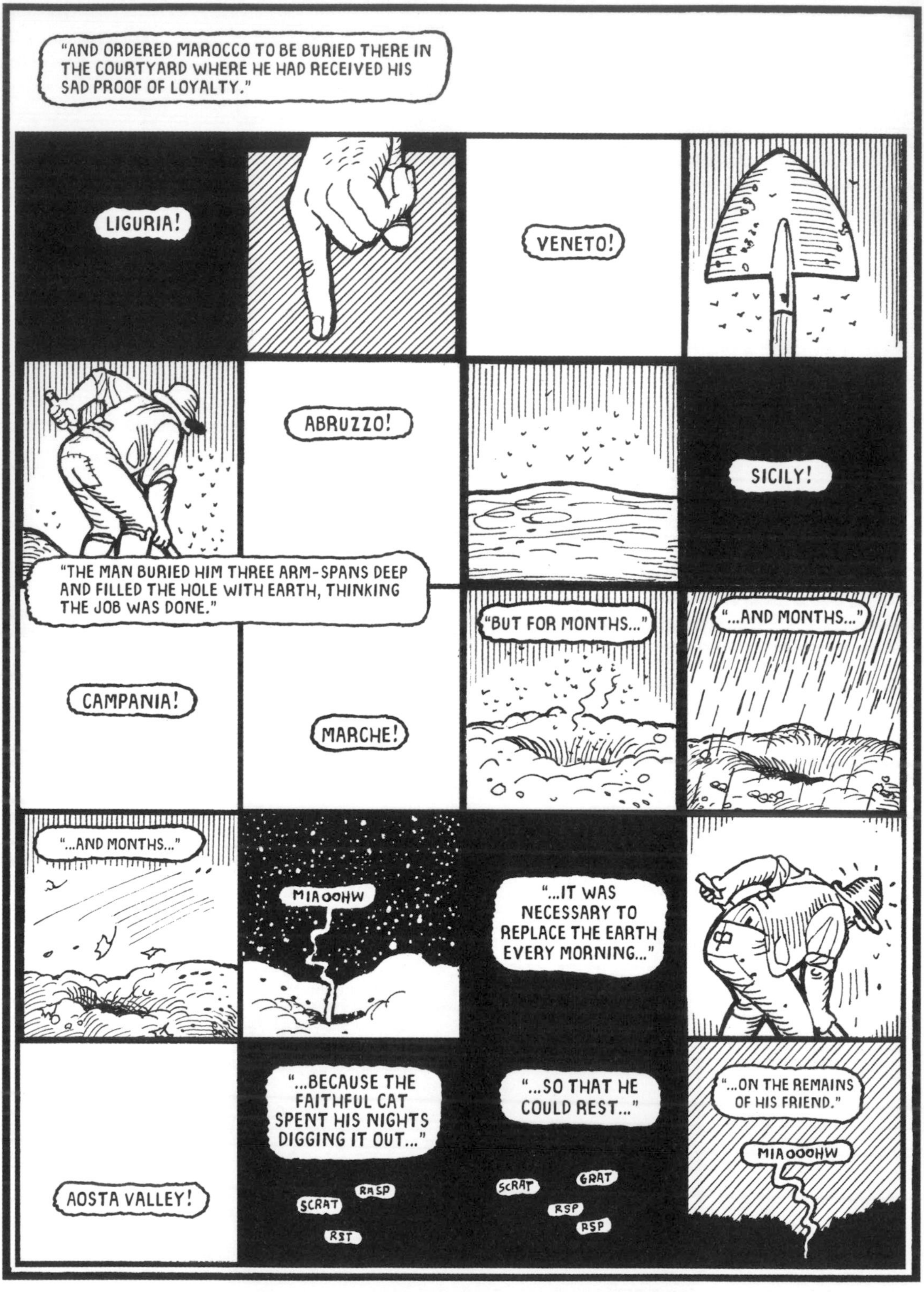
"AND ORDERED MAROCCO TO BE BURIED THERE IN THE COURTYARD WHERE HE HAD RECEIVED HIS SAD PROOF OF LOYALTY."
LIGURIA!
VENETO!
ABRUZZO!
SICILY!
"THE MAN BURIED HIM THREE ARM-SPANS DEEP AND FILLED THE HOLE WITH EARTH, THINKING THE JOB WAS DONE."
CAMPANIA!
MARCHE!
"BUT FOR MONTHS..."
"...AND MONTHS..."
"...AND MONTHS..."
MIAOOHW
"...IT WAS NECESSARY TO REPLACE THE EARTH EVERY MORNING..."
AOSTA VALLEY!
"...BECAUSE THE FAITHFUL CAT SPENT HIS NIGHTS DIGGING IT OUT..."
RASP
SCRAT
RST
"...SO THAT HE COULD REST..."
SCRAT
GRAT
RSP
RSP
"...ON THE REMAINS OF HIS FRIEND."
MIAOOOHW

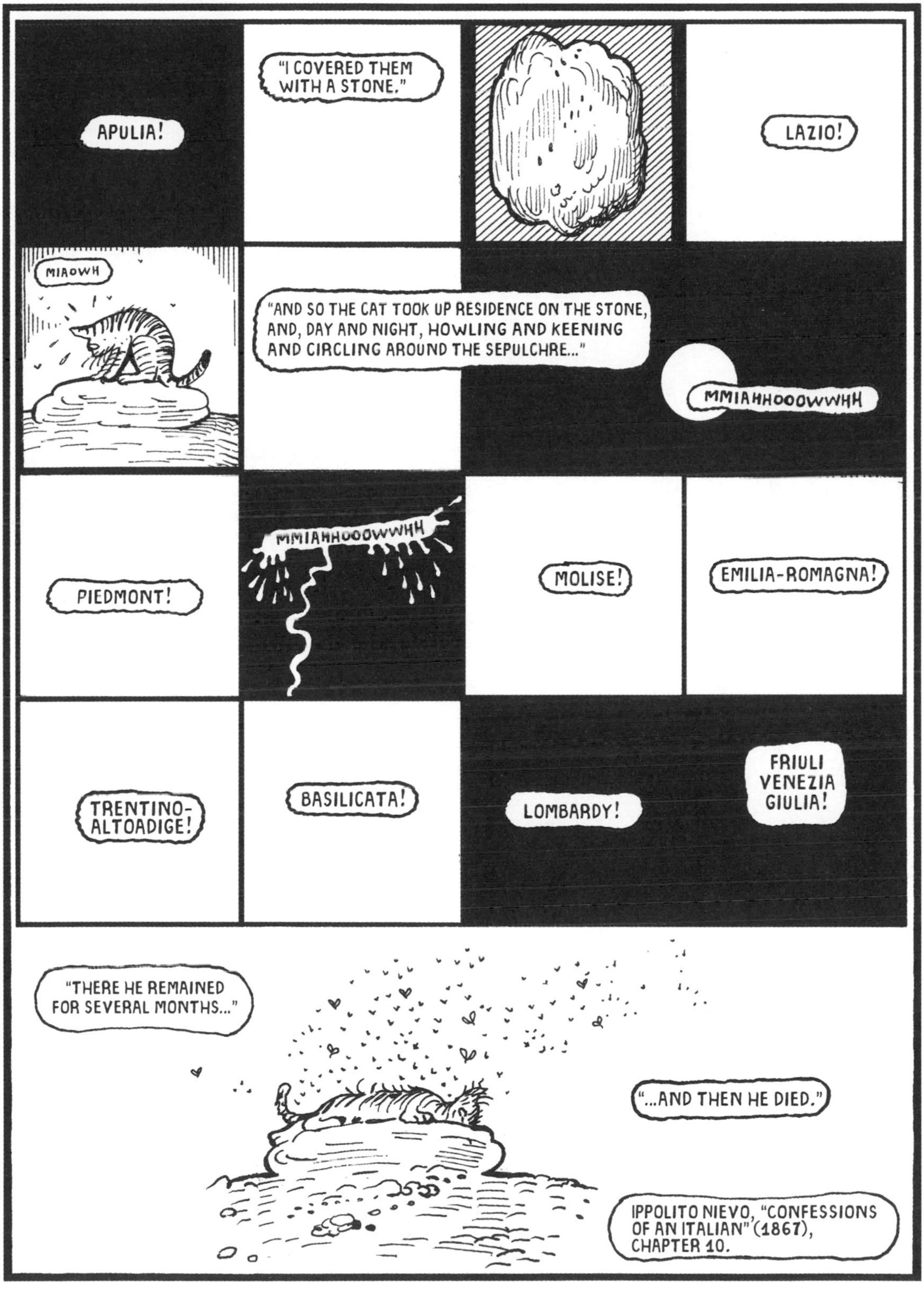

APULIA!
"I COVERED THEM WITH A STONE."
LAZIO!
MIAOWH
"AND SO THE CAT TOOK UP RESIDENCE ON THE STONE, AND, DAY AND NIGHT, HOWLING AND KEENING AND CIRCLING AROUND THE SEPULCHRE..."
MMIAHHOOOWWHH
PIEDMONT!
MMIAHHOOOWWHH
MOLISE!
EMILIA-ROMAGNA!
TRENTINO-ALTOADIGE!
BASILICATA!
LOMBARDY!
FRIULI VENEZIA GIULIA!
"THERE HE REMAINED FOR SEVERAL MONTHS..."
"...AND THEN HE DIED."
IPPOLITO NIEVO, "CONFESSIONS OF AN ITALIAN" (1867), CHAPTER 10.

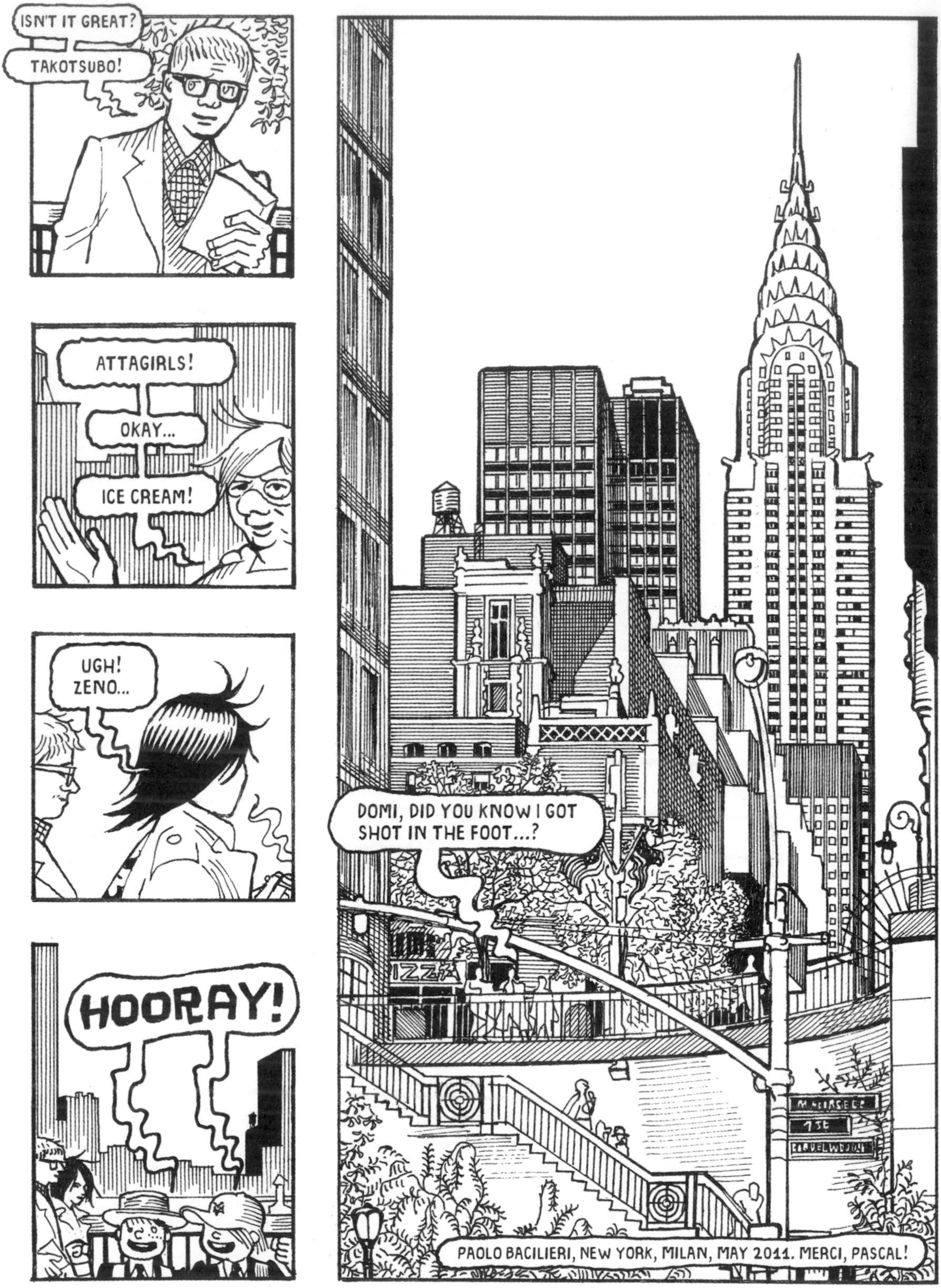

ISN'T IT GREAT?
TAKOTSUBO!
ATTAGIRLS!
OKAY...
ICE CREAM!
UGH! ZENO...
HOORAY!
DOMI, DID YOU KNOW I GOT SHOT IN THE FOOT...?
PIZZA
PAOLO BACILIERI, NEW YORK, MILAN, MAY 2011. MERCI, PASCAL!

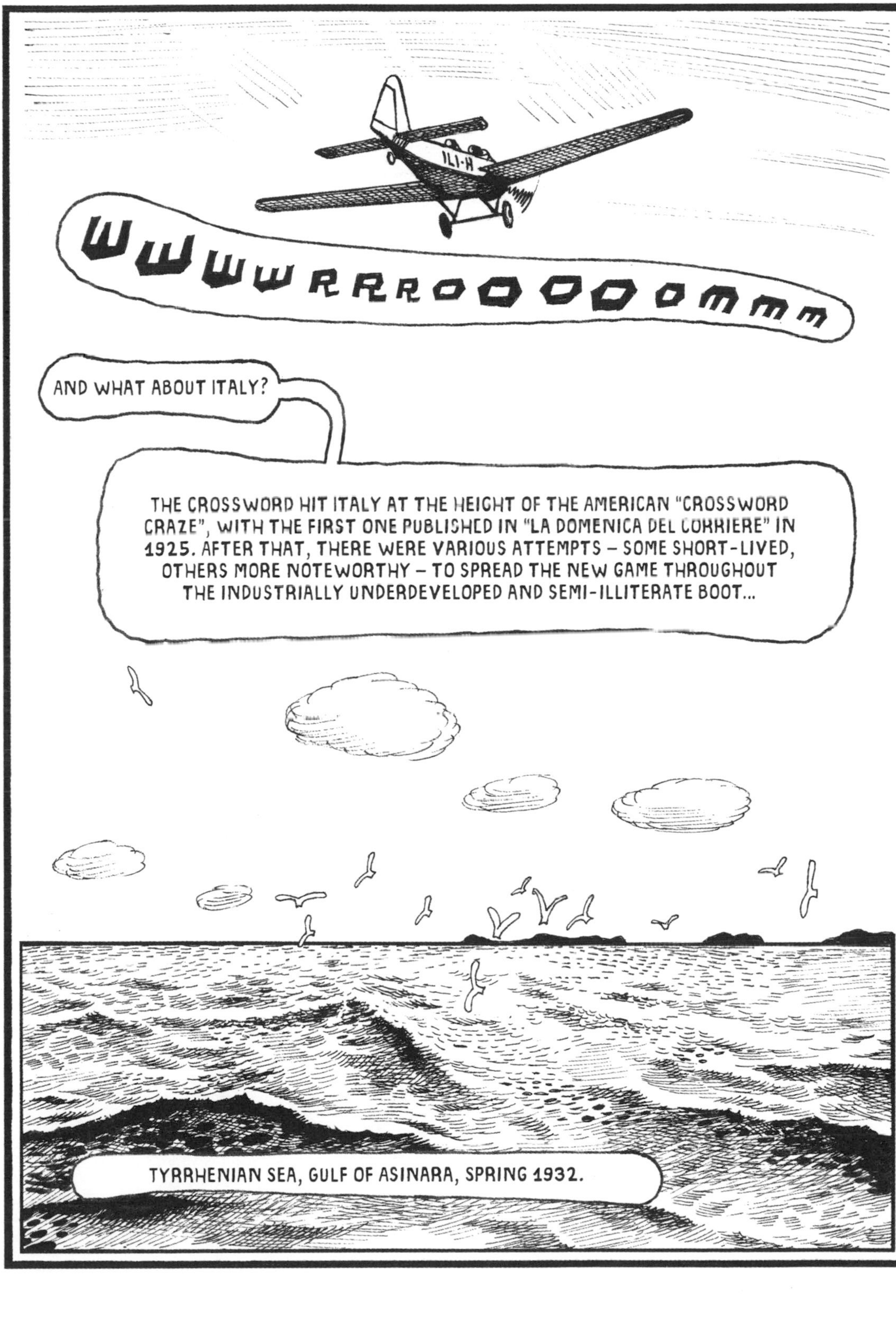
WWWWWRRRROOOOOOMMMM
AND WHAT ABOUT ITALY?
THE CROSSWORD HIT ITALY AT THE HEIGHT OF THE AMERICAN "CROSSWORD CRAZE", WITH THE FIRST ONE PUBLISHED IN "LA DOMENICA DEL CORRIERE" IN 1925. AFTER THAT, THERE WERE VARIOUS ATTEMPTS – SOME SHORT-LIVED, OTHERS MORE NOTEWORTHY – TO SPREAD THE NEW GAME THROUGHOUT THE INDUSTRIALLY UNDERDEVELOPED AND SEMI-ILLITERATE BOOT...
TYRRHENIAN SEA, GULF OF ASINARA, SPRING 1932.

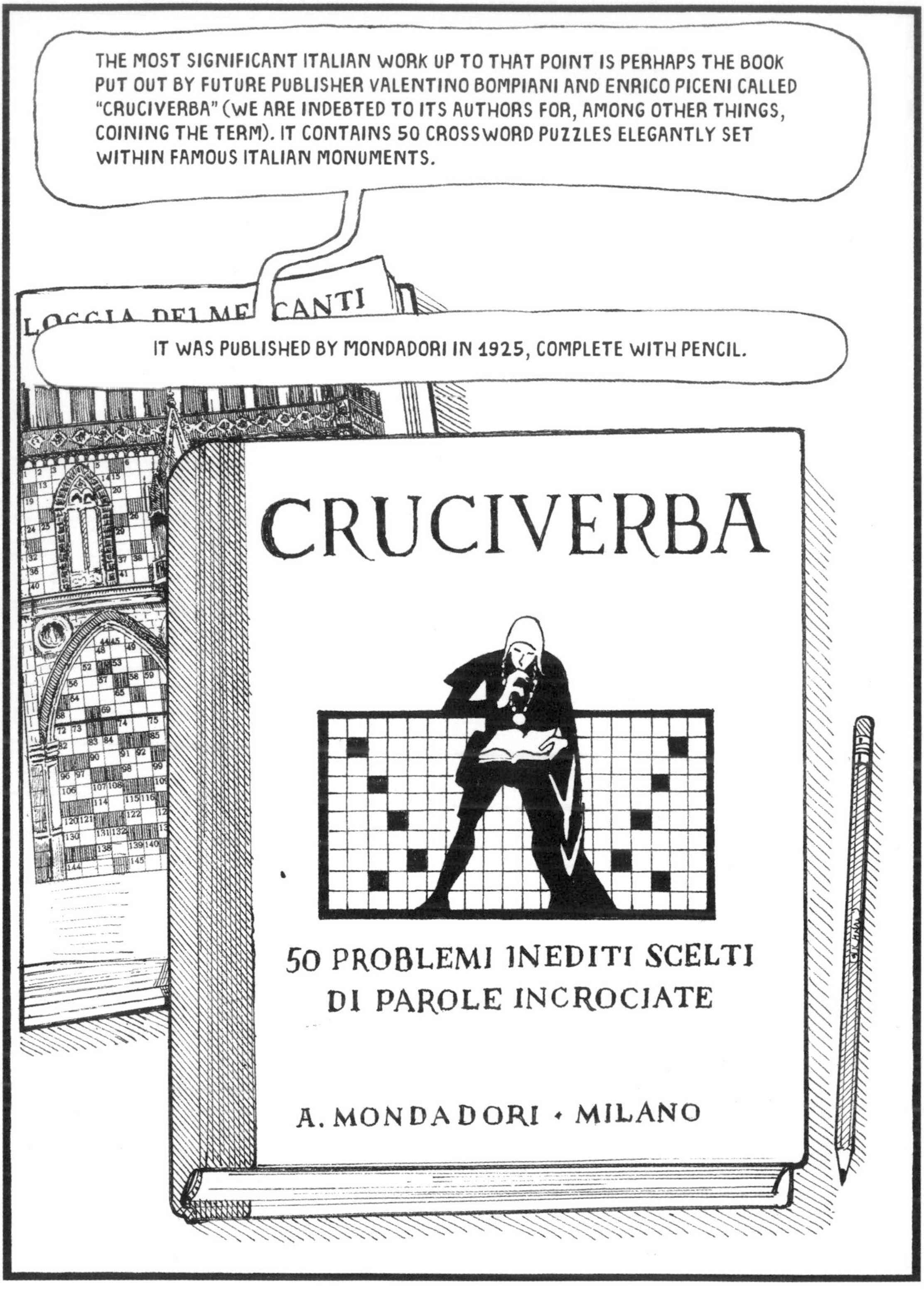
THE MOST SIGNIFICANT ITALIAN WORK UP TO THAT POINT IS PERHAPS THE BOOK PUT OUT BY FUTURE PUBLISHER VALENTINO BOMPIANI AND ENRICO PICENI CALLED "CRUCIVERBA" (WE ARE INDEBTED TO ITS AUTHORS FOR, AMONG OTHER THINGS, COINING THE TERM). IT CONTAINS 50 CROSSWORD PUZZLES ELEGANTLY SET WITHIN FAMOUS ITALIAN MONUMENTS.
IT WAS PUBLISHED BY MONDADORI IN 1925, COMPLETE WITH PENCIL.
CRUCIVERBA
50 PROBLEMI INEDITI SCELTI DI PAROLE INCROCIATE
A. MONDADORI • MILANO

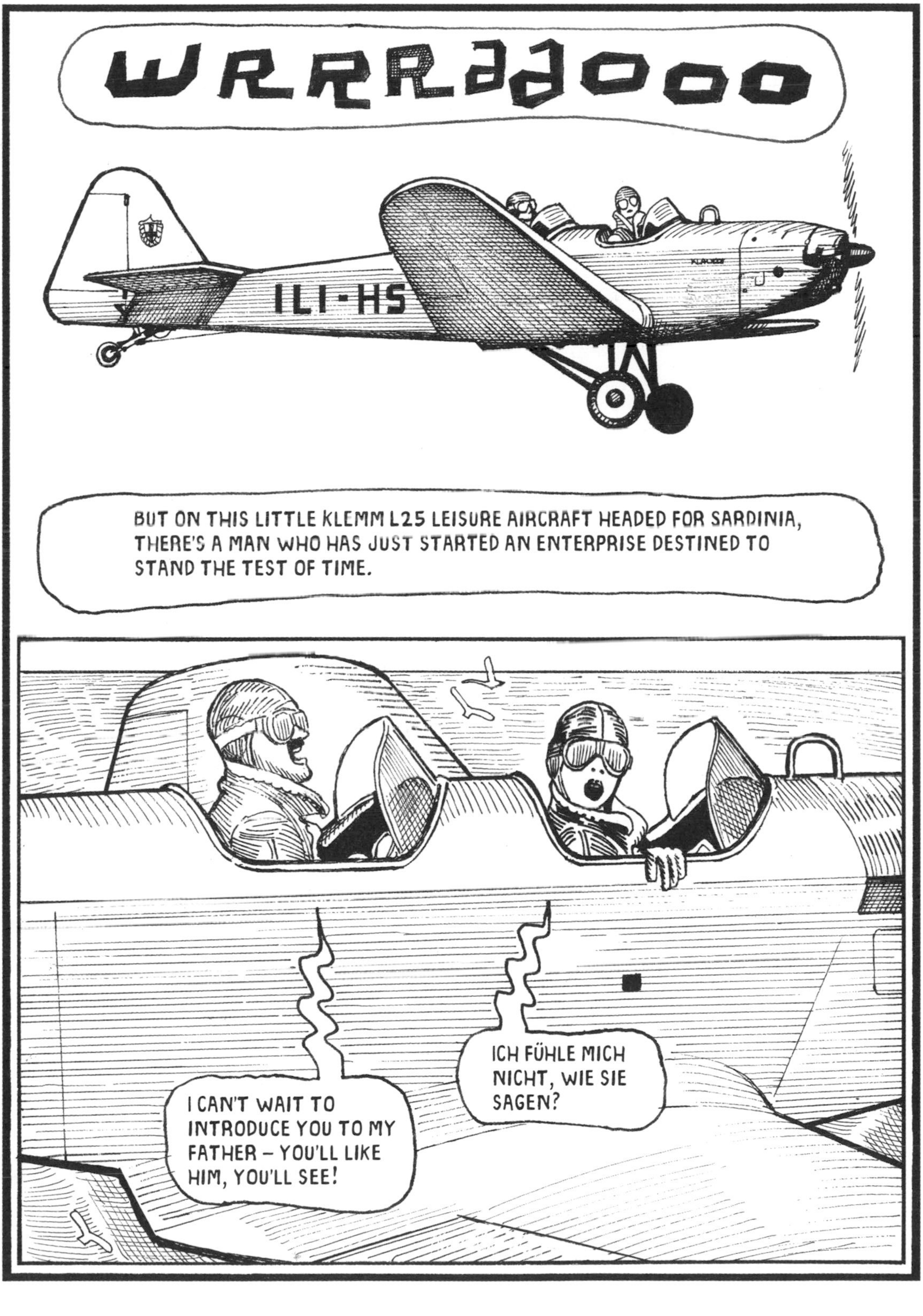
WRRRAAOOO
ILI-HS
BUT ON THIS LITTLE KLEMM L25 LEISURE AIRCRAFT HEADED FOR SARDINIA, THERE'S A MAN WHO HAS JUST STARTED AN ENTERPRISE DESTINED TO STAND THE TEST OF TIME.
I CAN'T WAIT TO INTRODUCE YOU TO MY FATHER – YOU'LL LIKE HIM, YOU'LL SEE!
ICH FÜHLE MICH NICHT, WIE SIE SAGEN?

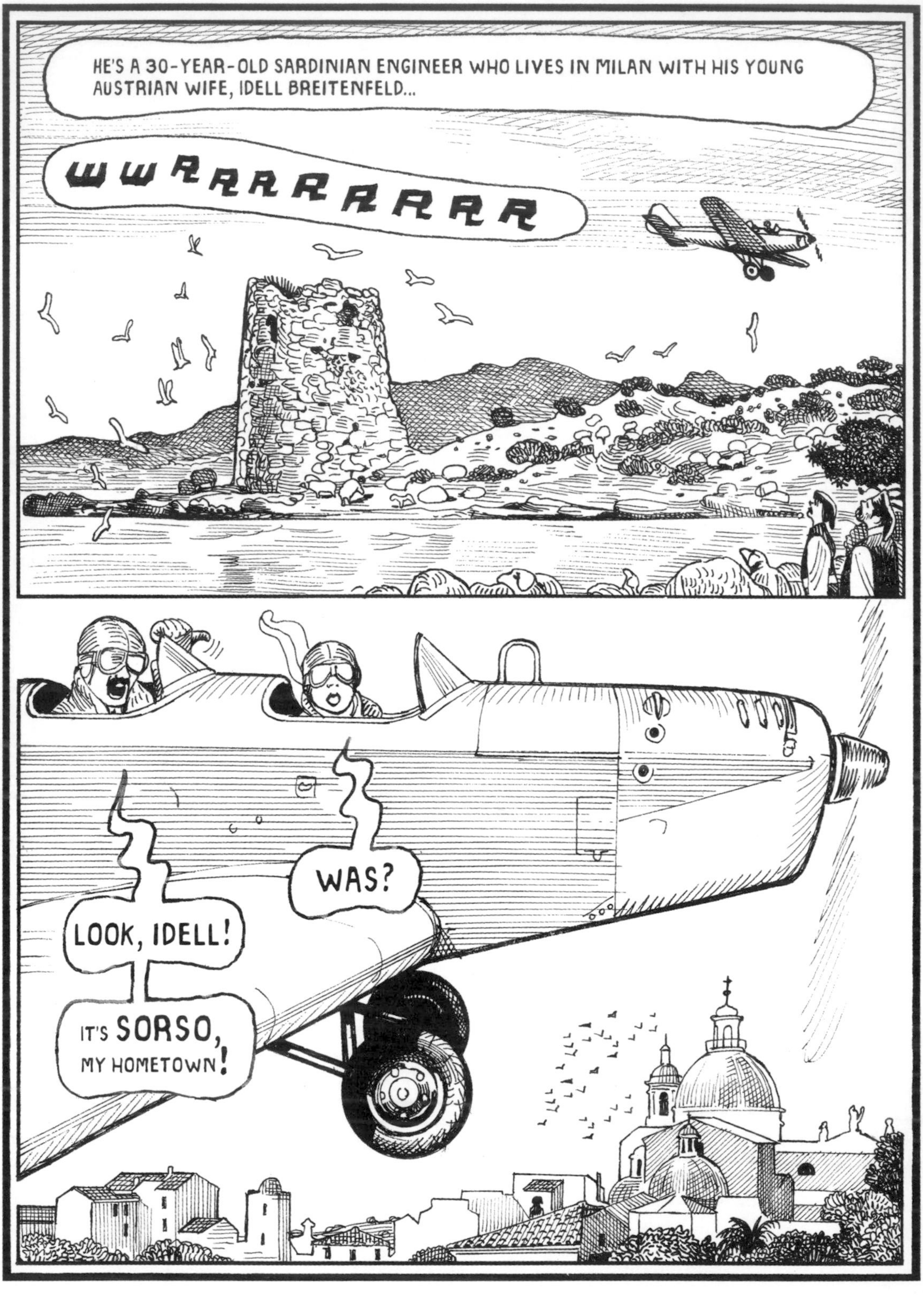
HE'S A 30-YEAR-OLD SARDINIAN ENGINEER WHO LIVES IN MILAN WITH HIS YOUNG AUSTRIAN WIFE, IDELL BREITENFELD...
WWRRRRRRRR
LOOK, IDELL!
IT'S SORSO, MY HOMETOWN!
WAS?

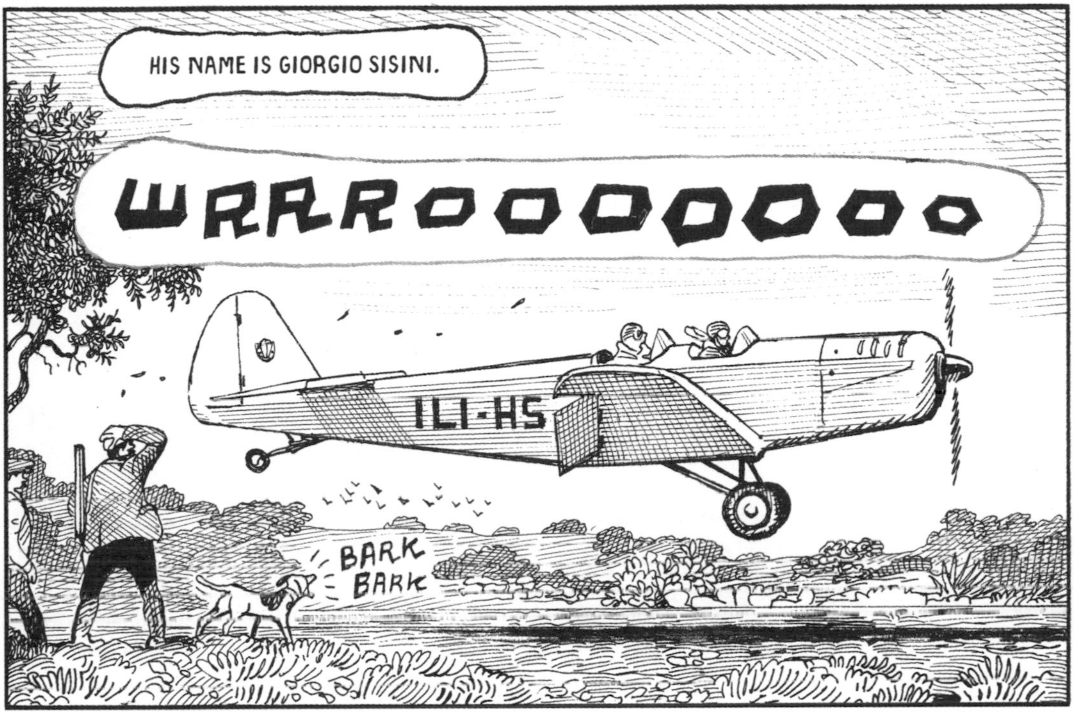
HIS NAME IS GIORGIO SISINI.
WRRROOOOOOOO
ILI-HS
BARK BARK

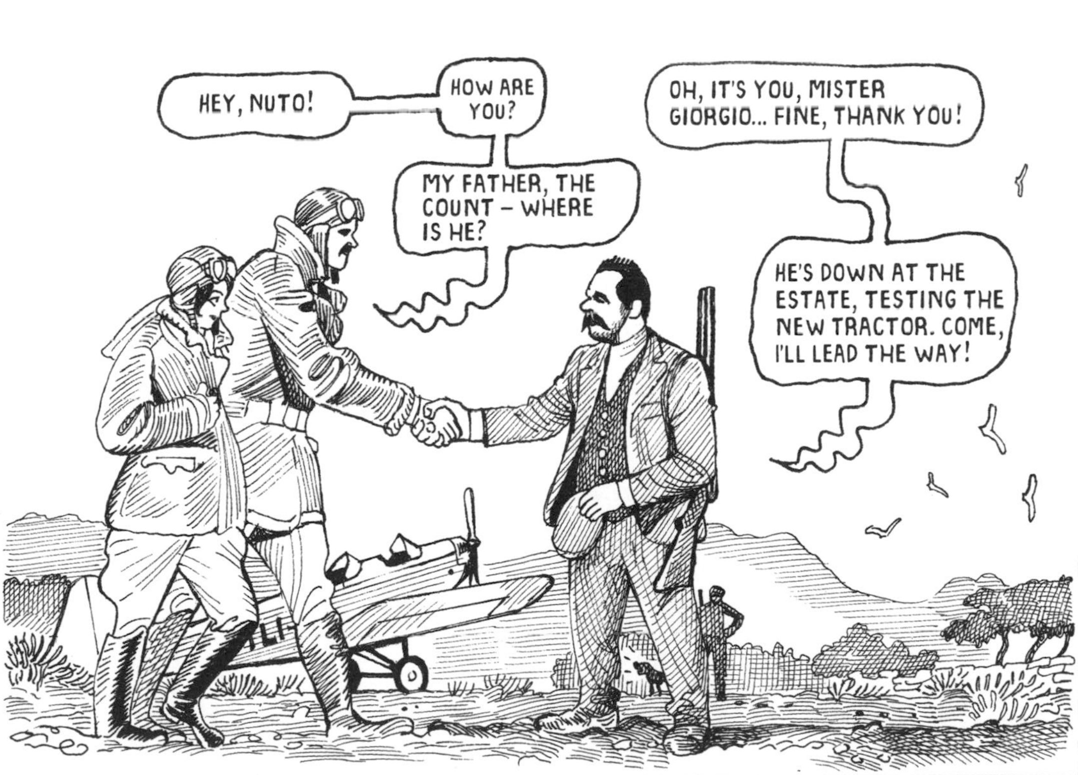
HEY, NUTO!
HOW ARE YOU?
MY FATHER, THE COUNT – WHERE IS HE?
OH, IT'S YOU, MISTER GIORGIO... FINE, THANK YOU!
HE'S DOWN AT THE ESTATE, TESTING THE NEW TRACTOR. COME, I'LL LEAD THE WAY!

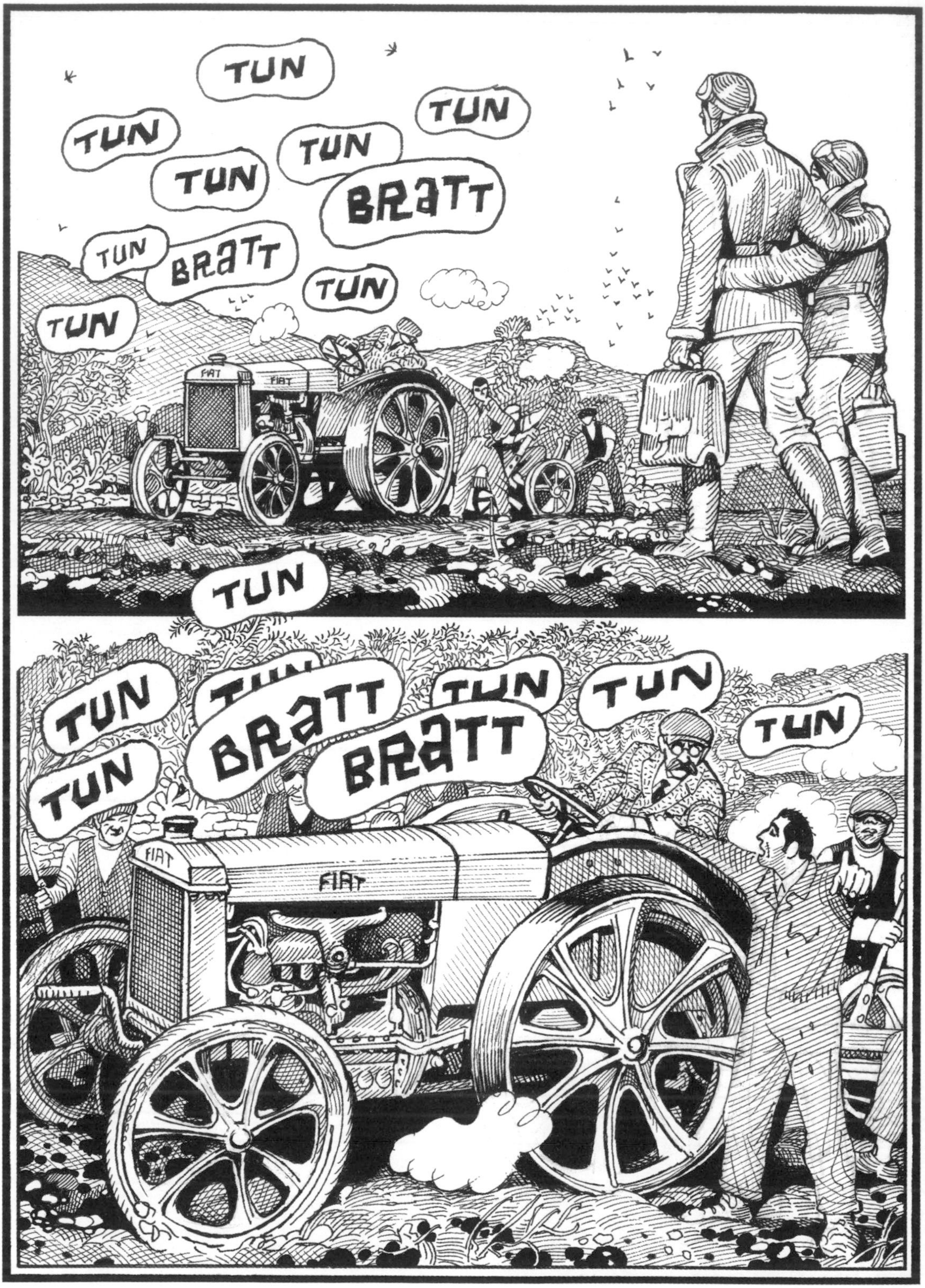
TUN
TUN
TUN
TUN
TUN
BRATT
TUN
BRATT
TUN
TUN
TUN
TUN
TUN
BRATT
BRATT
TUN
TUN

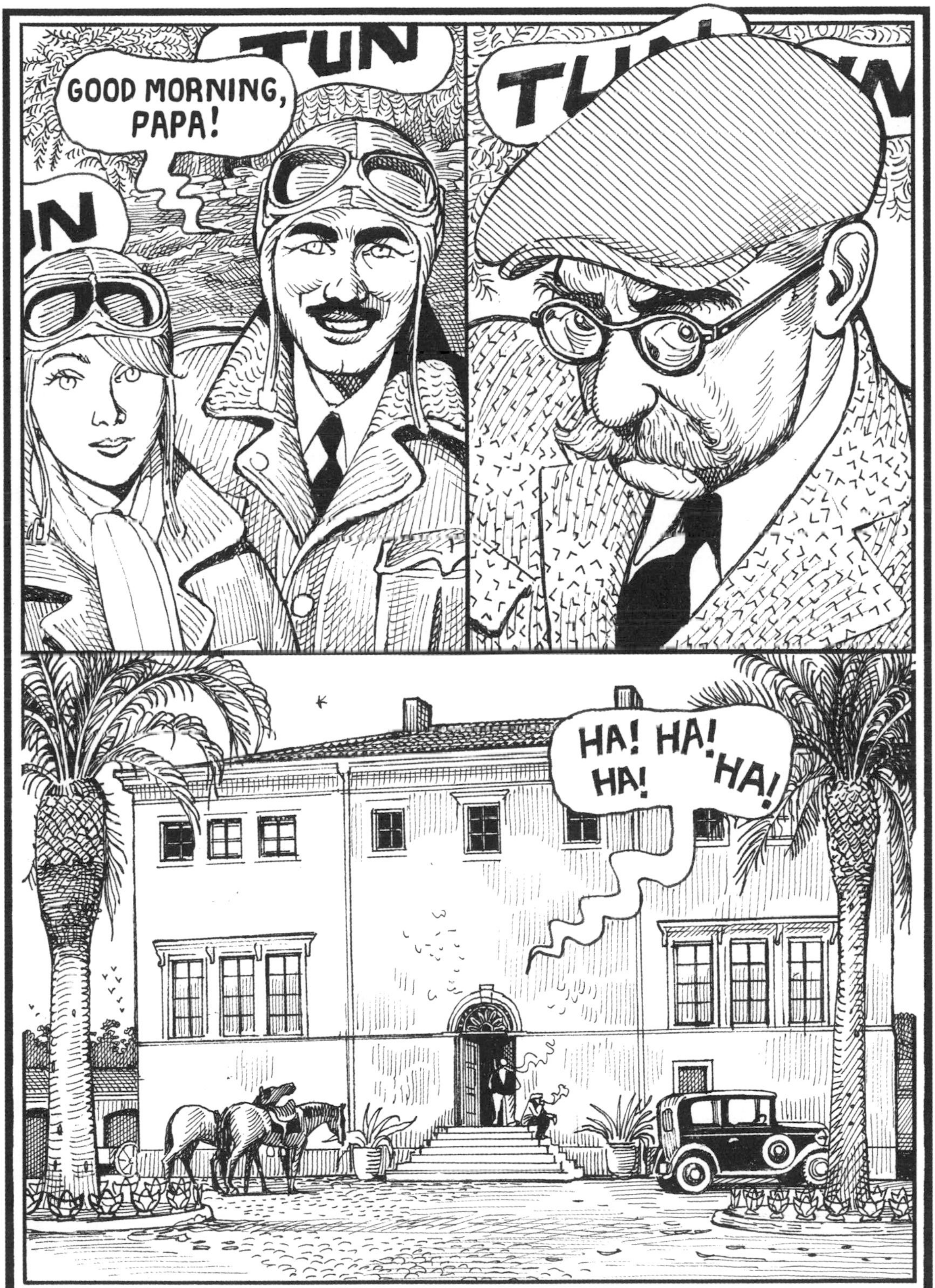
TUN
GOOD MORNING, PAPA!
UN
TUN
UN
HA! HA! HA! HA!

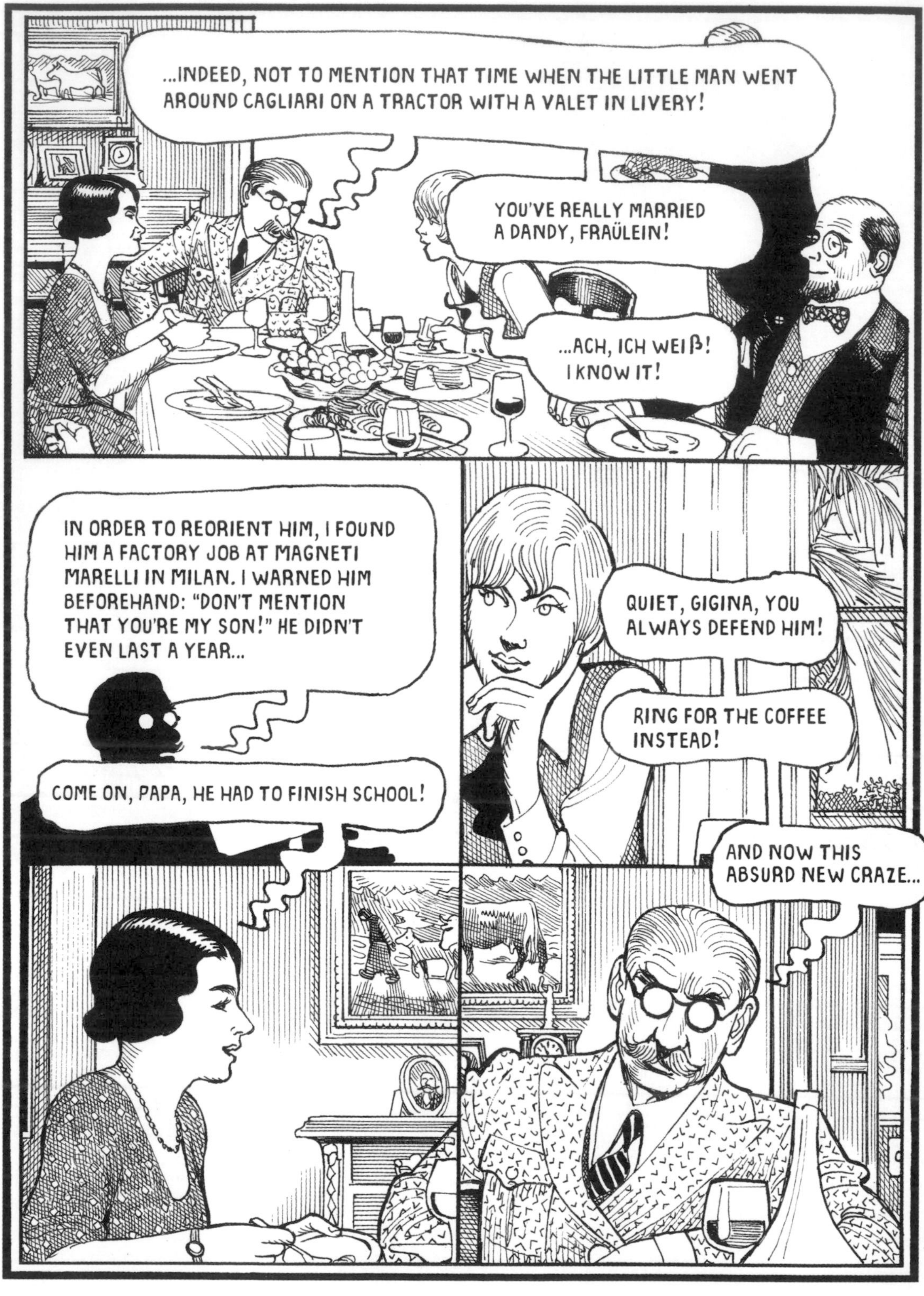
...INDEED, NOT TO MENTION THAT TIME WHEN THE LITTLE MAN WENT AROUND CAGLIARI ON A TRACTOR WITH A VALET IN LIVERY!
YOU'VE REALLY MARRIED A DANDY, FRAÜLEIN!
...ACH, ICH WEIß! I KNOW IT!
IN ORDER TO REORIENT HIM, I FOUND HIM A FACTORY JOB AT MAGNETI MARELLI IN MILAN. I WARNED HIM BEFOREHAND: "DON'T MENTION THAT YOU'RE MY SON!" HE DIDN'T EVEN LAST A YEAR...
COME ON, PAPA, HE HAD TO FINISH SCHOOL!
QUIET, GIGINA, YOU ALWAYS DEFEND HIM!
RING FOR THE COFFEE INSTEAD!
AND NOW THIS ABSURD NEW CRAZE...

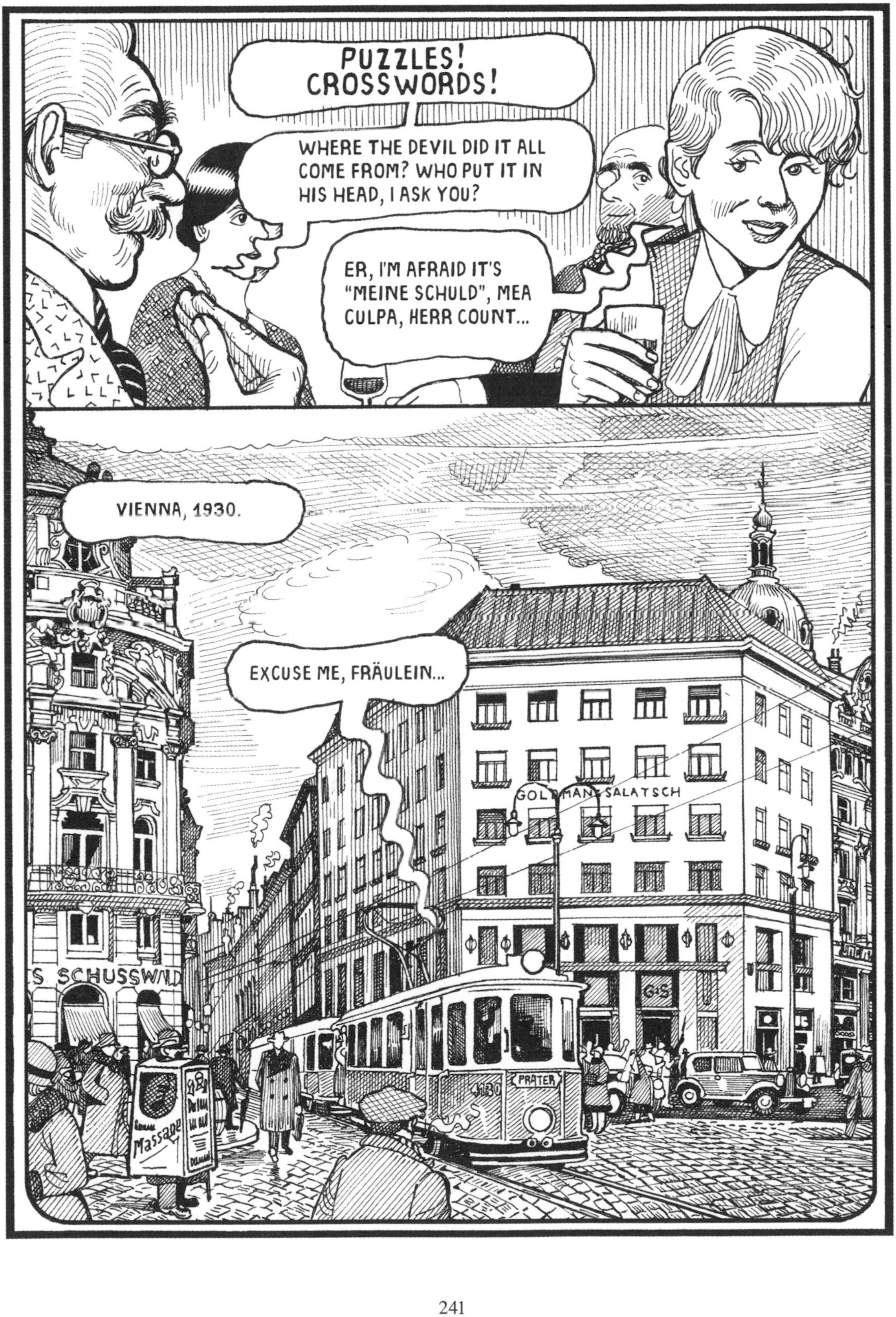
PUZZLES! CROSSWORDS!
WHERE THE DEVIL DID IT ALL COME FROM? WHO PUT IT IN HIS HEAD, I ASK YOU?
ER, I'M AFRAID IT'S "MEINE SCHULD", MEA CULPA, HERR COUNT...
VIENNA, 1930.
EXCUSE ME, FRÄULEIN...
GOLDMAN & SALATSCH
S SCHUSSWALD
G&S
PRATER
Massage

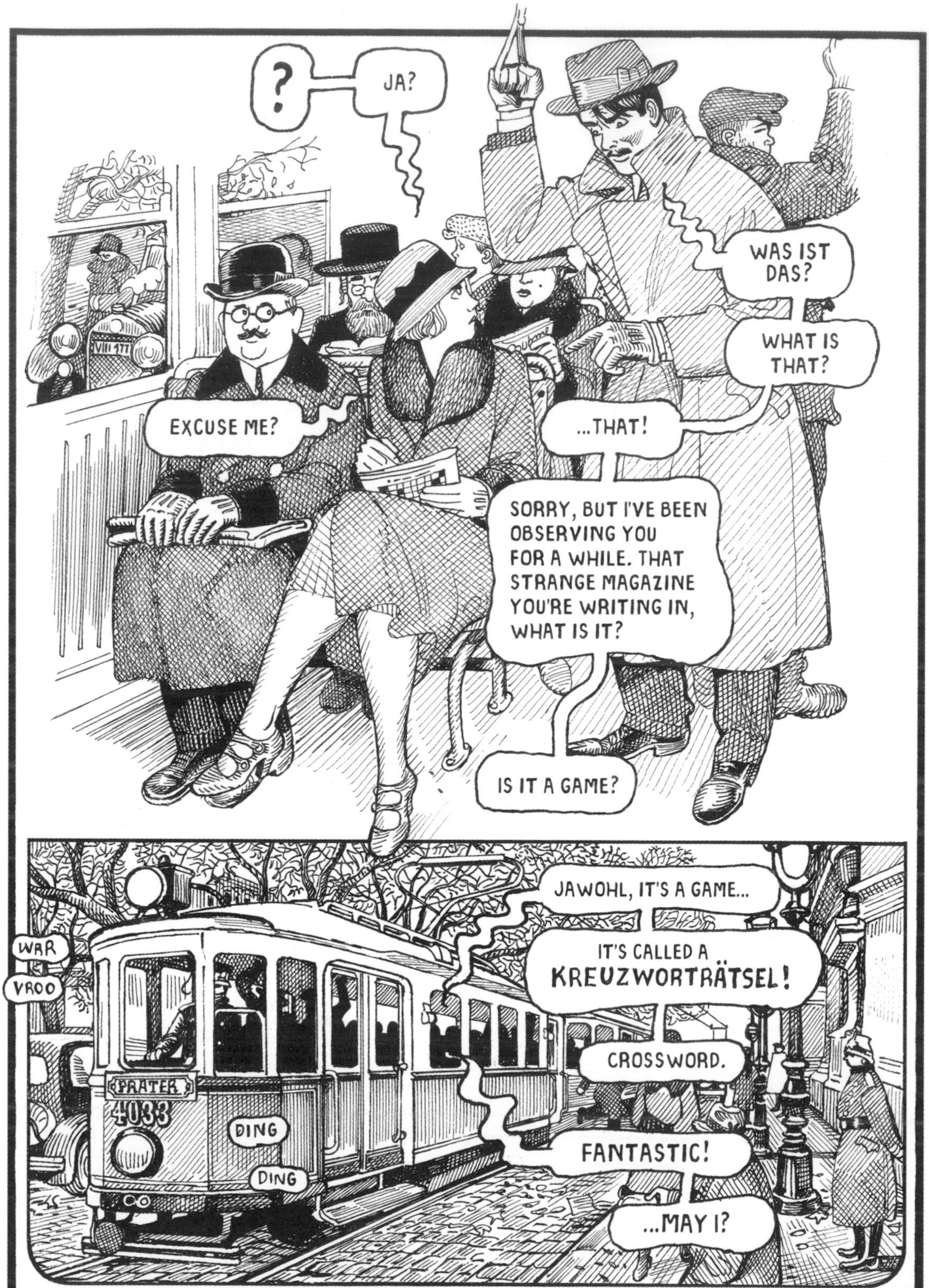
?
JA?
WAS IST DAS?
WHAT IS THAT?
EXCUSE ME?
...THAT!
SORRY, BUT I'VE BEEN OBSERVING YOU FOR A WHILE. THAT STRANGE MAGAZINE YOU'RE WRITING IN, WHAT IS IT?
IS IT A GAME?
WAR
VROO
PRATER
4033
DING
DING
JAWOHL, IT'S A GAME...
IT'S CALLED A KREUZWORTRÄTSEL!
CROSSWORD.
FANTASTIC!
...MAY I?

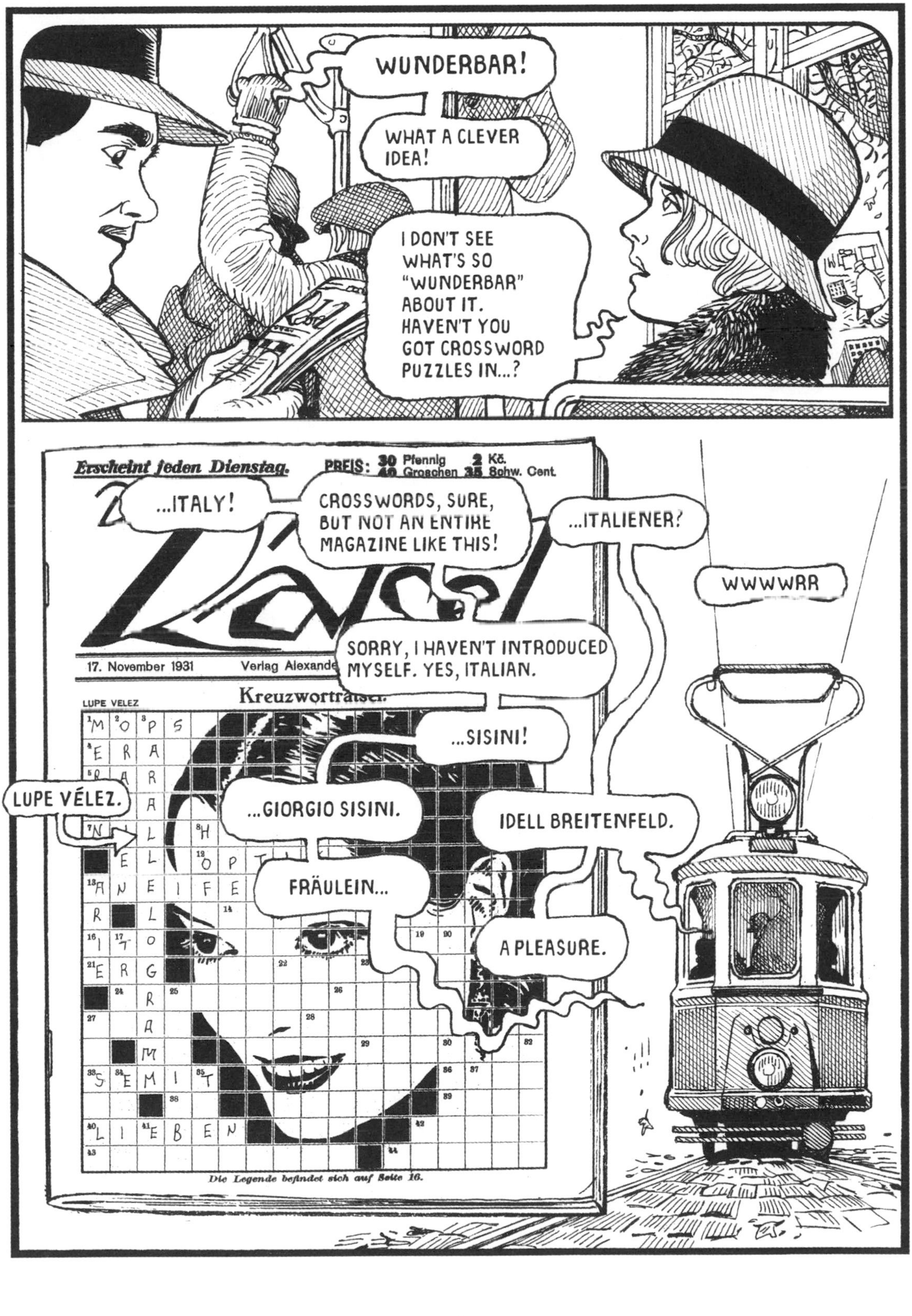
WUNDERBAR!
WHAT A CLEVER IDEA!
I DON'T SEE WHAT'S SO "WUNDERBAR" ABOUT IT. HAVEN'T YOU GOT CROSSWORD PUZZLES IN...?
Erscheint jeden Dienstag.
PREIS: 30 Pfennig 2 Kč. 40 Groschen 35 Schw. Cent
...ITALY!
CROSSWORDS, SURE, BUT NOT AN ENTIRE MAGAZINE LIKE THIS!
...ITALIENER?
WWWWRR
17. November 1931
SORRY, I HAVEN'T INTRODUCED MYSELF. YES, ITALIAN.
Kreuzworträtsel
LUPE VELEZ
...SISINI!
LUPE VÉLEZ.
...GIORGIO SISINI.
IDELL BREITENFELD.
FRÄULEIN...
A PLEASURE.
Die Legende befindet sich auf Seite 16.

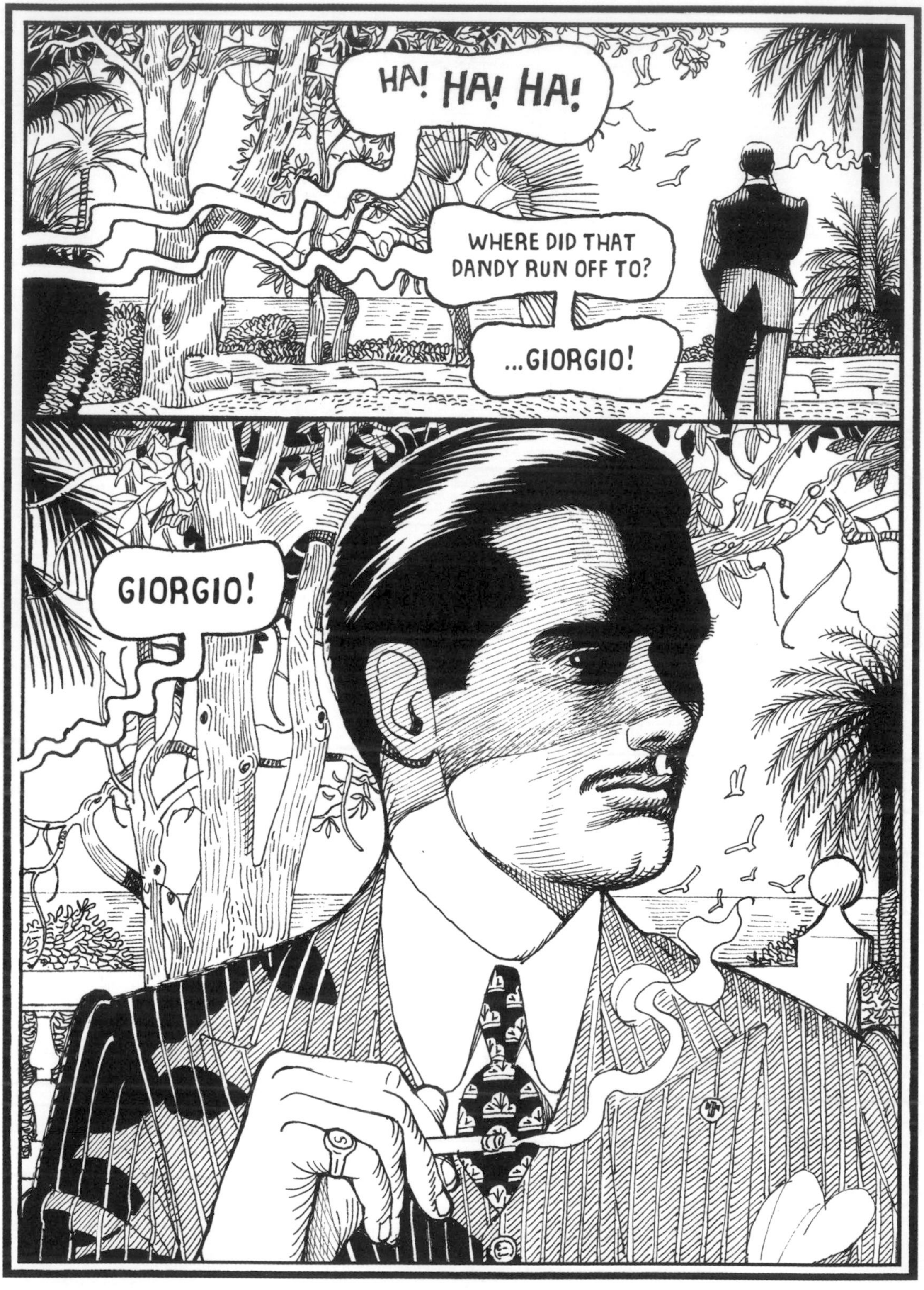
HA! HA! HA!
WHERE DID THAT DANDY RUN OFF TO?
...GIORGIO!
GIORGIO!

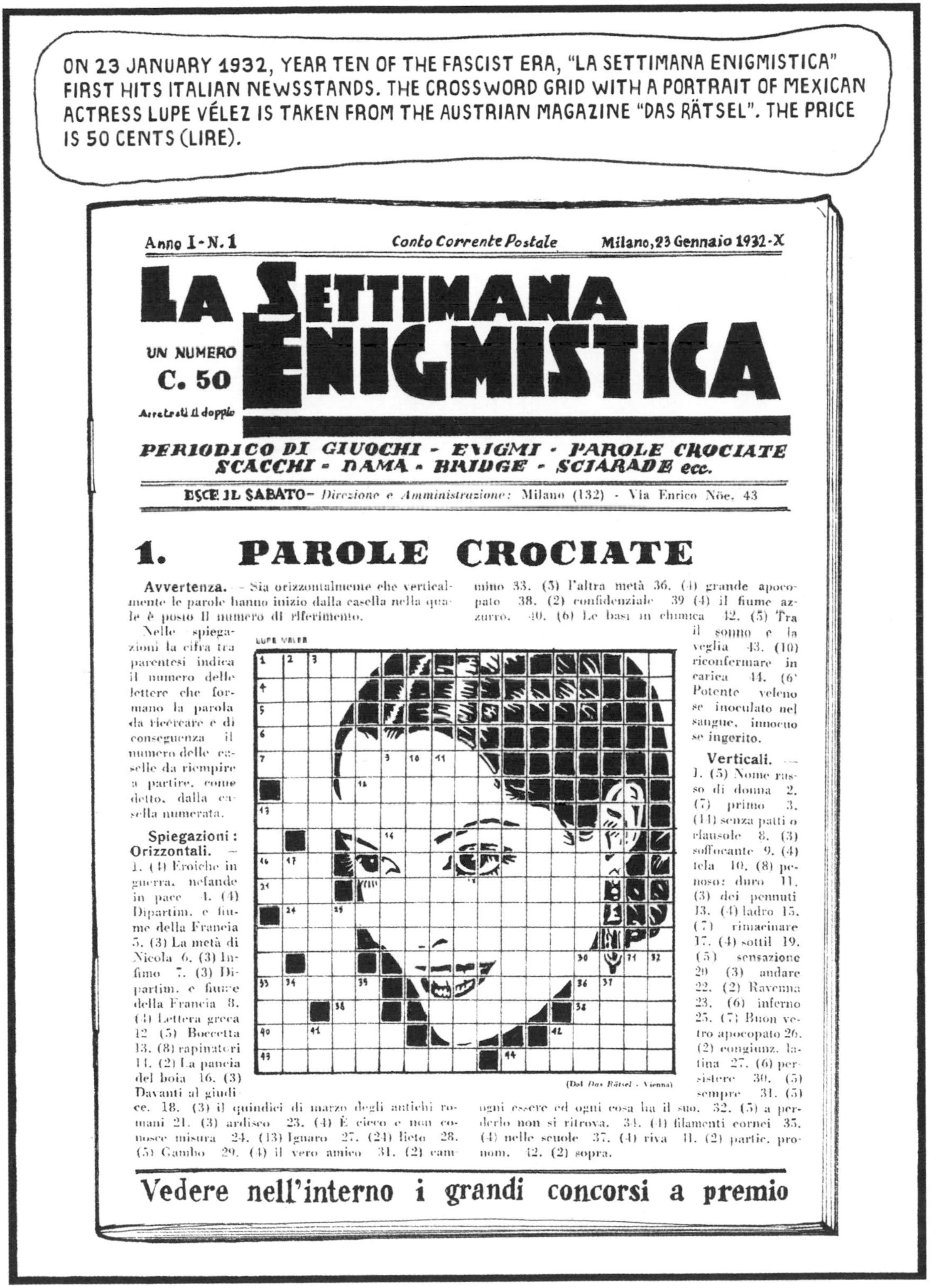
ON 23 JANUARY 1932, YEAR TEN OF THE FASCIST ERA, "LA SETTIMANA ENIGMISTICA" FIRST HITS ITALIAN NEWSSTANDS. THE CROSSWORD GRID WITH A PORTRAIT OF MEXICAN ACTRESS LUPE VÉLEZ IS TAKEN FROM THE AUSTRIAN MAGAZINE "DAS RÄTSEL". THE PRICE IS 50 CENTS (LIRE).

Anno I - N. 1 *Conto Corrente Postale* Milano, 23 Gennaio 1932-X

LA SETTIMANA ENIGMISTICA

UN NUMERO
C. 50
Arretrati il doppio

PERIODICO DI GIUOCHI - ENIGMI - PAROLE CROCIATE SCACCHI - DAMA - BRIDGE - SCIARADE ecc.

ESCE IL SABATO - *Direzione e Amministrazione:* Milano (132) - Via Enrico Nöe, 43

1. PAROLE CROCIATE

Avvertenza. — Sia orizzontalmente che verticalmente le parole hanno inizio dalla casella nella quale è posto il numero di riferimento.

Nelle spiegazioni la cifra tra parentesi indica il numero delle lettere che formano la parola da ricercare e di conseguenza il numero delle caselle da riempire a partire, come detto, dalla casella numerata.

LUPE VALEZ

(Dal *Das Rätsel* - Vienna)

Spiegazioni: Orizzontali. — 1. (4) Eroiche in guerra, nefande in pace 4. (4) Dipartim. e fiume della Francia 5. (3) La metà di Nicola 6. (3) Infimo 7. (3) Dipartim. e fiume della Francia 8. (4) Lettera greca 12 (5) Boccetta 13. (8) rapinatori 14. (2) La pancia del boia 16. (3) Davanti al giudice. 18. (3) il quindici di marzo degli antichi romani 21. (3) ardisco 23. (4) È cieco e non conosce misura 24. (13) Ignaro 27. (24) lieto 28. (5) Gambo 29. (4) il vero amico 31. (2) cammino 33. (3) l'altra metà 36. (4) grande apocopato 38. (2) confidenziale 39 (4) il fiume azzurro. 40. (6) Le basi in chimica 42. (5) Tra il sonno e la veglia 43. (10) riconfermare in carica 44. (6) Potente veleno se inoculato nel sangue, innocuo se ingerito.

Verticali. — 1. (5) Nome russo di donna 2. (7) primo 3. (14) senza patti o clausole 8. (3) soffocante 9. (4) tela 10. (8) penoso: duro 11. (3) dei pennuti 13. (4) ladro 15. (7) rimacinare 17. (4) sottil 19. (5) sensazione 20 (3) andare 22. (2) Ravenna 23. (6) inferno 25. (7) Buon vetro apocopato 26. (2) congiunz. latina 27. (6) persistere 30. (5) sempre 31. (5) ogni essere ed ogni cosa ha il suo. 32. (5) a perderlo non si ritrova. 34. (4) filamenti cornei 35. (4) nelle scuole 37. (4) riva 41. (2) partic. pronom. 42. (2) sopra.

Vedere nell'interno i grandi concorsi a premio

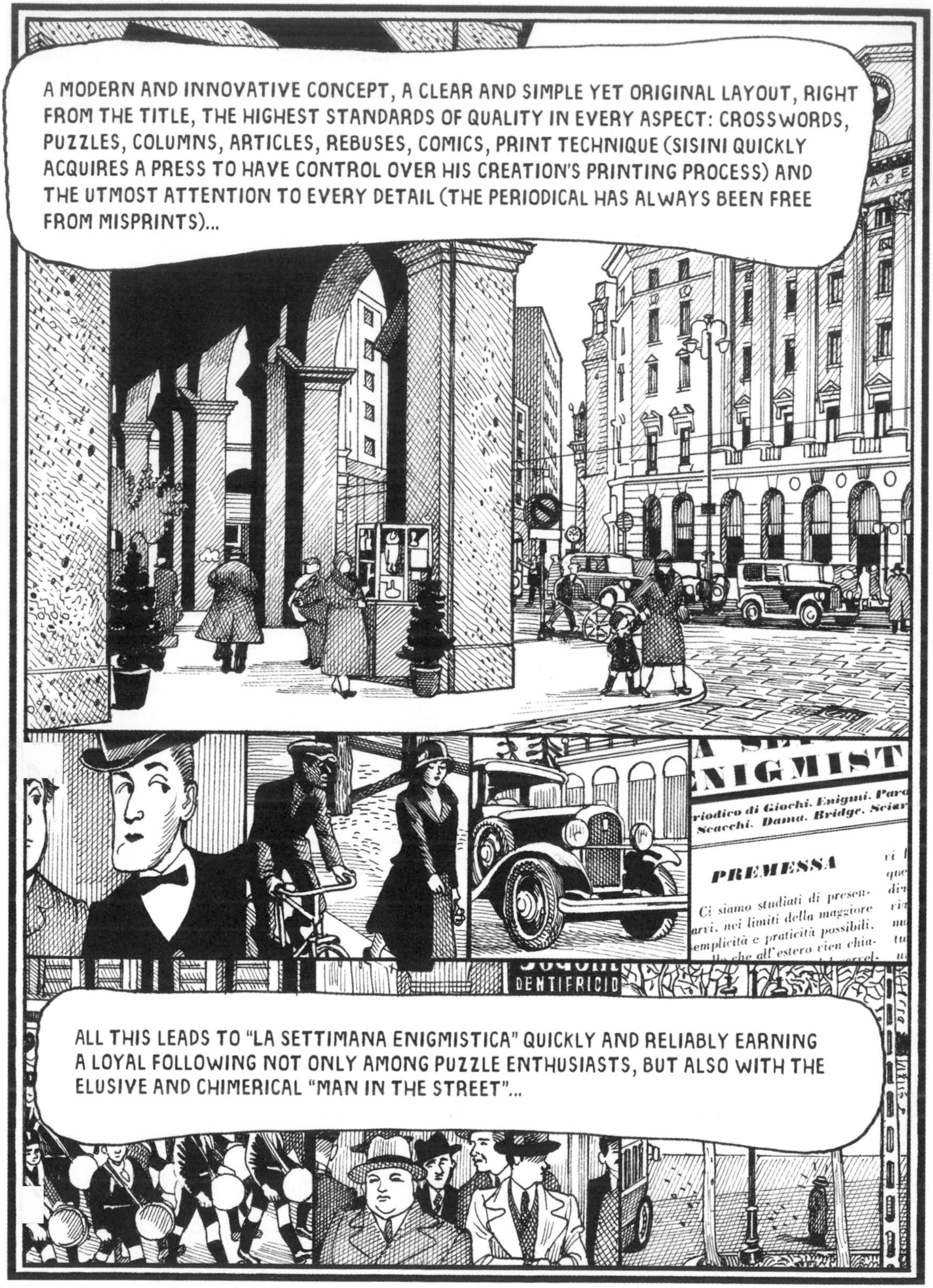
A MODERN AND INNOVATIVE CONCEPT, A CLEAR AND SIMPLE YET ORIGINAL LAYOUT, RIGHT FROM THE TITLE, THE HIGHEST STANDARDS OF QUALITY IN EVERY ASPECT: CROSSWORDS, PUZZLES, COLUMNS, ARTICLES, REBUSES, COMICS, PRINT TECHNIQUE (SISINI QUICKLY ACQUIRES A PRESS TO HAVE CONTROL OVER HIS CREATION'S PRINTING PROCESS) AND THE UTMOST ATTENTION TO EVERY DETAIL (THE PERIODICAL HAS ALWAYS BEEN FREE FROM MISPRINTS)...
PREMESSA
Ci siamo studiati di presen-
DENTIFRICIO
ALL THIS LEADS TO "LA SETTIMANA ENIGMISTICA" QUICKLY AND RELIABLY EARNING A LOYAL FOLLOWING NOT ONLY AMONG PUZZLE ENTHUSIASTS, BUT ALSO WITH THE ELUSIVE AND CHIMERICAL "MAN IN THE STREET"...

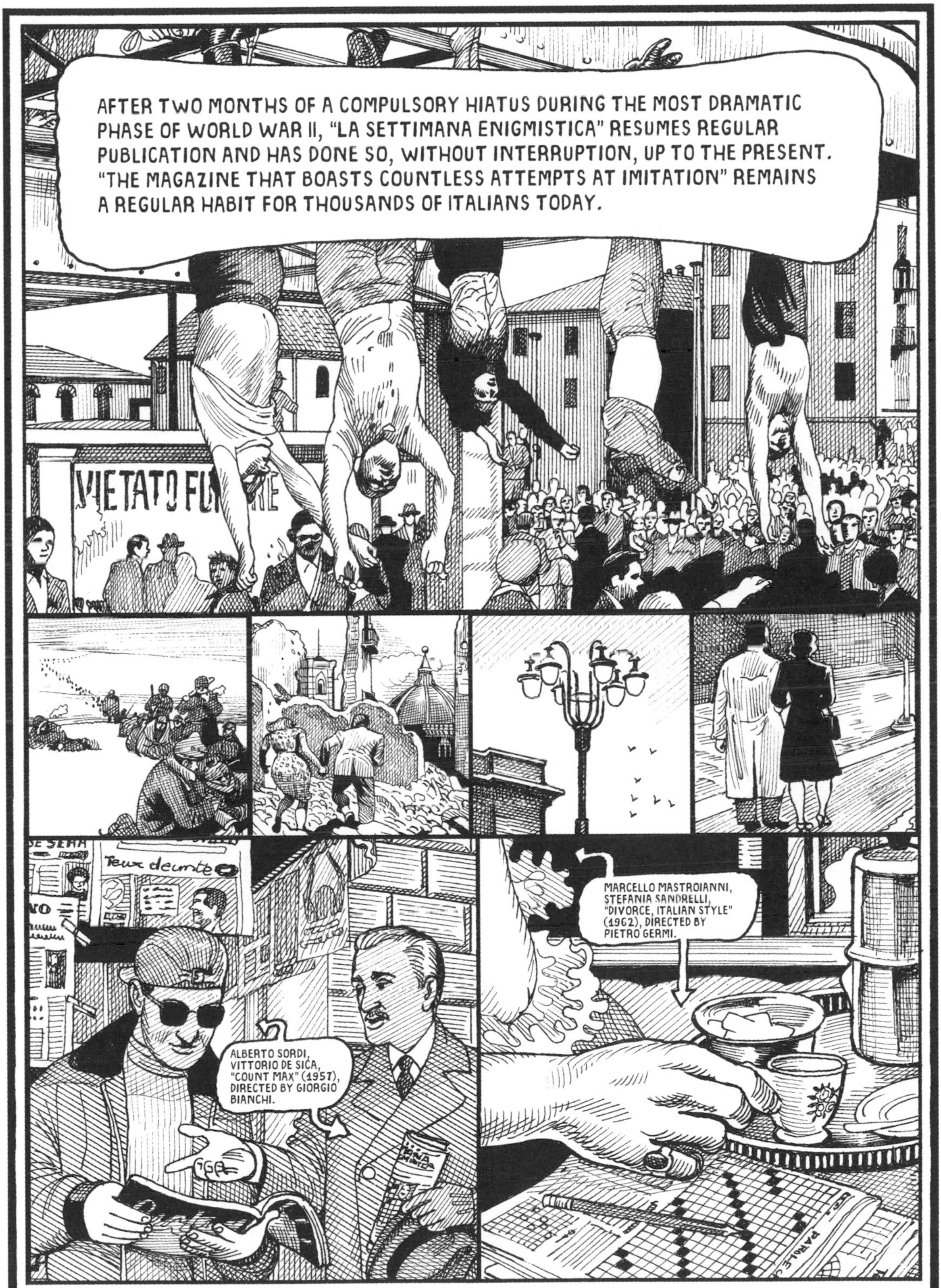
AFTER TWO MONTHS OF A COMPULSORY HIATUS DURING THE MOST DRAMATIC PHASE OF WORLD WAR II, "LA SETTIMANA ENIGMISTICA" RESUMES REGULAR PUBLICATION AND HAS DONE SO, WITHOUT INTERRUPTION, UP TO THE PRESENT. "THE MAGAZINE THAT BOASTS COUNTLESS ATTEMPTS AT IMITATION" REMAINS A REGULAR HABIT FOR THOUSANDS OF ITALIANS TODAY.
VIETATO FU RE
ALBERTO SORDI, VITTORIO DE SICA, "COUNT MAX" (1957), DIRECTED BY GIORGIO BIANCHI.
MARCELLO MASTROIANNI, STEFANIA SANDRELLI, "DIVORCE, ITALIAN STYLE" (1962), DIRECTED BY PIETRO GERMI.

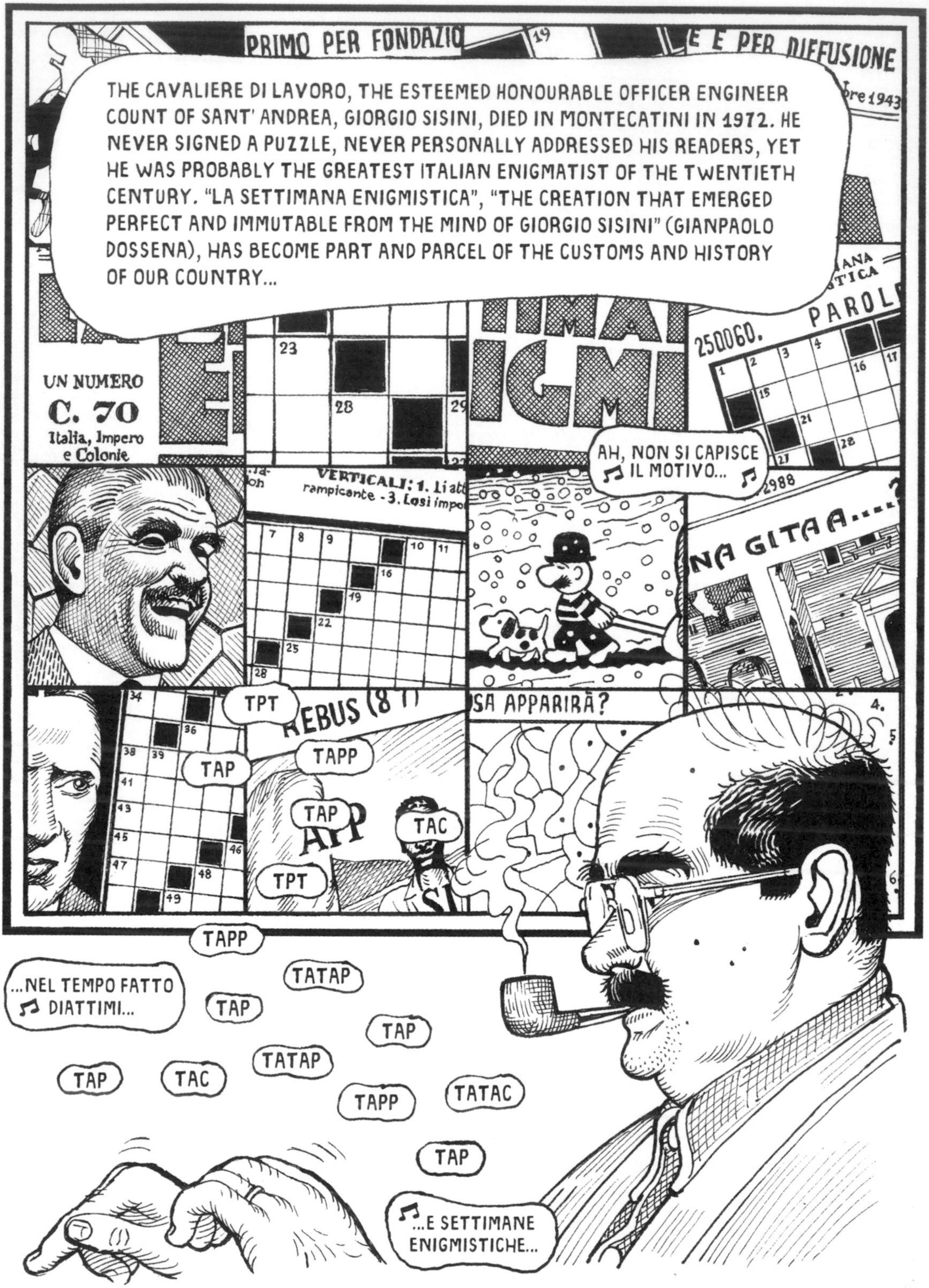

PRIMO PER FONDAZIO
E E PER DIFFUSIONE
THE CAVALIERE DI LAVORO, THE ESTEEMED HONOURABLE OFFICER ENGINEER COUNT OF SANT' ANDREA, GIORGIO SISINI, DIED IN MONTECATINI IN 1972. HE NEVER SIGNED A PUZZLE, NEVER PERSONALLY ADDRESSED HIS READERS, YET HE WAS PROBABLY THE GREATEST ITALIAN ENIGMATIST OF THE TWENTIETH CENTURY. "LA SETTIMANA ENIGMISTICA", "THE CREATION THAT EMERGED PERFECT AND IMMUTABLE FROM THE MIND OF GIORGIO SISINI" (GIANPAOLO DOSSENA), HAS BECOME PART AND PARCEL OF THE CUSTOMS AND HISTORY OF OUR COUNTRY...
UN NUMERO
C. 70
Italia, Impero e Colonie
PAROLE
AH, NON SI CAPISCE IL MOTIVO...
VERTICALI: 1. Li att rampicante - 3. Losi impo
NA GITA A....?
REBUS (8 7)
SA APPARIRÀ?
TPT
TAP
TAPP
TAP
TAC
TPT
TAPP
...NEL TEMPO FATTO DIATTIMI...
TATAP
TAP
TAP
TATAP
TAP
TAC
TAPP
TATAC
TAP
...E SETTIMANE ENIGMISTICHE...

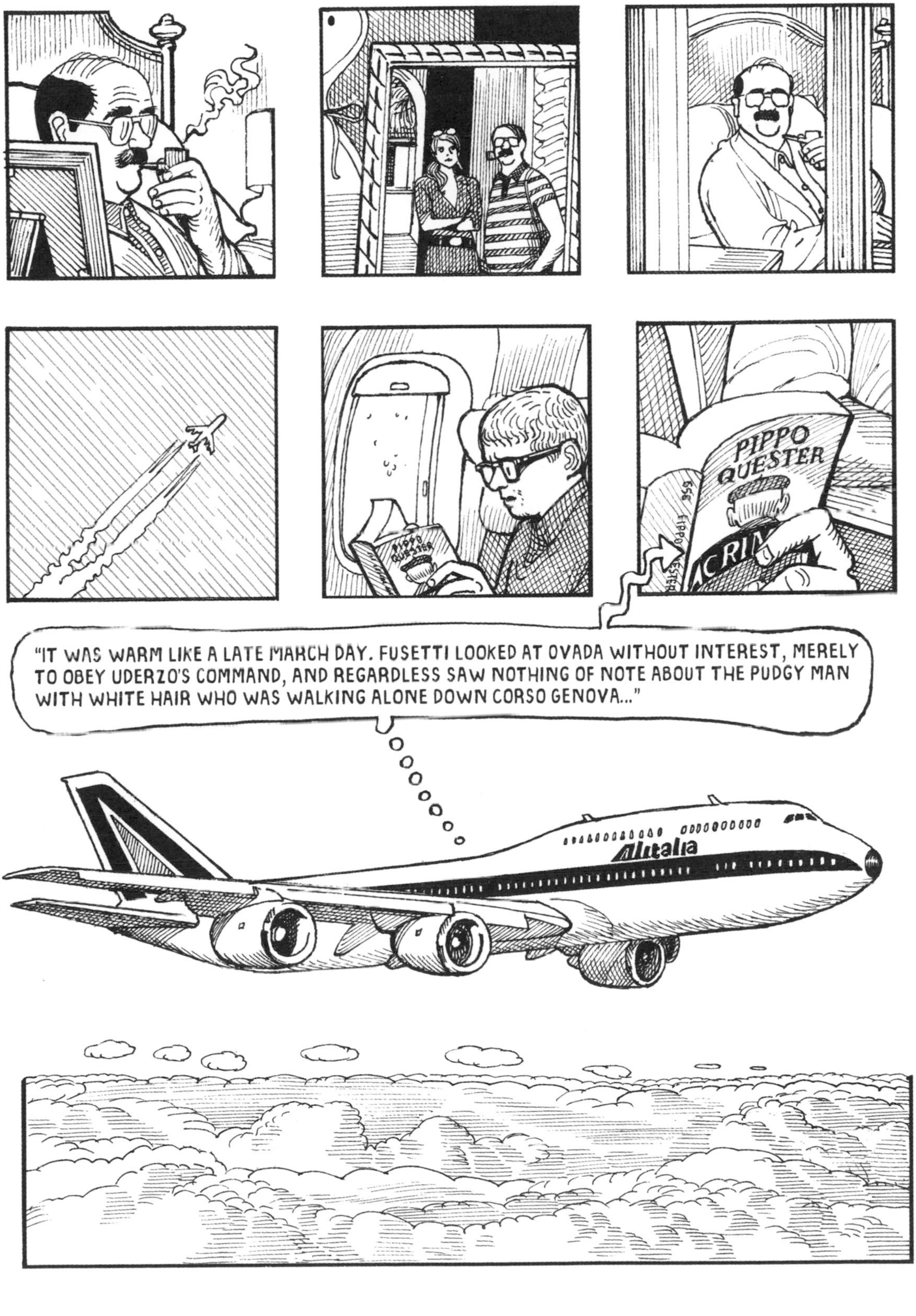
PIPPO QUESTER
"IT WAS WARM LIKE A LATE MARCH DAY. FUSETTI LOOKED AT OVADA WITHOUT INTEREST, MERELY TO OBEY UDERZO'S COMMAND, AND REGARDLESS SAW NOTHING OF NOTE ABOUT THE PUDGY MAN WITH WHITE HAIR WHO WAS WALKING ALONE DOWN CORSO GENOVA..."
Alitalia

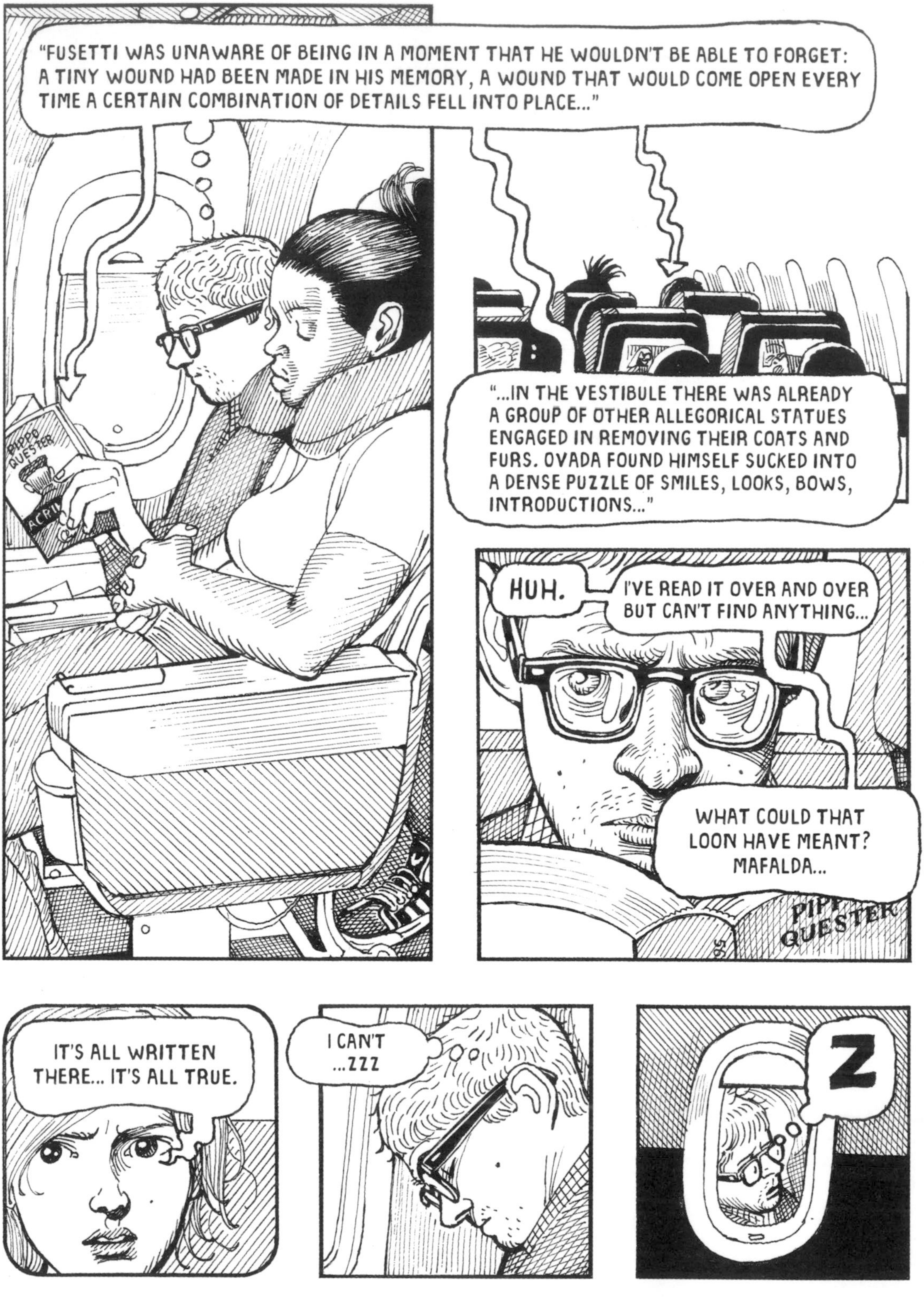
"FUSETTI WAS UNAWARE OF BEING IN A MOMENT THAT HE WOULDN'T BE ABLE TO FORGET: A TINY WOUND HAD BEEN MADE IN HIS MEMORY, A WOUND THAT WOULD COME OPEN EVERY TIME A CERTAIN COMBINATION OF DETAILS FELL INTO PLACE..."
PIPPO QUESTER
"...IN THE VESTIBULE THERE WAS ALREADY A GROUP OF OTHER ALLEGORICAL STATUES ENGAGED IN REMOVING THEIR COATS AND FURS. OVADA FOUND HIMSELF SUCKED INTO A DENSE PUZZLE OF SMILES, LOOKS, BOWS, INTRODUCTIONS..."
HUH.
I'VE READ IT OVER AND OVER BUT CAN'T FIND ANYTHING...
WHAT COULD THAT LOON HAVE MEANT? MAFALDA...
QUESTER
IT'S ALL WRITTEN THERE... IT'S ALL TRUE.
I CAN'T ...ZZZ
Z

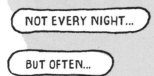

NOT EVERY NIGHT...

BUT OFTEN...

UMBERTO...

MILANESE ACCOUNT MANAGER, IN HIS FORTIES, AND HIS GIRLFRIEND GRAZIELLA, AN INTERN...

SHE WOKE UP IN THE MIDDLE OF THE NIGHT SCREAMING, IN THE GRIP OF TERRIFYING NIGHTMARES.

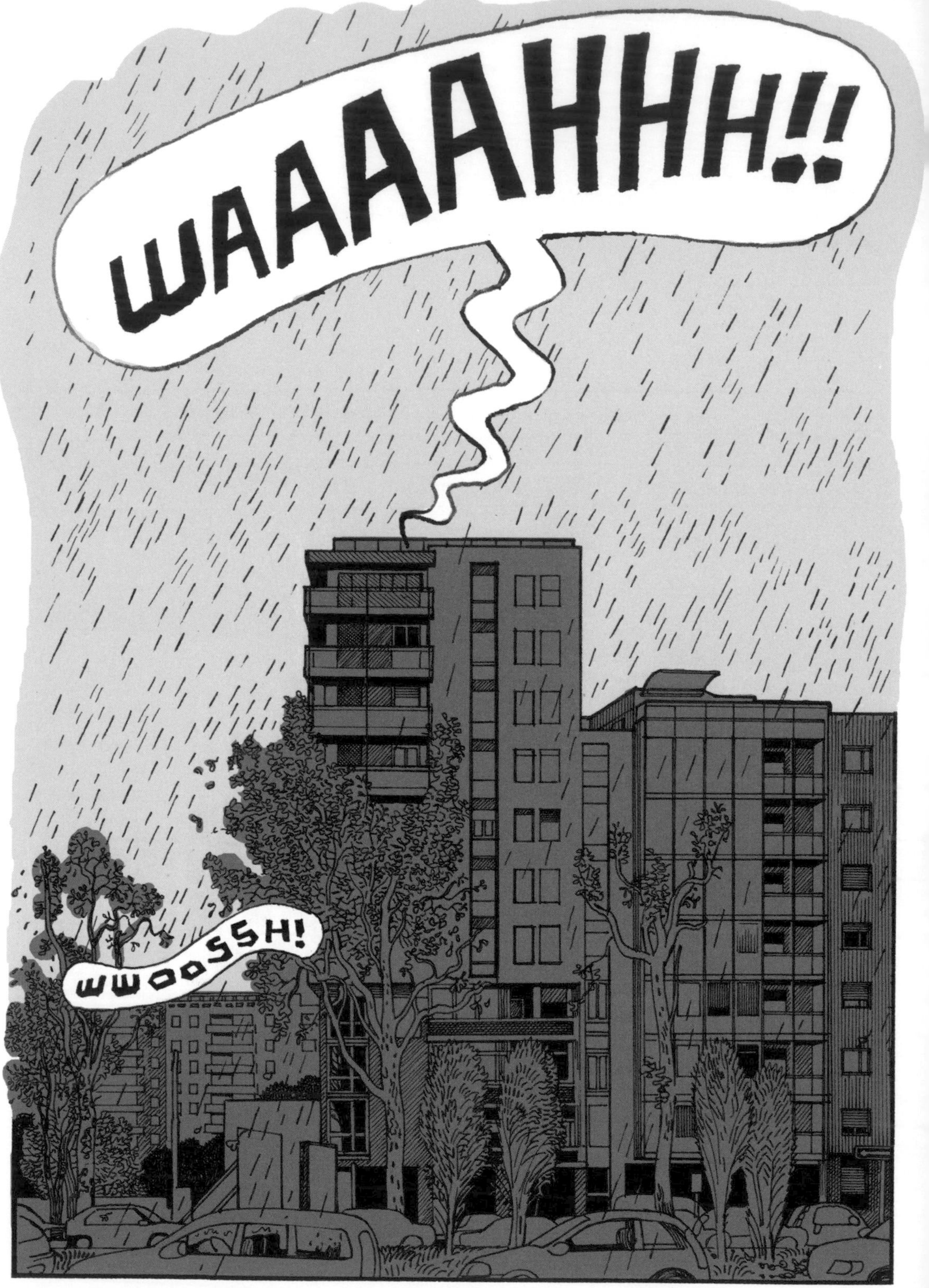
WAAAAHHH!!
WWOOSSH!

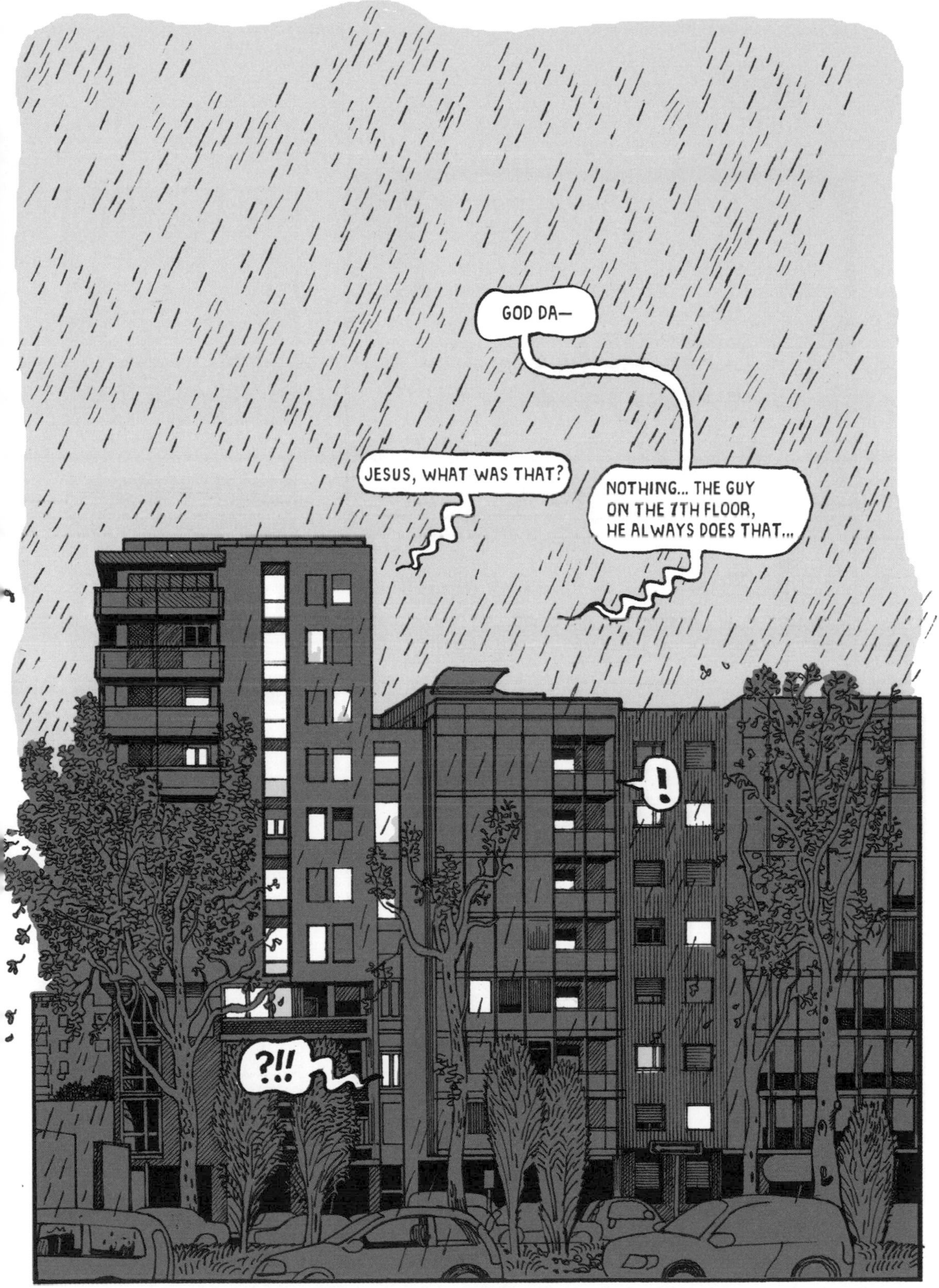
GOD DA—
JESUS, WHAT WAS THAT?
NOTHING... THE GUY ON THE 7TH FLOOR, HE ALWAYS DOES THAT...
!
?!!

CLICK!

WE WERE AT YOUR PARENTS' HOUSE ON THE LAKE. WE WERE ABOUT TO SIT DOWN TO EAT WHEN THERE WAS AN EXPLOSION... THE LIGHT, THE MUSHROOM CLOUD... AND THEN THE FIERY SHOCK WAVE THAT SWEPT EVERYTHING AWAY... YOUR MOTHER'S FLOWERS... THE DOG... THE KIDS...

YOUR MOTHER!

VERY FUNNY...

ZZZ

HIS LIFE WASN'T BAD, ALL IN ALL...

BUT...

ONE SPRING MORNING...

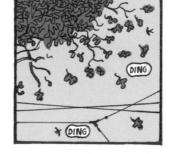

DING

DING

I HAVE SOMETHING TO TELL YOU.

...I SLEPT WITH SOMEONE ELSE.

THERE, I SAID IT.

NO, I'M STAYING WITH HIM TONIGHT.

I'M NOT COMING BACK, UMBERTO.

THERE, I SAID IT.

BETTER IF YOU DON'T CALL ME ANY MORE, UMBERTO...

THERE, I SAID IT.

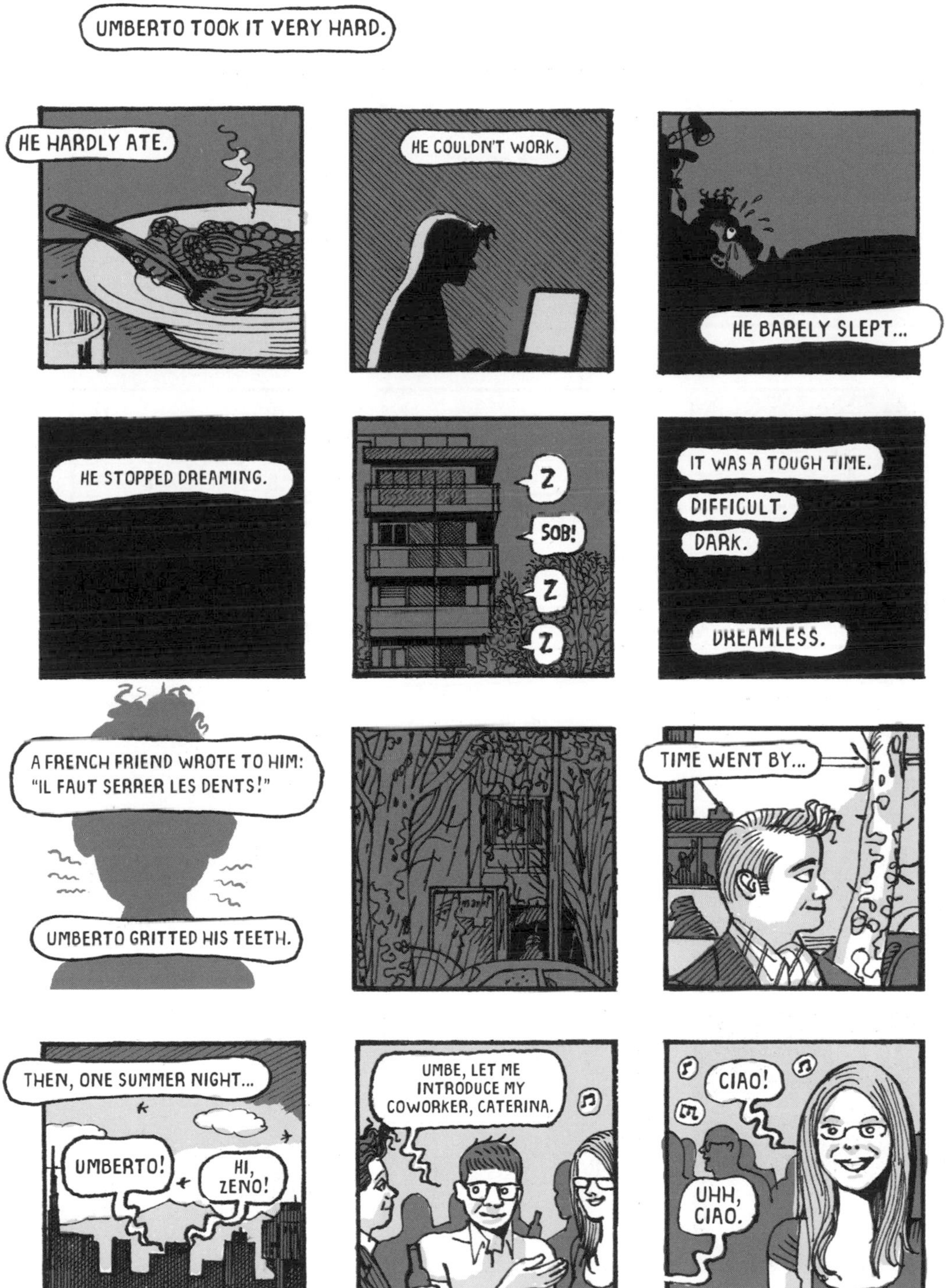
UMBERTO TOOK IT VERY HARD.
HE HARDLY ATE.
HE COULDN'T WORK.
HE BARELY SLEPT...
HE STOPPED DREAMING.
Z
SOB!
Z
Z
IT WAS A TOUGH TIME.
DIFFICULT.
DARK.
DREAMLESS.
A FRENCH FRIEND WROTE TO HIM: "IL FAUT SERRER LES DENTS!"
UMBERTO GRITTED HIS TEETH.
TIME WENT BY...
THEN, ONE SUMMER NIGHT...
UMBERTO!
HI, ZENO!
UMBE, LET ME INTRODUCE MY COWORKER, CATERINA.
CIAO!
UHH, CIAO.

TWO DAYS LATER, CATERINA AND UMBERTO SAW EACH OTHER AGAIN...

THEY WENT OUT TOGETHER.

THEY WENT ON VACATION TOGETHER.

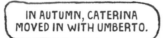

IN AUTUMN, CATERINA MOVED IN WITH UMBERTO.

AND, FINALLY ...

ONE WINTER NIGHT...

MMH...

NO, NO...

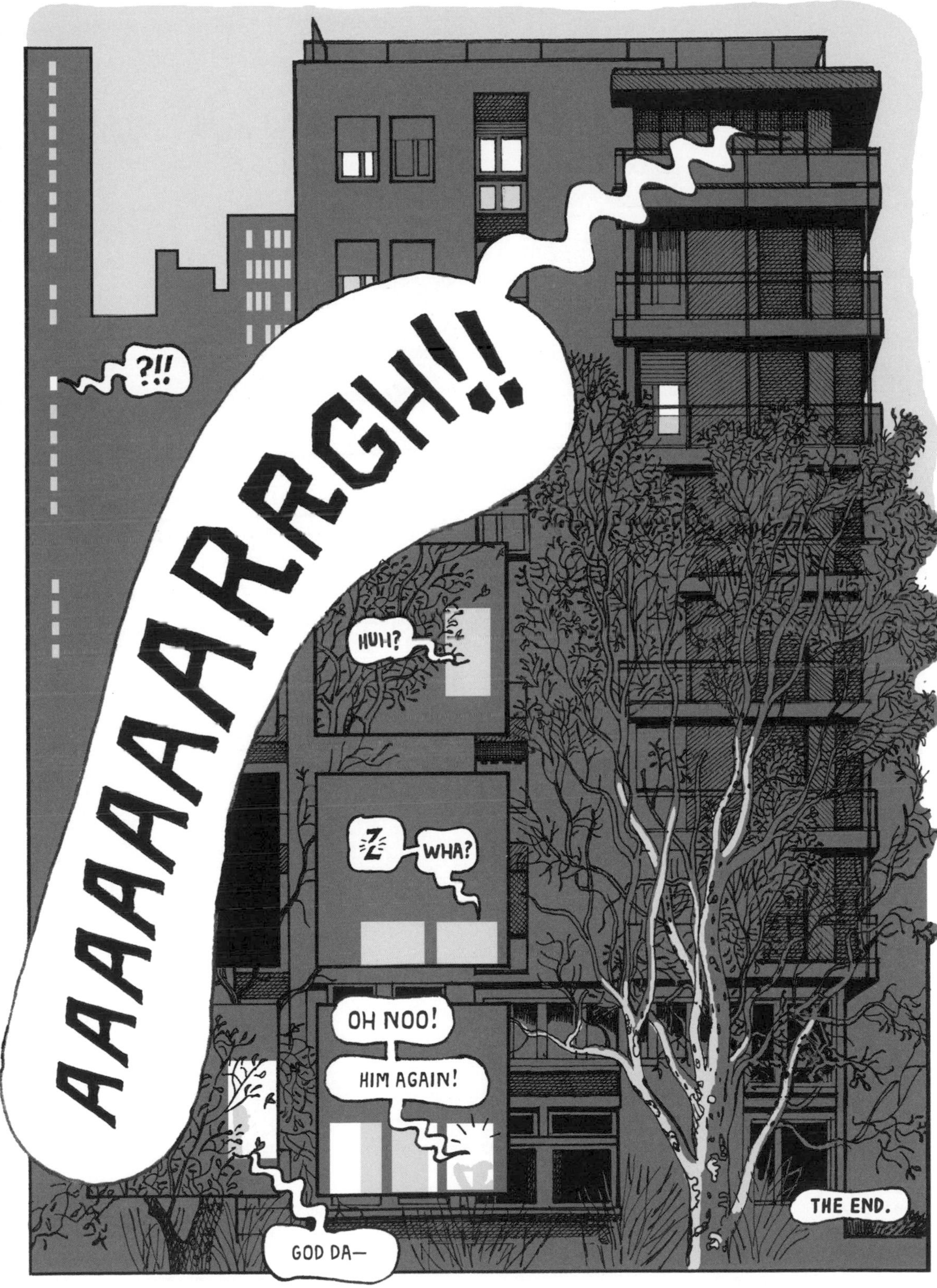

AAAAARRGH!!
?!!
HUH?
Z
WHA?
OH NOO!
HIM AGAIN!
GOD DA—
THE END.

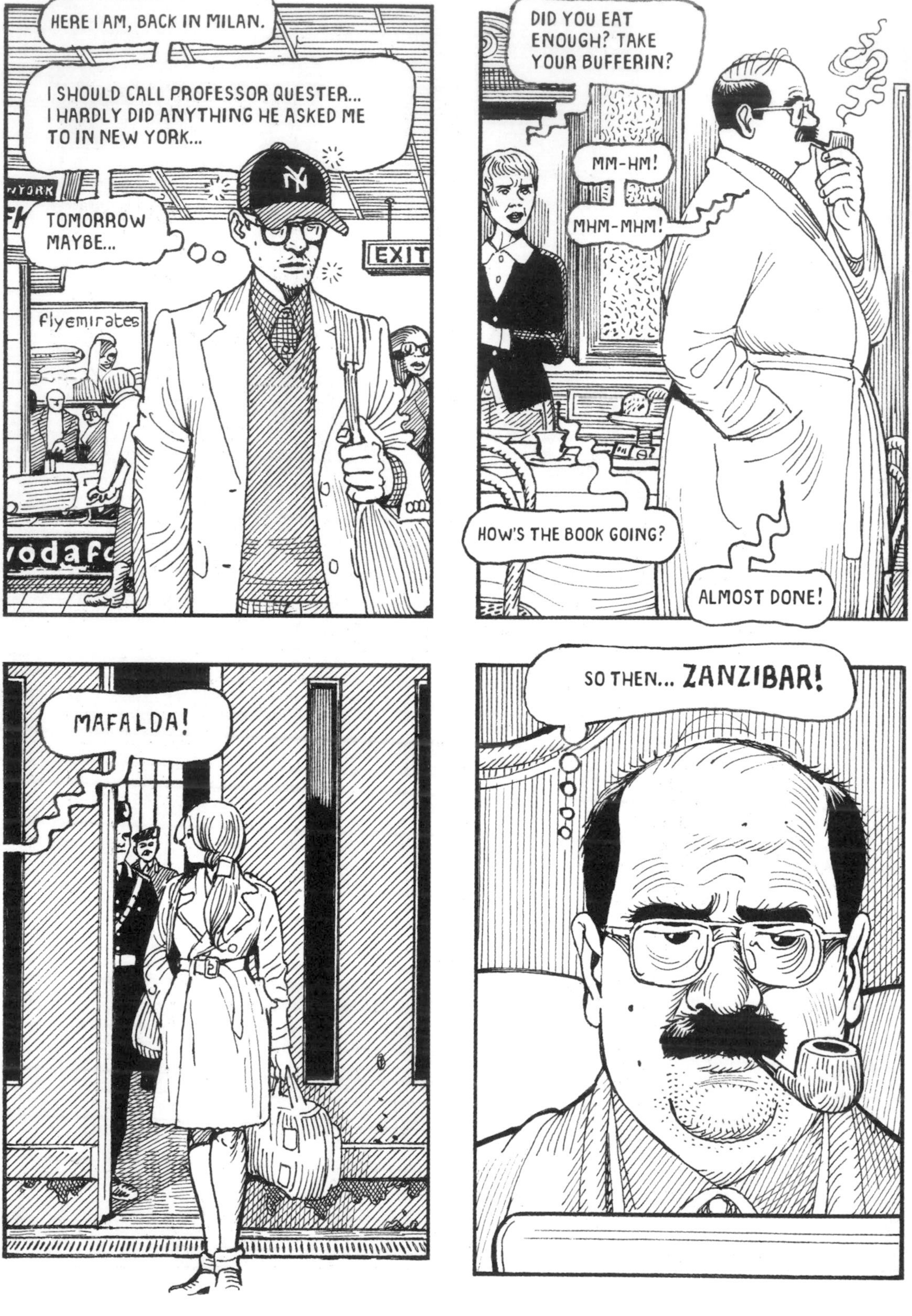
HERE I AM, BACK IN MILAN.
I SHOULD CALL PROFESSOR QUESTER... I HARDLY DID ANYTHING HE ASKED ME TO IN NEW YORK...
TOMORROW MAYBE...
EXIT
flyemirates
vodafo
DID YOU EAT ENOUGH? TAKE YOUR BUFFERIN?
MM-HM!
MHM-MHM!
HOW'S THE BOOK GOING?
ALMOST DONE!
MAFALDA!
SO THEN... ZANZIBAR!

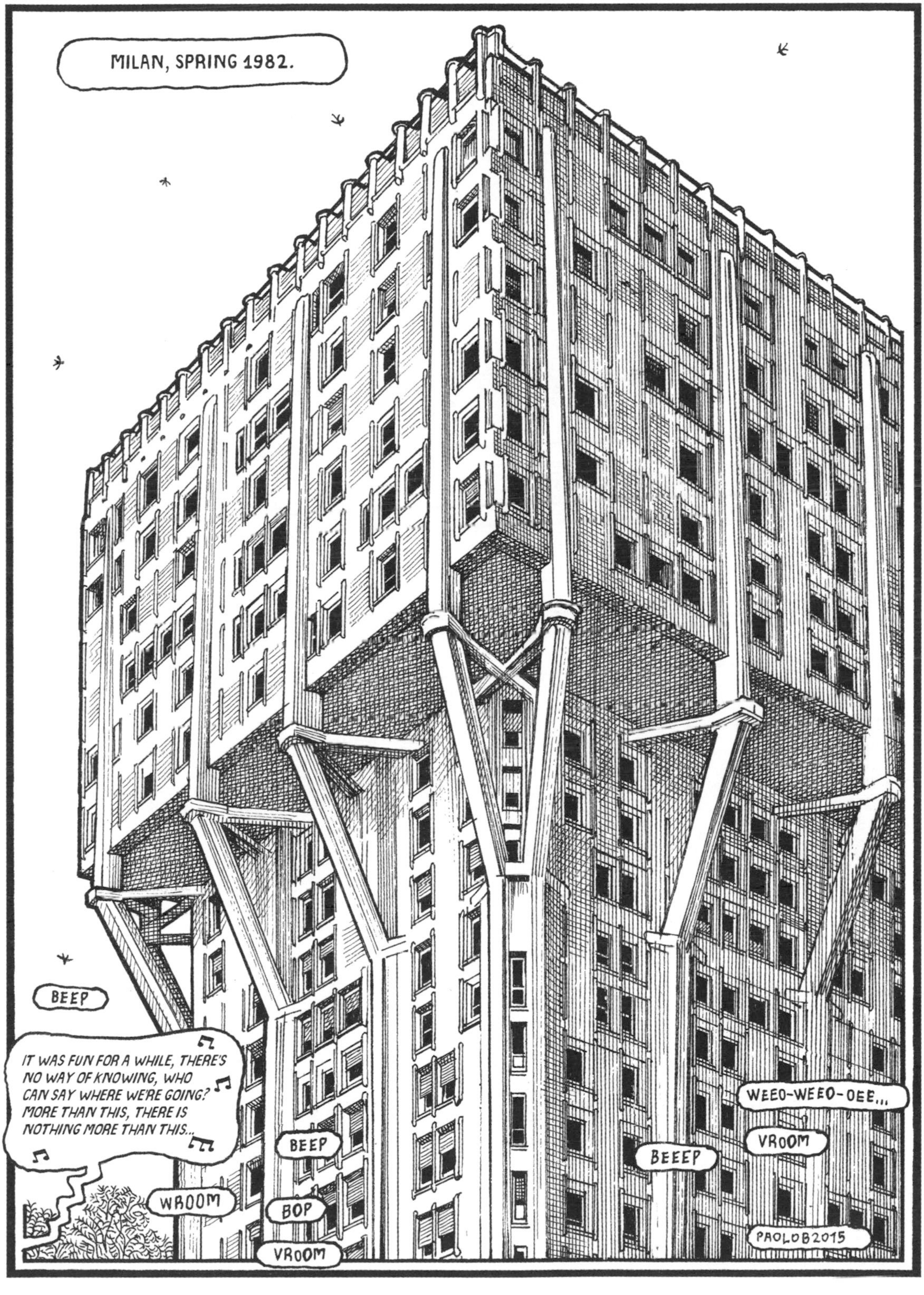
MILAN, SPRING 1982.
BEEP
IT WAS FUN FOR A WHILE, THERE'S NO WAY OF KNOWING, WHO CAN SAY WHERE WE'RE GOING? MORE THAN THIS, THERE IS NOTHING MORE THAN THIS...
WROOM
BEEP
BOP
VROOM
BEEEP
VROOM
WEEO-WEEO-OEE...
PAOLOB2015

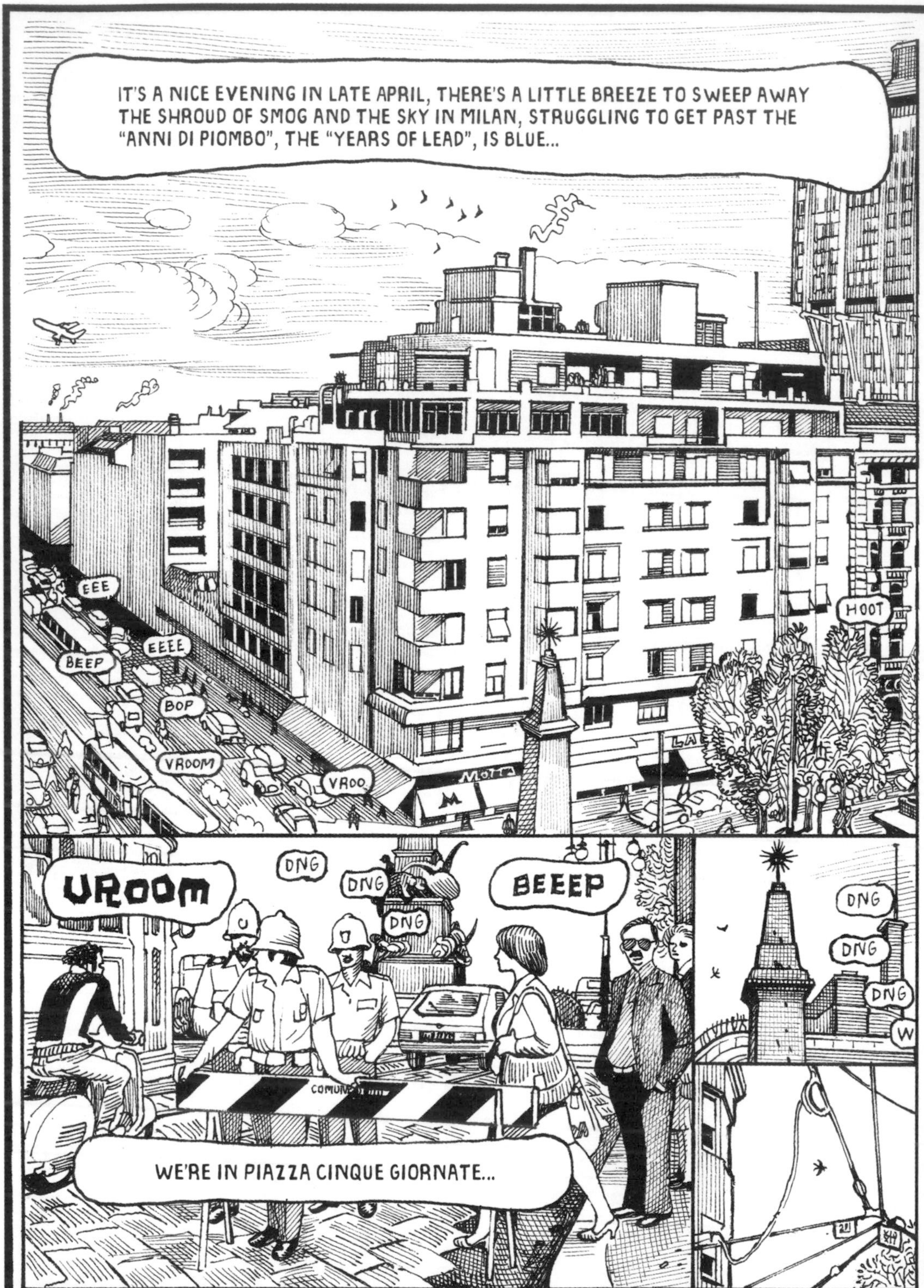
IT'S A NICE EVENING IN LATE APRIL, THERE'S A LITTLE BREEZE TO SWEEP AWAY THE SHROUD OF SMOG AND THE SKY IN MILAN, STRUGGLING TO GET PAST THE "ANNI DI PIOMBO", THE "YEARS OF LEAD", IS BLUE...
EEE
EEEE
BEEP
BOP
VROOM
VROO
HOOT
UROOM
DNG
DNG
DNG
BEEEP
DNG
DNG
DNG
W
WE'RE IN PIAZZA CINQUE GIORNATE...

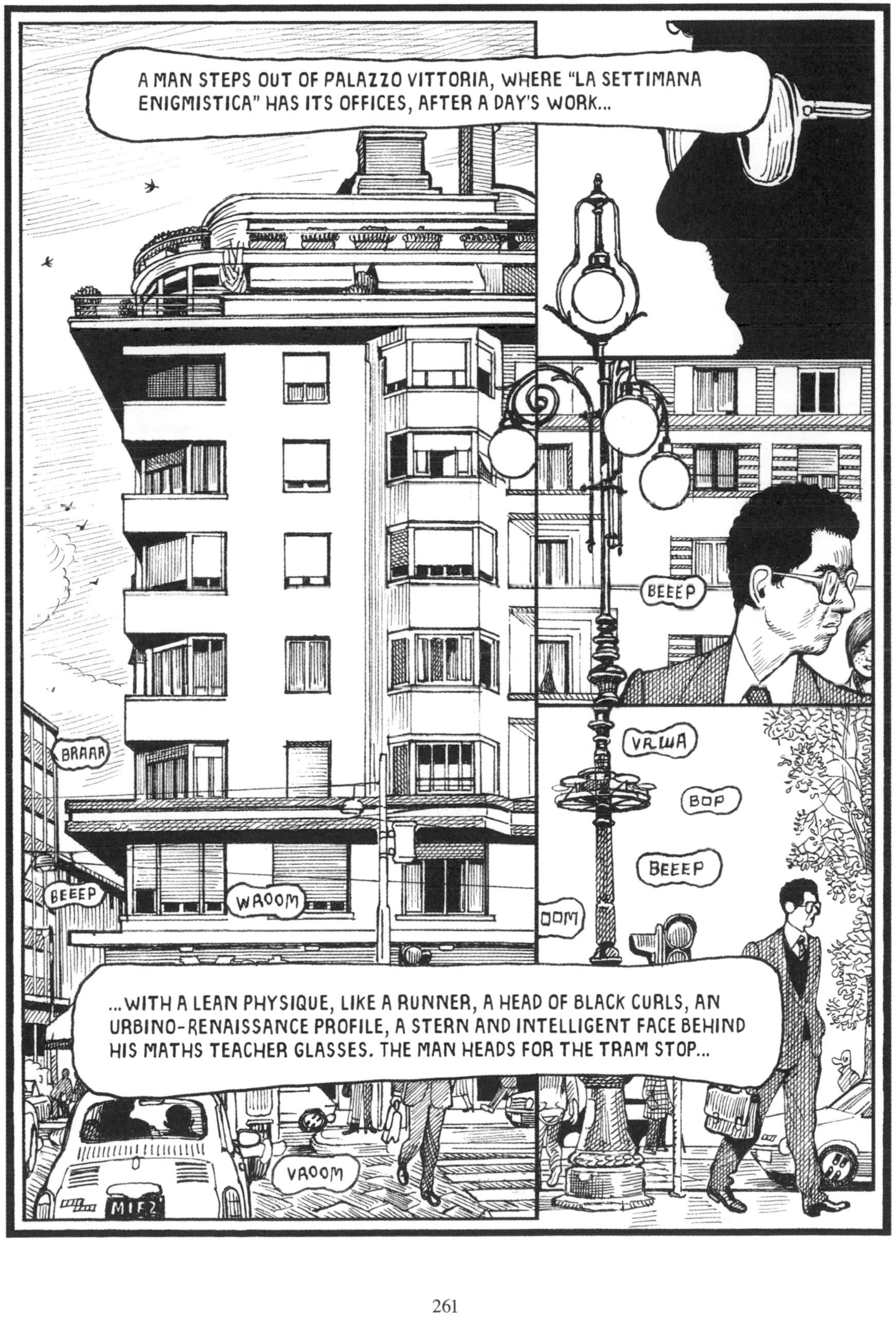
A MAN STEPS OUT OF PALAZZO VITTORIA, WHERE "LA SETTIMANA ENIGMISTICA" HAS ITS OFFICES, AFTER A DAY'S WORK...
BEEEP
BRAAA
BEEEP
WROOM
VRWA
BOP
BEEEP
OOM
...WITH A LEAN PHYSIQUE, LIKE A RUNNER, A HEAD OF BLACK CURLS, AN URBINO-RENAISSANCE PROFILE, A STERN AND INTELLIGENT FACE BEHIND HIS MATHS TEACHER GLASSES. THE MAN HEADS FOR THE TRAM STOP...
VROOM

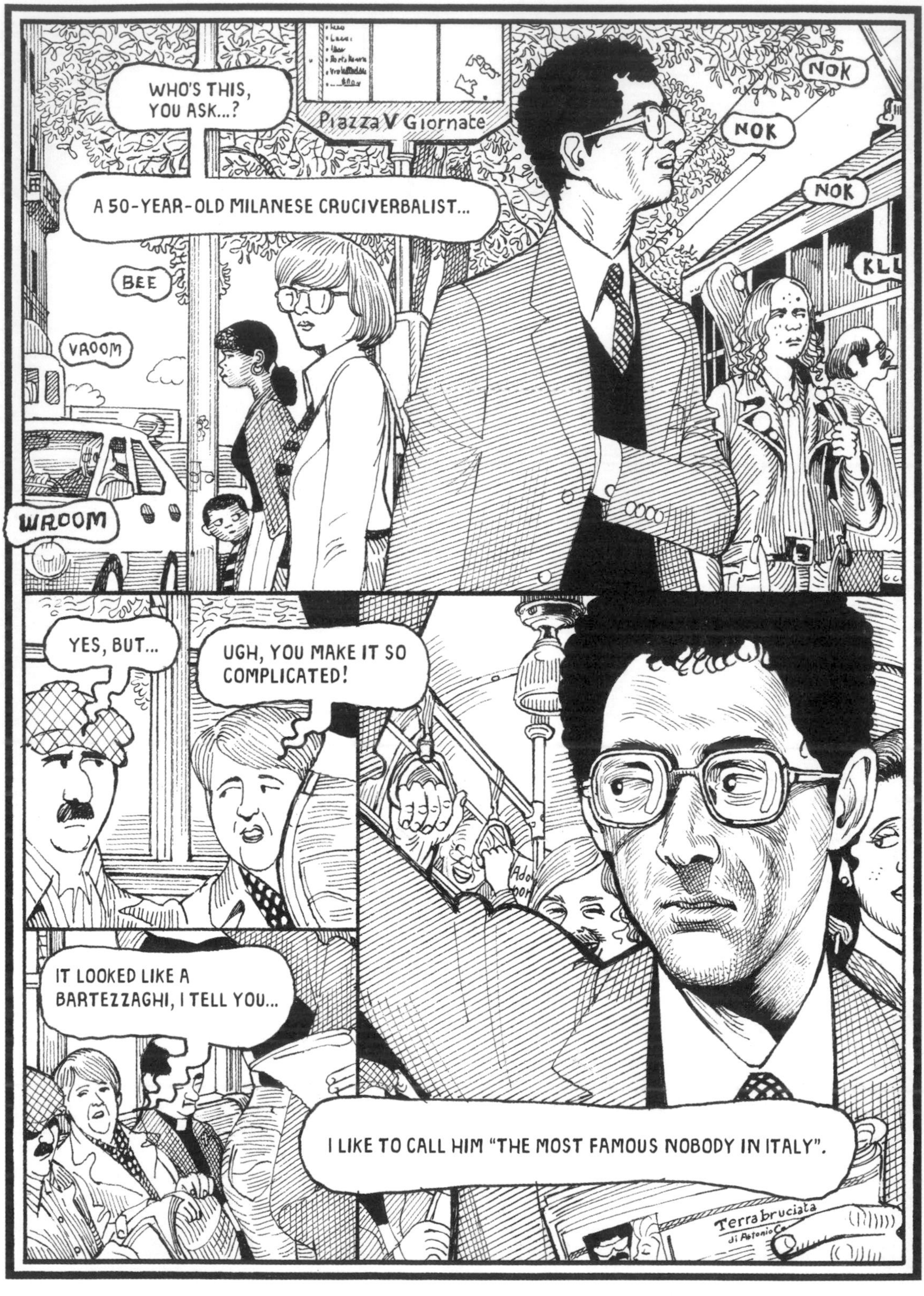
WHO'S THIS, YOU ASK...?
Piazza V Giornate
NOK
NOK
NOK
A 50-YEAR-OLD MILANESE CRUCIVERBALIST...
BEE
VROOM
WROOM
YES, BUT...
UGH, YOU MAKE IT SO COMPLICATED!
IT LOOKED LIKE A BARTEZZAGHI, I TELL YOU...
I LIKE TO CALL HIM "THE MOST FAMOUS NOBODY IN ITALY".
Terra bruciata

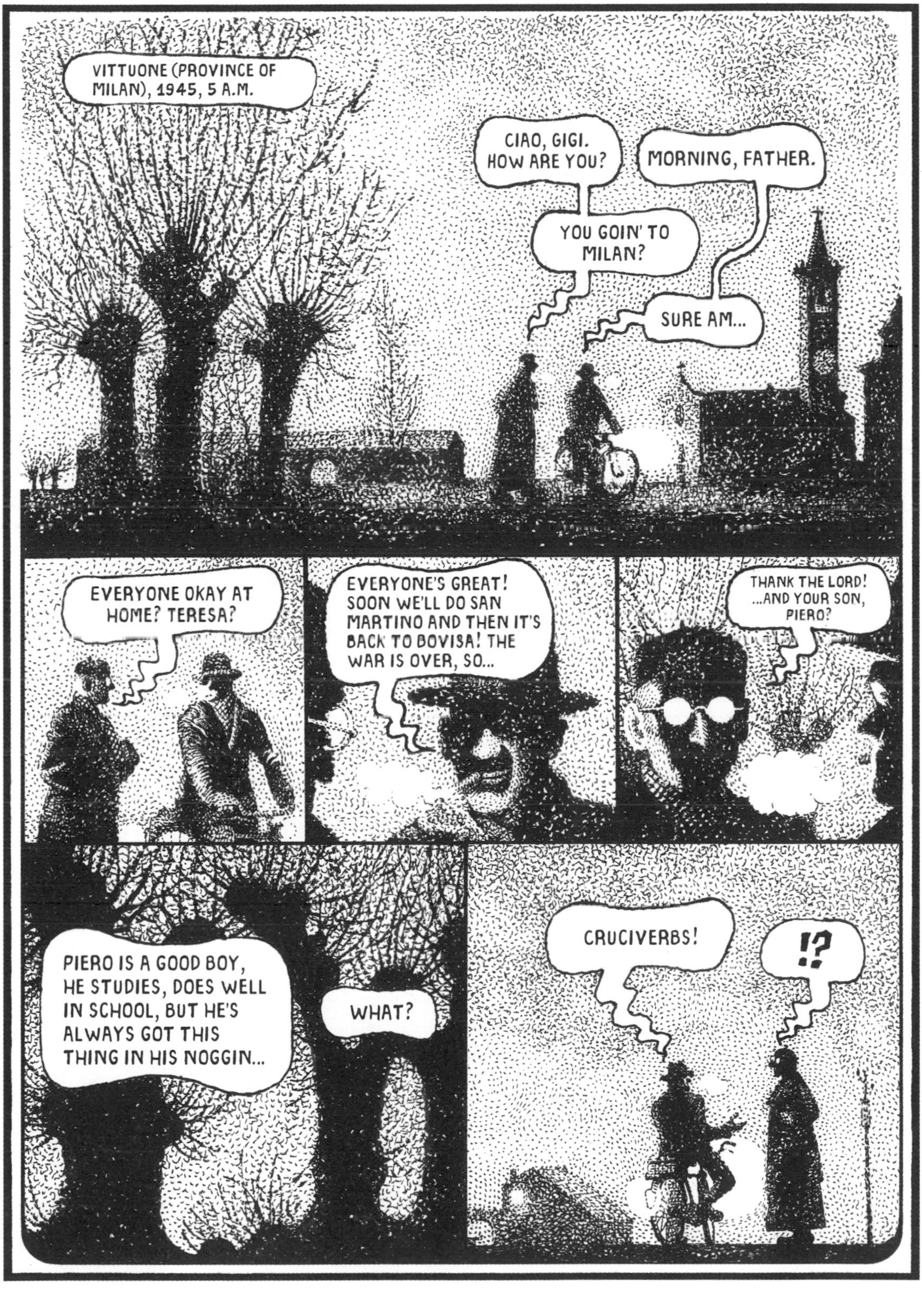

VITTUONE (PROVINCE OF MILAN), 1945, 5 A.M.
CIAO, GIGI. HOW ARE YOU?
MORNING, FATHER.
YOU GOIN' TO MILAN?
SURE AM...
EVERYONE OKAY AT HOME? TERESA?
EVERYONE'S GREAT! SOON WE'LL DO SAN MARTINO AND THEN IT'S BACK TO BOVISA! THE WAR IS OVER, SO...
THANK THE LORD! ...AND YOUR SON, PIERO?
PIERO IS A GOOD BOY, HE STUDIES, DOES WELL IN SCHOOL, BUT HE'S ALWAYS GOT THIS THING IN HIS NOGGIN...
WHAT?
CRUCIVERBS!
!?

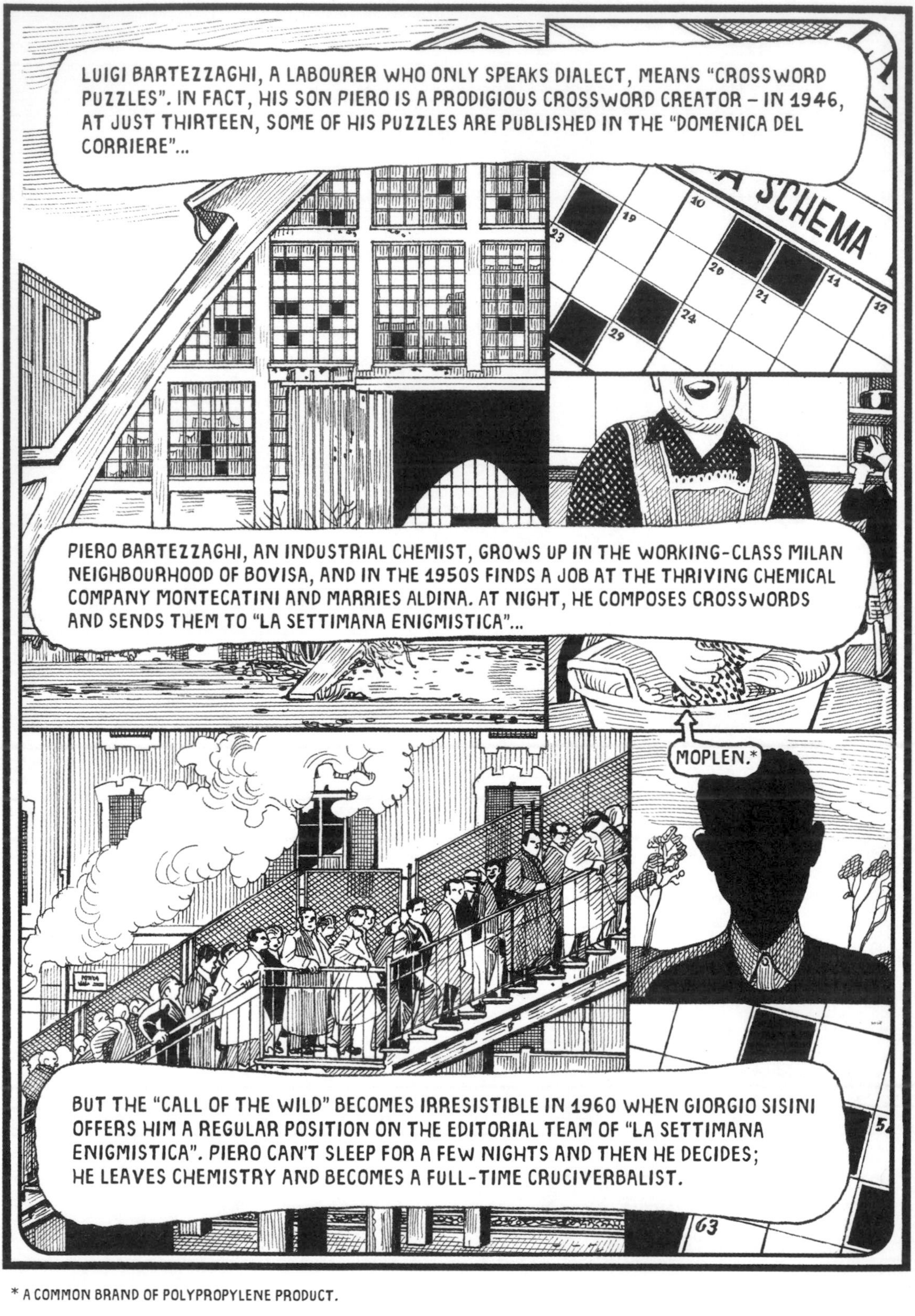
LUIGI BARTEZZAGHI, A LABOURER WHO ONLY SPEAKS DIALECT, MEANS "CROSSWORD PUZZLES". IN FACT, HIS SON PIERO IS A PRODIGIOUS CROSSWORD CREATOR – IN 1946, AT JUST THIRTEEN, SOME OF HIS PUZZLES ARE PUBLISHED IN THE "DOMENICA DEL CORRIERE"...
SCHEMA
PIERO BARTEZZAGHI, AN INDUSTRIAL CHEMIST, GROWS UP IN THE WORKING-CLASS MILAN NEIGHBOURHOOD OF BOVISA, AND IN THE 1950S FINDS A JOB AT THE THRIVING CHEMICAL COMPANY MONTECATINI AND MARRIES ALDINA. AT NIGHT, HE COMPOSES CROSSWORDS AND SENDS THEM TO "LA SETTIMANA ENIGMISTICA"...
MOPLEN.*
BUT THE "CALL OF THE WILD" BECOMES IRRESISTIBLE IN 1960 WHEN GIORGIO SISINI OFFERS HIM A REGULAR POSITION ON THE EDITORIAL TEAM OF "LA SETTIMANA ENIGMISTICA". PIERO CAN'T SLEEP FOR A FEW NIGHTS AND THEN HE DECIDES; HE LEAVES CHEMISTRY AND BECOMES A FULL-TIME CRUCIVERBALIST.

* A COMMON BRAND OF POLYPROPYLENE PRODUCT.

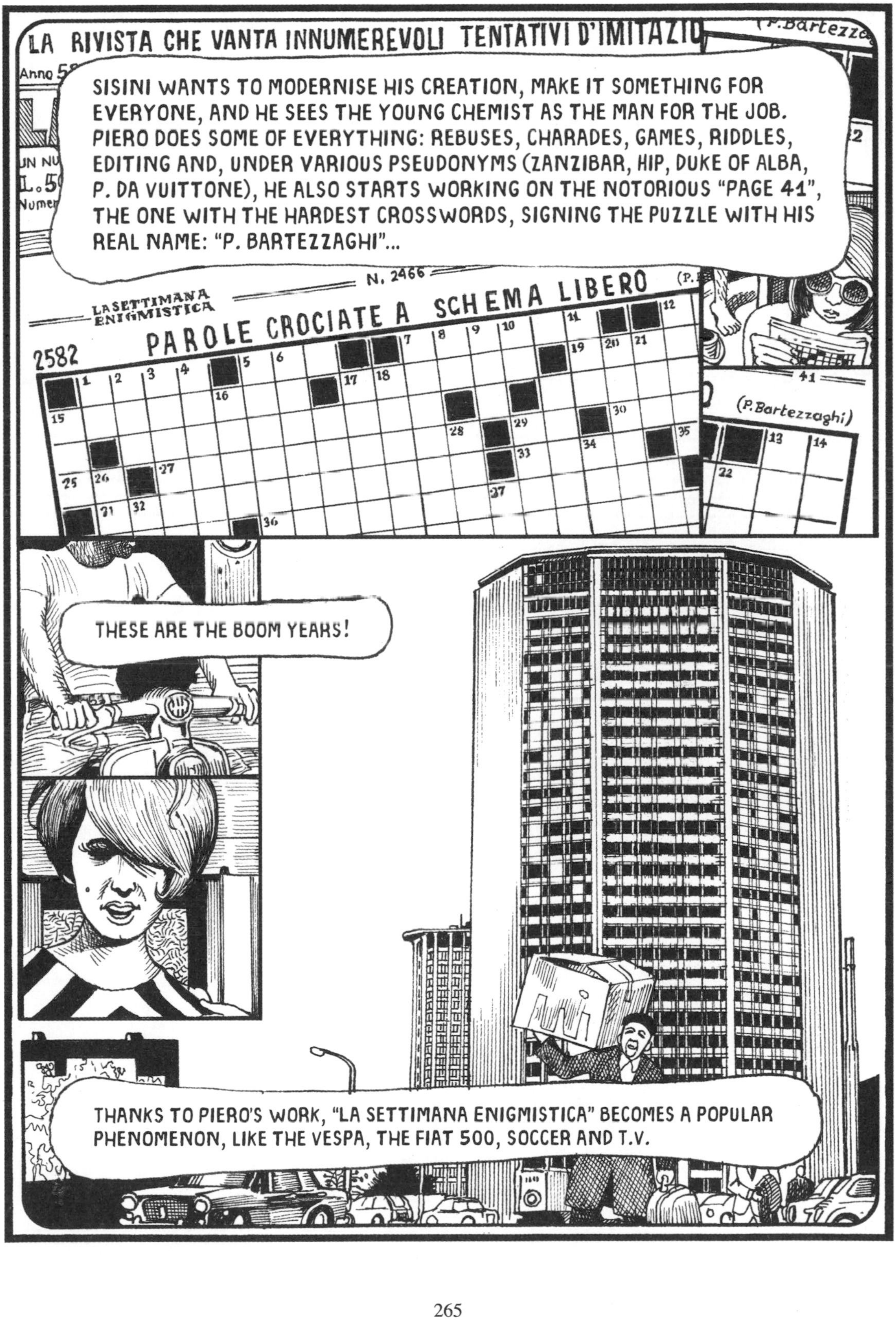
LA RIVISTA CHE VANTA INNUMEREVOLI TENTATIVI D'IMITAZIO
SISINI WANTS TO MODERNISE HIS CREATION, MAKE IT SOMETHING FOR EVERYONE, AND HE SEES THE YOUNG CHEMIST AS THE MAN FOR THE JOB. PIERO DOES SOME OF EVERYTHING: REBUSES, CHARADES, GAMES, RIDDLES, EDITING AND, UNDER VARIOUS PSEUDONYMS (ZANZIBAR, HIP, DUKE OF ALBA, P. DA VUITTONE), HE ALSO STARTS WORKING ON THE NOTORIOUS "PAGE 41", THE ONE WITH THE HARDEST CROSSWORDS, SIGNING THE PUZZLE WITH HIS REAL NAME: "P. BARTEZZAGHI"...
LA SETTIMANA ENIGMISTICA
N. 2466
2582
PAROLE CROCIATE A SCHEMA LIBERO
(P.Bartezzaghi)
THESE ARE THE BOOM YEARS!
THANKS TO PIERO'S WORK, "LA SETTIMANA ENIGMISTICA" BECOMES A POPULAR PHENOMENON, LIKE THE VESPA, THE FIAT 500, SOCCER AND T.V.

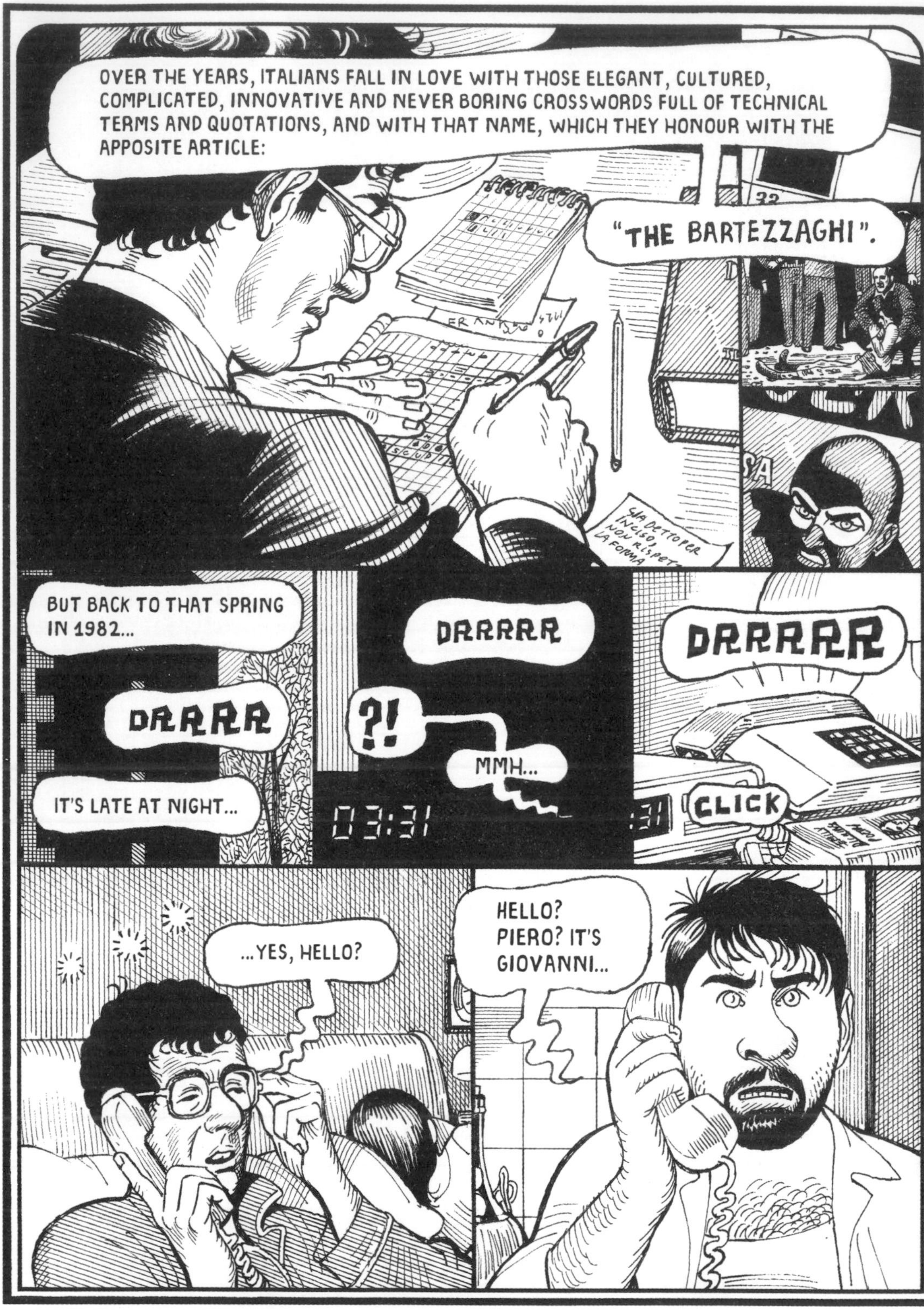

OVER THE YEARS, ITALIANS FALL IN LOVE WITH THOSE ELEGANT, CULTURED, COMPLICATED, INNOVATIVE AND NEVER BORING CROSSWORDS FULL OF TECHNICAL TERMS AND QUOTATIONS, AND WITH THAT NAME, WHICH THEY HONOUR WITH THE APPOSITE ARTICLE:
"THE BARTEZZAGHI".
BUT BACK TO THAT SPRING IN 1982...
DRRRR
IT'S LATE AT NIGHT...
DRRRRR
?!
MMH...
03:31
DRRRRR
CLICK
...YES, HELLO?
HELLO? PIERO? IT'S GIOVANNI...

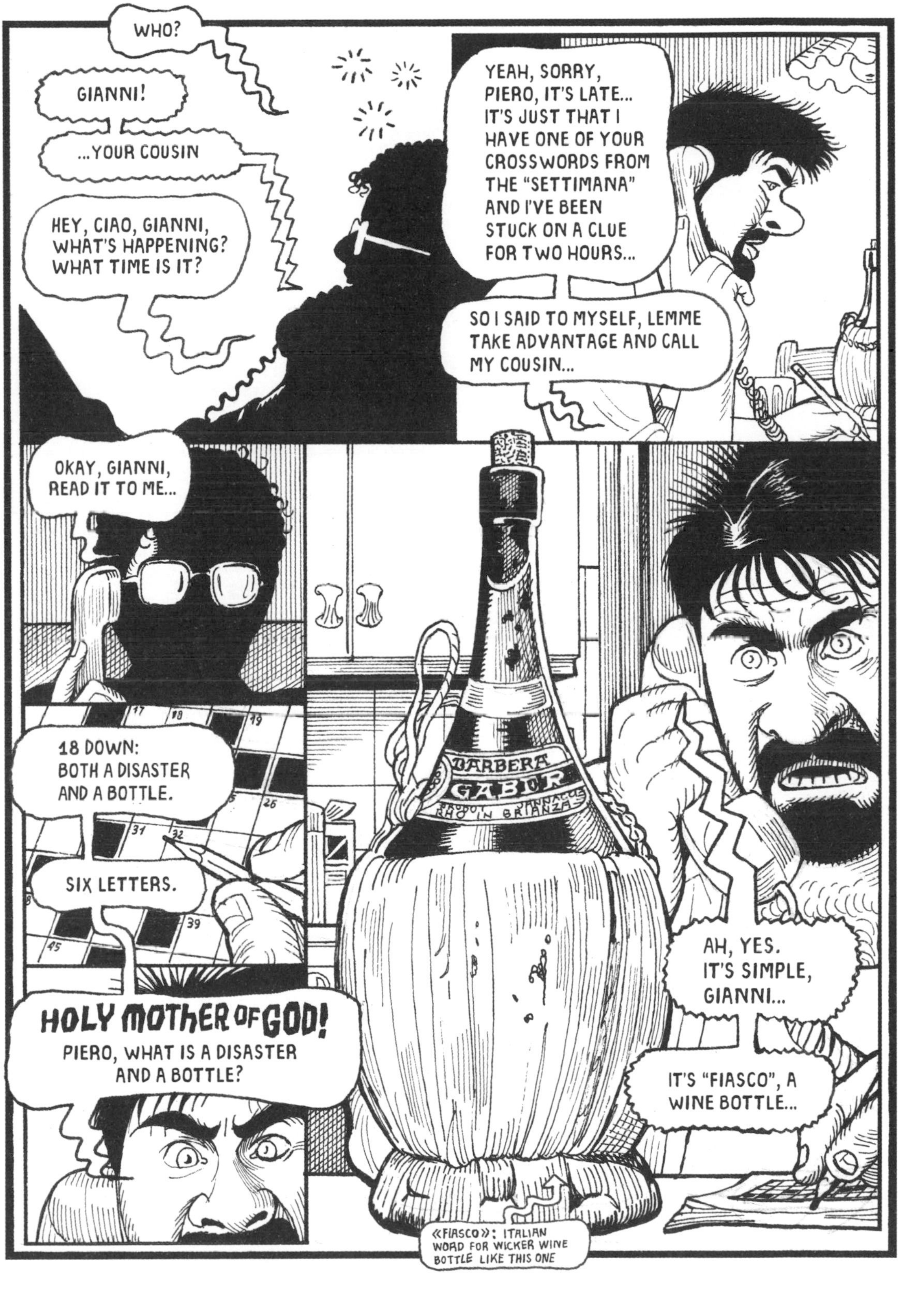
WHO?
GIANNI!
...YOUR COUSIN
HEY, CIAO, GIANNI, WHAT'S HAPPENING? WHAT TIME IS IT?
YEAH, SORRY, PIERO, IT'S LATE... IT'S JUST THAT I HAVE ONE OF YOUR CROSSWORDS FROM THE "SETTIMANA" AND I'VE BEEN STUCK ON A CLUE FOR TWO HOURS...
SO I SAID TO MYSELF, LEMME TAKE ADVANTAGE AND CALL MY COUSIN...
OKAY, GIANNI, READ IT TO ME...
18 DOWN: BOTH A DISASTER AND A BOTTLE.
SIX LETTERS.
HOLY MOTHER OF GOD!
PIERO, WHAT IS A DISASTER AND A BOTTLE?
BARBERA
GABER
AH, YES. IT'S SIMPLE, GIANNI...
IT'S "FIASCO", A WINE BOTTLE...
«FIASCO»: ITALIAN WORD FOR WICKER WINE BOTTLE LIKE THIS ONE

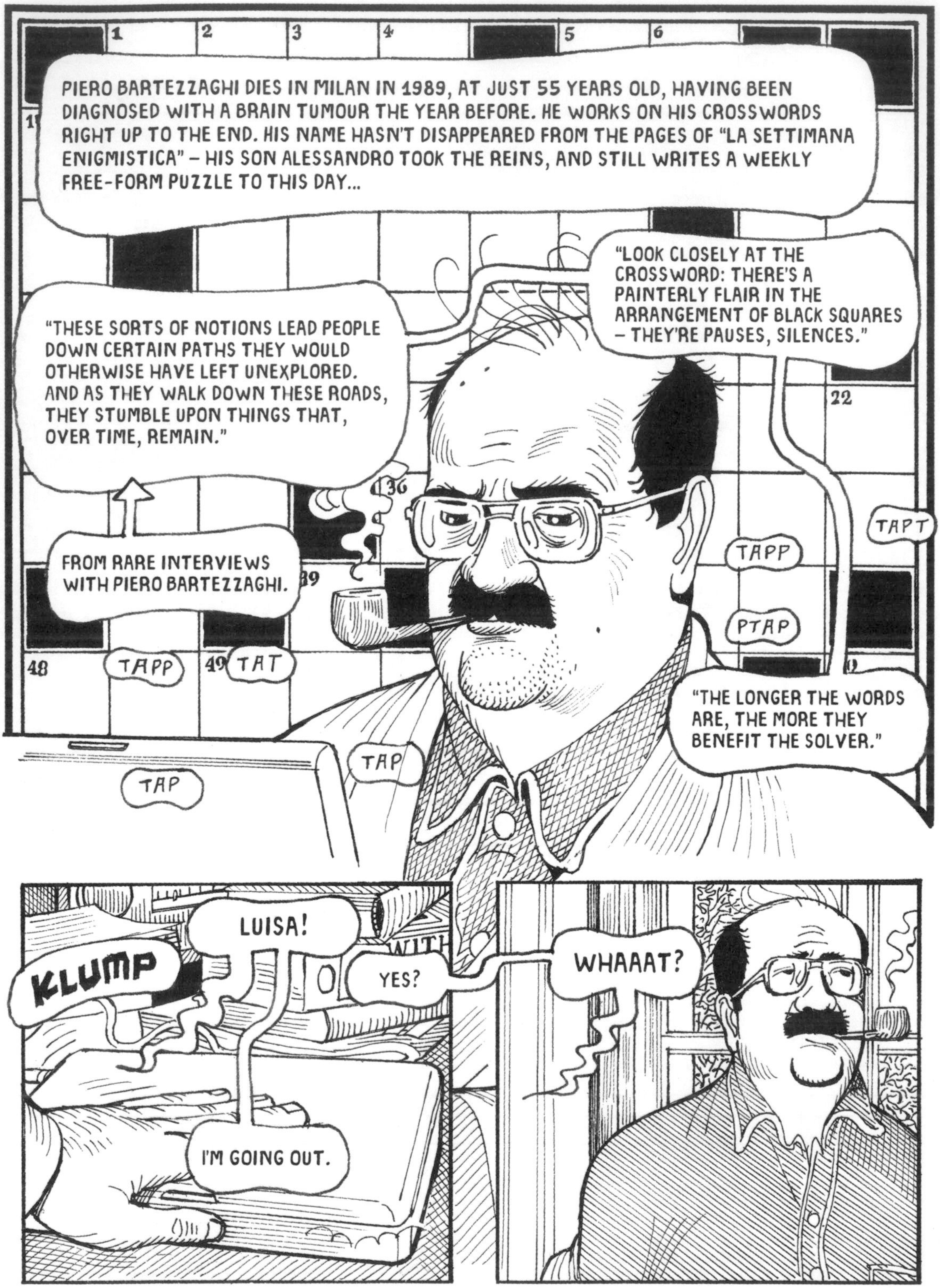
PIERO BARTEZZAGHI DIES IN MILAN IN 1989, AT JUST 55 YEARS OLD, HAVING BEEN DIAGNOSED WITH A BRAIN TUMOUR THE YEAR BEFORE. HE WORKS ON HIS CROSSWORDS RIGHT UP TO THE END. HIS NAME HASN'T DISAPPEARED FROM THE PAGES OF "LA SETTIMANA ENIGMISTICA" – HIS SON ALESSANDRO TOOK THE REINS, AND STILL WRITES A WEEKLY FREE-FORM PUZZLE TO THIS DAY...
"THESE SORTS OF NOTIONS LEAD PEOPLE DOWN CERTAIN PATHS THEY WOULD OTHERWISE HAVE LEFT UNEXPLORED. AND AS THEY WALK DOWN THESE ROADS, THEY STUMBLE UPON THINGS THAT, OVER TIME, REMAIN."
"LOOK CLOSELY AT THE CROSSWORD: THERE'S A PAINTERLY FLAIR IN THE ARRANGEMENT OF BLACK SQUARES – THEY'RE PAUSES, SILENCES."
FROM RARE INTERVIEWS WITH PIERO BARTEZZAGHI.
TAPT
TAPP
PTAP
TAPP
TAT
"THE LONGER THE WORDS ARE, THE MORE THEY BENEFIT THE SOLVER."
TAP
TAP
KLUMP
LUISA!
YES?
WHAAAT?
I'M GOING OUT.

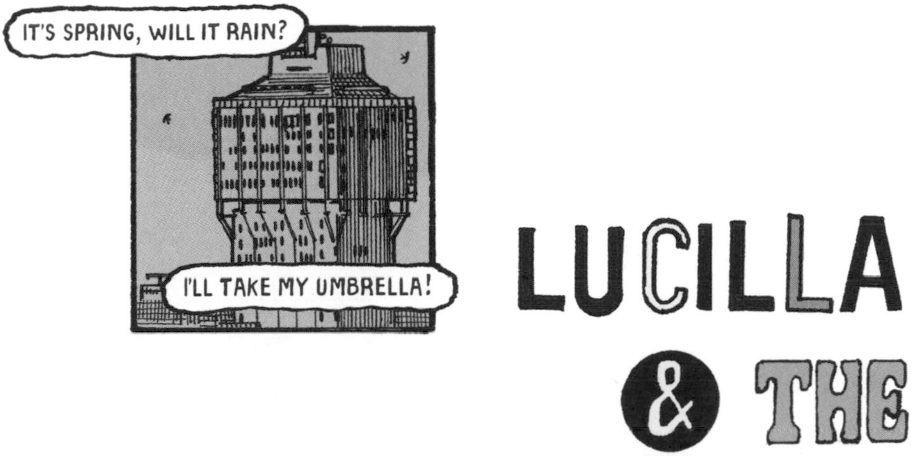
IT'S SPRING, WILL IT RAIN?
I'LL TAKE MY UMBRELLA!

LUCILLA & THE RAINBOW

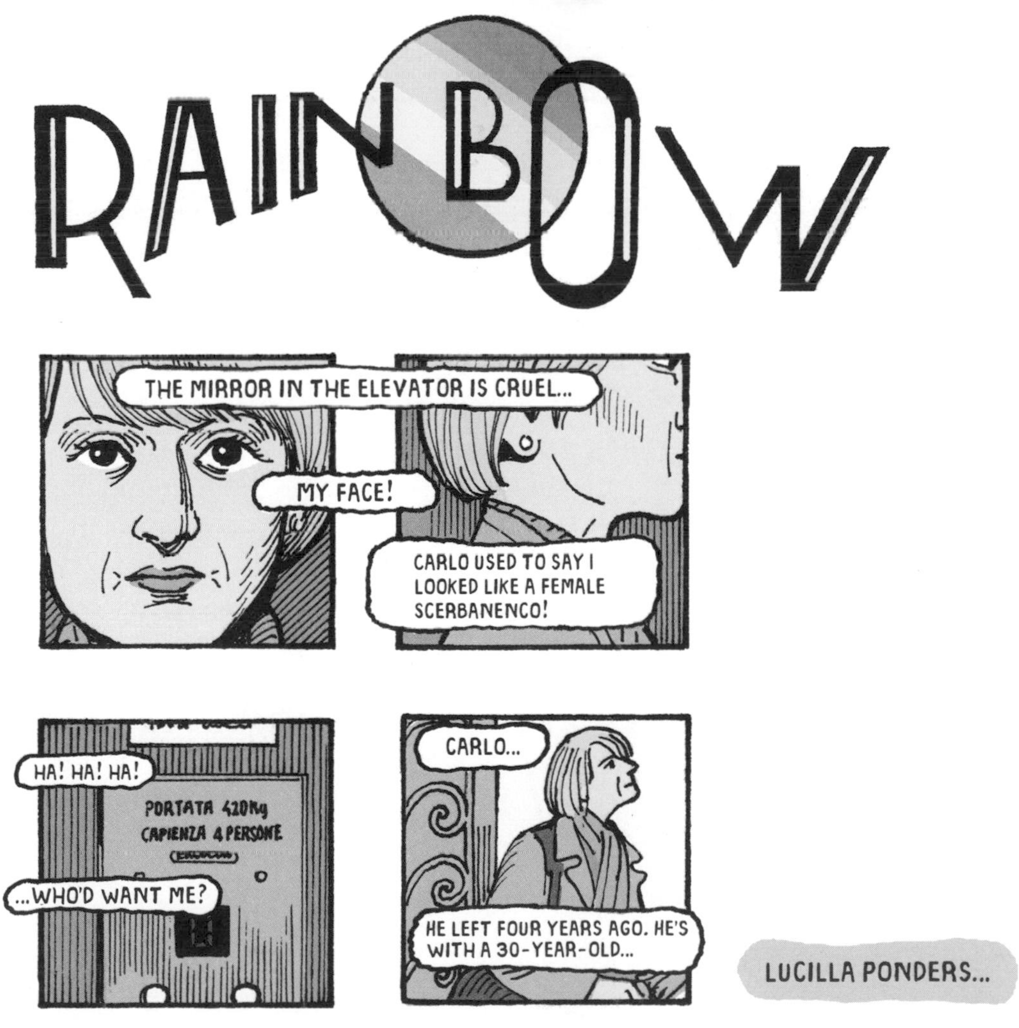
THE MIRROR IN THE ELEVATOR IS CRUEL...
MY FACE!
CARLO USED TO SAY I LOOKED LIKE A FEMALE SCERBANENCO!
HA! HA! HA!
PORTATA 420Kg
CAPIENZA 4 PERSONE
...WHO'D WANT ME?
CARLO...
HE LEFT FOUR YEARS AGO. HE'S WITH A 30-YEAR-OLD...
LUCILLA PONDERS...

FRIDAY, 29 MAY 2011.

LUCILLA LAMBERTI.

EDITOR AND READER AT AUDACE EDIZIONI, CHILDREN'S BOOK DIVISION.

BIRTHPLACE: MILAN.

DATE OF BIRTH: 15 DECEMBER 1959.

SEPARATED.

STUDIED MODERN LITERATURE AT THE UNIVERSITY OF MILAN.

TODAY, SHE GOT UP EARLIER THAN USUAL...

BEFORE WORK, SHE STOPS BY HER MOTHER'S IN GARIBALDI...

SHE IS 91. PILAR, HER CARE-WORKER, IS WITH HER. PILAR IS ALWAYS ON THE PHONE.

WWW...

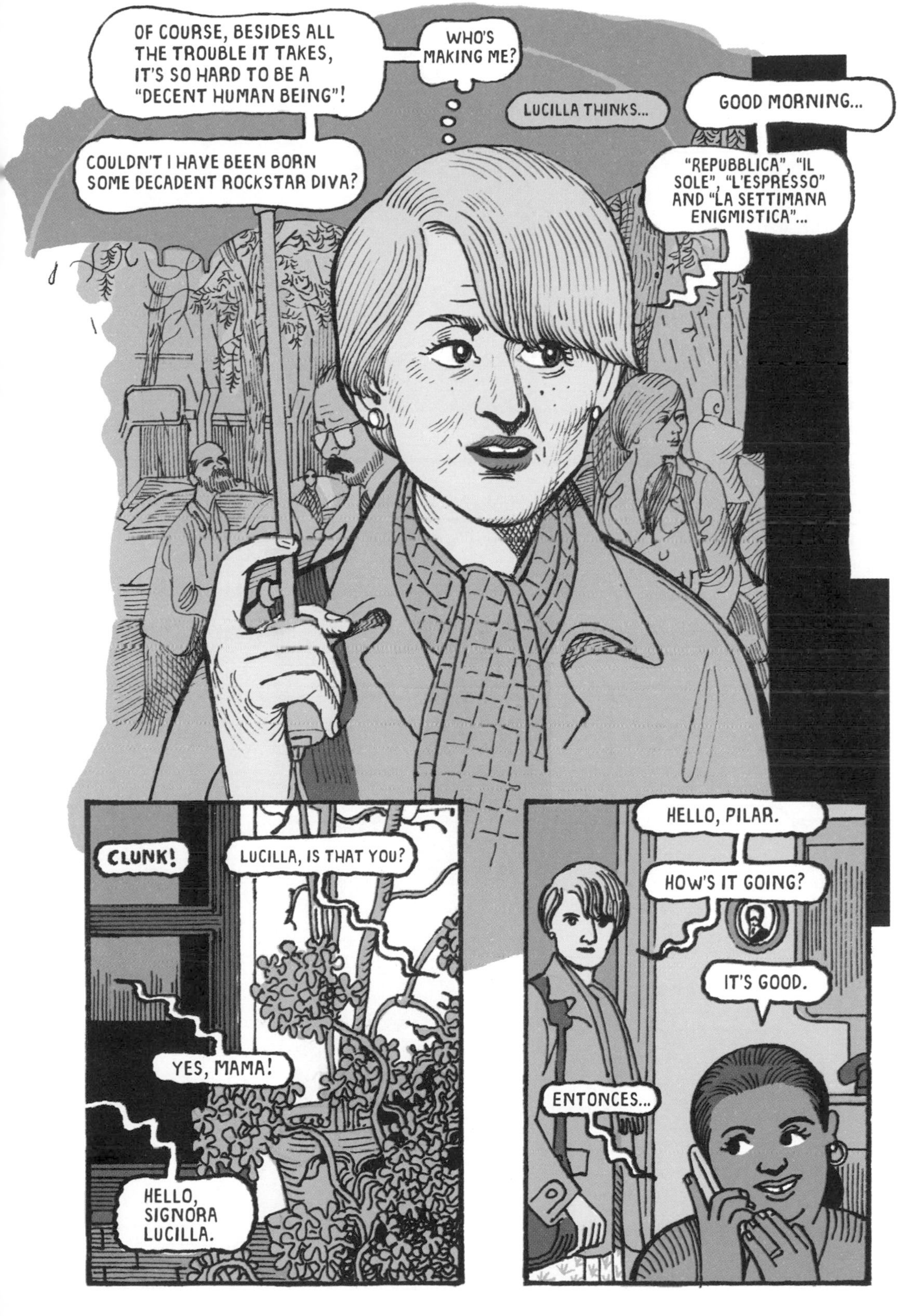
OF COURSE, BESIDES ALL THE TROUBLE IT TAKES, IT'S SO HARD TO BE A "DECENT HUMAN BEING"!
COULDN'T I HAVE BEEN BORN SOME DECADENT ROCKSTAR DIVA?
WHO'S MAKING ME?
LUCILLA THINKS...
GOOD MORNING...
"REPUBBLICA", "IL SOLE", "L'ESPRESSO" AND "LA SETTIMANA ENIGMISTICA"...
CLUNK!
LUCILLA, IS THAT YOU?
YES, MAMA!
HELLO, SIGNORA LUCILLA.
HELLO, PILAR.
HOW'S IT GOING?
IT'S GOOD.
ENTONCES...

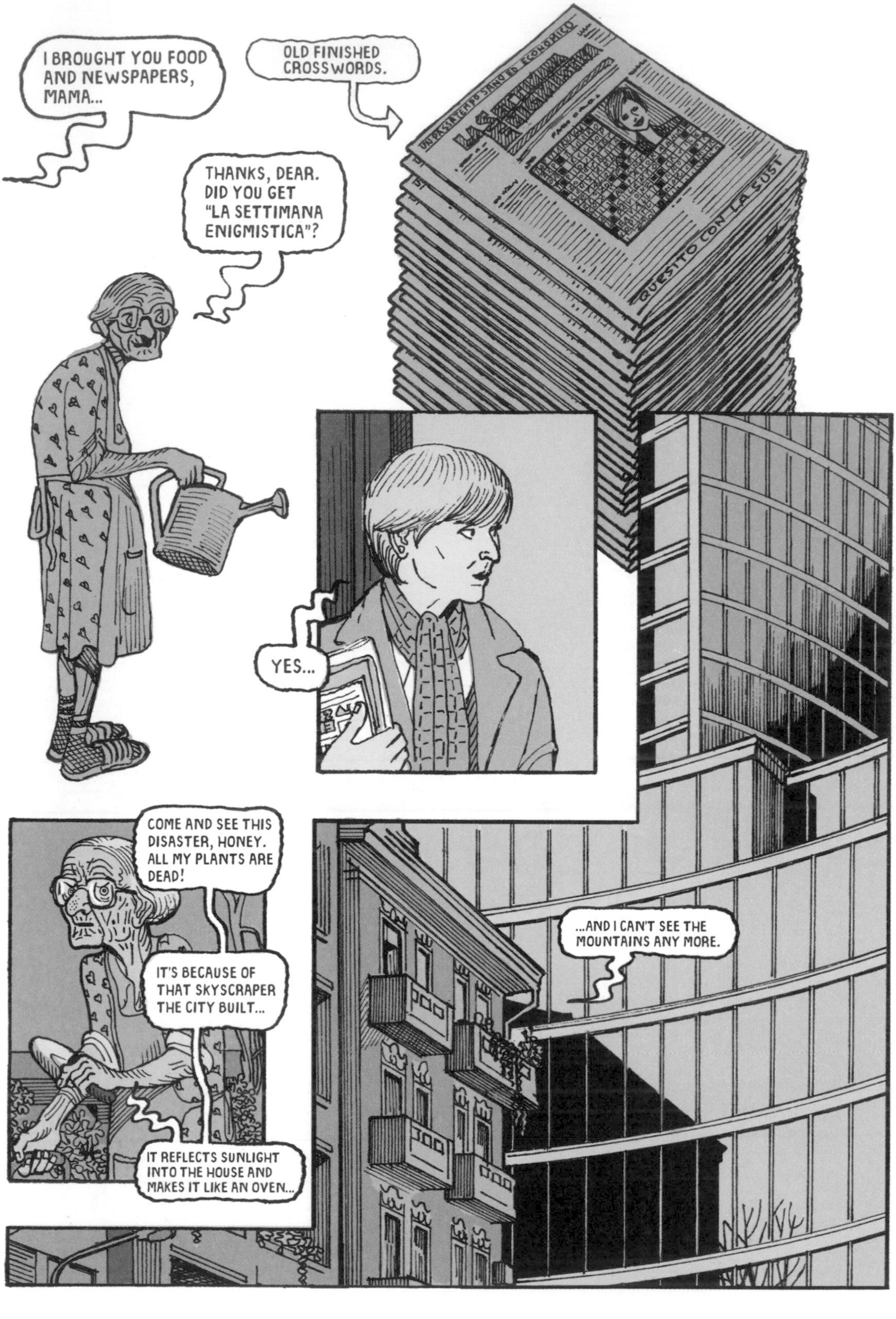
I BROUGHT YOU FOOD AND NEWSPAPERS, MAMA...
OLD FINISHED CROSSWORDS.
THANKS, DEAR. DID YOU GET "LA SETTIMANA ENIGMISTICA"?
QUESTO CON LA SUSI
YES...
COME AND SEE THIS DISASTER, HONEY. ALL MY PLANTS ARE DEAD!
IT'S BECAUSE OF THAT SKYSCRAPER THE CITY BUILT...
IT REFLECTS SUNLIGHT INTO THE HOUSE AND MAKES IT LIKE AN OVEN...
...AND I CAN'T SEE THE MOUNTAINS ANY MORE.

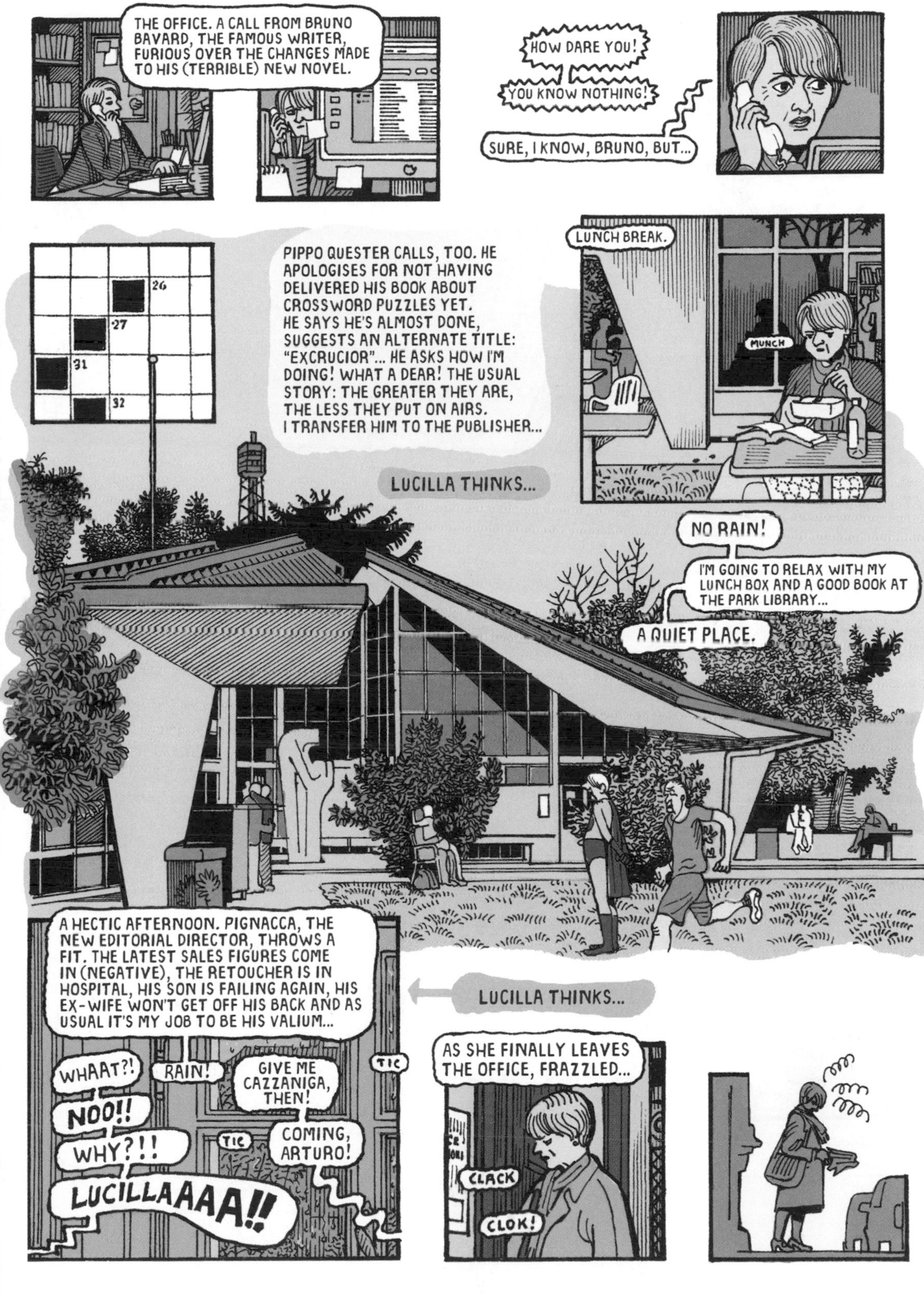

THE OFFICE. A CALL FROM BRUNO BAVARD, THE FAMOUS WRITER, FURIOUS OVER THE CHANGES MADE TO HIS (TERRIBLE) NEW NOVEL.
HOW DARE YOU!
YOU KNOW NOTHING!
SURE, I KNOW, BRUNO, BUT...
26
27
31
32
PIPPO QUESTER CALLS, TOO. HE APOLOGISES FOR NOT HAVING DELIVERED HIS BOOK ABOUT CROSSWORD PUZZLES YET. HE SAYS HE'S ALMOST DONE, SUGGESTS AN ALTERNATE TITLE: "EXCRUCIOR"... HE ASKS HOW I'M DOING! WHAT A DEAR! THE USUAL STORY: THE GREATER THEY ARE, THE LESS THEY PUT ON AIRS. I TRANSFER HIM TO THE PUBLISHER...
LUNCH BREAK.
MUNCH
LUCILLA THINKS...
NO RAIN!
I'M GOING TO RELAX WITH MY LUNCH BOX AND A GOOD BOOK AT THE PARK LIBRARY...
A QUIET PLACE.
A HECTIC AFTERNOON. PIGNACCA, THE NEW EDITORIAL DIRECTOR, THROWS A FIT. THE LATEST SALES FIGURES COME IN (NEGATIVE), THE RETOUCHER IS IN HOSPITAL, HIS SON IS FAILING AGAIN, HIS EX-WIFE WON'T GET OFF HIS BACK AND AS USUAL IT'S MY JOB TO BE HIS VALIUM...
LUCILLA THINKS...
WHAAT?!
RAIN!
GIVE ME CAZZANIGA, THEN!
TIC
NOO!!
WHY?!!
TIC
COMING, ARTURO!
LUCILLAAAA!!
AS SHE FINALLY LEAVES THE OFFICE, FRAZZLED...
CLACK
CLOK!

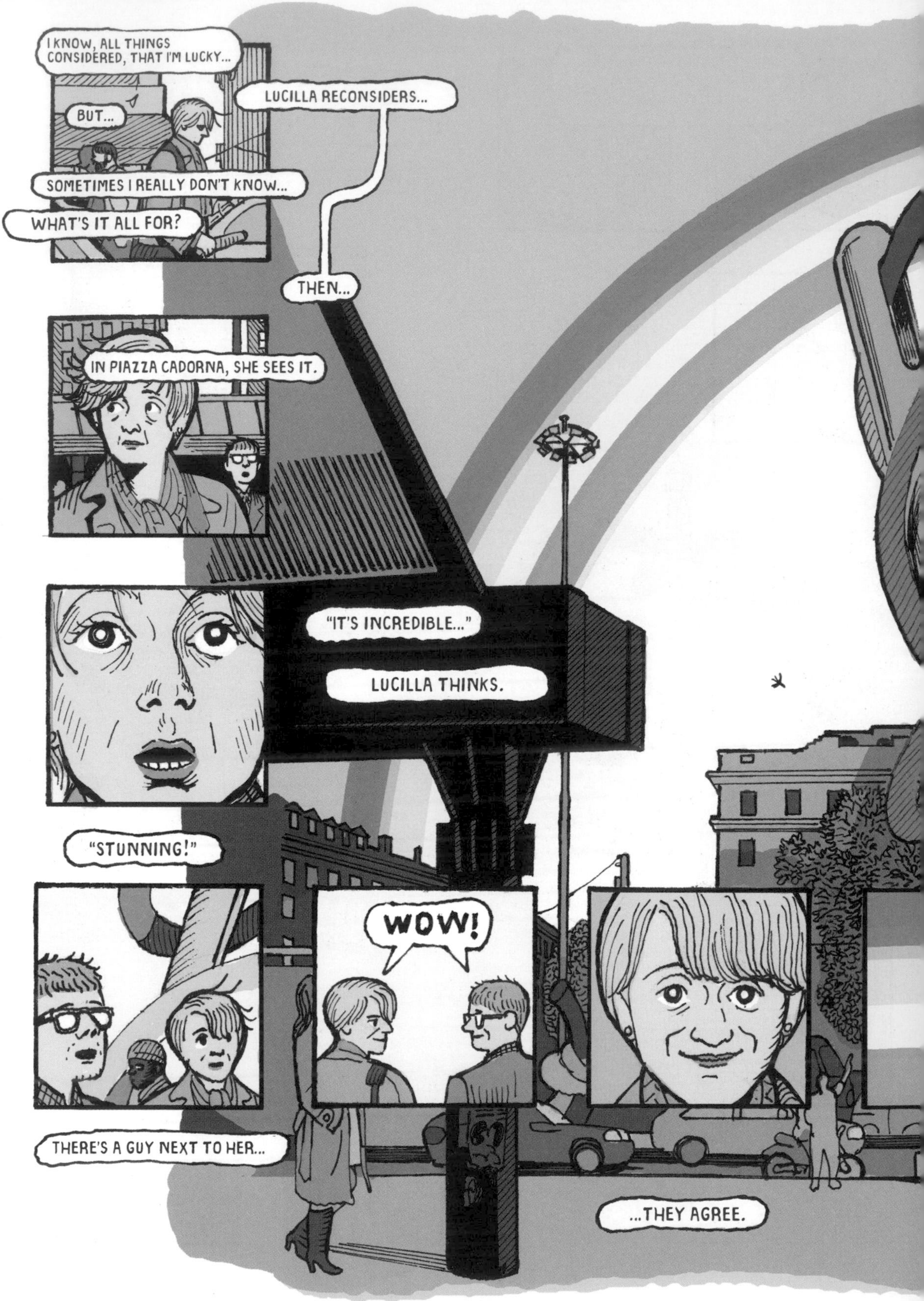

I KNOW, ALL THINGS CONSIDERED, THAT I'M LUCKY...
BUT...
SOMETIMES I REALLY DON'T KNOW...
WHAT'S IT ALL FOR?
LUCILLA RECONSIDERS...
THEN...
IN PIAZZA CADORNA, SHE SEES IT.
"IT'S INCREDIBLE..."
LUCILLA THINKS.
"STUNNING!"
THERE'S A GUY NEXT TO HER...
WOW!
...THEY AGREE.

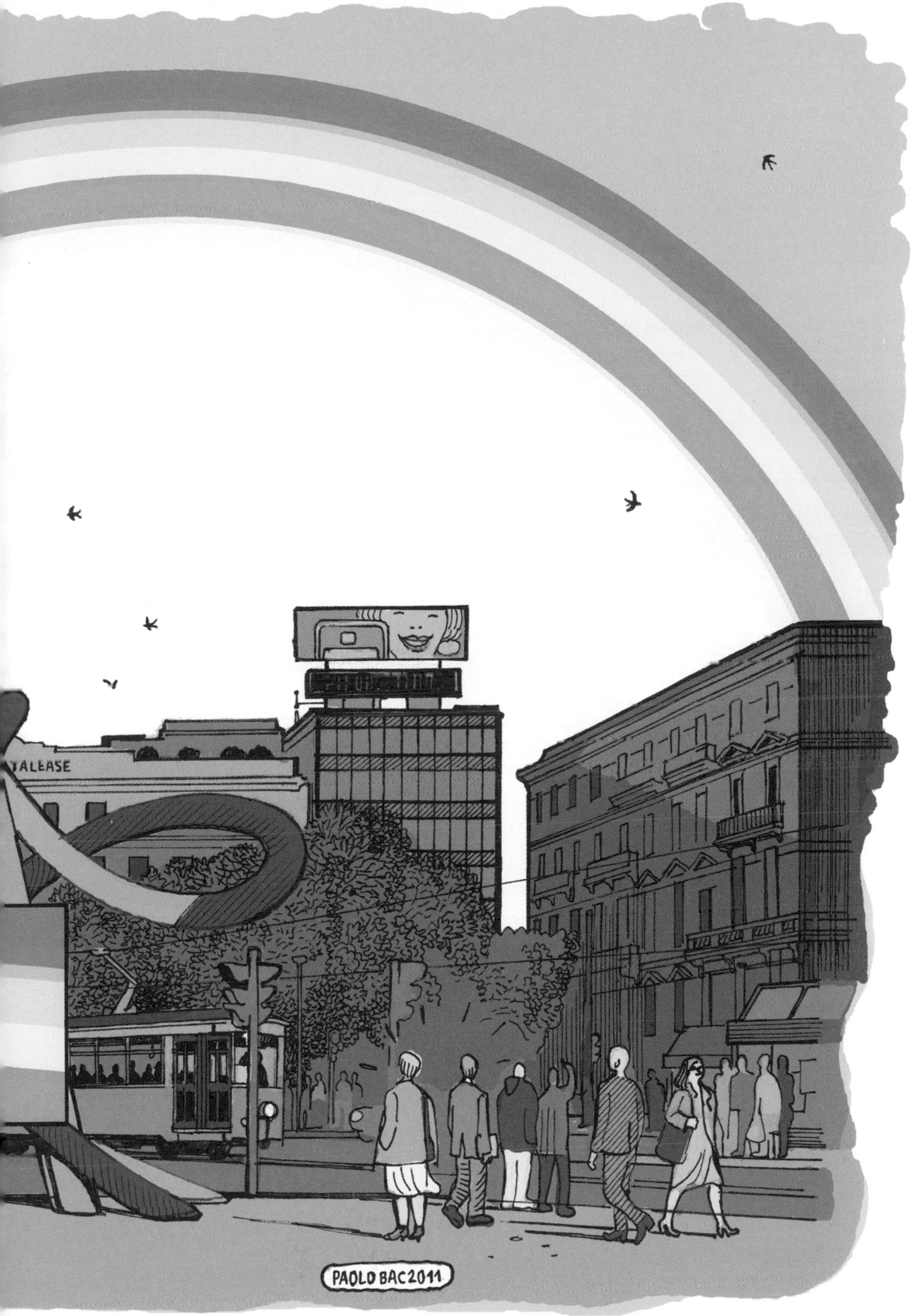
TALEASE
PAOLO BAC 2011

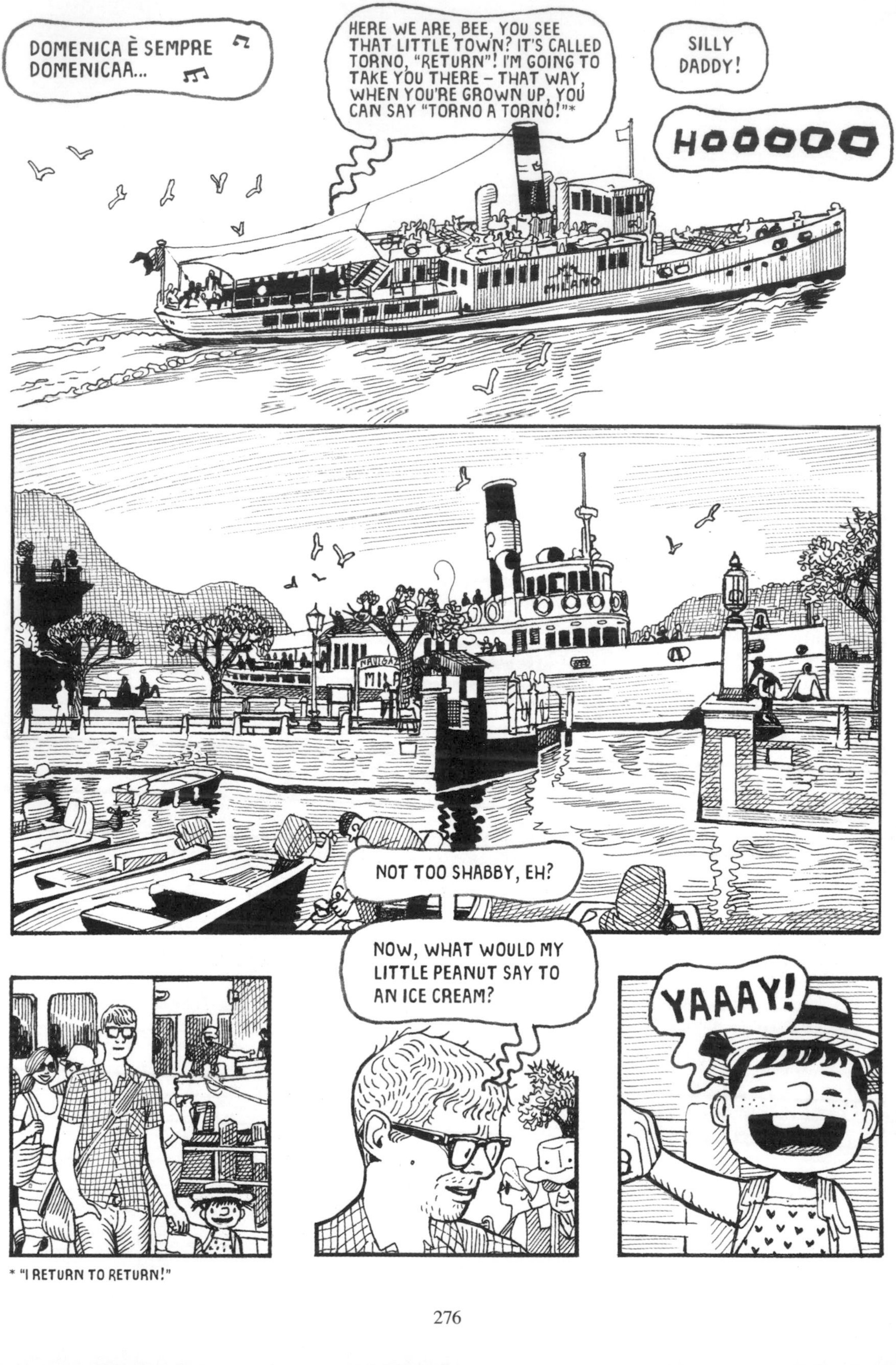
DOMENICA È SEMPRE DOMENICAA...
HERE WE ARE, BEE, YOU SEE THAT LITTLE TOWN? IT'S CALLED TORNO, "RETURN"! I'M GOING TO TAKE YOU THERE – THAT WAY, WHEN YOU'RE GROWN UP, YOU CAN SAY "TORNO A TORNO!"*
SILLY DADDY!
HOOOOO
NOT TOO SHABBY, EH?
NOW, WHAT WOULD MY LITTLE PEANUT SAY TO AN ICE CREAM?
YAAAY!

* "I RETURN TO RETURN!"

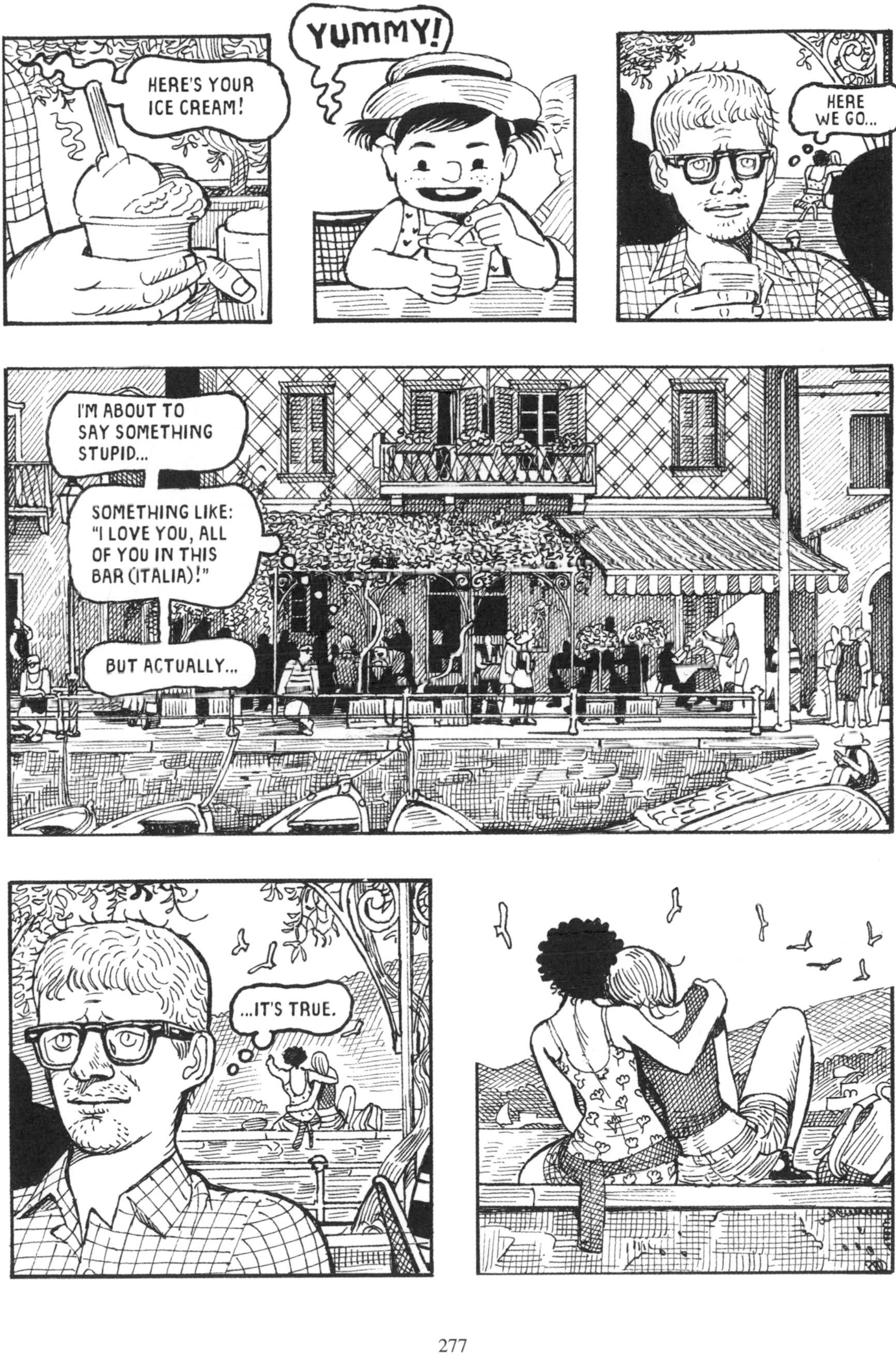
HERE'S YOUR ICE CREAM!
YUMMY!
HERE WE GO...
I'M ABOUT TO SAY SOMETHING STUPID...
SOMETHING LIKE: "I LOVE YOU, ALL OF YOU IN THIS BAR (ITALIA)!"
BUT ACTUALLY...
...IT'S TRUE.

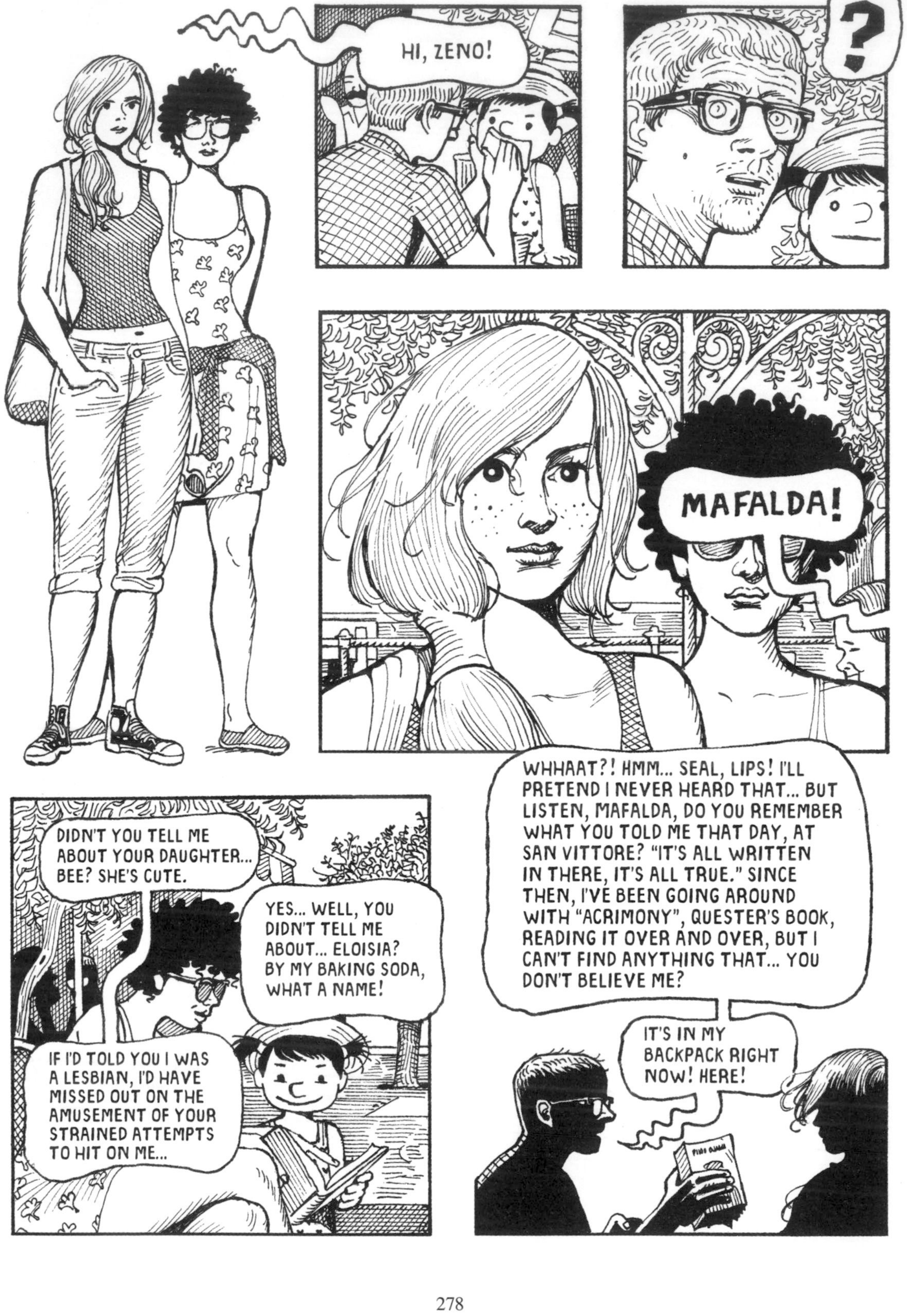
HI, ZENO!
?
MAFALDA!
DIDN'T YOU TELL ME ABOUT YOUR DAUGHTER... BEE? SHE'S CUTE.
YES... WELL, YOU DIDN'T TELL ME ABOUT... ELOISIA? BY MY BAKING SODA, WHAT A NAME!
IF I'D TOLD YOU I WAS A LESBIAN, I'D HAVE MISSED OUT ON THE AMUSEMENT OF YOUR STRAINED ATTEMPTS TO HIT ON ME...
WHHAAT?! HMM... SEAL, LIPS! I'LL PRETEND I NEVER HEARD THAT... BUT LISTEN, MAFALDA, DO YOU REMEMBER WHAT YOU TOLD ME THAT DAY, AT SAN VITTORE? "IT'S ALL WRITTEN IN THERE, IT'S ALL TRUE." SINCE THEN, I'VE BEEN GOING AROUND WITH "ACRIMONY", QUESTER'S BOOK, READING IT OVER AND OVER, BUT I CAN'T FIND ANYTHING THAT... YOU DON'T BELIEVE ME?
IT'S IN MY BACKPACK RIGHT NOW! HERE!

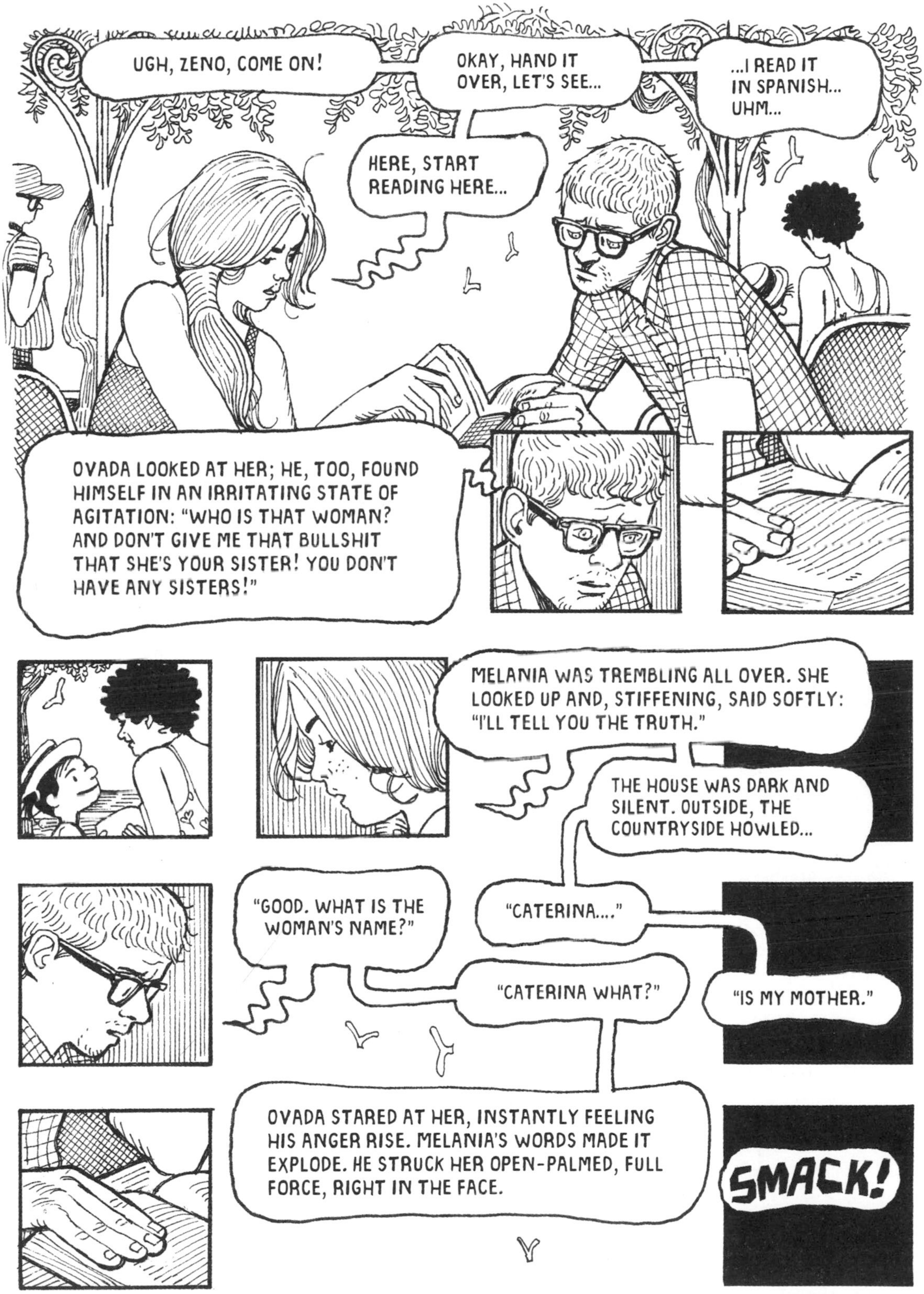
UGH, ZENO, COME ON!
OKAY, HAND IT OVER, LET'S SEE...
...I READ IT IN SPANISH... UHM...
HERE, START READING HERE...
OVADA LOOKED AT HER; HE, TOO, FOUND HIMSELF IN AN IRRITATING STATE OF AGITATION: "WHO IS THAT WOMAN? AND DON'T GIVE ME THAT BULLSHIT THAT SHE'S YOUR SISTER! YOU DON'T HAVE ANY SISTERS!"
MELANIA WAS TREMBLING ALL OVER. SHE LOOKED UP AND, STIFFENING, SAID SOFTLY: "I'LL TELL YOU THE TRUTH."
THE HOUSE WAS DARK AND SILENT. OUTSIDE, THE COUNTRYSIDE HOWLED...
"GOOD. WHAT IS THE WOMAN'S NAME?"
"CATERINA...."
"CATERINA WHAT?"
"IS MY MOTHER."
OVADA STARED AT HER, INSTANTLY FEELING HIS ANGER RISE. MELANIA'S WORDS MADE IT EXPLODE. HE STRUCK HER OPEN-PALMED, FULL FORCE, RIGHT IN THE FACE.
SMACK!

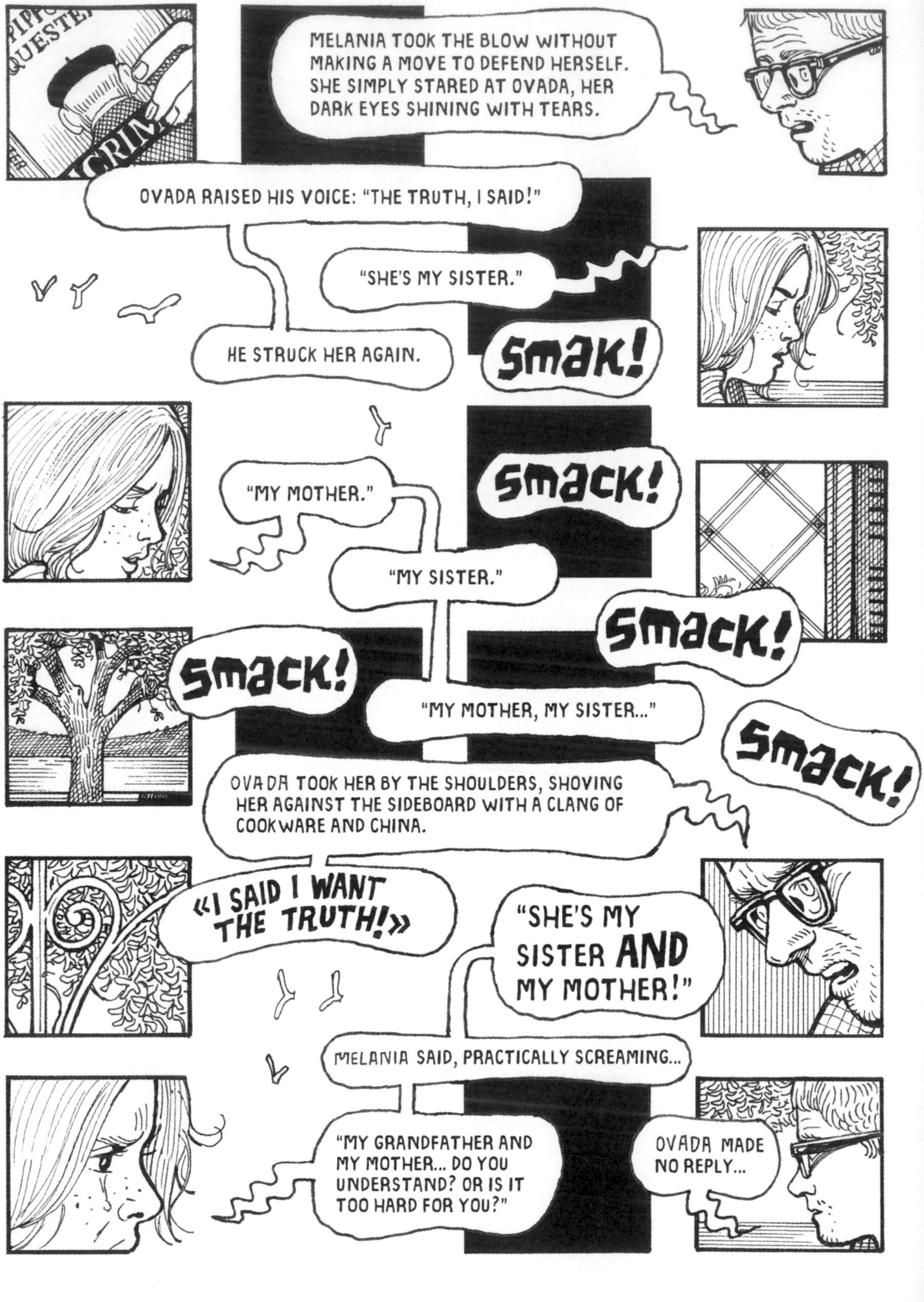
MELANIA TOOK THE BLOW WITHOUT MAKING A MOVE TO DEFEND HERSELF. SHE SIMPLY STARED AT OVADA, HER DARK EYES SHINING WITH TEARS.
OVADA RAISED HIS VOICE: "THE TRUTH, I SAID!"
"SHE'S MY SISTER."
HE STRUCK HER AGAIN.
SMAK!
SMACK!
"MY MOTHER."
"MY SISTER."
SMACK!
SMACK!
"MY MOTHER, MY SISTER..."
SMACK!
OVADA TOOK HER BY THE SHOULDERS, SHOVING HER AGAINST THE SIDEBOARD WITH A CLANG OF COOKWARE AND CHINA.
«I SAID I WANT THE TRUTH!»
"SHE'S MY SISTER AND MY MOTHER!"
MELANIA SAID, PRACTICALLY SCREAMING...
"MY GRANDFATHER AND MY MOTHER... DO YOU UNDERSTAND? OR IS IT TOO HARD FOR YOU?"
OVADA MADE NO REPLY...

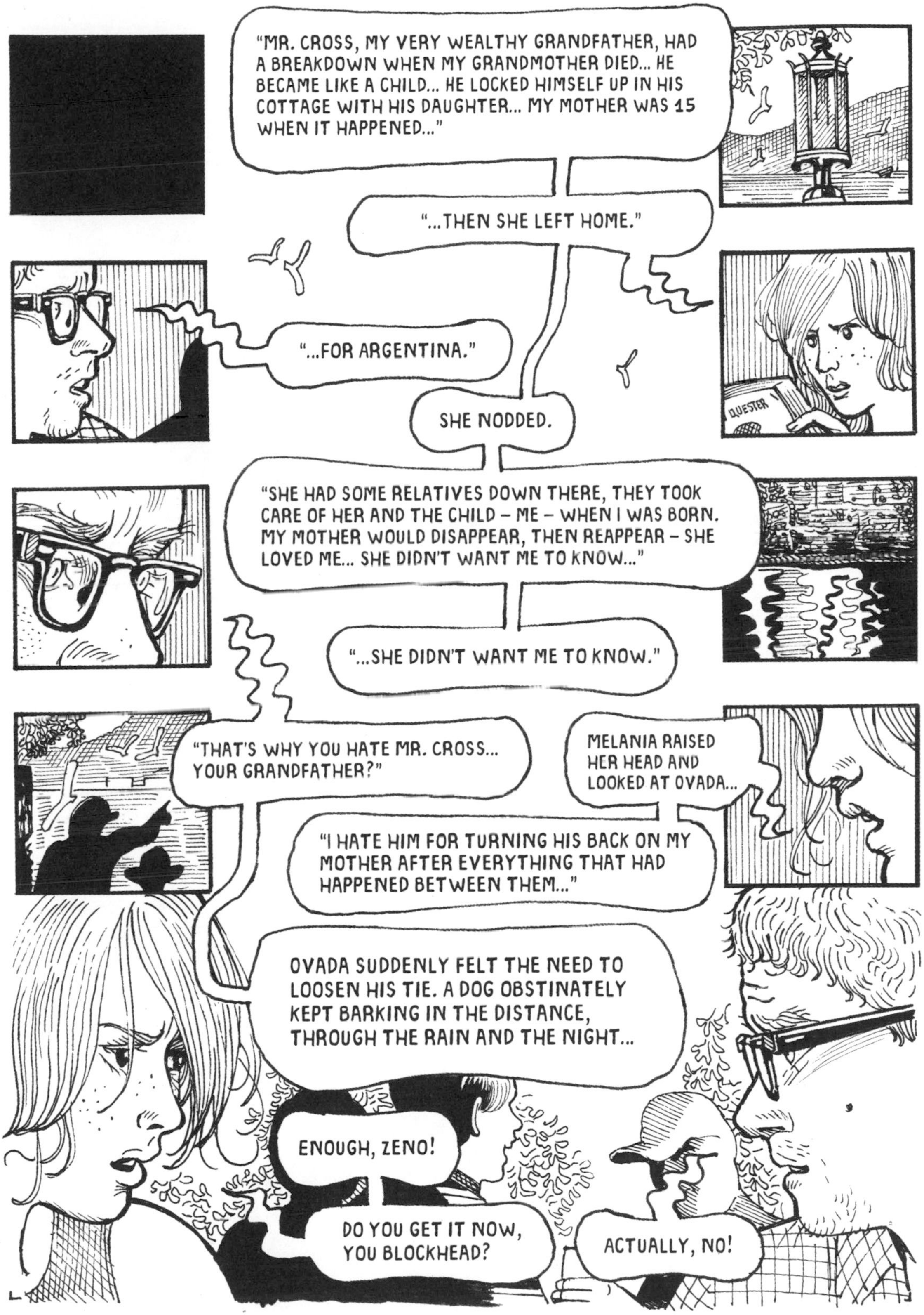
"MR. CROSS, MY VERY WEALTHY GRANDFATHER, HAD A BREAKDOWN WHEN MY GRANDMOTHER DIED... HE BECAME LIKE A CHILD... HE LOCKED HIMSELF UP IN HIS COTTAGE WITH HIS DAUGHTER... MY MOTHER WAS 15 WHEN IT HAPPENED..."
"...THEN SHE LEFT HOME."
"...FOR ARGENTINA."
SHE NODDED.
QUESTER
"SHE HAD SOME RELATIVES DOWN THERE, THEY TOOK CARE OF HER AND THE CHILD – ME – WHEN I WAS BORN. MY MOTHER WOULD DISAPPEAR, THEN REAPPEAR – SHE LOVED ME... SHE DIDN'T WANT ME TO KNOW..."
"...SHE DIDN'T WANT ME TO KNOW."
"THAT'S WHY YOU HATE MR. CROSS... YOUR GRANDFATHER?"
MELANIA RAISED HER HEAD AND LOOKED AT OVADA...
"I HATE HIM FOR TURNING HIS BACK ON MY MOTHER AFTER EVERYTHING THAT HAD HAPPENED BETWEEN THEM..."
OVADA SUDDENLY FELT THE NEED TO LOOSEN HIS TIE. A DOG OBSTINATELY KEPT BARKING IN THE DISTANCE, THROUGH THE RAIN AND THE NIGHT...
ENOUGH, ZENO!
DO YOU GET IT NOW, YOU BLOCKHEAD?
ACTUALLY, NO!

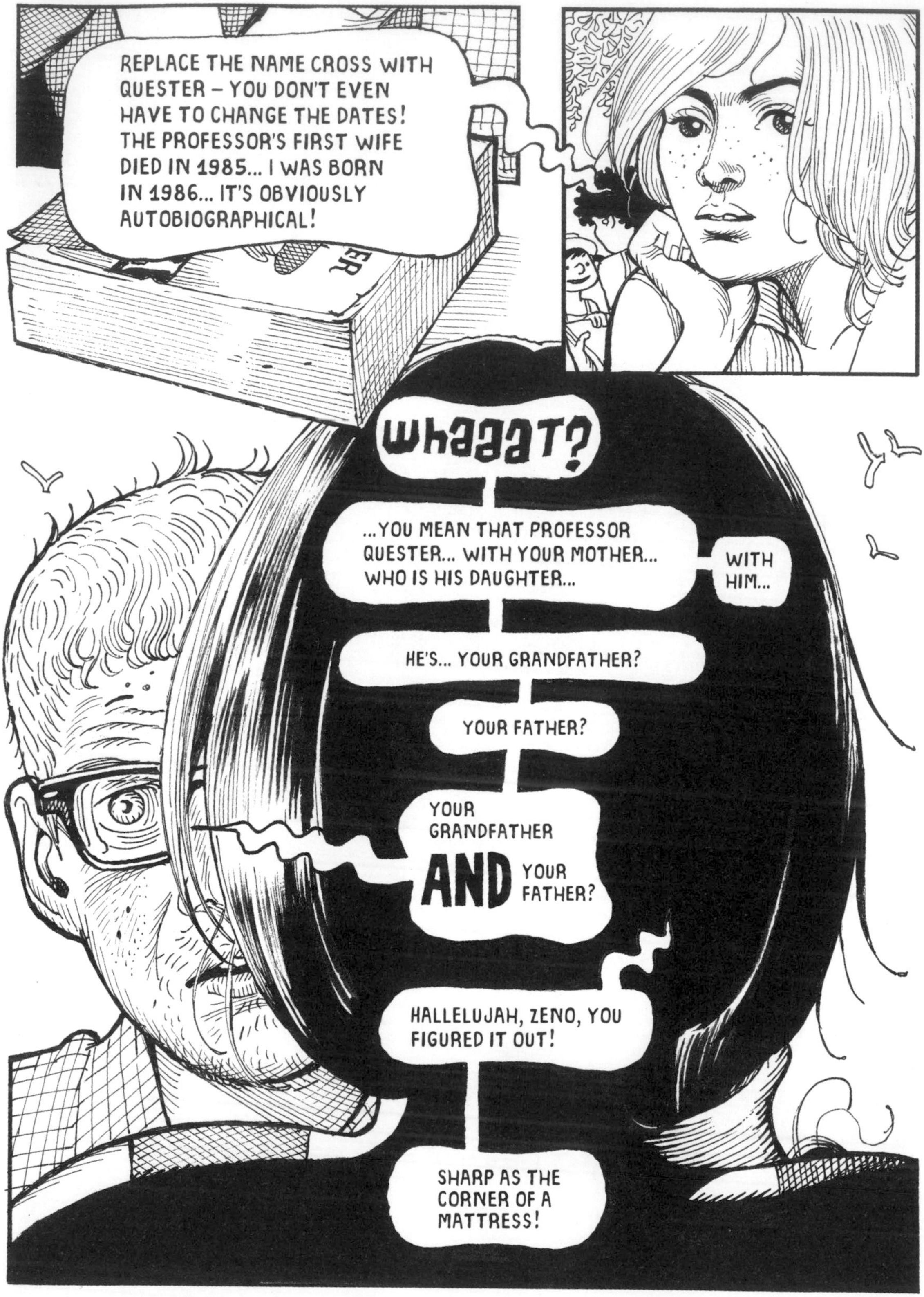
REPLACE THE NAME CROSS WITH QUESTER – YOU DON'T EVEN HAVE TO CHANGE THE DATES! THE PROFESSOR'S FIRST WIFE DIED IN 1985... I WAS BORN IN 1986... IT'S OBVIOUSLY AUTOBIOGRAPHICAL!
WHAAAT?
...YOU MEAN THAT PROFESSOR QUESTER... WITH YOUR MOTHER... WHO IS HIS DAUGHTER...
WITH HIM...
HE'S... YOUR GRANDFATHER?
YOUR FATHER?
YOUR GRANDFATHER AND YOUR FATHER?
HALLELUJAH, ZENO, YOU FIGURED IT OUT!
SHARP AS THE CORNER OF A MATTRESS!

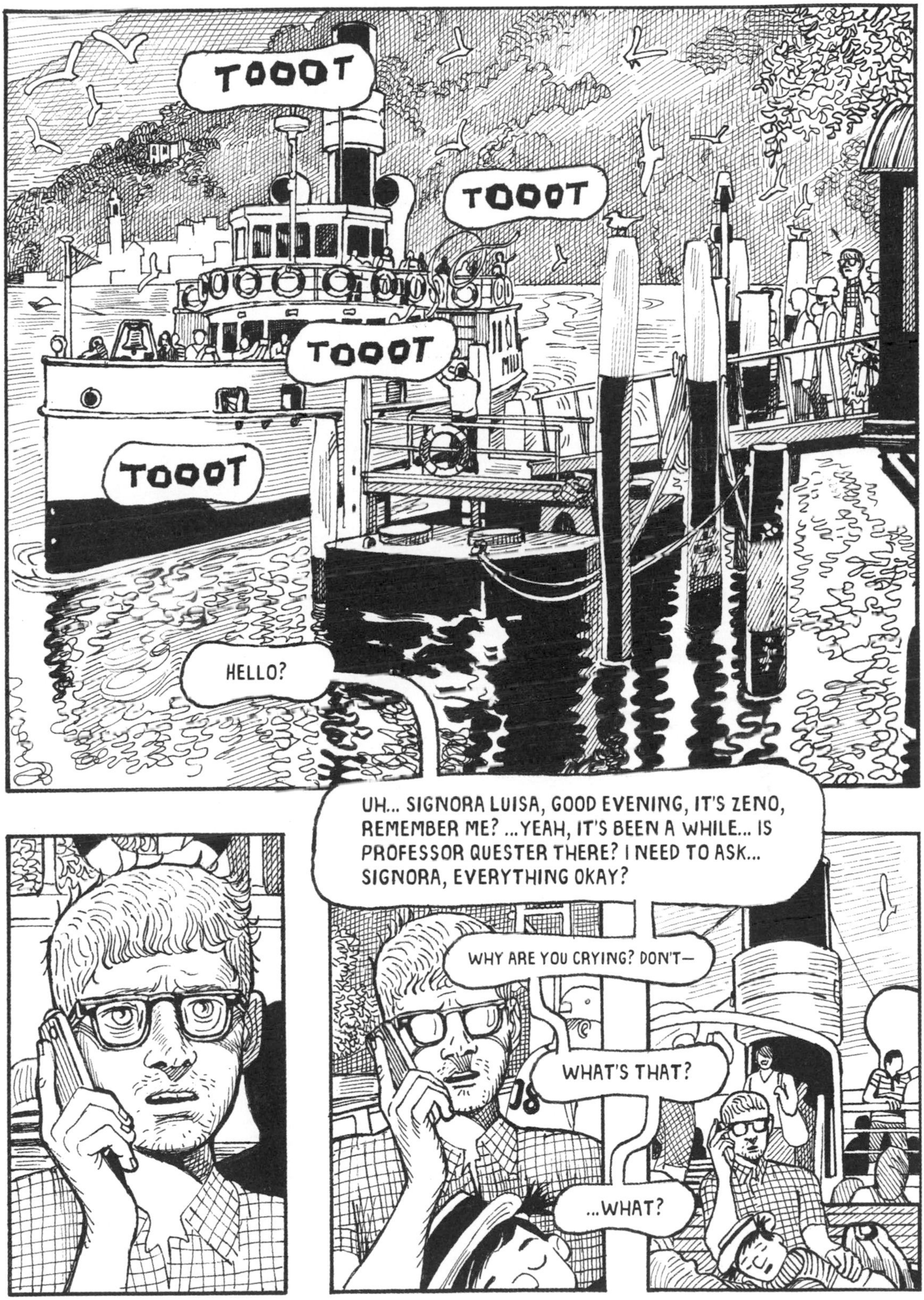
TOOOT
TOOOT
TOOOT
TOOOT
HELLO?
UH... SIGNORA LUISA, GOOD EVENING, IT'S ZENO, REMEMBER ME? ...YEAH, IT'S BEEN A WHILE... IS PROFESSOR QUESTER THERE? I NEED TO ASK... SIGNORA, EVERYTHING OKAY?
WHY ARE YOU CRYING? DON'T—
WHAT'S THAT?
...WHAT?

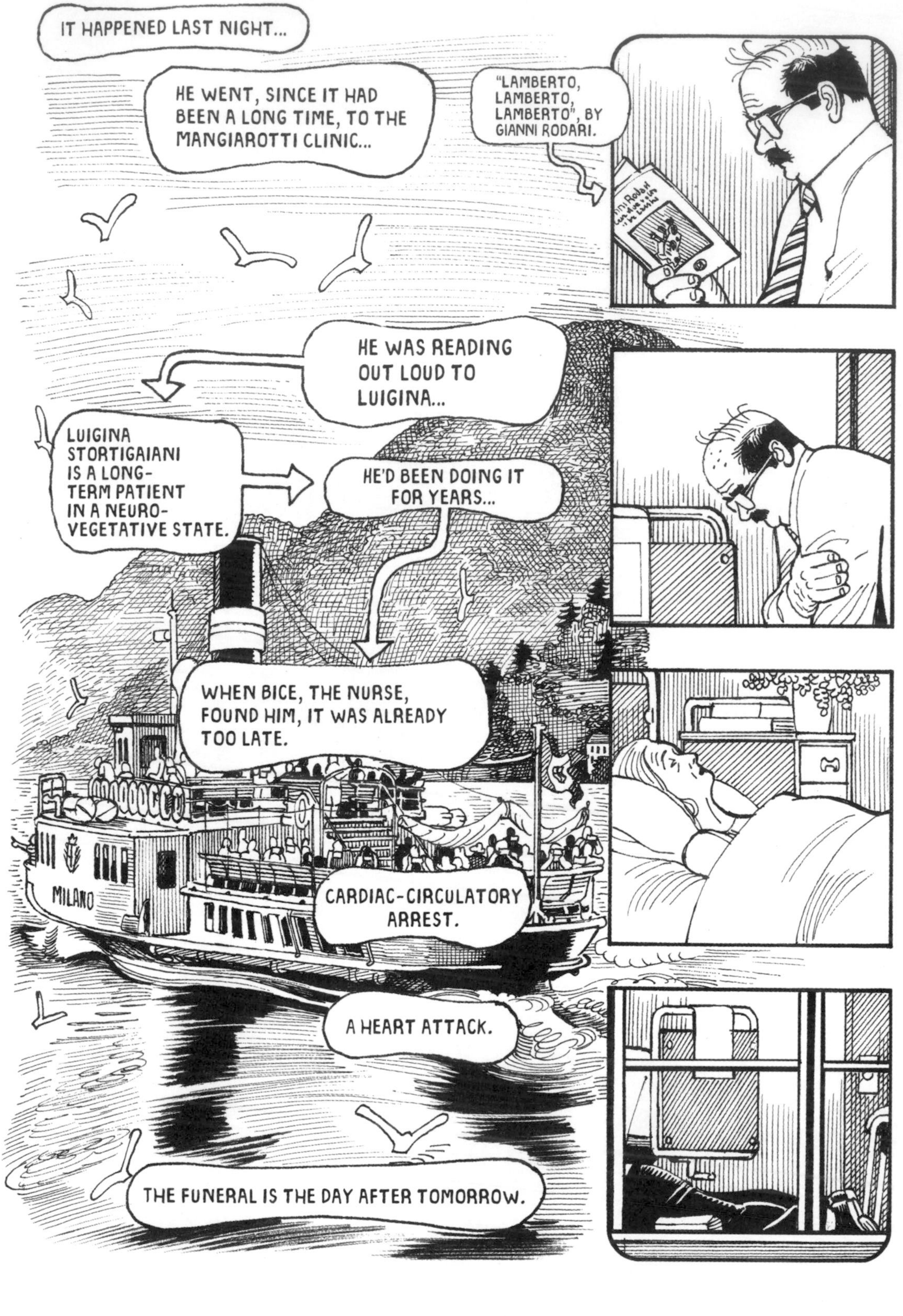
IT HAPPENED LAST NIGHT...
HE WENT, SINCE IT HAD BEEN A LONG TIME, TO THE MANGIAROTTI CLINIC...
"LAMBERTO, LAMBERTO, LAMBERTO", BY GIANNI RODARI.
HE WAS READING OUT LOUD TO LUIGINA...
LUIGINA STORTIGAIANI IS A LONG-TERM PATIENT IN A NEURO-VEGETATIVE STATE.
HE'D BEEN DOING IT FOR YEARS...
WHEN BICE, THE NURSE, FOUND HIM, IT WAS ALREADY TOO LATE.
MILANO
CARDIAC-CIRCULATORY ARREST.
A HEART ATTACK.
THE FUNERAL IS THE DAY AFTER TOMORROW.

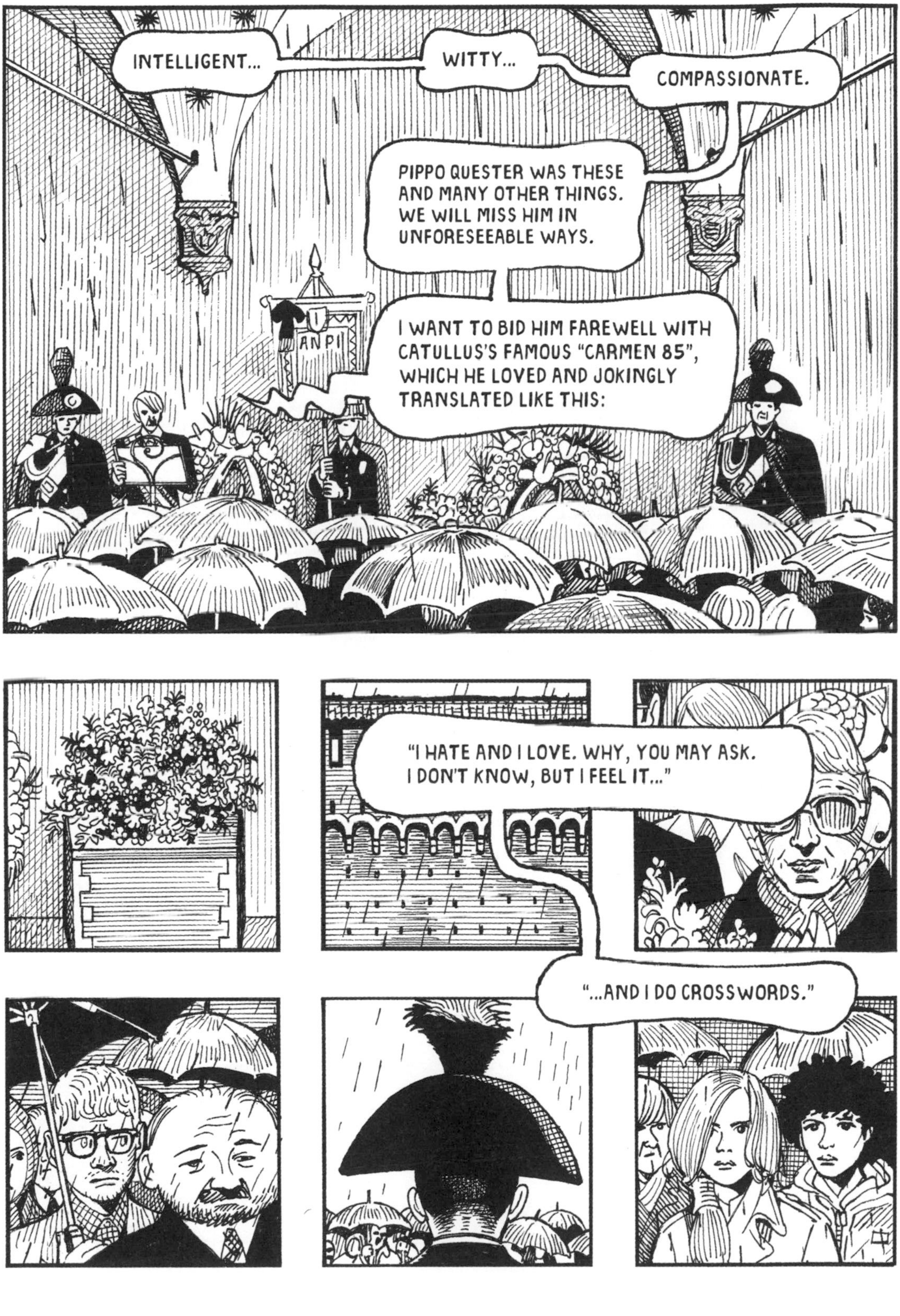
INTELLIGENT...
WITTY...
COMPASSIONATE.
PIPPO QUESTER WAS THESE AND MANY OTHER THINGS. WE WILL MISS HIM IN UNFORESEEABLE WAYS.
I WANT TO BID HIM FAREWELL WITH CATULLUS'S FAMOUS "CARMEN 85", WHICH HE LOVED AND JOKINGLY TRANSLATED LIKE THIS:
ANPI
"I HATE AND I LOVE. WHY, YOU MAY ASK. I DON'T KNOW, BUT I FEEL IT..."
"...AND I DO CROSSWORDS."

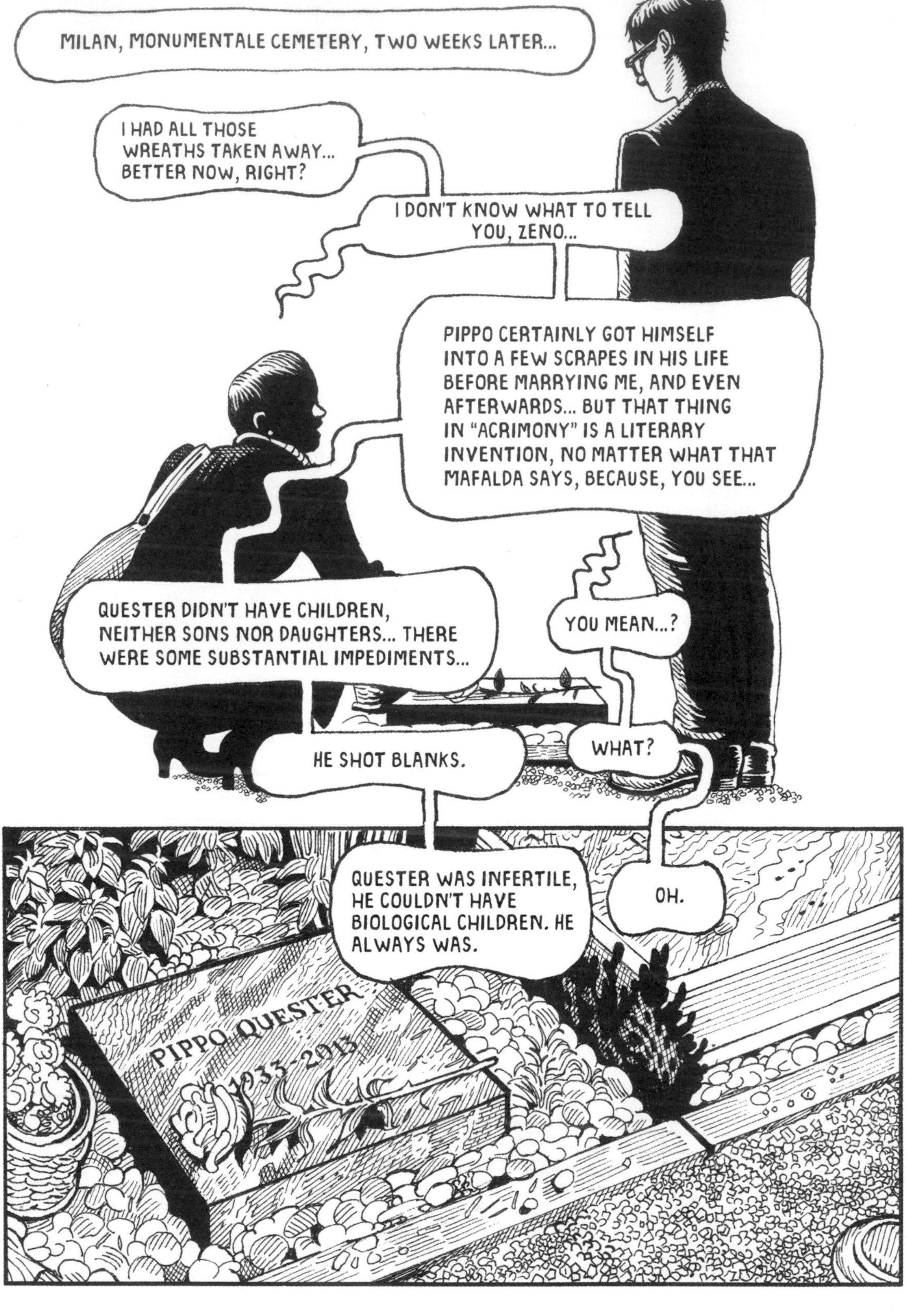
MILAN, MONUMENTALE CEMETERY, TWO WEEKS LATER...
I HAD ALL THOSE WREATHS TAKEN AWAY... BETTER NOW, RIGHT?
I DON'T KNOW WHAT TO TELL YOU, ZENO...
PIPPO CERTAINLY GOT HIMSELF INTO A FEW SCRAPES IN HIS LIFE BEFORE MARRYING ME, AND EVEN AFTERWARDS... BUT THAT THING IN "ACRIMONY" IS A LITERARY INVENTION, NO MATTER WHAT THAT MAFALDA SAYS, BECAUSE, YOU SEE...
QUESTER DIDN'T HAVE CHILDREN, NEITHER SONS NOR DAUGHTERS... THERE WERE SOME SUBSTANTIAL IMPEDIMENTS...
YOU MEAN...?
HE SHOT BLANKS.
WHAT?
QUESTER WAS INFERTILE, HE COULDN'T HAVE BIOLOGICAL CHILDREN. HE ALWAYS WAS.
OH.
PIPPO QUESTER
1933-2013

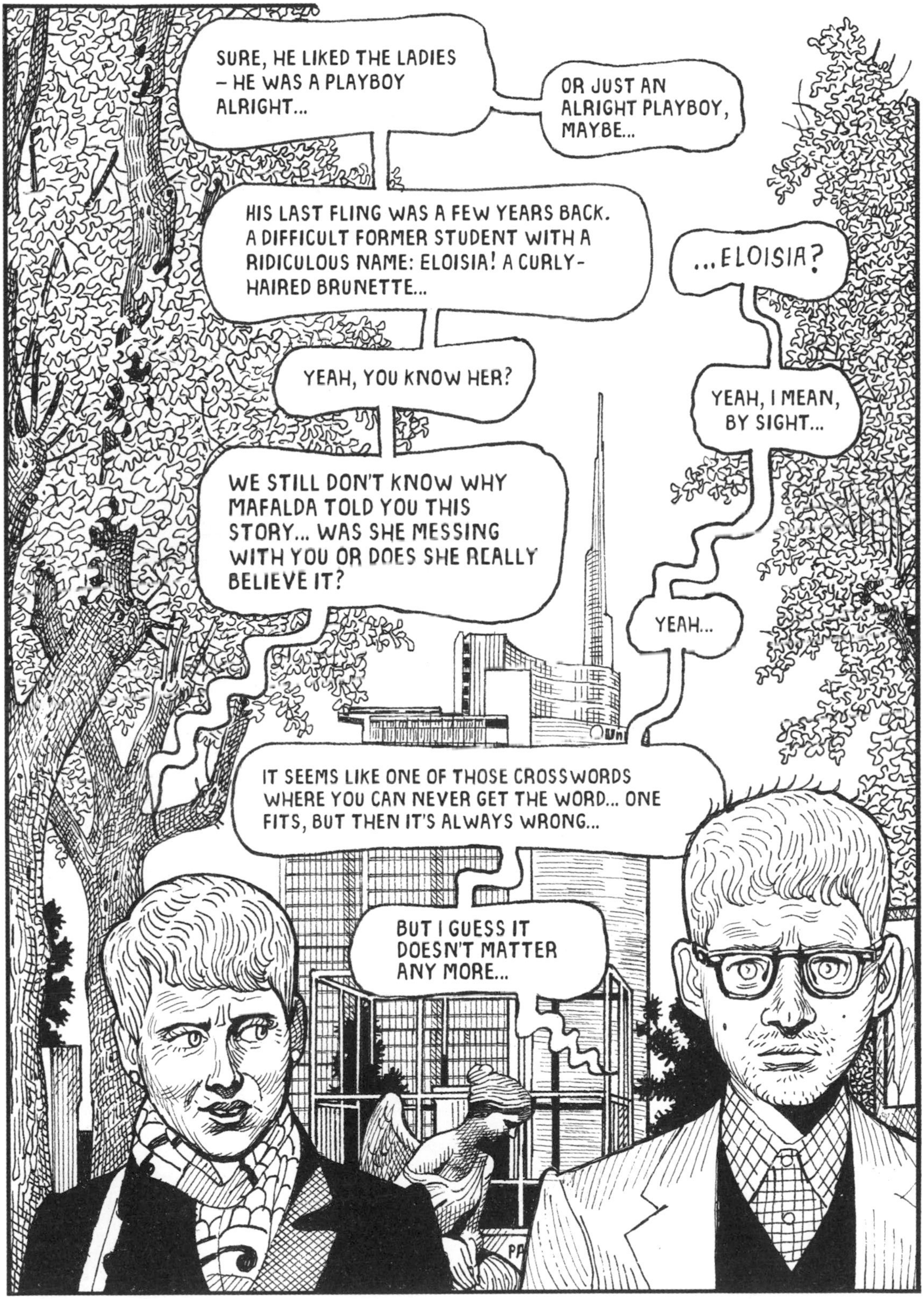
SURE, HE LIKED THE LADIES – HE WAS A PLAYBOY ALRIGHT...
OR JUST AN ALRIGHT PLAYBOY, MAYBE...
HIS LAST FLING WAS A FEW YEARS BACK. A DIFFICULT FORMER STUDENT WITH A RIDICULOUS NAME: ELOISIA! A CURLY-HAIRED BRUNETTE...
...ELOISIA?
YEAH, YOU KNOW HER?
YEAH, I MEAN, BY SIGHT...
WE STILL DON'T KNOW WHY MAFALDA TOLD YOU THIS STORY... WAS SHE MESSING WITH YOU OR DOES SHE REALLY BELIEVE IT?
YEAH...
IT SEEMS LIKE ONE OF THOSE CROSSWORDS WHERE YOU CAN NEVER GET THE WORD... ONE FITS, BUT THEN IT'S ALWAYS WRONG...
BUT I GUESS IT DOESN'T MATTER ANY MORE...

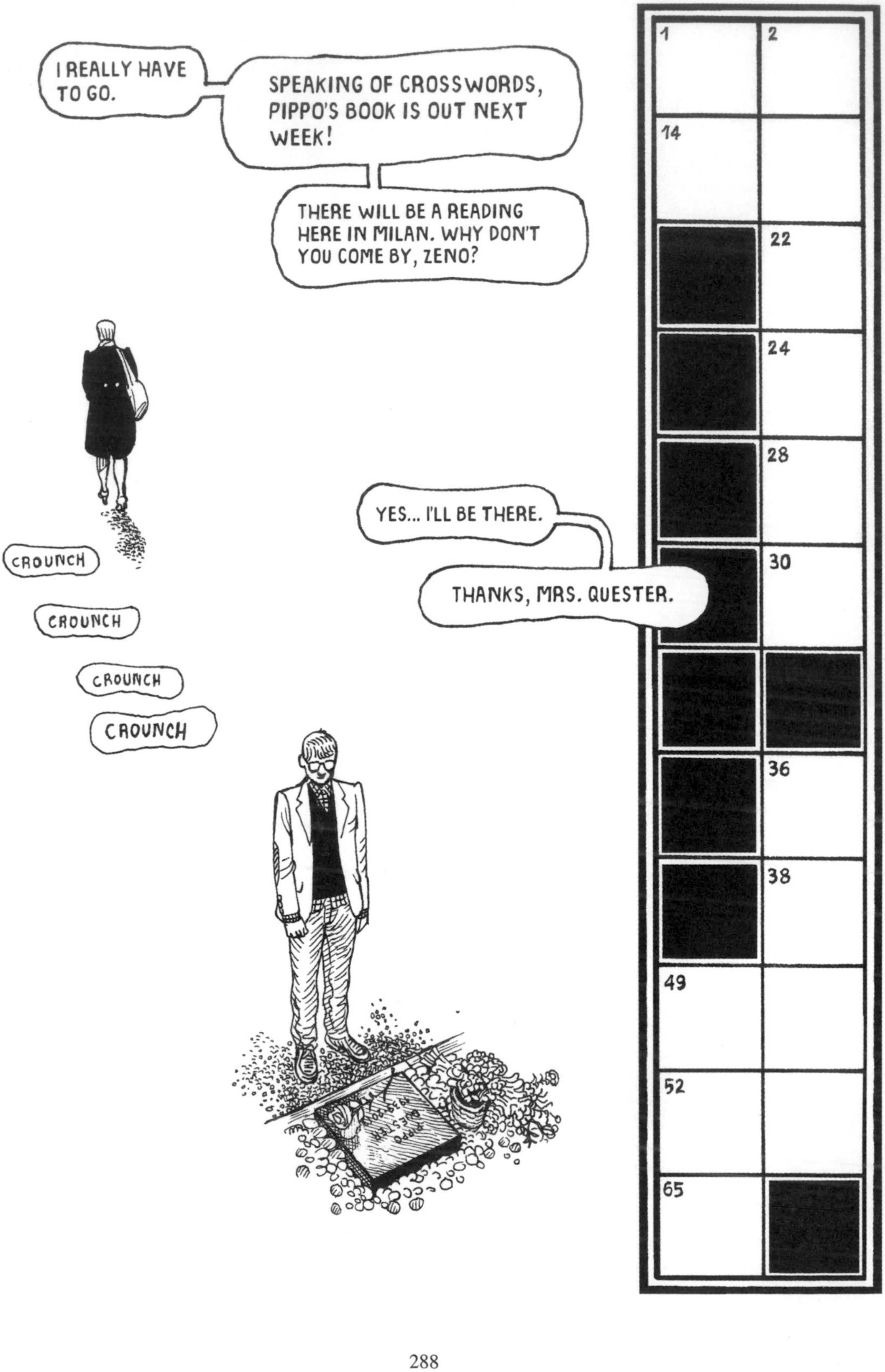
I REALLY HAVE TO GO.
SPEAKING OF CROSSWORDS, PIPPO'S BOOK IS OUT NEXT WEEK!
THERE WILL BE A READING HERE IN MILAN. WHY DON'T YOU COME BY, ZENO?
YES... I'LL BE THERE.
THANKS, MRS. QUESTER.
CROUNCH
CROUNCH
CROUNCH
CROUNCH
1
2
14
22
24
28
30
36
38
49
52
65

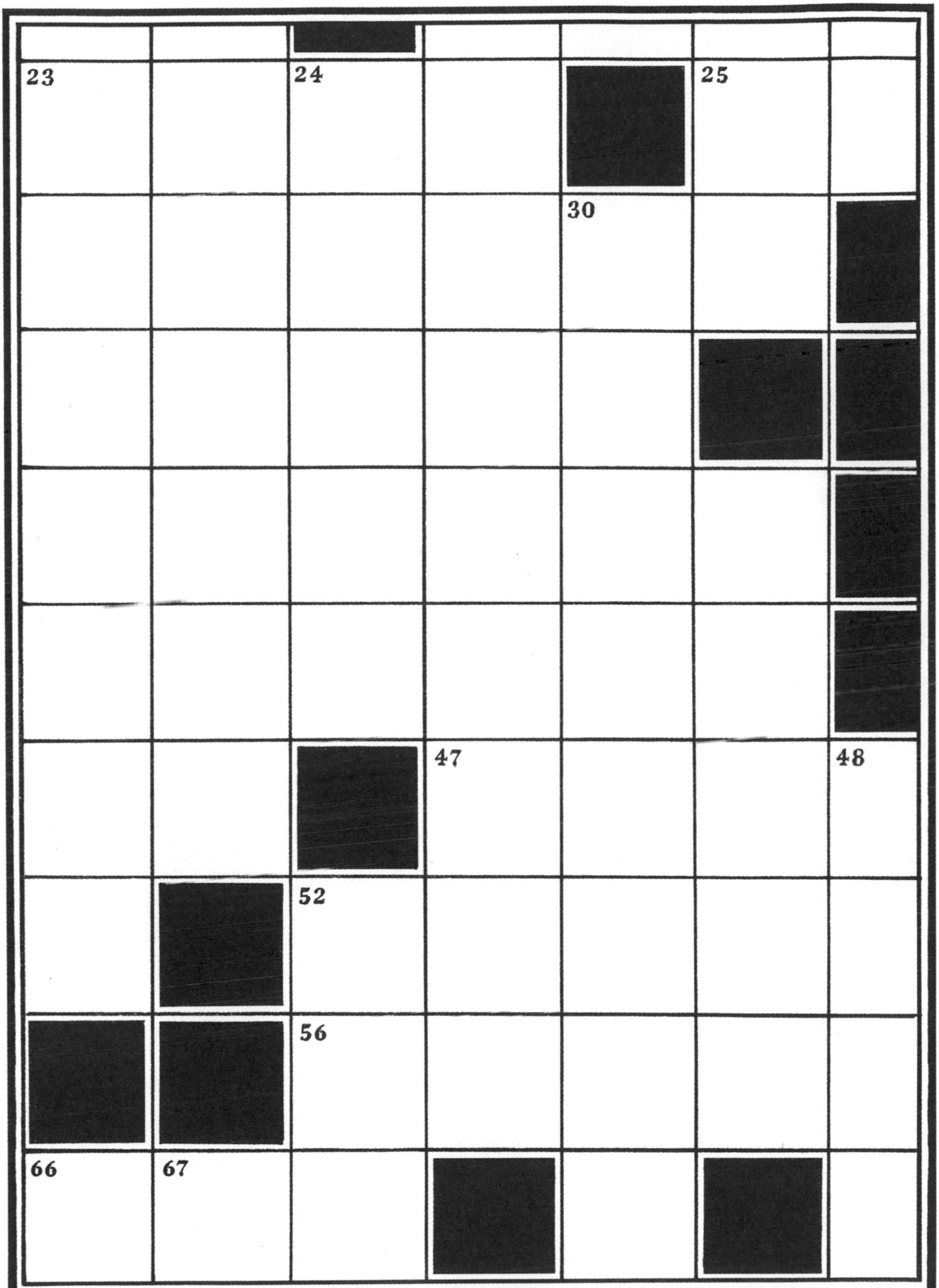
23
24
25
30
47
48
52
56
66
67

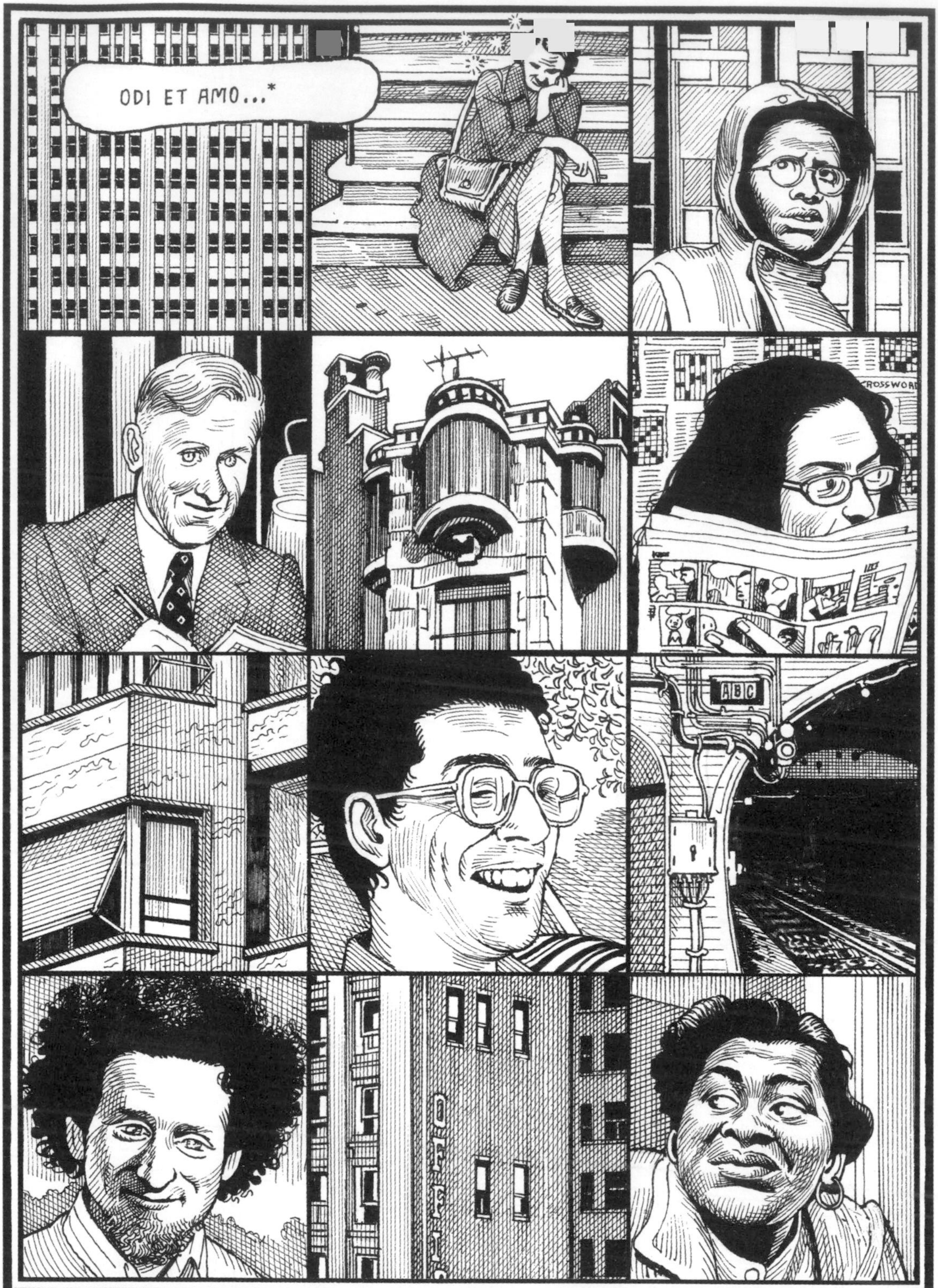
ODI ET AMO...*
CROSSWORD
ABC

* I HATE AND I LOVE...

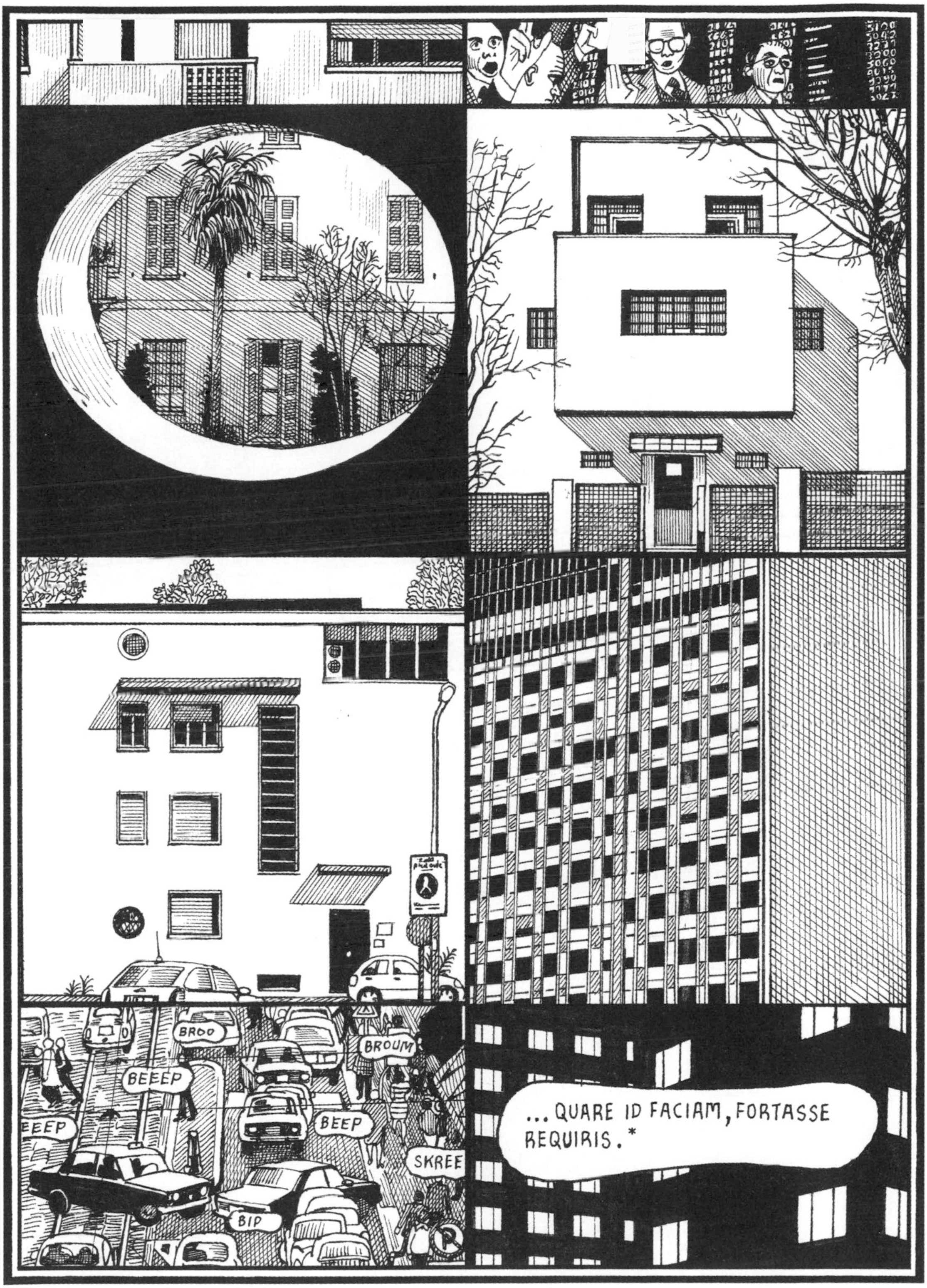
BROO
BROUM
BEEEP
EEEP
BEEP
SKREE
BIP
... QUARE ID FACIAM, FORTASSE REQUIRIS.*

* WHY, YOU MAY ASK.

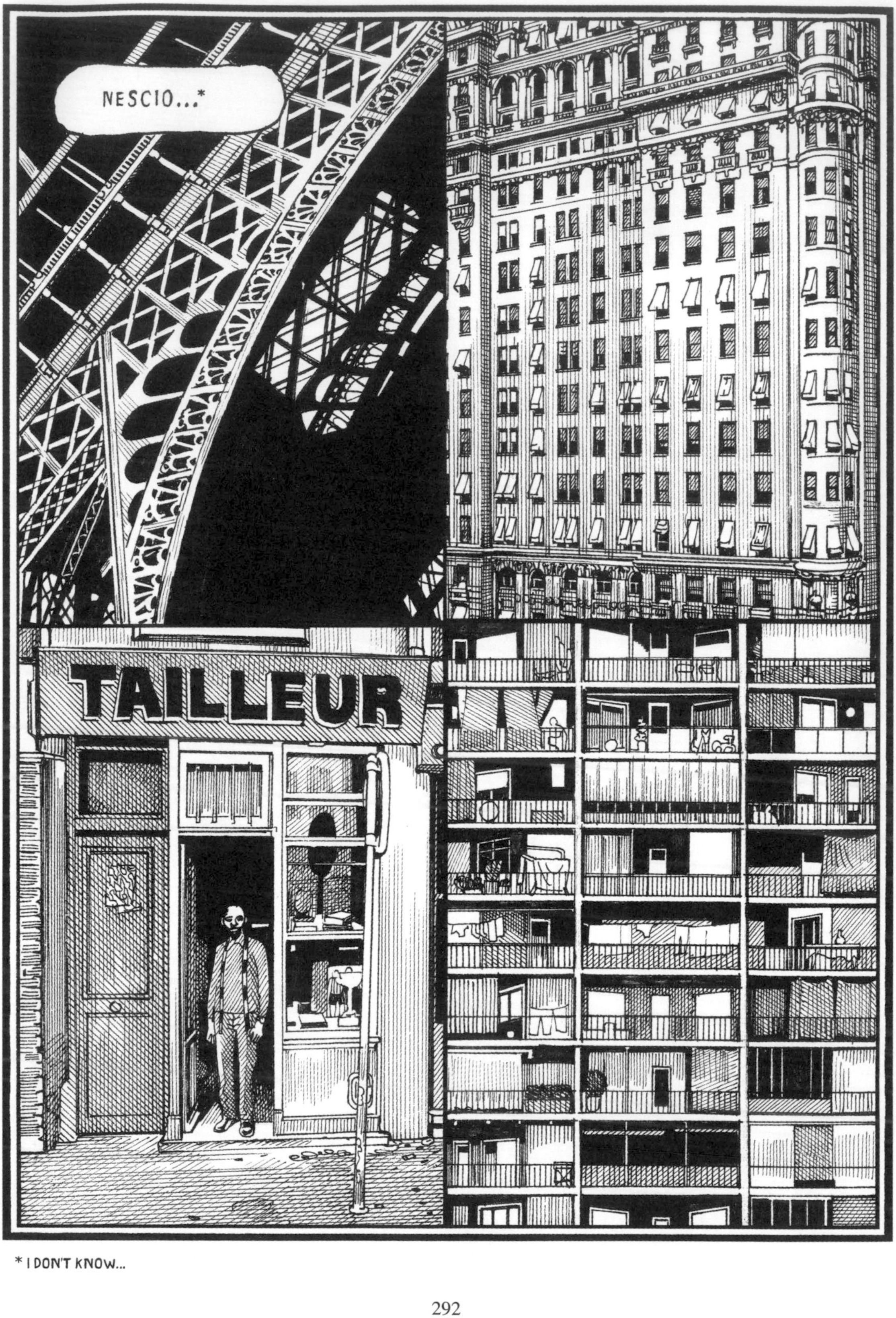
NESCIO...*
TAILLEUR

* I DON'T KNOW...

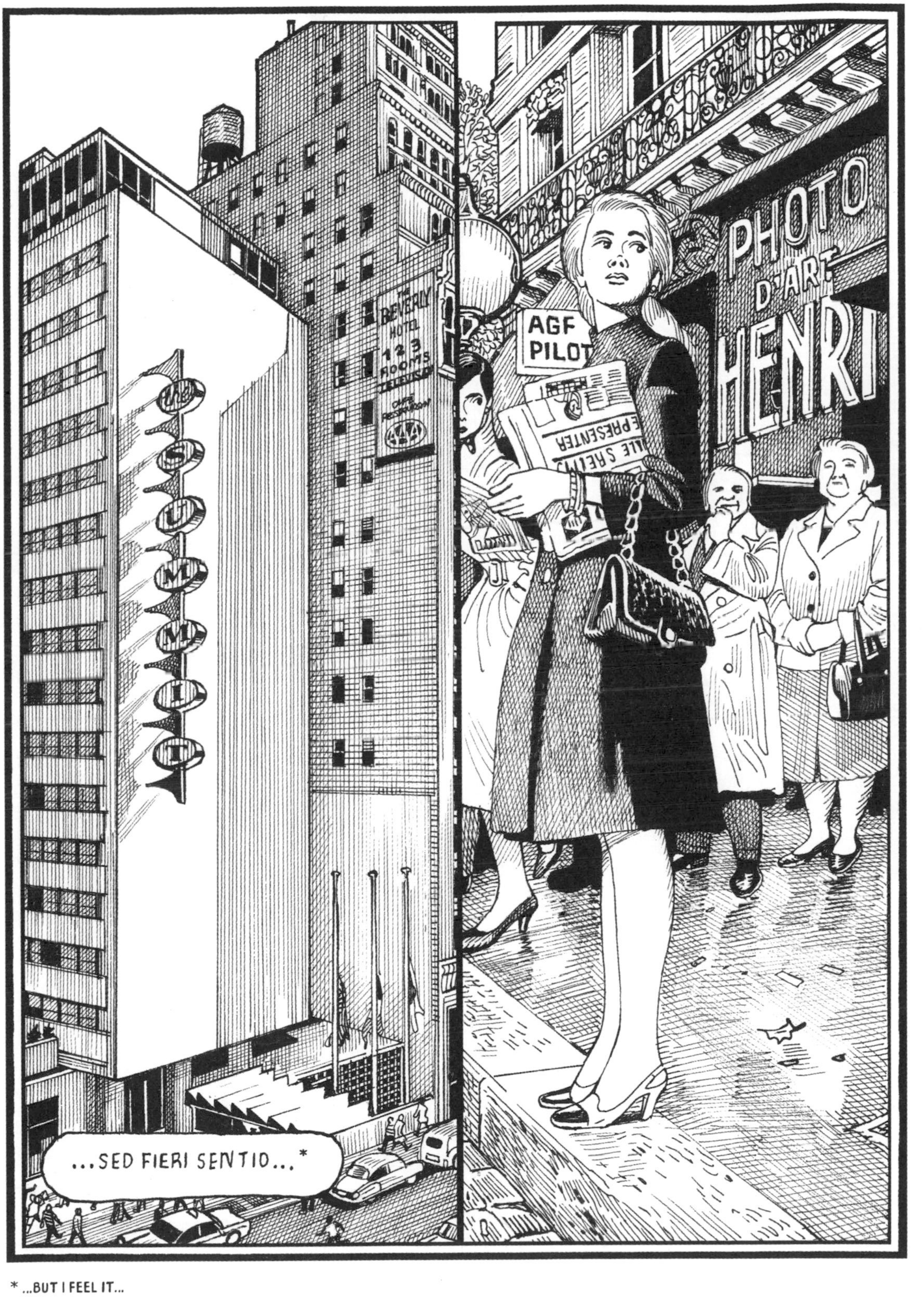
the SUMMIT
THE BEVERLY HOTEL
123 ROOMS
AGF PILOT
PHOTO D'ART HENRI
...SED FIERI SENTIO...*

* ...BUT I FEEL IT...

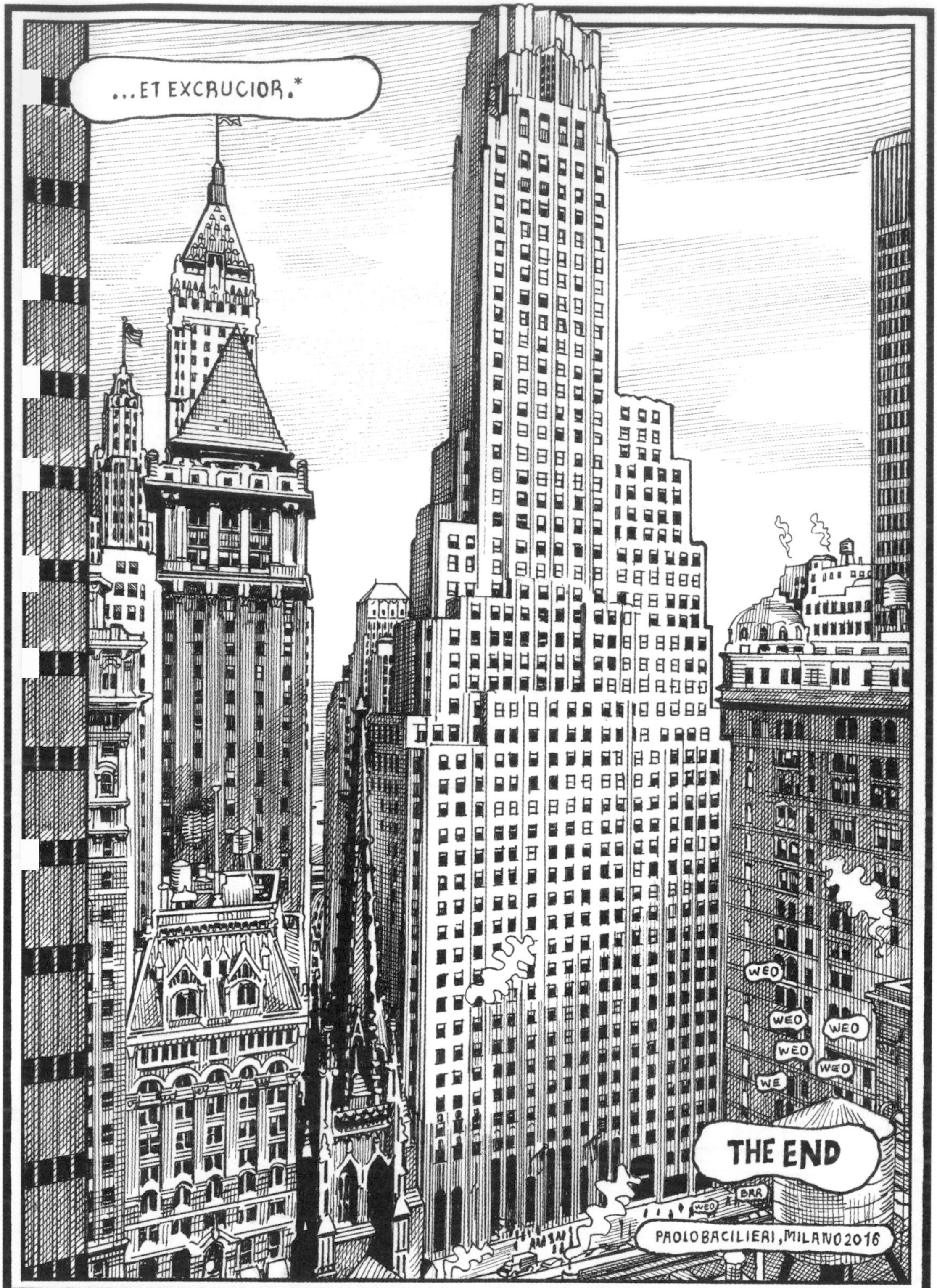
...ET EXCRUCIOR.*
WEO
WEO
WEO
WEO
WEO
WE
THE END
WEO
BRR
PAOLO BACILIERI, MILANO 2016

* ...AND IT'S EXCRUCIATING.

This book came out of a chat with Stefano Bartezzaghi, and the historical part is greatly indebted to his book *L'orizzonte verticale: invenzione e storia del cruciverba* [*The Vertical Horizon: Invention and History of the Crossword*] (Einaudi, 2007).

Thanks to:
Stefano Bartezzaghi, Daniela Melazzi, Giulia Salamon, Giuliano Tedesco, Igort, Viola Cagninelli, Orsola Mattioli, Tiziana Lo Porto, Giovanni Ferrara, Luca Baldazzi, Tiberino (Franco Diotallevi), Riccardo Secchi, Alessandra Straffi, Giuseppe (Pippo) Riva, Sara Vivan.

Bibliography

These are some of the books I consulted for *Fun* and *More Fun*.

Of course:
Stefano Bartezzaghi, *L'orizzonte verticale*, Einaudi 2007.

As well as:
Michelle Arnot, *What's Gnu? A History of the Crossword Puzzle*, 1981.
David Astle, *Cluetopia: The story of 100 years of the crossword*, 2013.
"50 years of Crw Puzzles", *The New York Times Magazine*, February 1992.
Piero Bartezzaghi, *Quello che volevo. Enigmi in versi*, 1999.
Giampaolo Dossena, *I giochi dei grandi*, 1979.
Chinatown, screenplay by Robert Towne, 1973.
Fruttero & Lucentini, *L'amante senza fissa dimora*, Mondadori 1986.
Graham Greene, *Il nocciolo della questione* [*The Heart of the Matter*], Mondadori 2001.
Raymond Chandler, *Addio, mia amata* [*Farewell, My Lovely*], Mondadori 1975.
David Bellos, *Georges Perec. Une vie dans les mots*, 2002.
Georges Perec, *W, ou Le souvenir d'enfance*, 1975.
Georges Perec, *Les mots croisés II*, P.O.L. 1979.
Georges Perec, *La vita, istruzioni per l'uso*, 1978.
Julio Cortázar, *Rayuela (Il gioco del mondo)*, Einaudi 2013.
Giuseppe Zichi, *Sisini, imprenditori di Sardegna*, ed. Fiesta 2013.
Alberto Fortis, *Il duomo di notte*, from the album by Alberto Fortis, 1979.
Paolo Conte, *Sotto le stelle del jazz*, from the album by Paolo Conte, 1984.
Gaio Valerio Catullo (Catullus), Carme LXXXV, from *Le poesie*,
    introduction and translation by Guido Paduano, Einaudi 1997.

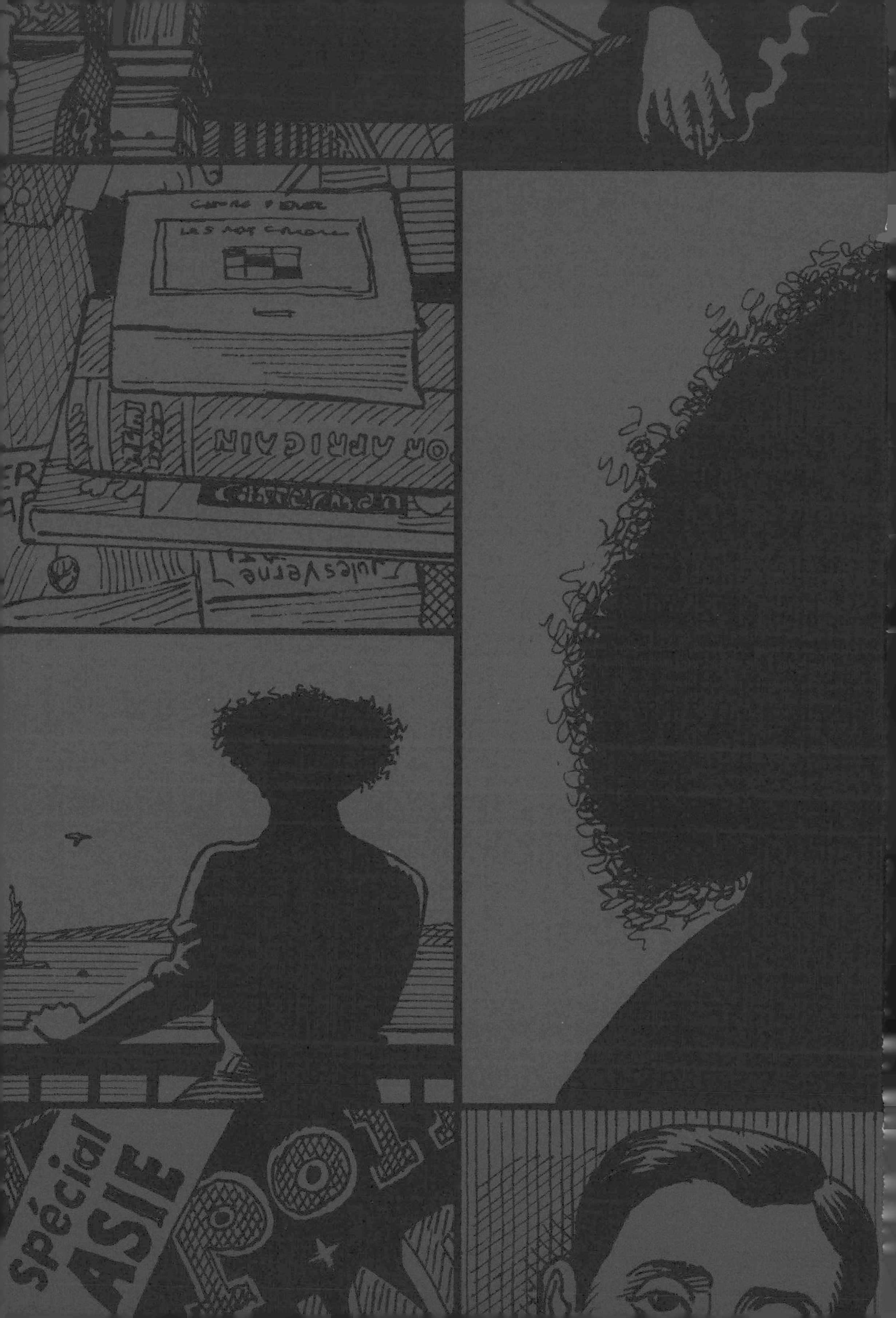
spécial
ASIE